THE PAPERS OF
BENJAMIN FRANKLIN

SPONSORED BY

The American Philosophical Society

and Yale University

Il a ravi le feu des Cieux.
Il faut fleurir les arts en des Climats sauvages.
L'amérique le place à la tête des Sages
La Grèce l'auroit mis au nombre de ses Dieux.

Dessiné et Gravé   par F.N. martinet

Benjamin Franklin: the Martinet engraving

THE PAPERS OF

Benjamin Franklin

VOLUME 20 *January 1 through December 31, 1773*

WILLIAM B. WILLCOX, *Editor*

*Dorothy W. Bridgwater, Mary L. Hart, Claude A. Lopez,
C. A. Myrans, Catherine M. Prelinger, and G. B. Warden,
Assistant Editors*

New Haven and London YALE UNIVERSITY PRESS, 1976

Funds for editing this volume of The Papers of Benjamin Franklin *have been provided by grants from three sources, for all of which the editors are most grateful: the Ford Foundation, the National Endowment for the Humanities, and the National Historical Publications and Records Commission, under the chairmanship of the Archivist of the United States, which is also generously providing a subsidy to the Yale University Press to compensate for unrecovered publishing costs. The support of the Commission and its Executive Director has been indispensable.*

Editor's Note

Two members of the staff left while this volume was on press: Gretchen Woelfle, who has been our secretary, typist, transcriber, and general factotum; and Gerard Warden, who for the past five and a half years has been assistant editor, and has contributed as much as any of us to the annotation and to the efficient functioning of the project. We wish them well and shall miss them both.

W.B.W.

Contents

CONTENTS

CONTENTS

List of Illustrations

Barbeu-Dubourg furnished François-Nicolas Martinet (b. 1731) with a copy of Fisher's popular mezzotint of Franklin, executed a decade earlier and reproduced as the frontispiece of Volume X, and asked him to make from it a frontispiece for the *Œuvres de M. Franklin*. Martinet took the commission seriously; he regretted not having met his subject and offered, if Franklin came to Paris in the summer of 1773, to redo the engraving from life. But the opportunity did not arise, and the print is the artist's interpretation of Fisher's interpretation of the original painting by Mason Chamberlain. When Franklin saw Martinet's work he recognized that Fisher's had suffered a sea change: "your old Husband," he remarked to his wife in his letter below of September 1, "... has got so French a Countenance, that you would take him for one of that lively Nation." See also Dubourg to Franklin below, under January 13, and Charles C. Sellers, *Benjamin Franklin in Portraiture* ... (New Haven and London, 1962), pp. 221–2. The engraving is reproduced by courtesy of the Yale University Library.

An oil by John Singleton Copley, painted between 1769 and 1771 and reproduced by courtesy of the Williams College Museum of Art. The Rev. Samuel Cooper, D.D. (1725–83), succeeded his father in the Brattle Street Church, of which he was the sole pastor for the last thirty-six years of his life. He was one of the leaders of the Bostonians' opposition to the crown, and until his death he played a prominent part in their public affairs.

The story of Franklin's invention or "philosophical experiment," as he described it in his letter to Dubourg below, January 22, is outlined in a note on that letter. This illustration of it is reproduced, by courtesy of the American Philosophical Society, from an engraving among his papers. The print has no information about when or by whom it was executed, and Franklin's description of the stove, as finally published in the Society's *Transactions* (11 [1786], 57–74), is illustrated with a slightly different print. This one, we are convinced, was what he sent to Dubourg with his letter below of June 29; and our reason is a sentence to Turgot on May 1, 1781 (University of Pennsylvania Library): "I did intend when in London to have published a Pamphlet," Franklin wrote, "describing the new Stove you mention, and for that purpose had a Plate engrav'd, of which I send you an Impression."

Where Franklin poured oil: Mount Pond, Clapham Common

facing page 466

The photograph was taken on January 3, 1967, by Dr. C. H. Giles of the University of Strathclyde, and is reproduced by his courtesy. Franklin's friend Henton Brown, Quaker and banker, had the pond made in the middle of the century as part of creating the common from a bog. Franklin's experiment was probably made shortly before 1773, but cannot be precisely dated. His only description of it, as far as we know, is in the letter that the photograph illustrates.

Contributors to Volume 20

The ownership of each manuscript, or the location of the particular copy used by the editors of each rare contemporary pamphlet or similar printed work, is indicated where the document appears in the text. The sponsors and editors are deeply grateful to the following institutions and individuals for permission to print or otherwise use in the present volume manuscripts or other materials which they own.

INSTITUTIONS

American Philosophical Society
Bodleian Library, Oxford
Boston Public Library
British Museum
Dartmouth College Library
First Federal Savings and Loan Association, Boston
Harvard University Library
Historical Society of Pennsylvania
Library of Congress
Linnean Society, London
Massachusetts Historical Society
Pierpont Morgan Library
National Archives, Washington
National Library of Scotland, Edinburgh

New England Historic, Genealogical Society, Boston
New-York Historical Society
New York Public Library
Pennsylvania Historical and Museum Commission, Harrisburg
Pennsylvania Hospital, Philadelphia
University of Pennsylvania Library
Public Record Office, London
The Royal Society
William Salt Library, Stafford
University of Virginia Library
Yale University Library

INDIVIDUALS

Mr. John H. Bradshaw, Lahaska, Pa.
The Earl of Dartmouth, London

Sir Francis Dashwood, Bart., West Wycombe

Method of Textual Reproduction

An extended statement of the principles of selection, arrangement, form of presentation, and method of textual reproduction observed in this edition appears in the Introduction to the first volume, pp. xxiv–xlvii. What follows is a condensation and revision of part of it.

Printed Material:

Those of Franklin's writings that were printed under his direction presumably appeared as he wanted them to, and should therefore be reproduced with no changes except what modern typography requires. In some cases, however, printers carelessly or willfully altered his text without his consent; or the journeymen who set it had different notions from his—and from each other's—of capitalization, spelling, and punctuation. Such of his letters as survive only in nineteenth-century printings, furthermore, have often been vigorously edited by William Temple Franklin, Duane, or Sparks. In all these cases the original has suffered some degree of distortion, which the modern editor may guess at but, in the absence of the manuscript, cannot remedy. We therefore follow the printed texts as we find them, and note only obvious misreadings.

We observe the following rules in reproducing printed materials:

1. The place and date of composition of letters are set at the top, regardless of their location in the original printing; the complimentary close is set continuously with the text.

2. Proper nouns, including personal names, which were often printed in italics, are set in roman except when the original was italicized for emphasis.

3. Prefaces and other long passages, though italicized in the original, are set in roman. Long italicized quotations are set in roman within quotation marks.

4. Words in full capitals are set in small capitals, with initial

letters in full capitals if required by Franklin's normal usage.

5. All signatures are set in capitals and small capitals.

6. We silently correct obvious typographical errors, such as the omission of a single parenthesis or quotation mark.

7. We close a sentence by supplying, when needed, a period or question mark.

Manuscript Material:

a. *Letters* are presented in the following form:

1. The place and date of composition are set at the top, regardless of their location in the original; the complimentary close is set continuously with the text.

2. Addresses, endorsements, and notations are so labelled and printed at the end of the letter. An endorsement is to the best of our belief by the recipient, a notation by someone else.

b. *Spelling* of the original we retain. When it is so abnormal as to obscure the meaning, we supply the correct form in brackets or a footnote, as "yf [wife]."

c. *Capitalization* we retain as written, except that every sentence is made to begin with a capital. When we cannot decide whether a letter is a capital, we follow modern usage.

d. Words underlined once in the manuscripts are printed in italics; words underlined twice or written in large letters or full capitals are printed in small capitals.

e. *Punctuation* has been retained as in the original, except:

1. We close a sentence by supplying, when needed, a period or question mark. When it is unclear where the sentence ends, we retain the original punctuation or lack of it.

2. Dashes used in place of commas, semicolons, colons, or periods are replaced by the appropriate marks; when a sentence ends with both a dash and a period, the dash is omitted.

3. Commas scattered meaninglessly through a manuscript are eliminated.

4. When a mark of punctuation is not clear or can be read as one of two marks, we follow modern usage.[1]

5. Some documents, especially legal ones, have no punctuation; others have so little as to obscure the meaning. In such cases we silently supply the minimum needed for clarity.

f. *Contractions and abbreviations* in general are retained. The ampersand is rendered as "and," except in the names of business firms, in the form "&c.," and in a few other cases. Letters represented by the thorn or tilde are printed. The tailed "p" is spelled out as per, pre, or pro. Symbols of weights, measures and monetary values follow modern usage, as: £34. Superscript letters are lowered.

g. *Omitted or illegible words or letters* are treated as follows:

1. If not more than four letters are missing, we supply them silently when we have no doubt what they should be.

2. If more than four letters are missing, we supply them conjecturally in brackets, with or without a question mark depending on our confidence in the conjecture.

3. Other omissions are shown as follows: [*illegible*], [*torn*], [*remainder missing*], or the like.

4. Missing or illegible digits are indicated by suspension points in brackets, the number of points corresponding to the estimated number of missing figures.

5. When the writer has omitted a word required for clarity, we insert it in brackets and italics.

h. *Author's additions and corrections:*

1. Interlineations and brief marginal notes are incorporated in the text without comment, and longer notes with the notation [*in the margin*] unless they were clearly intended as footnotes, in which case they are normally printed with our notes but with a bracketed indication of the source.

1. The typescripts from which these papers are printed have been made from photocopies of the manuscripts; marks of punctuation are sometimes blurred or lost in photography, and it has often been impossible to consult the original.

2. Canceled words and phrases are in general omitted without notice; if significant, they are printed in footnotes.

3. When alternative words and phrases have been inserted in a manuscript but the original remains uncanceled, the alternatives are given in brackets, preceded by explanatory words in italics, as: "it is [*written above:* may be] true."

4. Variant readings of several versions are noted if important.

Abbreviations and Short Titles

Académie des sciences, *Mémoires*	*Histoire de l'Académie royale des sciences ... avec les Mémoires de mathématique & de physique ...* (Paris, 1733–). Until 1790, when the title changed, the *Histoire* and *Mémoires* were paginated separately; our references, unless otherwise indicated, are to the second pagination.
Acts Privy Coun., Col.	W. L. Grant and James Munro, eds., *Acts of the Privy Council of England, Colonial Series, 1613–1783* (6 vols., London, 1908–12).
AD	Autograph document.[1]
ADS	Autograph document signed.
AL	Autograph letter.
ALS	Autograph letter signed.
Amer.	American.
APS	American Philosophical Society.
Archaeol.	Archaeological.
Assn.	Association.
Autobiog.	Leonard W. Labaree, Ralph L. Ketcham, Helen C. Boatfield, and Helene H. Fineman, eds., *The Autobiography of Benjamin Franklin* (New Haven, 1964).
Bargar, *Dartmouth*	Bradley D. Bargar, *Lord Dartmouth and the American Revolution* (Columbia, S.C., 1965).
BF	Benjamin Franklin.
Bigelow, *Works*	John Bigelow, ed., *The Complete Works of Benjamin Franklin ...* (10 vols., N.Y., 1887–88).
Board of Trade Jour.	*Journal of the Commissioners for Trade and Plantations ... April 1704 to ... May 1782* (14 vols., London, 1920–38).

---

1. For definitions of types of manuscripts see above, I, xliv–xlvii.

Bradford, ed.,
Mass. State Papers

Alden Bradford, ed., *Speeches of the Governors of Massachusetts, from 1765 to 1775; and the Answers of the House of Representatives* ... (Boston, 1818).

Burke's Peerage

Sir Bernard Burke, *Burke's Genealogical and Heraldic History of the Peerage Baronetage and Knightage with War Gazette and Corrigenda* (98th ed., London, 1940). References in exceptional cases to other editions are so indicated.

Butterfield, ed.,
John Adams Diary

Lyman H. Butterfield *et al.*, eds., *Diary and Autobiography of John Adams* (4 vols., Cambridge, Mass., 1961).

Candler, ed., *Ga. Col. Recs.*

Allen D. Candler, ed., *The Colonial Records of the State of Georgia* ... (26 vols., Atlanta, 1904–16).

Carter, ed., *Gage Correspondence*

Clarence E. Carter, ed., *The Correspondence of General Thomas Gage* ... (2 vols., New Haven and London, 1931–33).

Chron.

Chronicle.

Cobbett,
Parliamentary History

William Cobbett and Thomas C. Hansard, eds., *The Parliamentary History of England from the Earliest Period to 1803* (36 vols., London, 1806–20).

Coll.

Collections.

Crane, *Letters to the Press*

Verner W. Crane, ed., *Benjamin Franklin's Letters to the Press, 1758–1775* (Chapel Hill, N.C., [1950]).

Cushing, ed., *Writings of Samuel Adams*

Harry Alonzo Cushing, ed., *The Writings of Samuel Adams* ... (4 vols., New York, 1904–08).

DAB

Dictionary of American Biography.

Dartmouth MSS

Historical Manuscripts Commission, *The Manuscripts of the Earl of Dartmouth* ...: *Eleventh Report*, appendix, part 5; *Fourteenth Report*, appendix, part 10; *Fifteenth Report*, appendix, part 1 (3 vols., London, 1887–96).

DF	Deborah Franklin.
Dictionnaire de biographie	*Dictionnaire de biographie française* ... (11 vols. to date, Paris, 1933—).
DNB	*Dictionary of National Biography.*
DS	Document signed.
Duane, *Works*	William Duane, ed., *The Works of Dr. Benjamin Franklin* ... (6 vols., Philadelphia, 1808–18). Title varies in the several volumes.
Dubourg, *Œuvres*	Jacques Barbeu-Dubourg, *Œuvres de M. Franklin* ... (2 vols., Paris, 1773).
Ed.	Edition or editor.
Exper. and Obser.	*Experiments and Observations on Electricity, made at Philadelphia in America, by Mr. Benjamin Franklin* ... (London, 1751). Revised and enlarged editions were published in 1754, 1760, 1769, and 1774 with slightly varying titles. In each case the edition cited will be indicated, e.g., *Exper. and Obser.* (1751).
Gaz.	*Gazette.*
Geneal.	Genealogical.
Gent. Mag.	*The Gentleman's Magazine, and Historical Chronicle.*
Gipson, *British Empire*	Lawrence H. Gipson, *The British Empire before the American Revolution* (15 vols., New York, 1939–70; I–III, revised ed., N.Y., 1958–60).
Hinshaw, *Amer. Quaker Genealogy*	William W. Hinshaw, *Encyclopedia of American Quaker Genealogy* (6 vols. Ann Arbor, Mich., 1936–50).
Hist.	Historical.
Hutchinson, *History*	Thomas Hutchinson, *The History of the Colony and Province of Massachusetts-Bay* ... (Lawrence S. Mayo, ed.; 3 vols., Cambridge., Mass., 1936).
Jour.	*Journal.* The citation "Jour." is of Franklin's MS account book described above, XI, 518–20.
Kammen, *Rope of Sand*	Michael G. Kammen, *A Rope of Sand: the Colonial Agents, British Politics,*

	and the American Revolution (Ithaca, N.Y., [1968]).
Labaree, *Tea Party*	Benjamin W. Labaree, *The Boston Tea Party* (New York, [1968]).
Larousse, *Dictionnaire universel*	Pierre Larousse, *Grand dictionnaire universel du XIXe siècle* . . . (17 vols., Paris, [n.d.]).
Ledger	The Franklin MS described above, XI, 518–20.
Lee Papers	Paul P. Hoffman, ed., *The Lee Family Papers, 1742–1795* (University of Virginia Library *Microfilm Publication* No. 1; 8 reels, Charlottesville, Va., 1966).
Lewis, *Indiana Co.*	George E. Lewis, *The Indiana Company, 1763–1798: a Study in Eighteenth Century Frontier Land Speculation and Business Venture* (Glendale, Cal., 1941).
LS	Letter signed.
Mag.	*Magazine*
Mass. Acts and Resolves	Abner C. Goodell *et al.*, eds., *The Acts and Resolves, Public and Private, of the Province of Massachusetts Bay*. . . (21 vols., Boston, 1869–1922).
Mass. Arch.	Massachusetts Archives, State House, Boston.
Mass. House Jour.	*A Journal of the Honourable House of Representatives of His Majesty's Province of the Massachusetts Bay* . . . (Boston, 1715[–75]). The title varies, and each session is designated by date. The Massachusetts Historical Society is republishing the volumes (Boston, 1919–) and has reached 1767; for later years we cite by session and date the original edition, which is most readily available in microprint in Clifford K. Shipton, ed., *Early American Imprints, 1639–1800.*
MS, MSS	Manuscript, manuscripts.

Namier and Brooke, *House of Commons*	Sir Lewis Namier and John Brooke, *The History of Parliament. The House of Commons 1754–1790* (3 vols., London and N.Y., 1964).
N.J. Arch.	William A. Whitehead *et al.*, eds., *Archives of the State of New Jersey* (2 series, Newark and elsewhere, 1880–). Editors, subtitles, and places of publication vary.
N.Y. Col. Docs.	E. B. O'Callaghan, ed., *Documents Relative to the Colonial History of the State of New York* (15 vols., Albany, 1853–87).
Pa. Arch.	Samuel Hazard *et al.*, eds., *Pennsylvania Archives* (9 series, Philadelphia and Harrisburg, 1852–1935).
Pa. Col. Recs.	*Minutes of the Provincial Council of Pennsylvania* ... (16 vols., Harrisburg, 1851–53). Volumes I–III are reprints published in Philadelphia, 1852. Title changes with Volume XI to *Supreme Executive Council*.
Phil. Trans.	The Royal Society, *Philosophical Transactions*.
PMHB	*Pennsylvania Magazine of History and Biography*.
Priestley, *History*	Joseph Priestley, *The History and Present State of Electricity, with Original Experiments* ... (3rd ed.; 2 vols., London, 1775).
Proc.	*Proceedings*.
Pub.	*Publications*.
Rev.	*Review*.
Sabine, *Loyalists*	Lorenzo Sabine, *Biographical Sketches of Loyalists of the American Revolution* ... (2 vols., Boston, 1864).
Schofield, *Scientific Autobiog.*	Robert E. Schofield, ed., *A Scientific Autobiography of Joseph Priestley* ... (Cambridge, Mass., and London, [1966]).
Sibley's Harvard Graduates	John L. Sibley, *Biographical Sketches of Graduates of Harvard University*

	(Cambridge, Mass., 1873–). Continued from Volume IV by Clifford K. Shipton.
Smyth, *Writings*	Albert H. Smyth, ed., *The Writings of Benjamin Franklin* ... (10 vols., N.Y., 1905–07).
Soc.	Society.
Sparks, *Works*	Jared Sparks, ed., *The Works of Benjamin Franklin* ... (10 vols., Boston, 1836–40).
Stevens, *Facsimiles*	Benjamin F. Stevens, ed., *Facsimiles of Manuscripts in European Archives Relating to America, 1773–1783* (25 vols., London, 1889–98).
Sutherland, *East India Co.*	Lucy S. Sutherland, *The East India Company in Eighteenth-Century Politics* (Oxford, 1952).
Trans.	Translator
Trans.	*Transactions.*
Van Doren, *Franklin*	Carl Van Doren, *Benjamin Franklin* (N.Y., 1938).
Van Doren, *Franklin—Mecom*	Carl Van Doren, ed., *The Letters of Benjamin Franklin & Jane Mecom* (American Philosophical Society *Memoirs*, XXVII, Princeton, 1950).
Votes, N.J.	*Votes and Proceedings of the General Assembly of the Province of New-Jersey* ... (New York, Woodbridge, etc., 1711–). A separate volume was published for each session and is so designated, e.g., *Votes, N.J.* (Oct.–Dec., 1771).
W&MQ	*William and Mary Quarterly*, first or third series as indicated.
WF	William Franklin.
Wroth and Zobel, *John Adams Legal Papers*	L. Kinvin Wroth and Hiller B. Zobel, eds., *Legal Papers of John Adams* (3 vols., Cambridge, Mass., 1965).
WTF	William Temple Franklin.
WTF, *Memoirs*	William Temple Franklin, ed., *Memoirs of the Life and Writings of Benjamin Franklin, LL.D., F.R.S., &c.* ... (3 vols., 4to, London, 1817–18).

Introduction

Franklin's activities in 1773 were as multifarious as ever. He badgered the new comptroller of the American post office to send intelligible accounts. The first substantial consignment of Pennsylvania silk arrived in London, and he took care of having it auctioned. He watched, with the detachment born of long experience, the hopes of the Walpole Company brighten for a time only to be dashed once more, this time by the crown's law officers. He attended Lord North's installation as chancellor of Oxford, and mingled with celebrities. Lord Le Despencer invited him to West Wycombe and enlisted his help in a serious if fruitless effort to revise, or emasculate, the Book of Common Prayer. Other concerns during the year ran the gamut from old type to new printing methods, from the torpedo fish to Parmesan cheese, and from a stove that Franklin was perfecting to a treatise that he intended to write, but never did, on the common cold. Most of this bustle had little effect on his future, but two developments did. One was the growing impact on him and his London world of the shock waves emanating from Boston. The other was the impact on Europe of his works translated into French.

The shock waves in 1773 were greater than ever before; it may be argued, in fact, that they marked the beginning of the American Revolution. When that year opened the Governor and the House of Representatives were at loggerheads as usual, but the fundamental issues that underlay their squabbling were not yet clearly visible; and the packet containing Hutchinson's and Oliver's correspondence with Whately, enclosed in Franklin's letter of December 2, 1772,[1] was still crossing the Atlantic. By Christmas, 1773, three things had happened in Massachusetts. First, the Governor's debate with his opponents in the House and Council had forced them to hammer out, on the anvil of his logic, their ideas of colonial rights against the mother country; and the debate had revealed in London as well as America the full depth

1. See above, XIX, 401–13; the letters that BF enclosed are printed in the appendix of this volume.

of the chasm between two concepts of what the constitution was. Second, the legislature had learned of the Hutchinson letters and promptly moved from theory to action—a petition from the House, backed by resolutions of the Council, to have the Governor and Lieutenant Governor removed from office. Third, the East India Company's tea was sloshing in Boston harbor. Unless one side or the other retreated on fundamental issues, as neither had shown any sign of doing, force was the only arbiter left.

This argument is based on hindsight, the historian's pretence to wisdom, and would have made little impression at the time. The most astute observers would not have agreed that the quarrel by the year's end was beyond peaceful settlement. Franklin, aware as he was that matters were going from bad to worse, still kept the hope expressed in one of his essays, " 'tis never too late to mend."[2] When he heard that the letters he had sent had been published in Boston despite his strict injunction, he took the development in stride. When he received the formal demand from the House for the removal of Hutchinson and Oliver, he handled it as if it were a routine petition in which he had had no part. He watched with interest, but no great excitement, the developing scheme to market the East India Company's tea: his expectation that the Tea Act would include repeal of the Townshend duty was disappointed, and he believed that the new statute reasserted the principle of taxation behind that duty;[3] but he apparently had no inkling that tea, as symbol, would prove to be even more explosive than stamps eight years before. The sharpest eye can miss the shadow of coming events.

Franklin seems to have been equally unaware that a crisis in his own life was brewing. It resulted in part from what happened in Boston, in part from the role that he took in London. His connection with the Hutchinson letters was the only secret about that business that the Bostonians both knew and kept; before the year was out, nevertheless, he divulged it himself. In December two men suspected of complicity in the affair fought an inconclusive duel, and rumor had it that they would fight again; to prevent further bloodshed Franklin publicly avowed that he

2. Below, Sept. 14.
3. See the headnote on BF to Cushing below, June 4.

alone was responsible for obtaining the letters.[4] The revelation that he was behind the furor in Boston, of which the petition was the outcome, was sure to provoke the ministry, and was only the latest in a series of provocations that ran through the year. In February he wrote a preface to the resolutions—which the Governor called a declaration of independence—that the Boston town meeting had passed the previous November, and in June published both as a pamphlet, thereby associating himself with the radical cause.[5] In September he attacked British colonial policy in his two most famous satires, "Rules by Which a Great Empire May Be Reduced to a Small One" and the "Edict by the King of Prussia."[6] He was almost as busy as the Bostonians in antagonizing Whitehall, and he seems to have been no more concerned than they were with the danger of reprisal.

Although in what he published during the year he was still attempting, at least on the surface, to induce a more conciliatory mood in the British public, under the surface his mood seems to have been stiffening as his constituents' was. The change can be seen in his thinking about sovereignty. He had long held that the British people, and Parliament as their representative, were not sovereign in America, but that the crown was; it alone held the empire together. He had questioned the practical ways in which the royal prerogative was exercised; now he carried the questioning a step further by asking how that prerogative applied to settlers' right in land. He drew conclusions that challenged, by implication, the basis of royal authority. Colonists who bought or conquered land from the Indians, he contended, acquired thereby an indefeasible title; they needed no confirmation by the king and owed no quitrents to him. As for their government, he added at one point, they had the choice of accepting that of the Indians or retaining that of the crown or forming their own. This was said in private.[7] But in public he advanced arguments about land that pointed, though he did not quite make the point, to the same political corollary, that royal authority existed in the

4. See the headnote on BF's letter to the press below, Dec. 25.
5. See the headnote on the preface below, end of February.
6. Below, Sept. 11 and 22 respectively.
7. See the headnote on BF to WF below, July 14.

colonies only insofar as the colonists chose to accept it.[8] His idea of the prerogative was evaporating, and without it where was his idea of empire?

He apparently did not confront the question. His political thought tended to move by fits and starts in response to events; if he scrutinized its underlying implications, he did not say so. To judge by what he did say, or more accurately by what has survived of the thoughts that he committed to paper, he was much less the theorist than the pragmatist. He met problems as they came, investigated them for such solutions as expediency might suggest, and left first principles alone; when he encountered one, such as the nature of sovereignty, he fought shy of analyzing it. His political thinking, if this is a fair characterization of it, contrasted markedly with his scientific thinking. In politics he was concerned with experience as a guide to what was feasible; in science he examined and re-examined the data of experience in order to build a theoretical structure.

His renown as a scientist was by now international. Learned foreigners visiting England came to see him, he had written in 1772, because his reputation was "still higher abroad than here."[9] This was particularly true in France, where he had received in that year the accolade of election to the Académie royale des sciences; but he was not resting on such laurels. "M. Franklin est dans son automne, et c'est la saison des fruits."[1] Part of the fruit was maturing in 1773, as he finished and started to see through the press the fifth—and what proved to be the final—edition of *Experiments and Observations*. Another part was gathered in the late summer, when the first comprehensive French translation of his works appeared. Its preparation had entailed a long dialogue by letter between him and his editor and disciple, Barbeu-Dubourg; and extracts from their correspondence were included in the *Œuvres de M. Franklin*. Whatever the effect of this handsome two-volume edition may have been on raising Dubourg's reputation, its effect on raising Franklin's was unquestionable. Only small snippets of what he had written in the

8. "On Claims to the Soil of America," below, March 16.
9. Above, XIX, 259.
1. Dubourg's comment below, p. 432.

past two decades had become available to the French-speaking intelligentsia of Europe. Now the whole man, shrewd, wide-ranging, and voracious in his curiosity, was there to be seen; and his stature commanded recognition. At the moment when his political position in England was being eroded, his place in the Enlightenment was becoming more secure.

Chronology of 1773

January 3: The *Gaspee* commission begins its inquiry in Rhode Island.

January 6: Governor Hutchinson's speech to the Massachusetts House and Council opens a two-month debate on constitutional issues.

January 25: The Massachusetts Council answers the Governor's speech.

January 26: The House answers the Governor's speech.

February 16: The Governor replies to these answers in separate speeches to the House and Council.

Late February: BF writes a preface to the declaration of the Boston town meeting of November, 1772; he has copies printed and sent to America, but does not publish the pamphlet in London until June.

February 25: The Massachusetts Council answers the Governor's second speech.

March 2: The House answers the Governor's second speech.

March 6: The Massachusetts House petitions against the crown's paying salaries of local officials. Hutchinson delivers a final speech and prorogues the General Court.

March 12: The Virginia House of Burgesses appoints the first intercolonial committee of correspondence; other colonies soon follow suit.

March 16: The *Public Advertiser* publishes BF's "On Claims to the Soil of America."

April 26: The House of Commons debates the Tea Act.

May 10: The Tea Act becomes law.

May 14: BF presents the petitions of the Massachusetts House of July 14, 1772, and March 6, 1773, against the crown's paying officials' salaries.

May 26: The General Court reconvenes in Boston.

May 31: BF's second legitimate grandchild, William Bache, is born in Philadelphia.

June 2: The Hutchinson letters are laid before the Massachusetts House.

June 15: The Hutchinson letters are laid before the Massachusetts Council.

June 16: The House resolves that the letters were intended to subvert the constitution, and appoints a committee to draft a petition to the crown for Hutchinson's and Oliver's removal.

June 23: The House adopts the petition for removal.

June 25: The Council takes a position similar to that of the House on June 16, but does not join in the petition.

June 29: A joint committee of the Massachusetts House and Council writes a letter to Lord Dartmouth urging a return to the status quo of 1763. The General Court is prorogued.

July 7: BF is at Oxford for the installation of Lord North as chancellor of the University.

July 15: BF sends DF and Sally Bache cloth woven from Pennsylvania silk.

August 3: BF is at West Wycombe, where he and Lord Le Despencer complete their abridgment of the Book of Common Prayer.

August 20: BF and William Bollan forward to Lord Dartmouth the letter from the Massachusetts House and Council.

August 21: BF forwards to Lord Dartmouth the petition from the Massachusetts House for the removal of Hutchinson and Oliver.

September 8: The *Public Advertiser* publishes BF's "An Infallible Method to Restore Peace and Harmony."

September 11: The *Public Advertiser* publishes BF's "Rules by Which a Great Empire May Be Reduced to a Small One."

September 14: BF goes to Purfleet with the rest of the Royal Society's committee to inspect the completed system for protecting the powder magazines with lightning rods.

September 22: The *Public Advertiser* publishes BF's "Edict by the King of Prussia."

September 25: BF is again at West Wycombe.

Ca. October 15: BF experiments off Spithead with calming the waters with oil.

November 18: The Purfleet committee reports to the Royal Society its approval of the lightning rods installed to protect the magazines.

November 28: The *Dartmouth*, the first of three tea ships, arrives in Boston harbor.

December 11: John Temple and William Whately fight a duel.

December 16: The Boston Tea Party.

December 25: The *London Chronicle* publishes BF's avowal of his role in obtaining the Hutchinson letters.

THE PAPERS OF
BENJAMIN FRANKLIN

VOLUME 20

January 1 through December 31, 1773

A Committee of the Managers of the Pennsylvania Hospital to Franklin, David Barclay, and John Fothergill

Minutebook copy: Pennsylvania Hospital, Philadelphia

Esteemed Friends   Pennsylvania Hospital, 1 mo. 1st. 1773

We are now deputed by a Board of Managers of this Hospital to inform you, That it is agreed to draw on you for the further Sum of Four thousand pounds Sterling as Opportunities offer to dispose of our drafts,[1] and to put out the money on Interest on good and Sufficient Securities, which from our present prospect we expect will be Effected in a short time.

You will therefore be pleased to provide for the discharge of these drafts by selling out of the Stocks with the necessary Caution, a sufficient Sum for this purpose.

We have heretofore regularly advised you the particulars of our former drafts, and purpose to continue the like care in respect to the Bills intended to be drawn. We are Respectfully Your Obliged Friends

JOHN REYNELL
ISRAEL PEMBERTON
JAMES PEMBERTON

To Docr. John Fothergill Benjamin Franklin and David Barclay in London

The Managers of the Pennsylvania Hospital to Franklin, David Barclay, and John Fothergill

Minutebook copy: Pennsylvania Hospital, Philadelphia

⟨January 4, 1773: In accordance with the letter of Jan. 1 from their committee, they have drawn on the recipients for £700

---

1. For the Managers' earlier drafts on the funds that the Hospital had acquired from the defunct Pennsylvania Land Company see above, XIX, 145, 339–40, 366. The Board had recently decided to make the further withdrawal discussed here, provided that its bills could be sold at an exchange rate of 65%: Pa. Hospital minutebook, Dec. 28, 1772. For John Reynell see above, IX, 372 n, and for the Pemberton brothers the *DAB*.

sterling in four bills of exchange in favor of John Clark, three for £200 each and one for £100.[2]⟩

From Richard Bache   ALS: American Philosophical Society

Dear and Honoured Sir   Philadelphia Janry 4. 1773.

By the October Packet, I am favored by yours of 7. that Month,[3] am obliged to you for the pleasing Intelligence, that my Mother and Sisters were well, for it is some time since I heard from them. I am glad to hear, that the Bill I sent you was duly honored. I had really forgot the five Guineas you lent me, on the Morning I left you, or should have included them in the Bill. They shall be applied as you direct. My Note I received, inclosed in your Letter to my Mother[4] by the Novr. Packet.

I had the Pleasure when in Jamaica, of being acquainted with several Gentlemen, who had a smattering of Electricity, and were great Admirers of your Publication on that, and other Philosophical Subjects; but I never heard any such Report as you mention, of any Building being struck by Lightening, which had two Conductors, or any Conductor, tho' such a thing might have happened in a remote part of the Island, and I never hear of it. Mr. Ross of this Place was told some years ago by Captain Oswald Eve, whom I believe you know; and who has been in Jamaica, that such an Accident as you describe happened there, and Mr. Ross gave such credit to the Story, as to induce him to take down the Rod which he had put up at the Gavel End of his new House in Chestnut Street, because Mr. Lawrence had put up one at the end of his House, which is adjoining Mr. Ross', and indeed both Houses may be said to be under one Roof.[5] By

2. The Board was continuing its earlier policy of investing in mortgages; Clark had obtained one for £1,137 10s., Pennsylvania currency, on his plantation in Bucks County. The bills of exchange were at 62½%. Pa. Hospital minutebook, Jan. 4, 1773.

3. Above, XIX, 314–16. The matters discussed in this letter are, unless otherwise indicated, covered there.

4. The references here and hereafter, unlike the previous "my Mother," are to DF.

5. Ross was presumably John Ross, the prominent Philadelphia lawyer and friend of BF, for whom see above, XI, 531 n. Oswald or Oswell Eve was

4

first Opportunity, I shall write to my Friend Mr. Grant of Kingston, who is a sensible, intelligent Man, and desire him to inquire and let me know, if any such Accident ever happened in Jamaica, and to give me the particulars you require.

I am afraid I shall be obliged to sue Shuts' Estate for the Amount of your Note, as the Executors seem little disposed to liquidate it. Armbruster hath never paid any thing, nor is it likely that he ever will pay any thing, he has been in Jail, and is an idle, drunken good for nothing Fellow; The Types he had were distrained for Rent, and by my Mother replevied, in Consequence of which she was obliged to pay £35. to get possession of the Types, and it is a Doubt with me whether they are worth this Sum. Mr. Maugridge's Mortgage has been paid off, my Mother tells me some time ago, this is all I know of it.[6] I am afraid that the Insurance on your two Houses in Market Street, in front of us, expired some time ago, and hath not been renewed, if I find this to be the Case (which the Policies will declare, when my Mother finds them) I shall meet the Directors, and endeavor to get the Policies renewed, without forfeiture of premium, which I find is a penalty annexed to the failure of renewing them within a year after they expire.[7] I am glad your Bankers stood their Ground—I imagined you could not otherways be affected by the late Failures.

---

a Philadelphia merchant and sea captain, who fell on hard times and moved to the Caribbean in 1768; he returned temporarily in 1774, then took his family to the Bahamas. *DAB* under Joseph Eve; *PMHB*, v (1881), 19–20, 205. The story he told seemed to corroborate one that BF had heard in London and forwarded in the letter to which Bache is replying, but that turned out to be erroneous. Ross's neighbor, we assume, was Thomas Lawrence II, a civic-minded Philadelphia merchant, for whom see above, VI, 385, and Charles P. Keith, *The Provincial Councillors of Pennsylvania . . .* (Philadelphia, 1883), p. 433 of second pagination.

6. We do not know when Shütz died, but Bache had been working on his debt to BF since the previous spring: above, XIX, 144. For Anthony Armbrüster's debt see X, 289 n; XII, 342–5; XIX, 315; and for Maugridge's *ibid.*, pp. 315, 395.

7. The two houses "in front of us" must have been two of the three on Market Street that BF owned and rented; see the map above, XII, 285. We can only assume that he insured this property, as he certainly did his own house (XIII, 379–80), and that DF first forgot to keep up the policies and then forgot where she had put them.

I suppose my Mother, who writes you by this Conveyance, acquaints you of Mr. Hall's Death, he was a good Man and dies much lamented.[8] I hope we shall soon hear of the Completion of the Ohio Grant, numbers of People seem eager to become Setlers in that part, and many more Purchasers as they think it will be providing at least for Posterity.[9]

Sally and Ben join me in Love and Duty, and in wishing you and your new Neighbours in Craven Street the return of many happy Years. I have the Honor to subscribe myself Dear Sir Your Affectionate Son RICHD: BACHE[1]

From Thomas O'Gorman[2] ALS: American Philosophical Society

Sir   Paris 4th January 1773

I beg pardon for having been hitherto defficient in acquiting myself of my duty towards you and in returning you thanks for the many Civilities I have received from you While in London. Receive, I beseech you, tho late, my sincere acknowledgement thereon and be assur'd I shall for ever with pleasure embrace every opportunity of Shewing you the defference I have for the honour of your friendship. I profit of the departure of a friend for your City to Carry you this letter and I woud have Wrote to you before now, had I not been totally obsorbed these three Months past in preparing my eldest Son for his reception as page to the King and in tending my two other boys in the small pox, of which they have had, thank god, a looky riddance.

I Can with pleasure tell you that I have had a good ventage this Season and that I am able to Send choice Burgundy to my friends in London. I have mark'd before my departure from home a Hogshead of the right Sort for you, and shall have the pleasure to Send it you in March next. It gives me equal pleasure to hear

8. David Hall had died on Christmas Eve.

9. Bache was not directly involved in the Walpole grant, as far as we know, but was keenly interested in its progress; see his letter above, xix, 363–4. Some land in the tract had already been put on the market in anticipation of the grant (*ibid.*, p. 322 n), and would-be purchasers were clamoring for more.

1. Under the signature are unintelligible calculations, not BF's, about calendar dates.

2. For the Irish émigré and Burgundian wine-maker see Huske's letter to BF above, xix, 86 n.

that you and your friends have Succeeded to your wishes in your grand plan.[3] I wish you heartily great joy on it. I am Sure that in the hands of Such Spirited and opulent men it will become a mighty matter. Our friend Mr. Huske is laid up in the gout. He expects Soon to finish his affairs in this Country and to be able to embrace you in London. He desires in the mean time to be Most Kindly remembered to you. I shall be always glad to hear from you and to Cultivate the honour of your acquaintance and friendship. If any Commands you may have on this Side, pray dont Spare me. I have the honour to be with great defference Sir your most obedient and humble Servant   O'GORMAN

P.S. You'l please to direct to me at Tonnerre in Burgundy where I entend to go in a few days. You may hint to me with Caution and in a neutral manner What may be the thoughts of your friends upon what you and I have talked of.[4]

Addressed: Doctor Franklin at / Mrs. Stevenson's in Craven / Street—Strand / London

To Thomas Cushing

ALS and copy: Public Record Office; letterbook draft: Library of Congress

Sir,   London, Jan. 5. 1773
    I did myself the Honour of Writing to you on the 2d of December past inclosing some news papers to 30th november last[5]

3. A reference to the government's favorable action the previous August on the Walpole Company's grant (above, XIX, 244 n), a success that turned out to be transient.

4. They had discussed O'Gorman's scheme for wine-making in America. The Irishman had originally hoped for a large government subsidy; BF had discouraged that idea, but had suggested that something might be done on the land that the Walpole Company hoped to obtain. See Huske's letter just cited and BF's reply (*ibid.*, pp. 294–5). In talking with O'Gorman in London BF had apparently promised to sound out friends in the Company.

5. In the ALS "news papers to 30th november last" is in another hand and replaces words erased, which in BF's draft were "original Letters from Persons in Boston." Cushing was presumably responsible for the alteration, before he circulated this letter, to conceal BF's having sent the Hutchinson correspondence with his earlier letter of Dec. 2. See above, XIX, 403, 411.

which I hope got safe to hand. I have since received your Favour of Oct. 27. which containing in a small Compass so full an Enumeration of our Grievances, the Steps necessary to a Removal of them, and the happy Effects that must follow, I thought that tho' a private Letter,[6] it might be of Use to communicate it to Lord Dartmouth, the rather too, as he would there find himself occasionally mentioned with proper Respect, and learn that his Character was esteemed in the Colonies. Accordingly I wrote him a few Lines and enclos'd it,[7] a Day or two before I was to wait on his Lordship, that he might have a little time to consider the Contents. When I next attended him, he return'd me the Letter with much Complacence in his Countenance, said he was glad to find that People in America were dispos'd to think so favourably of him; that they did him but Justice in believing he had the best Dispositions towards them, for he wish'd sincerely their Welfare, tho' possibly he might not always think with them as to the means of obtaining that End. That the Heads of Complaint in your Letter were many, some of them requiring much Consideration, and therefore it could scarce be expected that a sudden Change should be made in so many Measures, supposing them all improper to be continued, which perhaps might not be the case. It was however his Opinion that if the Americans continued quiet, and gave no fresh Offence to Government, those Measures would be reconsidered and such Relief given as upon Consideration should be thought reasonable. I need not remark that there is not much in such general Discourse; but I could then obtain nothing more particular, except that his Lordship express'd in direct Terms his Disapprobation of the Instruction for exempting the Commissioners from Taxation; which, however, was, he said, in Confidence to me, relying that no publick Mention should be made of his Opinion on that head.[8]

6. Instead of "a private Letter" the draft reads "mark'd *private.*" The letter itself is missing, but the grievances must have had to do with the crown's paying the salaries of local officials. See the headnote on BF's preface to the declaration of the Boston town meeting below, under the end of February.

7. Above, XIX, 422–3.

8. The issue of taxing the customs commissioners' salaries had begun in 1768, and remained alive into the summer of 1773. See above, XVIII, 177–8;

In the meantime some Circumstances are working in our favour with regard to the Duties. It is found by the last Years Accounts transmitted by the Commissioners, that the Ballance in favour of Britain is but about £85 after Payment of Salaries, &c. exclusive of the Charge of a Fleet to enforce the Collection. Then it is observ'd that the India Company is so out of Cash, that it cannot pay the Bills drawn upon it, and its other Debts; and at the same time so out of Credit, that the Bank does not care to assist them, whence they find themselves obliged to lower their Dividend; the Apprehension of which has sunk their Stock from 280 to 160, whereby several Millions of Propery are annihilated, occasioning private Bankrupcies and other Distress, besides a Loss to the Publick Treasury of £400,000 per Annum which the Company by Agreement are not to pay into it as heretofore, if they are not able to keep up their Dividend at $12\frac{1}{2}$. And as they have at the same time Tea and other India Goods in their Warehouses to the Amount of Four Millions as some say, for which they want a Market, and which if it had been sold would have kept up their Credit, I take the Opportunity of remarking in all Companies, the great Imprudence of losing the American Market, by keeping up the Duty on Tea, which has thrown that Trade into the Hands of the Dutch, Danes, Swedes and French, who (according to the Reports and Letters of some Custom-House Officers in America) now supply by Smuggling the whole Continent, not with Tea only, but accompany that Article with other India Goods, amounting as suppos'd in the whole to £500,000 Sterling per Annum. This gives some Alarm, and begins to convince People more and more, of the Impropriety of Quarrelling with the Americans, who at that Rate might have taken off two Millions and a Half of those Goods

---

below, Cushing to BF, April 20, and BF's reply, July 7. This conversation with Dartmouth raises the fascinating question of what would have happened if the Americans had remained quiet. The administration, or at least the new Secretary, was reviewing American policy and considering more conciliatory measures; but developments in Massachusetts soon rendered such a course politically impossible. See Hutchinson, *History*, III, 276–7, and the second paragraph of BF to Cushing below, May 6.

within these 5 Years that the Combination has subsisted, if the Duty had not been laid, or had been speedily repealed.[9]

But our great Security lies, I think, in our growing Strength both in Wealth and Numbers, that creates an increasing Ability of Assisting this Nation in its Wars, which will make us more respectable, our Friendship more valued, and our Enmity feared; thence it will soon be thought proper to treat us, not with Justice only, but with Kindness; and thence we may expect in a few Years a total Change of Measures with regard to us; unless by a Neglect of military Discipline we should lose all our martial Spirit, and our western People become as tame as those in the eastern Dominions of Britain, when we may expect the same Oppressions:[1] For there is much Truth in the Italian Saying, *Make yourselves Sheep and the Wolves will eat you.*[2] In confidence of this coming Change in our favour, I think our Prudence is mean while to be quiet, only holding up our Rights and Claims on all Occasions, in Resolutions, Memorials, and Remonstrances, but bearing patiently the little present Notice that is taken of them. They will all have their Weight in Time, and that Time is at no great Distance. With the greatest Esteem,

9. In this paragraph BF is making substantially the same points that he had made a month earlier to Galloway: above, XIX, 419–20. He is greatly exaggerating the decline of the American tea market as a cause of the Company's troubles; a contributor to the *London Chron.* of Jan. 19–21 advanced the same argument, in such similar terms that it may have been part of BF's campaign. The government soon decided, as will appear later in this volume, that the situation could be remedied by reducing the price of tea while retaining the duty; and the remedy proved to be worse than the disease.

1. BF had once regarded the rising population and military potential of the colonies as a source of greater and greater strength to the empire, and had satirized the argument that such growth would endanger the mother country. See above, IV, 233; IX, 78–9; XIV, 131. Recently his position had been shifting closer to that which he had ridiculed; he was coming to believe that America would soon have the power to coerce Britain if need be. See also above, XVII, 7; XVIII, 27, 123. He clearly thought, along with many Englishmen, that India was powerless because its armies, in battles such as Plassey, had proved completely ineffectual.

2. This Italian proverb first appeared in English, as far as we know, in John Florio, *Florio's Second Frutes* . . . (London, 1591), p. 21.

I have the Honour to be, Sir, Your most obedient and most humble Servant   B FRANKLIN

Honble Thomas Cushing, Esqr

Endorsed: Dr Franklin   Jany 5   1773[3]

From William Franklin   ALS: American Philosophical Society

Honoured Father,   Burlington Janry. 5, 1773

   I am favoured with your Letters by the *October* and *November* Packets,[4] and want much for an Opportunity of writing to you *safely* on several Subjects, but I cannot venture to do it by the Packet, as your Letter by the *October* Packet came opened to me exactly in the same Manner that mine did to you. And Mr. Todd I hear has wrote to Mr. Foxcroft that his Letters [to] him by the New York Packet were broke open and new seal'd. This makes me now suspect that the Villainy is committed by some Person on this Side the Water;[5] though as Mr. W. told you he had seen all the same Accounts before (relative to the Virginia Claims) and did not chuse to let you read[6] those you received from me, I confess I suspected it was owing to his having had a Sight of my Letters to you, otherwise I think he would out of mere Curiosity have liked to have seen whether I wrote the same Sentiments as Mr. Foxcroft had done. I think the best way is to have the Direction of our Letters by the Packet wrote in a different Hand,

   3. The ALS was seized by the British in 1775, along with other letters to Cushing, and passed through the hands of Thomas Moffatt. The Loyalist appended his comment: "This opens with a Conference between the Earl of Dartmouth and him concluding with a malignant Instigating Depretiation of Great Britain compard with the Rising Power of America."
   4. Above, XIX, 321–3, 360–1.
   5. WF was echoing what he had written before (*ibid.*, p. 333), except that he was now persuaded by Foxcroft's experience that the interception was taking place in America; the Deputy Postmaster General's correspondence with the secretary of the Post Office, WF must have assumed, would be safe from tampering in England.
   6. "To him," we believe, should be inserted here; BF proposed to read documents aloud to Wharton as he did later (below, pp. 60–1). WF had previously discussed his father's conversation with Wharton: above, XIX, 349–51.

and sealed with a different Seal. If mine to you in that Way come safe do let me know. And if each Sheet is sealed it may be better.

I am glad to find that Lord D. has spoke so favourably of me, and am much obliged to you for mentioning me to him in the Manner you have done.[7] I have wrote to him by this Opportunity in favour of Mr. Skinner the Attorney General who requests an Augmentation of his Salary, and have taken Occasion to say a Word or two in my own Behalf. If you have an Opportunity of promoting our Application with his Lordship, Mr. Cooper, or any of our Friends I must beg you will do it.[8]

Enclosed is a Copy of a Letter I have just received from Lord Stirling[9] now in Virginia, who I requested to enquire particularly into the Virginia Claim.

I can only add that Betsy joins me in Duty and the Compliments of the Season. I am, in the greatest Haste Honoured Sir Your ever dutiful Son   WM: FRANKLIN

Addressed: To / Doctor Franklin / Craven Street / London / per Packet

From the Trustees of the Burlington Free School

LS: American Philosophical Society

Respected Friend   Burlington (January) 1st mo: 5th 1773

To a person of Doctor Franklins well known character, for humanity and benevolence, we think it scarcely necessary to enter into an apology for the freedom we have taken in enclosing

7. *Ibid.*, p. 360.

8. Cortlandt Skinner (above, XIII, 335 n) had recently been chosen again as speaker of the Assembly: 1 *N.J. Arch.*, XVIII, 298; his memorial to Dartmouth and WF's covering letter are in *idem.*, X, 383–5, 389–93. Grey Cooper was secretary of the Treasury. BF refused to have anything to do with his son's request for a raise: to WF below, April 6.

9. William Alexander, alias Lord Stirling, was an old acquaintance of BF: above, XIX, 191–2. The copy that WF enclosed, dated Dec. 5, 1772, is in the APS; Stirling discussed the western boundary of Virginia and concluded that "there will be no Room for Contention between this Colony and the New Colony." WF was not reassured. He had long been concerned about the Virginia grants, and continued to be. See above, XIX, 3–4, 334–5, 349–52, and to BF below, April 30.

the within Petition to the King, in presenting which we request thy friendly assistance.

Notwithstanding the *application* made by Lord Rochford for a *Grant of the Islands in Delaware* was thrown aside, at some future day, one similar may be revived. We therefore thought it a duty incumbent on us, as Guardians of an infant charitable seminary, to address the Throne for a confirmation of our Right; and no time we thought more favourable than the present, when the *application* abovementioned, may be supposed, very justly, to have alarmed us.[1]

The rents of the Island for about 26 years to come, will annually educate 25 poor children, and for 20 years then next succeeding

1. In 1682 the West Jersey Assembly had granted Burlington (alias Matinecunck or Stacy's) Island in the Delaware to the town of Burlington for the maintenance of a school. By 1767 the island was sufficiently settled so that revenue from its lands was appropriated for the tuition of some orphaned and indigent scholars, and eventually for the education of all the poor children of the town. I *N.J. Arch.*, X, 515–17; Evan M. Woodward and John F. Hageman, *History of Burlington and Mercer Counties* (Philadelphia, 1883), pp. 143–4; Nelson R. Burr, *Education in New Jersey* ... (Princeton, 1942), p. 56. But Burlington's title to the land was nonexistent: half a century earlier the King's law officers had decided that the riverine islands were crown property, not part of either Pennsylvania or New Jersey. At that time the Board of Trade had suggested that Burlington Island be transferred to New Jersey and granted to the town, but apparently nothing had come of the idea; and Lord Rochford's recent attempt to secure the islands for himself, even though unsuccessful, had brought to the fore the long dormant question of title. *Acts Privy Coun., Col.*, VI, 134; above, XIX, 276 n.

The petition that the trustees sent to BF went no farther; it is among his papers in the APS. It pointed out that the revenue from the island sufficed for twenty-five scholars, declared that the possibility of the land's being granted elsewhere alarmed the trustees "in behalf of the poor infant communicants," and begged the crown to confirm the original grant by the Assembly. BF's reason for not forwarding the petition can readily be conjectured. The whole method of granting crown land was under review at the time, and new rules were being promulgated; see A. Berriedale Keith, *Constitutional History of the First British Empire* (Oxford, 1930), pp. 321–2. In the previous August BF had advised Galloway to enter a caveat against any grant's being made in the islands before the property-holders had been heard: above, XIX, 277. He may well have advised the Burlington trustees, in a letter now missing, to do the same. If so they eventually took his advice, for their caveat came before the Board of Trade in November, 1775. *Board of Trade Jour.*, 1768–75, p. 451.

13

30 poor children; being lett out on a lease of 50 years, 4 of which are expired. But here a difficulty arises, our funds are wholly appropriated to this purpose, and if any considerable expence is likely to accrue in obtaining a confirmation of our Title, we have no way of defraying it, but by withdrawing the Scholars, till the rents make up the sum; as this would be an irreparable loss to a number of poor boys and girls, we would willingly hope some method may be fallen on to obviate any heavy expence, and we beleive no person would be more ready to devise, or more willing to execute, a plan suitable to the scanty state of our finances, than our worthy Agent. We therefore also beg a kind attention to this important point, and be pleased to inform us what may be likely to be the attendant charges. We humbly conceive that an *Instruction to the Governour to grant a Pattent* (as in New York and other Royal Governments) might answer every purpose,[2] and be attended with little or no expence, flattering ourselves that the pattenting Officers would generously give up their fees to so charitable a use.

As we serve entirely without pay, and have no private interest to promote, by this application, but only to procure some useful learning to those who might otherwise be destitute of it, we hope our desires of avoiding expence, wont be thought little or unreasonable. We remain with great respect on behalf of the Trust, Thy Friends[3]

> JOHN HOSKINS   SAML HOW
> ABRM. HEWLINGS   ELLIS WRIGHT
> RICHARD WELLS   SAML: ALLINSON

Doctor Benjamin Franklin

Endorsed: Letter from Trustees of Burlington School, concerning the Island.

2. Governors of royal provinces were normally authorized, with consent of their councils, to grant crown land by patent; but the trustees presumably wished to strengthen their shaky title by obtaining a royal command to WF to make the grant. Why they expected the crown to oblige, when the island had long since been declared to be outside the jurisdiction of New Jersey, we do not venture to guess.

3. The signers were for the most part Quakers. John Hoskins (1727?–1814) was prominent in the Burlington Society of Friends. Abraham

To Alexander Colden   ALS (letterbook draft): Library of Congress

⟨London, January 6, 1773. Returns two protested bills, Zeph-
[aniah] Turner on Barnes & Ridgate for £72 7s. 5d. and William
Taylor on Perkins, Buchanan & Brown for £15;[4] the charges
on each are 5s. 9d. Asks to have the bills acknowledged and to be
credited with £87 18s. 11d.⟩

To a Committee of the Managers of the Philadelphia
Silk Filature   ALS (letterbook draft): Library of Congress

⟨London, January 6, 1773. Has paid Mr. Wheeler twenty guineas,
pursuant to the instructions of November 16, and encloses
his receipt.[5]⟩

To Deborah Franklin

ALS: American Philosophical Society; letterbook draft: Library of
Congress

My dear Child,   London, Jan. 6. 1773.

I feel still some Regard for this Sixth of January, as my old
nominal Birth-day, tho' the Change of Stile has carried the real

---

Hewlings (d. 1785) had been a member of the New Jersey Assembly Committee of Correspondence: above, XVI, 256. Richard Wells (d. 1801) was an
English-born merchant who lived for several years in Burlington and then
moved to Philadelphia, where he subsequently served in the Assembly and
was secretary of the APS and a director of the Library Company. Samuel
Allinson (d. 1791) was a lawyer and former clerk of the Burlington corpo-
ration, who was commissioned in 1773 to prepare a new edition of the laws of
New Jersey; he and Hoskins were trustees of the Friends' Burial Ground in
Burlington. All we know about Samuel How is that he was at the time a
well-to-do landowner in the town; about Ellis Wright we know virtually
nothing. For these scraps of information see the following sources: Hinshaw,
Amer. Quaker Geneal., II, 177; *PMHB*, XVI (1892), 251; XXIV (1900), 57,
153; LXVI (1942), 417–18; *Geneal. Mag. of N.J.*, XIX (1944), 32–3; XXXVI
(1961), 51; Charles P. Keith, *The Provincial Councillors of Pennsylvania*
(Philadelphia, 1883), p. 33 of first pagination; George De Cou, *Burlington: a
Provincial Capital . . .* (Philadelphia, [1945]), pp. 46, 115.
    4. See above, XIX, 398.
    5. Richard Wheeler had been the agent for Evans and James in their land
purchase the year before; see above, XIX, 97–9, 168–9, 413, 421.

15

Day forward to the 17th, when I shall be, if I live till then, 67 Years of Age. It seems but t'other Day since you and I were rank'd among the Boys and Girls, so swiftly does Time fly! We have however great Reason to be thankful that so much of our Lives has pass'd so happily; and that so great a Share of Health and Strength remains, as to render Life yet comfortable.

I received your kind Letter of Nov. 16. by Sutton. The Apples are not yet come on shore, but I thank you for them. Capt. All was so good as to send me a Barrel of excellent ones, which serve me in the meantime.[6] I rejoice to hear that you all continue well. But you have so us'd me to have something pretty about the Boy, that I am a little disappointed in finding nothing more of him than that he is gone up to Burlington.[7] Pray give in your next as usual, a little of his History.

All our Friends here are pleas'd with your remembring them, and send their Love to you. Give mine to all that enquire concerning me, and a good deal to our Children. I am ever, my dear Debby, Your affectionate Husband   B FRANKLIN

To Joseph Galloway   ALS (letterbook draft): Library of Congress

Dear Friend,   London, Jan. 6. 1773

I have received your Favours of Oct. 18 and 30. I am oblig'd greatly to you and Mr. Rhoads for your friendly Interposition in the Affair of my Salary.[8] As I made never any Bargain with the House, I accept thankfully whatever they please to give me; and shall continue to serve them as long as I can afford to stay here: Perhaps it may be thought, that my other Agencies contribute more than sufficient for that purpose; but the Jersey Allowance tho' well-paid is a very small one; that from Georgia, £100 only, is some Years in Arrear; and will not be continued, as the

6. See BF's next letter to DF below, Feb. 2.

7. See above, XIX, 373. DF could scarcely have produced "something pretty" about the Kingbird in his absence; her tidbits were drawn from her own observation of the child.

8. Neither of Galloway's letters has survived to throw light on the mysterious business of BF's salary, for which see above, XIX, 338–9. Samuel Rhoads, re-elected to the Assembly in 1770, had been put on its committee of correspondence.

Appointment is by a Yearly Act, which I am told the Governor will not again pass with my Name in it.[9] And from Boston I have never receiv'd a Farthing, perhaps never shall, as their Governor is instructed to pass no Salary to an Agent whose Appointment he has not assented to.[1] In these Circumstances, with an almost double Expence of Living by my Family remaining in Philadelphia, the Losses I am continually suffering in my Affairs there through Absence, together with my now advanced Age, I feel renewed Inclinations to return,[2] and spend the remainder of my Days in private Life; having had rather more than my Share of publick Bustle. I only wish first to improve a little for the general Advantage of our Country, the favourable Appearances arising from the Change of our American Minister, and the good Light I am told I stand in with the Successor.[3] If I [can] be instrumental in [torn] Things in good train, with a Prospect of their [being?] on a better Footing than they have had for some Years past I shall think a little additional Time well spent, tho' I were to have no Allowance for it at all.

I must however beg you will not think of retiring from Publick Business.[4] You are yet a young Man, and may still be greatly serviceable to your Country. It would be I think something criminal, to bury in private Retirement so early, all the usefulness of so much Experience and such great Abilities. The People do not indeed always see their Friends in the same favourable Light; they are sometimes mistaken, and sometimes misled; but sooner

9. BF had received no salary from Georgia since 1770, but had continued to serve as agent and to charge the province for expenses incurred in transacting its business. Attempts in 1773 to reappoint him failed, if we read the evidence aright, because of Governor Wright's opposition. See below, the headnote on the letter to BF from the Commons House committee of correspondence, March 14, 1774, and his accounts with the province, May 2, 1774. Wright had been in England on leave in 1772, and had doubtless expressed his views to BF or some mutual acquaintance.

1. See above, XIX, 209–10 n.

2. BF here deleted "which I believe I shall execute the ensuing Summer, and hope the Assembly will not take it amiss."

3. Lord Dartmouth, who had succeeded Hillsborough the previous August.

4. In the aftermath of the election of 1772, which had been disastrous for him: above, XIX, 331 n.

or later they come right again, and redouble their former Affection. This I am confident will happen in your Case, as it often has in the Case of others. Therefore preserve your Spirits and persevere, at least to the Age of 60, a Boundary I once fix'd for my self, but have gone beyond it.

I am afraid the Bill, Wilcocks on Col. Alexander Johnstone for £166 15s. 3½d. must be return'd with a Protest.[5] I shall know in a Day or two.

I shall consult Mr. Jackson, and do in the Island Affair, what shall be thought best for securing your Interest and that of all concerned.[6]

By our Spring Ships I shall write you more fully. At present I can only add that I am, with unalterable Esteem and Affection, Yours most sincerely   B FRANKLIN

Jos. Galloway Esqr

To the Pennsylvania Assembly Committee of Correspondence.   ALS (letterbook draft): Library of Congress

Gentlemen,   London, Jan. 6. 1773

I have received your respected Favour of Oct. 16. with the enclos'd Resolve of the House appointing you the Committee of Correspondence for the current Year.[7] And you may rely on my faithful Observance of the Instructions transmitted to me by you, in opposing strenuously every thing that I apprehend may prejudice the Commerce or Rights of America, and promoting

5. See *idem.*, p. 418 n, and BF to Galloway below, Feb. 14.

6. Lord Rochford's attempt to secure title to islands in the Delaware had stirred up a controversy over their status. In the previous summer BF had argued to Galloway that the settlers were the rightful owners; and Richard Jackson, counsel to the Board of Trade, seems to have taken a similar position. Above, XIX, 276–7. Galloway must have continued the discussion in one of his missing letters, of Oct. 18 or 30. He may even have suggested a plan, to which BF is responding here, for confirming the rights of the inhabitants. For the conflicting claim of the Trustees of the Burlington Free School see their letter to BF above, Jan. 5.

7. The enclosure is not extant; for the letter and the members of the committee see above, XIX, 338–9.

by every means in my Power what may seem likely to restore that Harmony between Great Britain and her Colonies so necessary, as you justly observe, to their mutual Safety and Happiness.

Inclos'd is a List of thirty of your Acts, which were presented the 22d of December past. It becomes more important of late, to keep an exact Note of the Time of Presentment, as the Six Months is more frequently than heretofore suffered to expire without any Determination upon the Acts presented.[8] I shall attend them diligently while they are under Consideration, and use my best Endeavours in supporting them.

Be pleased to make my thankful Acknowledgements to the Assembly for the Allowance you mention,[9] and believe me to be, with sincere Esteem and Respect Gentlemen, Your most obedient humble Servant   B FRANKLIN

Jos Galloway, Saml Rhoads, Saml Shoemaker Wm Rodman, and Isaac Pearson Esqrs.

From Alexander Colden   ALS: American Philosophical Society

⟨General Post Office, January 7, 1773: Has received Franklin's letter of October 7 acknowledging receipt of several bills, and of Nov. 3 enclosing Mackie's bill on Molleson for £294 5s. 2d.[1] with the protest, which Colden will transmit to him. Encloses the second bill for £150 sterling by John Hancock on Haley & Hopkins in favor of Tuthill Hubbart;[2] the first was sent on Dec.

8. The thirty acts, passed in March and September, 1772, were referred to the Board of Trade on Jan. 15, 1773; in April the Privy Council allowed all but two. 8 *Pa. Arch.*, VIII, 7028–31; *Board of Trade Jour.*, 1768–75, pp. 334, 344, 347; *Acts Privy Coun., Col.*, V, 365–8. See also BF to Galloway below, Feb. 14, March 15. The Pennsylvania charter stipulated that all provincial laws became valid if the crown did not act upon them within six months, and legal opinion held that that period began when the laws were first presented to the Privy Council. George Chalmers, *Opinions of Eminent Lawyers . . .* (2 vols., London, 1814), I, 348–9.
9. A graceful way of acknowledging the cut in his salary, for which see above, XIX, 339 n.
1. BF's letters are above, XIX, 318, 359.
2. George Hayley (1723–81), the London merchant, alderman, and subsequently M.P., had been John Hancock's agent since 1767; his wife was the

2 by the *Halifax*, packet. Encloses a first bill for £100 sterling by Archibald Ritchie on Hyndman, Lancaster & Co. in favor of Joseph Williamson, postmaster at Hobbs Hole.[3] Will send by the next packet the printed advertisement about Mrs. Elizabeth Holland and an account of what he has done about it.[4]⟩

From Jane (Jenny) Mecom[5]   ALS: American Philosophical Society

My dear and Honourd Uncle   Boston Janry[6] the 9 1773

My Heart has ever been susceptible of the warmest greatitude for your frequent Benefactions to the whole of our Family, but your last KIND, unexpected as well as undeserved, NOBLE presant in particular to me, calls for a particular acknoledgement from me. Except then dearest Sir, my most Sinceare and hearty thanks, with a promise, that your kindness Shall ever be greatefully rememberd, and your donation be made the best use of; as it will be laid out by my Mamma and the good Mrs. Williams, who is

sister of John Wilkes and the widow of another Hancock agent, Samuel Storke (d. 1753). Hayley's mother was a Hopkins, and his partner, Edmund Hopkins (d. 1786), was probably a relative. See William T. Baxter, *The House of Hancock* . . . (Cambridge, Mass., 1945), pp. 47, 251–3 (where Hopkins is misnamed), 272–4, 279–87; Namier and Brooke, *House of Commons*, II, 602–3 (where Storke is misnamed); *Gent. Mag.*, LXVI (1786), 1001; 7 Mass. Hist. Soc. *Coll.*, IX (1914), 251–3; Horace Bleackley, *Life of John Wilkes* (London, 1917), pp. 21, 292, and the geneal. table facing p. 448. Tuthill Hubbart, the Boston postmaster and BF's stepnephew, has often appeared in previous volumes.

3. Ritchie (d. *c.* 1784) was a Scot who settled as a merchant in Tappahannock, Va., then known as Hobbs Hole; Hyndman & Lancaster was a mercantile firm in Gould Square, Crutched Friars. Charles H. Ambler, *Thomas Ritchie* . . . (Richmond, Va., 1913), pp. 9–11; *Kent's Directory* . . . (London, 1770).

4. For the missing heiress see above, XVIII, 157; XIX, 318–19. BF appended a note in the third person, dated March 3, asking Mr. Jesser to read and return the letter, and adding that the February packet was due in a week or two. Jesser was the agent of the London Hospital who was concerned with the Holland mystery.

5. Jane's daughter (C.17.9) and BF's niece.

6. The month is scrawled, and Van Doren misread it as July: *Franklin— Mecom*, p. 141. Jenny's history makes clear what her handwriting does not: she signed herself Mecom, and she married Peter Collas in March, 1773.

allways, ready with Mr. Williams, to give their friendly advice, and asistance on every occasion,[7] few are blessed, with Such friends as we are; how then can we be unhappy; I am not nor would I change conditions with one person living were I sure of fullfilling my most *ardent* wish, that every action of my life, may be a credit to my Uncle, my constant endeavours and earnest prayers, shall not be wanting. When dear Sir, shall I have the happiness, of thanking you in person, for all your kindness; god send it may be soon: till then, please to except this incorrect Scrawl and permit me to Subscribe myself, your Sincearly affectionate forever obliged, and ever dutifull Niece,

JENNY MECOM

P S the Man who will Share your goodness with me desires his most dutifull respects and Sincear thanks. J M

Addressed: To / Dr. Benjamin Franklin / Craven Street. / London.

From Jacques Barbeu-Dubourg

ALS (badly mutilated): American Philosophical Society

Monsieur et cher Ami, [Jan. 13?,[8] 1773]
Je n'ai encore reçu ni votre paq[uet ni votre lettre?] du 8e.[9] Je vous prie de me marquer [*torn*] ferez l'honneur de m'ecrire par la [*torn*] vous etiez servi pour les deux [*torn*] voyageans, je pourrois pour peu que [*torn*] decouvrir icy dans les hôtels garnis ou [*torn*] et si ce sont des françois domiciliés a Paris cela seroit encore plus simple, mais gueres plus sûr.
Si vous ne trouviez point d'inconvenient a communiquer au public l'explication que Miss s——n a proposée de la chaleur que l'eau de Bristoll aquert par l'action de la pompe, je pense que cela

7. BF had asked Jonathan Williams, Sr., to lay out £50 for him in furnishing the newlyweds' quarters under Jane Mecom's direction. Above, XIX, 363. Grace Harris Williams clearly intended to be in on the fun.
8. Or possibly the 15th; in the last extant line of his reply below, March 10, BF seems to be referring to a letter from Dubourg on each of these dates.
9. The "little Piece" sent on Dec. 4 and the letter of Dec. 8, both of which BF later said had miscarried: above, XIX, 437. The letter eventually arrived, for Dubourg printed an extract from it: *ibid.*, p. 422.

ne pourroit que faire plaisir au public.[1] J'ose encore mieux vous repondre qu'on seroit fort aise de sçavoir comment vous rendez raison de ce que le [torn] des rhumes, et que le linge [torn] mouillés n'en causent pas.[2] Si vous ne [torn] publier encore l'explication, je vous [torn] de la communiquer pour mon instruction.

[Torn] noircir les murs des espaliers a fruits [torn] fait executer, ou vu executé quelque [torn] il peut y avoir du pour et du contre. Les murs blanchis reflechissent plus de chaleur sur les fruits pendant le jour, et peuvent consequemment contribuer à avancer leur accroissement, et assurer leur parfaite maturité dans les climats un peu froids. Etes vous bien certain (même avant l'experience) que ce que les murs noircis pourront leur rendre pendant la nuit de leur reserve du jour, compensera avec surabondance ce qu'ils leur en auront absorbé de plus que les murs blancs ordinaires?[3]

Dans votre derniere lettre du 26e–30e. Xbre. vous avez la bonté de m'expliquer le mot chain en ces termes *a surveyor's chain meant here, is four pole, or* [66 feet.[4]] [*Torn*] des arpenteurs est de 4 perches [torn] est donc de 16 pieds et demi [torn] commode

1. Why the public should have been interested is not clear, because—as BF explained in his reply below, p. 103—he and Polly Stevenson concluded that the water was not warmed by pumping. See above, IX, 194, 212, 217–18, 296. Dubourg published extracts of two of BF's letters to Polly on the subject: *Œuvres*, II, 289–98.

2. This mutilated sentence was a response, we conjecture, to a comment from BF, perhaps in a missing part of his letter of Dec. 26, on wet clothes and colds, a subject in which he had long been interested; see above, IX, 339. If so, Dubourg's inquiry elicited the reply below, p. 103.

3. Dubourg was expanding on BF's suggestion (above, IX, 251) that "Fruit Walls being black'd may receive so much Heat from the Sun in the Daytime, as to continue warm in some degree thro' the Night, and thereby preserve the Fruit from Frosts, or forward its Growth." This idea aroused the Frenchman's curiosity (no difficult feat), for when he published the passage in the *Œuvres*, II, 309, he added the following note: "Le feu Lord Leicester avoit fait noircir les murs de ses jardins avec beaucoup de succès, quant à ce qui concerne la garantie des jeunes fruits contre le danger des dernieres gelées. Mais après que les fruits ont franchi ce terme, peut-être les murs blanchis feroient-ils plus favorables pour avancer leur maturité. C'est à l'expérience à en décider." For Leicester see below, p. 104 n.

4. Above, XIX, 438.

pour l'usage, je soupçonne [*torn*] par mégarde un chiffre pour l'autre [*torn*] la perche varie un peu d'une province à [l'autre et dans une province?] royale est de 22 pieds, ainsi 66 pieds [*torn*] je demande donc si vous n'auriez point [*torn*] 4 perches pour 3, ou 66 pieds pour [*torn*]. En examinant l'appareil electrique de M. Dalibard pour son experience de Marly la ville (tant la description que la figure) il me semble qu'il n'avoit pas bien pris ses precautions pour la sureté de son ami Coiffier, et que si le tonnerre eût eté tres fort, il auroit bien pu eprouver le meme sort que M Richman, puisque la verge de fer n'avoit point de communication etablie avec la terre, et portoit au contraire sur une planche isolée par des bouteilles.[5] Qu'en pensez-vous?

Permettez moi de vous addresser le petit memoire cy joint de M. Missa mon Confrere,[6] qui vous seroit fort obligé si vous pouviez sans [*torn*] procurer quelques eclaircissemens [*torn*.] [*Nihil*] *humanum à te alienum putas.*

[*Torn*] Mademoiselle Biheron depuis bien du [*torn*] beaucoup d'inquietude sur sa santé. Si [*torn*] ne lui est pas favorable, faites la [*torn*] la santé n'est point mauvaise, [*torn*] [intelli]gence, qui nous afflige tous, et [*torn*] Mademoiselle Basseporte malade.[7]

Votre graveur [prend?] votre portrait fort à coeur, et se flatte que s'il avoit eu le bonheur de vous voir dans un de vos precedens voyages, il auroit fait quelque chose de mieux que ce que je lui ai donné à copier et reduire.[8] Et il se propose de profiter de l'occasion que vous nous faites esperer l'été prochain pour le refaire à neuf. J'ai l'honneur d'etre avec un devouement à toute epreuve Monsieur et cher Ami Votre tres humble et tres obeissant serviteur   Dubourg

---

5. The experiment was actually performed in Dalibard's absence by Coiffier, a former dragoon; see above, IV, 302–10. Richmann was the Swede who was killed in an experiment with lightning: above, V, 155 n, 219–21.

6. Possibly Henri-Michel Missa, an editor of the *Jour. de médecine;* we have no clue to his memoir.

7. Mlles. Biheron and Basseporte were old friends of Dubourg, and the former had been in uncertain health for some time. See above, XV, 115 n; XIX, 347, 439.

8. The plate that Martinet, the engraver, did produce is the frontispiece of the *Œuvres* and of the present volume; and the provenance of his work is described in our list of illustrations.

From Noble Wimberly Jones

ALS: American Philosophical Society

Dear Sir   Savannah 13. Jany: 1773

I am realy ashamed at my remissness in neglect of Writing after your repeated favours, And this now can only serve as an Appology the Captn: being ready to go down. Your much esteemed of the 5th. May containing the curious Seed from India I received safe, also yours of the 3d. of August and a few days since that of the 7th. of October,[9] which repeated marks of kindness fills me with pleasure and gratitude, shall do all in my power that they may answer your laudable Intentions, the Rice there is little doubt of doing well, the others may fail for want of a proper knowledge of the kind of Land necessary the time of sowing and method of Treatment, tho hope they will succeed. I have not seen Mr. Jonathan Bryan since receiv'd your last, shall take care when I do that your and Mr. Ellis's request be fulfill'd which cant be many days, as our Assembly is to meet Monday next (of which he is a member)[1] am glad to hear tho he and I never agreed in politics that Mr. Ellis still thinks of us, and I heartily wish him well, the Province certainly throve under his Administration.[2] Our present Assembly met the 9th. Decr. last (tho many new Members) did me the Honour of Electing me Speaker which must gaul such arbitrary Men as we have been blest with but my private business making it so very inconvenient determined me to decline accepting, it gave me however real pleasure to see the sentiment of them and that they would not be dictated to.[3] I trust notwithstanding every obsticle that the

9. The letter of May 5 may well have ended with the fragment printed above. XVIII, 65, in which case we were wrong in accepting the date in the endorsement and right in guessing the recipient. BF's other letters are above, XIX, 226–7, 323–4.

1. For the gifts of seed and rice to Jones and Bryan see *idem.* Bryan was a member of the Georgia Council.

2. Jones, as BF pointed out in his reply below, Aug. 4, was confusing John Ellis, the naturalist, with Henry Ellis (1721–1806), the former governor of Georgia.

3. The perennial choice of Jones as speaker had long been both a cause and an effect of the ongoing quarrel between the Governor and the Assembly. See above, XIX, 55, 95–6. The quarrel was now in abeyance, though Jones did

Province will have the Hapiness of your continuance and Assist-ance.[4] Time Obliges to conclude with the Honour of subscribing myself with the greatest Respect Dear Sir Your Most Obedient and Very Humble Servant. N W JONES

The Managers of the Pennsylvania Hospital to Franklin, David Barclay, and John Fothergill

Minutebook copy: Pennsylvania Hospital, Philadelphia

⟨January 18, 1773: A copy of their previous letter is enclosed.[5] They have now drawn further on Franklin, Barclay, and Fother-gill for £1,250 sterling in three bills of exchange, one in favor, of Joseph Mitchell for £600 and two in favor of Joseph King[6] for £300 and £350 respectively.⟩

To Jacques Barbeu-Dubourg

Translated extract: printed in Jacques Barbeu-Dubourg, ed., *Œuvres de M. Franklin* . . . (2 vols., Paris, 1773), II, 118.

Londres, 22 Janvier 1773.

J'ai imaginé depuis quelques tems une nouvelle forme de chauffoir, ou espece de cheminée d'une construction différente, qui donne plus de chaleur, en consumant moins de bois; mais il lui manque quelques-uns des principaux avantages de ma premiere machine,

---

not admit it here; his faction had been weakened in the elections at the end of 1772, and the new Assembly was in a mood to abandon recriminations and get down to business. William W. Abbot, *The Royal Governors of Georgia, 1754–1775* (Chapel Hill, N.C., [1959]), pp. 157–8. This change in the political climate, rather than his own affairs, presumably led Jones to leave the speaker's chair.

4. The "obsticle" was to obtaining a salary for the agent; see BF to Gallo-way above, Jan. 6.

5. Presumably that of Jan. 4 above.

6. For the little we know about Joseph King see above, XIX, 367 n. About Joseph Mitchell, a new mortgager, we know nothing; he may or may not have been the man of that name who wrote BF in 1788 about other land transactions, and signed himself "a Decriped being this many years." 1 *Pa. Arch.*, XI, 253–5.

et elle a quelques inconvéniens que l'autre n'a pas;[7] d'ailleurs elle exige trop d'attention dans ses opérations pour etre gouvernée par des domestiques ordinaires, c'est pourquoi je ne puis en recommander l'usage, quoique je m'en serve pour moi-même. Ce n'est proprement qu'une curiosité, ou une expérience philosophique; la fumée s'y change toute insensiblement en flamme, au lieu de salir la cheminée; cette flamme descend, et sert à échauffer les plaques et la chambre; et en même-tems elle empêche les charbons qui avoient commencé à prendre feu, de se consumer. Je compte vous en envoyer dans quelque tems d'ici la figure, avec la description.[8]

From Isaac L. Winn   MS:[9] the Royal Society

Friday Morn. 22 Janry [1773]

Capt. Winn presents Respects to Dr. Franklin and sends Two Barrels of Apples from Mr. Theo. Bache[1] and begs leave to add one to them.

In August last Capt. Winn took the Liberty of sending Dr.

7. His first "machine" was the Pennsylvania fireplace that he perfected in 1744: above, II, 419–46.

8. This is BF's first mention of an old interest, and one that remained with him for years to come. The possibility of a smoke-consuming stove had intrigued him since 1766; see above, XIII, 197. A Frenchman whose name he forgot, writing at the close of the previous century, had first suggested the idea to him; and by 1771 he had a prototype stove that served him for three winters in London and one in America. In 1785, while at sea returning from France, he finally wrote the description of it that he promises in this letter, and in the following year the description was published. Smyth, *Writings*, IX, 443–62; APS *Trans.*, II (1786), 57–74. What he says here about the disadvantages of the stove doubtless accounts for his long delay in putting it before the public. He did send Dubourg an engraving of it, in confidence, with his letter below of June 29. The engraving is reproduced there; for further details see the list of illustrations. The stove did not appear in the *Œuvres* except in this extract. But Dubourg's curiosity was aroused—and remained unsatisfied. He twice asked for a description, in his letters below of Nov. 25 and Dec. 29, and never received one.

9. In the same hand as Winn's signed letter the previous August (above, XIX, 236–8), and hence presumably dictated.

1. See below, BF to DF, Feb. 2, and BF's acknowledgment to Theophylact Bache, Feb. 3.

Franklin some Observations on the Aurora Borealis, to which he would add that on Saturday Evening the 16 Instt., as Capt. Winn came to Town the Aurora was so bright that he found a Croud of People in the Minories gazing at it, which they took to be the Effect of a great fire about Bishopsgate Street,[2] the next day we had a hard Gale at SSW with Rain.[3]

[*Endorsed:*[4]] A further Note from the same Gentleman.

From François Rozier[5]

Printed circular letter with handwritten postscript: American Philosophical Society

The letter below is an interesting example of scientific communication in the period. The editor of a scientific journal in Paris was inviting

2. Bishopsgate St. is less than half a mile northwest of the Minories, which runs between Aldgate and the Tower.

3. The thesis of Winn's observations, in the 1772 letter just mentioned, was that the aurora presaged gales from the south or southwest. He here adds unusual corroboration, for auroral displays of such brilliance were rare in England; see Charles Hutton, *A Mathematical and Philosophical Dictionary* ... (2 vols., London, 1796), I, 175. When the Royal Society published Winn's 1772 letter, BF's comment on it and a truncated version of this letter were added as a note: *Phil. Trans.*, LXIV (1774), 132.

4. In BF's hand, presumably addressed to the Royal Society when he sent this letter with the material above, XIX, 236–9.

5. François Rozier (1734–93) was ordained to the priesthood and then, like many abbés of the period, devoted himself to secular pursuits. He administered a large country estate, explored new agricultural methods, wrote a prize-winning essay on the chemistry of wine-making, and even studied veterinary medicine. In 1771 he moved to Paris to edit a new monthly publication, *Observations sur la physique, sur l'histoire naturelle et sur les arts.* ... Eighteen issues in 12mo appeared between July, 1771, and December, 1772; the format then changed to 4to and the title to *Observations et mémoires sur la physique, sur l'histoire naturelle et sur les arts et métiers.* The first two 4to issues were apparently the gift to the APS mentioned in the postscript; each volume carried a note which, like this letter, asked for news of learned societies. Rozier continued to be an editor until he was killed during the Revolution. The periodical became a major forum for the exchange of scientific information, and was later rechristened the *Journal de physique, de chimie, d'histoire naturelle et des arts.* See Henry Guerlac, *Lavoisier—the Crucial Year* ... (Ithaca, N.Y., [1961]), pp. 59–65; *Nouvelle biographie générale* ... (46 vols., Paris, 1853–66), XLII, 827–30.

each of many learned societies in Europe to send him a periodic report of its current activities, which he would then broadcast within three months via his journal. After the letters of invitation were printed he seems to have decided to send with them, at least in some cases, sets of his own periodical to prove his bona fides and advertise his wares; he thereupon added to each letter a handwritten postscript explaining his gift. Franklin received the invitation and the volumes as president of the American Philosophical Society. He promised to do what he could to keep Europe informed, by this new medium, of the Society's work, and forwarded the books to Philadelphia.[6]

Monsieur,   Paris, ce 24 Janvier 1773.

Les Savans ne cessent de se plaindre de la tardive communication des découvertes et des nouvelles relatives aux Arts et aux Sciences: Nous croyons pouvoir obvier à cet inconvénient, si vous daignez concourir à une entreprise qu'une société d'amis et moi avons formée. Toute l'Europe sera instruite, dans l'espace de trois mois au plus tard, des travaux dont votre Compagnie se sera occupée. Pour cet effet, permettez que j'aie l'honneur de vous proposer les moyens suivans:

1°. De donner le titre des Mémoires qui auront été lus dans ses assemblées.

2°. Une simple notice, ou une petite analyse des articles essentiels qu'ils contiennent.

3°. Un abrégé de la vie des Académiciens que la mort ravira à votre Société, et sur-tout un tableau des Ouvrages qu'ils auront donnés et des découvertes qu'ils auront faites.

Ces Extraits ne sauroient nuire à l'impression de la Collection de vos Mémoires; ils serviront même de véhicule pour les faire desirer avec plus d'ardeur.

Chaque mois, à commencer à la fin de Janvier de cette année, je ferai remettre à l'Ambassadeur de votre Souverain résidant à Paris, un Exemplaire de mon Journal; et en cas de refus, je me servirai de quelqu'autre voie aussi prompte et aussi sûre: heureux si cet Ouvrage mérite l'approbation de votre Académie! Je vous prie de vous servir de la même voie pour me faire parvenir ce que

6. BF to Rozier below, June 22; APS, *Early Proc.* . . . . (Philadelphia, 1884), p. 83. Presumably as a result of this connection, the Society elected Rozier to membership in 1775: *ibid.*, p. 95.

vous aurez la bonté de me communiquer, ou bien de le faire remettre chez le Ministre de France résidant en votre Ville: Pour lors
il faudra, s'il vous plaît, faire une double enveloppe, et écrire sur
l'extérieure, *A Monseigneur le Duc d'Aiguillon, Ministre et Secre-
taire des Affaires Etrangeres en France;* et sur l'enveloppe intérieure,
écrire ces mots: *M. Rozier, Journal des Académies.*[7]

L'utilité de cette entreprise me fait espérer que votre Compagnie daignera l'encourager, et nommer spécialement un de
ses Membres pour se charger de cette correspondance, laborieuse
il est vrai; mais indispensable pour le progrès des Sciences. Je
suis avec respect, Monsieur, Votre très-humble et très-obéissant
serviteur, L'ABBÉ ROZIER
Place et Quarré Sainte-Genevieve.

p.s Ayez la bonté de presenter de ma part à Votre Illustre Societé
ces deux Volumes de mon Recueil, comm'un Obseque qui est
dû à la noble entreprise de votre Institut Philosophique: et de
recevoir pour vous meme les autres deux.

Outre les voyes que je viens de vous indiquer dans cette Lettre
pour les communications ci-dessus, peutetre vous sera-t-il
plus aisé de me les faire passer par les mains de Mr. le Docteur
Franklin *in Craven Street*, ou de Mr. Magalhaens *at no. 4. Old
North Street Red Lyon Square*, ou de Mr. Elmsley Bookseller
facing Southampton Street in the Strand, tous trois à *Londres*,
qui ont souvent des occasions pour me les envoyer à *Paris*.[8]

Notation: 1773 Rozier

7. Dubourg had suggested a forwarding arrangement that also involved
the duc d'Aiguillon: above, XIX, 385.
8. The list of three forwarding agents in London indicates that the postscript was for British correspondents, and the inclusion of BF in the list
suggests some earlier contact between him and Rozier of which we have
no record. For Peter Elmsley, the bookseller, see *idem.*, p. 343. Magalhaens
or Magellan, the Portuguese instrument-maker and scientist, appeared in
idem., p. 127, where we did not mention that he was acting at this time as an
agent for the French government in transmitting news of British scientific
and technological discoveries; see Guerlac, *op. cit.*, pp. 36–43, 63–5.

From William Brownrigg[9]

Extract: the Royal Society

Ormathwaite, January 27, 1773.

By the enclosed from an old friend, a worthy clergyman at Carlisle, whose great learning and extensive knowledge in most sciences would have more distinguished him had he been placed in a more conspicuous point of view, You will find that he had heard of your experiment on Derwent Lake, and has thrown together what he could collect on that subject; to which I have subjoined one experiment from the relation of another Gentleman.[1]

Extract of a Letter from the Revd. Mr. Farish,[2] to Dr. Brownrigg

I sometime ago met with Mr. Dun,[3] who surprised me with an account of an experiment you had tried upon the Derwentwater, in Company with Sir J. Pringle and Dr. Franklin. According to his representation, the water, which had been in great agitation before, was instantly calmed, upon pouring in only a very small quantity of oil, and that to so great a distance round the boat as seems a little incredible. I have since had the same accounts from others, but I suspect them all of a little exaggeration. Pliny mentions this property of oil as known particularly to the Divers, who made use of it in his days, in order to have a more

9. The north-country physician and scientist, whom BF and Pringle had visited the summer before and with whom they had experimented in pouring oil on Derwent Water; see above, XIX, 170. BF responded to this letter with a long disquisition on the use of oil for calming waves: below, Nov. 7.

1. The extract of Brownrigg's letter, which is in Fevre's hand, omitted this experiment.

2. James Farish was vicar of Stanwix, a village just outside Carlisle. He "possessed more knowledge in *several parts* of learning than the generality of scholars possess in *any one*," yet was so modest that he would publish nothing. William Jackson, ed., *Memoirs of Dr. Richard Gilpin . . . by the Rev. William Gilpin . . .* (London and Carlisle, 1879), p. 74.

3. Possibly Samuel Dunn, the Londoner of whom BF spoke in his letter to Galloway below, Feb. 14.

steady light at the bottom.* The sailors, I have been told, have observed something of the same kind in our days, that the water is always remarkably smoother in the wake of a ship that had been newly tallowed, than it is in one that is foul. Mr. Pennant also mentions an observation of the like nature made by the Seal Catchers in Scotland: *Brit. Zool.* Vol. IV. *Article Seal.*[4] When these Animals are devouring a very oily fish, which they always do under water, the waves above are observed to be remarkably smooth, and by this mark the fishermen know where to look for them. Old Pliny does not usually meet with all the credit I am inclined to think he deserves. I shall be glad to have an authentic account of the Keswick Experiment, and if it comes up to the representations that have been made of it, I shall not much hesitate to believe the old Gentleman in another more wonderful Phenomenon he relates of stilling a Tempest only by throwing up a little Vinegar into the Air.[5]

* Dr. Brownrigg's Note to Mr. Farish's Observations.

Sir Gilfred Lawson who served long in the army, at Gibraltar,[6] assures me that the Fishermen in that place are accustomed to pour a little oil on the sea in order to still its motion that they may be enabled to see the Oysters lying at its bottom; which are there very large, and which they take up with a proper instrument. This Sir Gilfred had often seen there performed, and said the same was practised on other parts of the Spanish Coast.

4. [Thomas Pennant,] *British Zoology* . . . (4 vols., London, etc., 1768–70), IV, 37–8.

5. This and the preceding reference to Pliny the Elder's *Natural History* are to Book II, respectively 132 and 234.

6. Lawson (*c.* 1709–94) began his military career in 1732, and his regiment was stationed at Gibraltar until 1749; how long he stayed with it we do not know. He succeeded as ninth baronet in 1762. *The Army List of 1740* . . . (Soc. for Army Hist. Research, Special No. III; Sheffield, 1931), p. 16; Chetwynd J. D. Haswell, *The Queen's Royal Regiment (West Surrey)* . . . (London, [1967]), p. 150; *Burke's Peerage*, p. 1502.

31

From Jacques Barbeu-Dubourg

Printed in Jacques Barbeu-Dubourg, ed., *Œuvres de M. Franklin* ... (2 vols., Paris, 1773), II, 226–7.

Monsieur,   [January?[7] 1773]

Ayant fait voir ces jours-ci les premieres épreuves de vos feuilles sur la Musique[8] à MM. G———, amateurs éclairés de tous les beaux arts, je crois devoir vous communiquer le résultat de ma conversation avec eux.

On ne doute point que ces airs Ecossois, que vous exaltez tant, ne soient excellens dans leur genre et parfaitement assortis aux paroles de ces anciennes ballades, telles que votre *Chevy-chase,* dont le Spectateur a fait un si bel éloge dans deux de ses feuilles.[9] On ne doute pas non plus que la plupart de vos Musiciens d'Angleterre, ainsi que ceux de bien d'autres Nations, ne se soient attiré de trop justes reproches par des compositions bruyantes, sans objet, sans expression, ou remplies de contresens. Mais d'un autre côté, il ne paroît pas raisonnable, et ce n'est surement pas votre intention d'assujettir les Musiciens à un seul genre de Musique, et de les renfermer dans un cercle plus étroit que leur art ne le comporte. Ils ne sauroient se donner un trop libre effort, lorsque le génie les éleve et que le goût les dirige. En Musique, comme en Poësie et en Peinture, il faut savoir exprimer énergiquement et distinctement tous les objets, tous les sentimens et toutes les passions généralement quelconques; il ne faut pas employer les mêmes tons à représenter une cabane, un naufrage, une noce de village, ou l'apothéose d'Hercule; il ne faut pas tout entasser confusément, mais faire un choix judicieux, et mettre à leur juste place les palais et les chaumieres, les héros et les bergers. Un grand Musicien doit savoir produire de doux sons, une mélodie agréable, former de beaux accords,

---

7. The letter may have been written at any time in the late winter or spring, when the proofs of Dubourg's edition were coming off the press. We assign it to the earliest likely date.

8. Dubourg published in the *Œuvres* (II, 209–14, 216–25) BF's description of his armonica in 1762 and a later extract and letter dealing with music; all had appeared in the 1769 edition of *Exper. and Obser.* and are printed above, X, 126–30; XI, 539–43; XII, 162–4.

9. *The Spectator*, nos. 70, 74 (May 21, 25, 1711).

une harmonie charmante, être varié, être abondant dans l'exécution d'un plan simple et aisé, et déployer à propos la grace et la force, le tendre et le terrible, le naïf et le sublime. Toutes ses compositions doivent être tellement assorties à leur objet qu'elles puissent plaire généralement à tout le monde, mais que chacune fasse plus spécialement les délices d'un certain ordre de personnes. Ainsi dans une ballade, ou un vaudeville destiné à l'amusement de l'universalité du peuple, le Musicien doit s'attacher à des modulations très-simples, et dont tous les rapports soient faciles à saisir; dans un opéra, ou un ballet qui doit être représenté devant des amateurs et des maîtres, qui ont le goût délicat et des oreilles exercées, le Musicien doit réunir plus d'harmonie, combiner un plus grand nombre de rapports, et chercher même du nouveau, pourvu qu'il ne s'écarte jamais du vrai. Mais il faut avouer qu'il est peu de Musiciens, comme il est peu de Peintres et de Poëtes assez favorisés de la nature, et dont les talens ayent été assez perfectionnés par l'art, et assez épurés par le goût, pour se pénétrer intimément de ces grands principes, les suivre constamment et les aggrandir successivement, comme vous le desireriez surement, ainsi que nous. J'ai l'honneur d'être, &c.

To Alexander Colden   ALS (letterbook draft): Library of Congress

London, Feb. 2 1773

I receiv'd yours of Dec. 2. enclosing a Bill Hancock on Haley & Hopkins for £150 for Account of the Gen. Post-Office.[1]

Inclos'd I return you the Bill, Dunn on Long, Drake and Long, for £100 Sterling, with the Protest which costs 5s. 9d.[2] I hope you are careful to give me Credit for these Protested Bills. I sent you two per last Packet, and one by that of November.[3] Present my Respects to your Good Father, and your very ingenious Brother David, whose Letter I have received. They shall hear from me by the next NYork Ships.[4] I am ever, with great Regard,

1. Discussed in the annotation of Colden's letter above, Jan. 7.
2. The bill had arrived the previous December: above, XIX, 398.
3. See above, BF to Colden, Jan. 6, and XIX, 359.
4. BF wrote David Colden on March 5 but did not, as far as we know, write the father, presumably because he could not bring himself to read the latter's treatise; see BF to Alexander Colden below, June 2.

Dear Sir, Your most obedient humble Servant   B FRANKLIN

Alexr Colden Esqr—per Packet

To Deborah Franklin   ALS (letterbook draft): Library of Congress

My dear Child,   London Feb. 2. 1773
    Since my last I have got the Apples on shore, and they come
out very good. Accept my best Thanks. Mr. Bache of NYork
has also kindly sent me two Barrels, Capt. Winn one, and Capt.
Falconer One. I told you before that Capt. All gave me one, so
that I am now plentifully supply'd.[5]
    I know you love to have a Line from me by every Packet;
so I write tho' I have little to say, having had no Letter from you
since my last of Jan. 6.
    In Return for your History of your *Grandson*, I must give you
a little of the History of my *Godson*.[6] He is now 21 months old,
very strong and healthy, begins to speak a little, and even to
sing. He was with us a few Days last Week, grew fond of me,
and would not be contented to sit down to Breakfast, without
coming to call *Pa*, rejoicing when he had got me into my Place.
When seeing me one Day crack one of the Philada. Biskets into
my Tea with the Nutcrackers, he took another and try'd to do
the same with the Tea Tongs. It makes me long to be at home to
play with Ben.
    My Love to him and our Children, with all enquiring Friends.
Mrs. Stevenson presents her affectionate Respects, and Sally her
Duty.[7] I am ever, my dear Debby, Your loving Husband

                                    B FRANKLIN

5. See above, BF to DF, Jan. 6, and Winn to BF, Jan. 22; also BF to Theophylact Bache below, Feb. 3. Six barrels, if DF sent only one, would seem to
be not so much a plentiful supply as a surfeit.
    6. William Hewson, Jr.
    7. Sarah Franklin (A.5.2.3.1.1.1), BF's distant cousin, was living in Craven
Street.

From Jane Parker Bedford[8] ALS: American Philosophical Society

Honoured Sir,   Woodbridge February 2d: 1773

At my Mamas perticular request I take the liberty of writing
to you, whom once I could address without ceremony, but the
unhappy Difference between our families render that perhaps now
more necessary, which would formerly have been looked upon as
an Act of Duty. You my Dear Sir, I was ever taught to look upon
as the Friend, the Benefactor of one of the best of Parents and tho'
he is now no more, and his memory and Actions too Soon forgot
by some, yet that hand which so kindly assisted him and thought
him worthy when here of friendship, we hope will not forget
his family now he is no more. When my Papa died he left
Something pritty behind him enogh to maintain Mama and for
his children to enter into the World upon.[9] His Estate was no
way incumbred, but with those Bonds to Mr. Franklin, as now
appears, but which my Mama have frequently heard him say
before his Death, were almost discharged, that he had remitted
s[ome mone]y to Mrs. Franklin to near the Amount of them,
and perti[cularly the?] last time he went frome home he told
Mama he believed he had Sufficient with him to Discharge them.[1]
However let that [be] as it will and owing to what cause it may
on either side there are now heavy Sums appear due on those
Bonds. We have seen Powers of Attorney in the hands of both
Governor Franklin and Mr. Bache to receive, and secure the Debt,
as soon as the Governor appeared we sent in our Account and
were ready to settle. Governor Franklin then took time to send
the Account over to you. When we called upon him again he said
he had nothing to do with the matter that Mr. Bache had come
with a later Power of Attorney, and that we must settle with him.
We [have] furnished Mr. Bache with the same Accounts as we had
the Gove[rnor] who in answer said he could not settle till he had
heard further from you. Since that we have Waited and called
upon him, again and again, but he says no news from home, and

8. James Parker's daughter has appeared briefly in earlier volumes: VII,
203 n; XI, 339 n; XVII, 204, 240. For her marriage to Gunning Bedford,
probably in late 1770, see above, XIX, 82 n.

9. For James Parker's estate see above, XVII, 204 n.

1. For the bonds see above, XIX, 81, and the references given there.

all must be let o[ver?] till then.[2] Mama thinks it very hard. If interest runs upon the Bonds they have almost consumed the Estate, tho this is what we principally want to know, papa in his Books mentions it, that if Interest is charged upon his Bonds to Mr. Franklin, he think it but reasonable he should have commissions upon the Business he did for him. Now what business he did, or what commissions to charge we know not as he kept no Account of it, and therefore we would wish to know from yourself wither or not we must pay Interest upon the Bonds and if we do, wither it is reasonable we should from the time [that?] we have been ready to settle them. It will make an odds in the Inte[rest] [*torn*] time upon so Great a sum. There was likewise [*line missing*] March 1770 to you by papa of which there is no mention made in the Account furnishd Govenor Franklin and Mr. Bache. I think he mentions the money arising from Books sold by Auc[tion] of which we should be glad to be informed of with the rest.[3]

In Mr. Coldens settling the Post Office Books there appears a Ballance due to Mama of betwen 20 and 30 pounds, and Mr. Foxcroft in a letter to her mention that in consequence of papas faithful discharge of his duty when in office, she is to be allowed the Sallary from the time of his Death to Mr. Coldens takeing the office. Mr. Colden likewise in a letter to mama mentions it and says that as Mr. Foxcroft had spoke to him about it, and had informed mama of it, he has only charged his Sallary from the third of October 1770, which was about a quarter after papas Death, he dying July 2d 1770, and has [kept the?] intervening Sallary to be receivd by the Board, and upon any orders [from] them he would immediately pay it to her. Now Good Sir, if you think Proper mama should receive the quarters Sallary, from papas Death to Mr. Coldens takeing the office and will

2. During the previous year BF, WF, and Richard Bache had talked about a settlement: *ibid.*, pp. 81, 143, 267. But since August BF had apparently done nothing about it, and Jenny's letter elicited only the vague promise in his reply below, April 9. In the late summer of 1774 the matter was almost settled: BF to WF below, Sept. 7, 1774.

3. The transactions not mentioned in the account were presumably those in Parker's letter of March 8, 1770: XVII, 92–3; for further references to the auction of Benjamin Mecom's books see *idem.*, pp. 55–6, 76–7, 130, 141.

make inter[est?] so far, as to have so much of it paid to you as will discharge [Mr.?] Potts his Account against the Estate for the London Chronicle, [from] the time papa began to take it October 10th 1768, to his Death Ju[ly 2] 1770 you will Greatly oblidge my Mama. Mr. Potts has cha[rged] his last Account to January 1773, but he must Charge Inslee for the money after papas Death til then, as we never received [*torn*] after, but Inslee and Carr has, who took his office.[4]

We should not have troubled or wrote to you, Good Sir was it not for mamas Great anxiety to have her affairs settled and her perticular desire that you should in some measure [be] concerned in them, that she may know from yourself what she must depend on as to your Accounts; as she finds much Difficulty in settling them in her present situation. She is now advanced in years and afflicted, and would Willingly live in peace and she thinks if those Bonds were discharged she could be ha[ppy?] as they are the only incumbrance on the Estate, but which tho we fear will eat the most of it up. She sincerely joins with me in much love and Gratitude for your many favours as would Mr. Bedford, the person whom I am so happy in calling Husband: were he present, a Gentleman tho unknown to you yet I flatter myself, whose Good qualities would recommend to your favour. Permit me therefore for him, with [myself?] to wish you many happy years, and a safe return to your Family and Friends. From Honoured Sir your affectionate Humble Servant   JENNY BEDFORD

Addressed in another hand: To / Dctr Benjamin Franklin / Craven Street / London

4. Alexander Colden, to judge by this evidence, was appointed in October, 1770, to succeed Parker as comptroller of the American post office. The salary for the quarter when the office was vacant was assigned, on BF's application, by the General Post Office to Parker's estate, but had not yet been paid; see BF's reply of April 9. Jenny was asking BF to use part of this sum for the subscription to the *Chron.*, which Samuel Potts, comptroller general of the Post Office, had been sending to Parker since 1767: XIV, 238–9, and subsequent volumes. Samuel Inslee and Anthony Carr, or Car, were former employees of Parker, who at his death leased the printing office from his son and for the next three years continued to publish the *N.-Y. Gaz.; or, the Weekly Post-Boy.* Clarence S. Brigham, *History and Bibliography of American Newspapers, 1690–1820* (2 vols., Worcester, Mass., 1947), I, 636.

To Richard Bache   ALS (letterbook draft): Library of Congress

Dear Son,   London, Feb. 3. 1773.

I received yours of Nov. 3.[5] with the Extracts from Mr. Hooper's Letter, and Remarks of Mr. Morgan which will come under Consideration in due time. As yet the Grant has not pass'd the Seals, tho' we are kept in continual Expectation. I am oblig'd to Mr. Baynton and you for the Communication.

The Demolishing Fort Pitt was a strange Measure. It might have been suffered to stand, tho' abandon'd, as a Refuge for the Inhabitants in Case of any sudden Emergency. But it is of a Piece with the late false Policy, of Discouraging all Settlements on the Ohio.[6] My Love to Sally and Ben. I am Your affectionate Father,   B FRANKLIN

Mr Bache

To Theophylact Bache

ALS (letterbook draft): Library of Congress

Dear Sir,   London, Feb. 3. 1773

I am much oblig'd by your Favour of Dec. 10. with the 2 Barrels of Apples which prove excellent, and are a great Refreshment to me. Please to accept my Thanks, and best Wishes for your Prosperity.

I thank you for your Kind Attention to Mr. Chysholme. I hope he will at last be fix'd to his Mind.[7]

Enclos'd is a Letter from your good Mother, which will

5. The people and matters that BF is discussing in this note are explained in Bache's letter above, XIX, 363–4.

6. Fort Pitt does not seem to have been demolished, as Bache and BF believed; by the time the troops departed little was left to demolish, and the Virginians subsequently reoccupied the post. John Shy, *Toward Lexington* . . . (Princeton, 1965), p. 330; Jack M. Sosin, *Whitehall and the Wilderness* . . . (Lincoln, Neb., 1961), pp. 222, 228. The army's abandoning the fort had long been under discussion as part of a general plan of retrenchment, not of discouraging settlers; the government had not agreed within itself that they should be discouraged.

7. See Bache's letter above, XIX, 423; we are still unable to identify Alexander Chysholm or Chysholme. As for the apples, BF was oversupplied; see his letter to DF above, Feb. 2.

inform you of her Welfare and your Sisters. With great Esteem, I am, Sir, Your most obedient humble Servant   B F.

Mr Theo. Bache

To William Franklin   AL (letterbook draft): Library of Congress

Dear Son,   London, Feb. 3. 1773
    I send you herewith some Seeds, and shall send more for your Friends, by the Philad. Ships, by whom I shall write more fully. They are Peas of a valuable Sort, and the Turnip Cabbage which abides the Frost of Winter, and therefore of great Use as Feed in the Spring before any other appears. They were given me by our good Friend Mr. Todd.[8]
    Yours of Oct. 29. Nov. 3. Dec. 1, and 4 are come to hand; but I hear nothing from Bristol concerning the Pork.[9] I shall write thither about it.
    I continue very well. Present my affectionate Respects to our good Friend Galloway. The Grant is not yet compleated. Love to Betsey. I am ever Your affectionate Father.

8. Turnip cabbage is kohlrabi, widely used for forage. Anthony Todd, who as secretary of the Post Office was in effect its head, seems to have been a go-between in delivering the seeds. The actual donor was Giovanni Francesco Fromond, a minor Lombard scientist who was in London at the time to perfect his training, and who subsequently returned to Milan as professor of optics and head of a laboratory of experimental physics. See Antonio Pace, *Benjamin Franklin and Italy* (Philadelphia, 1958), pp. 3–4, 36, 323. Almost three years after writing this letter BF mentioned that he had met Fromond in London and received the seeds from him, but by that time had forgotten what they were used for and how they were grown. To Philip Mazzei, Dec. 27, 1775, Dartmouth College Library.

9. The letter of Oct. 29, the only one that survives, says nothing about WF's gift of what must have been salt or pickled pork, which eventually arrived in a large consignment that was partly for BF and partly for John Sargent: BF to WF below, Feb. 14.

To John Bartram

ALS (letterbook draft): Library of Congress

My dear old Friend, London, Feb. 10. 1773

I am glad to learn that the Turnip Seed and the Rhubarb grow with you and that the Turnip is approved.[1] It may be depended on that the Rhubarb is the genuine Sort. But to have the Root in perfection, it ought not to be taken out of the Ground in less than 7 Years. Herewith I send you a few Seeds of what is called the Cabbage Turnip. They say that will stand the Frost of the severest Winter, and so make a fine early Feed for Cattle in the Spring when their other Fodder may be scarce.[2] I send also some Peas that are much applauded here.

I think there has been no good Opportunity of sending your Medal since I received it till now. It goes in a Box to my Son Bache with the Seeds. I wish you Joy of it.

Notwithstanding the Failure of your Eyes, you write as distinctly as ever. With great Esteem and Respect, I am, my dear Friend, Yours most affectionately   B FRANKLIN

Mr Bartram

To Anthony Benezet[3]

ALS (letterbook draft): Library of Congress

Dear Friend, London, Feb. 10. 1773

I received with Pleasure yours of Sept. 13. as it informed me of your Welfare. With this I send you one of Young's Night Thoughts, the largest Print I could find.[4] I thank you for the 4 Copies you sent me of your Translation of the French Book:[5]

1. Most of the matters BF refers to, here and below, are explained by the letter to which he is replying: above, XIX, 367–8.

2. For the provenance of the turnip seeds see the preceding document.

3. For the Quaker philanthropist see above, XIX, 112–13.

4. Either Benezet's eyesight was failing, of which we have no other indication, or he wanted the book for some one else; his September letter is missing. BF may have sent him one of the nine parts of Edward Young's *The Complaint: or Night-Thoughts on Life, Death, & Immortality*, which were published serially in 1742 and thereafter; more probably he sent one of the many collected editions listed in Henry Pettit, *A Bibliography of Young's Night Thoughts* . . . (Boulder, Colo., 1954), pp. 7–8.

5. The second edition of Benezet's translation of [Johannes Tauler,] *The Plain Path to Christian Perfection* . . . (Philadelphia, 1772).

I have given two of them to Friends here, whom I thought the Subject might suit. I have commenc'd an Acquaintance with Mr. Granville Sharpe, and we shall act in Concert in the Affair of Slavery.[6] The Accounts you send me relating to Surinam are indeed terrible.[7] Go on and prosper in your laudable [Endea]vours, and believe me ever, my dear Friend, Yours most affectionately   B FRANKLIN

I send you a few of a Pamphlet written at Paris by a Wellwisher to our Country. It is a little System of Morals, that may give distinct Ideas on that Subject to Youth and perhaps on that Account not unfit for a School Book. I will send you more if you desire it.[8]

Mr Antho Benezet / per Capt. All.

6. BF had been familiar with Sharp's work for at least the past three years; see above, XVII, 38–40. Benezet and Sharp, common crusaders against the slave trade, had begun a correspondence the previous spring that lasted during the Quaker's lifetime: George S. Brookes, *Friend Anthony Benezet* (Philadelphia, 1937), pp. 86–9. Benezet was helping to change BF's attitude on slavery, and may have been instrumental in bringing him and Sharp together.

7. The disappearance of Benezet's letter leaves us uncertain what accounts he had sent of the slave revolt. BF scarcely needed them, for news of the rising and of Dutch repressive measures had appeared frequently in the *London Chron.*: Oct. 20–22, Nov. 12–14, Dec. 24–26, 29–31, 1772.

8. The pamphlet was unquestionably Dubourg's *Petit code de la raison humaine*. BF may have sent copies of Polly Hewson's translation, which he had had privately printed in 1770 (above, XVII, 185–6); but the interval of time makes this unlikely. Benezet was a Frenchman by birth and a schoolmaster by profession, and had at one time taught French. Brookes, *op. cit.*, p. 30. The likelihood, therefore, is that the Quaker received the new French edition, dedicated to BF and printed for him in London; see above, XIX, 442 n. The bill from William Strahan, cited there and discussed below, Sept. 13, 1774, shows that the printing was done in December, 1772, and that errata followed in June and September, 1773. The absence of errata in copies we have located means that the original edition was published without them, presumably in December or January. BF, we believe, sent the pamphlet to Benezet and to the author at about the same time. Dubourg, when he acknowledged BF's assistance in his letter below of April 11, apologized for his delay in responding.

To a Committee of the Managers of the Philadelphia
Silk Filature   ALS (letterbook draft): Library of Congress

Gentlemen,   London, Feb. 10. 73

I duly receiv'd your Favour of [Nov. 17[9]] and have after a long Delay got the S[ilk f]rom the Custom House. The Throwsters[1] appointed to inspect it there, in order to ascertain the Bounty, valued it at 15*s.* the small pound the whole taken together, and afterwards wanted to buy it of me at that Price. But suspecting their Offer to be too low, I have shown it to others who say it is much undervalued. Our Friend Freeman advises its being sold by Auction as the last and recommends the same Broker.[2] Every one I have consulted are of the same Opinion. He will have a Sale about April next.

The Spitalfields Silk Business is very dead at present. The enormous Paper Credit which circulated so freely some time since, enabled the Master Manufacturers to employ more Men and make more Goods than the Market really required; and the Blow such Credit has lately received,[3] obliges them to stop their Work, till they can dispose of the great Quantity of Goods on hand, which some say is enough for a twelvemonth to come. So the disbanded Workmen are starving, tho' great Sums are collected to distribute among them in Charity. Several have apply'd to me to ship them to America, but having no Account that such Workmen were wanted there; I was obliged to refuse them. One came to me with the enclos'd Letter, and show'd me several written Characters from different Masters he had work'd with, all strongly in his favour for Ingenuity and Skill in his Business, as well as his Sobriety and Industry. He was a Quaker, and seem'd a sensible young Man, so that I was strongly inclin'd to send him till I understood he had a wife and young Family, which would

9. The date, lost in a tear, was clearly that of the letter above, XIX, 373–4, with which the Managers enclosed the present of silk that BF acknowledges at the end of this letter. See also the following document.

1. Those who throw or twist silk or, more broadly, are associated with the process of preparing silk for the weaver.

2. The broker, Boydell, is identified in *idem.*, p. 68; for Freeman see above, XVI, 250 n.

3. The financial crisis of 1772, for which see above, XIX, 315–16.

make it too expensive: Tho' he said his Wife was a Workwoman in the Business, and one Child could also be serviceable. He is endeavouring to get Subscriptions to pay the Passage Money, but I suppose will hardly succeed, as People here would rather maintain the Workmen idle, for a while, than pay towards sending them to America.[4]

I am much obliged to the Managers for their Present of 4 lb of the Silk, and shall consider what Purpose I can apply it to, that may best contribute to the Encouragement of the Produce.[5] Please to offer them my thankful Acknowledgements, and assure them of my most faithful Services. With great Esteem and Respect, I am, Gentlemen, Your most obedient humble Servant

B FRANKLIN

Messrs Abel James Benja Morgan

To Cadwalader Evans ALS (letterbook draft): Library of Congress

Dear Friend,   London, Feb. 10. 1773.

The Account of your Illness gave me great Concern, and I was glad to learn by yours of Nov 16. that you were mending. I hope by this time you are perfectly recovered.[6]

I have given you Credit for the Silk Committee's Bill of £152 2s. 9d. and have paid Wheeler the 20 Guineas you ordered.[7]

I was in the Country when the Truss was sent by Mr. Hewson, to the Coffee house made up in a Parcel directed to you. The Messenger remembers well the Delivery of it there, and that he saw it put into the Bag. But it is thought Osborne might be gone, and that it went in some of the other Ships.[8] I inclose you a List

---

4. The young man, Joseph Clark, did succeed in raising the money and left for Philadelphia; see BF to the Managers below, March 15.

5. See above, XIX, 374. BF decided that he could best encourage the produce by bedecking his womenfolk: he had the gift made into heavy corded silk for DF and Sally. To DF below, July 15.

6. The hope was not borne out; Evans was near the end of a lingering illness, and died on June 30: Pa. Gaz., July 7, 1773.

7. For the silk transaction and Wheeler's role see above, the preceding document and BF to the committee, Jan. 6.

8. See above, XIX, 203 n, 204, 272.

of them which I got from the Coffee house Books, that you may the better know how to make the Enquiry. The Master of the Coffee house is positive it was sent, no such thing remaining in his Care. Perhaps it may be come to hand before this time. I am ever, my dear Friend, Yours most affectionately   B F

I send you a Pamphlet on a Subject (Fix'd Air) that at present engrosses much of the Attention of Philosophers and Physicians here.[9]

Dr Cadwr Evans

To James Hunter[1]   ALS (letterbook draft): Library of Congress

Sir   London, Feb. 10. 1773

I duly received your Letter of Nov. 16. and in Answer acquaint you, that you may draw on me for Eighty-seven Pounds ten Shillings Sterling at 30 Days Sight, and the Bill shall be punctually paid. I am glad your Daughter is arrived at an Age when the Money may be of Use to her, and I wish her and you good Luck with it. When you draw send me a Letter of Advice with a Receipt expressing that the Payment of the Bill will be in full for the Principal of the Legacy, £50 and the Interest for 15 Years, at 5 per Cent and of all Demands. I am Sir, Your most obedient humble Servant   B FRANKLIN

Mr James Hunter

9. Joseph Priestley was investigating fixed air, or carbon dioxide, and had recently published two pamphlets on the subject: the brief *Directions for Impregnating Water with Fixed Air* ... (London, 1772) and the much longer and more important *Observations on Different Kinds of Air* ... (London, 1772), which also touched on the subject; the latter was a preprint of his paper in the *Phil. Trans.* discussed above, XIX, 214. BF sent this pamphlet to Rush with his letter below of Feb. 14, but his phrasing here suggests that he sent Evans the *Directions*.

1. A Philadelphian about whom we know nothing, except that he spoke of his "low sphere of life" in his reply below, April 24. He had married Mary Wheatley, the niece of an English clergyman whose will, in 1756, left a £100 legacy to her two sons, one by an earlier marriage and the other her eldest by Hunter. BF was named trustee, with discretion to pay the money in equal shares to them or for their use. Public Record Office, Prob. 11/823/

To James Johnston[2]   ALS (letterbook draft): Library of Congress

Sir,   London, Feb. 10. 1773

I received your Letter, with the Sample of N. American Senna, which I put into the Hands of a Friend who is a great Botanist as well as a Physician,[3] and has made some Trial of it. He tells me that to render it merchantable here, the Stalks should be pick'd out, and the Leaves pack'd up neatly, as that is which comes from the Levant. Perhaps among your Druggists you might see some of those Packages, and so inform yourself of the manner. He has not yet had sufficient Experience of it to be decisive in his Opinion of its Qualities in Comparison with other Senna, but thinks it likely that it may answer the same purposes. Of the Quantity that may be in demand here, I have yet been able to obtain no Intelligence. I am, Sir, Your humble Servant   B FRANKLIN

Mr James Johnston

------

155. He arranged to apprentice the older boy and take care of the other's schooling. But this younger son apparently died before anything was spent on him, and his £50 share devolved upon his surviving sister as his heir. Above, VII, 99, 378–9. Hunter must have told BF, in a letter since lost, that the girl was now old enough to use the money.

2. We have not the remotest idea who he was. The letter to which BF is replying has been lost, and the reply when sent was never delivered. BF addressed it to James Johnston (WF spelled it Johnson) at Philadelphia, and it turned up in the equivalent of the dead letter office because no one could identify the man. WF to BF below, April 30. The lists of unclaimed letters published that year in the *Pa. Gaz.* contain none to a Philadelphian of the name, however spelled. BF seems to have known little more about the man than we do.

3. Undoubtedly Dr. John Fothergill. Senna, as a purgative, was part of a doctor's pharmacopoeia.

From Jacques Barbeu-Dubourg

Printed in Jacques Barbeu-Dubourg, ed., *Œuvres de M. Franklin* . . .
(2 vols., Paris, 1773), II, 246–57.

Monsieur, 12 Février 1773.

J'ai trouvé votre Lettre à M. Néave beaucoup trop courte, parce que les choses excellentes qu'elle contient, m'ont appris à en desirer beaucoup d'autres dont je n'aurois peut-être jamais eu la moindre idée.[4] On ne m'a point fait apprendre à nager dans ma jeunesse, et je n'y ai gueres songé depuis. Je viens de chercher dans le grand Dictionnaire Encyclopédique, aux mots *nager*, *natation*, &c. tout ce qu'on y dit sur l'art de nager; et j'ai été surpris de voir combien on est peu avancé à cet égard. C'est cependant un objet si intéressant pour l'humanité, qu'il sembleroit mériter plus d'attention de la part des Physiciens, et même des Gouvernemens.

Après cet aveu que je vous ai fait de mon ignorance en cette matiere, il m'appartiendroit moins qu'à personne de la traiter; mais au moins me pardonnera-t-on de solliciter ceux qui sont en état de le faire; et je ne connois personne qui le puisse mieux que vous-même.

Je n'attens pas de vous un traité en forme, vous avez trop peu de loisir; mais entre une multitude de questions qui s'offrent en foule à mon esprit, je vous demande de jetter quelques traits de lumiere sur celles qui vous paroîtront mériter plus particuliére-ment votre attention.

Je les diviserai en trois Sections. La premiere roulera sur quelques notions préliminaires. La seconde sur les points princi-paux et essentiels de cet art. La troisieme enfin sur diverses conséquences, et autres considérations accessoires.

PREMIERE SECTION.

I. Le premier objet seroit, à mon avis, de déterminer le poids d'un pied cubique d'eau commune, puis successivement d'eau plus ou moins trouble, plus ou moins salée.

De déterminer également le poids ordinaire du corps humain,

---

4. For BF's famous letter to Neave on swimming see above, XV, 295–8. BF responded at some length to this treatise from Dubourg, and extracts of his reply are printed below under the end of March.

en pésant un homme adulte tant dans l'air que dans l'eau, afin
d'avoir la pesanteur moyenne d'un pied cubique de son corps;
de péser également une femme, un enfant, un viellard; d'en péser
même plusieurs, pour juger à quoi peuvent aller les différences
entr'eux à cet égard. Vous savez ce qu'on a avancé, il y a peu
d'années, dans les nouvelles publiques, au sujet d'un Prêtre de
Naples dont le corps n'enfonce, dit-on, aucunement dans l'eau.[5]

Peut-être donc se trouveroit-il des hommes dont le corps
flotteroit naturellement dans l'eau, comme la plupart des bois
ordinaires, et ce seroit, je crois, le plus grand nombre; d'autres,
en petit nombre, qui surnageroient comme le liége, ou qui
enfonceroient très-peu; et d'autres enfin, en plus petit nombre
encore, qui iroient tout-à-coup au fonds de l'eau, comme le
buis.

Tâcher de déterminer quelle quantité du volume total s'enfonc-
eroit dans l'eau, et quelle quantité seroit soutenue au-dessus de
l'eau dans un homme ordinaire.

Faire ensorte de déterminer le plus exactement qu'il seroit
possible, le rapport tant en volume qu'en pésanteur des différentes parties du corps humain. Le moyen qui me paroîtroit
le plus propre pour atteindre assez près de ce but, seroit de péser
d'abord tout le corps hors de l'eau, puis de le péser de nouveau
dans un grand vaisseau, où il auroit toutes les extrêmités inférieures dans l'eau et le reste hors de l'eau; puis successivement,
ayant tout le tronc du corps dans l'eau et les bras et la tête hors
de l'eau; ensuite ayant la tête seule hors de l'eau; et enfin ayant
tout le corps à la fois sous l'eau (ce qui ne seroit que l'affaire
d'un instant;) et au moyen d'un tube gradué, adapté au vaisseau
où l'eau seroit contenue, on auroit la mesure exacte de la quantité
d'eau déplacée par chacune des parties du corps, d'où résulteroit
la connoissance du volume de chacune, et par conséquent celle
des rapports de leur volume à leur poids, ce qu'on appelle leur
pésanteur spécifique.

II. Le second objet seroit de considerer la structure particu-
liere, et les différentes manoeuvres des animaux qui vivent
continuellement dans l'eau, ou qui la frequentent habituellement,

5. An editor's responsibility, in our opinion, does not extend to running
down Neapolitan miracles.

afin d'en tirer quelques inductions et de reconnoitre jusqu'à quel point on pourroit imiter par art ce que l'instinct leur fait faire.

Ainsi les tortues marchent au fond de l'eau, et peuvent y rester long-tems; mais enfin elles sont obligées de venir quelquefois respirer l'air. D'où vient qu'elles en ont si rarement besoin, tandis que nous en avons un besoin continuel? De ce que leur coeur n'a qu'un ventricule et que le nôtre en a deux, entre lesquels il y a une communication ouverte dans le foetus, par le *trou ovale* qui se bouche pour l'ordinaire peu de tems après la naissance, non pas pourtant si généralement qu'on ne le trouve quelquefois ouvert dans un âge assez avancé; on prétend, avec beaucoup de vraisemblance, que de tels sujets pourroient, comme les tortues, demeurer long-tems sous l'eau sans respirer: tel étoit vraisemblablement le fameux plongeur Pescecola, (ou Nicolas Poisson) en Sicile au 15e siecle, qui pouvoit rester deux ou trois heures sous l'eau;[6] sur quoi il a été proposé d'essayer si l'on ne pourroit pas procurer le même avantage à un enfant quelconque, en l'habituant dès sa naissance à passer chaque jour quelque tems dans l'eau, comme il y étoit dans le sein de sa mere.[7]

Si cette expérience paroit trop délicate, et trop hasardeuse, en voici une beaucoup plus simple, quoique fort embarrassante encore, et dont on cite divers succès: elle consiste à ménager à un plongeur une certaine provision d'air frais, en lui couvrant la tête en entier, et même au-delà, avec une espece de cloche portative dont la matiere ne seroit pas indifférente, quoique aucune ne soit capable de prévenir tout-à-fait une énorme condensation de l'air qui met les poumons fort mal à l'aise.

Tous, ou la plupart des poissons ont été pourvus par la nature d'une espece de vessie aërienne, en forme de double poche, qu'ils compriment ou dilatent à leur gré, pour se soutenir à différentes profondeurs entre deux eaux, descendre tout-à-fait au fond, ou s'élever à la surface. N'y auroit-il pas moyen d'imiter

---

6. Dubourg underestimated this legendary Italian: Nicholas the Fish was credited with the ability to remain under water an entire day. See Charles Steedman, *A Manual of Swimming* ... (London, 1873), pp. 148–52.

7. The proposal was in Jean F. Bachstrom, *L'Art de nager* ... (Amsterdam, 1741), pp. 13–14.

le mécanisme de ces sortes de vessies, qui seroient évidemment de la plus grande utilité? On assure que M. Baffert,[8] l'a en quelque sorte imité avec une espece de pompe.

Tous, ou la plupart des poissons ont reçu de la nature des nageoires pour frapper l'eau, et s'en faire un point d'appui qui les fasse avancer dans telle direction qu'il leur plait. Les oiseaux aquatiques ont les pattes tellement conformées qu'elles leur tiennent lieu de nageoires; les doigts en sont assemblés par des membranes qui s'ouvrent et se ferment en éventail, afin d'offrir plus ou moins de surface, plus ou moins de résistance à l'eau. Les oiseaux destitués de ces sortes de membranes craignent naturellement l'eau, quoique leur corps soit naturellement assez léger pour n'y pas enfoncer, parce qu'ils manquent d'un instrument propre à s'y mouvoir à volonté. L'art a imité en quelque sorte les nageoires et les pattes d'oye dans les rames des barques; mais ne pouvant donner à ces rames la flexibilité en éventail, on tâche d'y suppléer en tournant leur palette tantôt sur son plat et tantôt sur sa tranche, suivant le besoin. Les pattes d'oye ne sont pas difficiles à imiter avec des gants à éventail, qu'on peut faire de taffetas ciré.[9]

III. Le troisieme objet seroit de considerer spécialement quelles sont les parties du corps qui ont le plus de propension à prendre le dessous, et qui sont celles qu'il importe le plus de tenir au-dessus de l'eau.

De déterminer où est le centre de gravité du corps, et quelle des parties extérieures en est la plus proche, et en conséquence doit naturellement enfoncer la premiere.

La bouche et les narines étant manifestement les parties du corps qu'il est le plus nécessaire de tenir au-dessus de l'eau, de peur qu'il n'y entre de l'eau à chaque inspiration (pouvant pénétrer par cette voie dans l'estomac, dans les intestins, et peut-être même dans les poumons); considérer et avertir des divers moyens de tenir la face au-dessus de l'eau, dont le plus facile est vraisemblablement la position sur le dos.

8. Perhaps Nicolas-Marie Baffert (d. 1793), a well-known engineer and architect in Lyon. *Dictionnaire de biographie.*

9. [*Dubourg's note:*] C'est M. Dupont [de Nemours] qui m'en a suggéré l'idée.

2e. Section.

Venons maintenant au principal objet, c'est-à-dire, à ce qui constitue proprement l'art de nager, et pour plus de clarté, distinguons-y deux points essentiels, sçavoir les moyens de se soutenir à la superficie de l'eau, et les moyens de s'y mouvoir à son gré dans tous les sens. Chacun de ces points mérite d'être traité séparément.

I. Il est donc question en premier lieu d'examiner les divers moyens de se soutenir sur l'eau, ou de remonter du fonds de l'eau avec des secours accessoires, ou sans aide, ou même malgré quelques obstacles.

Il est aisé de concevoir que tout ce qui peut compenser l'excès de la pesanteur de nos corps sur la pesanteur de l'eau doit nous soutenir à la surface. Des corps légers fermement attachés à nos corps, et convenablement placés, peuvent très-bien remplir cet objet. Le liége tient le premier rang dans ce genre, attendu sa légereté naturelle avec une solidité suffisante. Les calebasses, les vessies, les bouteilles peuvent y suppléer, pourvu que leur intérieur soit vide, leur gouleau bien bouché, et que leurs parois ayent une force de résistance suffisante. Le scaphandre de M. l'Abbé de la Chapelle est (à ce qu'on m'a assuré) fort supérieur à tout cela dans le même genre;[10] mais j'ai entendu parler de certains corselets, ou soubrevestes, inventés en Angleterre, et qu'on prétend qui ne lui cédent en rien; c'est ce que vous êtes plus à portée que moi de verifier.

Mais supposons l'homme abandonné à lui-même, sans tous ces secours extérieurs, et supposons le au fond de l'eau, quelle ressource a-t-il pour remonter à la surface? Il en a une bien simple et immanquable. Qu'il fasse précisément ce qu'il feroit, s'il avoit les pieds dans un bourbier, pour s'y enfoncer davantage: qu'il fasse effort pour frapper la terre avec les pieds; son action ne sera point en pure perte. Ses pieds ne pouvant avancer suivant la direction qu'il leur aura imprimée, seront repoussés avec le même degré de force dans une direction diamétralement opposée,

---

10. Jean-Baptiste de la Chapelle (1710?–92) had described his invention in *Le Ventriloque, ou l'engastrimythe* . . . (Paris, 1772), pp. 3, 21–30. He subsequently devoted a book to it: *Traité de la construction . . . du scaphandre ou du bateau de l'homme* (Paris, 1775).

c'est-à-dire de bas en haut, et son corps se retrouvera presque dans l'instant à la surface de l'eau.

Arrivé ainsi à la superficie, il s'agit de s'y soutenir. Il faut donc considérer en quelle position il s'y trouve d'abord; ce qui résulte immédiatement de cette position, et ce qu'il a à faire en conséquence.

Il remonte à la surface dans une situation verticale, la tête sortante au-dessus de l'eau. Bientôt le poids de la tête la renverse sur l'eau, et les extrêmités inférieures continuant à s'élever, l'homme se trouve étendu à plat à fleur d'eau dans une situation horisontale. Dans cette position, son corps présente à l'eau sa surface la plus étendue, et ne peut enfoncer sans déplacer un très-grand volume d'eau.

Alors qu'il fasse effort de tout son corps pour l'enfoncer dans l'eau, en faisant agir de concert tous les muscles abdominaux, pectoraux, dorsaux, lombaires, &c., contre la couche inférieure de l'eau sur laquelle repose la masse de son corps; l'eau leur résistera avec la même force, et par sa réaction soutiendra le corps de l'homme, et tendra même à le soulever de plus en plus.

Le moyen que vous avez imaginé pour inculquer cette leçon, en proposant de jetter un oeuf au fond de l'eau, et de s'efforcer de l'en retirer promptement,[1] est on ne peut pas plus ingénieux, et tout-à-fait propre non-seulement à inspirer de la confiance dans la force de l'eau, mais encore à enseigner sans affectation le grand et seul vrai secret de mettre cette force à profit.

La peur, en pareil cas, n'empêche pas seulement de prendre à propos un bon parti, mais elle fait faire précisément le contraire de ce qui convient. L'homme effrayé se redresse de toute sa force, pour tâcher de remonter à la superficie. En relevant ses mains, il frappe l'eau de dessous en dessus, et en est repoussé en sens contraire, c'est-à-dire, de haut en bas. En abaissant ses pieds qui offrent à l'eau moins de superficie que son ventre ou son dos; ils font l'office de coins pour fendre l'eau, et l'homme est bientôt précipité au fond.

Il doit être sans contredit plus facile de nager tout nud qu'avec des habits, ou autres corps étrangers; ainsi il seroit bon de considérer les effets qui peuvent résulter tant de l'embarras des habits

---

1. In the letter to Neave.

que de leur pésanteur; les meilleurs expédiens, soit pour en supporter la charge, soit pour s'en débarrasser; et enfin de quel poids la prudence permet, ou ne permet pas à un bon et fort nageur de se charger, lorsqu'il a une riviere à traverser à la nage.

II. En second lieu, comme, à proprement parler, flotter sur l'eau ce n'est pas encore nager; il faut sçavoir donner à son corps un mouvement progressif sur l'eau, suivant telle direction que l'on juge à propos; il me semble que cette question peut se résoudre aisément par les mêmes principes que les précédentes.

Voyez un canard dans une piece d'eau, et considerez comment, avec ses pattes déployées, il chasse l'eau en arriere, pour en être rechassé, et se porter en avant.

Que vos mains allongées pointent, pour ainsi dire, en avant avec les doigts, et frappent l'eau avec leurs paumes en se rapprochant du corps. Que les plantes de vos pieds étendues, poussent fortement l'eau en arriere. L'eau de l'avant cédera à vos mains, l'eau de l'arriere réagira contre vos pieds avec une force presqu' égale à celle que vous aurez déployée; et vous avancerez à proportion.

Lorsque vous voudrez changer de direction, il vous suffira de tourner un peu la paume de vos mains er la plante de vos pieds, et d'en frapper l'eau à droite pour vous porter à gauche, ou à gauche pour vous porter à droite.

Il semble qu'on pourroit établir comme un théorême fondamental de l'art de nager qu'il faut faire agir ses pieds dans l'eau tout au contraire de ce qu'on feroit hors de l'eau; en frapper en arriere avec une force proportionnée à l'élan que l'on veut se donner en avant, en frapper l'eau à gauche pour aller à droite, et à droite pour aller à gauche, s'attendre en un mot que leur action sera contrariée en tout par la réaction de l'eau, faire fonds sur cette force répulsive, et se gouverner en consequence.

Ces principes admis, il s'agit de discuter les moyens les plus convenables et les moins fatiguans, soit pour se soutenir longtems sur l'eau, soit pour faire beaucoup de chemin en nageant.

De mettre en parallele les avantages et les inconvéniens des différentes positions du corps, dont les deux principales sont d'être couché sur le ventre, ou d'être couché sur le dos en nageant. La petite voute que le dos forme en-dessous n'est-elle d'aucune utilité? Quoiqu'il en soit, l'élévation de la face dans cette derniere situation semble une grande raison de préférence en sa faveur: sçavoir si, et jusqu'à quel point elle est balancée d'ailleurs?

Comparer les forces respectives des mains et des pieds pour frapper l'eau, les différentes manieres de les déployer, et de les faire agir conjointement ou séparément, en même tems ou alternativement, en battant l'eau ou en la pressant simplement. Les pieds ne peuvent servir que pour avancer en frappant de leur plante en arriere: les mains peuvent servir pour se soutenir et pour avancer, suivant qu'on en tourne la paume constamment en-dessous, ou qu'on la retourne en arriere.

Rechercher comment on peut se retourner lorsqu'on le juge à propos du dos sur le ventre, et comment on peut s'empêcher de tourner involontairement.

Combien de tems il est possible de se soutenir à flot en ménageant ses forces, et quel est le plus grand espace qu'un nageur puisse parcourir sur un canal dans un tems donné.

Comment on peut résister à un courant plus ou moins fort, et quel courant on peut entreprendre de traverser en croisant l'eau avec ses bras alternativement.

III. Examiner en troisieme lieu, s'il est plus utile de se tourner tantôt sur le dos et tantôt sur le ventre, ou de conserver toujours la même position.

Quelle est la profondeur de l'eau la plus favorable aux nageurs, &c.

IV. En quatrieme lieu, prévoir tous les accidens qui peuvent arriver dans l'eau, comme des coups, des crampes, des défaillances, &c.

Aviser aux ressources qui peuvent rester en pareils cas; comme pourroit-être quelquefois de marcher au fond de l'eau et de remonter de tems en tems à la surface, tant pour respirer que pour s'orienter.

3e. Section.

I. Considerer en premier lieu le plaisir du bain, et de l'exercice dans l'eau.

A quel âge à-peu-près on peut le procurer aux jeunes gens.

S'il seroit absurde de le procurer même aux personnes de l'autre sexe.

53

II. En second lieu, rechercher l'utilité de l'art de nager, et ne point se dissimuler les inconvéniens.

S'il devroit faire partie de l'éducation ordinaire de la jeunesse.

A quelles professions il paroit plus spécialement nécessaire.

S'il n'est pas sur-tout nécessaire aux Militaires.

III. Considérer en troisieme lieu les effets salutaires du bain, et de l'exercice dans l'eau.

Les degrés de chaleur ou de froid qui rendent le bain et l'exercice de nager plus ou moins sain ou malsain.

A quelles heures il convient de se baigner.

Combien il est essentiel que ce soit plutôt avant qu'après le repas.

Si l'on peut se permettre de prendre quelques boissons ou quelques alimens dans l'eau, et en quelle quantité.

Si l'on doit éviter d'entrer dans le bain étant fort échauffé, et quel en est le danger.

IV. En quatrieme lieu, considérer s'il est aisé d'apprendre de soi-même à nager, et de combien il est plus aisé de l'apprendre avec un bon maître.

Combien on s'y fortifie par l'habitude et l'exercice fréquent.

Et si on peut l'oublier faute de l'exercer.

V. En cinquieme lieu, donner des instructions simples et faciles à se rappeller pour ceux à qui il arriveroit de tomber dans l'eau sans sçavoir nager.

Indiquer des précautions peu dispendieuses à ceux qui ayant à voyager sur l'eau, sont exposés à ces sortes d'accidens.

Rechercher particulierement de quelle matiere, et en quelle forme on pourroit se faire des habillemens moins à charge, et moins embarrassans dans l'eau que ceux qui sont communément en usage.

VI. En sixieme lieu, savoir lorsqu'on apperçoit quelqu'un en danger de se noyer, comment on peut le secourir.

Quels sont les moyens les plus efficaces pour cet effet, et les attentions convenables pour ne pas s'exposer soi-même.

VII. En septieme lieu, considérer l'état des noyés et la cause formelle de leur mort.

Ce qui peut les faire croire morts lorsqu'ils ne le sont pas encore.

Quels sont les secours les plus prompts et les plus puissans qu'on puisse leur donner en pareils cas.

VIII. En huitieme lieu, rechercher tout ce qui a rapport à cet objet dans les anciens Auteurs, et discuter s'il y avoit dans les gymnases des peuples les plus célebres de l'antiquité, des maîtres pour apprendre à la jeunesse à nager, et si l'on nous a transmis quelques-uns de leurs préceptes.

Analyser ou critiquer sans prévention les différens écrits des modernes sur cette matiere.

S'informer aux voyageurs, si, et jusqu'à quel point l'art de nager est spécialement cultivé dans tels ou tels pays.

IX. En dernier lieu, aviser aux établissemens qui peuvent être à desirer, ou à proposer relativement à cet objet, principalement dans de grandes villes situées sur des rivieres, comme Paris, Londres, &c. afin de procurer plus de sureté contre ces sortes de dangers à quantité de citoyens, et plus d'assurance à tous contre la crainte même de ces dangers, dont l'idée seule fait frissonner quantité de personnes.

Si la gare à Paris,[2] ne seroit pas commode pour cela?

Je suis, &c.

To Richard Bache   ALS (letterbook draft): Library of Congress

Dear Son,   London, Feb. 14. [1773]

By Capt. All I send a Box directed to you containing a Number of Parcels for different People, which I request you to take care of that they may be carefully delivered. Among the rest there are 5 Doz Maps in a Roll with your Name on the Outside, of which you may take 6 for yourself, send Six to your Brother at Burlington, and give the rest to my Cousin Davenport.[3]

Mrs. Stevenson desires me to tell you, that as the Lace was tarnished and unfit for farther wear, she had burnt and sold it,[4]

2. The docking area on the Seine.
3. See the following document.
4. She must have melted down what was often called bullion lace, probably silver guipure, which was made of threads of that metal and would naturally tarnish. See Fanny M. Palliser, *History of Lace* (M. Jourdain and Alice Dryden, eds.; 4th ed., London, 1902), pp. 36–40, 90–1, 211–12, 349.

and with the Money bought you a fashionable Trimming to a new Wastecoat which goes in the Box. There is also a Gown, for your Wife and some Trifles for Ben, that he too may have his Parcel.

Your good Mother and Sisters were well last Week, as I learn by a Letter I then receiv'd from Preston.

I wrote to you a few Lines per Packet.[5] I am ever, Your affectionate Father   B FRANKLIN

Mr Bache

To Josiah Davenport   ALS (letterbook draft): Library of Congress

Although Franklin's nephew has often appeared in these volumes, he remains a shadowy figure; his only clear characteristic is that he drew financial troubles to him like his cousin, Benjamin Mecom. Davenport had been for a time a baker in Philadelphia, then a storekeeper and Indian agent in Pittsburgh.[6] By 1766 he was back in Philadelphia, where he tried and failed to establish a coffee house. Next he opened a tavern, the Bunch of Grapes on Third Street, which was a gathering place for merchants.[7] It failed, and he turned to a bookshop. Franklin heard of this development, and also that Davenport wanted a position in the Post Office; the news probably came from Josiah's son Enoch, who had been in London the year before[8] and may have stayed on, and who at some point doubtless visited his great-uncle. In any case Franklin sent, for the bookshop, the small contribution mentioned below, and minced no words in turning down the idea of a postal appointment. Before his letter was written, however, Josiah's circumstances had changed: his bookstore in turn had failed, and William Franklin had taken pity on him and brought him to Burlington as his private secretary. Soon the Governor was asking his father to intercede

5. Above, Feb. 3.

6. See above, I, lx, and the scattered references to him in *PMHB*, xxxvii (1913) and LXXI (1947).

7. Between April 7 and Oct. 27, 1767, he sent three petitions about the coffee house to the Mayor's Court. APS. For references to the tavern see the *Pa. Gaẓ.*, Sept. 27, Oct. 4, 1770, and *PMHB*, xiv (1890), 43, and for its name and location John T. Scharf and Thompson Westcott, *History of Philadelphia* . . . (3 vols., Philadelphia, 1884), II, 996. While he was keeping the tavern Josiah seems to have sold prints on the side; see above, XVI, 4.

8. Above, XIX, 42.

with Lord North for a customs post for Davenport, a suggestion that the senior Franklin rejected as brusquely as he had the earlier one.[9] After burning his fingers with Benjamin Mecom, as he says here, he had no intention of getting involved with another ne'er-do-well nephew.

Loving Cousin,   London, Feb. 14—73

I was sorry to hear of your Failing in your Business. I hear you now keep a little Shop and therefore send you 4 Doz of Evans's Maps,[1] which if you can sell you are welcome to apply the Money towards Clothing your Boys or to any other Purpose. Enoch seems a solid sensible Lad, and I hope will do well. If you will be advis'd [do not?] think of any Place in the Post Office. The Money you receive will slip thro' your Fingers, and you will run behind-hand, imperceptibly, when your Securities must suffer, or your Employers. I grow too old to run such Risques, and therefore wish you to propose nothing more of the kind to me. I have been hurt too much by endeavouring to help Cousin Ben Mecom. I have no Opinion of the Punctuality of Cousins. They are apt to take Liberties with Relations they would not take with others, from a Confidence that a Relation will not sue them. And tho' I believe you now resolve and intend well in case of such an Appointment, I can have no Dependence that some unexpected Misfortune or Difficulty will not embarras your Affairs and render you again insolvent. Don't take this unkind. It is better to be thus free with you, than to give you Expectations that cannot be answered. I should be glad to see you in some Business that would require neither Stock nor Credit, and yet might afford a comfortable Subsistence, being ever I am, Your affectionate Uncle   B F

Mr Josia Davenport

9. See below, WF to BF, May 4, and BF to WF, July 14.

1. They were sent to Bache (see the preceding document) and were copies of a pirated edition, an inaccurate reissue by Carington Bowles in 1771 of Evans' 1755 map. Thomas Pownall held the original plates in trust for Amelia Evans; she was BF's goddaughter, and he was encouraging an enterprise that competed with her father's work. See Henry N. Stevens, *Lewis Evans: His Map of the Middle British Colonies* . . . (3rd ed., London, 1924), p. 25; Lawrence H. Gipson, *Lewis Evans* . . . (Philadelphia, 1939), pp. 81–2.

To Nathaniel Falconer   ALS (letterbook draft): Library of Congress

Dear Friend,   London, Feb. 14. 1773

I thank you heartily for your very kind Present of Nuts and Apples, they are both excellent, and very much refresh me. We were sorry to miss you at Christmas. If you will not come and keep it with us, we must e'en go and keep it with you.

If the Land Affair is ever compleated, (which God only knows whether it will be or not) you may rely on my taking as much Care of your Interest as of my own.[2] Some People are very confident of seeing a speedy End to the Sollicitation, but they seem to me to hollow before they are out of the Wood. The less we talk of the Business the better. With great and sincere Respect, I am, my dear Friend, Yours very affectionately   B FRANKLIN

Capt. Falconer

To Deborah Franklin   ALS (letterbook draft): Library of Congres s

My dear Child,   London, Feb. 14. 1773

I wrote to you a few Days since by the Packet.[3] In a Box directed to Mr. Bache I send a striped Cotton and Silk Gown for you, of a Manufacture now much the Mode here. There is another for Sally. People line them with some old Silk Gown, and they look very handsome. There goes also a Bedstead for Sally, sent on Capt. All's telling Mrs. Stevenson that you wish'd it had been sent with the Bed.[4] She sends also some little Things for Benny-boy.

2. See above, XIX, 292, 371–2. Falconer announced in his reply below, May 13, that he had sold his right to the Whartons, for the implied reason that he wanted nothing more to do with them. Another reason seems to have been that this letter from BF discouraged him: below, p. 306.

3. Undoubtedly the letter of Feb. 2 above; that was a Tuesday, and mail for the New York packet was made up on the first Wednesday of the month.

4. BF had written the previous summer that the bedstead, according to Mrs. Stevenson, should not have a cornice: above, XIX, 267. Sally was consulting her on the current fashion, we take this to mean, and BF did not realize until All's message that she wanted the bedstead made in London rather than Philadelphia.

Now having nothing very material to add, let us trifle a little. The fine large grey Squirrel you sent, who was a great Favourite in the Bishop's Family, is dead. He had got out of his Cage, in the Country, and was rambling over a Common 3 Miles from home, when he met a Man with a Dog. The Dog pursuing him, he fled to the Man for Protection; running up to his Shoulder who shook him off, and set the Dog on him, thinking him to be, as he said afterwards, *some Varment or other*. So poor *Mungo*, as his Mistress call'd him, died. To amuse you a little, and nobody out of your own House, I enclose you the little Correspondence between her and me on the melancholy Occasion. Skugg, you must know is a common Name by which all Squirrels are called here, as all Cats are called *Puss*. Miss Georgiana is the Bishops youngest Daughter but one. There are five in all. Mungo was buried in the Garden, and the enclos'd Epitaph put upon his Monument. So much for Squirrels.[5]

My poor Cousin Walker in Buckinghamshire is a Lacemaker.[6] She was ambitious of presenting you and Sally with some Netting of her Work: But as I knew she could not afford it, I chose to pay her for it at her usual Price 3*s*. 6*d*. per Yard. It goes also in the Box. I name the Price, that if it does not suit you to wear it, you may know how to dispose of it.

I have desired Miss Haydock to repay you £8 6*s*. o*d*. Sterling, which I have laid out for her here, on Account of her Silk. I think it is not the Colour she desired. I suppose her Relation Mrs. Forster, who took the Management of it, will give her the Reason.[7] My Love to Sally and the dear Boy. I am ever, Your affectionate Husband   B FRANKLIN

5. For the tragedy of Mungo and the epitaph on him see *idem.*, pp. 300–2. DF dutifully replaced him: to BF below, Oct. 29.

6. Hannah Farrow Walker, BF's indigent relative, has appeared often before, most recently in her letter the previous December: XIX, 436.

7. For the involved business of the silk see BF to Rebecca Haydock below, Feb. 14, and the references there.

To William Franklin   ALS (letterbook draft): Library of Congress

Dear Son,   London, Feb. 14. 1773

Your late Letters of Oct. 13, 29, Nov. 3, Dec. 1. and 4. lying all before me, I shall answer the Particulars in order; such I mean as I have not answered by other Opportunities.

I have written to Mr. Bolton of Birmingham for a Plated Tea Urn, he being by far the best Maker, and his Work of the newest Fashion.[8] If it does not come in time to go by this Ship, I shall send it per Sutton.

I see Mr. Wharton of late but seldom. When I receiv'd your Account of the Virginia Transactions, I mention'd it to Mr. Strahan, and told him I purpos'd to communicate it to Mr. Walpole. But being much taken up with some other Business I did not immediately do it, and in the mean time he spoke of it to Mr. Wharton. This brought him and Major Trent to me, with a Pocket full of Papers to satisfy me that there was nothing in it, all their Grants being either out of our Boundaries or Void.[9] The first Paper he put into my hands was an Extract of a Letter from Col. Washington to the Govr. which I read aloud, and when I came to the Part where he says the propos'd New Colony will deprive Virginia of a great deal of Territory and take in such and such prior Grants, the Major said that was all nothing, the Letter being written before Col. Washington knew what our Boundaries were; but on reading a little farther it appeared that he knew our Boundaries, for he recited them verbatim to prove what he had advanc'd.[1] I remark'd this to the Major and he said no more: But Mr. W. to show that he knew all the Virginia Proceed-

8. Only WF's two October letters have survived. For the tea urn see above, XIX, 336 n, and BF to WF below, March 3 and 15, July 14.

9. The conference BF is describing was held on Jan. 30, and left Samuel Wharton bitter against both BF and WF; see Wharton's letter quoted in Gipson, *British Empire*, XI, 481–2. WF's "Account of the Virginia Transactions" was the paper he enclosed in his second October letter: above, XIX, 350.

1. Washington's letter was to Gov. Botetourt of Oct. 5, 1770; it complained that the proposed Walpole grant would be a fatal blow to Virginian interests, and would deprive officers and soldiers of land guaranteed them in compensation for their past services, John C. Fitzpatrick, *The Writings of George Washington* . . . (39 vols., Washington, [1931–44]), III, 26–9. For this guarantee to veterans see above, XIX, 3–4 n.

ings before, (for he knows every thing *before*[2]) put another Paper into my hand that contain'd the Resolutions of Assembly, repeating what he had once told me before, and what I suppose he has told the other Partners, that the £2,500 paid by Virginia for the Purchase of the Cherokees, or for the Line, was not Money belonging to the Province but to the King, being out of the Quitrents, and therefore did not give that Province any equitable Claim against a Grant of the Crown to us. This Fact I knew your Paper contradicted, and therefore I ran over his Paper with my Eye to see if it was omitted, but unluckily for him I found the Resolve of the House there among the rest, and reading it to him, he blush'd! and was a little confus'd, saying only, that it was Money granted to the King, and so became the King's Money the same as the Quitrents, and therefore if the King bought Land with it he might sell that Land to us.[3] Then he show'd me the List of Grants, which he said were most of them void as being beyond the Limits prescrib'd by the Proclamation of 1763; and he had written in the Margin against almost every one of them *Void, Void*, or *not in our Limits*, or *laps'd*. On casting my Eye over them, I remark'd to him that most of them were prior to the Proclamation of 1763, and therefore it should seem could not be affected by that Proclamation. He then said, they were however contrary to prior Instructions, but those Instructions he had not with him to show me.[4] It seems probable that what he said to me has been his Discourse to others, and thereby become so habitual to his Tongue, that he repeated it as of course,

2. And BF had said this before: *ibid.*, p. 349.

3. For the Virginia proceedings and WF's paper, which contradicted Wharton's claim that the £2,500 came from quitrents, see above, XIX, 350 n. When the actual cost of the negotiations amounted to £2,900, the difference did come out of quitrents; but Gov. Botetourt, doubtful that this would be allowed, offered if need be to pay the extra £400 from his own pocket. John P. Kennedy, ed., *Journals of the House of Burgesses* . . . , 1770–72 (Richmond, 1906), p. xiv. Wharton was probably right that the payment to the Cherokees, whatever its source, gave Virginia no claim against a royal grant to the Walpole Company.

4. The list containing Wharton's marginal notes is discussed above, XIX, 335 n. The "prior Instructions" were, we assume, those issued to Gov. Dinwiddie in 1754, limiting future individual grants west of the Alleghenies to a maximum of 1,000 acres apiece. See Bailey, *op. cit.*, pp. 247–8.

without adverting that he put into my Hands at the same time Papers that contradicted him. A Thought then struck me to give him your Paper to peruse, and leave it in his Hands a Week or two before I mention'd it to Mr. Walpole, that I might see whether he would be honest enough to communicate it. And that he might not have it to say I had discourag'd that important Friend. Accordingly he took it with him. They went away seemingly not very well satisfy'd with their Visit; but Mr. W. has told Mr. Strahan since that he had satisfy'd me. Mr. S. begins to entertain a very indifferent Opinion of him. And now to finish this Subject, I will just remark, that 7 Months are elaps'd since the Report in favour of the Grant, and we have not got one Step further, whence I begin to think that my *Auguring* (to use Botetourt's Phrase) in a Letter of Aug 17. will be verified, and upon the very Principles there conjectur'd.[5] If so you will see the Prudence of our never reckoning upon it as a done thing; and the Folly of others in claiming beforehand all the Merit of a *fruitless and expensive* Negociation.

The Pork is arrived safe and well from Bristol. I deliver'd the two Casks AH and IH to Mr. Sargent agreable to your Desire, who call'd to pay me for them, but I refus'd to take any thing, and he will write to thank you.[6] I am much oblig'd by your ready Care in sending them, and thank you for the Cranberries, Meal, and dry'd Apples. The latter are the best I ever saw. I have given Mr. S. a Copy of your Directions for keeping the Pork, and retain'd the Original. Yesterday we had a Piece at Table, and it was much admired.

I send you in a Box to your Brother Bache, the Seeds I mention'd in my last. Mr. Small sends a large Parcel of Seeds in a great Tin Canister solder'd close. You must have a hot Poker to open it. I know not what the Sorts are that he sends; nor

5. The report favoring the grant was the order in council of Aug. 14, 1772, and BF's pessimistic auguring had been in his letter three days later: above, XIX, 243–4. Pessimism was well founded. In May the Board of Trade reported favorably on the grant; the Privy Council referred the report to the law officers of the crown, and in July they raised objections. See below, BF to Foxcroft, July 14, and to WF, July 25.

6. For the pork see BF to WF above, Feb. 3; John Sargent, the banker, was an old friend of both men.

whether they are for you or Mr. Odell, or both.[7] His Letter will explain that, as well as who the Books are for, which came to me without any Direction, and I have directed them to you. They are in the same Box, and also a Parcel of Magazines and Reviews; and a Parcel on Canada Government from Mr. Maseres,[8] all directed for you.

The Opposition are now attacking the Ministry on the St. Vincent's Affair, which is generally condemned here, and some think L. Hillsborough will be given up as the Adviser of that Expedition. But if it succeeds perhaps all will blow over.[9] The Ministry are more embarrass'd with the India Affairs; the continu'd Refusal of North America to take Tea from hence has

7. The donor was presumably Dr. Alexander Small, who had been in Philadelphia the previous summer (above, XIX, 230-1); this reference indicates that he had also visited Burlington and met the Rev. Jonathan Odell, WF's friend and pastor.

8. Undoubtedly copies of the two pamphlets that Maseres had sent BF: *ibid.*, pp. 445-6.

9. Trouble had been simmering in St. Vincent since 1769. After the cession of the island to Great Britain in the Peace of Paris, commissioners had been appointed to make uninhabited land available to settlement while protecting the rights of the native Caribs. The prerequisite was a survey, and the natives would have none of it. They refused to admit British sovereignty, and were supposedly encouraged by the French on nearby Martinique. The commissioners eventually called for troops to protect the surveyors, but the arrival of the military left the Caribs unimpressed. Hostilities lasted from September, 1772, until three days after the date of BF's letter, when a treaty was signed by which the natives accepted allegiance to the crown and the commissioners' right to oversee land transactions. Meanwhile the little war was aired in Parliament. The opposition tried to show that the government, at the behest of land-hungry settlers, was despoiling the natives. The ministry answered that the Caribs had been treated with all consideration but, in collusion with the French, had defied British authority and threatened the lives of British subjects. The debate concluded, on the day after BF wrote, with defeat of two resolutions of censure, and a third that demanded to know who had been responsible for sending the troops. Hillsborough had been American secretary at the time, and this resolution would have revealed whether he had been the prime ministerial mover in the affair. See [William Young,] *An Account of the Black Charaibs in the Island of St. Vincent's* . . . (London, 1795; London reprint, 1971); Bryan Edwards, *The History, Civil and Commercial, of the British Colonies in the West Indies* (4th ed.; 3 vols., London, 1807), I, 421-5; Cobbett, *Parliamentary History*, XVII (1771-74), 568-639, 722-41.

brought infinite Distress on the Company; they imported great Quantities in the Faith that that Agreement could not hold; and now they can neither pay their Debts nor Dividends, their Stock has sunk to the annihilating near three millions of their Property, and Government will lose its £400,000 a Year; while their Teas lie upon Hand. The Bankrupcies brought on partly by this means have given such a Shock to Credit as has not been experienc'd here since the South Sea Year. And this has affected the great Manufactures so much, as to oblige them to discharge their Hands, and 1000's of Spital-field and Manchester Weavers, are now starving or subsisting on Charity.[1] Blessed Effects of Pride, Pique and Passion in Government, which should have no Passions.

Hayne's Wife came to me the Other Day, said her Husband was come home, had been very ill us'd, she had just been with Lord Dartmouth, to complain that the Officer in Jersey would not show her Husband the true Will; that there were two Salters, and one, her Father, dy'd worth £70,000 and that it was cruel to keep her out of it,[2] &c. That Lord D. had directed her to come to me, and desire from him that I would write to you for a Copy of the Will. In Discourse she pretended to have particular Information of many Circumstances that I was sure must be false, and refusing to tell me her Informers, I let her know my Opinion that the whole was an Illusion. *Why, Sir,* says she, *I hope you don't think I be mad: do ye?* That being the very thing I was then thinking, I e'en told her I was afraid she was so. She assur'd me she was perfectly in her Senses, and that I should soon know, threatning me and you and all the wicked People

1. The bursting of the South Sea Bubble in 1720 was the worst British financial crisis of the century. The difficulties of the East India Company, which stemmed in part from the American nonimportation agreements, came to a head in 1772 and deprived the Treasury of £400,000 a year; see above, XIX, 420. Times were still bad, and weavers in particular were suffering; see below, p. 203 n.

2. For Mary Hayne, her husband Richard and his trip to America, and their mythical New Jersey inheritance see above, XIX, 322 n. By "two Salters" we believe she meant two brothers. Judge Saltar, who she claimed was her father, left an estate valued at £1,268 1s. 10d.; his sons as executors sold part of the land in 1765 and another part in 1768. 1 *N.J. Arch.*, XXIV, 518; XXXIII, 370.

in New Jersey that keep her out of her Estate, with her Appearance against us before the Judgment Seat of God, where we should be made to suffer for our Wickedness, &c. I have not seen my Lord since, but shall next Wednesday. It is amazing how easily People delude themselves with these Fancies of Estates belonging to them in other Countries, without the least Foundation. My Love to Betsey. I am ever Your affectionate Father   B F

To Joseph Galloway   ALS (letterbook draft): Library of Congress

Dear Friend,   London, Feb. 14. 1773
    I wrote to you the 6th of last Month in answer to your Favours of Oct. 18 and 30. Since which I have no Line from you, the New York January Packet not being yet arrived.
    The Bill on Col. Johnston, which I mentioned as likely to be protested, is since paid.[3] The Gentleman trifled about it a good deal; first refus'd to accept it, then came to me and desired it might be sent to him again and he would accept it; then when it became due he wanted longer time. The Drawer I think should be inform'd of this, that he may be cautious. The Man seems honestly dispos'd, but appears embarras'd in his Money Affairs. This indeed is at present a more common Case than usual owing [to] the great Blow Paper Credit has received, which first fell upon the India Company, and by degrees became general.[4] Hence a great Stop of Employment among the Manufacturers, added to the Mischiefs mentioned in mine of Dec. 2. of which retaining the Duty on Tea in America, and thereby the Loss of that Market are now acknowledg'd to be the Cause. The Ministry now would have the Company save its Honour by petitioning for the Repeal of that Duty; and the Company has it under Consideration. They see Government will be oblig'd for its own sake to support them, and therefore must repeal the Duty whether they petition for it or not, and tis said they are not willing to ask it as a Favour, lest that should be made a Foundation for some additional Demand

3. See above, XIX, 418 n, and BF to Galloway, Jan. 6, 1773.
4. See above, XIX, 315–16, 419–20.

upon them.[5] A fine Hobble they are all got into by their unjust and blundering Politics, with regard to the Colonies. I thank you for proposing the two Members I mention'd.[6] I have now some others to propose viz. Dr. Barbeu Dubourg of Paris, a Man of very extensive Learning, and an excellent Philosopher, who is ambitious of the Honour, as is Lord Stanhope for himself and Son Lord Mahone who will be propos'd by Dr. Denormandie; there is also Mr. Samll. Dun, a very ingenious Mathematician, and universal Mechanic, very fond of America, and would be an Acquisition if we could get him there and employ him:[7] He writes to the Society, and is also very desirous of the

5. The Company, at a time when its affairs were under close scrutiny, was indeed reluctant to ask official favors. But it and not, as BF implies, the government was taking the initiative in attempting to change the duties on tea. These were of two kinds. One was the import duty in England, which for a time after 1767 had been in effect repealed, as it applied to sales in the colonies, by granting a total refund or drawback on exported tea; a statute of 1772, however, had reduced the drawback to 60%, and the Company wanted it raised again to 100%. The other was the Townshend duty, collected in America. In January and February, to judge by the minutes of the Court of Proprietors in the India Office Library, Foreign and Commonwealth Office, the Company was concerned with securing relief from the Townshend duty. The Directors sought Lord North's assistance, but he refused it; the most he would consider, the *London Chron.* reported on Feb. 11–13, was a 40% reduction. On the 12th, nevertheless, the Court agreed on a request to Parliament "that teas may be exported free of duty to America." *Ibid.*, Feb. 13–16. This key phrase, which was at the center of negotiations for months to come, is ambiguous. The two scholars who have recently dealt with it are Bernhard Knollenberg, *The Growth of the American Revolution* . . . (New York and London, [1975]), pp. 90–1, and Labaree, *Tea Party,* pp. 68–70. Both conclude that the phrase meant only restoration of the full drawback, and hence that the Company had abandoned the issue of the Townshend duty. Perhaps, but another interpretation seems to us equally plausible. India House had as much reason as ever for wanting to be rid of that duty, *and* for not saying so openly. The ambiguity of the phrase used may well have been intentional, and have represented a change of tactics rather than of policy. In any case BF believed, at this time and later, that the American duty was very much at issue in the Company's manoeuvering. For the next development see his letter to Cushing below, March 9.

6. Jean-Baptiste LeRoy and Baron Klingstädt: above, XIX, 278, 393.

7. Philip Stanhope, second Earl Stanhope (1714–86), F.R.S., was a distinguished mathematician, a lover of Greek, and a liberal in politics; his son Charles, at this time Lord Mahon (1753–1816), was a promising young

Honour. There is another Gentleman, who I believe would be pleas'd with it, tho' he has not mention'd it; I mean the President of the Royal Society, Sir John Pringle, Bart. It is usual for the Academy of Sciences at Paris always to chuse the President of the English Royal Society one of their Foreign Members, and it is well taken here as a Mark of Respect; and I think it would also be well taken by the Society if you should chuse him. By the way, is the Ten Shillings a Year expected of Foreign Members? I have been ask'd that Question. Here no Contribution is taken of them.

I send the Society some printed Pieces that will be indeed in the next volume of the Philosophic Transactions here: But as that will not come out till Midsummer, it may be agreable to have them sooner.

Enclos'd I send an Account of the presenting two more of your Acts to the King in Council. As yet I hear of no Objection to any of the former thirty, of which I sent a List per January Packet as presented Dec. 22.[8] With unalterable Attachment, I am ever, my dear Friend, Yours most affectionately

B FRANKLIN

Joseph Galloway Esqr

---

scientist and inventor, who subsequently fulfilled the promise while leading an active political life. *Burke's Peerage*, p. 2308; *DNB* under Charles Stanhope. The family was in Geneva at the time, which doubtless accounts for Mahon's being sponsored by Dr. John Denormandie, for whom see above, XIX, 332 n. Stanhope and Mahon were elected in January, 1774, Dubourg a year later. APS, *Early Proc.* . . . (Philadelphia, 1884), pp. 86, 95. Samuel Dunn (d. 1794) was a schoolteacher, astronomer, and mathematician who, although not an F.R.S., contributed a number of papers to the *Phil. Trans. DNB*. These contributions may well have brought him into contact with BF, who subsequently sent the APS a copy of Dunn's *New Atlas of the Mundane System* . . . (London, 1774): *Early Proc.*, p. 88. We have found no record of Dunn's election to the APS, but on the title page of the 1778 edition of his atlas he proclaimed himself a member.

8. The list was enclosed in BF's letter above to the Assembly's committee of correspondence, Jan. 6. All but two of the acts were allowed, as mentioned there. For one of those disallowed see BF to Galloway below, March 15.

To Rebecca Haydock [Garrigues⁹]

ALS (letterbook draft): Library of Congress

London, Feb. 14. [1773]

I send my young Friend's Silk in a Box [to] Mr. Bache, who will deliver it to her. Enclos'd is the Maker's Account and Sarah Forster's Receipt, for Eight Pounds Six Shillings, which you will please to repay to Mrs. Franklin. I did not well understand the first Account and therefore to explain it Mrs. Forster got the Maker to draw another more intelligible, which is also enclos'd.[1] I wish the Silk may please, and wear to your Satisfaction. I am, with Respects to your good Father and Mother,[2] Your most obedient Servant   B F

Miss Haydock

To the Managers of the Pennsylvania Hospital

ALS (letterbook draft): Library of Congress

Gentlemen,   London, Feb. 14. 1773

I received your Favours of Oct. 20. and Nov. 4. which I communicated to Mr. Barclay and Dr. Fothergill; and we have acted in Compliance with the Directions therein contained, by selling Part of the Stock and paying your Drafts.[3] I suppose Mr. Barclay has informed you of the Particulars. I wish you Joy of so considerable an Acquisition to the Hospital, which makes me the happier as I had some hand in advising the Appropriation of the

---

9. She had married, the month before, Samuel Garrigues, Jr., brother of the seafaring Isaac who appears above, XVIII, 21–2; see Hinshaw, *Amer. Quaker Genealogy*, II, 546.

1. See above, XIX, 43, 64–5, 231. BF had settled the bill the previous November. The maker of the silk, named Ireland, had charged for 41½ yards at 5s. 4d. the yard, in all £11 1s. 4d. But the rate apparently included the raw silk, which in this case was furnished and for which a reduction was made of £2 15s. 4d., bringing the total to the sum BF mentions. Jour., p. 44.

2. Eden and Elizabeth Haydock; for the father, a plumber, glazier, and house-painter, see above, XII, 14 n.

3. The Managers' letters above explain the transaction: XIX, 339–40, 366.

Money to that Institution, and hardly expected I should live to see it in Possession.[4] I hope Circumstances will admit of its being so dispos'd of as to produce a settled Revenue towards the Support of the House. With great Esteem and Respect, I am, Gentlemen, Your most obedient humble Servant   B FRANKLIN

Israel Pemberton, and others, Managers of the Hospital

To Humphry Marshall

ALS: Yale University Library; letterbook draft: Library of Congress

Sir,   London, Feb. 14. 1773
    A considerable Time after its Arrival I received the Box of Seeds you were so good as to send me the Beginning of last Year, with your Observations on the Spots of the Sun.[5] The Seeds I distributed among some of my Friends who are curious; please to accept my thankful Acknowledgements for them: The Observations I communicated to our Astronomers of the Royal Society, who are much pleas'd with them, and hand them about from one to another, so that I have had little Opportunity of examining them myself, they not being yet return'd to me. Here are various Opinions about the Solar Spots. Some think them vast Clouds of Smoke and Soot arising from the consuming Fuel on the Surface; which Clouds at length take fire again on their Edges, consuming and daily diminishing till they totally disappear. Others [think] them Spots of the Surface in which the Fire has

4. The act of Parliament establishing trustees to hold unclaimed shares of the Pennsylvania Land Company for a decade, and then turn over all undistributed funds to the Pennsylvania Hospital, was passed in 1760 during BF's first British mission. Above, XIII, 274 n. We have no other evidence than this letter that BF had a hand in this arrangement, but it is natural that he should have had.

5. The box of seeds, with the observations, was missing for some time; see above, XVIII, 255–6; XIX, 88, 92. The customs officers were to blame, it turned out, for the second paragraph of this letter in BF's draft began with two sentences that he deleted: "I have received but within these few Days your last Box of Seeds, which has been detain'd unreasonably at the Custom House. I am exceedingly oblig'd by the Present." The observations on sunspots were presumably included, but have been lost; for Marshall's illustrations of them see his letter below, May 3.

been extinguished, and which by degrees are rekindled. It is however remarkable that tho' large Spots are seen gradually to become small ones, no one has observ'd a small Spot gradually to become a large one; at least I do not remember to have met with such an Observation. If this be so, it should seem that they are suddenly form'd of the full Size: And perhaps if there were more such constant and diligent Observers as you, some might happen to be observing at the Instant such a Spot was formed, when the Appearances might give some Ground of Conjecture by what means they were formed. The Professor of Astronomy at Glasgow, Dr. Wilson, has a new Hypothesis.[6] It is this, That the Sun is a Globe of solid Matter, all combustible perhaps, but whose Surface only is actually on fire to a certain Depth, and all below that Depth unkindled, like a Log of wood whose Surface to half an Inch deep may be a burning Coal, while all within remains Wood. Then he supposes, that by some Explosion, similar to our Earthquakes, the burning Part may be blown away from a particular District, leaving bare the unkindled Part below, which then appears a Spot, and only lessens as the fluid burning Matter by degrees flows in upon it on all sides, and at length covers or rekindles it. He founds this Opinion on certain Appearances of the Edges of the Spots as they turn under the Sun's Disk or emerge again on the other side; for if they are such Hollows in the Sun's Face as he supposes, and the bright Border round the Edges be the fluid burning Matter flowing down the Banks in to the Hollow, it will follow, that while a Spot is in the middle of the Sun's Disk, the Eye looking directly upon the whole, may discern

6. The first theory, that sunspots were smoke, was initially promulgated by William Derham in the *Phil. Trans.*, XXVII (1710), 270–90. BF subscribed to a variant of this theory (above, IV, 300–1), and may be referring here either to his own views or to those of the Derham school. His belief that spots first appeared at full size, however, was a remarkable error: it had been known for more than a century that they could increase as well as decrease. Alexander Wilson was developing a theory of their nature that became before long the predominant one. (Charles Hutton, *A Mathematical and Philosophical Dictionary* . . . [2 vols., London, 1795], II, 62–3.) It grew out of observations begun in 1769, and was clearly arousing attention before he made it public in a paper read before the Royal Society in late April, 1773: "Observations on the Solar Spots," *Phil. Trans.*, LXIV (1774), 1–30. For Wilson, who achieved distinction as a type-founder as well as astronomer, see above, XVIII, 67 n.

that Border all round; but when the Hollow is moved round to near the Edge of the Disk, then, tho' the Eye, which now views it aslant, can see full the farthest Bank, yet that which is nearest is hidden and not to be distinguish'd; and when the same Spot comes to emerge again on the other Side of the Sun, the Bank which before was visible is now conceal'd, and that conceal'd which before was visible, gradually changing however till the Spot reaches the Middle of the Disk, when the Bank all round may be seen as before. Perhaps your Telescope may be scarce strong enough to observe this. If it is, I wish to know whether you find the same Appearances. When your Observations are return'd to me, and I have consider'd them, I shall lodge them among the Papers of the Society, and let you know their Sentiments.

As to procuring you a Correspondence with some ingenious Gentelman here, who is curious, which you desire, I find many who like to have a few Seeds given them, but do not desire large Quantities, most considerable Gardens being now supply'd like Dr. Fothergill's, with what they chuse to have; and there being Nursery-men now here, who furnish what Particulars are wanted, without the Trouble of a foreign Correspondence and the Vexations at the Customhouse. You will therefore oblige me by letting me know if in any other way I can be serviceable to you. With great Respect and Esteem, I am, Sir, Your most obedient humble Servant   B FRANKLIN

Mr Humphry Marshall

Addressed: To / Mr Humphry Marshall / of Bradford / Chester County / Pensylvania / per Capt All

To William Marshall[7]   ALS (letterbook draft): Library of Congress

Reverend Sir,   London, Feb. 14. 1773

I duly received your respected Letter of Oct. 30. and am very sensible of the Propriety and Equity of the Act passed to indulge your Friends in their Scruples relating to the Mode of Taking an

7. The Scots Presbyterian minister in Philadelphia, for whom see above, XIX, 354 n.

Oath which you plead for so ably by numerous Reasons. That Act with others has now been some time laid before his Majesty in Council. I have not yet heard of any Objection to it; but if such should arise, I shall do my utmost to remove them, and obtain the Royal Assent.[8] Believe me, Reverend Sir, to have the warmest Wishes for the Increase of Religious as well as Civil Liberty thro'out the World; and that I am, with great Regard, Your most obedient humble Servant   B FRANKLIN

Mr Wm Marshall

To Benjamin Rush

ALS: University of Pennsylvania Library; letterbook draft: Library of Congress

Dear Sir,   London, Feb. 14. 1773

In a Box to Mr. Bache I send you a Bundle of the Ephemerides; they came but lately to hand with Duplicates for me; tho' it appears by my Letter that they were sent from Paris last May was twelvemonth.[9] Where they have been all this time I have not learnt.

I send you also one of Dr. Priestly's Pamphlets, containing a Number of curious Experiments on what he calls fixed Air. The Subject at present engages a good deal of Attention here, and falls in your Way, I imagine, both as a Chemist and Physician.[1] Please to accept of it. Remember me kindly to your

8. The act, "for the Relief of such Persons as conscientiously scruple the taking of an Oath in the common Form," was one of the thirty that BF mentioned to the Pa. Assembly Committee of Correspondence above, Jan. 6. It was referred to the Board of Trade on Jan. 15, which reported favorably; the royal assent was given on April 7, and the Assembly was so informed on Oct. 15. 8 *Pa. Arch.*, VIII, 7025, 7028, 7030.

9. The long delayed bundle contained copies of Barbeu-Dubourg's publication, *Ephémérides du citoyen; ou bibliotheque raisonée des sciences morales et politiques*, the organ of the physiocrats. "My letter" was that from Dubourg of May 27, 1771, which had arrived with the bundle in October, 1772: above XVIII, 110–13; XIX, 357.

1. Rush's acknowledgment of this letter below, May 1, makes clear that BF sent him Joseph Priestly's *Observations on Different Kinds of Air* ... (London, 1772).

Brother,[2] and believe me ever Your affectionate Friend and humble Servant   B FRANKLIN

What is become of Mr. Coombe?[3]

Dr Rush

To Joseph Smith[4]   ALS (letterbook draft): Library of Congress

Sir,   London, Feb. 14. 1773
    I am much obliged by the Trouble you have taken in receiving the Salary for me.[5] You will shortly hear from me as to the Application of it. In the meantime please to accept my thankful Acknowledgements; and if I can here render you any Service, you will do me a Pleasure in commanding freely, Sir, Your most obedient humble Servant   B F

Mr Joseph Smith,

From Samuel Potts[6]   ALS: American Philosophical Society

Dear Sir   Genl. Post Office Monday 15 Febry. [1773[7]]
    I am very sorry as you have had the trouble of writing your Letters to acquaint you that we have no North American Boat on this side, consequently your Letters could not be forwarded as no mail was made up last Saturday night for New York.

    2. Jacob Rush had come to London in 1771 with letters of introduction to BF from DF and others, had spent two years at the Middle Temple, and must have returned only recently to Philadelphia. See above, XVII, 245 n.
    3. See Rush's answer below, May 1.
    4. For the former secretary of the N.J. Assembly's committee of correspondence see above, XVI, 256 n.
    5. For BF's salary as New Jersey agent see above, XVIII, 218–19; XIX, 73, 313; and Smith to BF below, May 13, 1774.
    6. Comptroller of the Inland Office in the Post Office. See Kenneth Ellis, *The Post Office in the Eighteenth Century: a Study in Administrative History* (London, 1958), pp. 83–4, 88, 108.
    7. The only years during BF's two British missions when Feb. 15 fell on a Monday were 1762, 1768, and 1773. This letter disclaims responsibility for supplying post horns, but in 1770 BF had charged them to the Post Office. (Jour., p. 24.) This he would scarcely have done if he had known that the charge would be disallowed; hence 1773 is the most likely year.

This Office does not supply the Post Boys with Horns, they are purchased by themselves, but I beleive the best place to get them is in Crooked Lane. I am with Truth Dear Sir Your Most Obedient and Humble Servant   SAM POTTS

From Jonathan Williams, Sr.

ALS: American Philosophical Society

Honoured Sir   Boston Feby 15th 1773
    I wrote you Decr. 27 by Capt: Jenkins,[8] and Inform'd you of a proposal made by Hall or rather Halls Friends, Who have advanced the Hundred pounds Sterling, and I have Received it, on this Condition, to Wait for the Remander Six and twelvemonths, to be paid in two equal payments from the above Date. I Wish I had your Orders in regard to the Disposition of the money as aunt Wants to be doing She Desires me to Invest fifty pounds of it in a Bill of Exchange and Send it home to you,

8. Master of the *Minerva*, and a relative of BF. Jenkins cleared Boston in late December and reached Falmouth in February: *Mass. Gaz.; and the Boston Weekly News-Letter*, Dec. 31, 1772; *Public Advertiser*, Feb. 13, 1773. BF was looking for him in March, and soon afterward had a visit from him and Seth Paddock. To Jane Mecom below, March 9, July 7. The visit must have been before April 6, when Jenkins left for Boston (*Public Advertiser*, April 8), carrying BF's letters below of April 3 to Cushing and Williams. Paddock was a Nantucketer (above, XVI, 250 n), and so was Jenkins. Nathan Folger (B.1.4.6), BF's first cousin, had a daughter Judith, who married Thomas Jenkins and bore him four sons, Seth, Benjamin, Thomas, and Charles. *Vital Records of Nantucket* . . . (5 vols., Boston, 1925–28), II, 207; III, 455; V, 383. All four were eventually sailors and called captain, but we believe that BF's visitor was Seth (1735–93) because he is the only one known to have been in the London trade. A Capt. Jenkins reappeared in England in January, 1774, this time as master of a Nantucket ship; and the following year Seth Jenkins brought letters from London to Nantucket. *London Chron.*, Jan. 25–27, 1774; William Lincoln, ed., *The Journals of Each Provincial Congress of Massachusetts in 1774 and 1775* (Boston, 1838), p. 434 n. For Seth's subsequent career, which had its adventurous moments, see Alexander Starbuck, *The History of Nantucket* . . . (Rutland, Vt., [1969]), pp. 198–200; *Ship Registers and Enrollments of Providence, Rhode Island, 1773–1939* . . . (2 vols., Providence, 1941), I, 381, 697, 1071; Anna R. Bradbury, *History of the City of Hudson, New York* . . . (Hudson, 1908), pp. 16–17, 20, 27, 34.

and She Will accompany it With an Invoice of Such Goods as She Wants to make a beginning With, the Remander She Wishes to reserve here (if agreeable to you) as She think it may be Improv'd to more advantage and I Belive it may.[1] So many failing in Business makes Good Sometimes Cheaper here then in London.[2] Capt. Symmes Sails for London in about 10 Days time by him We shall Send Said Bill and Invoice for your approbation.[3] My Wife Joines With our best Respects and I am With the Greatest Esteem Your Dutifull Nephew and Humble Servant

JONA WILLIAMS

Addressed: To / Doctr. Benjamin Franklin / Craven Street / London / per Capt Hatch

From Horace-Bénédict de Saussure[4]

ALS: American Philosophical Society

Monsieur   Naples le 23e. Févr. 1773.

J'ai reçu avec un extrême plaisir les deux lettres que vous m'avés fait l'honneur de m'écrire, l'une du 8e. Octobre, l'autre du 1er. Xbre de l'année dernière. Mais comme elles m'étoient l'une et l'autre adressées à Genève, et que j'en suis parti dès le commencement d'Octobre pour venir passer l'hyver en Italie, elles me sont parvenues extrêmement tard, et j'ai été ainsi privé de l'avantage de vous témoigner par une prompte réponse combien je suis flatté de l'honneur de votre correspondance.

La Lettre sur l'action des conducteurs pointus et le Mémoire

1. For Samuel Hall's debt and BF's assignment of it to Jane Mecom see above, X, 358; XVIII, 16, 219–20; XIX, 200, 291; and below, BF to Jane and to Williams, July 7.

2. The economic depression of 1772 (above, XIX, 101 n) was continuing in Boston unabated, with its concomitants of falling prices, surplus goods, and forced sales, and did not improve as the year wore on; by autumn merchants were "Desprate." Williams to BF below, Oct. 17.

3. The bill did not go as promised with Ebenezer Symmes in the *Mary Ann,* which sailed in March (*Boston Gaz.*, March 15, 1773), but with Williams' letter of April 15, which has since disappeared but which BF acknowledged on June 4.

4. For the Genevan physicist and scientist see above, XIX, 324 n.

qui l'accompagne, m'ont paru remplis d'expériences et de raisonnements absolument démonstratifs, et qui ne laissent aucun doute sur l'utilité de ces ingénieux Préservatifs. Si j'avois eu connaissance de ces Expériences nouvelles je m'en serois prévalu avec bien de l'avantage dans un petit Mémoire apologétique que je publiai au mois d'Octobre 1771. pour éclairer quelques personnes qui étoient effrayées d'un Conducteur que j'avois fait dresser à Genève devant la maison que j'habite.[5] Ce Mémoire eut cependant le succès que je desirois, il rassura tout le monde, et j'ai eu le plaisir d'observer l'Electricité des Nuages pendant tout le cours de l'Eté dernier. Plusieurs personnes ont même suivi cet Exemple et ont fait dresser des conducteurs ou sur leur maison même ou devant leur maison. M. de Voltaire a été un des premiers. Il a rendu à votre Théorie, Monsieur, la même justice qu'il rendit à celle de l'immortel Newton.[6]

Le projet de la Société Royale est bien digne du zêle de cet Illustre Corps pour l'avancement des connoissances utiles, et je serois bien flatté si je pouvois le séconder en quelque chose dans l'exécution de ce projet. Si j'avois été à Genève, je me serois fait un devoir et un plaisir d'aller faire un Voyage dans les Montagnes des environs pour déterminer avec exactitude les dimensions des Montagnes et des Vallées que je penserois les plus convenables pour l'exécution de ce projet. Je ne crois cependant pas qu'il y ait dans aucune de celles qui me sont connues aucun endroit vraiment propre à donner des lumières certaines sur l'objet qui fait le but de ces Recherches. Déja dans le Jurat il n'y a point de hauteur assez considérable puisque la Dole qui est la montagne la plus élevée au dessus du Niveau de notre Lac n'arrive pas à

5. For BF's letter, the enclosed memoir of his experiments, and de Saussure's pamphlet see *idem.*, pp. 324–7.

6. Voltaire's homage to the electrical theory was, we assume, the lightning rod itself; but he also mentioned BF and discussed rods at some length in his article on thunder in *Questions sur l'Encyclopédie* . . . (9 vols., [Geneva,] 1771–72), IX, 24, 27–9. As for Newton, Voltaire had championed his theories in *Elémens de la philosophie de Neuton* . . . (Amsterdam, 1738), *Reponse a toutes les objections principales qu'on a faites en France contre la philosophie de Neuton* (Amsterdam, 1739), and *La Métaphysique de Neuton* . . . (Amsterdam, 1740). On his Italian trip, incidentally, de Saussure had a letter of introduction from Voltaire: Theodore Besterman, ed., *Voltaire's Correspondence* . . . (107 vols., Geneva, 1953–65), LXXXIII, 50.

700 Toises au dessus de ce même niveau. Ensuite il faut considérer que le Jurat de même que les Alpes forment des chaines continues de Montagnes toutes liées les unes aux autres et situées du moins à de petites distances les unes des autres. Il n'y a, ou du moins je ne connois aucune montagne isolée d'une hauteur suffisante. On trouve fréquemment de profondes vallées bordées de hautes montagnes, mais ces montagnes ont derrière elles d'autres vallées et d'autres montagnes, en sorte que les déviations que l'on observeroit dans le fil à plomb seroient l'effet complexe des attractions réunies de toutes ces montagnes; et pour en déduire une comparaison entre la densité de la terre et celle de ces Montagnes il faudroit bien des travaux et bien des calculs. Autant que je puis en juger, il me paroit que quelque grand Rocher élevé en pleine mer, comme le Pic de Ténériffe seroit le lieu le plus convenable pour cette recherche.[7] J'ai fait passer à Genève à Mylord Stanhope le Mémoire que vous m'avés fait l'honneur de m'envoyer sur ce sujet afin qu'il puisse en conférer avec M. de Luc qui s'étant principalement occupé de la hauteur des Montagnes

7. Scientists had long been interested in improving Newton's calculations of the earth's density by estimating the mass of a mountain and then determining how much it deflected a plumb line. In 1772 Nevil Maskelyne urged the Royal Society to initiate experiments. On July 23, 1772, the Council appointed a committee consisting of BF, Maskelyne, Henry Cavendish, and others to investigate the matter; on Sept. 9, 1773, the committee was reappointed with the addition of William Watson. The members seem to have done little more, however, than arrange for the surveying of feasible sites and, when one was chosen, for Maskelyne to take charge of the investigation. MS Council minutes, the Royal Society, especially pp. 145, 205, 234–5, 242. BF, in his missing letter of Dec. 1, 1772, probably asked de Saussure about the feasibility of measurements in the Alps; but the committee seems to have had no such idea. A hill in Perthshire was eventually chosen, and in 1774–76 Maskelyne directed elaborate observations there. See the Rev. Nevil Maskelyne, "A Proposal for Measuring the Attraction of Some Hill in This Kingdom by Astronomical Observations" (1772), and "An Account of Observations Made on the Mountain Schehallien for Finding Its Attraction" (1775), printed together in *Phil. Trans.*, LXV (1775), 495–542; Sir John Pringle, *A Discourse upon the Attraction of Mountains* ... (London, 1775); Charles Hutton, "An Account of the Calculations Made from the Survey and Measures Taken at Schehallien ... ," *Phil. Trans.*, LXVIII (1778), part 2, 689–788; Charles H. Weld, *History of the Royal Society* ... (2 vols., London, 1848), II, 77–83; A. Stanley Mackenzie, ed., *The Laws of Gravitation: Memoirs by Newton, Bouguer and Cavendish* ... (New York, etc., [1900]), pp. 53–6.

à l'occasion de ses recherches sur le Baromètre, est l'homme du monde le plus propre à donner de bonnes lumieres sur ce sujet.

On n'ignore sans doute pas non plus que le Père Beccaria de Turin qui a mesuré un degré du Méridien au pied des Alpes, a eu occasion d'observer de grandes déviations du fil à plomb, et pourroit ainsi donner à la Société Royale des directions utiles.[8] J'ai le bonheur de voir souvent ici M. le Chevalier Hamilton qui a la bonté de me conduire dans les endroits les plus intéressans des environs de Naples, ceux qui établissent la Théorie sur les Volcans ancients et modernes, et qui prouvent que tout le Golphe de Naples depuis la Mer jusque aux Apennins a été lancé du fonds de la mer par les feux souterrains et est ainsi le produit des Volcans plustot que le théatre de leurs ravages. Nous nous occupons aussi beaucoup d'Electricité, la petite machine que lui a faite M. Nairne est réellement excellente, et de beaucoup la meilleure qu'il y eut jamais eue dans cette partie de l'Italie. M. Hamilton sçachant que j'avois l'honneur de vous écrire, m'a chargé de vous faire ses compliments.[9]

Je suis bien faché de ne m'etre pas trouvé à Genève pour y recevoir M. de Normandy,[10] j'aurois été charmé d'avoir cette occasion de vous prouver le cas que je fais de votre recommandation. Si vous aviés quelques ordres à me donner à Naples, je

8. For Lord Stanhope see BF to Galloway above, Feb. 14. Jean-André Deluc (1727–1817) was a Swiss meteorologist who had just published his *Recherches sur les modifications de l'atmosphère* . . . (2 vols., Geneva, 1772); he was well known for his portable barometer, with which he measured the altitude of mountains. *DNB*; Larousse, *Dictionnaire universel*. Giambatista Beccaria needs no introduction as an electrical experimenter, but he is less well known as a geographer. In 1759 he had been commissioned by the King of Sardinia to measure a degree of longitude in Piedmont, and in doing so had observed the deflection of the plumb line caused by the attraction of the Alps. *Ibid*.

9. Sir William Hamilton (1730–1803), K.B., F.R.S., had been the British envoy to the court of Naples since 1764. He was outstanding as a collector of ancient art, and was also a volcanologist and seismologist; his later claim to fame was as the husband of Lord Nelson's mistress. *DNB*; Brian Fothergill, *Sir William Hamilton, Envoy Extraordinary* (London, [1969]). Edward Nairne, the instrument-maker, was noted for his electrical machines; see BF to Ingenhousz below, Sept. 30.

10. For Dr. John Denormandie, a friend of Galloway who had gone to Geneva by way of London, see above, XIX, 332 n.

pourrois encore les y recevoir, et vous pourriés les adresser à M. Hamilton. Nous nous proposons de faire ensemble quelques Expériences sur l'électricité des Vapeurs du Vésuve, quoiqu'à dire le vrai, je ne les considère que comme des conducteurs qui établissent une communication entre la Terre et les régions supérieures de l'Atmosphère. M. Hamilton m'a fait aussi la grace de m'inviter à voir quelques expériences qu'il a faites sur la Torpedo, ces Expériences ne sont pas décisives parceque les poissons que nous avons eus étoient petits et ne donnoient que de foibles secousses, mais il n'a paru aucun signe quelconque d'électricité. Nous attendons d'en avoir de plus grosses pour continuer ces recherches suivant le plan que vous avés tracé vous même.[11]

Agréés les assurances des sentimens distingués de considération et d'estime avec lesquels j'ai l'honneur d'être, Monsieur, Votre très humble et tres obeissant serviteur   DE SAUSSURE

From Jacques Barbeu-Dubourg

ALS: American Philosophical Society

Monsieur et tres cher Ami   A Paris ce 24e. fr. 1773.

L'impression avança bien la semaine derniere, j'eus châque jour une feuille nouvelle (a corriger les epreuves). Le carnaval est cause que cette semaine cy ne m'a encore rien produit,[1] mais j'espere que cela va reprendre le même train sans interruption.

---

11. John Walsh's experiments the previous summer with the torpedo fish had demonstrated that its shocks were in fact electrical, but his findings were not widely known until the publication of his letter to BF below, July 1. BF's plan for experimental testing was presumably that printed above, XIX, 234–5; nothing else we know of fits the description. But in that case how did de Saussure know of the plan? BF, thinking him in Geneva, could scarcely have anticipated his interest in investigating the torpedo; hence we suspect that the Swiss learned about the fish from his companion. Hamilton had been on leave in England, and had begun his return in the fall of 1772. Fothergill, *op. cit.*, p. 121. At that time Walsh's discoveries were presumably the talk of the Royal Society; any one as curious about electricity as Sir William would have been likely to hear about the torpedo and BF's suggestions for testing it.

1. Lent began on the day he was writing, when production of the *Œuvres* resumed.

Je vous envoyai, il y a aujourd'huy 8 jours sous une simple envelope deux feuilles sortantes de la presse. Je comptois les mettre entre les mains de Mr. fowke et de Mr. Davies[2] qui m'avoient fait l'honneur de passer icy la veille, mais j'arrivai à leur hôtel deux minutes trop tard, ayant rencontré leur chaise de poste a 100 pas en deça.

Je vous en envoye cy jointes 4 nouvelles dans lesquelles j'ai trouvé 2 fautes echappées (à mettre en *errata*) aux pages 58, et 68.[3]

Ne pensez vous pas que pour changer les poles de l'aiguille aimantée, un coup d'electricité positive appliqué au pole du sud ou un d'electricité negative appliqué au pole du nord, doivent produire le même effet, pourvu qu'ils soient l'un et l'autre suffisamment forts?[4]

Ne pensez vous pas que pour changer les poles de l'aiguille de l'electricité, non de simples aiguilles, mais jusqu'a des barres de fer? Et n'espereriez vous pas qu'on pourroit par ce moyen se procurer des aimants artificiels d'une force superieure à tous ceux que l'on a eus jusqu'a present, puisqu'il n'y a point de bornes à la force qu'il est possible de donner à l'electricité?

Ne jugeriez vous pas à propos de communiquer au public, la construction du petit appareil electrique portatif que vous vous etes fait?

Je vous supplie de me dire encore entre les differentes formes de machines electriques, qu'elle est celle que vous jugez la plus simple et la meilleure et de l'usage le plus commode et le moins

2. Arthur Fowke, John Walsh's nephew, had been studying at the Académie d'équitation at Angers; see above, XIX, 286 n. David Davies was his tutor; the two were back in London by Feb. 20. George R. Kaye and Edward H. Johnston, eds., *Minor Collections and Miscellaneous Manuscripts* (India Office Library, *Catalogue of Manuscripts in European Languages*, II, part 2; London, 1937), pp. 69, 71.

3. The errors were in the translation of BF's opinions about electricity printed above, IV, 9–34.

4. His question arose, we presume, because he was printing a letter from BF that described reversing the polarity of a needle by electric charges but did not stipulate what kind. Above, IV, 143–4. Dubourg appended a note to that letter, in which he discussed similar experiments with positive and negative charges by BF's old acquaintance Dalibard, the translator of *Exper. and Obser. Œuvres*, I, 85 n.

fatigant, tant a l'egard des roues et de leur monture, et de la disposition du coussin et du conducteur, qu'a l'egard des verres en plateau, ou en globe &c. Mr. Dalibard, qui m'a chargé de vous faire bien des complimens, a par luimême un moyen aisé de me procurer la franchise des lettres et paquets depuis la frontiere, ou le port de mer, jusqu'à Paris. Je joins icy l'instruction qu'il m'a donnée à ce sujet. Je vous prie d'en faire usage pour m'envoyer, une ou plusieurs feuilles à la fois (4 à 5 a la fois) de votre nouvelle edition, ainsi que la brochure de Mr. Du Pont (de qui j'ai aussi mille complimens à vous faire aussi bien que de M. Le Marquis de Mirabeau).[5] Je crois qu'il sera necessaire d'affranchir les ports de ces paquets jusqu'a Douvres. Je vous prie de vous en assurer, et en ce cas de vouloir bien en faire pour moi les avances, dont je vous tiendrai un fidele compte, ou pour le mieux que je prie et prierai Melle. Biheron[6] de vous rembourser immediatement. J'ai l'honneur d'etre avec un inviolable attachment Monsieur et cher Maitre Votre tres humble et tres obeissant serviteur   DUBOURG

Ma femme vous embrasse de toute son ame, et est penetrée comme moi, de la plus vive reconnoissance de toutes vos bontés pour notre bonne Amie, Melle. Biheron.

5. For Pierre-Samuel du Pont de Nemours and Victor de Riquetti, marquis de Mirabeau, see above, xv, respectively 118 n and 182 n. Du Pont's pamphlet may have been an English translation of *De l'Origine et des progrès d'une science nouvelle*, which he had sent to BF in 1768 (*ibid.*, p. 119 n); such a translation is said to have been made, but no copy is known: Gustave Schelle, *Du Pont de Nemours et l'école physiocratique* (Paris, 1888), p. 402 n. We conjecture that BF sent the same pamphlet to Cooper and Mather with his letters to them below, June 4.

6. Dubourg's letter above, under Jan. 13, mentioned that she was in poor health. Yet she had been making frequent visits to London, perhaps to prepare an exhibit of her anatomical curiosities that was announced in the *Public Advertiser*, April 5, 1773.

Preface to the Declaration of the Boston Town Meeting

Printed in *The Votes and Proceedings of the Freeholders and Other Inhabitants of the Town of Boston* . . . (London, 1773), pp. i–vi.

In July, 1772, the Massachusetts House of Representatives petitioned the crown to stop paying Governor Hutchinson's salary.[7] At the end of September rumor spread that the judges were to be similarly paid, and a month later the Bostonians began a series of town meetings to protest what they considered to be unconstitutional innovations. The protest quickly expanded into a broader indictment of British policy, and culminated in the adoption on November 20 of three resolutions, which constituted for Hutchinson a "declaration of independency."[8] He believed that he had to meet this challenge, and it touched off his long and acrimonious debate with the House and Council on the constitutional status of the province.

The resolutions or declaration substituted the law of nature, spelled out in Lockean terms, for the law of the constitution as the British conceived it. The colonists, like all men, were entitled to enjoy life, liberty, and property, the declaration argued; these natural rights they had retained on entering the civil state. Laws existed to protect their rights, and were administered by magistrates whom the community compensated according to its best judgment. No legislative or executive authority in London, where the colonists were unrepresented, might substitute its judgment for that of the local community. Parliament was too distant and too little concerned with Americans' interests to legislate for them, regulate their manufactures, or tax them; the claim to do so was a usurpation of their right to control their own property. The declaration went on to attack executive authority: the prerogative did not extend to appointing customs officers unauthorized by the charter, to maintaining troops in Boston in time of peace, to controlling the governor's acts by instructions, to paying him and other officials, or to issuing writs of assistance, establishing vice-admiralty courts, and transporting prisoners to England for trial. The Bostonians rounded out their grievances by charging the British government with transferring land from one province to another, thereby inflicting

7. See above, xix, 209.
8. To James Gambier, Feb. 19, 1773, Mass. Arch., xxvii, 448–9; see also Hutchinson, *History*, iii, 262–3, 266. For the issue of the judges' salaries and the genesis of the town meetings see above, xix, 381 n.

hardship on settlers, and with harboring designs for an American episcopate.[9]

The town meeting concluded its work by appointing a committee of correspondence to send the declaration to other Massachusetts towns, encourage them to set up similar committees, and so gain their adhesion to a common front. The arguments were now in the open, and the organization in the making, to elevate the quarrel with the mother country to new and more dangerous heights. Small wonder that Hutchinson called this act a declaration of independence. It demanded in 1772 almost the same status for the colonies that the British government brought itself to offer, after Saratoga and under the threat of a Franco-American alliance, in 1778; and it would have left the sovereign, as was said of the later offer, not "one jot more substantially King of America than King of France."[10]

On November 28 Cushing forwarded the declaration in printed form to Franklin, who received it in February. He had often urged his constituents in Massachusetts to protest firmly against grievances but to avoid a head-on challenge to the prerogative; now the challenge had come. The grievances were old, but the response to them was new; for Boston was now calling on the whole province to support its defiance. Whether Franklin found this action welcome or unwelcome, he lost no time in endorsing it. He wrote the preface below, had it printed with the declaration, and sent copies back to America, where it was circulating in early May and arousing considerable attention.[1] He withheld publication in London until June.

His handling of the matter was interesting in three respects. In the first place he wrote a preface that had little bearing on the contents of the declaration: he emphasized, not the violation of natural rights, but the practical economic consequences of antagonizing the Americans. He considered the declaration so provocative, perhaps, that his best course was to remind British readers of its historical background and the effects of the quarrel on their pocketbooks. In the second place the bone of contention that he particularly stressed was one that was not in the declaration, the duty on tea. In the third place he waited

9. We have discussed most of these grievances in earlier volumes. For those having to do with prisoners and settlers, see respectively Merrill Jensen, *The Founding of a Nation* . . . (New York, 1968), pp. 426–7; Gipson, *British Empire*, XI, 310–45.

10. Quoted in William B. Willcox, *Portrait of a General* . . . (New York, 1964), p. 220.

1. Crane, *Letters to the Press*, pp. 225–6.

four months, during which the newspapers were full of the constitutional debate in Massachusetts[2] and the Tea Act was going through Parliament, before bringing out the pamphlet in London. Why the delay? If the preface had appeared when written in February, it might have supported the efforts that the East India Company was then making to secure repeal of the Townshend duty; did he write it for immediate publication but, on second thought, withhold it for fear that what the Bostonians said would outweigh what he said, and turn the public against concession to America? Or did he withhold it for another reason, the hope that as the debate in Boston ran its course the public would become more receptive to American arguments?

When the pamphlet did appear in June, it was old news and did not arouse great interest. The position of the Massachusetts House, which was known by then, was essentially that of the town meeting and even more ominous; new radicalism stole the limelight from old. But Whitehall did not forget Franklin's sponsoring the old, and increasingly imputed its substance to him. He later concluded that this imputation, as much as his satires and the affair of the Hutchinson letters, was responsible for the assault on him before the Privy Council in January, 1774.[3] If he was right, the pamphlet had as much impact on his life as the declaration had in Massachusetts.

[February 1773[4]]

All Accounts of the Discontent so general in our Colonies, have of late Years been industriously smothered, and concealed here; it seeming to suit the Views of the American Minister to have it understood, that by his great Abilities all Faction was subdued, all Opposition suppressed, and the whole Country quieted.[5] That the true State of Affairs there may be known, and the true Causes of that Discontent well understood, the following

2. Hutchinson's speech, which opened the debate, was reported in the *Public Advertiser* on March 4; Arthur Lee replied to it in the same paper on the 5th and 9th. The answer of the House and the Governor's rejoinder were printed in the London press in April.

3. See the extract of a letter from London below, Feb. 19, 1774.

4. So dated in Strahan's ledger and BF's accounts: Crane, *Letters to the Press*, p. 225; Mass. Hist. Soc. *Proc.*, LVI (1922–23), 119.

5. BF's charge that Hillsborough censored American news was mere polemics. The Secretary made difficulties about communications from the Massachusetts House, but only on the ground that BF was not a properly constituted agent.

Piece (not the Production of a Private Writer, but the unanimous Act of a large American City) lately printed in New-England, is republished here. This Nation, and the other Nations of Europe, may thereby learn with more Certainty the Grounds of a Dissension, that possibly may, sooner or later, have Consequences interesting to them all.

The Colonies had, from their first Settlement, been governed with more Ease, than perhaps can be equalled by any Instance in History, of Dominions so distant. Their Affection and Respect for this Country, while they were treated with Kindness, produced an almost implicit Obedience to the Instructions of the Prince, and even to Acts of the British Parliament, though the Right of binding them by a Legislature in which they were unrepresented, was never clearly understood. That Respect and Affection produced a Partiality in favour of every thing that was English; whence their preference of English Modes and Manufactures; their Submission to Restraints on the Importation of Foreign Goods, which they had but little Desire to use; and the Monopoly we so long enjoyed of their Commerce, to the great enriching of our Merchants and Artificers.[6] The mistaken Policy of the Stamp-Act first disturbed this happy Situation; but the Flame thereby raised was soon extinguished by its Repeal, and the old Harmony restored, with all its concomitant Advantages to our Commerce. The subsequent Act of another Administration, which, not content with an established Exclusion of Foreign Manufactures, began to make our own Merchandize dearer to the Consumers there by heavy Duties, revived it again: And Combinations were entered into throughout the Continent, to stop Trading with Britain till those Duties should be repealed. All were accordingly repealed but One, the Duty on Tea. This was reserved professedly as a standing Claim and Exercise of the Right assumed by Parliament of laying such Duties. The Colonies, on this Repeal, retracted their Agreement, so far as related to all other Goods except that on which the Duty was retained. This was trumpeted *here* by the Minister for the Colonies as a Triumph; *there* it was considered only as a decent and equitable Measure,

6. BF is here echoing his statements before Parliament in 1766: above, XIII, 135.

shewing a Willingness to *meet* the Mother Country in every Advance towards a Reconciliation. And the Disposition to a good Understanding was so prevalent, that possibly they might soon have relaxed in the Article of Tea also. But the System of Commissioners of Customs, Officers without end, with Fleets and Armies for collecting and enforcing those Duties, being continued, and these acting with much Indiscretion and Rashness, giving great and unnecessary Trouble and Obstruction to Business, commencing unjust and vexatious Suits, and harassing Commerce in all its Branches, while that Minister kept the People in a constant State of Irritation by Instructions which appeared to have no other End than the gratifying his Private Resentments,[7] occasioned a persevering Adherence to their Resolution in that Particular: And the Event should be a Lesson to Ministers, not to risque, through Pique, the obstructing any one Branch of Trade, since the Course and Connection of General Business may be thereby disturbed to a Degree impossible to be foreseen or imagined. For it appears, that the Colonies, finding their Humble Petitions to have this Duty repealed, were rejected and treated with Contempt, and that the Produce of the Duty was applied to the rewarding with undeserved Salaries and Pensions every one of their Enemies, the Duty itself became more odious, and their Resolution to starve it more vigorous and obstinate. The Dutch, the Danes and French, took the Advantage thus offered them by our Imprudence, and began to smuggle their Teas into the Plantations.[8] At first this was somewhat difficult; but at length, as all Business improves by Practice, it became easy. A Coast, 1500 Miles in Length, could not in all Parts be guarded, even by the whole Navy of England, especially where the restraining Authority was by all the Inhabitants deemed unconstitutional, and Smuggling of course considered as Patriotism. The needy Wretches too, who with small Salaries were trusted to watch the Ports Day and Night, in all Weathers, found it easier and more profitable, not only to *wink*, but to sleep in their Beds, the Merchant's Pay being more generous than the King's. Other India

7. For BF's elaboration of these points see above, XIX, 220–6.
8. BF is repeating the substance of what he had already written to American friends: *ibid.*, p. 420; to Cushing, Jan. 5, 1773.

Goods also, which by themselves would not have made a Smuggling Voyage sufficiently profitable, accompanied Tea to Advantage; and it is feared the cheap French Silks, formerly rejected as not to the Taste of the Colonists, may have found their way with the Wares of India, and now established themselves in the popular Use and Opinion. It is supposed that at least a Million of Americans drink Tea twice a Day, which, at the first Cost here, can scarce be reckoned at less than Half a Guinea a Head *per Annum*. This Market, that in the five Years which have run on since the Act passed, would have paid 2,500,000 Guineas, *for Tea alone*, into the Coffers of the Company, we have wantonly lost to Foreigners. Meanwhile it is said the Duties have so diminished, that the whole Remittance of the last Year amounted to no more than the pitiful Sum of 85 Pounds for the Expence of some Hundred Thousands in armed Ships and Soldiers to support the Officers.[1] Hence the Tea and other India Goods that might have been sold in America, remain rotting in the Company's Warehouses, while those of Foreign Ports are known to be cleared by the American Demand. Hence in some Degree the Company's Inability to pay their Bills; the sinking of their Stock, by which Millions of Property have been annihilated; the lowering of their Dividend, whereby so many must be distressed; the Loss to Government of the stipulated 400,000 Pounds a Year, which must make a proportionable Reduction in our Savings towards the Discharge of our enormous Debt; and hence in part the severe Blow suffered by Credit in general, to the Ruin of many Families; the Stagnation of Business in Spital-Fields and at Manchester, through want of Vent for their Goods; with other future Evils, which, as they cannot, from the numerous and secret Connections in General Commerce, easily be foreseen, can hardly be avoided.

To Richard Bache   ALS (letterbook draft): Library of Congress

Dear Son   London, Mar. 3. 73
    I received yours of Jan. 4. per Packet but none from Mrs. Franklin, whom you mention as writing at the same time.

1. BF had made the same point to Cushing: *ibid.*

I lament the Death of my old good Friend Mr. Hall, but am glad to understand he has left a Son fit to carry on the Business, which wish he may do with as good a Character and as good Success as his Father.[2]

The Gentleman who reported that Story of the House struck in Jamaica which had Conductors on it,[3] has since sent me a Letter he received from thence, acquainting him, that before the Stroke the Conductors had been taken down in order to make some Repairs to the House; and the Knowledge that Conductors had been there, occasioned the Report among the People that a House with Conductors had been struck. And he now every where contradicts the Story. I shall be glad to know what Information you receive.

The Ohio Grant has not yet got the Seals affixed. 'Tis good not to expect with any degree of Certainty, what is still subject to Accidents. My Love to Sally and Ben. I am ever Your affectionate Father   B FRANKLIN

Your Mother and Sisters were well about a Month since.

Mr Bache

To Alexander Colden   ALS (letterbook draft): Library of Congress

⟨London, March 3, 1773: Has received Colden's letter of Jan. 7 enclosing Ritchie on Hyndman, Lancaster & Co. for £100, and hopes it will be paid, for "we have had too many bad ones of late."⟩

To John Foxcroft   ALS (letterbook draft): Library of Congress

Dear Friend   London Mar. 3. 73
    I am favoured with yours of Jan. 5. and am glad to hear that you and yours are well. The Flour and Bisket came to hand in

---

2. After David Hall's death his elder son, William, carried on the *Pa. Gaz.* with a younger brother, David, Jr. See above, XIII, 99–101; XVII, 101 n.
3. For the story see BF's inquiry above, XIX, 314, and Bache's reply that BF is acknowledging.

good Order. I am much oblig'd to you and your Brother for your Care in sending them.

I believe I wrote you before that the Demand made upon us on Account of the Packet Letters was withdrawn as being without Foundation.[4] As to the Ohio Affair, we are daily amus'd with Expectations that it is to be Compleated at this and t'other time, but I see no Progress made in it. And I think more and more that I was right in never placing any great Dependance on it. Mr. Todd has receiv'd your £200.

Mr. Finlay sail'd yesterday for New York. Probably you will have seen him before this comes to hand.

You misunderstood me if you thought I meant in so often mentioning our Account to press an immediate Payment of the Ballance. My Wish only was, that you would inspect the Account, and satisfy yourself that I had paid you when here that large supposed Ballance in my own Wrong. If you are now satisfy'd about it, and transmit me the Account current you promise, with the Ballance stated, I shall be easy, and you will pay it when convenient. With my Love to my Daughter, &c. I am ever Dear Friend, Yours most affectionately   B Franklin

Mr Foxcroft Per Packet Mar. 3.

To Deborah Franklin   ALS (letterbook draft): Library of Congress

My dear Child   London, Mar. 3. 1773

I had no Line from you per last Packet. But I had the Satisfaction of hearing you were well by Mr. Beache's Letter. I wrote to you per Capt. All, and sent you some little Things.[5] I continue

well, and am ever, Your affectionate Husband   B Franklin

4. This and the other matters mentioned below—Hugh Finlay's appointment as postal riding surveyor and the accounting with Foxcroft—are discussed in BF's letters to him above, XIX, 60–1, 272–3, 320, 359, 374–5, 414–15.

5. Bache's letter was that of Jan. 4 above, and BF's by Capt. All was, we assume, that of Feb. 14.

To William Franklin

ALS (letterbook draft): Library of Congress

Dear Son   London, Mar. 3. 1773

I wrote to you largely by Capt. All, and sent you several Books, some Seeds, &c mentioned in my Letter, and one thing more, viz. a plated Tea Boiler, of Bolton's make, which I hope will prove good and please. I have not yet got the Bill. I have since receiv'd yours of Jan. 5. which I shall answer largely by next Opportunity, which I suppose will be Sutton. The India Company have petition'd Parliament to take off the Duty on Tea to America. Inclos'd is Mr. Small's Letter which by Accident was omitted to be sent by Capt. All.[6] I can now only add Love to Betsey, and that I am ever, Your affectionate Father

B FRANKLIN

Ohio Grant has not yet got the Seals. The Peas I sent you are called the Penshurst Peas. They are much valued as great Bearers, and hardy to stand the Winter.

From John Winthrop

AL:[7] American Philosophical Society

Dear Sir,   Cambridge New England, March 4. 1773

I received your favor of Septr. 18. I return you many thanks for Dr. Priestly's Piece on impregnating water with fix'd air.[8] If this should prove an effectual remedy for the sea-scurvy, it would be indeed a most important discovery. I am extremely concerned to hear, that Dr. Priestly is so meanly provided for, while so many [blank] are rolling about here in gilt chariots, with very ample stipends. I admire his comprehensive genius, his perspicuity and vigor of composition, his indefatigable application, and his free, independent spirit; and wish it were in my power to do him any kind of service.[9] It would give me

6. For the seeds, the tea urn, and Small's letter see BF to WF above, Feb. 14; for the East India Company petition see BF to Galloway of the same date.

7. The absence of a closing salutation and signature suggests that the letter is incomplete.

8. *Directions for Impregnating Water with Fixed Air* . . . (London, 1772).

9. In his missing letter of Sept. 18, 1772, which Winthrop is acknowledging, BF must have mentioned Priestley's financial straits and inquired

great pleasure to see him well settled in America; tho' indeed I am inclined to think, he can prosecute his learned labors to greater advantage in England. A man of his abilities would do honor to any of the Colleges. At present there is no vacancy among them; but if there were, I believe Sir you judge perfectly right, that his religious principles would hardly be thought orthodox enough. Indeed, I doubt, whether they would do at Rhode Island any more than in the others; for this reason, among others: That College is intirely in the hands of the Baptists, and intended to continue so; and I never understood that Dr. Priestly was of their persuasion.[1] However, I cannot but hope, that his great and just reputation will procure something valuable for him, and adequate to his merit.

I have looked over his Treatise of Optics, which you were so good as to present to our Library,[2] with great Satisfaction; and met with many articles, especially from the foreign Publications which were new to me. It is indeed a most noble collection of every thing relating to that Science.

In my last, I ventured to mention a little slip concerning the satellites of Saturn. It would be miraculous, if, in so large a work,

about an academic berth for him in America. Soon after BF wrote, Lord Shelburne's handsome offer ended Priestley's difficulties. See above, XIX, 299–300, and BF's reply to this letter below, July 25.

1. The College of Rhode Island, which became Brown University, was a Baptist foundation; see William G. McLoughlin, *New England Dissent, 1630–1833: the Baptists and the Separation of Church and State* (2 vols., Cambridge, Mass., 1971), I, 491–501. Priestley was what is now called a Unitarian.

2. For Priestley's treatise and Harvard's acknowledgment of it see above, XIX, 157 n, 178. Winthrop doubtless sent the acknowledgment, and his missing letter referred to in the next paragraph, by his son Adam the previous June; see *idem.*, p. 175. BF's response was the letter of Sept. 18; it also is missing, but this reply reveals the gist of its contents: Winthrop offers American data on atmospheric electricity in general and lightning in particular, and hopes that BF will soon produce a fuller discussion of the subject than the world has yet seen. The September letter, therefore, must have had the same purpose as BF's inquiry of Bache about lightning in Jamaica (*ibid.*, p. 314): he was gathering information for the reply to Benjamin Wilson that he never wrote (*ibid.*, p. 429), and Wilson had argued in 1772 that instances in America supported his theory against BF's: *Observations upon Lightning . . .* (London, 1773), pp. 11–12, 50–6.

collected from such a number of books, and on such a variety of matters, there should not be many such. I noted the few that occurred to me in the chapters taken from those Authors I was most acquainted with, and beg leave to inclose a list of the principal of them. There are not above two or three of them that are of any consequence: however the list, such as it is, is at Dr. Priestly's service, if you think it worth sending to him. It may help to remove a few trifling inaccuracies from that valuable work.[3]

I cannot forbear remarking to you Sir on a passage in Castillioneus's Life of Sir Isaac Newton. It appears to me a gross mistake, and derogates from the honor of that great man. If it has never yet been publicly animadverted on, I should be willing to have this remark communicated, provided you judge it proper; for which end I write it on a separate paper. But tho' it is addressed to the Royal Society, I would be understood, to leave it intirely to your judgment whether to present it to them or not; as I know you can judge much better of the propriety of it than I can.[4]

I have inclosed the news paper you mention, that gave an account of the thunder storm we had here a few years ago. As you are collecting facts on this subject, I look'd over my old almanacks, where I had made some memoranda relating to your admirable lightning-bells. I think it would not be worthwhile to transcribe them all, nor can I collect any thing from them but what is commonly known. In general, it seems that the bells hardly ever ring, in the summer, without a shower; they sometimes ring when there is no thunder or lightning, but do not always ring when there is; when there is a thunder shower, they generally ring most briskly while the cloud is yet at some distance, and cease as soon as it rains hard. In winter, they frequently ring

3. Winthrop's lost letter must have referred to the same work on optics, which mentions the satellites of Saturn only in passing. Because it never went into a second edition, in which Priestley might have remedied the inaccuracies, we have no way of identifying them.

4. BF submitted the paper, which was read at a meeting of the Society on Jan 20, 1774, and published in the *Phil. Trans.*, LXIV (1774), 153-7. Winthrop was criticizing a minor point in the life of Newton that Jean de Castillon had appended to his *Isaaci Newtoni ... opuscula mathematica, philosophica et philologica ...* (3 vols., Lausanne and Geneva, 1744).

briskly in snow storms; and twice they have done so, after the weather was cleared up, and while the new-fallen snow was driving about with the wind; as you have done me the honor already to publish.[5] But I will transcribe two or three of these memoranda.

1762 . July 18. Excessive hot. Spirit Thermometer of Royal Society's Scale was $6\frac{3}{10}$ above O. It has never been higher in the course of 30 years, except on 17 and 18 June Old Style 1749. when the spirit half fill'd the bubble at the top of the tube. I take it, that this would have answer'd to 99 of Fahrenheit's Scale. $6\frac{3}{10}$ above O answers to 93. About 6. P.M. wind comes NW and sharp lightning and thunder shower to the N. Bells ring briskly for an hour, and sparkle or snap sometimes. After they had ceased, a gentle shower, with scarce any lightning or thunder.

1762. July 24. P.M. extreme hot. Royal Society's thermometer $4\frac{2}{10}$ above O, answering to 91 of Fahrenheit. Bells ring, and then a shower, with much lightning and thunder, but not hard here. It set a barn on fire, on Jamaica Plain, by the pond, (about 4 miles S. from hence) and kill'd a woman at Hampton-Falls (about 50 miles N) who was standing near some shelves of pewter. Having occasion, soon after, to take a journey that way, I called at the house, and committed to writing the information I got, which I will transcribe in a separate paper; as also some other accounts of damage by lightning, where any circumstances were mentioned.

In looking for the News-paper before mentioned, I met with another, which gives an account of damage done by lightning in some places in Connecticut, in July 1771. As perhaps you have not seen it, I inclose it with the other, also, a Letter sent me, with another account.[6] In my almanacks I found also a few

5. In the 1769 edition of *Exper. and Obser.*: above, X, 150.

6. The letter has been lost, along with the separate paper that is mentioned again at the end of the letter. The newspapers enclosed were unquestionably the *Mass. Gaz.; and the Boston Weekly News-Letter* of Aug. 9, 1770 (see above, XVII, 263), and of Aug. 8, 1771, and perhaps the *Conn. Jour., and New-Haven Post-Boy* of Aug. 2 and 9, 1771. The accounts in the latter year were of two storms in Connecticut. In one, on July 28, lightning damaged a house in North Haven and a church in Stratfield, now Bridgeport, where

minutes, relating to some uncommon appearances of the Aurora borealis. I do not know that they can be of any use; but if they will afford you the least amusement, I will readily transcribe them.

In addition to my News-paper account, I would mention, that besides the strokes of lightning on the College[7] and the Elm tree July 2. 1768, there was another discharge that afternoon on a corn-field, at a little distance from the College towards the S.[W?] It spoiled the corn, which was of some hight, in a circle of about 24[?] feet diameter. That near the centre was burnt down to the roots, I was inform'd by the owner. I did not hear of it till some days after; and when I saw the place, it had been replanted with cabbage. The corn near the circumference of the circle was only scorched and I saw the leaves wither'd and drooping. The place struck was about midway between a tree on one side, and the well-pole[?] and chimney of the house on the other, and as I judge about 80 feet distant from each; and there was nothing near so high on the other sides, for a considerable distance. Hence, their protection did not extend 80 feet. If a person had been standing in the corn, I suppose there is no doubt but that he would have been killed. And therefore a person in the midst of an open plain is by no means secure from the stroke of lightning. The best security seems to be, to have something high, as a tree, for example near him, but not too near; perhaps from 30 or 40, to 10 or 15 feet or rather, to be near two such trees. But I have ventured a little too far. I hope you will be able to ascertain all such circumstances, with a good degree of exactness; and that the world will soon be favor'd with a more complete account of this violent meteor than it has ever yet seen. Thus, there were three explosions here that afternoon, within a small distance from each other; but at what distances of time [?] I cannot say. Some of our Scholars measured the distances between the places that were struck, and found that from the N.E. corner of Hollis to the Elm tree was 211 yards; from the Elm to the middle of the cornfield

---

two men were killed; in the other, four days later, churches were struck in Wallingford and Hartford.

7. The lightning caused considerable damage to Hollis Hall; Speaker Cushing and several students and faculty members had a narrow escape. *Boston Chron.*, June 27–July 4, 1768.

418 yards; and from the middle of the corn field to the corner of Hollis, 480 y[ards.]

I owe great acknowledgments to the Rev. Dr. Price for his goodness in sending me his curious Papers on the aberration; and have now the satisfaction to say, that I see clearly the source of the fallacy in the last p[aper?] I troubled you with.[8] Before I receiv'd Dr. Price's Papers, I had look'd into a Memoire of the famous M. Clairaut, in Acad. Sciences for 1746. on this subject, who seems to have made strange work with it.[9] He makes the visible aberration [of] Longitude of the superior planets to be greatest when in opposition to the sun (and greatest of all, if at the same time in perihelion) and least, when in conjunction, in opposition it being the sum, and in conjunction the difference, of their respe[ctive] aberrations and the Earth's: tho' as to the inferior planets, when in superior conjunction, he rightly makes it to be the sum of their aberrations and the Earth's. [But?] what he has said of the superior planets, seems to me contrary to the most evident principles of aberration.

Please to turn to the paper on Damage by Lightning.

Dr. Franklin

Endorsed: This Letter to be return'd to B.F. after Drs Price and Priestly have perus'd it.[1]

To David Colden

ALS: New-York Historical Society; letterbook draft: Library of Congress[2]

Dear Sir,   London, March 5. 1773

I received your obliging Favour with the Account of your Drill Plough, which appears to me very ingeniously contriv'd

8. For our attempt to reconstruct the scientific exchange between Winthrop and Price on the aberration of light see above, XVII, 264 n.

9. The paper was by Alexis-Claude Clairaut (1713–65), the noted mathematician and astronomer: "De l'aberration de la lumière des planètes, des comètes, et des satellites," Académie des sciences, *Mémoires* (for 1746; Paris, 1751), pp. 539–68.

1. This reminder to his friends, as might be expected, is in BF's hand.

2. The draft, dated March 3, differs from the final letter in details too inconsequential to note.

the Construction simple and easily executed, and the Description perfectly clear and intelligible. I put it into the Hands of Mr. Arbuthnot, who is a great Connoisseur in such Matters, and seem'd to like it much.[3] He will lay it before the Society of Arts. Kalm's Account of what he learnt in America is full of idle Stories, which he pick'd up among ignorant People, and either forgetting of whom he had them, or willing to give them some Authenticity, he has ascrib'd them to Persons of Reputation who never heard of them till they were found in his Book. And where he really had Accounts from such Persons, he has varied the Circumstances unaccountably, so that I have been asham'd to meet with some mention'd as from me. It is dangerous Conversing with these Strangers that keep Journals.[4]

With this I send you some Philosophical Papers, that will appear in the next Volume of the Transactions indeed; but as that is not to be publish'd till Midsummer, you will hereby see them so much sooner. Priestly's Experiments on Fix'd Air is the Subject of much Conversation here at present.[5]

3. BF is replying to Colden's letter above, XIX, 390–2. The drill plough or seed drill permitted sowing in even rows, as far apart as desired, and produced a greater yield than previous methods. John Arbuthnot of Mitcham, Surrey, a pioneer in agricultural methods and implements, was in Arthur Young's opinion a "real genius in Husbandry," "upon the whole the most agreeable, pleasant and interesting connection which I ever made in agricultural pursuits." *On the Husbandry of Three Celebrated British Farmers* . . . (London, 1811), p. 27; M. Bentham-Edwards, ed., *The Autobiography of Arthur Young* . . . (London, 1898), pp. 66–7. Arbuthnot, an F.R.S. since 1770 (above, VIII, 359), had by this time invented a number of ploughs and drills, which Young described with illustrations in *The Farmer's Tour through the East of England* . . . (4 vols., London, 1771), II, 510–20.

4. BF had had a quite different opinion when parting with Kalm in 1751. "I love the Man," he had written then, "and admire his indefatigable Industry." Above, IV, 113; for the information that Kalm derived from him see pp. 53–63. BF's change of view must have resulted from his first exposure to Kalm's writings, which were not accessible in England until Forster's translation in 1770–71: above, XV, 147–8.

5. The draft omits this sentence. One of the philosophical papers was undoubtedly Priestley's *Observations on Different Kinds of Air* . . . (London, 1772), which BF had sent to Rush with his letter above, Feb. 14. The paper was also published in the *Phil. Trans.*, LXII (1772), 147–264; but this volume, despite its date, did not actually appear until the latter part of 1773: *Monthly Rev.*, L (1774), 28.

I send you also some Penshurst Peas, much valued here for their great Bearing and Hardiness. Also some Turnip-rooted-Cabbage Seed, famous for bearing Winter Frosts and so affording early Food for Cattle when Fodder is scant and Grass not grown. And some Seed of the Scotch Cabbage.[6] My best Respects to your good Father, to whom I shall shortly write. With very great Esteem, I am, Dear Sir, Your most obedient Servant

B Franklin

D Colden Esqr

Addressed: To / David Colden, Esqr / New York / per Packet / with a Parcel / B Free Franklin

To William Cooper[7]

ALS and copy:[8] New York Public Library; ALS (letterbook draft): Library of Congress

Sir,   London, March 9. 1773

I received duly your Favour of Dec. 8. with a Copy for myself of the Proceedings of your Town Meeting, for which please to present my respectful Thanks to the Committee. I received also a Number more for different Persons, here, which I immediately deliver'd as directed. I have also reprinted the Pamphlet[9] to make your Grievances more generally known here,

6. Presumably some of the seeds from Anthony Todd that BF was distributing to American friends; see his letters above to WF, Feb. 3, and Bartram, Feb. 10.

7. William (1721–1809), the older brother of BF's regular correspondent, the Rev. Samuel Cooper, had represented Boston briefly in the House of Representatives, and during the Revolution did so again in the provincial congress. His long term as town clerk, which had begun in 1761 and continued till his death, made him an unofficial manager of the town meeting and a leader of the Boston Caucus and the Sons of Liberty. *New England Historical and Geneal. Register,* XLIV (1890), 56. "With 'Silver-Tongued Sam' speaking for the Deity in the General Court, and his brother William controlling Boston town meeting, it was said that the patronymic of the holy family was Cooper." *Sibley's Harvard Graduates,* XI, 197.

8. The copy is in the minutebook of the Boston Committee of Correspondence.

9. BF's draft here inserts "with a Preface." It is printed above, under the end of February, where the proceedings are identified.

97

a few Copies of which I send herewith. With great Esteem, I am, Sir, Your most obedient humble Servant   B FRANKLIN[1]

Wm Cooper   Esqr

Endorsed: London March 9, 1773 Dr. Benjamin Franklin's Letter to the Town Clerk recd. April 29. 1773 Recd

To Thomas Cushing   ALS (letterbook draft): Library of Congress

Sir,   London, March 9. 73

I did myself the Honour of Writing to you the 2d of December, and the 5th of January past. Since which I have received your Favour of Nov 28. inclosing the Votes and Proceedings of the Town of Boston, which I have reprinted here with a Preface.[2] Herewith I send you a few Copies.

Governor Hutchinson's Speech at the Opening of your Jany. Session, has been printed and industriously circulated here by (as I think) the ministerial People, which I take to be no good Sign. The Assembly's Answer to it is not yet arriv'd, and in the mean while it seems to make Impression on the Minds of many not well acquainted with the Dispute.[3] The Tea Duty however,

1. In his draft BF added and then deleted a postscript: "I have not yet seen Capt. Jenkins, but will enquire for him." Jenkins was presumably mentioned in the lost letter from Cooper of Dec. 8, and is identified in a note on Williams to BF above, Feb. 15.

2. Cushings' letter has disappeared. For the enclosure see the preceding document.

3. The declaration of the town meeting and the creation of a committee of correspondence persuaded Governor Hutchinson that he could no longer keep silent. He accordingly outlined to the General Court, when it met again on Jan. 6, what he conceived to be the position of Massachusetts in the empire. His speech was the fullest and most closely reasoned defense of the imperial constitution, as traditionally viewed, that appeared in America before the Revolution. It was also the indirect cause of BF's short but significant essay below, March 16, "On Claims to the Soil of America." When British subjects left the realm, the Governor argued, they retained their allegiance to the crown, and the lands they settled overseas became part of the crown's dominions; the very issuance of a charter was an assertion of royal authority over the colony so chartered. In leaving the realm, he continued, the colonists surrendered the right they had previously had to be governed by their

is under the Consideration of Parliament for a Repeal on a Petition from the East India Company; and no new Measures have been talked of against America as likely to be taken during the present Session;[4] I was therefore preparing to return home by the Spring Ships: But have been advis'd by our Friends to stay till the Session is over; as the Commission sent to Rhodeisland,[5] and the Discontents in your Province, with the Correspondence of the Towns, may possibly give Rise to something here, when my being on the Spot may be of Use to our Country. So I conclude to stay a little longer. In the mean time I must hope that great Care will be taken to keep our People quiet, since nothing is more wish'd for by our Enemies, than that by Insurrections we should give a good Pretence for increasing the Military among us, and putting us under more severe Restraints. And it must be evident to all that by our rapidly increasing Strength we shall soon become of so much Importance, that none of our just Claims of Privilege will be as heretofore unattended to, nor any Security we can wish for our Rights be deny'd us. With great

---

representatives in Parliament, because no practical means existed to provide such representation; but the surrender did not affect the right of Parliament to legislate for them. That right was undeniable, and if it was misused the remedy was not to deny it but to petition for redress. A state could not exist with two coequal legislatures: either Parliament was supreme, or the colonies were totally independent. Bradford, ed., *Mass. State Papers*, pp. 336–42; Hutchinson, *History*, III, 266–7. The speech was printed in the *London Chron.*, Feb. 27, and the *Public Advertiser*, March 4. If "ministerial People" were responsible, they presumably did not include Dartmouth, who was still averse to troubling the waters; see BF to Cushing above, Jan. 5, and Hutchinson, *History*, III, 276–7.

4. The Company's petition to Parliament, of which BF speaks, was based on the propositions adopted by the Proprietors on Feb. 12, for which see the note on BF to Galloway above, Feb. 14, and Labaree, *Tea Party*, p. 70. The petition as presented on March 2 contained the same ambiguous request as the propositions, to export tea to America free of duty. The subsequent Parliamentary debate did not make clear precisely what this request would entail, but BF still took it to mean, as he had in February, repeal of the Townshend duty. In fact, however, the government did not raise that possibility; see the headnote on BF to Cushing below, June 4.

5. To investigate the burning of H.M.S. *Gaspee*; see above, XIX, 379–80 and Cooper's and Cushing's letters to BF below, March 15, 24.

Respect, I have the Honour to be, Sir, Your most obedient
humble Servant   B FRANKLIN

Thos Cushing Esqr

To Jane Mecom   ALS (letterbook draft): Library of Congress

Dear Sister   London, March 9. 1773
I received your kind Letter of Dec. 30. and rejoice to find you
were well. I may possibly have the greater Pleasure of seeing you
before the Year is out[?]. I have desired Cousin Williams to give
you the Money he may recover from Hall.[6] I would only mention
to you, that when I was in Boston in 1754[?], Brother John then
living, an old Man whose Name I have forgotten, apply'd to me
with a Bond of our Father's of about 15 or 17 Pound if I remember
right, desiring I would pay it, which I declin'd with this Answer,
that as I had never receiv'd any thing from the Estate, I did not
think my self oblig'd to pay any of the Debts. But I had another
Reason, which was that I thought the Care of those Matters
belong'd more properly to my Brother. If you know that Person,
I wish you would now out of Hall's Money pay that Debt;
for I remember his Mildness on the Occasion, with some Regard.[7] My Love to Jenny, I am ever, Your affectionate Brother
                                               B FRANKLIN

I have not yet seen Capt. Jenkins, but will enquire him out when
I next go to the City.[8]

6. See the following document.
7. John Franklin (C.8), a tallow-chandler and soap-maker, had been
postmaster of Boston. Jane's reply to this letter, if she sent one, has been
lost; hence we do not know whether she could trace the innominate old man,
but we certainly cannot.
8. For Seth Jenkins, their relative, see Jonathan Williams to BF above,
Feb. 15.

To Jonathan Williams, Sr.

ALS (letterbook draft): Library of Congress

Dear Cousin, London, Mar. 9. 1773

I received your Favour of Dec. 27. with the Cask of Sowns and Tongues, which came very opportunely at the Beginning of Lent, and are very agreable to me. Mr. Stanley and your Brother have the others.[9] Accept my best Thanks.

I received also the Bill of Exchange for £27[1] for which have credited your Account. And shall soon send you a State of the whole from my Books.

I shall be satisfy'd with any Measures you take in the Affair of Hall, knowing you will act for the best. You may give the whole Sum recover'd to my Sister.[2] I have not now time to write as I would to Jonathan. Let him know that I recd. his of Dec. 26. and that I lately sent him the other 3 of Priestly's Book. I inclose Henry's Indentures. If you find it suitable, I could wish the Boy bound to his new Business.[3] My Love to Cousin Grace and all yours. I hear her Father is still living.[4] My Respects to him. I am ever, Your affectionate Uncle B FRANKLIN

Jonath Williams, Esqr

9. Cod's tongues and sounds, or air bladders, were delicacies of the period; the others who received them were John Stanley, the blind organist and former teacher of Josiah Williams, and Jonathan's brother John, the customs inspector. Lent began that year on Feb. 24.

1. Sheppard on King, listed above, x, 358; see also Jour., p. 47, and Ledger, p. 39.

2. BF is answering Williams' letter above, XIX, 290–1, which we should have dated Nov. 12; see BF to Williams below, July 7. For Samuel Hall's debt and Jane Mecom's windfall see the references in Williams to BF above, Feb. 15.

3. For the books see above, XIX, 200; the apprenticing of Henry Walker is discussed in his mother's letter to BF below, June 20.

4. William Harris, if he was indeed still alive, must have been in his eighties; he married Grace Williams' mother in 1712. Above, I, lvii.

To Jacques Barbeu-Dubourg

AL (mutilated and incomplete draft): American Philosophical Society; translated extract: printed in Jacques Barbeu-Dubourg, ed., *Œuvres de M. Franklin* ... (2 vols., Paris, 1773), II, 311.[5]

Dear [*torn*]   [March 10, 1773[6]]
  [*Torn*] Instant, [*torn*] read carefully [*torn*] much Importance [*torn*.]
Page 18.[7] line 14. [*torn*] électrisé en plus [*Torn*] line 20 and 21. read [*torn*.]
Page 24. line 25. for plus vîte, read plus tôt.
Pag. 25. l. 15. for *propre au verre*, read *proportionnée au quantité de verre*, or use some other words that are better French than those that I propose.
Pag. 30 l. 17. and 18. for *excédant les bords de la planche*, read *etant distant l'un de l'autre environ*, &c. Or it may be corrected by leaving the first Words as they stand and only for 4 read *14 pouces*. The Thi[mbles] in the Circumference were four Inches distant from each other, and there being 30 of them, it follows that the Circumference must be about 120 Inches, and the Radius of course about 20, whereas the Radius in the Translation is but about 10. viz, 6 Inches for half the Diameter of the Planche, and 4 Inches of an Arm of Glass extending from the Edge of the Planche. In fact the Strips of Glass were each 14. Inches long.
Page 31. line 3. for *quinze*, read *cent*. I imagine that you thought it incredible, that it should carry so great a Weight as 100 Piastres, each weighing 17. dwt 8. gr. or near an Ounce of Silver. But it is fact.
Page 36. delete the Words, *des deux côtés en même tems*, as not being in the Original; and the Experiment described in the

5. Smyth's retranslation (*Writings*, VI, 26) illustrates how BF's wording changed as it turned into French and back again.
6. Supplied from Dubourg's extract.
7. The page references that follow are to vol. I of the *Œuvres*, which contains misdated translations of the letters from BF to Collinson of July 28, 1747, and April 29, 1749, that are printed above, III, 156–64, 352–65; BF's comments are on experiments described in the second letter, pp. 359–60, 364–5. Dubourg received the suggestions too late for inclusion, but noted them in his corrigenda on p. [xxiii].

Note shows that the Spirits were [*torn*] on one side of the River only. The Words [*torn*] (*at the same time*) in the Original mean only at [*torn*] of the Party of Pleasure.

[*Torn*] more [*torn*] carefully, find [*torn*] 16. *on* for *ou*. [*Torn*] Arrear with your [*torn*].

[*Torn*] several Favours of January [*torn*] begging Pardon for the Delay, I will now endeavour to answer [*torn*] solution of the Question, why the [*torn*] is warmer after some time [*torn*] only this, that the Water which remain'd [*torn*] in the Trunk of the Pump, was cooled by its Nearness to the Air, and must be pumped out before the warm Water of the Spring below could be brought up.⁸

I do not attempt to explain why damp Cloaths cause Colds, because I now doubt the Fact, and apprehend they have no more that Effect than wet Clothes. I think Colds (the Disease so called) proceed from other Causes, and have no Relation to *Wet* or *Cold*. I purpose a Pamphlet on this Paradoxical Subject, as soon as I have a little Leisure.⁹ In the mean Time I must just mention one Thing to you, that suspecting [the common] Opinion not to be true that Cold closes the Pores [and obstructs Pers]piration, I prevailed with a young Physician,¹ who [was making] Experiments with the Sanctorian Ballance,² to try the different Quantities of Perspiration for an Hour sitting naked and another Hour warmly cloathed. He pursu'd the Experiment for eight successive days at all Hours, and constantly found the Perspiration near double in the Hours he was naked.³

8. This paragraph and the remainder of the fragment, until the last two lines, are in reply to Dubourg's letter above, under Jan. 13; the annotation there explains much of what BF is discussing.

9. See below, pp. 529–30.

1. William Stark: see above, XVI, 162 n, and BF to Dubourg below, May 4.

2. Santorio Santorio or Sanctorius (1561–1636), a physician and scientist at the University of Padua, was known for his work on perspiration; his balance was a device to measure changes in body weight. *Biographisches Lexicon der hervorragenden Ärtze* ... (5 vols., Berlin and Vienna, 1929–34), v, 21; Henry A. Skinner, *The Origin of Medical Terms* ... (2nd ed., Baltimore, 1961), p. 363.

3. This paragraph, which is Dubourg's extract, appears partly in the margin of the draft and is badly defaced; we have supplied missing words in

5. Black Walls were used by the late Lord Leicester, with good Success in this Particular, that the young Fruit was better secur'd by them from the Mischief of late Frosts. But when they are over, perhaps the ripening would best be forwarded by white Walls. Experience must decide this.[4]

Our Pole or Perch is really $16\frac{1}{2}$ feet, so that 4 of them make the Chain of 66 feet.

In M. Dalibard's Apparatus at Marli, it is true there was no fix'd Communication between the Iron Rod and the Earth, yet Coiffier was safe in touching it with the Ring of the Wire fastned to the Glass Phial by way of Handle, especially if the other End of that Wire went into the Earth.[5] And if not, yet I think he could receive no greater Stroke than the Shock of so much charged Glass as his Hand was apply'd to.

I hope I have answered in some preceding Letter what relates to the Memoir you mention of M. Missa; if not, I am very sorry and much ashamed; because I have lost or mislaid the Memoire, if I ever had it, and can remember nothing of it.[6] Therefore if I have not answer'd it, pray let it be repeated. Multiplicity of Business can hardly in this Case excuse me.

I must have written to you since the Receipt of yours of Jan 13. because I find in that of Jan. 15. the Verses of your young Poet, [*remainder missing.*]

---

brackets from the French translation. The latter has numerous verbal differences from the draft; the only substantial one is that "eight successive days at all Hours" becomes "huit heures de suite."

4. See Dubourg's letter above, Jan. 13. Thomas Coke (1697–1759), created Earl of Leicester in 1744, was postmaster general for a quarter-century before his death, but devoted himself principally to cultivating his estate at Holkham in Norfolk. See Romney Sedgwick, *The House of Commons, 1715–1754* (2 vols., London, 1970), I, 564–5. He was the great-uncle of the more famous Coke of Holkham, Thomas William (1752–1842). We have no idea why this paragraph is numbered, or what BF meant by a marginal note that he appended to it: "transpose this between 4 and 6 in Page 5."

5. See Dubourg's letter just cited.

6. Our guess about Missa (*ibid.*) adds that we are as ignorant of his memoir as BF was.

To Jacques Barbeu-Dubourg

Translated extract: printed in Jacques Barbeu-Dubourg, ed., *Œuvres de M. Franklin* . . . (2 vols., Paris, 1773), I, 277–9.[7]

De Londres, le 10 Mars 1773.

Quant au magnétisme qui semble produit par l'électricité, mon opinion actuelle est que ces deux puissances n'ont aucun rapport l'une à l'autre, et que la production apparente du magnétisme n'est qu'accidentelle.[8] Voici comment on peut l'expliquer.

1°. La terre est un grand aimant.

2°. Il y a un fluide subtil, appellé fluide magnétique, qui existe dans toute espece de fer, également attiré par toutes ses parties, et également répandu dans toute sa substance, à moins qu'il ne soit forcé à l'inégalité par un pouvoir supérieur à l'attraction du fer.

3°. Cette quantité naturelle de fluide magnétique contenue dans un morceau de fer, peut y être mise en mouvement au point d'être plus raréfiée dans un endroit et plus condensée dans l'autre, mais elle ne sçauroit en être tirée par aucune force à nous connue jusqu'ici, au point de laisser la totalité dans un état négatif, ou de moins, relativement à sa quantité naturelle; non plus qu'il ne sçauroit y en être introduit d'ailleurs au point de la mettre dans un état positif, ou de plus: en quoi le magnétisme diffère de l'électricité.

4°. Un morceau de fer tendre souffre que le fluide magnétique contenu dans sa substance soit mis en mouvement par une force médiocre, de sorte qu'étant dirigé parallelement, ou tourné vers le pôle magnétique de la terre, il acquert immédiatement la qualité d'aimant, son fluide magnétique étant tiré, ou poussé d'une de ses extrêmités à l'autre, et cela continue ainsi tant qu'il demeure dans la même position, l'un de ses bouts devenant positivement magnétique et l'autre négativement. Cet aimant

---

7. An English retranslation may be found in Smyth, *Writings*, VI, 23–6. We have a strong suspicion, but no proof, that the extract and the preceding document, and perhaps the further extracts below under the end of March, are from one and the same letter.
8. See Dubourg's letter above, Feb. 24.

passager cesse de l'être dès qu'on le tourne est et ouest, son magnétisme ne tardant gueres à se répandre également dans le fer comme auparavant.

5°. Si le fer est durci, comme l'acier, son fluide magnétique est plus difficile à mettre en mouvement; il faut une force plus grande que le magnétisme de la terre pour l'émouvoir; et lorsqu'il a été poussé d'une extrêmité vers l'autre, il ne lui est pas aisé de rétrograder; ainsi une barre d'acier devient un aimant durable.

6°. Une grande chaleur épanouissant sa substance, et éloignant davantage ses parties les unes des autres, elles donnent passage au fluide électrique qui se remet en équilibre, après quoi la barre ne paroit plus un aimant.

7°. Une barre d'acier, qui n'est pas aimant, étant mise dans une position pareille à celle que prend une aiguille flottante, relativement au pôle magnétique de la terre, et dans cette position étant chauffée et refroidie subitement, devient un aimant durable. Par la raison que tandis que cette barre étoit chaude, sa quantité naturelle de fluide magnétique a été facilement poussée d'un bout sur l'autre par la vertu magnétique de la terre, et que l'endurcissement et la condensation produite par le refroidissement subit, l'y a retenue, sans lui laisser la liberté de retourner à sa premiere place.

8°. De violentes vibrations des parties d'une barre d'acier, sur laquelle on frappe à grands coups tandis qu'elle est dans cette même position, séparent tellement ses parties durant leur vibration, qu'elles laissent passer une portion de fluide magnétique poussée par le magnétisme de la terre, et qui y est si bien retenue par le rapprochement des parties lorsque la vibration cesse, que la barre devient un aimant durable.

9°. Un choc électrique traversant une aiguille dans une semblable position, et la dilatant pour un moment, en fait par la même raison un aimant durable; non pas en lui donnant du magnétisme, mais en donnant occasion à son propre fluide magnétique de s'y mettre en mouvement.

10°. Ainsi il n'y a pas réellement plus de magnétisme dans un morceau d'acier après qu'il est devenu aimant, qu'il n'y en avoit auparavant. La quantité naturelle est seulement déplacée, ou repoussée. Et delà vient qu'une forte garniture d'aimants peut changer des milliers de barres d'acier en autant d'aimants sans leur rien communiquer de son propre magnétisme; elle ne fait que mettre en mouvement celui qui étoit déja dans ces barres. C'est à cet excellent Philosophe de Pétersbourg, M. Aepinus, que j'ai principalement l'obligation de cette hypothese, qui me paroit également ingénieuse et solide. Je dis *principalement*, parce que comme il y a plusieurs années que je n'ai lû son livre [9] que j'ai laissé en Amérique, il peut se faire que j'y aye changé ou ajouté quelque chose; et si j'y ai mis quelque chose de travers, la méprise doit être sur mon compte.

Si cette hypothese vous paroit admissible, elle servira de réponse à la plupart de vos questions, je n'ai qu'une chose à ajoûter, c'est que, quelle que soit la puissance du magnétisme que vous ayez à y employer, vous ne sçauriez faire d'un certain morceau d'acier qu'un aimant d'une certaine force déterminée par sa puissance à tenir son fluide magnétique là où il est placé, sans le laisser rétrograder: or cette puissance est différente en différentes especes d'acier, et limitée dans toutes ses especes quelconques.

To a Committee of the Managers of the Philadelphia Silk Filature   ALS (letterbook draft): Library of Congress

Gentlemen,   London, Mar. 15. 1773

In mine of Feb. 10. I mentioned a Silk weaver who was desirous of going to America; and endeavouring to get Subscriptions among his Friends to defray the Expence of his and Family's Passage. He now tells me they have been so kind as to double the Sum he requested, and that he is to go in Sutton. He takes with him a good Certificate from the Meeting; and I beg leave to recommend him to the Notice and Encouragement of the Silk Committee, as far as they may find him deserving. For tho' it may be most advantageous for our Country, while the Bounty continues so high, to send all our raw Silk hither; yet as the Bounty will gradually diminish and at length cease,[1] I should think it not

---

9. *Tentamen theoriae electricitatis et magnetismi* . . . (St. Petersburg, [1759]). For Aepinus see above, VIII, 393 n, and for his development of BF's theories of magnetism and electricity I. Bernard Cohen, *Franklin and Newton* . . . (Philadelphia, 1956), pp. 537–43.

1. See above, XVI, 80–1.

amiss to begin early the laying a Foundation for the future Manufacture of it; and perhaps this Person, if he finds Employment, may be a means of raising Hands for that purpose. His Name is Joseph Clark.[2]

By the enclos'd you will see when the Silk will probably be sold. I hope to send you a good Account of it;[3] and am, with great Esteem, Gentlemen, Your most obedient humble Servant

B F

Messrs Abel James and Benja Morgan

To Deborah Franklin

ALS: American Philosophical Society; letterbook draft: Library of Congress

My dear Child,   London, March 15. 73.

I wrote to you by Capt. All, and by the last Packet. By Capt. All I sent a Box containing sundry Parcels for my Friends. Among the rest were your Neighbour Miss Haddocks Silk, and Gowns for you and Sally.[4] I hope they will get safe to hand. I continue well, and hope now soon to have the Pleasure of seeing you and Home. My Love to all. I am ever, Your affectionate Husband   B FRANKLIN

Addressed: To / Mrs Franklin / Philadelphia / per Capt. Sutton.

2. Clark, his wife, and their son arrived in Philadelphia with a certificate from the Devonshire House Meeting in London, and were admitted to the Philadelphia Meeting in June, 1773. If Clark was ever a pioneer in American silk-weaving, it was not for long; in 1774 he became a schoolteacher in Rahway, N.J., and joined the meeting there. Hinshaw, *Amer. Quaker Genealogy,* II, 486; Geneal. Soc. of Pa. *Pub.,* XIV (1942–44), 274.

3. We have not located the enclosure; it was presumably a newspaper notice of the sale in which BF expected the Pennsylvania silk to be included. For his account of the sale itself see his letter to the committee below, July 14.

4. The letter by All was that above of Feb. 14, when BF, as his habit was, disposed of a large amount of correspondence on one day. Most of it, at least, went by Isaac All in the *Richard Penn;* see the two letters following this one. The ship had a slow passage; the *Pa. Gaz.* reported her arrival on April 21. BF's letter "by the last Packet" was presumably a missing one sent in the *Mercury,* which had sailed a few days before: *Public Advertiser,* March 13.

To William Franklin ALS (letterbook draft): Library of Congress

Dear Son,   London, March 15. 1773

I wrote you pretty largely by Capt. All, and sent you sundry things, particularly the plated Boiler you wrote for.[5] I have nothing to add, but to let you know I continue well. Enclos'd I send you the Boston Pamphlet with my Preface.[6] I grow tired of my Situation here, and really think of Returning in the Fall. My Love to Betsey. I am ever Your affectionate Father

B FRANKLIN

To Joseph Galloway ALS (letterbook draft): Library of Congress

Dear Sir,   London, Mar. 15. 1773.

I wrote to you pretty fully per Capt. All, and have little to add. Mr. Jackson told me Yesterday at Court, that he had return'd the 30 Acts to the Board of Trade with his Approbation to every one. But to day Mr. Bollan, Agent for the Council of the Massachusetts, tells me, the Board object to one, viz, that for dissolving a Marriage.[7] I shall enquire about it to-morrow, and endeavour to support it; as it would be very inconvenient to be oblig'd to come here with Evidences to obtain such Dissolutions. The Ministry are a good deal chagrin'd with the Boston Proceedings, but seem not to know what to do with them. Inclos'd I send you the Edition printed here with my Preface.

5. For the tea urn see BF's letter above, Feb. 14.

6. The preface to the town meeting's declaration in *Votes and Proceedings* is printed above under the end of February. BF, as mentioned in the headnote there, did not publish the pamphlet in London until June, but sent it to America months before; WF and Galloway (see the next document) were receiving two of these advance copies.

7. For the thirty acts see BF to the Assembly's committee of correspondence above, Jan. 6. Richard Jackson gave a long-winded and guardedly favorable report to the Board of Trade on the act that Bollan mentioned. But the Board recommended against it on the ground that colonial legislation dissolving a marriage, particularly when no ecclesiastical court had rendered a verdict, was either improper or unconstitutional. The act, along with another that the Board had questioned, was eventually disallowed. 8 *Pa. Arch.*, VIII, 7031–4; *Acts Privy Coun., Col.*, V, 365–8. See also William R. Riddell, "Legislative Divorce in Colonial Pennsylvania," *PMHB*, LVII (1933), 175–8.

I see Mr. Wharton but seldom.[8] Mr. Walpole, on whom I most rely, tells me that tho' many Delays have been thrown in our Way, he thinks he shall overcome all Difficulties, and soon get our Affair finished. But Men are too apt to expect what they wish. I continue to appear quite indifferent about it, and have never to this day ask'd as a Favour the Friendship of any Minister or Minister's Friend towards the Accomplishment of it. Partly because I would not in that way be oblig'd: And partly, because, as we are to pay the Value, and run all Risques of future Profit, I think it no Favour.[1] With unalterable Esteem and Affection, I am, my dear Friend, Ever Yours,   B FRANKLIN[2]

Mr Galloway

From Samuel Cooper   ALS: American Philosophical Society

Dear Sir   Boston N.E. 15th March, 1773.

I have been confin'd to my House great Part of this Winter by my valetudinary State, and been little able to see and converse with my Friends, and less to write to them.[3] A Line from you would have greatly refresh'd me in this Confinement, as your Letters have ever been one of the greatest Entertainments of my Life: but I do not mean to complain, having been so greatly indebted to you.

Till of late there has been little remarkable in our public Affairs for more than a Year. The Appointment of Ld. Dartmouth to the American Department was receiv'd here with a general Joy, which was soon check'd by his Official Letter to the Governor of Rhode-Island, respecting the Court of Inquiry into the Burning of the Gaspee and the Directions therein given to send the accused with the Witnesses to Great Britain for Trial; as also

8. For his conference with Wharton and Trent on Jan. 30 see his letter to WF above, Feb. 14.

1. BF subsequently elaborated this point in his letter of ostensible withdrawal from the Company: to Thomas Walpole below, Jan. 24, 1774.

2. BF added and then deleted a postscript: "I am come to a Resolution of returning in some of our Fall Ships."

3. Cooper is said to have suffered from mental troubles induced by overindulgence in Scottish snuff: *Sibley's Harvard Graduates*, XI, 211.

Samuel Cooper

by the Account of the Provision made by the King for the Support of the Justices of our Superior Court. These Events made a deep Impression on the Mind of People thro the Province. The latter, it is known, took Place before Lord Hillsborough's Removal; but the former was more unexpected, as the Disposition of Ld. Dartmouth to serve the Colonies, and to promote mild Measures was not doubted.[4]

Soon after the Appointment for the Superior Justices was known, the Town of Boston had a Meeting. Their Committee drew up a State of the public Grievances, which was accompanied with a Letter to evr'y Town in the Province, desiring their Breth-

4. For the salaries of the Superior Court judges see above, XIX, 381 n. The government's decision to pay them was taken while Hillsborough was still in office, and the warrants were issued just when he was leaving it: Oliver M. Dickerson, "Use Made of the Revenue from the Tax on Tea," *New England Quarterly*, XXXI (1958), 238–41; Bernhard Knollenberg, *Growth of the American Revolution, 1766–1775* (New Haven and London, [1975]), pp. 87–8. For the *Gaspee* affair see above, XIX, 379, and Knollenberg, pp. 83–6. Cooper is echoing popular disenchantment with Dartmouth, which was the result largely of propaganda. The Secretary seems to have opposed bringing prisoners to England for trial (*ibid.*, p. 347 n 47), but he had no choice about implementing governmental policy. His official letter to Gov. Joseph Wanton of Rhode Island, Sept. 4, 1772, outlined the procedure that the Privy Council had laid down for the investigative commission: to gather information about the causes of the affair, and about whether the King's officers had contributed to the outcome; to determine whether sufficient evidence existed to convict specific persons of attacking the ship; and if so to ask the civil authorities to apprehend such persons and deliver them to the navy, which would take them to England for trial. The King was determined on the one hand, the letter added, to protect his officers in performing their duties, and on the other hand to punish any of them who interfered unnecessarily with the commerce of his subjects in Rhode Island. Gov. Wanton laid the letter before the House of Deputies, and an extract of it was forwarded to Massachusetts (where it was promptly published) and to other colonies. The extract, which omitted the King's concern for local commerce, fanned the flames of a campaign that the Rhode Island press had begun against the commission as soon as its existence was known. Cushing, ed., *Writings of Samuel Adams*, II, 389–95; John R. Bartlett, ed., *Records of the Colony of Rhode Island* ... (10 vols., Providence, 1856–65), VII, 102–4; William R. Leslie, "The Gaspee Affair: a Study of Its Constitutional Significance," *Mississippi Valley Hist. Rev.*, XXXIX (1952), 238–45; David S. Lovejoy, *Rhode Island Politics and the American Revolution, 1760–1776* (Providence, R.I., 1958), pp. 160–3.

ren to express their own Sense of these important Matters. Tho this Measure was oppos'd by a Number of the most respectable Friends to Liberty in the Town, among which were three out of four of the Representatives of Boston, from an Apprehension that many Towns, for various Reasons might not chuse to adopt it, and in that Case, the Attempt might greatly prejudice the Interest it was design'd to promote, and tho the Governor and his Friends in ev'ry Place did not fail to avail themselves of this and evr'y other Circumstance to frustrate it, yet it had an Effect thro the whole Province beyond the most sanguine Expectations of it's Friends: And the public Acts of a great Majority of the Towns, whatever may be thought of the Manner of Expression in some of them, clearly demonstrates that it is not a small Faction, but the Body of the People, who deem themselves in a State of Oppression, and that their most essential Rights are violated. The Pamphlet containing the Proceedings of Boston has already been sent you, and I should enclose those of some other Towns, had I a sure and easy Way of Conveying such large Papers, without Fear of Burdening when I meant to entertain you.[5]

Upon the Convening the General Assembly, the Governor opened with a long Speech in Defence of the absolute Supremacy of Parliament over the Colonies, inviting both Houses to offer what they had to object against this Principle. His Prudence however, in this Step, and whether he will be thanked for it by Administration, is doubted.[6] By the Replies of the two Houses, perfectly united in the main Principles, the Governor and his Friends received a Shock which they could not conceal; while the People are greatly confirm'd in their Sentiments, and en-

5. Of the Boston representatives in the House, only Samuel Adams served on the committee of correspondence that the town meeting created; Thomas Cushing, John Hancock, and William Phillips declined. For the background of the meeting's declaration, the letters from the committee, and the response they evoked, see the headnote on BF's preface above, under the end of February, and Richard D. Brown, *Revolutionary Politics in Massachusetts* ... (Cambridge, Mass., 1970), pp. 59–61, 66, 92–121, 141.

6. The note on BF to Cushing above, March 9, discusses Hutchinson's speech on Jan. 6. Cooper's doubt that London would welcome it was well founded; see BF to Cushing below, May 6, July 7.

courag'd to support them.[7] I will venture to mention in Confidence to you, that the Governor appearing uneasy after he had received the second Reply of the Council,[8] employ'd his utmost Influence to have it reconsidered and altered. Having endeavor'd privately to prepare the Minds of some Influential Members for this, He enclos'd it in a Letter to one of the Board, requesting him to introduce the Reconsideration in Council: Presently He appears there himself, and argues strenuously in Favor of this. The Vote for the Reply, as it had been deliver'd, was however unanimous, except two, who desir'd to be excused from voting either Way. Oppos'd as he now stands to both Houses, and the Body of the People, an undisguis'd and zealous advocate for ev'ry Thing we account a Grievance, how far his Situation resembles that of his Predecessor, I leave you to judg.[9]

7. The Council and House answered the Governor's speech, just mentioned, separately and at length. The Council denied that Parliament had unlimited authority—only God had that—and argued that the colonists inherited all the limitations put on the taxing power from Magna Carta to the Bill of Rights. "Life, liberty, property, and the disposal of that property, with our own consent, are natural rights . . . . The preservation of these rights, is the great end of government." Bradford, ed., *Mass. State Papers*, p. 350. The House agreed with this position, and cited Hutchinson's own historical works to show how often the province had challenged his view of the constitution. The colonies were by their charters, the House asserted, distinct states under a common sovereign. If the Governor expected a line to be drawn between their independence and the supremacy of Parliament, that was a matter for them all to determine in a congress. *Ibid.*, pp. 342–64; Hutchinson, *History*, III, 267–70.

8. In February Hutchinson opened the second round of debate; see the chronology on p. xxxvi. He urged the Council, or Board, to oppose Parliament's use of power as inexpedient, not unconstitutional, to which the Council replied by reasserting its position. He delivered the House a disquisition on feudal tenure, to show that the colonists held from the crown and owed allegiance under their charters to the crown in Parliament. Feudal allegiance was owed solely to the crown, the House answered, and was limited by property rights that the settlers' own efforts had secured; Hutchinson's argument, furthermore, flouted logic as well as history, for consent of the governed alone made laws binding. *Ibid.*, pp. 270–3; Bradford, *op. cit.*, pp. 368–96.

9. The member of the Council through whom Hutchinson worked for reconsideration of its answer was undoubtedly its president, Samuel Danforth, whom he considered his closest supporter. Mass. Arch., XXVII, 481; for Danforth see BF's letter to him below, July 25. The Governor also

The Opposition here to the hard and oppressive Measures of the British Administration, never appear'd to me founded so much in Knowledg and Principle, never so systematical, deliberate and firm as it is at present. I may be mistaken in this opinion, but it leads me most earnestly to wish, for the Sake of both Countries, for some Pacification—some Lines to be drawn—some Bill of Rights for America—some Security against the unlimited Supremacy, and unbounded Pow'r not only of our Sovereign, but also of our Fellow Subjects in Britain over us: and unless something of this [sort?] soon takes Place, there is Danger that Things will run into Confusion.[10] Knowing your past Services to the Province, and being perswaded both of your ability and Inclination still to serve it in the best Manner that the State of Things will allow, I hope all Obstruction to your receiving the Grants made for you by the House will soon be removed.[11]

Our congregation are now engag'd in building an House of Worship, that will cost £6000. Sterling and be finish'd by Midsummer. The Dimensions within the Walls 80 by 65 Feet. The

---

lobbied with Bowdoin, on the Council, and with several members of the House. Butterfield, ed., *John Adams Diary*, II, 77; *Sibley's Harvard Graduates*, XI, 531–2. The debate united the Council and House, and did indeed emphasize the opposition between their view and the Governor's. To them the colonial legislature, although technically subordinate, was independent of Parliamentary control; to him the sovereignty of Parliament was supreme, absolute, and unlimited. The result was an even more complete impasse than that between Gov. Bernard and the House in 1768, the year before his recall. "If you are still of Opinion that two Jurisdictions, each of them having a Share in the Supreme Power, are compatible in the same State," Hutchinson told the legislators when proroguing them on March 6, "it can be to no Purpose to Reason or Argue . . . " *The Speeches of His Excellency Governor Hutchinson to the General Assembly . . . with the Answers of His Majesty's Council and the House of Representatives . . .* (Boston, 1773), p. 115. For fuller summaries of the debate see Gipson, *British Empire*, XII, 51–5; Bernard Bailyn, *The Ideological Origins of the American Revolution* (Cambridge, Mass., [1967]), pp. 219–22, and *The Ordeal of Thomas Hutchinson* (Cambridge, Mass., 1974), pp. 207–11.

10. See below, Cooper to BF, June 14, and BF to Cooper, July 7.

11. For the ongoing dispute over BF's salary as agent of the House see above, XVIII, 127, 153 n, 242; XIX, 209 n; and BF to the House and to Cushing below, July 7.

Building is of Brick. It is thought necessary to warm it in the Cold and damp Seasons of the Year, by some Machine, but what Kind, we are at a Loss. We have heard of Buzaglo's Inventions, but not been particularly inform'd. You will do us all a very great Favor if you would write me, what Machine you think most convenient and decent for this Purpose, the Price, the Manner of putting up, the Place where, and how the Smoke is convey'd away. We should be extremely glad of your Information Time etc. and[?] if it might ser[ve?] to send our Order for it, and have it put up early in the Fall.[1] I have been told that you and some others have lately obtain'd thro much opposition a Grant of Land for a new Province. If this be true,[2] and your Prospect agreable, You have no Friend that takes a warmer Part in it thro your large Circle, than your obedient humble Servant

SAMUEL COOPER.

On Claims to the Soil of America

Printed in *The Public Advertiser*, March 16, 1773;[3] incomplete draft: American Philosophical Society

This essay contains the first hint that in one crucial area, land tenure, Franklin was abandoning his earlier view of the crown as the centrip-

1. The old Brattle St. meeting house was being replaced by a new church; out of the £6,000 John Hancock contributed £1,000 for the interior. The congregation had asked Cooper to find a way to heat the building, but he was unsuccessful. *Sibley's Harvard Graduates*, XI, 195–6. BF did not help, for he discouraged the use of any stove; see his reply below, July 7. Abraham Buzaglo, a merchant of St. Catharine St., the Strand, had patented a "machine" for heating rooms by coal in 1765. Lord Botetourt subsequently ordered from him a special, enormous stove as a present to the Virginia House of Burgesses; Buzaglo created what he considered a masterpiece. It apparently arrived soon after Botetourt's death in 1770, and its elegance and size created a stir in the American press. *Kent's Directory . . .* (London, 1770); Bennet Woodcroft, *Alphabetical Index of Patentees of Inventions . . .* (London, [1969]); *Va. Gaz.*, Nov. 22, 1770, supplement; *Va. Hist. Register and Literary Companion*, VI (1853), 42–4; Henry C. Mercer, *The Bible in Iron . . .* (Doylestown, Pa., 1914), p. 131.
2. It was far from true; see BF to WF above, Feb. 14.
3. The next day's issue carried two minor textual corrections, which we have silently incorporated.

etal force in the empire. His thinking fed on controversy, which developed it a little here, a little there, until he was on new ground. In this case the controversy was the clash of ideas in Massachusetts, as reflected in recent letters to a London newspaper; and the new ground appears in a few sentences that are irreconcilable with the British concept of the crown and its dominion. Later in the year Franklin moved further, to the radical idea that colonists had an option about accepting royal sovereignty over their land.[4]

The background of the essay was Bostonian. In Hutchinson's opening speech to the General Court on January 6, which the *Public Advertiser* printed on March 4, the Governor argued that colonists carried Parliamentary jurisdiction with them when they emigrated to the crown's dominions overseas.[5] On March 5 "Junius Americanus," alias Arthur Lee, disagreed in the same newspaper. The issue, he contended, was not Parliament's authority as such, but whether that authority included taxation: taxing unrepresented colonists was a novel usurpation of the one power over them that the legislature did not possess, for taxation and representation were inseparable. This letter evoked an angry rejoinder on March 9, in which the anonymous writer made two points. First, British subjects at home were on a different level from those in the colonies, because the former held their land in their own right, whereas the latter held theirs from the crown and were therefore subject to its dominion exercised through Parliament. Second, taxation and representation were separable even in England, where many taxpayers were unrepresented; why then should colonists claim an exemption that their fellow-subjects did not claim?

This essay was Franklin's reply. The contentions that the king's American subjects were on a lower level than his British subjects, and that taxation was unrelated to representation, had annoyed him for years.[6] He attacked them here by a line of reasoning that had little novelty until it led him to adumbrate a query about the king's right in land. Questioning that right meant, in the last analysis, questioning the right of the crown in Parliament to govern the colonies.

The doctrine of royal sovereignty in British possessions outside the realm had been fully developed at law. The root of the doctrine, as it applied to colonies that had previously been uninhabited or peopled

---

4. See the headnote on his letter to WF below, July 14. His "Edict by the King of Prussia" (below, Sept. 22) is essentially a *reductio ad absurdum* of the idea that the sovereign has title to his subjects' land outside the realm.

5. See BF to Cushing above, March 9, n. 3.

6. Above, XIII, 220–1, 231–2; XV, 36–8; XVI, 246, 279, 324; XVII, 321, 324–5, 388, 399.

only by savages, was the king's position as universal landlord. He might grant land in one form of tenure or another, and delegate more or less of his jurisdiction; but final title remained his. When his subjects settled the American wilderness they carried with them, along with their allegiance, such of his law as was applicable to their circumstances; and statutes passed after their emigration affected them only when so specified. They could not conquer or purchase Indian land for themselves, or set up their own form of government; for government inhered in land, and their land was the crown's. The king conferred upon them such right as they had to govern themselves, and whatever measure of autonomy they derived from his prerogative was irrevocable by prerogative alone: he might not tax a colony, for instance, after vesting that power in the local assembly. But any such powers that the colony had acquired might be modified or revoked by the crown in Parliament. In this sense the colonists, being under an omnicompetent authority in which they had no part, were on a different level from their fellow-subjects at home. This in outline was the doctrine expounded by lawyers, if we read them correctly,[7] of royal dominion in America.

But Franklin was no lawyer. He was "somewhat of a Civilian," as he remarked to his son, and his views went "a little farther" than those of the jurists.[8] Indeed they did. Although in this essay he accepted quitrents, which expressed the crown's right in land, he proceeded to suggest that the right was nonexistent. The crown granted land to subjects only to exclude other subjects from it, he argued, and the grant entailed no responsibility for securing the grantees in possession; they themselves secured that possession by purchase or conquest from the Indians, and thereby obtained title to their land *"at their own Charges."* The emphasis was his, although half-concealed in the body of the essay; his point that settlers establish title by their own efforts, rather than by grant, was not hammered home as he knew how to do,

7. Our outline is based primarily upon the following: George Chalmers, *Opinions of Eminent Lawyers* . . . (2 vols., London, 1814), I, 29–140, 143–65, 195, 222–4, 232–3, 294; II, 44–5, 209, 246, 287; Sir Johns Comyns, *A Digest of the Laws of England* (5 vols., London, 1762–67), IV, 147–8, 220, 388, 403–404; and Joseph Chitty, *A Treatise on the Law of the Prerogatives of the Crown* . . . (London, 1820), pp. 30–4, 205. See also A. Berriedale Keith, *Constitutional History of the First British Empire* (Oxford, 1930), pp. 3–17, and Stanley G. Hardinge, first Earl of Halsbury, *The Laws of England* . . . (3rd ed.; 42 vols., London, 1952–63), V, 460, 544, 548–53, 697, 702; VII, 208–9, 240.
8. To WF below, July 14.

either because he did not realize its full implications or because he was too politic to develop them. But he did express here in public what he had hitherto suggested only in the privacy of his marginalia.[9] He thereby took issue, though unobtrusively, with the legal concept of the crown and its dominion.

To the Printer of the Public Advertiser.

SIR,

YOUR anonymous Correspondent in last Tuesday's Paper calls it *Arrogance* to place the Subjects in America and the Subjects in Great Britain upon a Level; and to prove it, asks and answers "from whom do the People of Great Britain hold their Lands? From no People under Heaven. From whom do most of the Inhabitants in North America hold their Lands? NOT FROM THEMSELVES, but from Great Britain. Does one Foot of Land on the Banks of the Missisippi belong to the American Colonists? No, the Lands on the Eastern Bank of the Mississippi, for the Extent of 1000 Miles, *are the* PROPERTY of the People of Great Britain, or of the King, as Trustee for the People of Great Britain." Thus far your positive Correspondent. To me, however it seems, that the Subjects in the two Countries are more upon a Level than he imagines. Britain was formerly the America of the Germans. They came hither in their Ships; found the *Cream* of the Land possessed by a Parcel of Welsh Caribbs,[10] whom they judged unworthy of it, and therefore drove them into the Mountains, and sat down in their Places. These Anglo-Saxons, our Ancestors, came *at their own Expence*, and therefore supposed that when they had secured the new Country, they held it of themselves, and of no other People under Heaven. Accordingly we do not find that their Mother Country, Germany, ever pretended to tax them; nor is it likely, if she had, that they would have paid it.[11] So far then the Level is clear; for unless Great Britain had a Property in the Lands of America before the Colonists went thither, it does not appear how they could take Lands of her

9. See above, XVI, 291–2; XVII, 385.

10. The sentence would have been clear enough to BF's readers because of the recent excitement over St. Vincent. The Caribs there, according to the opposition, were being treated in the same way. See above, p. 63 n. 9.

11. This is a foretaste of the idea that BF expanded in his "Edict by the King of Prussia" below, Sept. 22.

to hold on any Terms. Now the Fact is well known, that Britain had not a Foot of Land in New-England; and that when the first Settlers went into that Country, they found it possessed by various Tribes of Indians, from whom they either purchased or conquered what they now enjoy. European Nations have indeed pretended, some, that the Pope could give them a Right to the Lands of America; others, that, sailing along a Coast there, landing on some Beach unseen by the Natives, and branding a Post with the Arms of their own Country, created a Right to as much of the internal Territory as they should afterwards think proper to claim. But "one would hardly imagine" as your Writer says, "that such Nonsense could find Advocates." And yet he himself tells us, "the Lands on the Eastern Bank of the Mississippi are *the Property* of the People of Great Britain." That is, the French claimed them because one of their Nation discovered them by sailing down that River in a Canoe, and at the End of the last War gave up that Claim to the English. Whatever Right this Conquest conferred, give me Leave to say, is as much a Right of the Colonies as of Great Britain; for they had Man for Man with her in the Armies that fought for it.

But if Englishmen should come with this Parchment Right in their Hands, and bid an Indian Nation, settled there, remove in Consequence of it, I believe they would say, what your Correspondent says on the other Side of the Question, "that it is directly contrary to the Nature of Things and to Common-sense." Thus, Cassini, the French Astronomer, discovered with his Telescope that District in the Moon, which, in Honour of his Sovereign, he called Louisiana.[12] By a successful War, perhaps, we might oblige Louis to give it up, and agree that it should henceforth, in all Maps of the Moon be called Nova Britannia, and be held by King George as Trustee for the People of Great Britain. But if Englishmen could *fly* as well as *sail*, and arriving there should

12. The draft begins with "Cassini." BF was unquestionably referring to Jean-Dominique (1625–1712), the founder of a dynasty of French astronomers that lasted for more than a century. We have failed to find a lunar Louisiana, but assume that it was on the map of the moon that he presented to the Académie in 1679. See Charles J. E. Wolf, *Histoire de l'Observatoire de Paris* . . . (Paris, 1902), pp. 168–70.

claim the Country upon that Right, the native Inhabitants, to acknowledge and submit to it must be *Lunatics* indeed.

In Fact, neither the Grantor nor the Grantees of these chimerical Rights, ever understood more by them than that they were an Exclusion of other Englishmen from the respective Boundaries of each Grant. The Grantees, to obtain some Title, were obliged to purchase of the Indians, or conquer them *at their own Charges*. And if they had insisted that the Crown should put them in Possession of what it granted, the Grant would probably never have been made. This Purchase and Conquest, with the Expence of settling and clearing the Lands, have occasioned many of the Grants to be relinquished, as not worth holding. And most of those who went thro' with their Undertakings find they have dearly earned or paid for what they now possess. And yet, notwithstanding what this Writer says, I believe he cannot produce an Instance since the Settlement of the Country, of any one Colonist's Refusal to pay the stipulated Quit-rent to the Crown, on any Pretence whatever.[1] His Accusation, therefore, in this Point is injurious and quite without Foundation.

Since a good Understanding between the Parts of a great Empire is the Strength of the Whole, what beneficial End can it answer to represent the Colonists here as unreasonable and unjust, if they object to a Compliance with Exactions they think un-constitutional? Perpetual Abuse and false Representation, may exasperate and alienate on both Sides. It may divide. It can never unite. This Writer says, "The Colonists will most graciously accept of Land from Great Britain for nothing; but should Great Britain *ask for* a small Part of the Produce of those Lands to help to defray the Public Expence, the Colonist immediately cries out he is treated as a Slave, and robbed of his Property." Now it happens that FACTS shew this Charge also to be groundless; and that the Writer does not, in his own Phrase, use "the Words of *Truth* and Soberness." The Grant of Lands *for nothing*, I have already spoken to; and I here add, that Great Britain never

---

1. Many objections were raised to quitrents, but BF seems to be correct that the crown's right to them was not challenged; see Beverley W. Bond, Jr., *The Quit-Rent System in the American Colonies* (New Haven and London, 1919), pp. 219–460, especially p. 457.

asked for a small or any Part of the Produce of those Lands to help defray the Public Expence, but it was immediately, voluntarily and freely *given*, in Proportion to the Abilities of the People. But there is some Difference between *asking* and *taking by Force.* The *old* Way, and the best, in my humble Opinion, was for the Crown to *ask* Supplies, and then they were granted to an Extent beyond its Expectations. The new Way is to make an Act of Parliament to levy Duties on the Colonies without asking, and send a Fleet and Army to enforce it. A Landlord engaged in an expensive Law-suit may borrow Money[2] of his Tenants who respect him, or by shewing them that their Interest in the Event is the same with his, he may receive their voluntary Contributions towards the Support of his Litigation; but if he should declare that he has a Right to take from them whatever he thinks proper, and should go from House to House among them with a Parcel of armed Servants, extorting Money Sword in Hand, perhaps it might be justly called *Robbery*; at least it would be manifest that the Want of Money was not his only Want—that he wanted Honesty—and it would be found in the End that he also wanted Understanding.

As a Friend to both Countries, being connected with both, I wish Governor Hutchinson had thought of some other Subject for his Speech, and not revived needlessly a Dispute that can end in nothing but Mischief. I am sure he could not expect to convince an Individual there by such known false Facts and sophistical Reasoning. Here the Discourse appears plausible by chiming in with national and ministerial Prejudices, and therefore I think it written to recommend himself here, and not to do Service there. It has been industriously printed and circulated here before the Assembly's Answer could come over. To that however I leave it, only reminding its Readers of the equitable Rule, *Audi et alteram partem.*

The hacknied Argument of your Correspondent, that all the Freeholders in America ought to be taxed by Parliament, though they have no Share in the Choice of its Members, because many

---

2. The draft ends here. BF's plea for returning to the "*old* Way" was one that he had often made before; see the conclusion of the headnote on Cushing's letter below, June 30.

People in England are so taxed without having any Share in that Choice, seems to be arguing from bad to worse. If any here are unjustly deprived of that Privilege, restore it. Do right at home, if you please, and then make that a Precedent for doing right abroad: But never think that doing wrong at home will justify your doing wrong all the World over.[3] The Argument is a Confession indeed, but contains not the least Shadow of a Justification. I am, Sir, A NEW ENGLAND-MAN

Note on Franklin's Marginalia in Benjamin Wilson, *Observations upon Lightning*

[After March 21 and before March 30?,[4] 1773]

Benjamin Wilson was a hardy controversialist. When he lost his case against Franklin in the Purfleet committee in the summer of 1772, he carried it first to the Surveyor General of the Ordnance, then to the Royal Society, and finally to the public by printing his *Observations upon Lightning, and the Method of Securing Buildings from It's Effects, in a Letter to Sir Charles Frederick, &c.* (London 1773).[5] The Yale University Library has Franklin's copy of this pamphlet, which he must have read with care; for he marked numerous passages and made several comments. One on p. 23, a mere "Qu[ery]," does not make clear what is being queried; another on p. 48, on the increase in resistance as the number of surfaces increases, is cramped, smudged, and impossible to decipher.[6] Only two are both legible and of any significance. At one point Wilson remarked (p. 4 n) that none of the members of the Purfleet committee, when Franklin read them a report of experiments, expressed doubt "of the difference in the effects between pointed and blunt metal [rods] being as 12 to 1"; here Franklin

3. This echoes one of BF's marginalia above, XVII, 330–1.
4. The first date is Wilson's in the preface to the pamphlet. The second is that of BF's letter to LeRoy below, March 30, in which he said that he intended to write an answer; the intention makes it seem likely to us that he had already examined and marked his copy.
5. See above, XIX, 424–30.
6. BF used a pencil, and the writing has faded; some of it has also been lost in later cropping.

wrote "Attempt to mislead."[7] At another point Wilson concluded (p. 56) that buildings made of fir, containing no metal, were least likely to be struck by lightning; here Franklin wrote "supposing them never wet. Masts of Ships." These fragmentary marginalia were first jottings, presumably, for the reply to Wilson that he intended to write but never did.

From Thomas Cushing   ALS: Library of Congress

Sir   Boston, March: 24th: 1773

I have just received your Favor of the 2d. December last with the several papers Inclosed for which I am much oblidged to you. I have communicated them to some of the Gentlemen you mentioned.[8] They are of opinion, that though it might be inconvenient to publish them, yet it might be expedient to have Copys taken and left on this side the water as there may be a necessity to make some use of them hereafter, however I read to them what you had wrote me upon the occasion, and told them I could by no means Consent Copys of them or any part of them should be taken without your express Leave, that I would write you upon the subject and should strictly Conform to your directions.[9] I have also been favoured with yours of the 5th Jany. Am glad to find that Lord Dartmouth is so well disposed towards America. I think you have done me great Honor in thinking my Letter[1] of Consequence enough to lay before his Lordship. I am perswaded what I then wrote you were the Sentiments of nine Tenths of the People, I thought it might not be amiss to let you

7. For the experiments see *idem.*, *loc. cit.* and p. 261 and ns. It is not clear in context whether BF was castigating Wilson for attributing the 12:1 ratio to him rather than to Henly, or for twisting the evidence; probably the latter.

8. Also to John Adams, who had not been mentioned but who saw the letters on March 22, and to others as well. See Butterfield, ed., *Adams Diary,* II, 79–81, and our next note.

9. On April 20 Cushing repeated his request to take copies, but it was much ado about nothing. The original letters and copies in John Hancock's possession, he reported to BF on June 14, had been laid before the House; secrecy was gone.

1. The missing letter of Oct. 27, 1772, referred to in the opening of BF's letter above of Jan. 5, about the grievances of Massachusetts.

know it for your own Government. I apprehended it was high Time the Controversy was Settled and thought *that* was as good a Time as any, and that any further delay would render it more difficult: I found the People were greatly disturbed at the Independency of the Governor and the Judges and at the late Act passed for securing his Majesty Dock Yards &c.[2] I foresaw a Storm arising and the breach awidening. It is in Vain for administration to flatter themselves that the People here will rest quiet, when they find the Ministry are depriving them of their charter by peace meal and there is not a year passes without one Essential Clause or another's being rendered null and Void. The People think they have a right upon such occasions to represent their Grievances and to Petition to his Majesty for releif and cannot conceive how their Petitions and representations can be considered by the Administration as a measure that will give fresh offence to Goverment. Neither can they possibly imagine that a Kind Parent would ever be offended with his Children for making known to him their Grievances; if the Colonists are reduced to this deplorable Situation, that every new Petition they prefer is to be Considered as a fresh offence to his Majesty, what have they left to do? to whom are they to apply for releif? will it not throw them in to State of Despair?[3] And what the Consequence of such a state must be I leave to a Gentleman of your Good Sense to Determine. I observe you had consented that Lord Dartmouth should delay Delivering the House's petition till you should receive fresh Orders. As by this Conveyance you will receive another Petition from the House to be laid before his Majesty, and also a Letter to Lord Dartmouth containing a full representa-

2. The governor's and judges' "Independency" was of the legislature; see n. 4 below on the petitions from the House. The Dockyards Act (12 Geo. III, c. 24) made the burning of a naval vessel in a dockyard a felony punishable by death and, if the crime was committed in the colonies, gave the king the option of bringing the accused to England for trial. Gipson, *British Empire*, XII, 28–9. This statute, like the earlier move to revive the Treason Act (above, XVI, 248), was disturbing because it was Parliamentary interference with the subject's right to be tried in a local court.

3. Cushing is answering Dartmouth's argument, as reported in BF's letter of Dec. 2, against forwarding the Massachusetts petition of the previous July, and is using much the same terms as BF's to the Minister; see above, XIX, 409–10.

tion of our Greivances You will be able to form some judgement of the temper of the House since the change made in the American Administration and consider it as Equall to receiving fresh directions with respect to the former Petition and consequently prevail with Lrd. Dartmouth to lay all our Complaints before his Majesty at once.[4] The House is not now Sitting so I cannot consult them upon this Matter, what directions they would give you I cannot say, but, as a private Individual I think, from their Proceedings the last sessions you may easily judge what their resolutions and directions would be in the next. I have no Authority to give any orders relative to this Matter and as there will not be another sessions till the latter End of May next, it must be left with you therefore to form a judgement what Course to take from the proceedings of the last sessions. I write in Confidence and pritty freely and therefore should not chuse to have my name mentioned upon this occasion. I conclude with great Respect Your most humble Servant   THOMAS CUSHING

(Private)

Benjamin Franklin Esqr

Addressed: To / Benjamin Franklin Esqr   L L D / London

4. For BF's handling of the July petition see *ibid.*, pp. 410–11. The second petition, dated March 6, 1773, applied to the judges the same argument that the earlier one had applied to the governor: the charter authorized the legislature to support government by levying taxes, and the judiciary was part of government; royal salaries would make the judges completely dependent on the crown, especially while they held office only during the king's pleasure, and would thereby endanger the impartial administration of justice on which the community's well-being depended. The accompanying letter to Dartmouth was, as Cushing says, a full enumeration of grievances; see Gipson, *op. cit.*, XII, 56–7. The texts of the two documents are in the *Lee Papers*, roll 2, frames 141–6. For Whitehall's reaction see Dartmouth to BF below, June 2.

From Jacques Barbeu-Dubourg

Printed in Jacques Barbeu-Dubourg, ed., *Œuvres de M. Franklin* …
(2 vols., Paris, 1773), I, 309–11; copy:[5] American Philosophical Society

Monsieur,   A Paris, 25 Mars 1773.

Si j'ai bien saisi vos principes, il faut que le verre qui doit servir à l'expérience de Leyde réunisse ces deux conditions: 1°. qu'il soit impénétrable au fluide électrique; 2°. qu'il ne soit pas impénétrable à l'énergie de ce fluide; ou, pour exprimer la même chose en d'autres termes, il faut que le fluide électrique ne puisse traverser d'une surface à l'autre, mais il faut que son affluence dans une des surfaces du verre puisse exciter une effluence dans la surface opposée.[6]

Le verre réunit communément ces deux conditions, mais non pas toute sorte de verre; il se trouve même des verres que le fluide électrique traverse presqu'aussi librement qu'il court dans les métaux. C'est une propriété naturelle à quelques verres, et accidentelle à d'autres. Il paroitroit étonnant qu'aucun Physicien n'eût encore songé à rechercher les causes de toutes ces différences, si la Physique ordinaire y suffisoit; mais elle a besoin du concours de la Chymie, qui ne se refusera pas sans doute à l'éclaircissement d'un point aussi intéressant.

Je ne proposerois pas aux Chymistes de faire l'analyse des différens verres perméables ou imperméables à l'électricité; mais de chercher à les imiter, ce qui leur seroit beaucoup plus aisé.

Une terre vitrifiable pure est sans doute l'unique ingrédient du crystal de roche, qu'on peut regarder comme un véritable

---

5. The copy appears to be of an early draft of the letter; it is not in Dubourg's hand. The only substantial departure from the printed version is noted below.

6. The first condition is phrased differently in the copy, but with the same purport. The second condition reads: "que l'effort du fluide électrique, pour se répandre dans une de ses surfaces, puisse faire sur la surface opposée une impréssion capable d'en chasser une semblable quantité de ce même fluide. Il faut, en deux mots, que le verre soit impénétrable à l'électricité, mais qu'il soit pénétrable à son énergie; ou en d'autres termes encore (car on ne sçauroit se retourner de trop de façons pour faire entendre une chose si éloignée des idées communes) il faut que l'action du fluide électrique se communique d'une surface à l'autre, mais que le fluide même ne puisse s'y communiquer."

verre naturel; mais l'art n'est point encore parvenu à pouvoir nous procurer un verre aussi simple, et on a même très-peu d'espérance de pouvoir jamais atteindre à une telle perfection. On ne connoit point de terre si vitrifiable qu'on n'ait besoin de quelque fondant auxiliaire pour en faciliter la vitrification. Or on distingue des fondans de trois principaux genres, qui sont les fondans salins, les fondans métalliques, et les fondans terreux; car il y a différentes especes de terres qui, quoique réfractaires chacune en particulier, se servent mutuellement de fondant les unes aux autres, comme il y a également plusieurs especes de sels, plusieurs especes de métaux qui peuvent servir de fondans aux terres vitrifiables, et qui peuvent se combiner en différentes proportions avec ces mêmes terres. On ne doit pas être plus surpris de trouver des verres plus ou moins perméables à l'électricité que d'en trouver de perméables et d'imperméables à la lumiere. Puisqu'il y a des verres transparens et des verres opaques, ou diversément colorés, pourquoi n'y auroit-il pas des verres conducteurs et non-conducteurs d'électricité?

Ce n'est pas un problème difficile à résoudre pour un Chymiste, mais ce seroit pourtant l'objet d'un assez long travail que de nous donner une série comparative de verres doués de l'une ou de l'autre de ces qualités à tous les différens degrés. Les places mêmes où viendroient se ranger tant votre verre verdâtre d'Amérique que le verre blanc de Londres indiqueroient au premier coup-d'oeil la mixtion des ingrédiens respectifs dont ils sont composés.

D'un autre côté, comme la violence de la chaleur que la matiere du verre éprouve soit dans sa cuite, soit dans sa recuite, peut causer une évaporation d'une partie de ces ingrédiens, et que cette chaleur n'est pas de la même violence dans toutes les parties du fourneau, il est peu étonnant que vous ayez trouvé une différence considérable entre plusieurs globes de verre de la même fabrique, comme vous l'annoncez, page 181.[7]

7. Here and in the preceding paragraph Dubourg is referring to the Œuvres, I, 181–2, where he reprints BF's discussion in a letter to John Lining in 1755 (above, v, 521) of the difference between American and English glass. BF says nothing there about differences in the products of the same glassworks, but he discusses the matter at some length in the postscript of his reply to this letter below, May 28.

Indépendamment des qualités naturelles de tels ou tels verres, résultantes de leur composition spécifique, il peut encore résulter de très grandes différences de la diversité de l'épaisseur de leurs masses, ne fût-ce que par cette seule considération que la chaleur n'a pu être exactement la même, ni la promptitude du refroidissement égale à beaucoup près, entre les différentes couches d'un verre fort épais; sans compter qu'il semble presqu'impossible que l'action du fluide électrique en mouvement se porte efficacement d'une surface à l'autre d'un corps trop massif.

Enfin il est également aisé de concevoir qu'un degré de chaleur considérable, en raréfiant la substance d'un verre mince, peut ouvrir son tissu au fluide électrique; mais que ce degré de chaleur doit être relatif à l'épaisseur de ce verre; et que M. Kinnersley a pu n'avoir besoin que d'une chaleur de 210 degrés (ce qui est le degré de l'eau bouillante au thermometre de Fahrenheit,) pour rendre perméable au choc électrique le verre très-mince d'un flacon de Florence, tandis que M. Cavendish a eu besoin d'une chaleur de 400 degrés pour rendre perméable au courant ordinaire un verre un peu plus épais.[8]

Ce qui me fait desirer que quelque Chymiste veuille bien nous éclairer sur tous ces points, c'est qu'on ne sauroit avoir trop d'attention à épargner de fausses dépenses aux Amateurs de la Physique; parce que cela peut en arrêter tout-à-fait quelques-uns, et refroidir un peu le zele de beaucoup d'autres. Je suis, &c.

To Jacques Barbeu-Dubourg

Translated extract: printed in Jacques Barbeu-Dubourg, ed., *Œuvres de M. Franklin*... (2 vols., Paris, 1773), II, 313.[1]

Londres, 27 Mars 1773

Je compte que notre Poke-Weed est ce que les Botanistes appellent PHYTOLACCA. Cette plante porte des bayes grosses comme des pois: la peau en est noire, mais elle contient un suc cramoisi. C'étoit ce jus évaporé au soleil en consistence d'extrait que l'on

8. For the experiments of Ebenezer Kinnersley and Lord Charles Cavendish see above, respectively, IX, 283–4; X, 41–2.
1. An English retranslation is in Smyth, *Writings*, III, 87 n.

employoit. Il causoit beaucoup de douleurs, mais on disoit que quelques personnes en avoient été guéries. Je ne suis pas assuré des faits: tout ce que je sçais, c'est que le Docteur Colden en avoit bonne opinion.²

To Jean-Baptiste LeRoy

ALS (draft): American Philosophical Society

Dear Sir   London, March 30 [1773]

You punish my delay of writing to you very properly by not writing to me. It is long since I have had the Pleasure of hearing from you: But it is my fault: and I must for my own sake write to you oftener tho' I have little to say, or you will quite forget me.

I thank you for your Advice to send an English Copy of my Writings to the Academy, and shall do it as soon as the new Edition now in hand here is finish'd.³

I am glad you see some Weight in the Experiments I sent you concerning pointed Rods. Mr. Wilson is grown angry that his Advice was not follow'd in making them blunt, for the Public Magazines of Gunpowder, and has published a Pamphlet reflecting on the R. Society, the Committee and myself, with some Asperity; and endeavouring to alarm the City with the supposed Danger of Pointed Rods drawing the Lightning into them and blowing them up. I find it is expected from me that I make some Answer to it, and I shall do so, tho' I have an extreme Aversion to Public Altercation, on philosophic Points, and have never yet disputed with any one who thought fit to attack my

2. Pokeweed juice had been tried as a cure for cancer more than a decade earlier, and BF and Cadwallader Colden had been hopeful about it: above, IV, 280–1, 301. See also BF to Dubourg below, April 23.

3. BF's most recent surviving letter was the previous April, and LeRoy's the following September: above, XIX, 111, 306–9. To judge by this sentence, however, the Frenchman must have written again, despite BF's opening remark, to suggest sending a copy of *Exper. and Obser.* to the Académie royale des sciences. The fifth edition was published in the late summer of 1774: *Public Advertiser*, Sept. 9, 1774.

Opinions.[4] I am oblig'd to you for the Experiment of the Point and Ring.

There is no being sure of any thing before it happens; but considering the Weight of your Reputation, I think there is little Reason to doubt the Success of your Friends Endeavours to procure for our Society here the Honour of adding you to their Number at the next Election.[5] In the mean time will you for my sake confer the same kind of Honour on my young Society at Philadelphia? When I found that our first Volume of American Transactions was favourably receiv'd in Europe, and had procur'd us some Reputation, I took the Liberty of nominating you for a Member, and you were accordingly chosen at a full Meeting in Philadelphia, on the 15th of Jany. last. I sent a Copy of that Volume to the Academy of Sciences at Paris when it first came out, but I do not remember to have heard that they ever receiv'd it. I think it was Mr. Magelhaens who undertook to convey it.[6] If it miscarried I will send another; and by the first Opportunity one for your self.

Two Ships are now fitting out here, by the Admiralty, at the Request of the Royal Society, to make a Voyage to the North Pole, or to go as near to it as the Ice will permit. If they return safe, we shall probably obtain some new Geographical Knowledge, and some Addition to Natural History.[7] With the greatest Esteem and Respect I am, ever, Dear Sir, Your most obedient humble Servant   B F

M LeRoy

4. BF's aversion overcame his resolve; he never rebutted Benjamin Wilson's *Observations upon Lightning* ... (London, 1773). For the long argument between them over the Purfleet magazine see above, XIX, 153–4, 260–2, 424–5, 429–30.

5. LeRoy was elected to the Royal Society on June 10.

6. For the distribution of the first volume of the APS *Trans.* see above, XIX, 147–9, and for J. H. Magalhaens or Magellan BF to Rozier above, Jan. 24.

7. The Royal Society made its request in February through Sandwich, the First Lord, and the King approved; the navy assigned and refitted two bomb ships for the expedition. It sailed in May, was turned back north of Spitzbergen by pack ice, and accomplished little. See Constantine J. Phipps, second Baron Mulgrave, *A Voyage towards the North Pole Undertaken by His Majesty's Command, 1773* (London, 1774).

To Jacques Barbeu-Dubourg

Translated extract: printed in Jacques Barbeu-Dubourg, ed., *Œuvres de M. Franklin* . . . (2 vols., Paris, 1773), II, 258–61.[8]

[March?,[9] 1773]

J'appréhende bien de ne pouvoir trouver le tems de faire sur cette matiere toutes les recherches et les expériences qui seroient à désirer. Je me bornerai donc à faire ici quelques remarques. La pesanteur spécifique de quelques corps humains, par comparaison avec celle de l'eau, a été examinée par M. Robertson, dans nos *Transactions Philosophiques*, Volume 50, page 30, pour l'année 1757. Il prétend que les personnes grasses qui ont les os menus, sont celles qui flottent le plus aisément. . . . La cloche pour les plongeurs est aussi décrite exactement dans nos Transactions. . . .[1]

Dans ma jeunesse, je m'étois fait moi-même deux petites palettes ovales, chacune d'environ 10 pouces de long, sur 6 de large, avec un trou pour y passer le pouce, afin de la tenir appliquée sur la paume de ma main. Elles avoient assez l'air de palettes de peintre. En nageant, je les poussois en avant par leur tranche, et je frappois l'eau du plat de leur surface en les retirant. Je me souviens très-bien que je nageois plus vite au moyen de ces palettes, mais elles me fatiguoient les poignets. Je m'étois fait aussi des especes de semelles pour appliquer à la plante de mes pieds, mais je n'en fus pas content, parce que j'observai que le coup se donne en partie avec le côté interne des pieds et des chevilles, et non pas uniquement avec la plante des pieds. . . .

Nous avons ici des camisoles de nageurs, qui sont faites d'un double canevas matelassé avec de petits morceaux de liége piqués entre deux. . . .

8. A retranslation may be found in Smyth, *Writings*, v, 542–5.
9. BF was replying to Dubourg's letter above, Feb. 12, the annotation of which explains many of the references in these extracts. The extracts themselves, and those above of March 10, may all have been from one long communication on many subjects.
1. BF's references are to John Robertson (for whom see above, XIV, 351 n), "An Essay towards Ascertaining the Specific Gravity of Living Men," *Phil. Trans.*, L (1757–58), 30–5, and to Martin Triewald, "A Letter . . . Concerning an Improvement of the Diving Bell," *ibid.*, XXXIX (1735–36), 377–83.

131

Je ne connois point du tout le scaphandre de M. de la Chapelle. . . . Je sais par expérience que c'est un soulagement pour un nageur, qui a beaucoup de chemin à faire, de se tourner quelquefois sur le dos, et de diversifier à d'autres égards les moyens de se procurer un mouvement progressif. . . . Lorsqu'il prend une crampe dans une jambe, le moyen de la dissiper c'est de donner aux membres affectés une secousse subite, vigoureuse et violente, ce qui peut se faire dans l'air lorsqu'on nage sur le dos. . . . Dans les grandes chaleurs de l'été, il n'y a aucun danger à entrer, quelque chaud que l'on ait, dans des rivieres qui ont été bien échauffées par le soleil. Mais de se jetter dans une eau de source froide lorsqu'on a le corps échauffé par l'exercice au soleil, c'est une imprudence qui peut être funeste. J'ai eu connoissance d'un exemple de quatre jeunes hommes qui, ayant travaillé à la moisson dans la chaleur du jour, se plongerent pour se rafraîchir dans une fontaine d'eau froide; il en mourut deux sur la place, un troisieme mourut le lendemain matin, et le quatrieme eut beaucoup de peine à en guérir. . . . Une ample boisson d'eau froide, en de semblables circonstances, a souvent produit les mêmes effets dans l'Amerique Septentrionale. . . . L'exercice de la nage est le plus agréable et le plus sain qu'il soit possible de faire. . . . Après avoir nagé une heure ou deux le soir, on dort fraîchement toute la nuit, dans les plus grandes chaleurs de l'été. Peut-être que les pores étants néttoyés, la transpiration insensible est plus abondante, et occasionne cette fraîcheur. . . . Il est certain que de beaucoup nager, c'est le moyen d'arrêter un dévoiement, et même d'occasionner une constipation. A l'égard de ceux qui ne savent point nager, ou qui ont une diarrhée dans une saison qui ne permet pas d'aller nager, un bain chaud, en néttoyant et purifiant la peau, leur fait beaucoup de bien, et souvent les guérit radicalement. J'en parle d'après ma propre expérience souvent répétée, et celle des autres à qui je l'ai recommandé.

Vous trouverez bon que je termine ces remarques faites à la hâte, en vous certifiant que comme la maniere ordinaire de nager se réduit à ramer avec les bras et les jambes, et est conséquemment laborieuse et fatiguante lorsqu'on a un grand espace à parcourir, il est un moyen par lequel un nageur peut passer à de grandes distances avec beaucoup de facilité à l'aide d'une voile; c'est à quoi j'ai réussi par aventure de la maniere que je vais vous raconter.

Etant petit garçon, je m'amusois un jour à faire voler mon grand cerf-volant; et étant arrivé au bord d'un étang qui avoit près d'un mille de large, comme il faisoit très-chaud, j'attachai la ficelle à un poteau, et le cerf-volant s'éleva fort haut par dessus l'étang, tandis que j'y étois à nager. Au bout de quelques tems, voulant m'amuser avec mon cerf-volant, et jouir en même-tems du plaisir de nager, je retournai sur mes pas, et ayant détaché la ficelle du poteau avec le petit bâton auquel elle étoit attachée, je rentrai dans l'eau, où je trouvai qu'étant couché sur le dos et tenant le bâton entre mes mains, j'étois tiré au travers de l'eau fort agréablement. Alors ayant obtenu d'un autre petit garçon de transporter mes habits en tournant autour de l'étang, à un endroit que je lui indiquai de l'autre côté, je me mis à traverser l'étang avec mon cerf-volant, qui me porta tout au travers, sans la moindre fatigue et avec le plaisir le plus délicieux qu'il vous soit possible d'imaginer. Je fus seulement obligé de m'arrêter quelques fois tant soit peu pour résister à son mouvement en avant, lorsqu'il me paroissoit qu'en le suivant trop vîte j'avois trop fait baisser le cerf-volant; et en arrêtant ainsi, je le faisois relever davantage. Je n'ai point pratiqué depuis ce tems cette méthode singuliere de nager, mais j'imagine qu'un homme pourroit au besoin traverser ainsi à la nage de Douvre à Calais. . . . Cependant une barque vaut encore mieux.

From Jacques Barbeu-Dubourg

Printed in Jacques Barbeu-Dubourg, ed., *Œuvres de M. Franklin . . .* (2 vols., Paris, 1773), I, 314–20; two incomplete copies:[2] American Philosophical Society

Monsieur,   A Paris, premier Avril 1773

Depuis six mois que je suis occupé presque sans relâche de la traduction et de l'édition de vos Oeuvres, je me suis un peu familiarisé avec l'Electricité. Il faudroit avoir l'esprit bien bouché

2. They appear to be of two different drafts of the letter, and are in the same hand as the copy of Dubourg's earlier one of March 25.

pour ne pas devenir Electrician avec vous. Mais dans ce genre de science, comme en toutes autres, vous voulez qu'on cherche de préférence, ce qu'elles ont de plus utile, et par une admirable institution du Créateur, ce plus utile est toujours constamment le plus aisé et le moins abstrait. Mon goût naturel et la médiocrité de mes talens s'accommodent très-bien de cela.

Depuis que vous avez démontré la possibilité de tirer et de conduire le feu du tonnerre, et que la solidité de vos principes a été confirmée par l'expérience de Marly-la-Ville[3], et par une infinité d' autres, le tonnerre a encore produit beaucoup de malheurs qu'il auroit été possible de prévenir.

Vous avez parfaitement dévelopé les moyens de garantir de la foudre les maisons, les églises, les vaisseaux, et spécialement les magasins à poudre. Quantité de Physiciens ont répété vos leçons de toutes parts; et cependant hors de l'Amérique, le public en a très-peu profité.

Vous avez indiqué aux personnes qui appréhendent le tonnerre, et qui se trouvent pendant un orage dans une maison dénuée de conducteurs électriques à l'extérieur, quelles sont les situations les plus favorables, et les précautions les plus sages qu'ils puissent prendre pour leur sureté en cette occasion.[4]

On a proposé en Hollande de distribuer un certain nombre de verges électriques, de distance en distance, avec de bons conducteurs des unes aux autres, à l'entour et au travers d'une ville entière, pour garantir généralement du tonnerre et tous ses bâtimens, et tous ses habitans. Je vous laisse à discuter l'efficacité de la méthode que l'on a proposée à cet effet; mais ne resteroit-il pas encore différens cas particuliers qui méritent quelque considération, et dont personne ne paroît s'être occupé jusqu'ici?

1°. De se faire en son particulier un asyle assuré de l'appartement même auquel on est borné dans une maison dont on ne dispose pas en entier, et où le propriétaire a négligé de prendre toutes les mesures qui seroient à desirer.

2°. Lorsqu'on voyage en voiture, savoir si, et quelles précautions l'on auroit à prendre pour la voiture, tant à l'égard de la forme que de la matiere de sa construction?

3. See above, IV, 302–10.
4. See above, XIV, 264.

3°. Lorsqu'on est obligé de sortir à pied, soit à la ville, soit en campagne, dans des tems où les orages sont à craindre, n'y auroit-il pas quelques moyens de se garantir aussi-bien du tonnerre que de la pluie et du soleil?

Quant au premier point, il semble qu'un lit tout de bois, sans aucun métal, et dont les quatre pieds porteroient sur quatre tabourets électriques, et une table et une chaise isolées par de semblables tabourets, seroient des expédiens assurés pour manger, travailler et dormir en dépit des orages avec la plus parfaite tranquillité d'esprit. Il seroit bon cependant d'ajouter à cela la précaution de n'avoir dans l'appartement aucune sorte de métal qui ne fît portion d'une espece de cercle électrique sans interruption, aboutissant de part et d'autre en dehors.

Quant au second article, qui est celui des voitures préservatives, la théorie peut aisément s'en déduire des mêmes principes; mais le détail des différentes applications qu'on en peut faire me meneroit trop loin, et seroit déplacé ici.

3°. Enfin j'ai à vous proposer pour les voyageurs à pied, pour qui j'ai toujours pris un intérêt de prédilection, une espece de Paratonnerre, s'il est permis de s'exprimer ainsi, que je vais soumettre à votre jugement.

Cette machine ne differe presque d'un parasol, que par quelques petits accessoires, qui s'y adaptent aisément en cas d'orage.

La partie principale, qui fait le corps du Parasol, comprend

1°. un taffetas bombé à l'ordinaire en forme de dôme, mais dont l'une des coutures est recouverte en dessus d'une tresse, ou petit galon d'argent.

2°. Un bâton, ou manche d'un bois léger, d'environ 2 pieds de long.

3°. Une tringle de fer, d'un demi pouce de diametre, et de 8 à 10 pouces de long, placée en dessus à l'opposite du manche, et terminée supérieurement par un écrou.

4°. Un anneau, des baguettes et un ressort de cuivre, également placés en dessus; cet anneau glissant sur la tringle de fer, pour servir tant à plier qu'à déplier les baleines, et par leur moyen étaler le taffetas, ou le refermer.

5°. Neuf à dix baleines, chacune de deux pieces, arcboutées à l'ordinaire, mais placées au-dessus du taffetas; l'une de ces baleines, attenant le galon d'argent, armée d'un bout de cuivre terminé par un écrou.

Les accessoires comprennent,

1°. Une verge de cuivre mince longue d'un pied, terminée supérieurement par une pointe fine, et inférieurement par une vis, qui s'adapte aisément quand on veut à l'écrou de la tringle de fer.

2°. Un gros fils de laiton d'un pied et demi de long, terminé par une petite vis, qui peut s'adapter au besoin à l'écrou du bout de cuivre, dont nous avons dit que l'une des baleines étoit armée, et pointant obliquement de-là en en bas.[5]

4°. Un cordonnet d'argent, pendant au bout inférieur de ce fil de laiton, et terminé par une petite houpe de frange de la même matiere, trainante un peu en terre.

Avec ce Paratonnerre bien monté, un homme peut passer sans crainte sous des nuées orageuses, ou sous des cucurbites électrisées; étant bien certain que, dès qu'il approchera de la distance du choc, la pointe de la verge supérieure attirera sur elle seule tous leurs redoubtables feux, qui seront conduits de-là innocemment tout le long de la tringle, du galon, du bout de cuivre, du fil de laiton, du cordonnet, et de la houppe, tous excellens conducteurs métalliques, jusqu'à la terre qui est le grand réservoir commun du feu électrique, dont il ne passera pas la moindre parcelle dans, ni au travers du taffetas, qui n'a aucun attrait pour lui.

Lors donc que l'on croît voir un orage imminent, ou lorsque cet orage paroît entierement dissipé, on peut en moins d'une minute joindre ou disjoindre les deux parties de cette machine, et convertir son parasol en paratonnere, ou réduire son paratonnere en l'état d'un simple parasol.

5. One of the two drafts has a different version of this sentence and includes the missing third accessory:

"2°. Deux gros fils de laiton chacun d'un pied et demi [de] long, attachés ensemble par un bout, et écartés par le bout opposé ou ils sont terminés par deux petites vis qui peuvent s'adapter au besoin aux écrous des bouts de cuivre, dont nous avons dit que deux des baleines étoient armées.

"3°. Un fil de laiton de la même longueur, attaché [par] un bout à l'angle de réunion des précédents et pointant obliquement de là en embas."

Dubourg actually had a "paratonnerre" constructed; see the final note on BF's reply to this letter below, May 28.

Après avoir travaillé premierement pour soi-même, il convient de chercher à faire part aux autres des avantages que l'on a sçû se procurer; jouir seul de quelque bien que ce soit, c'est n'en jouir qu'à demi. J'attens de mon paratonnerre une satisfaction plus complette; je me flatte que chaque machine de cette espece, étant capable de dépouiller un petit nuage électrisé, et d'en repousser en même-tems plusieurs autres semblables, suffira pour garantir une certaine étendue à la ronde, et pour la garantir pendant un certain tems, quoique je ne puisse assigner ni les limites de l'espace, ni celles de la durée.

Pour bien concevoir ceci, supposons 1°. un grand tube de métal fortement électrisé, et une douzaine de personnes rangées de côté et d'autre presqu'à la distance du choc, c'est-à-dire, tant soit peu plus loin qu'il ne faudroit qu'elles fussent pour en tirer des étincelles. Si l'on présente la pointe d'un stylet, non-seulement à la même distance de ce tube, mais même à une distance plus grande du double, elle en attirera tous les feux sur elle et le déchargera entierement.

Supposons 2°. comme dans une de vos belles experiences,[6] plusieurs flocons de coton peu serrés, pendants au-dessous de ce même tube, et attachés ensemble par de petits bouts de fils; plus on électrisera fortement le tube, plus ces flocons tendront à s'écarter; ils s'allongeront et se fileront pour ainsi-dire d'eux-mêmes, et le dernier tombera fort bas. Dans cette position, si l'on en approche un peu la pointe d'un stylet, il tirera l'électricité du dernier flocon, qui la tirera du suivant, et ainsi de proche en proche, de sorte que tous se resserreront, se raccourciront, et remonteront vers le tube, comme si une puissance occulte leur avoit imprimé une forte impulsion de bas en haut.

Voilà quel doit être constamment l'effet de la verge d'un Para-tonnerre sur de petits nuages chargés de l'électricité céleste. Elle dépouillera celui qui se trouvera le plus à sa portée, et en le faisant réagir sur les autres, elle en forcera plusieurs à se relever vers les régions supérieures de l'atmosphere.

Mais que deviendra le feu ainsi tiré?[7] N'en soyons pas en peine,

6. [*Dubourg's note:*] Voyez ci-devant, page 129 [the experiment that BF described to Collinson in 1753: above, v, 78].

7. [*Dubourg's note:*] Que deviennent les feux de ce qu'on appelle des étoiles tombantes?

pourvû que nous lui fassions trouver de bons conducteurs pour le faire repasser au grand réservoir commun d'où il a été pompé, et où il doit aller se reperdre. Or les métaux sont les meilleurs de tous les conducteurs, l'eau vient ensuite, et les corps animaux en troisieme lieu. Ayant donc eu soin de ménager des conducteurs métalliques au feu électrique attiré par la verge du paratonnerre, on est parfaitement assuré 1°. qu'il les suivra jusqu'au bout, sans que rien soit capable de l'en écarter; 2°. qu'ils l'épancheront définitivement dans le sein même de la terre, où tout fluide électrique se remettant de lui-même en équilibre, perd sur le champ toute son activité. Tous les fils de la frange d'argent qui traine jusqu'en terre peuvent être regardés comme autant de pointes fines, et l'on sçait que les pointes ne sont pas moins propres à répandre le feu électrique qu'à le recevoir.

Il n'en est pas d'un torrent de feu comme d'un torrent d'eau: celui-ci ne peut être que détourné, celui-là peut également être détourné, ou être tout-à-fait éteint. Le feu électrique s'allume plus rarement, et s'éteint plus promptement encore que le feu commun; il se laisse conduire plus aisément, a plus de disposition à reprendre son équilibre, et ne causa jamais d'aussi grands ravages. Donnons cependant un exemple du pouvoir de l'art pour manier même le feu commun.

Si par un beau soleil d'été l'on dirige sur une balle de plomb le foyer du grand miroir ardent imité d'Archimede par M. de Buffon,[8] elle se mettra aussi-tôt en fusion, et sera évaporée dans un instant. Si on avoit placé cette même balle en de-çà ou au de-là du foyer, quoique dans la même direction, les mêmes rayons solaires non encore réunis dans l'un de ces cas, ou déjà éparpillés dans l'autre, n'auroient produit sur elle absolument aucun effet sensible. Voilà à-peu-près comment le changement d'une légere circonstance peut faire éclater la foudre avec la plus grande impétuosité, ou la dissiper sans le moindre fracas, en la réduisant, pour ainsi-dire, à zéro.

On pourroit, s'il en étoit besoin, confirmer par mille autres

8. Archimedes is supposed to have built his mirror to set fire to Roman warships approaching the walls of Syracuse. The comte de Buffon's imitation was a lens intended to determine how far the sun's heat penetrated sea water; see William Smellie, trans., *Natural History, General and Particular by the Count de Buffon* (2nd ed.; 9 vols., London, 1785), IX, 267–8.

exemples cette prodigieuse différence entre les effets des mêmes élémens assemblés ou dispersés. Ainsi les caracteres d'imprimerie, suivant la différence de leurs arrangemens, peuvent donner une Bible, ou un Alcoran; mais ils peuvent également ou être à l'aventure, ou être distribués dans des casses, de maniere à ne former aucun sens quelconque; et s'il faut beaucoup de tems pour en former une Iliade, il ne faut pas une minute pour la faire rentrer dans le chaos, tant la matiere est dépendante de la forme.

To Thomas Cushing

ALS: Public Record Office;[9] letterbook draft: Library of Congress

Sir   London, April 3. 1773
    My last was of the 9th past, since which nothing material has occurr'd relating to the Colonies. The Assembly's Answer to Gov. Hutchinson's Speech is not yet come over; but I find that even his Friends here are apprehensive of some ill Consequences from his forcing the Assembly into that Dispute, and begin to say it was not prudently done, tho' they believe he meant well. I inclose two Newspapers in which it is mentioned.[1] Lord D: the other Day express'd a good deal of Concern to me, at the growing Uneasiness in N England, wishing some Means could be fallen upon to heal the Breach.[2] I took the Freedom to tell him, he could do much in it if he would exert himself. I think I see Signs of

9. This was one of the letters that later went through the hands of the Rhode Island Loyalist, Thomas Moffatt, who commented on the cover that it "Contains some Strictures upon the Massachusetts Assemblys Reply to Govr. Hutchinsons Speech written only to keep alive the fewel of Strife and Discontent in the Province." We assume that "written" modifies "Strictures," and that the Assembly's reply crept into the sentence by mistake.
    1. For Hutchinson's speech see the annotation of BF to Cushing above, March 9. In his draft BF added here, and then deleted, "The Paper sign'd a New England Man is of my Writing." One of the two newspapers, then, was the *Public Advertiser* of March 16, which printed "On Claims to the Soil of America." The other was probably the March 9 issue of the same paper, which contained the letter that evoked BF's reply; see the headnote on that reply above.
    2. BF's draft, after the deleted sentence noted above, continued: "Lord

Relenting in some others. The Bishop of St. Asaph's late Sermon to the Society for Propagating the Gospel, is much talk'd of for its Catholic Spirit and favourable Sentiments relating to the Colonies. I will endeavour to get a Copy to send you, tho' it is not yet publish'd.[3] With great Esteem and Respect, I have the Honour to be Sir, Your most obedient humble Servant   B FRANKLIN[4]

Honble. Thos Cushing, Esqr.

Private

Addressed: To / The honble. Thomas Cushing, Esqr / Boston

Endorsed: Benja Franklin London April 13. 1773 private

To Jonathan Williams, Sr.   ALS: Massachusetts Historical Society

Dear Cousin,   London, April 3. 1773.
    I wrote to you on the 9th. of March. I have not since heard from Boston. This is just to let you know I am well, and to cover a Newspaper containing one of my Scribblings, which please to

---

Dartmouth express'd his Wishe to me that some Means," etc. The interview seems to have been devoted to the affairs of New Jersey as well as New England; see BF to WF below, April 6.

    3. Jonathan Shipley, *A Sermon Preached before the Incorporated Society for the Propagation of the Gospel in Foreign Parts . . . February 19, 1773* (London, 1773), pp. 1–17. For a modern reprint, with an introduction, see Paul H. Smith, ed., *English Defenders of American Freedoms, 1774–1778: Six Pamphlets Attacking British Policy* (Washington, 1972), pp. 9–27. Shipley advocated more moderation in dealing with the colonies and emphasized the role that the Society might play in promoting reconciliation; to that end, presumably, he refrained from any mention of an American episcopate. The sermon was published by April 6, when BF sent copies to Coombe and Galloway, and it elicited articles from Arthur Lee in the *Public Advertiser* on April 13 and 15. In America it sold like hot cakes. It was reprinted in Boston in June, and soon afterward in Newport, Norwich, New York, and Philadelphia. Thomas R. Adams, *American Independence: the Growth of an Idea* (Providence, 1965), pp. 77–9; see also below, Cushing's acknowledgment of June 14 and BF to Shipley, Aug. 21.

    4. BF's draft has a deleted memorandum, "Wrote by the same Conveyance Capt. Jenkins, to Coz. Williams," the letter that follows.

give to my Sister with my Love:[5] I have not now time to write to her. Love to Cousin Grace and your Children. I am ever, Your affectionate Uncle   B FRANKLIN

To Richard Bache   ALS (letterbook draft): Library of Congress

Dear Son,   London, April 6. 1773.
The Bearer Mr. Robert Hare visits Philadelphia with a View of establishing himself there or at New York in the Porter-brewing Business. He bears an excellent Character among his Friends here as a very honest, ingenious, amiable Man.[6] I therefore recommend him warmly to your Civilities; and doubt not but you will give him the best Advice and Information in your Power. My Love to Benny-boy. I am ever Your affectionate Father   B FRANKLIN

Mr Bache

per Loxley

To Sarah Franklin Bache

ALS (letterbook draft): Library of Congress

Dear Sally,   London, April 6. 1773
I received your pleasing Letter of Jan. 5. I am glad you have undertaken the Care of the Housekeeping, as it will be an Ease to

5. Undoubtedly the essay printed above, March 16, "On Claims to the Soil of America." Jane Mecom may or may not have been interested in the subject. But five years earlier she had asked him for any contributions of his to the newspapers (above, XV, 204); and he was not backward about honoring such a request.

6. Robert Hare (1752–1812) was a young Londoner destined for considerable prominence in Philadelphia, where he arrived in June, 1773. Two and a half years later he married Margaret Willing, of the Shippen clan, and by the time the British occupied the city in 1777 he was sufficiently Americanized to flee to Virginia. He was subsequently a trustee of the University of Pennsylvania and speaker of the state assembly. Charles P. Keith, *The Provincial Councillors of Pennsylvania* ... (Philadelphia, 1883), p. 129 of first pagination. For his letter of thanks to BF see below, Oct. 28. This connection, we cannot resist adding, was subsequently useful to Hare's son of the same name, a famous chemist, who late in life secured endorsement of his electrical theories from BF's ghost. *DAB*.

your Mother, especially if you can manage to her Approbation; *that* may perhaps be at first a Difficulty. It will be of Use to you if you get *a Habit* of keeping exact Accounts; and it will be some Satisfaction to me to see them.[7] Remember, for your Encouragement in good Œconomy, that whatever a Child saves of its Parents Money, *will be its own another Day*. Study Poor Richard a little, and you may find some Benefit from his Instructions. I long to be with you all, and to see your Son. I pray God to bless him and you: being ever Your affectionate Father   B FRANKLIN

Mrs. Stevenson and Daughter send their Love to you. The latter is near lying-in again.[8] Her Boy, my Godson, is a very fine Child, and begins to talk.

per Packet

To Thomas Coombe[9]   ALS (letterbook draft): Library of Congress

Dear Friend,   London, April 6. 1773
    I receiv'd a few welcome Lines from you acquainting me with your safe Arrival at Philada. and promising me a long Letter, which I suppose has miscarried. So I know nothing of your Reception and Engagements,[1] your Views, Pursuits or Studies, or what would please you best from hence, new Poetry or new Sermons; for the better Chance therefore of hitting your Taste, I send you a Sample of each perhaps the best we have had since Pope and Tillotson. The Poetry is allow'd by the Wits here, to be neat classical Satyr. Finding a vacant Niche in it, I have with my Pen stuck up there a certain Enemy of America.[2] The just, liberal,

7. For years DF had been trying and failing to keep accurate accounts: above, VII, 167–8; X, 100–1; XII, 193–4; XVIII, 90–2. She proved to be even more obdurate than BF had supposed about surrendering the management of the household; see Sally's letter below, Oct. 30.
    8. For Polly Hewson's second son see BF to DF below, July 15.
    9. BF's young clerical friend, who has appeared frequently in recent volumes, had returned to America in 1772.
    1. BF had some trouble in putting this tactfully; instead of the two nouns he wrote and deleted, "Station in the Church" and then "Connections."
    2. BF undoubtedly sent one or the other of two recent poems by Thomas H. Delamayne (*c.* 1718–*c.* 1773), an Irishman and former barrister. *The Senators* ... (London, 1772) satirized the principal speakers in the House of

and benevolent Sentiments in my Friend the Bishop's Sermon do honour both to his Head and Heart; and the more, as he knows the Doctrine cannot be relish'd at Court, and therefore cannot conduce to his Promotion.[3] My Respects to your good Father, and believe me ever Your affectionate Friend   B FRANKLIN

Give me leave to recommend to your Acquaintance and Civilities, the Bearer Mr. Robert Hare, who bears an excellent Character here, and has Views of Settling in America.[4]

Mr Coombe

per Loxley

To Cadwalader Evans

ALS (letterbook draft): Library of Congress

Dear Friend,   London, April 6. 1773
It is some time since I have had the Pleasure of hearing from you. I hope your Health is thoroughly established.[5] Mr. Small often speaks of you with great Regard: I am glad to see by the News Papers that our Society have chosen him a Member.[6] No Man more deserves it.

Our Silk will be sold next Thursday. The Broker was with me yesterday and tells me he thinks it improv'd in the Winding Part,

---

Commons; it ran through several editions during the year. *The Patricians* . . . (London, 1773), which did the same for speakers in the House of Lords, was published early in the year: *London Chron.*, Feb. 20–23, 1773. We suspect that BF found his vacant niche in the latter work, in the wide margin of the passage (pp. 28–30) in which Delamayne wrote in relatively mild terms of Lord Hillsborough. For the poet and his satires see David J. O'Donoghue, *The Poets of Ireland* . . . (Dublin and London, 1912), p. 103.

3. For Shipley's sermon see BF to Cushing above, April 3.

4. See BF to Richard Bache above, April 6.

5. BF was repeating the hope he had voiced on Feb. 10, and it must have been small comfort to Evans if it ever reached him. The *Carolina*, which carried this letter, arrived in Philadelphia early in June (*Pa. Gaz.*, June 9); and he died on the 30th.

6. Dr. Alexander Small was elected to the APS on Jan. 15. APS, *Early Proc.* . . . (Philadelphia, 1884), p. 75. For his visit to Evans in Philadelphia see above, XIX, 272.

and that some of it is equal to almost any brought to Market here. He has sorted it into 4 Parcels, according to his Opinion of its Difference in Perfection. I inclose his Advertisement, and as soon as I can get it shall send his Account of Sales.[7]

Mr. Robert Hare, who does me the favor of carrying this Letter, is a young Gentleman of excellent Character among all that know him here.[8] He visits America with Views of establishing either at Philada. or New York, a Porter Brewery, being a thorough Master of that Business. I take the Liberty of recommending him to your Civilities, and request you would favour him with such Information and Advice as you may judge useful to him. With great Esteem, I am ever, my Dear Friend, Yours most affectionately   B FRANKLIN

Dr Evans

per Loxley per Packet

To Deborah Franklin

ALS: American Philosophical Society; letterbook draft: Library of Congress

My dear Child   London, April 6. 1773
I received yours of Dec. 28 and Jan. 6. and am glad to find you were so well.

I do not recollect the Miss Moore's you mention, whom Ben visited before they went away.[9] As to Mrs. Wright, I have done all I could to serve her here; but I have somehow or other, I know not which way, displeas'd her of late, so that she does not now come near me.[1] I wish her well.

7. The broker was undoubtedly one of the two Boydell brothers mentioned in *idem*, p. 68. See also BF to the silk committee above, Feb. 10, March 15.

8. See BF to Richard Bache above, April 6.

9. The letters from DF to which he was replying, if they had survived, might have thrown light on the Moore sisters. We are inclined to think that they were the same pair who had appeared at a party of Sally's six years before: above, XIV, 137.

1. BF's draft here inserts a delightful sentence: "Some Folks Friendship is of such brittle Stuff, it costs more than it is Worth to keep it in repair." For Patience Wright see above, XIX, 93.

I condole with you on the Death of our good Friend Mr. Hall.[2] My old Friends so drop off one after another, that I am afraid, when I come home, I shall find myself a Stranger in my own Country.

Your Accounts of your Kingbird please me exceedingly. I hope soon to see him and you. Last Night I was at Mr. West's. They desire to be remember'd to you. Their youngest Boy, my Godson, is a very fine one,[3] as is also my other Godson, young Hewson. I continue well, Thanks to God, and am ever, my dear Debby, Your affectionate Husband   B FRANKLIN

P.S. Since writing the above I have receiv'd yours of March 2. per Packet.[4] Mrs. Stevenson and Polly send their Love. Sally her Duty. She is to be married and leave us next Week.[5]

Addressed: To / Mrs Franklin / at / Philadelphia / via N York / per Packet / B Free FRANKLIN

To William Franklin   ALS (letterbook draft): Library of Congress

Dear Son,   London, April 6 [–9]. 1773

I received yours of Feb. 2. with the Papers of Information that accompany it.

I know nothing of Col. Mercer's being appointed Surveyor of the new Colony: Indeed the Proprietors, if they ever are to be such, are not yet in a Situation to appoint or promise any Places, the Grant not being compleated.

I never heard of Jones; or his Chief Justiceship in Eyre. Nor do I know any thing of General Lyman's Project or Grants.[6]

2. The news was probably in DF's letter of Dec. 28, for David Hall died on the 24th.

3. Benjamin West, Jr. These sentences about the Wests were an afterthought, omitted in the draft.

4. Also lost. BF's postscript must have been written some time after his letter, because the packet, the *Duke of Cumberland*, reached Falmouth on April 6: *Lloyd's Evening Post*, April 5–7, 1773.

5. The bridegroom was a farmer, James Pearce; see above, XIX, 395 n.

6. WF's missing letter must have asked about a number of rumors that he had heard. George Mercer, responsible for merging the Ohio Co. of Virginia with the Walpole Co. in 1770 (above, XVII, 136), was mentioned before long

No Proposal has been made to me of being their Agent, which indeed I should not undertake, being about to quit all Agencies, and return home to settle my own Affairs.

I have ordered a Jack for you, and will send it by the first Opportunity.[7]

I have sent to Mr. Galloway one of the Bishop of St. Asaph's Sermons to your Society for propagating the Gospel. I would

---

not as the surveyor but as the governor of the new colony: BF to WF below, July 14. The colony had been in the planning stage since the previous summer (above, XIX, 244 n), and was now taking form on paper; it was to include the Walpole grant and also large tracts outside its borders. The Board of Trade discussed the matter frequently in April, called in Samuel Wharton on the 5th, and issued a favorable report on May 6. *Board of Trade Jour.*, 1768–75, pp. 351–356; Kenneth P. Bailey, ed., *The Ohio Company Papers* ... (Arcata, Cal., 1947), pp. 263–79; Clarence W. Alvord, *The Mississippi Valley in British Politics* ... (2 vols., Cleveland, O., 1917), II, 150–2. The colony had already been named. "It was proposed at first to call the Province Pittsylvania," Samuel Wharton wrote his brother Thomas and Joseph Galloway on April 9 (APS); "But in Compliment to the Queen, it will be called Vandalia; as her Majesty is descended from the Vandals."

Nathaniel Jones had been appointed chief justice of New Jersey in 1759, only to find his office occupied by another claimant, and had been actively campaigning ever since for some kind of recompense. WF may have had an inquiry about him from Dartmouth, to whom Jones had addressed a memorial. *Dartmouth MSS*, II, 124; *DAB* under Robert Hunter Morris; 1 *N.J. Arch.*, XX, 417–24 n; Jerome J. Nadelhaft, "Politics and the Judicial Tenure Fight in Colonial New Jersey," 3 *W&MQ*, XXVIII (1971), 52, 54–5, 58. Gen. Phineas Lyman (above, XIII, 414 n) was still advancing claims for himself and his veterans. In 1768 he had petitioned unsuccessfully for land later included in the Walpole Co.'s application. *Acts Privy Coun., Col.*, V, 139–40; *Board of Trade Jour.*, 1768–75, pp. 77, 89–91. In the autumn of 1772 he was hoping for a grant on the east bank of the Mississippi from its mouth to the mouth of the Ohio; his hope was widely publicized as a fait accompli, and two expeditions were setting out to explore the grant he had "obtained." *The Conn. Jour., and the New-Haven Post-Boy*, Dec. 4, 1772; see also Alvord, *op. cit.*, II, 92–3, 173–6; Shaw Livermore, *Early American Land Companies* ... (New York and London, 1939), pp. 99–100. WF may have elided Lyman's two schemes, and in any case must have inquired about what he took to be still another threat, complete with explorers, to the Walpole grant.

7. BF bought it for £9 (Jour., p. 47), but what it was we cannot say because the word was used for a variety of implements; our guess is a mechanical kitchen jack for turning a spit.

have sent you one, but you will receive it of course as a Member. It contains such liberal and generous Sentiments relating to the Conduct of Government here towards America, that Sir J. P. says it was written in compliment to me. But from the Intimacy of Friendship in which I live with the Author, I know he has express'd nothing but what he thinks and feels; and I honour him the more, that thro' the mere Hope of doing Good; he has hazarded the Displeasure of the Court, and of course the Prospect of farther Preferment.[8] Possibly indeed the Ideas of the Court may change; for I think I see some Alarm at the Discontents in New-England, and some Appearance of Softening in the Disposition of Government, on the Idea that Matters have been carry'd too far there. But all depends upon Circumstances and Events. We govern from Hand to Mouth. There seems to be no wise regular Plan.

I saw Lord Dartmouth about 2 Weeks since. He mention'd nothing to me of your Application for additional Salary, nor did I to him, for I do not like it. I fear it will embroil you with your People.[1] I told him I look'd upon Mrs. Haine to be out of her Senses, and that there was no Foundation for her Pretensions; at which he seem'd to wonder, her Story, he said, was so circumstantial. He has given a Letter to the Chief Justice, which is gone by an Attorney sent by Hayne.[2]

While I am writing comes to hand yours of Mar. 2. My Letter by the October Packet must have been sent as usual, to the Office by the Bellman. That being, as you inform me, rubb'd open as some of yours to me have been, gives an additional Circumstance

8. For the Bishop's sermon see BF to Cushing above, April 3. Sir John Pringle's comment was indeed wide of the mark: Shipley had the courage of his convictions, and in consequence was never promoted from St. Asaph.

1. See WF to BF above, Jan. 5. BF's fear, based on developments in Massachusetts, was not borne out: the New Jersey Assembly was more interested in keeping down expenditures than in the issue of principle. It refused to raise WF's salary on the ground that any increase should be paid out of the Townshend duties, in other words by the crown. 1 *N.J. Arch.*, X, 389–93; XVIII, 299–300, 306–9.

2. We have found no trace of Hayne's emissary, but Dartmouth himself sent one: below, p. 313. For the Hayne affair see also above: XIX, 321–2; BF to WF, Feb. 14, 1773.

of Probability to the Conjecture made in mine of Dec. 2. For the future I shall send Letters of consequence to the Office when I use the Pacquet-Conveyance, by my Clerk.[3]

Your Accounts of the Numbers of People, Births Burials, &c. in your Province, will be very agreable to me and particularly so to Dr. Price. Compar'd with former Accounts, they will show the Increase of your People, but not perfectly, as I think a great many have gone from N Jersey to the more Southern Colonies.[4]

I have scarce seen Mr. Wharton twice in the last 12 mo. and know little of his Proceedings.[5] Mr. Strahan and Mr. Todd and Mr. Walpole tell me our Business is going on, and they have good Hopes of seeing it soon compleated. But the two first know as little of Circumstances as I do; who have never ask'd a Question about it of any Minister for reasons formerly mention'd. I think however to speak of it to Lord Dartmouth next time I see him, and learn where it sticks.

The Parliament is like to sit till the End of June, as Mr. Cooper tells me. I had thoughts of returning home about that time. The Boston Assembly's Answer to the Governor's Speech, which I have just received,[6] may possibly produce something here to

3. For BF's conjecture see above, XIX, 416–17, and for his French clerk *ibid.*, p. 438 n.

4. Each governor had standing instructions to report annually on the increase or decrease of population in his colony. Leonard W. Labaree, *Royal Instructions to British Colonial Governors, 1670–1776* (2 vols., New York and London, [1935]), II, 746–7. Richard Price had earlier used New Jersey statistics of 1738 (above, XVI, 103–4), and was sure to be interested in the census that WF was trying to take. But the Governor ran into difficulties with the county assessors, who refused to do the work gratis; the returns, which WF eventually sent to Dartmouth in 1774, were therefore incomplete. In 1775 the Assembly authorized paying the assessors, but nothing seems to have been accomplished. See 1 *N.J. Arch.*, X, 445, [452–3]; Samuel Allison, ed., *Acts of the General Assembly of ... New Jersey ...* (Burlington, N.J., 1776), p. 491; Evarts B. Green and Virginia D. Harrington, *American Population before the Federal Census of 1790* (New York, 1932), pp. 8, 108.

5. BF described to WF above, Feb. 14, his interview with Wharton on Jan. 30.

6. Grey Cooper was secretary to the Treasury. "The Assembly's Answer" was to the Governor's speech of Jan. 6; see the note on Cooper to BF above, March 15. The replies of the House and Council were singularly slow in arriving; BF had been expecting them since his letter to Cushing of March 9.

occasion my longer Stay. I am, Your affectionate Father

B FRANKLIN

PS. Apr. 9. Your Jack is shipt in Loxley.

To Joseph Galloway ALS (letterbook draft): Library of Congress

Dear Sir, London, April 6. 1773.

I wrote to you of the 14th Feby. and 15th of March, since which I have receiv'd no Line from you.

This just serves to cover a Sermon of my Friend the Bishop of St. Asaph. You will find it replete with very liberal Sentiments respecting America. I hope they will prevail here, and be the Foundation of a better Understanding between the two Countries. He is the more to be honour'd by us for this Instance of his Good Will, as his Censure of the late Conduct towards the Colonies, however tenderly express'd, cannot recommend him at Court, or conduce in the least to his Promotion.[7]

The Parliament is busy about India Affairs, and as yet see no End of the Business. It is thought they will Sit till the End of June. An Alliance with France and Spain is talk'd of; and a War with Prussia.[8] But this may blow over. A war with France and Spain would be of more Advantage to American Liberty: Every Step would then be taken to conciliate our Friendship, Our Grievances would be redress'd and our Claims allow'd. And this will be the Case sooner or later. For as the House of Bourbon is most vulnerable in its American Possessions, our hearty Assistance in a War there must be of the greatest Importance.

The Affair of the Grant goes on, but slowly. I do not yet

7. BF said much the same thing in the preceding document.
8. For the affairs of the East India Co. see above, BF to Galloway, Feb. 14, and to Cushing, March 9; and the headnote on BF to Cushing below, June 4. Parliament had been debating those affairs since early March, and the "End of the Business" did not come until the statutes passed in May and June: 13 Geo. III, c. 44, 63, 64. The opposition, to provide a red herring for the public, was circulating the rumor that North sought a French alliance against the three powers that were engaged in partitioning Poland. Thomas W. Copeland et al., The Correspondence of Edmund Burke (9 vols., Cambridge and Chicago, 1958–70) II, 429.

clearly see Land. I begin to be a little of the Sailors Mind when they were handing a Cable out of a Store into a Ship, and one of 'em said, 'Tis a long heavy Cable, I wish we could see the End of it. D—n me, says another, if I believe it has any End: Somebody has cut it off.[9]

I beg leave to recommend to your Civilities Mr. Robert Hare[1] who does me the Favour to carry this Letter. He bears an excellent Character among all that know him here, and purposes Settling in America to carry on there the Brewing Business. With the sincerest Esteem and Affection I am ever Yours,

B FRANKLIN

Mr Galloway

per Loxley

The Managers of the Pennsylvania Hospital to Franklin, David Barclay, and John Fothergill

LS (minutebook copy): Pennsylvania Hospital, Philadelphia

⟨Pennsylvania Hospital, April 6, 1773: Notification that ten bills, nos. 23 through 32, have been drawn on Franklin, Barclay, and Fothergill, to be paid from the account of the contributors to the Hospital.[2] The bills are: two of Feb. 6 in favor of Charles Stewart, £365 sterling in all; one of Feb. 19 and three of March 12 in favor of Joseph King, £1,500 in all; one of April 6 in favor of William

9. Galloway told this story to Thomas Wharton, who soon afterward sent him a covering note to enclose the letter to both of them from Samuel Wharton of April 9, 1773. The note has been lost, but WF copied an extract of it at the foot of Samuel's letter (APS). "I hear Dr. Franklin has wrote his Son more favourable of the Prospect in finishing the Affairs of the New Colony," Thomas wrote Galloway, "and that there was some Hopes of getting to the '*End of the Cable*.' I am sure he knows Nothing of the Matter but from Second Hand, therefore do not admire at the Intimations from Time to Time given." BF indeed was out of touch with developments; see the next to last paragraph of the preceding document.

1. See BF to Richard Bache above, April 6.

2. The Managers were continuing to liquidate the windfall discussed in their letter above, Jan. 1.

Logan, £75;[3] three in favor of King, £300 in all. The total is
£2,240. Signed by Isaac Jones, Joseph Morris, Israel and James
Pemberton, John Reynell, Samuel Rhoads, Daniel Roberdeau,
and Thomas Wharton.[4]⟩

From Richard Bache

ALS (fragment): American Philosophical Society

[April 6, 1773[5]]
[*Beginning mutilated*] I wrote you a few lines of the Mar[*torn*] that
we were all well. We have continued so [*torn*] at this Time made
happy by the Company of the Burlington Family who have been
with us a few days, and intend making some Stay with us.
Having disposed of almost all my dry Goods, and found them but
a sorry Concern, I have determined to employ my Money in
another Branch of Business, which few have failed in, in this Place,
Vizt. the Wine and Grocery Business. I am now fitting up a Store
for this Purpose, and have made a purchase of some old Wines,
which I purpose selling by the Gallon or otherwise, and Sugar &c.
by the small or great Quantity.[6] To this Plan of Business, which I
expect will yield me some Profit [*torn*] into his Place. I [*torn*: can

3. Charles Stewart we cannot identify. For King see above, XIX, 367 n, and
for William Logan, the Quaker merchant, III, 456 n; XII, 97 n. Stewart and
Logan were undoubtedly new mortgagers.

4. All the signers except Roberdeau are identified above, XVIII, 93 n and
XIX, 340 n. For Daniel Roberdeau see XVII, 81 n, where the back reference
should be to XIII, 274 n.

5. In replying to Bache's letters below, July 15, BF mentioned one of April
6. DF on that date spoke of having "all our children in town"; see the
following document. The visit must have been from WF's Burlington family,
to which Bache refers here.

6. Bache advertised his wine store, on the south side of Market between
Third and Fourth Sts., in the *Pa. Gaz.* of May 12, 1773. He had been restless
for some time in his dry goods business. When he toyed with the idea of a
governmental post, BF counseled against it, helped to finance his son-in-law,
assured him that times would improve, and urged him to stick with his trade.
Above, XIX, 42–3, 45, 46–7, 143–5, 267. Now Bache, it seems, felt no need
to explain his change of trade. If so his self-confidence had made giant strides
since the fall of 1771, when the young man had been on tenterhooks before
his first meeting with BF. Above, XVIII, 258.

not be any more?] particular as the post is just agoing. I remain with Sally and Ben's joint Love and Duty Dear sir Your Affectionate Son

RICHD. BACHE

Remember me to Dr. Small and Friends in Craven Street.

From Deborah Franklin ALS: American Philosophical Society

My Dear child   Aprill the 6 1773
I did reseve yours by the laste packit dated Jan 6. I due in tend to write by Capt. All if it ples got [God] to preserve him Safe back a gen. I did in tend to say [sum]thing a boute Ben Franklin Beache but Billey told me he had mens[honed him?] to you in his letter yester day, I had thought I had bin two trubel sum [*torn*] as you had told me that he was two much or he was master of the house and then told me but I leve of[f] Leaste I shante due as I should say what I shold due as plese you well I know what such littel cretuers gain the afeckshon of those thay live with so the young Jentelman you wrote to of[7] I muste leve of[f] leste I shold not due writs. Capt. All cold [could] tell you [*illegible*] you have bin in formed we have all our children in town. Be so kind to remember me to Dr. Small and all that remember me. Capt. orrey if re-member[8] as I am Cald on So Subscrib my Self your afeckshonet wife   D FRANKLIN

From Anthony Todd AL: American Philosophical Society

General Post Office April 6th: 1773
Mr. Todd presents his Compliments to Dr. Franklin and as he understands he has received his Accounts by this Days Mail he would be glad if the Accountant General could have them to

---

7. Undoubtedly BF's godson, William Hewson, Jr. DF must have received, although she does not specifically mention it, BF's letter above of Feb. 2.

8. Lewis Ourry was an old friend, and Alexander Small had recently called on DF in Philadelphia. Above, VII, 62 n; XIX, 140–1. BF returned their greetings to DF in his reply below, July 15.

examine next Wednesday that if there should be any Errors in them they may be wrote about by this Month's Mail.[9]

To Alexander Colden ALS (letterbook draft): Library of Congress

⟨London, April 7, 1773: Has just received the accounts,[1] but has not had time to examine them. Has also received Christie on Molleson for £338 17s. 2d., and the papers for Mr. Jesser.[2] Will write by the next packet to Colden and also to Foxcroft, to whom his affectionate respects.⟩

To Jane Parker Bedford

ALS (photocopy): American Philosophical Society; letterbook draft:[3] Library of Congress

Dear Jenky   London, April 9. 1773

For so I must still call you, tho' you seem a little angry with me.[4] I received your Letter of Feb. 2.[5] and shall examine the Accounts that are sent me from your Books, and write to you fully upon them very soon. In the mean time, you and Mrs. Parker may be assured that nothing will be expected or desired on my Part inconsistent with the Regard I always had for her and you, and the ancient Friendship that so long subsisted between Mr. Parker and me, whose Memory as an honest worthy Man I shall

9. For the accounts see the following document. The 6th was a Tuesday; Todd must have wanted them submitted on Wednesday week, the 14th. In any case they were mislaid in the office of the accountant general, who did not act on them for months: BF to Colden below, June 2.

1. The amended accounts for 1771–72 that BF had demanded in December: XIX, 399, 414–5. See the preceding document for what happened to them.

2. Christie was James Christie (Jour., p. 47), presumably the Baltimore merchant who appears in Sabine, Loyalists, I, 312. Molleson, Jesser, and the papers—relating to Mrs. Holland—are all mentioned in Colden to BF above, Jan. 7.

3. The ALS, which appears to have been lost without a trace, differed markedly from the draft; and the significant differences are noted below. Jane's letter posed a problem, and BF's handling of it changed between the draft and the final version of his answer.

4. The draft begins "Dear Madam" and omits the first sentence.

5. Her letter above explains most of what BF discusses in this reply.

always honour. The Power of Attorney you mention and seem to take amiss, was a general one, to settle Accounts for me with any Person in my Absence. But since your Accounts are sent to me, I will endeavour to settle them myself: And desiring nothing but what is just, shall be more pleas'd to find little due to me than much. In a Letter some Years since to Mr. Parker, I gave my Reasons for expecting his Bond, bearing Interest, whenever I advanc'd considerable Sums of Money for him; viz. because to serve him I took my Money out of other Hands where it bore Interest; and when I bought Goods for him here, and paid my Money for them, I charg'd no Profit or Commissions upon them, being no Merchant.[6] Any Business he did for me, I always was and shall be willing to allow for, to Satisfaction,[7] in Money; as well as to return Kindness for Kindness: But I think it contributes to the Duration of Friendship, to keep *its* Accounts, and those of Business, distinct and separate, and that as exact Justice in Pounds Shillings and Pence should be observed between Friends as between Strangers. I always intended making Mr. Parker an Allowance for the *Time* he spent and the Trouble he took in settling my Accounts with Mr. Hall after I left America.[8] This is the only thing I at present recollect unsatisfy'd. But if Mrs. Parker, or you, or I myself, can find or recollect any thing else, it shall be allow'd for. And not withstanding what is said above, of Interest, I think with Mrs. Parker that from the Time she render'd the Accounts, and offer'd as you say to pay the Ballance, no Interest should be charged. I received also for him here £64 3s. 0d. Sterling, on Jan 14. 1772 from which time the Interest of that Sum must be struck off in the Bonds.[9] It was upon my Application here that the Quarter's Salary after your good Father's Death, was allowed, and if it is not yet paid, it will be. I suppose Mr. Potts has desired Mr. Colden to receive for the Newspapers. If so, I

6. The draft omits the participial phrase.
7. The draft omits much of what follows: "to Satisfaction. The Time he spent . . . is the only thing," etc.
8. For Parker's examination of these accounts see above, XII, 176–82; XIII, 87–99.
9. The draft omits this sentence. The payment was from the customs commissioners for salary still due Parker from his position as land waiter: Jour., p. 39.

think you had better pay it there out of the Money you are to receive from the Office. If not, I will pay him here, as you desire it. Present my affectionate Respects to your good Mother, and my Compliments to Mr. Bedford tho' unknown, to whom with yourself I wish all Happiness in your Marriage; being ever, with sincere Regard Your affectionate Friend   B FRANKLIN

PS. The £135 0s. 0d. remitted in March 1770, was part of a Bill of £250 Sterling Watts & McEvers on Messrs. Harley and Drummond, dated Feb. 28. 1770. concerning which your Father thus writes to me in his Letter of March 8. . . . [1] I suppose you may find by his Books how this Account was closed.   B F

You speak of a Difference between our Families. I have never heard of such a Thing but in your Letter, and wonder at it.

Mrs Bedford

To Richard Woodward[2]

ALS (draft[3]): American Philosophical Society

Reverend Sir   London, April 10. 1773

Desirous of being reviv'd in your Memory, I take this Opportunity by my good Friend Mrs. Blacker, of sending you a printed Piece, and a Manuscript, both on a Subject you and I frequently convers'd upon, with similar Sentiments, when I had the Pleasure of seeing you in Dublin.[4] I have since had the Satisfaction to

1. BF quoted here, almost verbatim, the first paragraph of Parker's letter (after the opening sentence) above, XVII, 92–3. The draft omits the postscripts entirely.

2. Woodward (1726–94), Dean of Clogher since 1764 and Chancellor of St. Patrick's, Dublin, since 1772, was the stepson of a better known dean, Josiah Tucker, but unlike him rose in time to be a bishop. Woodward was best known for advocating a compulsory system of poor relief in Ireland. *DNB*.

3. A few words in the MS, now illegible, have been supplied in brackets from the printed version in Sparks, *Works*, VIII, 42.

4. For the elusive Mrs. Blacker, née Martin, see above, XIX, 40. If the subject of BF's conversation with the Dean was slavery, as seems likely, the printed piece may well have been either BF's "Conversation on Slavery" or "The Sommersett Case and the Slave Trade": above, respectively, XVII, 37–44; XIX, 187–8.

APRIL 10, 1773

learn that a Disposition to abolish Slavery prevails in North
America, that many of the Pennsylvanians have set their Slaves at
liberty, [and] that even the Virginia Assembly have petitioned
[the] King for Permission to make a Law for preventing the
Importation of more Slaves into that Colony. This Request
however, will probably not [be gr]anted, [as their former laws
of that kind have always been repealed,] and as the Interest of a
few Merchants here has more Weight with Government than that
of Thousands at a Distance. Witness a late Fact. The Goal
Distemper being frequently imported and spread in Virginia, by
the Ships transporting Convicts, occasioning the Death of many
honest innocent People there, a Law was made to oblige those
Ships arriving with that Distemper to perform a Quarantine. But
the two Merchants of London, Contractors in that Business,
alledging that this might increase the Expence of their Voyages,
the Law was at their Instance repealed here.[5] With great Esteem
and Respect, I have the Honour to be, Reverend Sir, Your most
obedient humble Servant   B FRANKLIN

Dean Woodward

To William Deane[6]   ALS (draft): American Philosophical Society

Dear Sir,   London, April 11. 1773
    Miss Martin that was, now Mrs. Blacker, being about to return

5. The Virginia House of Burgesses had tried in 1769 to tax the local slave
trade out of existence, but the act had been disallowed as a result of mercantile pressure. In April, 1772, the House passed another, accompanied by an
address to the crown requesting permission for the governor to permit such
taxation in future (*ibid.*, p. 116 n). On the issue of quarantining convicts
the House was equally obstinate. An act for that purpose in 1767 was
disallowed; a similar act followed in 1772, which the contractors in London
insisted would stop their exporting convicts to the colony, and thereby
contravene a Parliamentary statute. Both efforts of the House died in
Whitehall. *Board of Trade Jour.*, 1768–75, pp. 39, 333, 342–4; *Acts Privy
Coun., Col.*, v, 163–4, 287–8, 362–3.
    6. An Irish friend that BF had made during his visit in 1771. To judge by
the tone of this letter, the friendship was still very much alive; but Deane
(d. 1793) has not appeared before and, to the best of our knowledge, does not
appear again. He was a solicitor and officer in the Irish Court of Chancery,

156

to Dublin,[7] I cannot omit the Opportunity it gives me of chatting a [little] with one, whose Conversation afforded me so much pleasure and Instruction while I was there.

I know of nothing new here, worth communicating to you, unless perhaps the new Art of making Ca[rriage] W[heels,] the Fellies of one Piece bent into a Circle and sur[rounded] by a Hoop of Iron, the whole very light and strong, there being no cross'd Grain in the Wood, which [is also?] a great Saving of Timber. The Wood is first [steam]'d in the Vapour from boiling Water, and then bent by a forcible Machine, I have seen Pieces so bent of 6 Inches wide, and $3\frac{1}{2}$ thick into a Circle of 4 feet diameter.[8] These

---

but was better known as an amateur scientist and one of the owners of a factory that made bottles and window glass; he was also a founding member of the Royal Irish Academy. He received a B.A. from Trinity College in 1757 and an honorary L.L.D. in 1779, and at his death left chemical apparatus and a planetarium to his alma mater. 4 Royal Hist. and Archaeol. Assn. of Ireland *Jour.*, VII (1885–86), 448; M. S. Dudley Westropp, *Irish Glass* . . . (London, [1920]), pp. 46–7, 51; George D. Burtchaell and Thomas U. Sadleir, eds., *Alumni Dublinenses* . . . (Dublin, 1935), p. 219; *The Gentleman's and Citizen's Almanack* . . . (Dublin, 1774), pp. 58–9, 94; *Gent. Mag.*, LXIII (1793), 1152.

7. BF was attempting to renew, through letters she carried, two friendships he had formed; see the preceding document.

8. The advent of the turnpike had created a traffic problem of increasing magnitude, and a demand for greater Parliamentary control. In 1772 a committee of the House of Commons issued its report on revising earlier legislation. The following year the report was implemented in two statutes (13 Geo. III, c. 78, 84), one for highways and one for turnpikes. Both regulated the relationship between wheel width and the number of horses used, and the second regulated the wheels themselves. The subject aroused considerable public attention (see for example the *Public Advertiser*, March 12, 19, April 3, 1773), and mechanics became interested in new ways of making wheels. BF suggested one to Joseph Jacob, a partner of his friend John Viny (above, XVII, 72 n) in a carriage-building firm: make the wheel in one piece, as New Jersey farmers did by bending a sapling into a circle. Jacob thought the idea impractical, but Viny took it up. Saplings were unavailable in England, and BF worked with Viny until they devised a method of making a circular felly with dry wood. That was the account Viny gave John Adams and Thomas Jefferson in 1786, when they visited his factory. BF, he made clear, originated "the new Art of making Carriage Wheels"—for which he takes no credit in this letter—and worked on implementing it; Viny "spoke of him with love and gratitude." Julian P. Boyd *et al.*, eds., *The Papers of Thomas Jefferson*

for Duration can only be exceeded by your Iron Wheels. Pray, have you compleated that ingenious Invention?

W[hat is] become of honest Mr. Kettilby?[9] Does he go on with his Printing Schemes, or has he got into some better Employment?

Th[ey tell] us here that some Person with you has discovered a new moving Power, that may be of Use in mechanical Operations; that it consists in the Explosion of Iron Tears chill'd suddenly from the melting State in Cold Water. That Explosion I have often seen in Drops of Glass with Wonder, understanding it no more than they did in the Time of Hudibras, who makes a Simile of it, which I repeat because tis probably long since you read it,

> *Honour*, is like that glassy Bubble,
> That gives Philosophers such Trouble
> Whose least part crack'd, the whole does fly,
> And Wits are crack'd to find out why.

May I ask you if you know any thing of the Application of this Power, of which I have not at present the smallest Conception?[1]

(19 vols. to date, Princeton, N.J., 1950–), XI, 43–4; see also Butterfield, ed., *Diary of John Adams*, III, 186–7; Smyth, *Writings*, VII, 222. It was not Viny but Jacob, however, who patented the new method, apparently in 1771. He described it in general terms in a pamphlet two years later, and soon afterward announced that specimen wheels were on display at the factory on Blackfriars Road, Christ Church. Bennet Woodcroft, *Alphabetical Index of Patentees of Inventions...* (London, [1969]); Jacob, *Observations on the Structure and Draft of Wheel-Carriages* (London, 1773), pp. 81–3, and *Animadversions on the Use of Broad Wheels...* (London, [1774]), pp. 23–4. The partners subsequently quarreled over the patent rights, and the firm went bankrupt in 1778. Viny continued to operate the factory for the creditors, and before long controlled it. By 1783 he was being supported by seven-year subscriptions, to the tune of £1,800; three dukes were on the list. But BF had the reputation of having devised "the best wheels Ever Invented." William James to BF, June 7, 1783, APS; see also *Gent. Mag.*, XLVIII (1778), 440; Mary Hewson to BF, Jan. 11, 1779, APS; John Viny to BF, May 21, 1783, APS.

9. J. G. Kettilby was an innovative printer; doubtless he was also honest, but we know nothing about him except for a single letter: above, XVIII, 85–7.

1. We have no more conception than BF had. On the back of the page is a drawing, badly blotted and with no evidence of who drew it, that may be somehow related to BF's inquiry of Deane about the drops of iron, but even conjecturing how would require a wild stretch of imagination; the drawing shows a circle containing a pattern of triangles of equal size, arranged

I have compleated my Stove, in which the Smoke of the Coal is all turn'd into Flame and operates as Fuel in heating the Room. I have us'd it all this Winter; and find it answer even beyond my Expectation. I purpose to print a little Description of its Use and Construction and shall send you a Copy.[2]

I hope *Billy and Jenny* continue and will always continue as happy as when I knew them. My best Wishes attend them, being ever, with sincere Esteem, Dear Sir, Your most obedient humble servant   B F

Wm Deane Esqr

From Jacques Barbeu-Dubourg

ALS (incomplete): American Philosophical Society

11e. avril 1773.[3]

[*Beginning lost.*] M. Dalibard avoit un tableau magique tres bon, et une grande cucurbite dont il s'etoit fait une bonne bouteille de Leyde.[4] L'un et l'autre sont devenus tout a fait conducteurs. Il en a trouvé la raison sensible dans l'alteration de la colle qui avoit servi a faire tenir l'etamure, et qui s'est trouvée aigrie et corrompue. Il seroit a desirer pour les progrès ulterieurs de l'electricité que l'on fit une bonne suite d'experiences sur les verres de differentes natures, c'est a dire, dans lesquels entrent les differentes

---

eccentrically, and a sequence of numbers. The curiosity of glass drops that provided Samuel Butler with his metaphor in *Hudibras* ([John Wilders, ed.; Oxford, 1967], p. 137) evoked more serious attention in the eighteenth century; see Claude le Cat, "A Memoir on the Lacrymae Batavicae or Glass-Drops...," *Phil. Trans.*, XLVI (1752), 175–88. The "Explosion of Iron Tears," however, is something else again; it resembles the way in which leaden buckshot and bullets were made at the time, but no one would have called that process "a new moving Power."

2. BF did not print the description for more than a decade; see the story of the stove in the note on BF to Dubourg above, Jan. 22.

3. The date is at the end. Dubourg never, as far as we know, plunged into a letter without salutation; we are therefore convinced that the MS is incomplete.

4. Dalibard, the physicist and botanist, was repeating Ebenezer Kinnersley's game with the electrified "magical picture," for which see above, III, 358–9. The cucurbit had originally been part of an apparatus for distilling.

especes de fondant tant salins que metalliques en differentes proportions; et sur chacun de ces verres a differens degrés de chaleur.[5]

Dans ce moment il vient de me passer par la tête une idée que vous trouverez peutetre bien folle. Je pourrai cependant vous la communiquer l'ordinaire prochain; mais il faut lui donner au moins ce tems là, soit pour mûrir ou pour pourrir.

Nous avons icy le Phytolacca, je me doutois que c'etoit le Pokeweed mais il y en a au moins 3 especes.[6] Quelle est la bonne?

Un de mes Confreres et moi sommes convenus de travailler en societé a traduire les Transactions philosophiques Americaines.[7]

Est-il possible est-il pardonable que je ne vous aye pas encore fait le moindre remerciment pour toutes les peines que vous avez daigné prendre pour l'impression du P. C.?[8] J'ai eté si petrifié de la trahison que j'ai eprouvée à l'occasion d'un exemplaire que j'en ai perdu le sens. Daignez en recevoir mes excuses aussi sinceres et humbles que tardives et disproportionnées à la faute. Tâchez aussi, je vous supplie, de me menager la continuation des bontés de Madame Hewson que j'honore de toute mon ame et envers qui je ne m'aquitterai pas facilement; mais je n'y negligerai rien si je puis en trouver l'occasion.

Quant a l'execution typographique de cette brochure, il est tres bien. Revoyons pourtant:

le frontispice est une page un peu uniforme.

dans l'epitre dedicatoire, Les deux Monsieur, encore un peu trop ressemblans.

preface, page 1. ligne 12. *son.* lisez *sont.*

page 13. ligne 16. *leur* jouissances. lisez *leurs.*

page 38. ligne 5. *né, libre.* effacez la virgule.

page 41. ligne 16. *d'engrossir.* separez ces deux mots *d'en grossir.*

page 52. *La fin.* effacez *la.*

---

5. See Dubourg's letter above, March 25.

6. He is replying to BF's letter above, March 27; see also BF's answer to this one below, April 23.

7. See BF's answer to his inquiry about the APS *Trans.*: above, XIX, 438.

8. *Petit code de la raison humaine.* . . . BF, just when he was receiving proofsheets of the *Œuvres*, was sending copies of the second French edition of the *Petit code*, which he had had printed in London; see above, XIX, 442 n; BF to Benezet, Feb. 10, 1773.

Le caractere *&c* me paroit un peu trop figuré et trop saillant.

Je ne sais ce que signifient certains chiffres au bas de quelques pages: comme 9. (page 8.) 6. (page 5.) 6. (page 10.) 7. (page 17.) 5. (page 30.) 4. (page 37.) 6. (page 44).[9]

Au reste les caracteres sont beaux, le papier assez beau, les articles bien disposés. En un mot je suis, comme je le vois penetré de vos bontés.

On reçut hier une lettre de Melle Biheron par la poste; mais celles qu'elle a ecrit par des occasions sont encore en chemin. Puissiez vous nous la ramener bientôt avec vous? Plût a Dieu. L'heure me presse de finir. Je joins icy 9 nouvelles feuilles.

J'ai l'honneur d'etre avec un attachment et une [*torn*] sans bornes, Mon cher Monsieur, Votre tres humble et tres obeissant serviteur   DUBOURG

From Jacques Barbeu-Dubourg

Printed in Jacques Barbeu-Dubourg, ed., *Œuvres de M. Franklin* . . . (2 vols., Paris, 1773), I, 322–6.

Monsieur,   Paris, 15 Avril 1773.

Moitié dormant, moitié éveillé, j'ai beaucoup rêvé la nuit derniere. Il faut vous dire sur quoi, et comment, afin que vous jugiez si ce sont des rêves, ou des rêveries; s'il faut s'y arrêter, ou les oublier.

J'ai songé à la vie, à la mort; mais plus à celle-ci qu'à celle-là. Je recherchois ce qui constitue proprement la mort, si ce n'est autre chose que la cessation de la vie; si c'est le dernier des maux du corps; les causes occasionnelles qui la procurent; les causes formelles qui la décident; les différentes causes formelles de la mort naturelle en vieillesse, de la mort anticipée par maladies internes, de la mort précipitée par violence externe; de l'approche et des suites de la mort quelconque.

De ces idées lugubres, je passois de tems en tems à des idées plus consolantes; des moyens aussi efficaces que peu communs de

---

9. The figures that puzzled the Frenchman were presumably press numbers, used at the time to identify a particular press or workman; see Thomas Landau, *Encyclopedia of Librarianship* . . . (3rd revised ed., New York, 1967), p. 354.

repousser dans bien des cas la mort imminente, et de ranimer la vie éteinte.

Mais ne vous semblera-t-il point que je rêve encore, en mettant une distinction entre la mort et l'extinction de la vie? Et ne regarderez-vous point comme autant de nouveaux rêves tout ce que je pourrai vous dire des maladies des cadavres, du bon état ou de l'altération des parties organiques d'un corps mort?

La vie consiste essentiellement dans le mouvement spontané du coeur, qui est le premier vivant et le dernier mourant en nous, et qui imprime le mouvement vital à tout le reste. Le mouvement du coeur paroît dépendre des nerfs dont il est pourvû; ce mouvement s'exerce sur le sang qu'il reçoit d'une part, et qu'il reverse de l'autre. Le coeur a deux cavités que le sang doit parcourir successivement, mais le sang ne sauroit passer de l'une à l'autre sans traverser les poumons, et il ne sauroit les traverser si leurs vésicules ne sont alternativement distendues et affaissées par un air élastique, entrant et ressortant tour-à-tour. Voilà ce qui constitue ce qu'on appelle proprement les fonctions vitales. Si quelqu'une de ces fonctions vient à cesser, par quelque cause que ce soit, la vie cesse aussitôt.

Or ces fonctions peuvent cesser par diverses causes, dont trois principales: soit parce que les organes qui y servent sont détruits, ou les fluides dissipés; soit parce que ces solides, ou ces fluides sont corrompus en tout ou en partie; soit enfin parce que ces solides, ou ces fluides, quoique sains et entiers, rencontrent des obstacles insurmontables à leur action.

Dans ce dernier cas, c'est-à-dire, lorsque les parties tant solides que fluides sont saines et entieres, mais qu'un obstacle au-dessus de leurs forces fait cesser en elles tout mouvement vital, la vie cesse, et on peut dire qu'elle est éteinte; mais peut-on dire que le corps soit encore mort, s'il reste quelque possibilité de lever l'obstacle fatal, et de redonner une impulsion à des organes bien disposés, et qui semblent n'attendre autre chose? N'en est-il pas de l'homme réduit en cet état comme d'une bougie nouvellement éteinte, dont la meche est encore rouge et fumante, et n'a besoin que d'un souffle pour se rallumer?

C'est une opinion que se répand assez généralement aujourd'hui, que beaucoup de noyés se trouvent dans ce cas-là, et en conséquence plusieurs grandes villes ont déjà pris de très-sages mesures pour les empêcher de mourir tout-à-fait, et on a réussi en divers endroits à en rappeller plusieurs à la vie.[1]

N'est-il pas bien-tôt tems de songer s'il seroit possible de porter des secours également efficaces aux personnes foudroyées? C'est mon avis; il faut tâcher de lui donner quelque vraisemblance. Pour y parvenir, il me paroît nécessaire de rechercher exactement la cause formelle de la mort de ceux que la foudre a frappés, cause qui n'est peut-être pas toujours constamment la même; et attendu l'importance de la matiere, j'espere que vous me permettrez toutes les digressions qui pourront tendre à y jetter quelques lumieres de reflet.

J'ai vû quelqu'un qui venoit de se couper la gorge, et j'ai dit sur le champ qu'il en mourroit, s'il n'étoit secouru; mais qu'il étoit aisé de le sauver, en supposant même une très-large ouverture à la trachée artere sur laquelle il avoit porté successivement trois divers instrumens pour en étendre l'incision. Mon jugement étoit fondé, d'une part sur ce qu'une ouverture à la trachée, plus grande que n'est celle de la glotte, rend impratiquable la respiration nécessaire à l'entretien de la vie; et d'autre part sur ce qu'une telle plaie étant très-curable et très-susceptible de cicatrice, on peut réduire par ce moyen à ses justes proportions le passage naturel de l'air pour entrer et ressortir de la poitrine et conséquemment rétablir la respiration, &c. C'est ce qui arriva effectivement.

J'ai vû crucifier quelques personnes, j'ai entendu crier au miracle de ce qu'une mort prompte ne s'en suivoit pas, et j'ai osé assurer devant des gens de qui l'imagination étoit fort échauffée sur cela, que je ne voyois aucune cause de mort dans cette opération, qui se réduisoit à percer d'outre en outre les mains et les pieds, et assez superficiellement l'un des côtés du ventre, parce que rien de tout cela n'est capable d'empêcher la continuation des fonctions vitales.

Il en est tout autrement des pendus; il semble même qu'il peut se réunir dans cette seule et même opération trois causes formelles de mort, et que c'est tantôt l'une, tantôt l'autre qui décide du sort de tel ou de tel sujet.

La cause la plus manifeste de l'extinction de la vie par rapport

---

1. See the concluding paragraphs of Dubourg's letter above, Feb. 12, and BF's reply below, under the end of April.

aux pendus, c'est la suffocation résultante de la compression de la trachée trop serrée par la corde pour permettre le passage de l'air; mais les parties organiques peuvent bien n'être pas détruites par-là, et les liquides encore moins altérés; d'où il est arrivé que plusieurs ont été rappellés à la vie. Une seconde cause, peut-être plus funeste, a lieu principalement à l'égard des sujets fort sanguins; c'est l'engorgement, ou la rupture des vaisseaux de l'intérieur de la tête, attendu que les veines qui doivent en rapporter le sang sont plus exposées à la compression de la corde, que les arteres qui y portent ce sang et qui sont situées beaucoup plus profondement. Enfin une troisieme cause plus prompte et plus funeste encore que l'étranglement, c'est la compression des nerfs de la moëlle épiniere par une luxation des vertebres du col, qu'on peut regarder comme le coup de maître des plus habiles bourreaux, et qui est suivie de la mort la plus soudaine.

Quant aux personnes tuées par la foudre, il ne me paroît pas possible de prononcer généralement sur la cause subite de leur mort, si c'est suffocation, brûlure, déchirement de fibres, paralysie de nerfs, corruption de liqueurs, &c. mais je pense qu'une suite de bonnes observations et d'expériences bien dirigées pourroient, en assez peu de tems, mettre la chose entiérement hors de doute, puisque l'identité de la foudre et de l'électricité est (graces à Vous) parfaitement démontrée.

On a de tems en tems occasion de charger du feu du ciel une, ou plusieurs bouteilles de Leyde; on est toujours à même d'en charger tant que l'on veut du feu électrique. On peut non seulement décharger tout-à-coup ces bouteilles sur tel animal que l'on voudra, mais même sur telle partie de l'animal, et dans telle direction qu'on jugera à propos; sur la tête, sur la colonne vertébrale, sur les poumons, sur le coeur, &c. ou sur plusieurs de ces parties à la fois; d'où il est à présumer que s'ensuivroient différens genres de morts plus ou moins promptes; et qu'il y auroit en plusieurs de ces cas un intervalle plus ou moins long entre l'extinction de la vie et la destruction des organes, qui fait la mort complette.

De-là s'ensuivroit une indication presqu'assurée des moyens les plus appropriés pour rappeller ces animaux à la vie dans chacune de ces circonstances. De-là enfin un juste motif d'employer en suite ces mêmes moyens avec quelqu'espérance de succès à l'égard des infortunés qui seroient frappés de la foudre.

Monsieur Tasker vous régala d'une petite trombe dans le Mariland, il y a 18 ans.[2] Que je serois flatté si je pouvois cette année vous régaler ici de quelque petite résurrection, ne fût-ce que d'un poulet, ou d'un dindon !

Je vous avouerai cependant que je serois plus flatté encore si je pouvois faire concevoir à tant de personnes qui sont si vivement affectées de la frayeur du tonnerre que, dans le cas même où ils auroient le malheur assez rare d'être frappés de la foudre, leur sort ne seroit pas encore tout-à-fait désespéré.

J'ajouterai enfin que si on se permettoit, comme il a été souvent proposé, de faire de tems en tems de grandes expériences de médecine sur des criminels, en réparation des maux qu'ils ont faits à l'humanité, ce seroit la moins cruelle de toutes les expériences qu'il soit possible de tenter sur ce principe, puisqu'il n'est point de mort plus douce que celle-là, comme vous l'avez très bien remarqué;[3] et qu'on ne les y condamneroit qu'avec un certain degré d'espérance de les rendre bientôt à la vie. J'ai l'honneur d'être, &c.

From William Henly   ALS: American Philosophical Society

This letter poses a remarkable problem of dating, and we cannot solve it. Henly's date is all too clear, and could not have been a slip: April 18 was a Sunday in 1773. Yet he makes a number of references that seem inapplicable to that year, and are definitely applicable to 1774. They were all related to the continuing controversy with Benjamin Wilson over lightning rods. Franklin had withdrawn from the fray in late 1772, and Henly had taken his place as chief protagonist.[4] Developments thereafter are the background of the dating problem.

2. In 1755 BF had chased a small whirlwind that his host, Col. Tasker, claimed to have ordered as a treat for him. Above, VI, 167–8. BF subsequently decided that his description of the episode had been obscurely worded: to Dubourg below, June 29.

3. Above, V, 525, where BF merely endorsed a comment made by his correspondent that electrocution would be the easiest of deaths.

4. In February, 1773, BF, Priestley, Price, Walsh, and others, perhaps in recognition of Henly's new role, nominated him for the Royal Society; and he was elected on May 20. Above, VIII, 359; Royal Society archives.

In March, 1773, Wilson published his *Observations upon Lightning*, which was an outgrowth of the arguments the year before about pointed versus blunt rods.[5] He subsequently developed his idea that the quantity of charge in a cloud could not be known, and might well be greater than any rods could conduct in safety to the ground. To test this possibility he suggested constructing a giant metal ring, sharpened on the upper edge, and placing it horizontally on top of St. Paul's, to see whether it would not draw more electricity from a thunderhead than any one dreamed the cloud could hold. He challenged whoever was skeptical—meaning Franklin—to try the experiment on a smaller scale: "I would ask the philosopher, whether he would chuse to put a crown of this kind upon his own head, and venture to walk or ride with it on, over Salisbury-plain, in the midst of a very violent thunderstorm; notwithstanding there should drag behind him a communication of metal from the crown itself to the earth, during the whole of his journey." Wilson, as far as we know, first publicized his idea and made this jibe at Franklin, without naming him, in a paper that he says he read before the Royal Society on February 24, 1774, and that he published unaltered as a pamphlet the following May.[6] On May 5 Henly responded, again before the Royal Society, to the wild idea of the ring by pointing out that a similar one existed, and had for more than a century without incident, on top of the Monument to the Great Fire.[7] When he subsequently obtained and read Wilson's pamphlet, he contented himself with scathing marginalia; the public controversy ended there.

This background suggests why the present letter is puzzling. In it Henly speaks of a paper read before the Royal Society the previous evening, April 17 (when the Society's records do not show any meeting), and virtually says that the paper was Wilson's and contained the jibe at Franklin. Wilson himself refers only to the later paper of

5. See above, XIX, 260–2, 424–9, and the note on BF's marginalia in Wilson's pamphlet, after March 21, 1773.

6. The Royal Society has no record of the February paper. Wilson mentioned it by date, and made his jibe at BF, in *Further Observations upon Lightning* . . . (London, 1774), pp. iii, 15.

7. "An Account of Some New Experiments in Electricity . . . ," *Phil. Trans.*, LXIV (1774), 413–14. The Monument, designed by Christopher Wren and built in 1671–77, is crowned by an urn of metal flames surrounded by an iron framework or ring; in the interior of the building is a spiral staircase. Henry B. Wheatley, *London Past and Present* . . . (3 vols., London, 1891), II, 557–9. The stair rail is of iron and connected with the ring, Henly makes clear, and would serve as a conductor.

February, 1774, which became his second pamphlet. Among Henly's marginalia in that pamphlet is one, on the taunt to Franklin, that is similar to what he says here.[8] The letter, in short, could not have been written when it was: it refers to Wilson's argument before the Royal Society and contains some of Henly's response; yet the paper was not presented until more than ten months later, according to its author, and Henly's response, in his paper and his marginalia, was later still. We have two alternative explanations, both implausible. One is that the final phase of the controversy that became public in the spring of 1774 was in rehearsal a year earlier. The other is that Henly dated his letter in the grip of some aberration.

Dear Sir   Sunday Evening Apl 18. 1773
    I am much pleased that I went to the Society last [night?] I am now sensible what the crown is, which Mr. [Wilson?] informed me he had prepared for you. As you [are to?] wear it on horseback on Salisbury plain, and a [chain?] is to hang dangling from behind; when you next experiment permit me to request the honour of [being] *your trainbearer.* I think it will add a little [to the] state with which you'l take your ride. B[ut for?] the greater pomp I could wish to recommend a person to precede you on foot, equip'd as follows. He should have *a cap of metal,* furnished with a pair of ears *of a very considerable length* standing upright, and terminated by large round balls; which besides making a handsome appearance upon the cap, would (as I learn from a *curious* paper read last night,) make so great a resistance to a stroke of lightning, as effectually to preserve the head (suppose Mr. W—s) within it from harm. On second thoughts I believe it will be scarce worth our while to take this trouble, for I recollect a building called the monument whose head is adorned with much such a kind of hoop as my friend W— has proposed, and the hoop is surrounded by 1000 points to represent flames of fire. The Iron twist rail (which is carried to the bottom,) may very well serve to represent your dangling chain: but this building which hath stood very near a century, happens never to have been struck by lightning at all; I think therefore we may as well content [us;] were I to

8. "Quere, would not a cap of metal, with *a pair of long ears,* suit some electricians as well?" The comment is on p. 15 of Henly's copy of *Further Observations,* Yale University Library.

conclude by inference from the experiments [I] have already made; it would be thus. Supposing such a force used as would strike the Knob *in contact with the coatings* at $4\frac{1}{2}$ Inches from the insulated body. In that case I suspect that the point could not be struck at more than 2 Inches, for I cannot help thinking that the point lessens the force of explosion as the distance increases to *a certain quantity,*[9] and after that hath no more influence than Knobs.[1] I should imagine this experiment (which I own *to me,* seems demonstration,) must convince every one who repeats it (except those who are determined not to be convinced,) of the preference due to *pointed* Conductors, rather than those terminated by a Knob.

I beg your indulgence in the liberty I now take, and that you would believe me to be with real regard Dear Sir your obliged and obedient Servant   W HENLY

Addressed: To / Dr. Franklin / Craven-street / Strand

From Jean-Baptiste LeRoy   AL: American Philosophical Society

De Paris ce 19 Avril 1773

Vous vous plaigniez de moi Monsieur et cher confrere comme je me plaignois de vous.[2] Nos lettres se sont croisées car Jespere bien que vous avez reçu un Exemplaire de mon memoire sur les barres métalliques &c. que je vous ai envoyé dans le mois de mars.[3] Cependant par vos plaintes obligeantes sur mon silence je crains fort que vous n'ayez pas reçu une lettre que je vous écrivis au commencement de l'année. Quoiqu'il en soit je vous prie bien de

9. [*Henly's note:*] length, or distance.

1. [*Henly's note:*] With respect to Inviting or Attracting the Electricity, and this distance I believe is not v[ery gre]at.

2. He is replying to BF's letter above, March 30, where much of what follows is explained.

3. He enclosed, we assume, an early form of the paper that he read seven months later before the Academy: "Mémoire sur la forme des barres ou des conducteurs métalliques, destinés a préserver des édifices des effets de la foudre, en transmettant son feu à la terre," Académie des sciences, *Mémoires,* LXXV (1773), 671–86.

croire que lorsqu'il se passe du temps sans que je vous écrive c'est que des affaires indispensables me privent d'une occupation qui m'est si agreable.

Je vous suis doublement obligé et des bonnes esperances que vous me donnez pour l'élection prochaine du mois de may et de la nouvelle flatteuse que vous m'avez appris que la Société Philosophique d'amérique m'a choisi pour un de ses membres. Non seulement j'accepte avec grand plaisir cet honneur mais je me trouve très glorieux d'être d'une société qui a si bien debuté et qui donne de si grandes esperances elles sont dignes de son Président. Je vous prie de lui en écrire dans ces termes en attendant, que je lui en écrive moi même, car je compte bien lui écrire une lettre de remerciment que je vous prierai de faire passer les Mers.

Vous me faites plaisir de m'apprendre que vous faites une nouvelle édition de votre Ouvrage et je vous assurre que ce sera aujourdhui un présent très agréable. Je dis aujourdhui car on commence à y reconnoître toutes les Inepties et les pauvrités que l'abbé Nolet y a débitées sur l'Electricité. Un homme comme lui retarde comme je le fais entendre dans le mémoire que je vous ai envoyé le progrès d'une Science des demi siécles. Les trois quarts des gens dans ce pays cy en sont presqu'encore à l'abc sur l'Electricité ce qui m'a obligé comme je vous l'ai marqué a reprendre les choses de si haut dans mon mémoire. Je croyois que notre sécrétaire vous avoit remercié des mémoires de l'Académie de Philadelphie mais puisqu'il ne l'a pas fait je vous en remercie au nom de notre Académie car nous les avons reçus dans le temps.

Il me paroît que M. Banks se conduit on ne peut pas mieux pour tirer le plus grand parti possible du voyage au Pole que vous projettez. Son voyage en Hollande à ce sujet m'a fait grand plaisir.[4] Vous nous donnez souvent des leçons nous autres qui faisons tout à la hâte et en courant. Notre malheureuse vivacité gâte la plupart de nos entreprises et de nos recherches. On

4. Joseph Banks's trip to Iceland (above, XIX, 75 n) had ended the previous November. He was now gathering information for the polar expedition, mentioned in BF's letter to LeRoy of March 30, of his old friend Capt. Phipps, and had recently returned from a visit to Rotterdam to inquire about Dutch experience in the northern seas. Edward Smith, *The Life of Sir Joseph Banks* . . . (London, 1911), pp. 10–11, 32–4, 36.

pourroit presque toujours nous dire ce que disoit Bacon allons un peu plus doucement nous aurons plutot fini.[5]

Vous savez sans doute que mon frère ainé a remporté le prix de l'Académie sur les longitudes. Il paroit par le rapport qu'en ont fait les commissaires (MM. Pingré et Borda) que sa montre a donné la longitude a un quart de dégré près en six semaines justesse double de celle qu'exige l'acte du P[arlemen]t d'angleterre pour les 90000 livres. Et il y a toute apparence qu'elle auroit donné dans toute la campagne des preuves non équivoques d'une justesse semblable si par un malheur bien facheux pour mon frère il n'etoit tombé dessus des caissons qui lui ont fait éprouver un si rude choc que sa justesse en a eté sensiblement altérée pendant long-temps. Il faut que vous sachiez que tel a été ce choc qu'une autre montre de mon frère qui etoit aussi du voyage en a eu son Thermometre cassé de façon qu'il a fallu renoncer à l'observer le reste de la campagne. Notez que cet accident est arrivé au mois de mars c'est à dire presque à la moitié du Voyage[6] mais je ne sais si je ne vous avois pas deja entretenu de tout cela. Je vous envoye un programme de L'Académie comme à un confrère ou vous verrez le nouveau sujet que L'Académie propose pour prix de l'année 1775.[7]

Depuis que j'ai reçu votre lettre j'ai eu l'ecrit de M. Wilson mais malgré toutes ses raisons je suis toujours de meme sentiment et je pense que les verges ou barres doivent être en pointes cependant pas assez pour que la pointe soit facilement fonduë ou emportée par le feu de l'eclair parceque elle deviendroit par là peu propre à transmettre la matière fulminante dans un autre coup de tonnerre. Vous avez vu mon mémoire vous avez vu que j'étois un peu flottant. Mais vos raisons et les réflexions que j'ai faites depuis sur

5. "Sir Amice Pawlet, when he saw too much haste made in any matter, was wont to say, 'Stay a while, that we may make an end the sooner.'" Sir Francis Bacon, *Apothegms*, no. 76.

6. For Pierre LeRoy's chronometer, and the prize offered by Parliament in 1714, see above, XVII, 126 n. The prominent astronomers, Alexandre-Gui Pingré (1711–96) and Jean-Charles Borda (1733–99), sailed in 1771 on a voyage to test this and other chronometers.

7. The question proposed for the prize was how best to make and suspend magnetized needles and to explain their regular diurnal variations. "Ouvrages présentés à l'Académie," Académie des sciences, *Mémoires*, LXXV (1773), 77 of first pagination.

cette matiere importante m'ont convaincu qu'il falloit que les verges fussent pointuës au moins à un certain dégré parce que l'essentiel est ici que la pointe que vous elevez attire de preference à toutes les autres parties du bâtiment la matière fulminante ou au moins qu'elle lui presente une entrée facile. Or si cette pointe ou barre est courte et mousse par le bout ce sera presqu'un hazard ayant aussi peu d'avantage sur les parties circonvoisines si la matière fulminante s'y jette d'ou il suit qu'elle sera inutile &c. Il y a plus. Cette espece de choc qui constituë l'étincelle paroît tenir à ce qu'il y a une grande quantité de matière électrique qui passe ou qui est déchargée dans un Instant car voici une experience constante. Si vous voulez décharger un carreau vous pourrez le faire avec toute sureté sans craindre de choc ou de secousse violente en communiquant par une main avec une de ses super-ficies et en approchant de l'autre superficie avec l'autre main une aiguille longue très fine et très aiguë car alors vous ne sentirez le choc que très foiblement à moins que le carreau ne fut excessive-ment chargé. C'est une expérience que j'ai fait et que j'ai fait faire à d'autres cent fois. J'ose avancer de plus mais c'est ce que je n'ai pas fait que la fonte de l'or n'a [?] pas lieu si le morceau [de fer] ou la boule de cuivre par lequel se fait [?] le choc de l'Exp[érience] de Leyde et toutes les experiences que l'on fait avec ce choc n'auroient pu tiré [?] l'étincelle si trouvoit une[8] pointe très longue très deliée et très pointue. Les consequences de ces faits sont bien faciles à tirer pour les bâtimens garni de barres métalliques pré-servatives, pour éviter autant qu'il est possible que l'electricité soit dissipée par une etincelle ou un éclair au lieu de l'etre peu a peu et en silence.

J'ai tant rempli les 4 pages de ma lettre que je suis obligé de mettre ici que vous trouverez dans ce paquet la planche et les fig. du ms. que je vous ai envoyé où vous verrez comment je propose qu'on arrange les barres et même comment je suppose qu'il faut en mettre aux facades des batimens lorsqu'ils sont fort eleves.

8. Of the three preceding words only "trouvoit" is clear, and we can make no sense of it. LeRoy's hand is as difficult as his syntax is in this passage, our reading of which is highly conjectural. He means, we believe, that the gold is not melted unless the iron or copper that carries the charge is sharply pointed to draw the spark.

From Thomas Cushing

ALS: Library of Congress

Sir   Boston April 20. 1773

I wrote you in my last[9] that the Gentlemen, to whom I had communicated the papers you Sent me under Cover of your's of the 2d December last, were of opinion that they ought to be retained on this side the water to be hereafter improved as the Exigency of our affairs may require or at least that authenticated Copies ought to be taken before they are returned: I shall have, I find, a very difficult task properly to Conduct this matter unless you obtain leave for their being retained or Copied, I shall wait your directions upon this head and hope they will be such as will be agreable to all the Gentlemen who unanimously are of opinion that it can by no means answer any valuable purpose to send them here for the Inspection of a few persons barely to satisfy their Curiosity. I embrace this opportunity to transmit you a Pamphlet containing the Governor's Speaches and the answers of both Houses to the same upon the Supream authority of Parliament.[1] The Controversy has been carried on with great good temper and Calmness and on the part of the House with great reluctance. They were forced into the dispute and could not avoid it without tacitly conceding to sentiments and opinions that they held to be Erroneous and false; If this is a subject that Administration would have wished had not been Stirred at this juncture, I think, upon a reveiw of it, they must clear the House of any Blame respecting this Matter: however If it should be resented on your side the water and any high Measures should be taken with respect to this province, it ought well to be considered that this is a question that *nearly* and *Equally* affects all the Colonies and what is done by way of punishment to any particular Colony will be consider'd as if done to all and Consequently will be resented by all. It will throw us togather and as firmly unite us in measures to obtain redress as any one thing I can well conceive of. The House of Burgesses of the Government of Virginia, as you will find by the Inclosed paper, have upon this

9. Of March 24, above, acknowledging receipt of the Hutchinson correspondence; BF replied to that letter on June 2 and to this one on July 7.

1. For a résumé of the debate see above, BF to Cushing of March 9, n. 3, and Cooper to BF of March 15, n. 9; the latter cites the pamphlet.

occasion passed a Number of Resolves appointing a Standing Committee of Correspondence and Enquiry to Correspond and Communicate with their Sister Colonies in America respecting the Acts and resolutions of the British Parliament and have directed their Speaker to transmitt their resolutions to the Speakers of the different assemblys thro' the Continent and request them to appoint simular Committees.[2] There is no doubt the Most of the Colonies, if not all, will come into the like resolutions and some imagine, if the Colonies are not soon releived, a Congress will grow out of this Measure and perhaps render a settlement of this unhappy dispute still more difficult.[3] This Question, That the Governor has lately started and been so open and Explicit upon has arrested the attention of the whole Continent, we are continually receiving Letters from principal Gentlemen in the other Governments highly approbating the Answers of both Houses so that we have the happiness to find we are not singular in our Sentiments upon this Important Subject: I have lately seen the Governor and in the course of conversation told him that I apprehended the Instruction he had received relative to the Commissioners if not speedily withdrawn would occasion much Uneasiness and greatly Embarrass the Affairs of Government, that I beleived if he would Inform administration of the difficulties it would occasion, it was probable different Instructions might easily be obtained: he replyed that the difficulty with regard to this Instruction as also with respect to another by which he was

2. Agitation over the *Gaspee* inquiry (above, XIX, 379 n) provoked the Virginia resolves, which may be found in John P. Kennedy, ed., *Journals of the House of Burgesses of Virginia, 1773–1776* (Richmond, 1905), p. 28. The resolves, in turn, stimulated the Massachusetts House to form its own committee of correspondence in May. By the end of the year a network of such committees—in localities, mercantile groups, and legislatures—was developing throughout the colonies. Edward D. Collins, "Committees of Correspondence of the American Revolution," Amer. Hist. Assn., *Annual Report* . . . (for 1901; 2 vols., Washington, 1902), I, 245–71; Richard D. Brown, *Revolutionary Politics in Massachusetts* . . . (Cambridge, Mass., 1970), pp. 140–3, 150, 155, 165–6; Richard A. Ryerson, "Political Mobilization and the American Revolution: the Resistance Movement in Philadelphia, 1765 to 1776," 3 *W&MQ*, XXXI (1974), 565–88.

3. For BF's reception of this idea see his letters to Cushing and the House below, July 7.

directed not to Consent to the pay of any Agent not appointed by the whole Court[4] might be easily removed, for if he should receive a line from Lord Dartmouth intimating that in case he should sign a Tax Act wherein the Commissioners were not Exempted from Taxation as also consent to the pay of the Agent, it would not be disagreable to Administration and that he should not thereby come under any blame; he would, (notwithstanding his Instructions were Signed by the King and were very Peremptory and Explicit,) sign such an Act and Consent to the pay of such Agents immediately.[5] I mention this for your Government and that you may make such use of it as you may judge best, at the same time I desire my Name may not be mentioned relative to this or any other matter I have now wrote you upon. Before I conclude I would refer it to your Consideration whether, when you write me upon any affairs which it may be necessary to Communicate to the House, it would not be best to direct to me as Speaker and in my public Character and when you write in Confidence and what is to be Communicated only to a few in such Case to write to me in my private Character. I mention this at this time because in yours of the 2d December last, there were matters mentioned (particularly with regard the House's Petition to the King relative to the Governors Independency) which you desired fresh Instructions upon and which therefore must necessaryly be Com-

4. For the issues of taxing the customs commissioners and of BF's salary see above, XVIII, 177–80 and 242 n. The Speaker's interview with the Governor was the day before. Mass. Arch., XXVII, 480. Hutchinson, like Cushing, deplored the situation; the tax bills would soon expire, he wrote Dartmouth six days later, and his instructions debarred him from assenting to a new one. *Ibid.*, p. 485.

5. Hutchinson, if we read him aright, was merely saying that his instructions might be amended by a letter from the Secretary of State. But in the matter of the commissioners he may have had at the back of his mind another way of escape, which he had put forward in 1771. Let Whitehall permit him to pass the tax bill for a year in the usual form, he had suggested then, and see what happened: if the commissioners were not taxed, the dispute would evaporate; if they were, by virtue of the clause that made the trouble in 1769, his instructions might then be enforced. "State of the Proceedings Respecting the Commissioners of the Customs' Complaint of Being Taxed by the Boston Assessors," Dartmouth Papers, William Salt Library, Stafford. We are inclined to think that his suggestion was eventually adopted; see the note on BF's reply to this passage below, July 7.

municated to them. And in the same Letter there were Inclosed a Number of papers and your Observations upon the writers of them which I presume you by no means Intended I should communicate to the House as you laid me under the Strictest Injunctions to Communicate them only to a few. I remain with great respect Your most humble Servant   THOMAS CUSHING

Benjamin Franklin Esqr

From Jonathan Williams, Jr.

ALS: American Philosophical Society

Dear and Honored Sir   Boston April 20. 1773
I have wrote you several Letters, but have not as yet been honor'd with an answer, which I impute to the want of Time, occasioned by your more important Engagements: tho' should have been glad if you had mentioned your opinion of my conduct with regard to Henry, as I wish to see the Boy settled; his Master still likes him and he behaves very well.[6] I had the pleasure of seeing your good Lady, Mr. and Mrs. Bache with young Benjamin, about 6 weeks since, all of whom I left in good Health, I likewise called on the Governor and his Lady at Burlington who were also very well. I was happy to find on my return that my absence was no Injury to my Business, and by going I have settled a long Account for my Father, who finds the Phila. Trade in such a declining State, that he is about entering into the Commission Way, as at this Time of Life he is afraid of hazarding what he has acquired in the World, by any precarious Business, and his having a real Estate in the Town will make it safe for any person to trust their property in his hands:[7] and I flatter myself,

6. For Henry Walker's apprenticeship see above, XIX, 337, and his mother to BF below, June 20. BF's letter to Jonathan's father of March 9, above, had clearly not arrived yet.

7. For Jonathan's trip to Philadelphia see above, XIX, 440–1. A retailer operating "in the Commission Way," in the narrow sense, was selling on consignment from the supplier, who retained title to the goods until they were sold and assumed the entire risk. The phrase in a broad sense meant that the retailer acted, in return for a commission, as the supplier's agent in selling his goods, buying a return cargo, etc., and ran the risk of bad debts if

his Integrity and Capacity in Business, is undoubted by all who know him. If it should be in your power to recommend it among your Friends, in the mercantile way, to send Business to him it will greatly add to the Obligations we are already under; if It should answer in the course of some Time, he proposes to join me in a House with him, tho' shall keep up my Cloth Trade as well as ever, as this kind of Business will not interfere with it, and I wish to employ every moment of my Time for these purposes, as my Ambition leads me to hope for advancement in this Way, tho' do not intend my desire of increasing, should get the Better of my Caution in Transacting it.

In the papers I see that the East India Company are to be allow'd to send two Ships directly from India to America, and perhaps to this port. If so I shall be much obliged if you would recommend their Business, (as farr as is in your power) to My Father and Self. This may seem an aspiring request, but many things have been lost by being previously supposed unattainable, and I have reason to believe the Company does sometimes consign Goods to America for Sale. I hope you will not blame me, for mentioning it, as I rest it intirely on your Judgment, and if you should not think it proper, it will be sufficient to convince me we ought not to have it. I have taken the liberty to write to Mrs. Barwell, which I inclose unseal'd for your perusal, if you think it adviseable, please to deliver it, if not, please to destroy it.[8] Please

he was not promptly reimbursed for his purchases. Williams' fear of "any precarious Business" may suggest that he intended to sell on commission in the narrow sense.

8. For Mary Barwell and her connection with the East India Company see above, XVII, 194 n. Boston papers had recently reported the government's negotiations with the Company, as described in the London press through Feb. 20. Lord North had suggested not only a reduction in the Townshend duty but also that "the Company will be permitted to send Annually two Ships directly from China to America, laden with Teas, clear of all Duties." *Mass. Gaz.; and the Boston Weekly News-Letter*, April 16, 1773. The second suggestion accounts for the "aspiring request" to be consignees, which BF passed on to Miss Barwell; but nothing came of the idea. See below, BF to Williams, June 4, and to Jonathan, July 7. The Williamses' proposal, given the economic conditions at the time, is understandable. Colonial merchants had a hunger for sterling, which was in desperately short supply; a new source, such as the Company's tea, would assure solvency at a time when credit was hard to come by.

to make my best Respects to Mrs. Stevenson Mr. and Mrs.
Hewson and Mrs. Blunt with Compliments to all enquiring
Friends. I am with the greatest Respect Your dutifull and
Affectionate Kinsman   JONA WILLIAMS JUNR

Addressed: Doctr Franklin

From John Mervin Nooth⁹

Extract: printed in the Royal Society, *Philosophical Transactions* . . . ,
LXIII (1773), part 1, 333–9.

9. Doctor Nooth (1737–1828) was a Bond St. physician and scientist, who
subsequently rose high in the medical service of the army. Little is known
about his early life, except that he received his M.D. from Edinburgh in 1766
with a dissertation on rickets: *Tentamen . . . de rachitide . . .* (Edinburgh,
1766). A number of his acquaintances, BF among them, nominated him for
the Royal Society on Nov. 23, 1773, on the ground that he had "cultivated
several branches of natural knowledge with great diligence, and with equal
success," and cited in evidence the paper of which this is an extract; he was
elected the following spring. (Royal Society archives; see also above, VIII,
359.) What natural knowledge, aside from electrical, he had cultivated by
1773 is not clear; but he soon branched into chemistry and published a
method of carbonizing water that long remained in vogue: "The Description
of an Apparatus for Impregnating Water with Fixed Air . . . ," *Phil. Trans.,*
LXV (1775), part 1, 59–66. Priestley believed that Nooth's account of earlier
work belittled his own, and replied at some length in his *Experiments and
Observations on Different Kinds of Air* (2nd ed.; 3 vols., London, 1775–1786),
II, 269–76.

In the autumn of 1775 Nooth was commissioned as purveyor and physician
extraordinary in the British army in America, and two years later was in Rhode
Island. In 1779 he became superintendant general of all British military
hospitals in America; by then he was stationed in New York. After the war
he was in Canada, in charge of the hospitals in the province of Quebec. In
1799 he was appointed superintendant general of all hospitals maintained by
the army, a post that put him at the top of its medical hierarchy; but his
position seems to have been more honorary than onerous, for he is said to
have remained in Quebec. In 1807, back in England, he married and retired,
but retained his rank until his death. He left no issue. These scraps of information about his career come from the following sources: *Miscellanea
genealogica et heraldica,* new ser., II (1877), 9; Sir Robert Drew, *Commissioned
Officers in the Medical Services of the British Army, 1660–1960* (2 vols.,
London, 1968), I, xxxix, xli, 47; Maude E. Abbott, *History of Medicine in the
Province of Quebec* (Montreal, 1931), p. 43; *A List of the General and Staff
Officers . . . Serving in North-America . . .* (New York, 1777), p. 5; *A List of
the Officers of the Army . . .* (London, 1828), p. 388. Our search for bio-

[Before April 22, 1773[10]]

It must undoubtedly appear extraordinary, that, in the present age, when the study of electricity is become so general, and the advances that have been made in the science are so very considerable, I should attempt to recall your attention to the structure of the electrical machine. But I believe it must be allowed, that, notwithstanding the remarkable progress that has of late been made in electrical pursuits, the machine still remained the most imperfect part of the apparatus. The construction of it has been in general left to the workman, who has seldom been in a capacity of making those improvements in it, which it certainly admits of.

The subject, however, seems well worth the attention of the electricians themselves; as a knowledge of the means of correcting the capricious state of their machines will enable them to pursue their electrical inquiries with more certainty, success, and satisfaction.

A prospect of discovering the cause of the common uncertainty in the action of electrical machines, induced me, some months since, to make some observations on the appearance, produced by a machine in motion. Being well convinced, that the electric fire, which we receive from a machine, is derived from the cushion, and from such parts as communicate with it, I first attended to the effects which the glass and rubber had on each other.

My inquiries, however, were not directed towards an investigation of the cause of that accumulation of electric matter, in consequence of the friction of the glass on the rubber, as I looked on that circumstance as a secret in nature, no less impenetrable than gravitation itself; but I endeavoured to find out the best method of increasing the excitation of a glass, and of taking from it that fire for electrical purposes which might be collected on its surface.

It is evident, that the electric matter is excited in the instant that

---

graphical data was complicated by the existence of another John Mervin Nooth, also an army officer, who was a lieutenant by 1798 and died, a lieutenant colonel and C.B., in 1821. He does not appear in the geneaology of the Doctor's family.

10. The date when the Royal Society received the letter. For a contemporary opinion of it see the *Monthly Rev.*, LI (1774), 223–4.

the glass passes over the rubber, and that it becomes sensible to us by its adhering to the revolving surface of the glass. It likewise appeared to me highly probable, that the quantity of fire, which we find on the glass in motion, is not the whole of that which is excited by the passage of the glass on the rubber. The luminous appearance in the angles between the glass and rubber, and which is extremely distinct in a dark room, rendered it next to certain, that a part of the excited electric fluid returns immediately to the cushion without performing a revolution with the glass; and that, of course, a circulation of the fire is thus kept up in the substance of the cushion in the common method of constructing the machines.

To be certainly convinced of this, I attempted to make the passage of the fire from the glass to the anterior part of the cushion, or to that part which corresponds with the ascending side of the cylinder, demonstrable, by placing a piece of silk between the glass and cushion. This silk was larger than the cushion; and part of it was allowed to adhere, by the attraction of the electric fire, to the ascending part of the cylinder. My view in doing this was to cut off, in that part, the immediate communication between the excited glass and cushion, and by that means render the circulation of electric matter visible, which I suspected to take place in the machine; as it was thus forced to turn over the loose edge of the silk before it could return to the cushion. The event answered my expectation; and I then perceived, that the greatest part of the excited fluid was commonly re-absorbed by the forepart of the cushion without becoming sensible on the superior part of the glass.

Having thus verified my supposition by actual experiments with silken flaps of different sizes, I endeavoured to discover a method of preventing that circulation of the electric fluid, and, if possible, of obliging the whole, or the greater part of it, that is once excited, to make the revolution with the glass. This, indeed, the silk, when of considerable breadth, in some measure effected; but I thought that this obstruction to the immediate return of the fire might be rendered more complete by increasing the thickness of the silk, or by applying to it some nonconducting substance, that might confine the excited fluid more perfectly to the surface of the revolving cylinder.

Bees-wax being a nonconducting substance easily procured, I rubbed the silken flap with it, and found, as I expected, that the return of the fire to the cushion at the anterior part of the machine was by that means much diminished, and consequently the excitation of the glass was apparently increased. The addition, however, of more silk was still more effectual in confining the fire to the glass; and when it was employed ten or twelve times doubled, it seemed to deny any passage from the glass to the cushion.

As I thus discovered the method of remedying the common defect in the construction of the anterior part of the cushion, I next attended to that part which corresponds with the descending side of the cylinder. Being convinced that this part of the rubber was alone concerned in the excitation, I imagined that the reverse of what was necessary anteriorly should be adopted in the structure of the posterior part; that, instead of placing nonconducting substances between the glass and cushion, we should here make the afflux of the electric matter as great as possible, by the application of the most perfectly conducting bodies. Confining therefore the amalgam to that place where the glass first comes in contact with the rubber, I placed some tinfoil close to the amalgam and, bending it back, secured it to the metallic plate below the cushion. By this means the electric matter found an easy access to the place of excitation; and the effect of the machine was thereby incredibly increased. A piece of leather, covered with amalgam, and fixed to the posterior part of the rubber, in such a manner as to allow about an inch of it to pass under the cylinder, answered every purpose of the tinfoil; and, as it was not liable to be corroded by the mercury, like tinfoil, it was on that account much preferable.

From the above experiments it was apparent that the excitation was altogether performed by the posterior portion of the cushion; and that the anterior part, when made of conducting substances, re-absorbs the greater quantity of the excited matter. In the structure therefore of electrical machines, we should always have a free electric communication behind, to facilitate the excitation; and the most perfectly nonconducting substances before, to prevent the re-absorption. To answer these intentions, it will perhaps be adviseable to make the cushion of silk, stuffed with hair, and to lay some metallic conductor round the posterior part, that a free access might be allowed to the electric matter coming to the place of excitation from the inferior part of the machine. Cushions, made in this manner, and then covered with silk ten or twelve times doubled, are much more powerfully excitant than any others that I have yet tried. Various other methods, however, may be pursued in the construction of the rubber; but it should be an invariable rule, to place nonconducting bodies before, and conducting substances behind, the cylinder. From the preceding principles, it follows, that the support to the rubber should likewise have its conducting and nonconducting side. For this purpose, it may be necessary to employ baked wood, and to cover the posterior half with tinfoil. The place of excitation will be thus sufficiently supplied with electric matter; and the cylinder will not be robbed of a part of the excited fire, before that fire has made a revolution with the glass.

By attending to the place where the excitation is effected, it must appear evident, that the amalgam is only to be laid on the posterior part of the cushion; its presence, indeed, would be useless, if not injurious, in any other situation. It will, however, be found somewhat difficult to confine the pure amalgam to the posterior part of the rubber; but if it is mixed with a little hairpowder and pomatum, it pretty perfectly keeps its place. The strewing the amalgam thus prepared on the glass, as it revolves, is perhaps the best method of applying it; as, by that means, it is in a great measure prevented from passing on to the nonconducting substances that are placed before. Should any of the amalgam be carried forward by the revolution of the glass, it should be carefully removed. The necessity of keeping that part free from conducting bodies cannot be too much insisted on; and, when fresh amalgam is applied as before mentioned to the proper part of the rubber, the flap should be held down during half a dozen turns of the machine, lest it might collect some of the amalgam before it is properly fixed. It is a probable conjecture, that, when the flap of silk is covered with amalgam, part of the amalgam, which is not immediately subservient to the excitation, acts as a conductor in restoring the fire again to the cushion; and that thus, by an improper disposition of it, we suppress, instead of increasing, the quantity of the excited matter.

In short, when an electrician attends to the preceding principles in the construction of his rubber, and to the proper disposition of the amalgam, he has nothing to fear from the humidity of the atmosphere, as his machine will work equally well in all kinds of weather. The rest of the electrical apparatus may be made according to the directions that have been given by the different electrical writers. Each has had his favourite machine; and, perhaps, no one has been yet contrived that has not had its peculiar advantages.

Received April 22, 1773. An Extract of a Letter from Dr. Nooth to Dr. Franklin, F.R.S. on some Improvements in the Electrical Machine.

From Thomas Cushing
ALS: Library of Congress

Sir   Boston April 22. 1773
  Inclosed you have a number of the Pamphlets Containing the Governors Speaches and the Answers of the two Houses with which you may Accomodate some few of your Freinds.[1] I conclude with great Respect your most humble Servant
THOMAS CUSHING

Benjamin Franklin Esqr

Addressed: To / Benjamin Franklin Esqr

From Jonathan Williams, Jr.
ALS: American Philosophical Society

⟨Boston, April 22, 1773: Sends a letter from Henry that came too late to be enclosed with his.[2]⟩

1. BF's own copy had been enclosed with Cushing's letter of two days before.
2. Jonathan's letter was that of two days before. For Henry Walker's letter to his mother see hers to BF below, June 20.

To Jacques Barbeu-Dubourg

Translated extract: printed in Jacques Barbeu-Dubourg, ed., *Œuvres de M. Franklin* ... (2 vols., Paris, 1773), II, 313.[3]

Londres, 23 Avril 1773.

Vous verrez par le papier ci-joint du Docteur Solander, que cette herbe (Poke-Weed) dans laquelle on a trouvé un remede spécifique du cancer, est précisément l'espece la plus commune de Phyto-lacca (*Phytolacca decandra. L.*).[4]

From James Hunter

ALS: American Philosophical Society

Honoured Sir   Philadelphia 24 [April, 1773]

I Received yours of the 10th of February, by which I was told to Draw upon you for eighty seven pounds ten shillings sterling, pursuant to which I have Drawn upon you, for the said sum of eighty seven pounds ten shillings sterling, and have disposed of the Bill unto James Hunter Merchant of our City[5] on his order, to be paid on thirty Days Sight according to your order, and when the said Bill is paid it is in full for the Legacy of fifty pounds with

3. An English retranslation may be found in Sparks, *Works*, V, 288 n.

4. The idea that pokeweed was efficacious against cancer was an old one; see above, BF to Dubourg, March 27, and Dubourg's query of April 11. To the extracts of BF's earlier letter and of this one Dubourg appended a note: "Le Cancer est peut-être de tous les maux qui affligent l'humanité celui qui mene le plus tristement au tombeau. On ne sauroit donc répandre trop prompte-ment, ni trop universellement l'importante découverte d'un remede efficace à une si cruelle maladie. Ainsi le Public auroit la plus grande obligation au Docteur Solander, s'il vouloit bien nous apprendre à quelle dose, et avec quelles precautions on doit administrer l'extrait de Phytolacca, soit intérieure-ment, soit extérieurement." If he received and read correctly the "papier ci-joint" (which we are unable to identify) he must have been right in assuming that Daniel Solander, the famous botanist, had lent the authority of his name to the remedy. But BF's sentence in itself could mean only that Solander had classified pokeweed.

5. For the context of this letter see the one from BF that Hunter is acknowl-edging. The latter's namesake was in all likelihood the merchant of Straw-berry Alley, whose British correspondents in this period appear briefly in *PMHB*, XXVIII (1904), 104–5. The two James Hunters may or may not have been related; we know next to nothing about either.

interest for fifteen years and of all Demands. Worthy Sir it is not in my power, in my low sphere of life, to make you any restitution for your very great Kindness to us, I can only with my Wife and Daughter exert our Gratitude, in wishing you all Happiness and Success in all your Laudable purposes and undertakings and with great Humility subscribe my self Sir your Very Humble thankful and obedient Servant   JAMES HUNTER

Addressed: To / Dr / Benjamin Franklin / In London / These per Capt All

From William Franklin   ALS: American Philosophical Society

Honoured Father,   Philadelphia April 30th. 1773
    I wrote to you by Capt. All who left Town the day before Yesterday, and this morning I received a few Lines from you dated Mar. 15. by a Passenger in Sutton.[6] I was surprized to find that it contained nothing about the Ohio Grant, as the Whartons are quite elated with the glad Tidings they have received by that Opportunity from Mr. S. Wharton. The Old Man (who has become excessively absurd) sent one of his Sons to me Yesterday to demand of me whether I would Sell my Share of the Lands on the Ohio, and to make me an offer for the Purchase of it. I did not know the young man, but told him at once upon his asking the Question that I would not. *So you won't part with it then?* No, I have not any Thoughts of it at present; but pray Sir, what may be your name? He said it was *Wharton*, and instantly turn'd about making me a Sort of a half Bow and went away. Had I known him at first; I fancy I should have given him a somewhat different Treatment, for I could not look upon his coming in that Manner, and on that Business, as any other than an intended Insult. As I had never given out that I had any Inclination to dispose of it, he might with as much Propriety have demanded whether I would Sell my Watch or my Coach and Horses. His Brother Joe has since told Mr. Bache that he was sorry his Father had acted such a Part, but that neither he, nor his Brother Tom,

6. On April 28 the *Pa. Gaz.* announced Isaac All's departure in the *Richard Penn,* and on May 5 James Sutton's arrival in the *Catherine.*

had any hand in it. It was intirely owing to the Old Man's humour who would not be persuaded to the Contrary.[7]

Mr. Clement Biddle[8] (I am told by Doctr. Evans) is just returned from Virginia, and he says he saw a Patent which Lord Dunmore had lately given a Man for 3,000 Acres on the Great Kanawa. He thinks it was dated in Decemr. last. Mr. Foxcroft is of Opinion that Col. Washington and the Provincials are getting the Lands they Claim under Governor Dinwiddie's Proclamation (Viz the 200,000 Acres) all patented as fast as they can, which I think is very probable; but is it not extraordinary that Lord Dunmore should Venture to grant Patents in that Country after what he told Lord Stirling, Unless he has since received a particular Power for that Purpose; and, if he has, is not that as extraordinary?[9]

7. Samuel Wharton's "glad Tidings," we assume, were that his plan for the new colony of Vandalia was winning acceptance. He had explained it to Lord Dartmouth in December and was presumably discussing it with the Board of Trade, which adopted it in substance on May 6. The Whartons, elated by his news, were buying as many shares as possible in the Walpole Co.; by the time of the Revolution they held thirteen of the seventy-two. Peter Marshall, "Lord Hillsborough, Samuel Wharton and the Ohio Grant, 1769–1775," *English Hist. Rev.*, LXXX (1965), 733–5; see also Falconer to BF below, May 13. This was the second Wharton offer that WF turned down; the first, in 1772, was for his share in the claim of the "suffering traders": WF to Thomas Wharton, April 27, 1772, Hist. Soc. of Pa. The present offer from the "Old Man" (Joseph, Sr., alias the Duke) came through an unidentifiable son; there were ten living at the time, of whom Thomas was the eldest, then Samuel and Joseph, Jr.: Anne H. Wharton, "The Wharton Family," *PMHB*, I (1877), 326–7. For a year and more the family had been on bad terms with WF, partly because Samuel was claiming sole credit for success and denigrating BF's role. Above, XIX, 59.

8. Clement Biddle (1740–1818), the son of John and brother of Owen, was engaged with them in the shipping and importing business. *DAB; PMHB*, XLII (1918), 310.

9. Washington was indeed busy establishing claims for his veterans under the Dinwiddie proclamation of 1754, and Dunmore was patenting them. See above, XIX, 3 n, 335 n; BF to WF, Feb. 14, 1773; Douglas S. Freeman, *George Washington: a Biography* (7 vols., New York [1948–57]), III, 297–304. The reference to Lord Stirling is to his trip to Virginia mentioned in WF to BF above, Jan. 5. Stirling's letter, cited there, brought assurances from prominent men in the province that the Walpole grant would not be contested because the grantees had agreed to honor legitimate Virginia claims within their tract. Dunmore's patenting such claims on his own authority

Our good Friends Dr. Evans and Mr. Baynton are Still in a very declining State; I have but little hopes of the Doctor's Recovery, tho' perhaps he may be able to linger out a few Months longer.[1]

I am glad the Pork proved good, and was so acceptable to you and our worthy Friend Mr. Sargent. I have a Letter of Thanks from him which I shall answer by Osborne.[2]

I thought I had fully satisfied Haynes of there being no such Estate as he came in quest of. I am sure he appeared to be so, and very thankful for the Pains I took to procure him all the information that was necessary. Nor can I help thinking that he is himself quite convinced it was all a Illusion tho' perhaps he don't like to have it thought that he went so far on such an idle Errand.[3]

There is a Letter from you (per Capt. All) directed to one James Johnson at Philada. for which no owner can be found. There is a man of that name (who was formerly Clerk to Mr. Norris) but on opening it he said it was not for him.[4] Betsy joins in Duty with, Honoured Sir, Your ever dutiful Son

WM: FRANKLIN

Addressed: To / Dr: Franklin / Craven Street / London

---

made WF doubt Stirling's information, it seems, and wonder whether Whitehall countenanced the Governor's policy. Whitehall did not. Dunmore was acting counter to repeated instructions, and the government had just issued an order in council forbidding all colonial governors to make land grants until further notice, except to veterans who qualified under the provisions of the proclamation of 1763. *Acts Privy Coun., Col.,* v, 360–1; John R. Alden, *John Stuart and the Southern Colonial Frontier* . . . (Ann Arbor and London, 1944), pp. 286–9.

1. John Baynton died in the following May and Dr. Evans in June; see George Morgan to BF below, May 4, and the note on BF to Evans above, Feb. 10.

2. For the pork see BF to WF above, Feb. 3; Peter Osborne was master of the *Pa. Packet.*

3. For Richard Hayne's labors to obtain an inheritance for his wife see above, XIX, 321–2.

4. We have had no more success than the postal authorities in identifying the man; see BF to Johnston above, Feb. 10. Mr. Norris may have been either Charles (above, II, 376 n) or his older brother Isaac, both Philadelphia merchants who died in 1766.

From Daniel Wister[5]   ALS: American Philosophical Society

Dear friend,   Philada: April 30th: 1773

You have undoubtedly been inform'd of my unhappy situation for three years past. I had engag'd too largely in business, contracted many bad debts, to no less amount than £30,000 which unfortunate circumstances have disabled me from satisfying those persons in England who had supplied me with Merchandise. The consequence has been, that I have been a prisoner, not in the common jail, but in my own house, only six weeks short of three years. I cannot deny but my creditors have cause of being offended, for I was influenc'd, (but when at a distance from home, far from my friends) by the Attorney of D: and J Barclay and H & Powell, to give them security in preference, and to the great injury of others to whom I was as justly indebted.[6] But at the time I secured those two houses, I had no Idea of my not being able to satisfy every demand against me, but unhappily for me, a short time after a person, to whom I had given an unlimited credit, and of whose circumstances I was never doubtful, died, and his affairs were in so desperate a situation that I suffer'd a loss of £20,000. This added to numerous other misfortunes of the same nature, has put it out of my power to pay every man his own. I have not been able to influence my father to offer more than £1500 Sterling to my creditors, to induce them to give me a discharge.[7] This sum, some of them will not accept, and I know my father will not add thereto, consequently I am still confin'd,

5. A Philadelphia merchant of German extraction, who in his younger days had been BF's political ally; see above, XII, 277 n; XIII, 429. BF replied cordially (below, July 14), but we do not know how the story ended.

6. The Barclays, John and David, Jr., were major London merchants: above, IX, 190 n; the other firm was undoubtedly Harford & Powell, of Mincing Lane. Their attorney, John Gibson, announced in 1770 that Wister had assigned him all his assets, and promised to settle with his creditors and collect from his debtors. *Pa. Gaz.*, June 21, 1770.

7. His father, John Wister, was also a merchant: above, XII, 328 n. In the circumstances he was showing considerable generosity, for Daniel had brought disgrace on the family. Little more than a month after his bankruptcy he had been read out of the Friends Meeting for a variety of offenses, which ranged from keeping game cocks to paying a girl to strip naked. Carl A. and Jessica Bridenbaugh, *Rebels and Gentlemen* ... (New York, [1942]), pp. 182–3; Hinshaw, *Amer. Quaker Geneal.*, II, 690.

and cannot have a chance of doing any thing for them. If I could procure my liberty, I have no doubt of being able to satisfy every demand against me, in a few years, for my father is very willing to put me again into business, and I hope past misfortunes will make me more circumspect for the time to come. It is impossible I can make any attempt towards paying my debts, in my present situation, my creditors give up every chance of having their demands upon me satisfied, and a continuation of my condition must inevitably destroy me: for it is well known that want of air and exercise, will undo any constitution.

The occasion of my addressing you at this time is, to request the favour of you to interceed with my creditors on my behalf. The person principally averse to receiving what my father offers, is Moses Franks Esqr: of London, whom you may possibly influence to accept the offer.[8] If you think me worthy your friendship in my unfortunate circumstances, I shall be happy, and shall ever remember your kindness with gratitude. I have inclos'd you a list of the names of all my creditors in London, and shall be particularly obliged, if you'll speak to them all, but as I am inform'd, none of them are so much displeas'd as the Gentleman above named. If you cannot influence them to accept my father's proposal, I should be glad you would endeavour to get them to agree to give me a letter of licence,[9] for any number of years which may be thought reasonable, that I may at least have a chance of becoming so fortunate in the world, as to pay every man his due. I would observe, that tho' my father asks a discharge for me, upon his paying £1500 yet I should never look upon myself as discharg'd from the obligation I should be under of satisfying every man, if it ever should be in my power so to do.

I desire you will be kind enough to excuse my troubling you on this subject, your known willingness to assist the distressed, induc'd me to apply to you for assisstance, and in expectation thereof I am, Your real Friend   DANIEL WISTER

B. Franklin Esqr.

8. Moses Franks, like the Barclays, was a prominent London merchant: above, x, 73 n. He and BF had been, as Wister may have known, associates in the Walpole group since its formation: above, xvi, 166–8.

9. An agreement between a debtor and his creditors, permitting him to carry on his business either with or without stipulated conditions.

To Jacques Barbeu-Dubourg

Translated extract: printed in Jacques Barbeu-Dubourg, ed., *Œuvres de M. Franklin* . . . (2 vols., Paris, 1773), I, 327–9.[1]

[End of April?,[2] 1773.]

Vos observations sur les causes de la mort, et les expériences que vous proposez pour rappeler à la vie ceux qui paroissent tués par le tonnerre, montrent également votre sagacité et votre humanité. Il paroit que la doctrine de la vie et de la mort en général est encore peu connue.[3]

Un crapaud enseveli dans du sable peut vivre, dit-on, jusqu'à ce que le sable soit petrifié; et se trouvant alors renfermé dans la pierre, il peut encore y vivre, on ne sçait combien de siecles. Les faits que l'on cite a l'appui de cette opinion sont trop nombreux, et trop circonstanciés pour ne pas mériter un certain degré de confiance. Parce que nous sommes accoutumés à voir tous les êtres vivans manger et boire, il nous paroit difficile de concevoir comment un crapaud peut être nourri dans ce cachot. Mais si nous faisons réflexion que le besoin de nourriture pour les animaux, dans l'état ordinaire, provient de la déperdition continuelle de leur substance emportée par la transpiration, il paroîtra moins incroyable que quelques animaux, dans un état d'engourdissement, transpirant moins parce qu'ils ne font point d'exercice, ayent moins besoin d'alimens; et que d'autres qui sont couverts d'écailles ou de coquilles qui arrêtent la transpiration, comme les tortues, les serpens, et quelques poissons, puissent vivre long-tems sans nourriture quelconque. Une plante avec ses fleurs, se fane et meurt bientôt si elle est exposée à l'air, sans avoir de racines dans un sol humide, dont elle puisse pomper l'humidité pour suppléer à ce qui se dissipe de sa substance, et que l'air lui enleve continuellement. Mais peut-être que, si on l'enterroit dans du vif argent,[4] elle pourroit conserver longtems sa vie végétale,

---

1. An English retranslation may be found in Smyth, *Writings*, VI, 42–4. He, like previous editors, omitted the notes that appear in the *Œuvres*. These are clearly Dubourg's because they are italicized, his way of distinguishing his comments from BF's.

2. BF was replying to Dubourg's letter above of April 15.

3. [*Dubourg's note:*] Les limites n'en sont bien connues que de celui qui les a posées.

4. [*Dubourg's note:*] Ou seulement dans du sable fin.

son odeur et sa couleur. S'il en est ainsi, ce pourroit être un bon moyen pour faire venir des pays les plus éloignés des plantes délicates qui ne sçauroient soutenir l'air de la mer, ni se passer de soins et d'attentions particulieres. J'ai vu un example de mouches communes conservées par un moyen assez approchant. Elles avoient été noyées dans du vin de Madere, apparemment dans le tems qu'on le mettoit en bouteille en Virginie pour l'envoyer ici (à Londres). A l'ouverture d'une de ces bouteilles, chez un de mes amis où je me trouvois, trois mouches noyées tomberent dans le premier verre que l'on remplit. Ayant entendu dire que les mouches noyées se ranimoient au soleil, je proposai de l'essayer sur celles-là. On les exposa donc au soleil sur un tamis, au travers duquel on avoit passé le vin pour les en retirer; et en moins de trois heures, il y en eut deux qui revinrent peu-à-peu à la vie. Elles commencerent par quelques mouvemens convulsifs dans les cuisses, enfin elles s'éleverent sur leurs pieds, essuyerent leurs yeux avec leurs pattes de devant, battirent et brosserent leurs ailes avec leurs pattes de derriere, et s'envolerent à la fin, se trouvant dans l'ancienne Angleterre sans sçavoir comment elles y étoient venues. La troisieme resta morte jusqu'au soleil couché que, n'en espérant plus rien, on la jetta.

Je souhaiterois que vous pussiez déduire de-là un art d'embaumer les personnes noyées, desorte qu'on pût les rappeller à la vie quand on voudroit, au bout de tant de tems que ce fût: car ayant une extrême envie de voir et de reconnoître l'état de l'Amérique dans cent ans d'ici, je préférerois à une mort ordinaire d'être entonné avec quelques amis dans des muids de Madere[5] jusqu'à ce tems-là, pour être alors rendu à la vie par la chaleur du soleil de ma chere patrie. Mais comme nous vivons peut-être dans un siecle trop peu avancé, trop près de l'enfance des sciences, pour espérer qu'un tel art soit porté de nos jours à sa perfection, il faut me contenter pour le présent du régal que vous avez la bonté de me proposer de la résurrection d'un poulet, ou d'un dindon. Je suis, &c.   B. FRANKLIN.

5. [*Dubourg's note:*] Nombre d'yvrognes adopteroient volontiers ce nouveau genre de sépulture; mais seulement après leur mort.

190

From Jacques Barbeu-Dubourg

Printed in Jacques Barbeu-Dubourg, ed., *Œuvres de M. Franklin* . . . (2 vols., Paris, 1773), I, 330–1.

Monsieur,   A Paris, premier Mai 1773

J'étois monté sur un ton bien grave dans mes dernieres lettres; il sembloit que j'eusse respiré l'air d'Angleterre, on dira que vous m'aviez gâté l'esprit.[6] Il est vrai que l'électricité est de tous les pays, mais c'est bien la moindre chose qu'en France on l'habille à la Françoise; tout, sans exception, y subit l'empire de la mode. On n'oseroit espérer de vous y plier tout-à-fait, mais j'attens au moins un peu d'indulgence aujourd'hui de votre part, et peut-être n'aurez-vous pas à vous en repentir.

Je vous demande donc bien sérieusement, Monsieur, si l'on ne pourroit pas faire entrevoir à notre très-frivole nation dans les expériences électriques une utilité de luxe, qui les lui feroit accueillir avec beaucoup plus de vivacité. Si, par exemple, on pouvoit imaginer qu'un jour viendra, et qu'il n'est peut-être pas loin, où avec un appareil très-simple, et toujours sous la main, on fera en trois ou quatre minutes mortifier suffisamment les viandes des animaux fraichement tués, pour en manger sur le champ, comme si elles avoient été longtems gardées. Quel plaisir en arrivant à la campagne de n'avoir qu'à faire tuer un chapon et le mettre aussi-tôt à la broche, de n'avoir point à attendre toute une semaine un gigot de mouton, pour le trouver tendre !

Une jolie petite lettre sur une semblable matiere, pour terminer gayement le recueil de vos oeuvres le feroit voler aux nuës; nos petits-maîtres, et nos belles Dames en affolleroient pendant huit jours, et les provinces en retentiroient long-tems. Je ne sçais même combien de pays étrangers on ne pourroit pas ranger au nombre des provinces de notre frivolité. Je suis, &c.

P.S. M. Dalibard, ici arrivant, se joint à moi, pour vous demander votre avis sur cela.[7]

---

6. He doubtless had in mind his lugubrious letter of April 15; that of the 11th was cheerful enough.

7. See BF's reply below, under May 25.

From Benjamin Rush[8]

ALS: American Philosophical Society

Honored Sir   Philada: May 1st: 1773.

I am much Obliged to you for Dr. Priestley's Experiments. They have thrown a good deal of Light upon the subject of fixed Air, Altho' I can by no means assent to some of his inferences from them. The Experiment made with a Sprig of mint extends our Ideas of the Oconomy of Vegetables.[9] But is all the fixed Air which is discharged from its various sources Absorbed and applied to the Nourishment of Plants? Does not common Air possess a power of destroying it either by Diffusion or Mixture? Is not much of it destroyed likewise by being restored to its Elasticity so as to become common Air? What water is to vapor, fixed Air appears to be to common Air. How diffirent are the Effects of Water and Vapor upon Animals, Vegetables and Fires, and yet we all know they are of the same Natures. The former possesses no narcotic stimulating or poisonous Quality, and yet Animals expire, and fires are extinguished in it. May not all the peculiar Qualities in like manner of fixed Air be ascribed to its containing common Air in a fixed state and not to any adventitious Matter of a poisonous and stimulating Nature?

The Doctor deserves great Credit for his Application of fixed Air to Medicine. To his Remarks upon this Subject I would beg leave to add One More. A large Quantity of fixed Air is discharged in Perspiration. This is proved by a Candle's immediately ceasing to burn if it be put under the Bed Cloaths of a Person who is well covered in Bed. This fixed Air being of a recrementitious[1] Nature is no doubt of a septic quality. If this be the Case we learn the great Necessity of obliging Patients to sit up as much as possible in putrid Diseases, and to change their Linnen and Bed Cloaths every Day.[2]

8. For informative annotation of this letter see Lyman H. Butterfield, ed., *Letters of Benjamin Rush* (2 vols., Princeton, 1951), I, 80.

9. These sentences identify the pamphlet, enclosed in BF's letter above of Feb. 14, as Joseph Priestley, *Observations on Different Kinds of Air* ... (London, 1772). The other pamphlet that Priestley published the same year, on impregnating water with fixed air, contained no experiments with mint.

1. Capable of being reabsorbed into the body.

2. In his answer below, July 14, BF promised to pass on this comment to Priestley.

You will receive with this Letter a small Pamphlet which the public have ascribed to me. It was written at the Request of Anth: Benezet to promote and accompany a Petition to our Assembly to put a more complete Stop to the Importation of Negro Slaves into the Province.[3] I have sent a Copy of it together with all those News Papers which contain the late Dispute between Govr: Hutcheson and the Counsil and Assembly at Boston to our good Friend Monsr. Dubourg of Paris. They are directed to your Care. Please to forward them by the first Opportunity.[4]

When shall we have the Pleasure of seeing your Treatise upon Colds?[5] In Dr. Cullen's late ingenious Arrangement of Diseases he speaks of a great many Catarhs or Colds from Contagion, but includes with these One Species *a frigore*.[6] He does not say however that Moisture alone has any Share in producing them. I have found Shallopmen and Sailors in this City [who are] more subject to Intermitting fever, but much less to Colds than any Other People. With the sincerest Gratitude and the truest Respect I have the Honor to be Your Much Obliged Most Affectionate Humble Servant   B: RUSH

P.S. Our Revd. Friend Mr. Coombe is to be married in a few Days, not to Miss Ord, but to a Miss Badger, an amiable young Lady with a most sweet Temper.[7]

Addressed: To / Benjamin Franklin Esqr / London

3. The pamphlet was by Rush: *An Address to the Inhabitants of the British Settlements in America, upon Slave-Keeping* (Philadelphia, 1773). The petition that it supported had a transient success: an act was passed in February to double the duty on imported slaves, but was disallowed the following year. 8 *Pa. Arch.*, VIII, 6915–16, 6937, 6965–6; *Acts Privy Coun., Col.*, V, 398–9.

4. Rush wrote a covering letter to Dubourg, largely about the campaign against slavery; the Frenchman printed a lengthy extract from it in *Œuvres*, II, 315–16, which is retranslated and annotated in Butterfield, *op. cit.*, pp. 76–8.

5. The treatise was often discussed but never written. See above, XVIII, 203, and BF's notes below at the end of the year.

6. For Dr. William Cullen of Edinburgh see above, VII, 184 n; his *Synopsis nosologiae methodicae* (Edinburgh, 1769) went through a number of editions in Latin: *DNB*.

7. The Rev. Thomas Coombe, whom BF had known well during the young man's recent stay in London, married Sarah (Sally) Badger on May 13; she died five years later. 2 *Pa. Arch.*, VIII, 63; *PMHB*, V (1881), 30 n; VII (1883), 244.

From Humphry Marshall

Extract:[8] the Royal Society

May 3, 1773

Having for some time declined making any more Observations on the dark Spots that appear on the Sun's Disk, I now send a Copy of the Figures I drew of them, which I desire may be presented to the Royal Society.[9] Perhaps, some one or more of the Members may be pleased with them, in which case I shall not think my Labour lost. They were viewed with a Reflecting Telescope of [*blank*] Inches, and their Appearances I think pretty truly delineated, both as to Magnitude and Situation. Upon the whole, I am of Opinion, that the Spots are near the Sun's Surface (if not closely adhering thereto) for these Reasons; 1. That their Velocities are apparently greatest near the Center and gradually slower towards each Limb. 2. That the Shape of the Spots varies, according to their Position on the several Parts of the Sun's Disk; those that appear broad and nearly round when on the middle, seeming at their first Appearance on the Eastern Limb but as Lines, and as they advance towards the Center grow oval, then round, and in their Progress to the Western Limb, appear again as Ovals and Lines. My other Remarks were, that the Spots were twelve Days and an half, and about two or three Hours, in passing. That tho' some continued visible from one Limb to the other, a few would disappear after having been visible several Days, and others divided into parts. That scarce any Spots ever appeared beyond what may be called the Polar Circles of the Sun;

8. The letter was in response to BF's above of Feb. 14, and gave the thoughts that Marshall had promised long before: XVIII, 255.

9. The figures were not included, presumably because the observations were missing, when the extract was printed in *Phil. Trans.*, LXIV (1774), 194–5. A note on the MS reads:

"The figures of the Solar Spots mentioned in this Letter are Sketches with black-Lead Pencil, upon a very small Scale. They are accompanied with short notes of the state of the weather at the time of each observation and sometimes the Height of the Thermometer is mentiond. Among these meterological remarks the following seems the most extraordinary.

"'Febry 21st. 1773 [*an error in transcription?*]. Ther[mometer] at 3 degrees below O at Sunrise. This morning had there been a snow on the ground I believe would have been as cold as it was January 2d. 1767. when the Thermometer was 22 degrees below O, there being a large snow on the Ground at that time and none now.'"

and that the same Spot never appeared a second time on the eastern Limb, at least not in the same form and Position.

Notation: Extract of a Letter from Mr. Humphry Marshall, of West Bradford, in Chester County, Pensilvania, to B. Franklin, dated May 3, 1773, sent with Sketches of the Solar Spots.

Redde Febry 3d. 1773 [*i.e.*, 1774]. To be printed.

To Jacques Barbeu-Dubourg

Translated extract: printed in Jacques Barbeu-Dubourg., *Œuvres de M. Franklin* . . . (2 vols., Paris, 1773), II, 312.

4 Mai 1773.

Ce jeune Docteur est mort, et toutes les notes qu'il avoit faites de ses curieuses expériences ont été perdues par je ne sçais quel accident entre nos amis le Chevalier Jean Pringle, et le Docteur Huck; mais il paroit que ces Messieurs, s'ils ne retrouvent pas les papiers, comptent répéter les expériences eux-mêmes . . . .[1]

From William Franklin   ALS: American Philosophical Society

Honoured Father,   Burlington May [4, 1773[2]]

Enclosed is a Letter I wrote last Week at Phi[ladelphia] in order to go by Mesnard, but it happened to be too [late for] that Opportunity.[3]

1. The young doctor was William Stark, who had starved himself to death more than three years before: above, XVI, 162 n. For the experiments with perspiration that he had carried out before his death see BF to Dubourg above, March 10. Dr. Richard Huck (above, XV, 172 n) and Sir John Pringle apparently never did find the reports of those experiments and, as far as we know, never repeated them. They are not mentioned in the posthumous volume of Stark's writings: James Carmichael Smyth, ed., *The Works of the Late William Stark, M.D.* . . . (London, 1788).

Dubourg appended to the extract a puzzling note: "*Exoriare aliquis* . . . Virg.*" The quotation is from the *Aeneid*, IV, 625–9, part of Dido's curse that called down fire and sword on the departing Trojans. The relevance of this resounding imprecation, either to Stark or to Huck and Pringle, eludes us.

2. So dated in BF's reply below, July 14.

3. The enclosure was WF's letter above of April 30. The *Pa. Gaz.* announced on April 28 the departure of Thomas Mesnard in the *Mary and Elizabeth*.

Coz. Davenport is greatly obliged to you for [*torn*] you sent him.[4] As he could not make out to get a comfortable Living at Philadelphia, not having a sufficient Capital to carry on his Trade, nor able to procure any other Business for which he was qualified, I offered him two or three small Offices here, and to make him my private Secretary, which altogether might afford him a Maintenance until something better should turn up. This he accepted, and has been here ever since the first of January. It is not in my Power to make a handsome Provision for a private Secretary as the Govr. of New York,[5] and the Governors of some other Provinces can; for all the Offices of any Value are engrossed by the Provincial Secretary.[6] However, an Opportunity now offers of doing something for him which may afford him a lasting Support, and, with the other Offices he now has, will enable him to make a comfortable Provision for his Family. Mr. Chas. Read has proposed to resign to him the Office of Collector of the Customs for the Port of Burlington (in case he can make Interest to obtain the Commission) on Condition of his engaging to pay Mr. Read's Son Jacob £50 *Currency* per Annum for 3 Years.[7] The Salary is £30 Sterl. besides an Allowance of £9 16s. od. Sterling for an Office, Paper, Pens, Ink, &c. The Fees and Perquisites I think may if the Office is properly attended to, amount

4. The ne'er-do-well Josiah Davenport was presumably more obliged for the maps BF sent him than for the accompanying letter of Feb. 14.

5. WF here added a marginal note: "The Governor of N. York has given his private Secretary the Prerogative Office which is worth I suppose £5 or 600 per annum." The secretary was Edmund Fanning, who was busy recouping his fortune after losses in North Carolina; see above, XVIII, 44 n. The prerogative office, which exercised the powers vested in the governor and delegated by him, was customarily held by the provincial secretary, who was responsible for proving wills and issuing marriage licences; fees for the latter were particularly lucrative. The incumbent, when Tryon replaced him with Fanning, petitioned for and secured reinstatement. *Sibley's Harvard Graduates*, XIV (1968), 165; *Acts Privy Coun., Col.*, V, 47–9.

6. Maurice Morgann, secretary of New Jersey since 1767, never left England but acted through a deputy; see above, XIII, 430 n and, for all the offices Morgann engrossed, 1 *N. J. Arch.*, X, 2.

7. For Charles Read's career see above, X, 313 n. His son Jacob was irresponsible, shiftless, intemperate, and a great worry to his father; see Carl R. Woodward, *Ploughs and Politicks: Charles Read of New Jersey and His Notes on Agriculture* . . . (New Brunswick, 1941), pp. 39, 212–14, 218–19.

to about as much more; so that the Bargain is as favourable for Mr. Davenport as could reasonably be desired. Enclosed is a Letter from Mr. Read to Lord North, containing his Resignation, which you are authorized to deliver in case you find you can secure the Office for Mr. Davenport, but not otherwise. I well know your [reluc]tance to ask for any Office or Favour for any Relative [while] you continue Agent; but, if no better Method occurs [to y]ou of serving Mr. Davenport in this Matter, I think you might, as Agent, memorialize Lord North in my Name or Behalf, setting forth, That Mr. Davenport has for some Time past acted as my private Secretary, and that it is usual in the Colonies for the Govrs. to reward their Secretaries for their Services, with some Office or Offices which may be in their Gift, but that almost all the Offices which could with Propriety be executed by a private Secretary in this Province are already included in the Patent to Mr. Morgann Provincial Secretary; That the Governor's own Income is too small to make a proper Allowance out of it to a Gentleman qualified to execute an Office of such Trust and Importance, Therefore hopes and intreats that his Lordship would gratify his Secretary with an Appointment to the Collectorship of Burlington, which the present Collector is disposed to resign in his Favour, and which, tho' of too small Value to be worth the Acceptance of any Gentleman who does not already reside in the Province, will nevertheless be an acceptable Addition to the small Consideration he receives for his Trouble &c. &c. I only throw these out as Hints which you may, if you please, improve upon, as I doubt not but you will be as happy to be instrumental in procuring our Couzin a better Establishment in Life as, Honoured Sir, Your ever dutiful Son

WM: FRANKLIN

P.S. I suppose our Friends Mr. Cooper, and Mr. Jackson will give you their Assistance on this Occasion.[8]

8. Grey Cooper was secretary to the Treasury, of which North was First Lord, and Richard Jackson was counsel to the Board of Trade.

Addressed: To / Dr: Franklin / Craven Street / London / Seal'd so
to prevent pulling out at the Ends[9]   WF

From George Morgan[1]   ALS: American Philosophical Society

Sir   Philada May 4th 1773
Let me beg that the Distresses of Mr. Bayntons Family may
appoligize to you for the Trouble I now take the Liberty to give
you as the general Friend to Mankind and the particular Friend
of Mr. Baynton.

The sudden Turn of Mr. Bayntons Disorder[2] and the Post
going off in a few Minutes will prevent my being so particular as
I intended. By the first Vessel which sails from hence for London
I will take the Liberty of troubling you again. In the Interim
suffer me to request the favour of you to converse with Mr.
Wharton on the Subject of the inclosed Letter[3] and serve Mr.
Bayntons Family therein if possible. I am with the greatest
Respect, Sir Your most Obedient and most humble Servant
                                                          GEO MORGAN

Addressed: To / Doctor Benjamin Franklin / Craven Street / London

9. A precaution against prying eyes; see WF's letter above of Jan. 5.
1. A partner in the firm of Baynton, Wharton & Morgan and the son-in-
law of John Baynton; see above, XIII, 400 n. The troubles of the partners
were the background of this letter. The firm was organized in 1763, and soon
became heavily involved in western trading ventures that brought on
bankruptcy. To recoup their losses the partners, along with WF and others,
subsidized Samuel Wharton's trip to England to lobby for the Indiana
grant. When this was merged with the Walpole Co.'s claim, Wharton failed
to include Baynton and Morgan in the larger scheme; their resultant feud
with him was long, involved, and bitter. See Max Savelle, *George Morgan,
Colony Builder* (New York, 1932), *passim*; Lewis, *Indiana Co.*, pp. 65–7,
96–7, 107–8, 122–3, 142–3, 148, 192–4.
2. Baynton died on May 8. His business difficulties, according to an obituary
that Morgan wrote, were a major cause of death: *Pa. Gaz.*, May 12, 1773.
3. Baynton was at the point of death, Morgan wrote to Samuel Wharton,
and had declared before witnesses that his demise was due to Wharton's ill
usage of him. Morgan went on to demand an immediate accounting to BF of
what Wharton had received from his partner and how many shares in the
Walpole Company Baynton held in consequence. "As this is the only
Recompense you can now make to the much injured Family, let me beseech
of you to do it immediately and without further Hesitation." "Substance of a
Letter . . . May 5th or 6th . . . ," Letterbook A, p. 117, Baynton, Wharton &

To Thomas Cushing

LS (duplicate):[4] Public Record Office; letterbook draft: Library of Congress

Franklin's account in this letter of his interview with Lord Dartmouth indicates how little scope was left to either of them, two years before Lexington, to further reconciliation between Massachusetts and the mother country. Both the Englishman and the American wanted an end to the quarrel, yet neither could find a political solution that lay within the art of the possible. Governor Hutchinson's debate with his General Court had brought the constitutional issue into the open in starkest form, and it could not be concealed by wishful thinking born of good will. Franklin hoped against hope that Parliament would tacitly accept the principles that the Court had enunciated; Dartmouth hoped against hope that the Court would repudiate them. The first course was as unlikely in Westminster as the second was in Boston, and on both sides of the Atlantic time was running out. Four days after Franklin wrote his account of the interview, the fateful Tea Act became law; and within four weeks the General Court launched the attack on the Governor, based on his letters to Whately, that was intended to drive him from office.

Sir,   London, May 6. 1773.

I have received none of your Favours since that of Nov. 28. I have since written to you of the following Dates, Dec. 2; Jan. 5; March 9; and April 3. which I hope got safe to hand.

The Council and Assembly's Answers to Govr. Hutchinson's Speech, I caused to be printed here as soon as I received them. His Reply I see since printed also, but their Rejoinder is not yet come.[5] If he intended by reviving that Dispute to recommend

---

Morgan Papers, Division of Archives and MSS, Pa. Hist. and Museum Commission, Harrisburg. BF's reply to Morgan below, July 14, is considerably mutilated, but indicates that Wharton provided nothing more concrete than expressions of good will.

4. The letter is the first, or at least the first that survives, in the hand of BF's new French clerk, Louis Fevre, for whom see above, XIX, 438 n.

5. BF received in early April the answers of the House and Council to Hutchinson's speech of Jan. 6: to WF above, April 6. The House's answer and the Governor's reply to both houses on Feb. 16 appeared in the *Public Advertiser* between April 9 and 23. The rejoinders and Hutchinson's final speech at the end of the session were apparently not published in London,

himself here, he has greatly missed his aim; for the Administration
are chagrined with his Officiousness, their Intention having been
to let all Contention subside, and by Degrees suffer Matters to
return to the old Channel. They are now embarras'd by his
Proceedings; for if they lay the Governor's Dispatches containing
the Declaration of the General Court before Parliament, they
apprehend Measures may be taken that will widen the Breach;
which would be more particularly inconvenient at this Time,
when the disturbed State of Europe gives some Apprehensions of
a general War;[6] on the other hand, if they do not lay them before
Parliament, they give Advantage to Opposition against themselves on some future Occasion, in a Charge of criminal Neglect.[7]
Some say he must be a Fool; others that thro' some Misinforma-
tion, he certainly supposed Lord Hilsborough to be again in
Office.

Yesterday I had a Conversation with Lord D. of which I think
it right to give you some Account. On my saying that I had no
late Advices from Boston, and asking if his Lordship had any, he
said, None since the Governor's second Speech; but what Difficulties, says he, that Gentleman has brought us all into by his
Imprudence! Tho' I suppose he meant well, yet what can now be
done? It is impossible that Parliament can suffer such a Declaration

---

although copies of a pamphlet containing the entire debate were then on their
way to BF with Cushing's letter of April 22. These copies BF circulated
privately, as he told the Speaker on July 7, while Parliament was prorogued
for the summer.

6. Europe was disturbed by two interrelated developments, the Russo-
Turkish war and the initial partition of Poland. The first was going badly for
the Turks; the second had been arranged by treaty the previous year but was
still being resisted. Both had international implications, in part because
Poland and the Ottoman Empire were traditional spheres of French influence.

7. The government escaped this dilemma by postponement. In April
Dartmouth wrote Hutchinson that the Cabinet would give immediate
attention to the dangerous doctrines promulgated by the House and Council;
meanwhile the Governor was commanded to avoid all further discussion of
the subject. In June the decision was taken, Dartmouth informed him, to lay
the matter before the next session of Parliament, because in the present one
time was too short, and the affairs of the East India Co. too pressing, to
give the problem of Massachusetts the attention it deserved. Bernard
Donoughue, *British Politics and the American Revolution* ... (New York
and London, 1964), pp. 18–19.

of the General Assembly (asserting its Independency) to pass unnoticed. In my Opinion, says I, it would be better and more prudent to take no Notice of it. It is *Words* only. Acts of Parliament are still submitted to there. No Force is used to obstruct their Execution. And while that is the Case, Parliament would do well to turn a deaf Ear, and seem not to know that such Declarations had ever been made. Violent Measures against the Province will not change the Opinions of the People. Force can do no good. I do not know says he, that Force would be thought of; but perhaps an Act may pass to lay them under some Inconveniences till they rescind that Declaration. Can they not withdraw it? I wish they could be persuaded to reconsider the Matter, and do it of themselves voluntarily; and thus leave things between us on the old Footing, the Points undiscuss'd. Don't you think (continues his Lordship) such a thing possible? No, my Lord, says I, I think it impossible. If they were even to wish Matters back in the Situation before the Governor's Speech, and the Dispute obliterated, they cannot withdraw their Answers till he first withdraws his Speech; which methinks would be an awkward Operation, that perhaps he will hardly be directed to perform. As to an Act of Parliament laying that Country under Inconveniences, it is likely *that* will only put them as heretofore upon inventing some Method of incommoding this Country till the Act is repealed; and so we shall go on injuring and provoking each other, instead of cultivating that Good Will and Harmony so necessary to the general Welfare. He said, That might be, and he was sensible our Divisions must weaken the whole; for we are yet *one Empire*, (says he) whatever may be the Sentiments of the Massachusets Assembly; but he did not see how it could be avoided. He wondered, as the Dispute was now of publick Notoriety, Parliament had not already called for the Dispatches; and he thought he could not omit much longer the communicating them, however unwilling he was to do it, from his Apprehension of the Consequences. But what, (his Lordship was pleas'd to say) if you were in my Place, would or could you do? Would you hazard the being called to Account in some future Session by Parliament, for keeping back the Communication of Dispatches of such Importance? I said, his Lordship could best judge what in his Situation was fittest for him to do: I could only give my poor Opinion with regard to

Parliament, that supposing the Dispatches laid before them, they would act most prudently in ordering them to lie on the Table, and take no farther Notice of them. For were I as much an Englishman as I am an American, and ever so desirous of establishing the Authority of Parliament, I protest to your Lordship I cannot conceive of a single Step the Parliament can take to encrease it that will not tend to diminish it; and after abundance of Mischief they must finally lose it. The loss in itself perhaps would not be of much consequence, because it is an Authority they can never well exercise for want of due Information and Knowledge, and therefore it is not worth hazarding the Mischief to preserve it. Then adding my Wishes that I could be of any Service in healing our Differences, his Lordship said, I do not see any thing[8] of more Service than prevailing on the General Assembly, if you can do it, to withdraw their Answer to the Governor's Speech. There is not, says I, the least Probability they will ever do that. For the Country is all of one Mind upon the Subject. Perhaps the Governor may have represented to your Lordship, that these are the Opinions of a Party only, and that great Numbers are of different Sentiments which may in time prevail. But if he does not deceive himself he deceives your Lordship: For in both Houses, notwithstanding all the Influence appertaining to his Office, there was not, in sending up those Answers, a single dissenting Voice. I do not recollect, says his Lordship, that the Governor has written any thing of that kind; but I am told, however, by Gentlemen from that Country who pretend to know it, that there are many of the Governor's Opinion, but they dare not shew their Sentiments. I never heard, says I, that any one has suffered any Violence for siding with the Governor. Not Violence, perhaps, says his Lordship, but they are reviled and held in Contempt, and People don't care to incur the Disesteem and Displeasure of their Neighbours. As I knew Govr. Bernard had been in with his Lordship just before me, I thought he was probably one of these Gentlemen Informants, and therefore said, People who are ingaged in any Party or have advised any Measures, are apt to magnify the Numbers of those they would have understood as

8. In his draft BF here added, then struck out, "you can possibly do, that would be."

approving their Measures. His Lordship said, that was natural to suppose might be the present Case; for, whoever observed the Conduct of Parties here, must have seen it a constant Practice; and he agreed with me, that tho' a *Nemine Contradicente* did not prove the absolute Agreement of every Man in the Opinion voted, it at least demonstrated the great Prevalence of that Opinion.

Thus ended our Conference. I shall watch this Business till the Parliament rises, and endeavour to make People in general as sensible of the Inconveniences to this Country that may attend a Continuance of the Contest, as the Spitalfields Weavers seem already to be in their Petition to the King, which I herewith send you.[9] I have already the pleasure to find that my friend the Bishop of St. Asaph's Sermon is universally approved and applauded, which I take to be no bad Symptom.[1] With sincere Esteem and Respect, I have the honor to be, Sir, Your most obedient humble Servant,   B FRANKLIN

Honourable Thomas Cushing, Esqr

(Private)

Copy[2]

Endorsed: Benja Franklin May. 6. 1773 private.

Notation: Dr. Franklin May 6th. 1773

9. Venality and rapacity in high places, the petition asserted, had brought on the long contention between the colonies and the mother country, which was the immediate cause of the slump in trade that was reducing the petitioners to destitution. *Public Advertiser*, May 3, 1773. The silk weavers of Spitalfields and Bethnal Green had a long background of political agitation; see Simon Maccoby, *English Radicalism, 1762–1785: the Origins* (London, [1955]), pp. 453–5, 458–60.

1. For the sermon and its impact see the annotation of BF to Cushing above, April 3.

2. This and the preceding two lines, as well as the place and date at the head of the letter, are in BF's hand. The Speaker kept this LS among his papers, as its present location indicates. On the cover Thomas Moffatt commented, "This letter relates a long conference between Lord Dartmouth and him concluding with a panegyrick upon the Bishop of St Asaphs Sermon and a claim of friendship with that prelate."

From Thomas Cushing
ALS: Library of Congress

Sir   Boston May. 6. 1773

I transmit you by this Conveyance the Votes of the House for the last Year as far as they are printed. I also send you this days paper in which you will find the Town of Boston's Instructions to their Representatives.[3] How the dispute between the Governor and the two Houses is relished on your side the Water we have not yet heard. In justice to the Americans, I would observe, that the Colonies from the first of this dispute Acquiesced in the distinction between Taxation and Legislation and were disposed to Confine the dispute to that of Taxation only and entirely to wave the other as a subject of too delicate a Nature but the advocates for the Supream authority of Parliament drove us into it. They Strenuously asserted that the right of Parliament to Legislate for the Colonies (which they said we did not dispute) necessarily Involved in it the right of Taxation, that if they had a right to Legislate in one case they had in all. The Colonists were sinsible if this doctrine was true, they were nothing but abject Slaves at the Absolute will and disposal of Parliament, that it never could be the Intention of our Ancestors, when they first settled this Country, to put themselves in such a Condition and

3. The General Court had been prorogued in March and dissolved in April; the new Court was to meet as usual at the end of May. On May 5 the Boston town meeting re-elected Cushing, Hancock, Phillips, and Samuel Adams as its representatives, and appointed a committee chaired by Dr. Joseph Warren to instruct them. The instructions breathed defiance. The secret and capricious mode of governing by royal instructions, they declared, had undermined the representative system, and reduced all assemblies in America to such constitutional ciphers that the Bostonians had hesitated even to elect members to the House. They did so because their privileges under the charter must be defended at all costs. Those privileges included taxing themselves and legislating for themselves; here the instructions were almost a Declaratory Act in reverse. Massachusetts had outstanding grievances, which were listed, and other colonies were equally abused—notably Rhode Island by the *Gaspee* inquiry. In conclusion Boston's delegates were told to work toward implementing Virginia's proposal to obtain a "Union of Councils and Conduct" through intercolonial correspondence. W. H. Whittemore *et al.*, eds., *Reports of the Record Commissioners of the City of Boston* (30 vols., Boston, 1881–1909), XVIII, 132–4. For the Virginia resolves see the note on Cushing to BF above, April 20.

that it was directly inconsistent with their Charter which Entituled them to all the rights and priviledges of British Subjects, in short they Could find no Line between the Supream Authority of Parliament in all Cases whatsoever and a state of absolute Slavery, that therefore the Doctrine must be false and Unsupportable.[4] I have just received your Favor of the 9 March togather with Votes and Proceedings of this Town reprinted with a very judicious preface[5] much approved on here, for which I am Oblidged to you and am glad to hear of your determination to stay in England till the sessions is over as your Tarry there may be of service to this Country. With great Respect I subscribe myself Sir Your most humble Servant   THOMAS CUSHING

Benjamin Franklin Esqr.

Addressed: To / Benjamin Franklin Esqr LLD / In / London

From Jonathan Williams, Jr.

ALS: American Philosophical Society

Dear and honored sir   Boston May 6. 1773

Mrs. Walker wrote me a Letter and expressed great uneasiness about the welfare of her Son, which I have endeavoured to remove by the inclosed Answer,[6] and as I dont know of any other way to convey it to her hands, must beg you will be so kind as to forward it. With best Respects to Mrs. Stevenson Love to Sally Franklin[7] and all Freinds I remain as ever Your dutifull and affectionate Kinsman   JONA WILLIAMS JUNR

Addressed: To / Doctr Benja Franklin / at Mrs Stevensons In / Craven Street / Strand / London

4. Cushing's instructions as a Boston representative, outlined in n. 3, were a shade more overt in their defiance of Parliament than the position taken earlier by the House of Representatives in answering the governor, for which see above, pp. 113–14 ns. The Speaker is here summarizing, it seems, the House's phrasing.

5. The preface is printed above under the end of February.

6. The enclosure was undoubtedly the letter from Jonathan's mother for which Hannah Walker, writing BF below, June 20, expressed great thankfulness.

7. He had apparently not heard the news of Sally's marriage in April; see above, XIX, 395 n, and BF to DF, April 6, 1773.

From Nathaniel Falconer   ALS: American Philosophical Society

My Dear Friend   Philadla May the 13. 1773
   I Received yours of the 14 of Feb. by Capt. All about a week
after the arrival of the London Ships[8] the Grand Duke Gave him
self some verey unbecoming aiers to me about some person that
I think there Famiely are under Great obligations too. They
would people hear belive that a Certain man Can Turn out
pr[ime?] minnesters and put in at pleashur.[9] Our Debate became
so warm that I have sold my Right to the Family have got the
money advanced and Intrest with there obligation.[1] If you should
have paid aney money on my account before the Receipt of this
they are to Repay it before they have a deed maid.[2] I am verey
sorry my Dear Sir I have been so Troublesome to you on this
matter. I hope after this it will be no more Trouble as I have Sold
it among them selfs. My best Compliments to Mrs. Stevenson
Mrs. and Mr. Hewson Salley Franklin and master Temple. I am
Dear Sir with Great Respect your Friend and Humble Servant
                                   NATHL FALCONER

Addressed: Docter Franklin / in Craven Street Strand / London

8. Capt. All had arrived on April 13. The "London Ships" were the *Mary
and Elizabeth*, which docked about a week later, and the *Pa. Packet* and the
Catherine, which were in port by the beginning of May. *Pa. Gaz.*, April 14,
21, May 5, 1773.
   9. The Grand Duke, Joseph Wharton, may have been putting on airs about
the family's relationship with either Thomas Walpole or Samuel Wharton.
The latter, we believe, was the one credited with power to unseat ministers,
an illusion born of Hillsborough's ouster. Wharton was becoming unpopular
with his colleagues, BF reported two months later, for taking to himself sole
credit for everything: to WF below, July 14. See also Morgan to BF above,
May 4.
   1. The Wharton family had also tried to get WF's shares in the Walpole
Co., had aroused almost equal annoyance, and had failed: WF to BF above,
April 30. For Falconer's right see his letter above, XIX, 292.
   2. See also Falconer's later letter above, *ibid.*, pp. 371-2.

Franklin's Contributions to a History of the British Colonies in America

Printed in *The History of the British Dominions in North America from the First Discovery of That Vast Continent by Sebastian Cabot in 1497, to Its Present Glorious Establishment as Confirmed by the Late Treaty of Peace in 1763* ... (London, 1773); draft of one paragraph: American Philosophical Society

In the spring of 1773 William Strahan published a volume of American history, presumably in the hope of capitalizing on the current interest in the colonial question. The book is essentially a compilation of the work of earlier writers.[3] Franklin contributed a few passages and subsequently marked them in his copy, which is now in the Boston Public Library. The passages are printed below with a bracketed résumé of the context in which each appears, and bracketed pagination.

[Before May 20, 1773[4]]

[During the French and Indian War a naval force was created on Lake Ontario, and the colonies from Virginia northward raised between them more than ten thousand men.] Although the union of the Colonies was a measure recommended to them by the crown, yet when a plan for that purpose was so readily concerted by the commissioners, it seems that a jealousy arose, lest such an union might in time render them formidable even to the mother-country. Their plan, therefore, which was to form a general council composed of deputies from the assemblies of all the Colonies, wherein should preside a governor-general to be appointed by the crown, with a power in the council to lay and levy general taxes, and raise troops for the common defence, and to annoy the enemy, was not approved by the ministry. But a new one was projected in England, wherein it was proposed, that the provincial governors appointed by the crown should be impowered to meet, and order such troops to be raised, forts built, expeditions undertaken, and other expences incurred, as they should judge necessary; for which they should draw on the treasury in England, which should be reimbursed by future taxes on the Colonies, to be raised by act of parliament. This the

---

3. See the long and unenthusiastic review in *The Monthly Rev.*, XLIX (1774), 18–22.
4. The date when publication was announced in the *London Chron.*

Colonies did not approve of; so neither of them were carried into execution.[5] Had the first been agreed to, probably no farther expence on the part of Britain would have been necessary than what related to the fleet, as by land the Colonies united would have been much too strong for the French, when their succours from Europe were intercepted or prevented. [Pp. 24–5.]

[Virginia and North Carolina were unrepresented at the Albany Congress, but their Governors strongly recommended that the assemblies grant supplies and enter a union for mutual defense.] The assembly of Virginia granted £30,000 Maryland £6,000 and North Carolina £8,000 toward the common cause: the assembly of Pennsylvania also passed a bill for granting £25,000; but their governor, who is appointed by the Penns, proprietors of that province, and instructed by them, refused his assent to it, unless they would exempt the proprietary estate from taxation towards that sum. This they thought unjust and unreasonable, as the proprietary estate was to be defended as well as the estates of the people. The grant, therefore, was rendered ineffectual; but the assembly nevertheless gave, out of money they could dispose of, £5,000 to trustees, to be by them laid out for purchasing fresh victuals, and such other necessaries as they should think expedient, for the use of the king's troops: and £10,000 more for the general service of the crown, and then adjourned. But the danger became so alarming before the end of the next year, that the proprietors consented to contribute, and the assembly granted £60,000 more, and established a militia in the Colony.[6] [P. 26.]

[The colonists have many privileges: (1) they make their own

5. For BF's involvement in the Albany Plan of Union see above, V, 344–55, 357–92, 397–417. Near the end of his life he elaborated on his statement here by adding that Whitehall rejected the scheme as too democratic: *ibid.*, p. 417. His statements are misleading. The plan was indeed "not approved by the ministry," for the reason that it was never formally submitted; the Board of Trade forwarded it to the crown, but it was not acted upon because the colonial legislatures unanimously turned it down. The colonies never saw the British counterproposal; it originated in the Board of Trade, went to the crown, and was never heard of again. Robert C. Newbold, *The Albany Congress and Plan of Union* . . . (New York, [1955]), pp. 173, 177.

6. BF was writing from memory, which was inaccurate in some details. For the aspects of the controversy that he mentions see above, V, 280–1, 528; VI, 129–130, 140–1, 257 n, 273–4, 433–5.

laws, provided that their acts do not conflict with those of Parliament; (2) they tax themselves; (3) a Parliamentary statute made after the colonies were founded applies to them only when so stipulated,] and even that is disputed, some contending that no British act is in force there, unless expressly adopted by some act of their own.[7] [P. 70.]

[Transportation by land and sea is far more economical in New York than in Pennsylvania, and farming is consequently thirty percent more profitable.] Such is the account given of the advantage of their situation by the New York writers. But when these facts are considered, that New York was a well-advanced colony long before William Penn began to settle his province; that though there have been always in the territory of New York great tracts of land unsettled, strangers have rather chosen to sit down in Pennsylvania; that numbers of families, particularly the Germans, have actually abandoned the former for the latter; that most of the emigrants from New England crossed the province of New York to settle beyond it; that Pennsylvania now far exceeds it in population; and that wheat, though equally good, is generally cheaper at Philadelphia market than at that of New York; it seems as if those boasted advantages were either much exaggerated, or over-balanced by some disadvantages accompanying them, or by greater advantages in Pennsylvania, which these writers do not mention.[8] [P. 78.]

[The Quakers, soon after they first appeared in Massachusetts in 1656, began to foment opposition to the secular and religious order established in the colony; military defense, they claimed, was unlawful for Christians.] This doctrine was deemed particularly dangerous to an infant state surrounded by Indian enemies: on which account[9] they were imprisoned, and their books ordered to be publickly burnt. [P. 119.]

7. See A. Berriedale Keith, *Constitutional History of the First British Empire* (Oxford, 1930), pp. 48, 106, 183–6.

8. This is the paragraph of which BF's draft survives. It differs from the printed version only in a few inconsequential details.

9. A questionable conclusion: the Quakers appear to have been persecuted more for their political and religious views than for their military scruples. See Charles E. Park, "Puritans and Quakers," *New England Quarterly*, XXVII (1954), 69–73; Hutchinson, *History*, I, 167–75.

From Rebecca Haydock Garrigues

ALS: American Philosophical Society

Esteem'd Freind   Philadelphia 5th Mo 20th 1773
   Thy favour of Captain All came safe to hand with the Silk in
good Order, which merits my sincere Thanks. I shall always
esteem myself much obliged by Doctor Franklin's kindness, in
taking so much Trouble as he has done in getting the Silk made.
My Father has paid Neighbour Franklin the ballance on account
of the Silk, agreeable to thy Order.[10] I am very respectfully Thy
assured Freind   REBECCA GARRIGUES

Addressed: To / Benjamin Franklin Esqr. / Craven Street / York
Buildings / London. / Favord by Capt. Sutton

To Jacques Barbeu-Dubourg and Thomas-François Dalibard[1]

Translation printed in Jacques Barbeu-Dubourg, ed. *Œuvres de M.
Franklin* . . . (2 vols., Paris, 1773), I, 332–4.[2]

Mes Chers Amis,   [On or before May 25, 1773[3]]
   Ma réponse à vos questions sur l'attendrissement des viandes
par l'électricité ne peut être fondée que sur des conjectures; car je
n'ai pas des expériences suffisantes pour garantir les faits.[4] Tout

---

   10. See BF's letter to her above, Feb. 14.
   1. In his humorous letter above of May 1, on the possibility of an electrical
tenderizer for meat, Dubourg had associated Dalibard with his request for a
reply in kind that would help to sell the French edition: "une jolie petite
lettre sur une semblable matiere, pour terminer gayement le recueil de vos
oeuvres le feroit voler aux nuës . . . ." The serious tone of BF's response must
have been disappointing, as he realized it would be; see the following
document.
   2. An English retranslation may be found in Smyth, *Writings*, VI, 44–7.
   3. BF sent the letter, he said in the following document, by "last Tuesday's
packet"; that was the day when mail for the Dover-Calais packet was made
up in London. Hence he must have written on or shortly before Tuesday the
25th.
   4. The only experiment we know of was certainly inadequate: in 1750 he
had killed a turkey by electricity (and almost killed himself), and found the
flesh unusually tender. Above, IV, 82–3, 112–13, 141.

ce que je puis donc dire pour le présent, c'est que je suppose qu'on peut employer l'électricité pour produire cet effet, en vous donnant ce qui suit comme des observations ou des raisons qui me le font présumer.

On a observé que le tonnerre, en raréfiant et réduisant en vapeurs l'humidité contenue dans un bois solide, un chêne, par exemple, a séparé par force ses fibres, et les a brisées en filandres: qu'en pénétrant intimement les plus durs métaux comme le fer, il en a séparé les parties en un instant de façon à faire d'un solide, un liquide. Il n'est donc pas hors de vraisemblance que la même matiere subtile, en traversant des corps animaux avec rapidité, ait une force suffisante pour produire dans leur substance un effet à-peu-près semblable.

La chair des animaux récemment tués à la maniere ordinaire est ferme, dure, et peu en état d'être mangée, parce que leurs parties adhérent fortement les unes aux autres. Au bout de quelques tems leur union est affoiblie, et en avançant vers la putréfaction qui tend à une séparation totale, la viande est dans un état que nous appellons tendre, ou au point le plus convenable pour être apprêtée en aliment pour notre usage.

On a souvent remarqué que les animaux tués par le tonnerre se putréfient tout d'un coup. Ce ne peut pas être toujours le cas, parce qu'une quantité de tonnerre suffisante pour tuer peut bien n'être pas assez considérable pour déchirer et diviser les fibres, et les parcelles des chairs, et leur procurer ce tendre qui est le préalable de la putréfaction. De-là vient qu'entre les animaux tués ainsi, les uns peuvent se garder plus long-tems que d'autres. Mais la putréfaction a été quelquefois d'une promptitude surprenante. Un homme de considération m'a assuré qu'il avoit une parfaite connoissance d'un exemple remarquable en ce genre. Tous les moutons d'un troupeau rassemblés en foule sous un arbre en Ecosse, ayant été tués par un grand coup de tonnerre, le soir un peu tard, le propriétaire voulant en sauver quelque chose, envoya le lendemain matin des gens pour les écorcher; mais la pourriture étoit si grande et l'infection si abominable que les gens n'eurent pas le courage d'exécuter cet ordre, desorte que les corps furent enterrés avec leurs peaux. . . . Il y a lieu de présumer qu'entre leur mort et le terme de cette putréfaction, il y eut un tems où leur chair auroit pu ne se trouver que tendre, et tendre au degré le plus propre pour être servie sur table. Ajoutez à cela, que quelques personnes qui ont mangé des volailles tuées par notre drôle de petit tonnerre, (l'électricité,) et accommodées sur le champ, ont certifié qu'elles en avoient trouvé la chair singulierement tendre. Le peu d'utilité de cette pratique a peut-être fait qu'on ne s'est pas beaucoup occupé de la suivre plus loin. Car quoiqu'il arrive quelques fois qu'une compagnie survenant tout-à-coup dans une maison de campagne où l'on ne s'y attendoit pas, ou une quantité extraordinaire de voyageurs dans une auberge, mette dans la nécessité de tuer des animaux, pour les apprêter tout de suite; cependant comme les voyageurs ont ordinairement bon appétit, on n'a pas fait grande attention à l'inconvénient des viandes dures. Néanmoins comme cette espece de mort est la plus subite et conséquemment la plus douce de toutes, si c'étoit un motif pour la faire préférer par les personnes compatissantes pour les animaux qui doivent être immolés à leur service, voici comment on pourroit s'y prendre.

Ayant préparé une batterie de six grandes jarres de verre (contenant chacune vingt à vingt-quatre pintes) comme pour l'expérience de Leyde, et établi une communication de l'intérieur de chacune au premier conducteur, comme à l'ordinaire; et les ayant chargées en plein (ce qui peut être exécuté en peu de minutes avec une bonne machine, et vérifié au moyen d'un électrometre) il faut prendre une chaîn communiquante avec leur extérieur, et en entourer les cuisses de la volaille; après quoi l'opérateur la tenant par les ailes renversées et rejointes ensemble sur le dos, doit l'élever autant qu'il faut pour que la tête reçoive le choc du premier conducteur. Elle meurt dans l'instant. Qu'on lui coupe alors la tête, pour la faire bien saigner; cela fait, on peut la plumer et la faire cuire aussitôt. On suppose cette quantité d'électricité suffisante pour un dindon de dix livres pesant, et peut-être pour un agneau. L'expérience seul peut nous instruire des proportions requises pour des animaux de différentes tailles, et de différens âges. Il en faut peut-être autant pour attendrir un petit oiseau, s'il est fort vieux, que pour un gros qui seroit plus jeune. Il est facile de donner des quantités d'électricité aussi différentes qu'on le desire, en y employant plus ou moins de jarres.

Mais comme six jarres déchargées à la fois sont capables de donner un terrible coup, celui qui fait l'opération, doit être trèscirconspect, crainte qu'il ne lui arrive, par accident, ou par inadvertance, de mortifier sa propre chair au lieu de celle de sa poularde. Je suis, &c.   B. FRANKLIN

To Jacques Barbeu-Dubourg

ALS (incomplete draft): American Philosophical Society; incomplete translated extract: printed in Jacques Barbeu-Dubourg, ed., *Œuvres de M. Franklin* ... (2 vols., Paris, 1773), I, 321.

Dear Sir,   London, May 28 [–June 1]. 1773
    I have received your Favour of the 13th Instant with several Packets of the Sheets. I have examined more of them, and hope to finish examining the rest before next Post, when I shall send you what Remarks have occur'd to me, towards furnishing your Errata.[5]
    I much like the Letters you propose to insert, as written from you to me; and am oblig'd to you for them, as they will adorn my Work. An Answer to one of them went in Tuesday's Packet; but I am afraid 'tis written with too serious an Air. Mould it as you please.[6] Some Observations on the others may soon follow. At present I confine myself, to what you seem most desirous of having immediately, my Remarks on the Translation of the Papers relating to the Powder Magazines.[7] The Difficulty lies in the technical Terms used by Builders. To explain these, I must try to make a little Sketch of one of the Magazines.

[The drawing on page 214 follows here in MS.*]*

    aa is what in my Papers is called the Ridge of the House, and what appears you would call in French *Sommet*, ou *faîte*, and not *corniche*, as that would go along under the Eaves, as at *bb*.
    The Shaded part from *a* to *a*, represents the bent Plate of Lead

5. The promised letter was presumably either the missing one of June 22 or that of the 29th below.
    6. See above, under May 25. Dubourg clearly refrained from "moulding" the letter.
    7. The letter to Dawson and the report of the Royal Society's committee on the Purfleet magazine (above, XIX, 154–6, 262–5) were printed in Dubourg, *Œuvres*, I, 280–7.

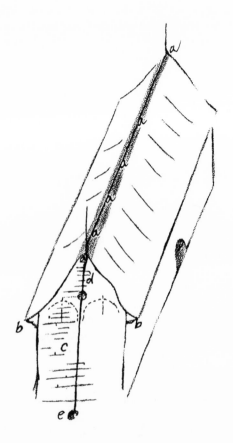

22 Inches wide which covers the Ridge, from End to End, 11 Inches on each side, to prevent the Entrance of Rain where the Slates meet at top. This Plate of Lead, which in English we call a *Coping*, I suppose you would call *Plaque* or *chaperon* perhaps and not *entablement*. *c* is the Wall. *d* the Conductor [*in margin:* extending above the Ridge, but well united with the Plate of Lead at *a*].

Thus I imagine you would say at the Beginning of Section 2d of the Letter to Major Dawson, (but in better French than mine) "Que le batiment qui a une plaque [ou chaperon] de plomb le long du Sommet [ou faîte] peut être garanti, &c. communiquant

avec cette plaque [ou chaperon]" &c.[8] And at the End of the
same Section; instead of *le plomb qui couvre la corniche,* say, *la
plaque du plomb qui couvre le sommet du comble.* In the 3d
Section, where mention is made of *corniches revetues de plomb,*
perhaps it may be right instead of *corniches* to say, *faîtes,* ou
sommets. And near the End, instead of *entablements* to say
plaques, and instead of *corniche,* to say *faîte, ou sommet.* But as I
am not Sure that I understand your Term *arcboutans,* I have
endeavoured to give you the Form of these 4 Roofs, by a Sketch,
wherein *ab* is the Ridge covered with Lead; *ca* and *da* are what
we call the *Hip-Joints,* or Joinings of the Sloping Roof of the End
with the sloping Roof of the Sides, which Joinings are also
covered with Lead, to prevent the Entrance of Rain where the
Slates meet. In this Form of Roof, the Proposal is, that the Iron
Conductor should rise from the Wall *e,* as high as *f,* and thence
extend its Arms to c and d. Thus the pointed Rod being erected at
a would communicate with the Iron Conductor by means of the
leaden Coping on the Hip Joints *ac* and *ad.*

[*The drawing on page 216 follows here in* MS.]

In the Note after the Letter to Major Dawson, I would omit the
Words *à faire le frais du reste.* The Idea of the Board being only
this that they should be better justified in the Public Opinion, if
they obtain'd the Sentiment of the Royal Society in favour of the
Project, than if they acted upon the Advice of a single Person. As
to the Expence, it was entirely in their own Power.

In the Report of the Committee near the Beginning of the
second Paragraph for *entablement de plomb,* I suppose it should be
plaque de plomb; and in the same line, for *corniche,* say *faîte,* or
sommet du comble. Again in the 4th Paragraph, for *entablement de
plomb le long des goûtières,* perhaps it might be, *plaques de plomb
le long les jointures du toit, jusques les goutieres, qui sont aussi de*

8. Dubourg had written (p. 280) "que le batiment qui a un entablement de
plomb le long de la corniche . . . peut etre garanti . . . communiquant avec
cet entablement . . . " In his errata he changed *entablement* to *chaperon* and
corniche to *faitière.* The suggestions that follow he embodied in the text,
improving on BF's French in the process. Brackets in this paragraph are in
the original draft.

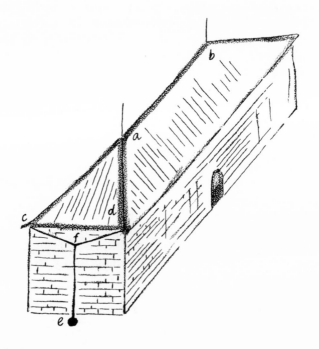

plomb, d'ou descendent, &c. I see my French must be abominable, but I hope you will understand it better than my English. Near the End of the 7th Paragraph, for *corniche* read *sommet* twice. In the 8th Parag. for *grosseur* read *roideur,* for *corniche* read *sommet,* and perhaps for *l'entablement,* read *plaque;* but I begin to think I do not rightly comprehend the meaning of your Word *entablement;* and that it may be proper in this Place. Towards the End of the 9th Paragraph for *étendûë sur le comble,* &c. read, *étendûë sur le toit,* [or, au travers du toit] avec *la plaque de plomb du sommet, cette plaque de plomb étant absolument semblable a celle du sommet.* In Paragraph 10. for *corniche,* read *faîte,* twice. All the rest seems to be right.

I suppose you have Copies of the Translations, you sent me, and that therefore I need not return them, as they would swell the Packet. I am, ever, with Love to Mrs. Dubourg, Your affectionate humble Servant   B FRANKLIN

P.S. June 1. [I] wish with you, that some Chymist, (if he is at the same time an Electrician, so much the better) would, from the excellent Hints in your Letter,[9] work on Glass with your Views. With a thorough Knowledge of that Substance as to its electric Qualities, we might go to work with greater Certainty in making our own Experiments, and in repeating those made by others in different Countries; which latter have I think, often succeeded differently, by the Use of different kinds of Glass, and thereby occasioned Misunderstandings and a Contrariety of Sentiments.

There is another Desideratum in Glass, that it should not be liable to break through when highly charg'd in the Leiden Experiment. In 20 Bottles discharg'd together I have known 8 so destroy'd, in 35, 12. The Loss on these Occasions is very discouraging to Electricians that would accumulate a large Force, necessary for some Experiments. What the Cause is, of this Rupture, has not yet been explained.[1] The first Thought naturally is, that the Positive Electricity accumulated on one Side of the Glass, bursts through to supply the Deficiency on the other and restore the Equilibrium. But I conceive this cannot be the Case, when I consider, that where a Number of Bottles are so united that they may be charg'd and discharg'd together, the Bursting of one alone would discharge the whole Number; and therefore, that if it depended on some Weakness in the Glass, it is not probable that 8 should have precisely the same degree of Weakness, so as all to break at the same Instant, but that the weakest would break first and thereby secure the rest. That when a certain Effect is to be produced, by the whole Quantity passing in the destin'd Circuit, as the Melting of a Wire for Instance, if the Charge instead of passing in the Circuit should burst thro' the Sides of the Bottles the intended Effect must fail, which however does not happen. For these Reasons, I suspect that there is in the Substance of the Glass either some little Air Bubble, or some Particle of unvitrified Sand or Salt, into which a Quantity of the Electric Fluid may be forced during the Charge, and there confin'd, till the general Discharge, when the Force being suddenly taken off, its elasticity acts on the confining Glass from which it cannot

9. Of March 25 above.
1. See above, XVIII, 181.

so soon escape and therefore bursts it. This I offer only as a Conjecture for others to examine.

The Globe I had which could not be excited, tho' from the same Glass house with others that were excellent, was not out of the same Pot.[2] The common Glass made there was a little Greenish, and work'd up chiefly for Windows and Bottles. But the Workmen once attempted to make a Pot of White Glass, and the above-mentioned Globe was out of that Pot. The Glass prov'd not of a clear white, was therefore not lik'd, and therefore they gave over that Attempt. I suspected that there was too much Salt in the Composition; but I am ignorant of those matters.

Your *Para Tonnerre* is ingeniously contrivd.[3] And tho' the Chance is small that any one Person walking abroad shall be struck by Lightning, yet as it sometimes happens, and some may think the Chance, small as it is, worth guarding against, I know not how they can do better than use your Contrivance. Perhaps [*remainder missing*.][4]

M. Dubourg.

2. See above, v, 521.
3. It is described in Dubourg's letter above, April 1.
4. The printed extract, which begins with this paragraph, gives more of the sentence but breaks off in the middle of it: "Peut-être pourriez-vous simplifier encore votre instrument, et vous contenter de faire adapter à un parasol ordinaire vos . . . ." Dubourg here appended the following note:
"J'ai fait en conséquence, non-seulement au Paratonnerre, mais encore à la lettre qui l'annonçoit, un petit changement dont l'objet n'est pas assez intéressant pour en rendre compte ici plus au long; mais j'ai cru devoir persister à mettre tout ce qu'il y a de métallique en-dessus, pour tranquilliser d'autant plus les esprits prévenus de terreurs paniques, qu'on ne peut pas déraciner en un jour.
"J'ai fait faire ce Paratonnerre, par un de mes voisins, qui l'a tres-bien exécuté à mon gré. (Le Sieur Bairin de la Croix, Ingénieur du Cabinet de Physique et d'Optique du Roi, demeurant rue Copeau, à Paris)."

From Edmé-Louis Daubenton[5]

AL: American Philosophical Society

au jardin du Roy ce 31. may. [1773]

M. Daubenton le jeune a l'honneur de presenter son hommage à Monsieur franklin et de l'assurer de son respect en lui envoyant les nouveaux Cayers des oiseaux enluminés qui lui manquent pour completer son exemplaire. Il aura grand soin de mettre a part ceux qui restent à faire et de les envoyer à Monsieur franklin.

Addressed: A Monsieur / Monsieur franklin / membre de plusieurs academies / pres de la Muette / à Passy[6]

From William Strahan

ALS: American Philosophical Society

Dear Sir   New Street Thursday Afternoon [May, 1773?[7]]

Dont forget your Appointment tomorrow at 3, or soon after. I send you herewith the 10th. Vol. of the Statutes; but the

5. Known as Daubenton le jeune (1732–85) to distinguish him from his older and far more famous relative, Louis-Jean-Marie, who collaborated for years with the comte de Buffon in the Jardin du roi; see above, xv, 141–2 n. The younger man, employed in the same collections, began in 1765 to publish a series of colored engravings of birds by François-Nicolas Martinet (b. 1731), designed to illustrate Buffon's monumental *Histoire naturelle des oiseaux.* Between 1770 and 1786 this work appeared in four different formats. Two were illustrated with line engravings; the other two had references for inserting the colored plates, which were completed in 1780 in forty-two fascicles containing more than a thousand illustrations. Noël Mayaud, "Les éditions originales de l'*Histoire naturelle des oiseaux* de Buffon," *Alauda: revue trimestrielle d'ornithologie* . . . 3rd ser., xi (1939), 19–20. Daubenton was enclosing some of these fascicles for BF's copy of the *Histoire.*
6. The home of Jean-Baptiste LeRoy, who was forwarding the plates to BF; see Daubenton's second note below, July 20.
7. So dated on the assumption the "American Tea Act" to which Strahan refers was not the minor statute of 1772 but the famous one, 13 Geo. iii, c. 44, which became law on May 10, 1773; Strahan, according to custom, printed it as a separate pamphlet. The tenth volume of *Statutes at Large,* to which he also refers, had been published more than two years earlier: *London Chron.,* March 19–21, 1771.

American Tea Act is not yet printed, but will be done in a Day or two. I am Dear Sir Most affectionately Yours   WILL: STRAHAN

Addressed: To / Dr. Franklin / Craven Street

[*In another hand*] At Mr Nelson's / In Bush Lane / Scotch Yard / Cannon Street.

To Alexander Colden   ALS (letterbook draft): Library of Congress

Dear Sir   London, June 2. 1773.

I received yours of April 7. inclosing Coningham and Nesbit's Bill on D. Harvey & Co for £200[8] with which your Account is credited. In my last I acknowledged the Receipt of Christie's renew'd Bill for £338 17s. 2½d.

I am glad the last Years Accounts are to come by the next Packet, for then we shall have the whole settled and pass'd together,[9] there having been a Delay for some time occasioned by the Mislaying of a preceding Account at the Office. If at the Settlement, any thing new should be required in the Mode of rendring your Accounts I shall acquaint you with it.

I admire your good Father's rare Felicity in retaining so long his Health, and Spirits, and particularly that Vigour of his mental Faculties which enables him still to amuse himself with abstruse philosophical Disquisitions. For my own part, every thing of difficult Discussion, and that requires close Attention of Mind, and an Application of long Continuance, grows rather irksome to me; and where there is not some absolute Necessity for it, as in the Settlement of Accounts, or the like; I am apt to indulge the Indolence usually attending Age, in postponing such Business from time to time: tho' continually resolving to do it. This has been the Case with regard to your Father's Philosophical Piece on the

8. John M. Nesbitt (*c.* 1730–1802) and Redmund Conyngham had been in partnership since 1756; the firm was one of the most prosperous in Philadelphia. *DAB* under Nesbitt. David Harvey was a merchant of Lawrence Lane, Cheapside: *Kent's Directory* . . . (London, 1770).

9. In other words the accounts for 1771–2 and 1772–3. The latter, of which this is the first mention, had been sent on May 5 and arrived before July 14: below, Colden to BF, June 2; BF to Foxcroft, July 14.

Principles of Vital Motion, which he did me the Honour some time since to desire my Opinion of. I have read it cursorily and long intended to read it with close Attention, and still intend it, but what with Business that takes up so much of my Time, Interruptions of various kinds, and the Indolence I have above confessed, I have hitherto put it off. In my Voyage home, which I am now preparing for, I promise my self to study it thoroughly,[1] so that if I have the Happiness once more of meeting him, we may discourse of it together. In the mean time, present my best Respects to him, and believe me, with great Regard, Dear Sir, Your most obedient humble Servant   B F

Mr Colden

To Thomas Cushing

AL (copy[2]): Public Record Office; ALS (letterbook draft): Library of Congress

Sir,   London, June 2. 1773.

Since my last, which was of the 6th past, I have been honour'd with yours of March 6. and 24. inclosing a Petition to the King, and a Letter to Lord Dartmouth.[3] On considering the whole, I concluded that a longer Delay of presenting the first Petition and Remonstrance was not likely to answer any good Purpose,[4] and therefore immediately waited on Lord Dartmouth, and deliver'd to him the Letter, and the second Petition, at the same time redelivering the first, and press'd his Lordship to present them to his Majesty, which he promised to do. Enclos'd I send you the

1. The promise may have given BF second thoughts about the voyage: he had no desire to tackle Cadwallader Colden's "Inquiry in the Principles of Vital Motion," despite prodding from the old man, and for more than two years had resisted studying it. Above, XIX, 94 n, 392 n.

2. At the head of BF's letter below, June 4; the original has been lost. Cushing's answer to both letters is below, Aug. 26, and Thomas Moffatt's comment on both is appended to that of June 4.

3. Cushing's letter of March 6 is missing; see that of March 24 for the second petition and the letter to Dartmouth.

4. In his draft BF added here, and then struck out, "since the new one would probably be full as disagreeable."

Answer I have just received from him,[5] this Day's Pacquet, (the Mail for which is to be made up and dispatch'd in a few Hours) being the earliest Opportunity, as the Ships for Boston do not sail till the Beginning of next Week. By one of them I shall send a Copy with what Observations occur to me on the Occasion, which the Time will not now permit me to write.[6] In the mean while I would just beg leave to say, that I hope the House will come to no hasty Resolves upon it. The longer they deliberate, the more maturely they consider, the greater Weight will attend their Resolutions. With great Respect, I am, &c.

From Lord Dartmouth   Copies:[7] Public Record Office

Since the previous summer the grievances of Massachusetts had been working their way toward the throne. The petitions from the House of Representatives in July, 1772, and March, 1773, had arraigned the Townshend Acts and their implementation as violating the colony's charter, and had demanded a return to the old system whereby the General Court controlled officials' salaries. The demand revealed how hollow was the dream, long shared by Franklin and other Americans, that the empire was a league of states with a common sovereign and coequal legislatures. The empire was not, and could not be without profound constitutional change at home. In British eyes the King had no option about implementing a Parliamentary statute; refusing to do so would have revived the dispensing power and defied the Bill of Rights. Crown and Parliament were in this respect inseparable, and the claim that a colonial charter limited their sphere of action was one that no British government could accept.

Once the claim was raised, as Dartmouth was well aware, it could not be compromised. He had therefore persuaded Franklin to delay delivering the first petition, in the faint hope that the House would

5. See the following document.

6. When he sent the copy with his letter of June 4, he was again too hurried to make any observations.

7. The letter appears here, out of the usual order, because BF enclosed it with the preceding document. The original and the copy that he sent Cushing on June 4 have disappeared. The two copies that survive are virtually identical; this one was the office draft, as the docket indicates, and was subsequently entered in the secretary's letterbook.

reconsider; instead a second petition was added to the first.[8] The Secretary had no alternative to forwarding both, and the letter that follows was the King's reply. It was categorical: the supreme and unlimited imperial authority was the crown in Parliament.[9]

Sir,   Whitehall June 2d: 1773.

I have not failed to lay before the King the Petition and Remonstrance to His Majesty of the late house of Representatives of the Province of Massachuset's Bay, resolved upon in general Assembly on the 14th. of July 1772. and also their Petition to His Majesty resolved upon in general Assembly on the 6th. of March last, which Petitions and Remonstrance you delivered to me on the 14th. instant.

His Majesty commanded me to read them to Him, and having well weighed and considered the Subject Matter thereof, and the Expressions contained therein, was graciously pleased to declare, that as on the one hand His Majesty would ever attend to the humble Petitions of His Subjects, in all parts of His Dominions, and be most forward to redress, as far as depended upon him, every real Greivance they might have to complain of, so on the other hand His Majesty was determined to support the Constitution, and to resist with firmness every Attempt to derogate from the Authority of the Supreme Legislature.

That His Majesty considered His Authority to make Laws by and with the Advice and Consent of the Lords Spiritual and Temporal, and Commons of Great Britain in Parliament assembled, of sufficient Force and Validity to bind His Subjects in

---

8. For the nature and progress of the petitions see above, XIX, 209, 409–11; Cushing to BF, March 24, 1773; and the preceding document.

9. The reply did not end all possibility of compromise. Asserting constitutional principles was one thing; enforcing them was another. Before the end of the month Dartmouth began his remarkable private letter to Cushing (below, p. 377 n), in which he expressed the wish that the controversy might become dormant and the crown abandon the innovation of paying salaries. The innovation would be abandoned and judges accorded tenure during good behavior, he said a few weeks earlier in a letter to Hutchinson that was drafted but apparently not sent, if the House provided royal officials with adequate permanent salaries. *Dartmouth MSS*, II, 152–3; Hutchinson, *History*, III, 298. The Minister may have thought this suggestion conciliatory, but it was unrealistic; it did not touch the petitioner's central claim to control royal officials by paying them. See above, XIX, 381 n.

America in all Cases whatsoever,[1] as essential to the Dignity of the Crown, and a Right appertaining to the State, which it was His Duty to preserve entire and inviolate, and therefore His Majesty could not but be greatly displeased with the Petitions and Remonstrance of the late Representatives of the Province of Massachuset's Bay, in which Petitions and Remonstrance that Right is drawn into question.

That His Majesty was unwilling to suppose that the Sentiments of His faithful Subjects in general in the Province of Massachuset's Bay corresponded with the unwarrantable Doctrines held forth in the said Petitions and Remonstrance, but imputed the same to the Artifices of a few who seek to create groundless Jealousy and Distrust, and to disturb that Harmony and Union, the Preservation of which is so essential for the mutual Interest both of the Mother Country and of the Colonies.[2] I am &c.   DARTMOUTH

Dr. Franklin, Agent for the late Representatives of the Province of Massachuset's Bay.

Notation: Drat. to Dr. Franklin, Agent for the late Represenves: of the Province of Massachuset's Bay.[3] Whitehall June 2d: 1773.

Entd.

To Deborah Franklin   ALS: Yale University Library

My dear Child,   London, June 2. 1773.

I received yours per Capt. All.[4] This is just to let you know I am well, as all our other Friends here are: I have been so hindred

1. A paraphrase of the Declaratory Act.
2. The idea that the "unwarrantable Doctrines" were the creation of a few trouble-makers was deeply rooted in Whitehall; BF and Dartmouth had skirted it in their interview the month before: above, p. 202.
3. The "late" representatives, as in Dartmouth's first sentence, were in the house that had since been dissolved.
4. The letter was DF's of April 28, now lost, which BF mentioned in writing her on July 15. Capt. All in the *Richard Penn* cleared from Philadelphia in early May: *Pa. Gaz.*, May 5, 1773. He did not reach London, however, until mid-June: *Lloyd's Evening Post*, June 14–16, 1773. BF's acknowledging on June 2 a letter sent by a ship that arrived almost two weeks later is an obvious impossibility; either he dropped a digit from the date, or the *Richard Penn* put the mail ashore at a Channel port and then made slow progress to London.

to day, that I can only add my Love to our Children, and that I am ever, Dear Debby, Your affectionate Husband   B FRANKLIN

From Alexander Colden   ALS: American Philosophical Society

⟨General Post Office, New York, June 2, 1773: Wrote him on May 5 and sent the accounts through April 5 last; also sent first bills of exchange, of which he now encloses seconds: John Bonfield on Quarles Harris, £80; Thomas Boylston on Champion & Dickason, £100; George Erwin on Lane, Son & Fraser, £120; Benjamin Ogles on James Anderson, £83 10s. 3d.; William Maxwell on Rowland [?] Williams, £67; total, £450 10s. 3d. Also encloses a first bill of Willing & Morris on Harris & Co. for £15, "being the Bill Mr. Foxcroft sent me for Wm. Taylors Protested Bill which you returned me, and I mentioned Mr. Foxcroft had Omitted to Endorse."[5] The *Lord Hyde*, packet, has not arrived.⟩

5. Two of the American bills were drawn by Thomas Boylston, the prominent Boston merchant, and Willing & Morris, the equally prominent Philadelphia firm. George Erving, as BF spelled the name (Jour., p. 49), was undoubtedly the Bostonian who was Bowdoin's brother-in-law: above, XVII, 243. Ogles may well have been Benjamin Ogle (1749–1809), a Marylander who was the son of a former governor and later became himself governor of the state; he was suing at the time for recovery of his plantation. Louise J. Hienton, *Prince George's Heritage: Sidelights on the Early History of Prince George's County* . . . [Baltimore, 1972], pp. 105–9. Ogle's finances may have been precarious; in any case the bill was protested: BF to Colden below, Aug. 3. John Bonfield could have been the merchant, John Bondfield, who was later U.S. consul at Bordeaux and will appear often in subsequent volumes. Little is known of his early career, but the fact that John Adams knew him in America suggests that he was a Bostonian; see Butterfield, ed., *John Adams Diary*, II, 294 n. Some of the English merchants were Quarles Harris of Crutched Friars; Champion & Dickason of Bishopsgate St. Within; Lane, Son & Fraser of Nicholas Lane; and Herries & Co.—as BF spelled the name (Jour., p. 50)—of Jeffrey's Square, St. Mary Axe. James Anderson may have been either the man of that name on Lamb's Conduit St., Holborn, or the firm of James and William Anderson, Tower Hill. *Kent's Directory* . . . (London, 1770).

To Samuel Cooper

ALS: British Museum; letterbook draft: Library of Congress

Dear Friend,   London, June 4. 1773.

I can now only acknowledge the Receipt of your much esteem'd Favours of March 15 and Apr. 23. which gave me great Satisfaction. By the next Opportunity I purpose to write to you fully, and among other Things give you my Thoughts on the Warming of your Meeting-house.[6]

I send you a french Pamphlet containing some liberal Sentiments on Taxes, Commerce, &c. And another that contains a little System of Morals; both written by Friends of mine in Paris.[7] With best Wishes for the Establishment of your Health, and with sincere Esteem, I am ever, Dear Sir, Yours most affectionately

B FRANKLIN

Revd Dr Cooper.

To Thomas Cushing

ALS: Public Record Office; letterbook draft: Library of Congress

In the paragraph of this letter that deals with the Tea Act, Franklin implies that the purpose of the statute was "to keep up the Exercise of the Right" to tax the colonies. This idea was sure to be a red rag to the Bostonian bull. All that is known about the passage of the act, however, indicates that the ministry avoided the question of right and concentrated upon the need to obtain revenue and ease the financial crisis of the East India Company.[8]

6. The April letter is missing; that of March 15 BF answered below, July 7, with gloomy advice on the heating problem.

7. The pamphlet with liberal sentiments, we conjecture, was an English translation of one by du Pont de Nemours, for which Dubourg had asked in his letter above of Feb. 24, and in which the author did deal in general terms with taxes and commerce; but for other possibilities, in the writings of BF's physiocratic friends at the time, see Henry Higgs, *The Physiocrats* . . . (London, 1897), pp. 53–8, 61–6. The system of morals was undoubtedly Dubourg's *Petit code*, perhaps Polly Hewson's translation but more likely the French edition that BF had recently had printed; see his letter to Benezet above, Feb. 10.

8. For this crisis see above, XIX, 420 n and Gipson, *British Empire*, XII, 12–17.

Since early March the Company's affairs had absorbed Parliament. Attention focused on two closely related issues, the Directors' request for a loan and government's determination to force a measure of control upon them. Their desire to market more tea in America was a relatively minor political issue, and perhaps for that reason was settled before the larger ones. On April 26 the House of Commons debated, and the next day adopted, ten resolutions relating to the Company, of which the last three were promptly embodied in a bill that became the Tea Act. It provided for a drawback, on tea exported to America, of the total import duty paid in England; the Townshend duty in the colonies was left unchanged.[9] On May 3, when the bill had its second reading, the House received the propositions that were later turned into the Regulating Act; on the same day a select committee concluded its report on conditions in India, and Lord Clive opened his defense of his conduct there. Tea, it is safe to say, did not receive undivided attention.[1]

The one full-scale debate on the question was on April 26, when the resolutions were introduced in the House. A few opposition speakers immediately raised the issue of the Townshend duty of 3d. a pound. Repealing it, they argued, would not decrease revenue any more than the drawback would, and offered the only way to increase American consumption. "I tell the Noble Lord now," said William Dowdeswell, Rockingham's lieutenant, "if he don't take off the duty they won't take the tea." The duty was being kept, he asserted, to maintain the right to tax;[2] and this assertion may have been the basis for Franklin's remark.

But North refused to be drawn into a discussion of right. The most he admitted was that there were "political" reasons for retaining the duty, and the adjective had many possible meanings. An increased market for tea in America would mean an increased yield from the duty, and hence more money for paying official salaries; and the lowered cost would operate to discourage smuggling. North may have had

9. This was a return to the situation, as it related to tea, that had prevailed from 1767 to 1772. Retention of the Townshend duty reflected a change in North's views, for in February he had considered reducing it by 40%; see the note on BF to Galloway above, Feb. 14.

1. Lucy Sutherland, in her detailed account of the session (*East India Co.*, chap. ix), devotes only a sentence to the Tea Act, p. 252. For excellent descriptions of its passage see Labaree, *Tea Party*, pp. 70–3, and Bernhard Knollenberg, *Growth of the American Revolution, 1766–1775* (New York and London, [1975]), pp. 90–4.

2. *Ibid.*, p. 92.

such political considerations in mind, but he did not elaborate. Although the issue of right was certainly in the background, just as certainly it did not come to the fore; one speaker even pointed out, with questionable accuracy in view of Dowdeswell's remarks, that it had never once been raised.[3] The government, as Franklin says, was acting on the principle of interest and, as he does not say, was apparently unaware that its action would stir another principle to life. The warning that it would fell on deaf ears.

Sir,   London, June 4. 1773.

The above is a Copy of mine per Packet, inclosing the Original of His Majesty's Answer to our Petitions and Remonstrance.[4] I now send an exact Copy of the same, which I did intend to accompany with some Observations, and my Sentiments on the general State of our Affairs in this Country, and the Conduct proper for us to hold on this Occasion. But, beginning to write, I find the Matter too copious, and the Subject, on Reflection, too important to be treated in a hasty Letter; and being now told the Ships will sail tomorrow, I must postpone it to another Opportunity.

It was thought at the Beginning of the Session, that the American Duty on Tea would be taken off. But now the Scheme is, to take off as much Duty here as will make Tea cheaper in America than Foreigners can supply us; and continue the Duty there to keep up the Exercise of the Right. They have no Idea that any People can act from any Principle but that of Interest; and they believe that 3*d*. in a Pound of Tea, of which one does not drink perhaps 10 lb in a Year, is sufficient to overcome all the Patriotism of an American!

I purpose soon to write to you very fully. As to the Letters I communicated to you, tho' I have not been able to obtain Leave to take Copies or publish them, I have Permission to let the Originals remain with you as long as you may think it of any Use to have them in Possession.[5] With great Esteem and Respect, I

3. Labaree, *Tea Party*, p. 72.

4. In his draft BF here added, then deleted, "as I receiv'd it from Lord Dartmouth. Inclos'd I now send," etc. The letters in question are above, BF to Cushing and Dartmouth to BF, June 2.

5. BF is responding to Cushing's request above, March 24, to be able to make better use of the Hutchinson letters. But by this time no permission was relevant; for the secret was out; see Cushing's letter below, June 14.

have the Honour to be, Sir, Your most obedient humble Servant
                                                        B FRANKLIN

Honble. Thos Cushing Esqr.⁶

To Samuel Mather⁷   ALS (letterbook draft): Library of Congress

Reverend Sir,   London, June 4. 1773
    I received your respected Favour of March 18. with the valuable
Pamphlets it enclosed for which I thank you: By the next Opportunity I shall do myself the Honour of writing to you fully.⁸ At
present I can only add that I am, with great Esteem and Respect,
Reverend Sir, Your obliged and most obedient humble Servant
                                                        B FRANKLIN

[*In the margin:*] I send you a Pamphlet, that shows the Spirit of
some Missionaries towards the Colonies that encourage them.
And a French one wherein you will find some liberal Sentiments
on Commerce, Taxes, &c.⁹

Mr Mather

    6. Thomas Moffatt made two notes, which we elide, on this and the June 2
letter: "Both relate to Petitions from the Massachusetts General Assembly to
His Majesty. The second letter imparts the design of lowering yet continuing
three pence duty upon Tea and finishes with an Extravagance or Encomium
upon American Virtue and Patriotism . . . [which] may well pass as another
Specimen of the Writers Modesty Sincerity and Gratitude to Administration
for some favour conferrd upon himself."
    7. The Rev. Samuel Mather (1706–85), Governor Hutchinson's brother-
in-law, was third and last in the family line of distinguished Congregational
clergymen. Like his father and grandfather, Cotton and Increase, he was for
a time minister of the Second Church in Boston; but he was dismissed in 1741
and founded a church of his own. He was a man of greater erudition than
intellectual power. *DAB*.
    8. Below, July 7, where BF discussed two of Mather's pamphlets.
    9. The first pamphlet we cannot identify; the second was the one that BF
sent to Cooper with his note of June 4, above.

To Jonathan Williams, Sr.

ALS (letterbook draft): Library of Congress

Dear Cousin   London, June 4. 1773
I have just time to acknowledge the Receipt of yours of April
15. with the £50 Bill, (Ross and Mills) part of the Money you
receiv'd for me of Hall. I have purchased the Things for my
Sister directed in her Invoice, and they go by this Ship.[1] I shall do
you every Service in my Power relating to the Commission
Business, &c. Tell Jonathan I received his Letter, and deliver'd
that to Miss Barwell, who will serve him whenever she can;[2] as
will also Your affectionate Uncle   B F

I write in great haste. Love to my dear Sister and to your Family.
The Invoices are in the Trunk.

Mr Williams
Per Capt Hatch, the Nicholas

1. The letter of April 15, now missing, enclosed the bill that Williams had
promised in his letter above, Feb. 15. It was drawn by T. Russell (above, x,
358), who was doubtless the Charlestown and Boston merchant lauded at his
death by John Warren: *An Eulogy on the Honourable Thomas Russell* . . .
(Boston, 1796). Ross & Mill was a mercantile firm in Botolph Lane: *Kent's
Directory* . . . (London, 1770). BF entered the bill in May, and the next month
paid out £55 4s. 5d. for haberdashery for Jane. Jour., p. 48. In early August
Williams acknowledged, through his son, the arrival of the goods; see the
postscript to the letter from Jonathan, Jr., below, July 29.

2. For the commission business and the appeal to Mary Barwell see Jonathan to BF above, April 20, and BF's reply below, July 7. The Williamses'
request to be consigned tea from India was made before the Tea Act, and
Miss Barwell apparently did not try to get them consignments under the act.
Competition for those consignments was intense. Three interrelated Boston
firms won out, thanks to backing in London: Hutchinson's commercial
agent recommended to India House the Governor's two sons, Thomas and
Elisha; Jonathan Clarke, then in England, persuaded the Company to
choose his family firm, Richard Clarke & Sons; and a London house consulted by the Company suggested its Boston correspondents, Benjamin
Faneuil and Joshua Winslow. See Francis S. Drake, ed., *Tea Leaves: Being
a Collection of Letters and Documents Relating to the Shipment of Tea to the
American Colonies in the Year 1773* . . . (Boston, 1884), pp. 189–91, 209–11,
214–15, 222–3, 238. The Williamses had no such friends at court.

From Edward Rowe Mores[3]

ALS: American Philosophical Society

Sir,   Leyton, Essex. 7 June. 1773.

Mrs. James is so teazing that I am constrained to apply to you for relief. I could write a volume of grievances; but as our time is not to be bestowed upon trifles I shall trouble you with no more than two.

The first is, Mrs. James before I was concerned in the foundery employed a printer because he owed her money, and now she is desirous that I should get rid of him, which I cannot attempt to do as he was not employed by me, and his behaviour has been such as I cannot object to. But I cannot approve of his workman-ship, which, in Mrs. James's case more especially, should be performed with the greatest nicety. I enclose a bit for your judgement, and if you are pleased to tell me that it will do I will correct it and send him more copy.

The second, Sir, I mention with reluctance, fearful lest it should transpire and obstruct my scheme, but I trust I am writing to a gentleman who will keep my secret. I am desirous, and have reason to think my desire will be gratified, that Her Majesty of Russia should purchase the foundery. So the foundery will be preserved entire, Mrs. James obtain a better price for it than she can obtain in England and our own people be pleased that it is gone out of the kingdom.[4] And Mrs. James is angry that I will not disclose to her my design.

---

3. An eccentric antiquary (1730–78), who had built himself a bizarre house on the French model and was beginning, at about the time of this letter, a book on the history of type-founding. *DNB*.

4. Mrs. James was the widow of the famous type-founder, John James, for whom see above, XVIII, 87 n. We offer no conjecture about "our own people" or why they should be pleased to have the foundry go overseas; the better price for it was probably because the domestic value of James's type, some of which dated from the fifteenth century, was decreasing as Caslon's founts became more popular. After James's death in 1772 Mores is said to have bought much of the type, presumably when it was auctioned in December, 1773, and to have acquired thereby a proprietary interest in the business. Talbot B. Reed, *A History of the Old English Letter Foundries . . .* (new ed., A. F. Johnson, ed.; London, [1952]), p. 215; Mores, *A Dissertation upon English Typographical Founders and Founderies . . .* (Harry Carter and

The only use I entreat you, Dear Sir, to make of this information is, to Mrs. James (if that I say shall merit your approbation)
that I have communicated my design to you, and that you
approve of it, to me (if you do not approve of it) that you will be
kind enough to tell me so, who am, Sir, your obedient humble
servant   EDWARD ROWE MORES.

Addressed: To / Dr Franklyn.

From Samuel Cooper

AL (incomplete): American Philosophical Society; ALS (draft): British
Museum[5]

Dear Sir,   Boston 14th[–15]. June. 1773.
  I wrote you on the 15th. March and 23d of April last, and
mention'd in these Letters, which I hope you have receiv'd, the
most important Political Occurrences among us, particularly
the grand Discussion, in the last Session of Assembly between
the Governor and both Houses, and the great Effect it had
upon the Minds of the People. I have seen[6] high Eulogiums
upon the Replies of our Council and Commons from Gentlemen
of the most respectable Characters in the other Colonies, where
there evidently appears an increasing Regard for this Province,
and an Inclination to unite for the common Safety.
  Virginia has led the Way, by proposing a Communication and
Correspondence between all the Commons Houses thro the
Continent. The Letter from their Committee for this Purpose

Christopher Ricks, eds.; Oxford Bibliographical Soc. *Pub.*, new ser., IX,
Oxford, 1961), p. lxi. This letter suggests, however, that Mores had such an
interest—managerial or financial or both—before his purchase; otherwise he
would not have been judging a printer, or hoping to keep the collection
entire by selling it to Catherine the Great. When the hope was disappointed
and the stock auctioned, Mores was not the only buyer. BF also acquired
some; see his letters below to Baskerville, Sept. 21, 1773, and to Bache,
Feb. 17, 1774.
  5. The letter that was sent, which we print according to our usage, is torn
as well as incomplete; we have silently supplied missing portions from the
draft and have noted where the two MSS differ in wording.
  6. The draft reads "We have receiv'd." Cooper's letter of March 15 is
above; that of April 23 is missing.

was receiv'd here with no little Joy, and the Proposal agreed to in the most ready and respectful Manner. Rhode-Island, Connecticut, and N. Hampshire have already chosen Committees, so that all N. England is now united with Virginia in this salutary Plan, and the Accession of most if not all the other Colonies is not doubted.[7] This opens a most agreable Prospect to the Friends of our common Rights.

In my last I mention'd to you my having had a Sight of some Letters that had been sent to the Speaker, with Leave to communicate them to me and some others in Confidence. I soon apprehended from the Nature of the Contents, and the Number of Persons to whom they were directed to be shewn, that they could not long remain secret. However, I have preserv'd inviolate the Trust reposed in me. Some, not named by you as Confidents, had Hints from London that such Letters were come, or on their Way to us, and began to suspect they were concealed in Favor of the Writers.[8] The Secret was kept till the Meeting of the General Court, when so many Members had obtain'd such general Intimations of it as to render them extremely inquisitive and sollicitous. At last it was thought best to communicate them, to the House with the Restrictions that accompanied them here. The House could not act upon them with these Restrictions; but the Substance of them was now known ev'ry where, and the Alarm given. Soon after Copies of them were brought into the House, said to have come from England by the last Ships. Many Members scrupled to act upon these Copies while they were under such public Engagements to the unknown Proprietor of the Originals. As the Matter was now so publick, and the Restrictions could answer no good End, no View of the Sender, but on the contrary might prevent in a great Measure a proper Improvement of the Letters for the public Benefit, and for weakning the

7. See Cushing to BF above, April 20. By February, 1774, New York, New Jersey, Maryland, Delaware, Pennsylvania, North and South Carolina, and Georgia had joined the New England colonies and Virginia in forming committees of correspondence. Gipson, *British Empire*, XII, 34–7.

8. By late April a number of Bostonians other than those pledged to secrecy knew of the letters' existence; see the note on Cushing to BF above, March 24, and the document following this one. We have annotated the latter, when it deals with the same events that Cooper discusses, because Cushing's account was somewhat more circumstantial.

Influence and Power of the Writers and their Friends[9] it was judg'd most expedient by the Gentlemen to whom they were first shewn to allow the House such an Use of the Originals, as they might think necessary to found their Proceedings for the common Safety. By whom, and to whom they were sent is still a Secret, known only to three Persons here, and may still remain so, if you desire it.[1] I forgot to mention that upon the first Appearance of the Letters in the House they voted by a Majority of 101 to 5, that the Design and Tendency of them was to subvert the Constitution and introduce arbitrary Powr.[2] Nothing could have been more seasonable than the Arrival of these Letters. They have had great Effect: they make deep Impressions wherever they are known. They strip the Mask from the Authors who under the Profession of Friendship to their Country[3] have been endeavoring to build up themselves and their Families upon it's Ruins. They and their Adherents are shock'd and dismay'd. The Confidence reposed in them by many is annihilated; and Administration must soon see the Necessity of putting the Provincial Pow'r of the Crown into other Hands.[4] This is at present almost the Universal Sentiment. The House have this Day sent up the Letters to the Board which I believe will concur with them in the Substance and Spirit of their Proceedings.[5]

9. The draft added "and disarming their Revenge."

1. BF's response to Cooper's implied question was in his letter of July 25 below.

2. The vote was on June 2; see the following document. The draft here added, "Their Committee upon this Matter, reported this Day a Number of Resolutions, which are to be printed by to Morrow Morning, and ev'ry Member furnish'd with a Copy, that they may compare them with the Letters, and to Morrow 3 o Clock p. m. is the Time appointed to decide upon the Report; The Acceptance of it by a great Majority is not doubted. Should the Vessel that is to carry this Letter, tarry long eno' I will send you a Copy of the Resolutions." Cooper's use of "this Day" proves that he was writing on June 15, when the committee of the House reported on the Hutchinson letters; see Cushing to BF below, June 16.

3. The draft added, "now plainly appear to." For the authors of the letters see above, XIX, 401–2, 403 n.

4. The draft added, "if they mean it should operate to any good Effect."

5. On the 15th the House sent the Council copies of the letters, and soon afterward the originals to be compared and returned. *Mass. House Jour.,*

We are highly indebted to our Friends in London, and to you Sir in particular, for so important a Communication, and hope while it supports the Cause of Truth and Justice, and promotes the Deliverance of this abused and oppressed Country, it will be attended with no Disadvantage to them. The Inconveniences that may arise accidentally from such generous Interpositions, are abundantly compensated by the Reflection that they tend to the Security and Happiness of Millions. I trust, however, that Nothing of this Kind will occur to disturb the agreable Feelings of those, who in this Instance, have done such extensive Good. I write in great Hast not having had early Notice of this Opportunity and am with great Esteem and Affection &c. Your &c

S. COOPER

From Thomas Cushing

ALS: Library of Congress

Sir   Boston June. 14. 1773.

I am now to Acknowledge the receipt of your Favors of the 9th March and the 3d. of April togather with the News Papers and the Bishop of St. Asaph's Sermons for which I am much obliged to you. The reply to the observations made upon a Speculation signed Junias Americanus is highly approved of; The Bishop's Sermon is also much liked as it discovers a Catholic Spirit and sentiments very favourable respecting America.[6] I have endeavoured inviolably to keep to your Injunctions with respect to the papers you sent me, I have shewn them only to such Gentlemen as you directed, no one person excepting Dr. Cooper and one of the Committee of Correspondence know from whom they Come or to whom they were sent. I have constantly avoided mentioning your name Upon the Occasion so that it never need be known (if you incline to keep it secret) who they Came from or to whom they were sent and I desire so far as I am Concerned my name may not be mentioned, for as I hold an office in the Government

first session, May–June, 1773, pp. 55–6. The Council did not act until the 25th, when it passed concurrent resolutions; see the note on Williams to BF below, June 28. The Council and House then appointed a joint committee to write to Lord Dartmouth; see Cushing to BF below, June 30.

6. See the annotation of BF's letter above, April 3.

subject to the Governor's negative, it may be a damage to me. Notwithstanding all my Care and precaution it is now publicly known that such Letters are here; the Governor suspects they were brought over by Mr. William Storey;[7] Considering the number of Person's who were to see them (not less than Ten or fifteen) it is astonishing to me they did not get Air before. When I first received them I was in great doubt whether to Communicate them to one single person or not, for when I considered the number of Persons I was directed to Communicate them to, I apprehended, it would be almost Impossible to Keep them secret, however I considered further that they Contained matters of Importance that very nearly affected the Government, that they were sent as much to the Persons named in your Letter as to my self and consequently that they had as good a right to determine what Improvement was to be made of them. Besides one of the Gentlemen to whom they were to be Communicated had advice of their being sent before they were Communicated to him, if not before their arrival, and it was strongly suspected for some time by his Informer that they were secreted on purpose to preserve the Governor,[8] so that If I had determined it not to be prudent to reveal them under the restrictions I was laid, it would have been out of my power to have prevented it's being known that such Letters were sent, however they were kept very secret till the annual Election when it generally got abroad that such Letters were come and as some of the Persons to whom they were sent were members of the Court they thought they were Obliged to mention that they had seen such Original Letters, this made the rest of the Members very sollicitous to have a sight of them and they talked of moving the House to send for Persons and papers as they said they had a right to such knowledge and Intelligence as very nearly and Essentially affected the public and rather than have any public

7. The suspicion was groundless: Story left London months before the letters were sent. He could have seen them in England, however, and even alerted BF to their existence; see above, XIX, 24 n.

8. The gentleman to whom they were to be communicated, not one of those BF had named, was Jeremiah Dummer Powell, a member of the Mass. Council; his informer in Boston was supposedly John Temple's brother Robert. Butterfield, ed., *John Adams Diary*, II, 81.

order about it and by that means let the House have the Entire possession of the Letters, it was thought adviseable by those to whom they were sent to Communicate them to the House provided they would engage they should not be printed nor Copied in whole or in part and that they Should return them again after a Convenient time when called for, which Engagement the House Entered into and they were read, upon which the House resolved it self into a Committee of the Whole House and after due Consideration the Committee reported to the House that it was their opinion that it was the design and Intention of these Letters to overthrow the Constitution of this Government and to Introduce arbitrary Power within this Province, which report was accepted by the House—101 Members for it, but 5 against it, and then the Letters were Committed to a Committee of nine to Consider what was proper to be done thereupon. While this matter was under Consideration of the House several Vessells arrived from London by Whom, it was reported, that Copies of these very letters were arrived and Wednesday the 9th Instant Mr. Hancock Informed the House that he had received a Number of Letters which were said to be Copies of those that were before the House, and as the House were under some Engagements with respect to the Letters that had been Communicated to them, he moved that the Copies he had received might be Compared with those before the House and if they proved to be true Copies the House might have them and make what use of them they thought proper. This was a great releif to the House as they were under some Difficulty about proceeding upon the other Letters under their present Engagements as they were thereby prevented from taking any Copys of them in whole or in part.[9] What determinations the House will

9. For Cooper's version of these events see the preceding document. The principal victim wrote his account much later: Hutchinson, *History*, III, 287–9. Cushing's references require amplifying the chronology at the beginning of the volume. On June 2 Samuel Adams revealed the existence of the Hutchinson letters to the House; the committee of the whole made the report mentioned, and referred the matter to a committee of nine that was chosen the next day. *Mass. House Jour.*, first session, May–June, 1773, pp. 26–8. Meanwhile the vessels were arriving from London: John Hancock's *Lydia* on May 29, and on June 6–7 the *Minerva*, *Neptune*, and *Dartmouth*. *Mass. Gaz.*; and the *Boston Weekly News-Letter*, June 3, 10; *Boston Gaz.*,

Enter into I cannot at present say, but it is universally appre-hended that the G—v—r will never be able to recover the Confidence of this People and that his Usefullness is at an End. I have done all in my power strictly to Conform to your restrictions, but from the Circumstances above related you must be sinsible it was Impossible to prevent the Letters being made public and therefore hope I shall be free from all Blame respecting this Matter. I conclude with great respect Your most humble Servant

THOMAS CUSHING

Benja Franklin Esqr.

Addressed: To / Benjamin Franklin Esqr LLD / Craven Street / In / London

From Thomas Cushing

AL: Massachusetts Historical Society; copy: Library of Congress

Sir: Boston June 16. 1773

Inclosed you have a report of a Committee upon the Letters lately laid before our House of Representatives, they have not as yet pass'd upon them. The Time assigned for Considering this Report is at 3 o Clock this afternoon. It is probable the most if not all of them will Pass by a great Majority.[1]

To Benj Franklin Esq.

Notation: Thos Cushing to Dr. Franklin June 16. 1773

June 7. On the 9th Hancock informed the House that he had copies of what he supposed was the correspondence in question, and they were compared with the originals. On the 10th the House appointed a separate committee to consider how the restrictions put upon the letters could be honorably cir-cumvented; the same day the committee reported that, because copies were already abroad and being read, the person who had furnished the letters—Cushing—consented to have the House use them as it pleased, provided the originals were returned. *Mass. House Jour.* just cited, pp. 41, 43–4; see also Hutchinson, *History,* III, 289. In BF's reply below, July 25, he dismissed the rumor that the copies had come from England, and asserted that they were made in Boston and used to soothe the conscience of the House.

1. They did indeed. On June 15 the committee of nine delivered the report that Cushing enclosed. It contained a number of resolutions, which the

From Hannah Walker

ALS: American Philosophical Society

Most Honoured Sir   Westbury June [20, 1773]

I return you thanks for your Goodness in freeing[2] my Letters. I Should have wrote before now but I have been quite ill and quite uncapable of all things. At Sometimes notwithstanding I Strove to keep my Spirits up but it was not in my Power. Trouble would overcome them but hope I Shall now get the Better for as my Son has wrote to me and Seems to like his trade and Place at Present and hope he will behave himself well and Mrs. Willams has wrote me so kind a Letter that I find great consolation in my Self for She is so kind to let me know they gave him his choice to return to England or to choose a trade and She Sees him often and Desires him if he wants for any thing to let her know and She has talked with his Master Several times and Says She has the Pleasure to acquaint me that his Master gives him a very good Charracter.[3] Sir I Humbly beg the Favour of your goodness to do

---

House adopted on the 16th by a vote of eighty-three to twenty-eight. Hutchinson, *History*, III, 291; see also pp. 289–90. An extract of the resolutions, now incomplete, is among BF's papers in the APS. They declared that the letters were designed to influence British policy by turning it against Massachusetts and preventing redress of grievances; the writers were trying to further their own fortunes through implementation of the Townshend Acts, by the military force that had destroyed the peace of the colony and subverted its morals and good government. The letters from the two Rhode Islanders, Moffatt and Rome, were malicious slanders on the administration of that colony. Whitehall had received and acted upon inflammatory and self-serving letters from individuals and, on the pretext that BF was not a duly constituted agent, had prevented the remonstrances of the House from reaching the throne. Hutchinson and Oliver had lost the confidence of the people, and the King should be asked to remove them. Smyth, *Writings*, VI, 276–9. The resultant petition was enclosed in Cushing to BF below, June 25.

2. Franking; BF had responded to her request above, XIX, 436. See also the document following this one, from which we have supplied the day of the month.

3. Young Henry Walker's troubles as a Boston apprentice, which distressed his mother at the time, are clear in outline though not in detail. He was apparently indentured at the start to both Jonathan Williams, Jr., and his brother Josiah, and after the latter's death in August, 1772, worked for Jonathan. When the boy was in some way "unfaithful," Jonathan found him a new master; and before he was apprenticed the indentures were sent to

me the Favour to Send these Letters to Boston my Husband joyns me in begging the acceptance of our Humble Duties to your Self and good Mrs. Stevenson from your most Humble and most obedient Servant HANNAH WALKER

From Thomas Walker

ALS: American Philosophical Society

Most Honour'd Sir June the: 20th. [1773]

I this day Carried these Letters to the Post and was so happy as to receive a letter from good Mr. Williams[4] that gave us So good a Charicter of Henry that it is great Satisfaction and Comfort to Us, he says that he is hapily Situated with a good Master and to a good Trade and that he is very ingenious and that his Master likes him Very well. From Your Most Humble and Most Obedient Servant THOS: WALKER

Addressed: To / Docter Franklin / at Mrs. Stevensons Craven Street / Strand / London

To Jean-Baptiste LeRoy

ALS (draft): American Philosophical Society

London, June 22. 1773

However glad I am of the Occasion, I forbore indulging my self in the Pleasure of congratulating by the first Post my dear double

---

England for his mother's and BF's approval. Above, XIX, 337, 436. BF returned the documents to Jonathan's father with his letter above, March 9. By the following May Henry was doing well, and by the end of the summer was on his way, Jonathan believed, to mastering his trade. Jonathan to BF above, April 20, and below, before Sept. 21. Mrs. Walker's uneasiness about him, apparent in this letter, went back for months. She expressed it in a letter to Jonathan (see his note to BF above, May 6), which evoked two replies. On April 22 Jonathan forwarded BF one from Henry, and on May 6 another—the letter from Mrs. Williams, we are convinced, that is described here.

4. The letter was from Mrs. Williams (see the preceding document); it had arrived earlier and not, as he appears to be saying, when he delivered to the post "these Letters"—his own, his wife's, and those she enclosed to be forwarded. They all seem to have been in a single envelope, which is stamped "free"; BF was franking the Walkers' correspondence with him and with Boston.

Confrere, on his Election into our Royal Society; because Mr. Walsh undertook to give you the Information,[5] which would make a Second Expence unnecessary, and I saw I should soon have this opportunity by the favour of M. Poisonnier.[6] I rejoice in the Event, as you seemed anxiously concern'd about it, and we have done ourselves Honour, in distinguishing and associating a Merit so universally known and acknowledg'd.

I am pleas'd to hear you are engag'd in the Consideration of Hospitals.[7] I wish any Observations of mine could be of Use to you, they should be at your Service. But 'tis a Subject I am very, little acquainted with. I can only say, that if a free and copious Perspiration is of use in Diseases, that seems, from the Experiments I mention'd to M. Dubourg,[8] to be best obtain'd by light covering and fresh Air continually changing: The Moisture on the Skin when the Body is warmly covered, being a Deception and the Effect not of greater Transpiration, but of the Saturation of the Air included under and in the Bedclothes, which therefore can absorb no more, and so leaves it on the Surface of the Body. From those Experiments I am convinc'd of what I indeed before

5. LeRoy, a leading member of the Académie royale des sciences, had been elected to the APS in January: above, XIX, 278. On Sept. 5, 1772, he had been nominated for the Royal Society by some of its French members; a number of F.R.S. in England, including John Walsh and BF, supported the nomination, and he was elected on June, 10, 1773. From the letter of nomination in the Royal Society. Walsh doubtless brought the letter when he returned to England on Sept. 17 (above, XIX, 295 n), and wrote LeRoy after the election.

6. For Poissonnier see above, XIX, 328 n. He also took Dubourg a letter from BF and a packet from Rush; see below, BF to Dubourg, June 29, and to Rush, July 14.

7. BF must be referring to a LeRoy letter, now lost, later than that of April 19. As a physician the Frenchman was particularly interested in the condition of hospitals, a matter that was at the moment much to the fore. The Hôtel-Dieu in Paris had been partially burned in December, 1772, and the following May the King had ordered the hospital transferred to two others. These developments led LeRoy to work on a project, which dragged on for years and never came to fruition, for rebuilding the Hôtel-Dieu on a novel design. Louis S. Greenbaum, "Tempest in the Academy: Jean-Baptiste Le Roy, the Paris Academy of Sciences and the Project of a New Hôtel-Dieu," *Archives internationales d'histoire des sciences*, XXIV (1974), 122–40.

8. In his first letter to Dubourg above, March 10; see also Rush to BF, May 1.

suspected, that the Opinion of Perspiration being check'd by Cold is an Error, as well as that of Rheums being occasion'd by Cold. But as this is Heresy here, and perhaps may be so with you, I only whisper it, and expect you will keep my Secret. Our Physicians have begun to discover that fresh Air is good for People in the Small Pox and other Fevers. I hope in time they will find out that it does no harm to People in Health.

We have nothing new here in the philosophic Way. I shall like to hear how M. Lavoisier's Doctrine supports itself as I suppose it will be controverted.[9] With the greatest Esteem, I am ever, Dear Sir Yours most affectionately   B FRANKLIN

Enclos'd I send you some Pamphlets relative to our American Affairs for your Amusement. Sir Jno Pringle bids me present his Compliments. He interested himself much in the Election.

M. Le Roy.

To François Rozier[1]

ALS (letterbook draft): American Philosophical Society

Sir   London, June 22. 1773
I am much oblig'd by your very polite Letter and Present of your valuable Collection. Please to accept my hearty Thanks. I had before purchased of M. Magalhaens all the Numbers of small

---

9. The "Doctrine" was indeed controversial, and turned out to be epoch-making. Priestley's work, about which LeRoy had been skeptical the previous autumn (above, XIX, 308), stimulated Lavoisier in his now famous experiments on combustion; they demonstrated that substances which increase in weight when burned do so by absorption from the atmosphere. His sealed note of this discovery, deposited with the Académie in November, 1772, was opened and read on May 5, 1773, after further experiments had confirmed its findings. Douglas McKie, *Antoine Lavoisier* ... (New York, [1952]), pp. 101–3. Those findings were irreconcilable with the phlogiston theory, of which Priestley was the outstanding protagonist; hence BF's interest in the controversy.

1. BF is replying to the circular letter from Rozier above, Jan. 24, which explains the contents of this note.

Form.[2] I think it must prove a useful Work to Science in general, and I wish it Success. When any thing occurs to me that may be suitable for it I shall not fail to communicate it in the manner you desire. With much Respect, I am, Sir, Your most obedient humble Servant
B F.

Monsr Rozier

From Thomas Cushing

Reprinted from Jared Sparks, ed., *The Works of Benjamin Franklin* . . . (10 vols., Boston, 1836–40), VIII, 52–3.

Sir,　　　　　　Province of Massachusetts Bay, 25 June, 1773
The House of Representatives have lately had divers letters, signed Thomas Hutchinson, Andrew Oliver, &c., laid before them, attested copies of which, you have enclosed;[3] and, after maturely considering their contents, they have voted as their sense, that the tendency and design of said letters appear to have been to overthrow the constitution of this government, and to introduce arbitrary power into this province; and have passed sundry resolves respecting these letters, which accompany this letter.[4] They have also agreed upon and passed a petition to his Majesty, which you will receive with this enclosure, praying that his Excellency Thomas Hutchinson, governor, and Andrew Oliver, lieutenant-governor, of this province, be removed from the posts they hold within this government;[5] which petition you

2. *I.e.*, 12mo; for a detailed description of the eighteen issues published in 1771–2 see Douglas McKie, "The '*Observations*' of the Abbé François Rozier . . . ," *Annals of Science* . . . , XIII (1957), [73–]89. BF seems to have deferred payment until the following August, when he entered £3 2s. "for Abbé Rossier's Collection": Jour., p. 50.

3. Because Cushing wrote in his official capacity, he maintained the fiction that the attested copies were BF's first contact with the Hutchinson letters.

4. Cushing had already enclosed, in his letter of June 16, the committee report accepted on that day; he now enclosed the resolutions of the House.

5. After the failure of delaying tactics the petition for removal was adopted on June 23. More than half of those who had opposed the resolutions on the 16th (see the note on Cushing's letter of that date) now apparently abstained, for the vote was eighty to eleven. *Mass. House Jour.*, first session, May–June, 1773, p. 75. The petitioners did not mince words. The

are desired, as soon as possible, to present to his Majesty; and, as the persons aforenamed have by this their conduct rendered themselves very obnoxious, and have entirely lost the confidence of this people, you are desired to use your interest and influence to support said petition, that it may have its desired effect; and you are further directed to employ Arthur Lee as counsel upon this occasion, and any other counsel you may think proper.[6]

You are desired also to take effectual care, that the several petitions, relative to the governor and judges of the Superior Court receiving their support from the crown, independent of the grants of the people, may be (if they have not already been) immediately laid before his Majesty, and strenuously supported; as they are matters that very nearly and essentially affect our happy constitution, the preservation of which in a great measure depends upon their meeting with a favorable reception and answer.[7] I have the honor to be, &c.

THOMAS CUSHING, *Speaker.*

---

quarrel between the colonies and the mother country, which they feared might prove fatal to both, had been abetted by evil men in the province, who would destroy its rights to advance their own fortunes. Hutchinson and Oliver were responsible for alienating the King and his ministers from his loyal subjects in Massachusetts, for preventing their situation from being recognized and their grievances from reaching the throne, and for introducing armed force into the colony. They had forfeited the confidence of the people and rendered themselves obnoxious to them. The petitioners therefore begged for their removal. Smyth, *Writings*, VI, 279–80.

6. On the 16th the House, on Samuel Adams's motion, named Lee as sole counsel. The next day a question was raised whether he was yet qualified to practice (it turned out that he was not), and BF was authorized to use other counsel if need be. Cushing, ed., *Writings of Samuel Adams*, III, 48–9; Richard Henry Lee, *Life of Arthur Lee* . . . (2 vols., Boston, 1829), I, 267. BF forwarded the petition with his letter to Dartmouth below, Aug. 21. The result was the hearing before the Privy Council on Jan. 29, 1774; on the day of the hearing Lee, as his contribution to the cause, published in the *Public Advertiser* a pseudonymous open letter to Dartmouth defending the position of Massachusetts.

7. The petitions against royal salaries had already been presented and rejected; see Dartmouth to BF above, June 2.

From Marie Catherine Biheron[8]

ALS: American Philosophical Society

Monsieur,   de Paris ce 26 juin 1773

J'ay remit à notre Amis le depots de papie dont vous m'aviez fait l'honneur de me charger concernant la Traduction de vos excelents ouvrages de phisique.[9] Jespert en proffiter des premiere. Cette étude me sera d'autant plus agreable que je la tiendray de vous et de notre amis Dubourg. Lui et sa chere Epouse Mademoiselle Bassenporte, Mr. Dalibart[1] et tous ceux qui ont le bonheur de vous connoitre vous presente leurs compliments. Je vous suplie de ne me pas oubliés auprès de Monsieur Pringle et de penser quelque fois à celle qui au dela des mers conservera éternelement le souvenir de vos attantions pour elle. Mesdames Stevenson, Hewson, et Monsieur Hewson voudrons bien agrer compliments et remerciment de l'amities qu'il m'ont marque et dont je suis tres reconnoisante.

Mes balots[2] ont passé la mer tres heureusement et son partis de Calais pour paris le 18e du courant pour arriver demain dimanche. Monsieur Dalibart paroît enchanté de laquisition que vous lui avez fait sans l'avoir encore vüe. En vous remerciant il saisira loccasion la plus prochaine pour vous faire tenir le montant de cette glasse.[3]

---

8. The maker of wax reproductions, an old friend of BF and Dubourg, who had just returned from a prolonged visit to England. See above, xv, 115 n and subsequent volumes. Her spelling is bizarre, to use the kindest adjective; we have changed it only when necessary to avoid ambiguity. She also ran her sentences together, and as usual we have separated them when confident of her meaning.

9. "Notre Amis" was Dubourg, and "le depots de papie" presumably contained further detailed comments from BF, now lost, on the text of the *Œuvres*, like those he sent Dubourg above, May 28–June 1, and below, June 29.

1. All these were, like Mlle. Biheron herself, acquaintances that BF had made during his visit to Paris in 1767. For Mlle. Basseporte, the engraver, and Dalibard, the translator of the first edition of *Exper. and Obser.*, see above, respectively, xv, 115 n; IV, 302 n.

2. *Ballots*, trunks or luggage.

3. BF had presumably sent Dalibard, perhaps in her luggage, a scientific instrument that contained a mirror, or the mirror alone; see Dubourg to BF below, Nov. 25.

Il y à un jeune chirugien de beaucoup de merite qui se propose de partir pour Londres au commancement de la semaine prochaine pour profiter des lumieres de vos artistes en se genre. Joze le recommander à Mr. Hewson. Jay l'honneur de vous avertir en confidance que Mademoiselle Guion de St. Marie est tres peut connu à Paris et que quelqu'un qui s'enterresse à vous est venu me trouvé pour vous engagé à vous en méfier. Elle paroît avoir dupée le pere Bertier par sa langue. Un de nos ministre à diton écrit à Mr. le Conte de Guine[4] pour faire revenir un homme de condition agée de trente ans que jay vüe avec elle qu'elle détourne depuit du temps d'une famille à qui il semble tres cher à les en croire. Comme nous n'avont pas besoin d'ens savoir d'avantage vous en feray l'usage que votre prudance vous dictera. Je vous suis trop attaché pour ne pas vous informé de cela en vous re-iterant les assurances de mon attachement. Croyés moi pour la vie, Monsieur, votre tres heumble et obeisante servante   BIHERON

Permeté sil vous plait que je salue Mr. fevre.[5]

From Jonathan Williams, Jr.

ALS: American Philosophical Society

Honoured Sir   Boston June 28. 1773
My Father received your Favour the Evening before last, and accordingly delivered your Letter to the Speaker.[6] Altho' you will no doubt receive from him the Resolves and proceedings of our Council relative to the Governors conduct &c &c, I inclose the Gazette, having it in my hand, as the more ways a thing is sent,

4. The French adventuress and her runaway companion have eluded us. The man whom she supposedly duped was Joseph-Etienne Bertier, who called himself "Bertier frankliniste": above, XVI, 56. The comte de Guines was French ambassador to St. James's.
5. For BF's French clerk see above, XIX, 438 n.
6. The letter to Williams is missing; that to Cushing of May 6 is above. We have no other indication that BF was using Williams to forward letters to the Speaker, but he could have made a habit of it—to reduce the chance of their being opened—without our being any the wiser. Unless an envelope is marked with a stamp or some indication of a particular ship, there is no way to tell whether it was sent by itself or as an enclosure.

the more likely it is to arive Safe.[7] I shall be obliged if you will please to present my duty to my Uncle, and let him have the perusal of the Inclosed Papers, with those I sent in my last.[8] I then desired you would please to give directions for the Making of a hand Organ, such an one as you had made for Mr. Foxcroft, and also that you would please to collect a number of Pieces according to your own fancy to be put on the Barrells, which I shall be much oblig'd if you will please to do for me.[9] I am with the greatest Esteem and Respect Your dutiful and affectionate Kinsman

JONA WILLIAMS JUNR

Addressed: To / Benjamin Franklin LLD FRS / at Mrs Stevensons / in / Craven Street / Strand / London

Endorsed: Jona. Williams jun   June 28. 73

7. He enclosed the *Boston Gaẓ.* of June 28. It described proceedings in the Council on the 25th, on the report of a committee, including James Bowdoin and John Winthrop, that had been appointed to consider the correspondence. The report first analyzed Hutchinson's six letters in great detail and Oliver's more briefly, and then concluded that both men should be removed from office because they were responsible for arousing the King's displeasure, expressed in sending troops to Boston and refusing redress of the colony's grievances. The Council then passed its own resolutions; they contained an abbreviated analysis of the letters, and a slightly expanded argument for removal. Court records, legislative Council (State House, Boston), xxx, 110, 112–28. The Council, in other words, concurred in the judgment of the House but stopped short of resolving to petition.

8. Presumably a missing letter after his of May 6 above. The uncle was John Williams, the customs inspector, to whom BF forwarded the papers with his note below, Aug. 15. He apparently sent this letter as well, for on the verso is written, in what seems to be another hand, "To/John Williams Esq./ at M[rs.?] Wilkes's."

9. BF had purchased Foxcroft's organ for £15 6s. in 1770, while Williams was in London (Jour., p. 26), and promptly carried out the second commission: to Williams below, Oct. 6. It was for a hand or barrel organ, an instrument which had long been popular in England. Each piece of music was pricked out in pins and staples on a wooden cylinder, or barrel, to be inserted in the instrument; Jonathan is asking BF to select music for these barrels. See his letters below, July 29, Dec. 11.

To Jacques Barbeu-Dubourg

ALS (draft): American Philosophical Society

Dear Friend,   London, June 29. 1773
    I wrote to you by favour of M. Poissonnier, on the 22d Instant, since which I have received yours of the 20th. with some more Sheets.[1]

    I have now gone through all that are come to hand, and the following are all the Corrections that occur to me to propose for your Errata, some of which are scarce worth Notice.

Premiere Partie

Page 295   line 11. from the Bottom, *choc*, in the same Sense you sometimes use *coup*, which methinks is better, but you know best.

—   300   line 8. from the Bottom, for *moins*, read, *plus*. This is a material Error, as it totally alters the Sense. The Discharges being more frequent is the Reason that the Quantity is less at each Discharge.[2]

Seconde Partie.

Page   4.   line 5. for *reçoivent*, read, *donnent à l'air*, another material Error.[3]

—   26. — 4. for *tube*, read, *cuve*.

—   29 — 20. for *tube*, read, *cuve*.

—————— 21 for *tube*, read *cuve*.[4]

    It seems to me that *tube* conveys the Idea of a small narrow Vessel, and my Meaning is a Vessel of large Diameter, to give room for a Current from the Circumference to the Center.

---

1. See BF to LeRoy above, June 22. The letters that BF mentions here have been lost.

2. The page references here and hereafter are to the two vols. of the *Œuvres*. Dubourg preferred *choc* to *coup*; *plus*, noted in his errata, we have incorporated in the text printed above, XIX, 255.

3. Dubourg had rendered "may be taken up from the Lungs" (above, IV, 237) as "nos poumons reçoivent."

4. BF's "tub" (*ibid.*, pp. 431, 434) had been transformed into "tube."

— 35 — 19. *lumiere,* does that Word express *Lightning?*[5]
— 76 — 17. *et quand je vis,* &c. to the End of the Paragraph. On examining the Original I see that my English is obscure, and therefore you might easily mistake the Meaning, which is this. It had been a common Opinion that a Shot fired thro' a Whirlwind would break it. I try'd to break the little one by striking my Whip thro' it, which had no Effect. And I afterwards saw when it grew larger that great Trees passing thro' the Body of it, did not break it. The Trees indeed stand still and the Whirlwind has the progressive Motion, but their Effect on the Whirl, if any, must be the same whether they move to it, or it to them. If you look once more at the English, page 357 line 3 from the Bottom, and consider the word *which* as relating to *Whirl,* (the immediate antecedent,) and not to *Trees,* you may perceive what I intended.[6]
— 79 — 14. for 9, read 11. This is a material Error, as it takes away the Ground of the Observation.[7]
— 80 — 11, 12, for *de derriere,* read, *qui entre. back to the Door,* signifies not behind the Door but back against the Stream that moves from the Door to the Chimney.[8]
—————————— 21, 22. for *nord-ouest au sud-est,* read, *nord-est au sud-ouest.*
— 81 — 2, from the bottom, for *on,* read *ou.*
— 87 — 14. *fraîcheurs,* does this french Word express the Distemper we in English call *a Cold?*[9]

5. "Flashes of Lightning" (*ibid.,* p. 440) had become "traits de lumiere."
6. BF amended his phrasing in the next edition of *Exper. and Obser.;* see above, VI, 168 and n.
7. *I.e.,* eleven o'clock (IX, 111). BF had been trying to determine the movement of a storm along the northeastern seaboard.
8. The air next the chimney moved toward it when a fire was lighted, and then the rest of the air "quite back to the Door." *Ibid.,* p. 112.
9. Dubourg translated "Colds in the Head" (above, II, 425) as "fraîcheurs à la tête."

If a Person has a swell'd Face, with a Pain in the Jaws, we call it *a Cold* in the Head. But our Ideas of *a Cold* are so various and so inconsistent, that I do not wonder if the French Language should scarce afford adequate Expressions for them.

— 94 — 12. for *comble*, read, *front.*

— 109 — 8 from the bottom, delete *en entrant.*

— 115 — 17. I know not whether *mine de plomb*, is French for *black Lead*; what we call by that Name is not the *Ore of Lead*, it cannot be flux'd and reduc'd to any Metal, and is unfit for crucibles; it is what Pencils are made of, for Drawing: I think you call it *Crayon*. It is mention'd again line 5 from the bottom.

— 116. — 2, from the bottom, The motive for turning the Smoke down behind the Air Box was to heat the other Side of it, and so obtain more Heat to the Air that passes thro' it. I mention this only to account for it to you, not to propose any Erratum here.[1]

Page 161, line 14. for *d'usage*, read, *utile.*[2]

— 183 — 16. for *evavorant*, read, *evaporant.*

— 199 — 9. from the bottom, for *800*, read *80*. This is a material Error. I believe no Mine in the World ever went so deep as 800 fathoms below the Sea. If this were to pass, I should seem to romance exceedingly.[3]

— 272 — 10 for *industie*, read, *industrie*

— 279 — 5, for *concentriques*, read, *excentriques.*

— 291 — 7. for A, H, F, G, read A, H, F.

The English Edition was sold for half a Guinea in boards, or what you call *broché*; but yours contains more Pieces, and more Plates.

1. A comment on Dubourg's comment in the *Œuvres* on the Pa. fireplace.
2. BF had written that it is "of Use" to consider what people will think as well as what they ought to think: v, 443.
3. See above, XIX, 368.

Franklin's new stove

I have not time now to write what I intend upon the Cause of Colds, or Rheums, and my Opinions on that Head are so singular here, that I am almost afraid to hazard them abroad.[4] In the mean time, be so kind as to tell me, at your leisure, whether in France, you have a general Belief that moist Air, and cold Air, and damp Shirts or Sheets, and wet Floors, and Beds that have not lately been used, and Clothes that have not been lately worn, and going out of a warm Room into the Air, and leaving off a long worn Wastecoat, and wearing leaky Shoes, and sitting near an open Window or Door, or in a Coach with both Glasses down, are all or any of them capable of giving the Distemper we call *a Cold*, and you a *Rheum* or *Catarrh*? Or are these merely *English* Ideas?

Inclos'd I send you the Engraving of my new Stove: The Description must be postpon'd for want of Time, and I had rather it should not be published at present.[5] It is fit only for burning Pit-coal, and therefore can be of little or no Use with you who generally burn Wood.

If M. LeRoy means that *some* Glass is permeable to the Electric Fluid, I have acknowledg'd it in several Places. If he means *all* Glass, I doubt it.[6] Tho' I would not be positive; Experience must determine.

My Love to your good Spouse and to Mlle. Biheron. I hope she had an agreable Journey, and arrived in good Health.[7] I am ever, with the greatest Esteem and Respect, Dear Sir, Your most obedient humble Servant   B F

M Dubourg

4. See above, BF to LeRoy, June 22, and below, to Rush, July 14, and BF's notes below at the end of the year.

5. For BF's reluctance to describe the stove see the note on his letter to Dubourg above, Jan. 22. The reason for supposing that BF's enclosure was the engraving reproduced here is explained in the list of illustrations.

6. Jean-Baptiste LeRoy, we suspect, had remarked on the postscript of BF's letter to Dubourg above, May 28, and Dubourg had passed on the comment in his missing letter of June 20. BF held in general that glass was impermeable; the only exception he acknowledged, as far as we know, was when the glass was heated. See above, IV, 25–32; V, 522–3; X, 40–1; XI, 254.

7. The journey, presumably back to Paris from London, was that mentioned in her letter above of June 26, which BF had not yet received.

From Thomas Cushing ls (duplicate) and als[8]: Library of Congress

With the letter below Speaker Cushing enclosed another, from the two houses of the General Court to Lord Dartmouth. On June 28 the houses, as their last act of the session, appointed a drafting committee; the letter was composed the following day and dispatched the day after.[9] Its purpose seems to have been to shake Dartmouth's conclusion, which Franklin had reported in his letter of May 6, that the houses had declared their independence of British authority. The trouble between the colony and mother country began, the letter asserted, after Bernard's appointment as governor: he and his coterie used their influence to secure Parliamentary taxation and prevent remonstrances against it from being heard; the working of this influence had just come to light in Hutchinson's and Oliver's letters. When Parliament seemed to be moving toward repeal of the Townshend Acts under Dartmouth's guidance, furthermore, Hutchinson challenged the House and Council on fundamentals of the constitution. Ignoring his challenge would have meant tacitly accepting a status akin to slavery; hence he left them no choice but to contradict him, sorry as they were to do it. The people of the province were loyal subjects, the letter continued, who would rejoice to see harmony reign again. But that could not happen until their charter rights, particularly that of paying royal officials, were respected again as they had been at the end of the last war. The houses pinned their faith on Dartmouth to work for this end, and to frustrate the machinations of Bernard "and other known enemies of the peace of Great Britain and her colonies."[1]

The point underlying these arguments, if we read them correctly, was that Whitehall's view of the situation was the reverse of the truth. Controversy in Massachusetts was due not to a small group of radicals, as Hutchinson and other officials had persuaded the government, but to those very officials and their henchmen, who out of self-interest

8. The als lacks the second postscript; with that exception the two texts are virtually identical.

9. Thomas Cushing, Samuel Adams, and Robert Treat Paine represented the House on the committee, and James Bowdoin and John Winthrop the Council; Thomas Flucker signed the letter as secretary of the province. Bowdoin's draft is in 6 Mass. Hist. Soc. *Coll.*, ix (1897), 302–5; the text of the letter as sent is in Bradford, ed., *Mass. State Papers*, pp. 398–400.

1. *Ibid.*, p. 399. The letter was in essence an amalgam of the resolutions that the House and Council had already passed, for which see above, 239 n, 247 n.

were hoodwinking the King and his ministers to turn them against a loyal province. Hutchinson had first labored surreptitiously for this end and then, when repeal of the Townshend Acts seemed imminent, had made repeal politically impossible by forcing a confrontation with the houses. Here was a hint that exposing his letters offered, as Franklin contended, the means of bringing peace.[2] The Governor and his coterie were trying to destroy peace, which could be restored only by undoing their evil work and returning to the traditional status quo. This hope of curing the ills of the present by resurrecting the past was not new. Abandon Parliamentary taxation and revert to the old ways, Franklin had said over and over again, and all would be well.[3] The two houses concurred, and the hope proved to be long-lasting. It survived the Coercive Acts and came to the fore in the first two Continental Congresses; it underlay Burke's and Chatham's and North's eleventh-hour efforts to avoid conflict. Until 1776 many men, in England and America, believed that the only way to save the empire was to put back the clock.

Sir   Boston June 30 [–July 7] 1773

I have received your Favour of the 6th: of May last, am obliged to you for the Intelligence therein Contained. I communicated the same to some few Freinds with a caution not to divoulge the contents, but one of them inadvertently mentioned to some of the members his having seen such a Letter and it soon got among the members that I had received a Letter from you relative to our publick affairs and it being a Time of general expectation and the members being very sollicitous to hear in what manner our dispute with the Governor the last session was received at home. Especially as you had wrote no Letter to the House I expected to have no rest till I had given them some inteligence or another. I therefore thought it best, in order to keep the conversation you had with Lord D. as secret as possible, to give them an extract of your Letter containing only the first and last Paragraphs; which satisfied the House and kept the other part of it from publick

2. For BF's argument see above, XIX, 407–9, 412.

3. Above, XIII, 137–40; XV, 4–5, 187–8; XVI, 17, 243–6; XVII, 29, 325–7. BF made the same point in "An Infallible Method to Restore Peace and Harmony" below, Sept. 8; see also his letter to Cushing of Nov. 1. A committee of the House had taken the same position three years before: above, XVII, 301–2.

Veiw.[4] I hope the necessity I was under, at such a critical time to communicate some parts of the Letter will be a sufficient apology for my going thus far; before I leave this Subject I would just mention that it would be very agreeable to the House more frequently to hear from you while matters of so interesting a nature are depending at the Court of Great Britain, and this amoung others was one reason why I communicated to the House such parts of your Letter of the 6 May last as I did. I conducted it in such a manner as to have it considered as a publick Letter as by that means I apprehended I should place you in a more favourable light with the House.[5]

By this Conveyance the Secretary will forward to you or mr. Bollan a Letter from the Two Houses to Lord Dartmouth which is of a conciliating nature and hope will have a happy affect and tend to extricate his Lordship and the rest of the administration out of their Embarrasements on account of our late Dispute with the Governor upon the Supream authority of Parliament. His Lordship was mistaken in saying we had asserted our Independency of G. Britain, it is True we gave the opinion of our Forefathers upon this Subject but carefully avoided Expresly declaring our own and his Excellency in his reply takes notice of it and says he was glad to find we avoided it.[6] In great haste I conclude with Sincere regard and respect Your Most humble Servant

THOMAS CUSHING

P.S. You was quite right in informing his Lordship that it would

4. The "first" paragraph of BF's letter was in fact the second. The House would scarcely have been pleased with one passage withheld from it, in which BF referred to its declaration as "*Words* only." According to Hutchinson (Mass. Arch., XXVII, 503) parts of BF's letter, presumably the same ones, were read to the Council. This departure from usual custom was doubtless to underscore the Governor's lack of support in London, as preparation for the Council's indictment of him in its resolutions of June 25.

5. BF's standing with his constituents needed improving. He had already been criticized, in a letter now lost, for not keeping the House informed of relevant Parliamentary legislation; see Cooper to BF below, Nov. 10. BF replied to this charge in his private letter to Cushing below, July 7.

6. What Cushing meant by "this Conveyance" is discussed in the headnote on BF and Bollan to Dartmouth below, Aug. 20. The reference to Dartmouth's comment on "Independency" is to BF's report of his interview with him: above, pp. 200–1.

be impossible for us to withdraw or rescind our answer to the Governor till he withdrew or rescinded his Speach, it can never be done, the Sentiments contained in those answers were well weighed and thoroughly considered before they were delivered.

July. 7. 1773

Inclosed you have an attested Copy of a Letter from both Houses dated June 29. 1773 to Lord Dartmouth which I wish safe to hand.

Copy

Addressed: To / Benjamin Franklin Esqr LLD / In / London / per Capt. Moth

To Jonathan Shipley

ALS:[7] Yale University Library

[June?[8] 1773]

Extract from Kalm's Travels into America.

"It has been found repeatedly that these Trees [Peach Trees] can stand the Frost much better on Hills than in the Vallies; insomuch that when those in a Valley were killed by the Frost, those on a Hill were not hurt at all. It is remarkable that in cold Nights, all the Leaves to the height of 7 and even of 10 feet from the Ground, have been killed by the Frost, and all the Top remained unhurt. Further it is observable that the cold Nights which happen in Summer never do any hurt to the high Grounds, damaging only the low and moist ones." Vol. II. page 83.[9]

7. The absence of place, date, and salutation suggests at first glance that the beginning of the letter is lost. But BF's opening sentence after the extract, it may be argued, is a salutation.

8. BF declines an invitation to Twyford which we know he received before mid-July: to WF below, July 14. He mentions that he has not yet heard the American reaction to Shipley's sermon, and his tone implies to us that he was expecting to hear; he had sent copies to Coombe and Galloway on April 6, and could not have looked for word to reach him before the middle of June. Hence the letter was probably written at some time between then and early July.

9. From John Reinhold Forster's translation of Peter Kalm, *Travels into North America* ... (3 vols., London, 1771), II, 83–4. The brackets are BF's.

The above Extract shows that the Phenomenon mentioned by my dear good Friend is not uncommon in North America. I remember to have once travelled thro' a Valley there, on both sides of which the Leaves on the Trees were killed to a certain height, the Line of the Blast appearing very even and level as far as the Eye could reach, all below the Line being blasted, and all above green. I think I have heard it observed here, that Frost in a dry Night does not hurt so much as when the Leaves have been wet. Fogs sometimes lie on low Grounds, and one can see over them from the Side of a Hill. Perhaps a Frost with such a Fog may affect the Trees immers'd in it more than those above it. In a hilly Country, too, tho' the Valleys are warmest in the Day-Time, while the Sun shines, from the many Reflections of his Rays; yet as soon as he is set, the contrary takes place; the cooler Air of the Hills settles into the Vallies, and the warmer Air of the Vallies ascends to the Hills: This I have frequently observed in little Excursions from Philadelphia in the Summer Season. Riding out in the Day I have been swelter'd in the Vallies, notwithstanding the Thinness of my Dress, and refresh'd when passing over the Hills. Returning in the Evening, the same Thinness of Dress made me sensible of a chilling Coolness in the Vallies, while the Air on the Hills was agreeably warm.

Your very kind Invitation to Twyford, with the strong Impression I have from Experience, of the Happiness I might enjoy there, in a Family I so truly love, almost staggers my Resolution of visiting America this Summer. But I grow exceedingly homesick. I long to see my own Family once more. I draw towards the Conclusion of Life, and am afraid of being prevented that Pleasure. Besides, I feel myself become of no consequence here. I find I cannot prevent nor alter Measures that I see will be pernicious to us all. But there, where my Opinion and Advice is a little more regarded, I imagine I may still be of some Use, in diminishing or retarding the Mischief. It is true my Country pays me well for residing here: But I think a meer Labourer, tho' paid as usual for a Days-work, would not be satisfied to turn a Grindstone all Day, where nothing was to be ground.

Please to present my respectful Compliments to good Mrs. Shipley, and all the amiable young Ladies, with your valuable Son, who, I hear by Mr. and Mrs. Jackson, is at present with you.[10] I had a little of the Pleasure of their Company before they set out for Spa.

I have not yet heard from America how the Sermon was received there: But expect it will have several Editions in different Places, and be greatly applauded,[1] as indeed it is here among all the Friends of Liberty and the Common Rights of Mankind. I think even the New Englanders will for once have a good Opinion of a Bishop. With the sincerest Esteem and most affectionate Respect, I am, My Lord, Your much obliged and most obedient humble Servant   B FRANKLIN

Bishop of St. Asaph

To Matthew Maty[2]

ALS (letterbook draft): American Philosophical Society

Sir,   Craven street, July 1. 1773
Our ingenious and worthy Brother Mr. Walsh, having long had an Intention of drawing up from his Minutes a full Account of the numerous Experiments he made on the Torpedo, which Intention his other Avocations have not permitted him to execute, it is but lately that I have obtain'd his Permission to lay before the Society what he had in the meantime been pleased to communicate to me on that very curious and interesting Subject, or I should sooner have put it into your Hands for that purpose: I wish you may now have time to read them before the Recess.[3] With great Esteem, I am, Sir, Your most obedient humble Servant
                                              B FRANKLIN

Dr Maty, Secry. to the Royal Society.

10. For the Shipleys' children see above, XVIII, 199–202. The Jacksons were an Irish couple whom we cannot identify: *ibid.*, pp. 203, 266 n.

1. BF was quite correct; see the annotation of his letter to Cushing above, April 3.

2. The secretary of the Royal Society and, since 1772, the principal librarian of the British Museum. *DNB*.

3. BF unquestionably enclosed the following document, perhaps in rougher form than the published text that we print, and it was supposedly read the same day before the Royal Society: *Phil. Trans.*, LXIII (1773–74), part 2, 461.

From John Walsh

Printed in the Royal Society, *Philosophical Transactions* ..., LXIII (1773–74), part 2, 461–77.[4]

Dear Sir,   Chesterfield-Street, July 1, 1773.

I am concerned that other engagements have prevented me from giving to the Royal Society, before their recess, a complete account of my experiments on the electricity of the Torpedo; a subject not only curious in itself, but opening a large field for interesting inquiry, both to the electrician in his walk of physics, and to all who consider, particularly or generally, the animal œconomy.

To supply the deficiency in the best manner I am now able, I will request the favour of you to lay before the Society my letter from la Rochelle, of the 12th July 1772, and such part of the letter I afterwards wrote from Paris, as relates to this subject. Loose and imperfect as these informations are, for they were never intended for the public eye, they are still the most authentic, and so far the most satisfactory I can at present offer, since the notes I made of the experiments themselves remain nearly, I am sorry to say it, in that crude and bulky state in which you had the trouble to read them.

Letter from Mr. Walsh to Dr. Franklin, dated la Rochelle, 12th July 1772 ...

Extracts of a letter from Mr. Walsh to Dr. Franklin, dated Paris, 27th August, 1772 ...[5]

4. For the background of this report see above, XIX, 160–2. Walsh printed his letter as a pamphlet, *Of the Electric Property of the Torpedo* ... (London, 1774), and the Royal Society included it in *Three Tracts Concerning the Torpedo* ... (London, 1775). Seignette, the Mayor of La Rochelle, had it translated into French for the *Jour. de physique*, IV (1774), part 2, 205–19; see Jean Torlais, "L'Académie de la Rochelle et la diffusion des sciences au XVIIIe siècle," *Revue d'histoire des sciences* ..., XII (1959), 120.

5. Both letters appear under their dates above, XIX, 204–6, 285–9. They were slightly revised for the *Phil. Trans.*, but in style rather than substance. In the first one a note was added referring to Lorenzini's engravings of the torpedo's electrical organs in his *Osservazioni*. "Redi seems to be the first," the note continued, "who remarked these singular parts of the Torpedo in 1666. Franc[esco] Redi, *Exper[imenta circa res diversas] Nat[urales* ..., Amsterdam, 1675]."

258

A clear and succinct narrative of what passed at one of the public exhibitions, alluded to in the last letter, appeared in the French Gazette of the 30th October 1772. As it came from a very respectable quarter, not less so from the private character of the gentleman, than from the public offices he held, I must desire leave of the Society to avail myself of such a testimony to the facts I have advanced, by giving a translation of that narrative.

Extract of a Letter from the Sieur Seignette, Mayor of la Rochelle, and second perpetual Secretary of the Academy of that City, to the publisher of the French Gazette.[6]

"In the Gazette of the 14th August, you mentioned the discovery made by Mr. Walsh, Member of the parliament of England, and of the Royal Society of London. The experiment, of which I am going to give you an account, was made in the presence of the Academy of this city. A live Torpedo was placed on a table. Round another table stood five persons insulated. Two brass wires, each thirteen feet long, were suspended to the ceiling by silken strings. One of these wires rested by one end on the wet napkin on which the fish lay; the other end was immersed in a basin full of water placed on the second table, on which stood four other basins likewise full of water. The first person put a finger of one hand in the basin in which the wire was immersed, and a finger of the other hand in the second basin. The second person put a finger of one hand in this last basin, and a finger of the other hand in the third; and so on successively, till the five persons communicated with one another by the water in the basins. In the last basin one end of the second wire was immersed; and with the other end Mr. Walsh touched the back of the Torpedo, when the five persons felt a commotion which differed in nothing from that of the Leyden experiment, except in the degree of force. Mr. Walsh, who was not in the circle of conduction, received no shock. This experiment was repeated several times, even with eight persons; and always with the same success. The action of the Torpedo is communicated by the same mediums

6. Seignette was writing, we conjecture, to correct the earlier report in the *Gaz. de France* mentioned above, XIX, 286 n.

as that of the electric fluid. The bodies which intercept the action of the one, intercept likewise the action of the other. The effects produced by the Torpedo resemble in every respect a weak electricity."

This exhibition of the electric powers of the Torpedo, before the Academy of La Rochelle, was at a meeting, held for the purpose in my apartments, on the 22d July 1772, and stands registered in the journals of the Academy.

The effect of the animal was, in these experiments, transmitted through as great an extent and variety of conductors as almost at any time we had been able to obtain it, and the experiments included, nearly, all the points, in which its analogy with the effect of the Leyden Phial had been observed.[7] These points were stated to the gentlemen present, as were the circumstances in which the two effects appeared to vary. It was likewise repre- sented to them, That our experiments had been almost wholly with the animal in air: That its action in water was a capital desideratum: That indeed all as yet done was little more than opening the door to inquiry: That much remained to be examined by the Electrician as well as by the Anatomist: That as artificial electricity had thrown light on the natural operation of the Torpedo, this might in return, if well considered, throw light on artificial electricity, particularly in those respects in which they now seemed to differ: That for me, I was about to take leave of the animal, as nature had denied it to the British seas; and that the prosecution of these researches rested in a particular manner with them, whose shores abounded with it.[8]

The Torpedo, on this occasion, dispensed only the distinct, instantaneous stroke, so well known by the name of the electric shock. That protracted but lighter sensation, that Torpor or Numbness which he at times induces, and from which he takes

7. Testing this analogy was the principal purpose of BF's instructions in *idem.*, pp. 234–5.
8. Walsh subsequently found that he was mistaken about British seas: *ibid.*, p. 287. His challenge to the Rochellais apparently left them unmoved, but others soon became interested. Ingenhousz was experimenting with the torpedo at Leghorn in January, 1773, and Sir William Hamilton at Naples soon afterward. See BF to Ingenhousz below, Sept. 30, and de Saussure to BF above, Feb. 23.

his name, was not then experienced from the animal; but it was imitated with artificial electricity, and shewn to be producible by a quick consecution of minute shocks. This, in the Torpedo, may perhaps be effected by the successive discharge of his numerous cylinders, in the nature of a running fire of musketry: the strong single shock may be his general volley. In the continued effect, as well as in the instantaneous, his eyes, usually prominent, are withdrawn into their sockets.

The same experiments, performed with the same Torpedos, were on the two succeeding days repeated before numerous companies of the principal inhabitants of La Rochelle. Besides the pleasure of gratifying the curiosity of such as entertained any on the subject, and the desire I had to excite a prosecution of the inquiry, I certainly wished to give all possible notoriety to facts, which might otherwise be deemed improbable, perhaps by some of the first rank in science. Great authorities had given a sanction to other solutions of the phœnomena of the Torpedo; and even the Electrician might not readily listen to assertions, which seemed in some respects, to combat the general principles of electricity. I had reason to make such conclusions from different conversations I had held on the subject with eminent persons both at London and Paris. It is but justice to say, that of all in that class you gave me the greatest encouragement to look for success in this research, and even assisted me in forming hypotheses, how the Torpedo, supposed to be endued with electric properties, might use them in so conducting an element as water.

After generally recommending to others an examination of the electric powers of these animals when acting in water, I determined, before I took my final leave of them, to make some farther experiments myself with that particular view; since, notwithstanding the familiarity in which we may be said to have lived with them for near a month, we had never detected them in the immediate exercise of their electric faculties against other fish, confined with them in the same water, either in the circumstance of attacking their prey, or defending themselves from annoyance: and yet that they possessed such a power, and exercised it in a state of liberty, could not be doubted.

A large Torpedo, very liberal of his shocks, being held with both hands by his electric organs above and below, was briskly plunged into water to the depth of a foot, and instantly raised an equal height into air; and was thus continually plunged and raised, as quick as possible, for the space of a minute. In the instant his lower surface touched the water in his descent, he always gave a violent shock, and another still more violent in the instant of quitting the water in his ascent; both which shocks, but particularly the last, were accompanied with a writhing in his body, as if meant to force an escape. Besides these two shocks from the surface of the water, which may yet be considered as delivered in the air, he constantly gave at least two, when wholly in the air, and constantly one and sometimes two, when wholly in the water. The shocks in water appeared, as far as sensation could decide, not to have near a fourth of the force of those at the surface of the water, nor much more than a fourth of those intirely in air.[9]

The shocks received in a certain time were not, on this occasion, counted by a watch, as they had been on a former, when fifty were delivered, in a minute and a half, by the animal in an insulated and unagitated state: But from the quickness, with which the immersions were made, it may be presumed there were full twenty of these in a minute; from whence the number of shocks, in that time, must have amounted to above an hundred. This experiment, therefore, while it discovered the comparative force between a shock in water and one in air, and between a shock delivered with greater exertion on the part of the animal and one with less, seemed to determine, that the charge of his organs with electricity was affected in an instant, as well as the discharge.

The Torpedo was then put into a flat basket, open at top, but secured by a net with wide meshes, and, in this confinement, was let down into the water, about a foot below the surface; being there touched, through the meshes, with only a single finger, on one of his electric organs, while the other hand was held, at a distance, in the water, he gave shocks, which were distinctly felt in both hands.

The circuit for the passage of the effect being contracted to the finger and thumb of one hand, applied above and below to a

9. Henry Cavendish later achieved the same results by simulation, and reported them in "An Account of Some Attempts to Imitate the Effects of the Torpedo by Electricity," *Phil. Trans.*, LXVI (1776), 209–13.

single organ, produced a shock, to our sensation, of twice the force of that in the larger circuit by the arms.

The Torpedo, still confined in the basket, being raised to within three inches of the surface of the water, was there touched with a short iron bolt, which was held, half above and half in the water, by one hand, while the other hand was dipped, as before, at a distance in the water; and strong shocks, felt in both hands, were thus obtained through the iron.

A wet hempen cord being fastened to the iron bolt, was held in the hand above water, while the bolt touched the Torpedo; and shocks were obtained through both those substances.

A less powerful Torpedo, suspended in a small net, being frequently dipped into water and raised again, gave, from the surface of the water, slight shocks through the net to the person holding it.

These experiments in water manifested, That bodies, immersed in that element, might be affected by immediate contact with the Torpedo; That the shorter the circuit in which the electricity moved, the greater would be the effect; And that the shock was communicable, from the animal in water, to persons in air, through some substances.

How far harpoons and nets, consisting of wood and hemp, could in like circumstances, as it has been frequently asserted, convey the effect, was not so particularly tried as to enable us to confirm it.[1] I mention the omission in the hope that some one may be induced to determine the point by express trial.

We convinced ourselves, on former occasions, that the accurate Kæmpfer,[2] who so well describes the effect of the Torpedo, and happily compares it with lightning, was deceived in the circumstance, that it could be avoided by holding in the breath, which we found no more to prevent the shock of the Torpedo, when he was disposed to give it, than it would prevent the shock of the Leyden Phial.

Several persons, forming as many distinct circuits, can be

---

1. The shocks suffered by fishermen who did not actually touch the torpedo had long defied explanation; see above, XIX, 161.

2. [*Author's note:* Engelbert] Kaempfer[er,] *Amoen[itatum] Exot[icarum politico-physico-medicarum fasciculi V . . .* , (Lemgo),] 1712, p. 514.

affected by one stroke of the animal, as well as when joined in a single circuit. For instance, four persons, touching separately his upper and lower surfaces, were all affected; two persons likewise, after the electricity had passed through a wire into a basin of water, transmitted it from thence, in two distinct channels, as their sensation convinced them, into another basin of water, from whence it was conducted, probably in an united state, by a single wire. How much further the effect might be thus divided and subdivided into different channels, was not determined; but it was found to be proportionably weakened by multiplying these circuits, as it had been by extending the single circuit.[3]

Something may be expected to be said of the parts of the animal immediately concerned in producing the electrical effect. The engraving, which accompanies this letter, while it shews the general figure of the Torpedo, gives an internal view of his electric organs. The Society will, besides, have a full anatomical description of these parts from the ingenious Mr. John Hunter, in a paper he has expressly written on the subject at my request.[4] It would therefore be superfluous for me to say any thing either in regard to their situation or structure.

I have to observe, however, That in these double organs resides the electricity of the Torpedo, the rest of his body appearing to be no otherwise concerned in his electrical effect than as conducting it: That they are subject to the will of the animal; but whether, like other double parts so controlable, they are exercised, at times, singly as well as in concert, is difficult to be ascertained by experiment: That their upper and under surfaces are capable, from a state of equilibrium with respect to electricity, of being instantly thrown, by a meer energy, into an opposition of a *plus* and *minus* state, like that of the charged Phial: That, when they are thus charged, the upper surfaces of the two are in the same state of electricity; as are the under surfaces of the two, though in a contrary to that of the upper; for no shock can be obtained by an insulated person touching both organs above, or both below: And that the production of the effect depends solely

3. Cavendish reported the same results: *op. cit.*, pp. 197–8, 210–11.
4. John Hunter's "Anatomical Observations on the Torpedo" was read to the Royal Society on the same day as this letter, July 1, and published with it in the *Phil. Trans.*, LXIII (1773–74), part 2, 481–8.

on an intercourse being made between the opposite surfaces of the organs, whether taken singly or jointly.

All the parts bordering on the organs act, more or less, as conductors, either through their substance or by their superficies. While an insulated person, placing two fingers on the same surface of one or both organs, cannot be affected; if he removes one of his fingers to any such contiguous part, he will be liable to a shock: but this shock will not be near, perhaps not half, so violent, as one taken immediately between the opposite surfaces of the organ; which shews the conduction to be very imperfect.

The parts, which conduct the best, are the two great lateral fins bounding the organs outwardly, and the space lying between the two organs inwardly. All below the double transverse cartilages scarcely conduct at all, unless when the fish is just taken out of water and is still wet, the mucus, with which he is lubricated, shewing itself, as it dries, to be of an insulating nature.

The organs themselves, when uncharged, appeared to be, not interiorly we might suppose, but rather exteriorly, conductors of a shock. An insulated person touching two Torpedos, lying near one another on a damp table, with fingers placed, one on the organ of one fish, and another on the organ of the other, was sensible of shocks, sometimes delivered by one fish, and sometimes by the other, as might be discovered by the respective winking of their eyes. That the organs, uncharged, served some way or other as conductors, was confirmed with artificial electricity, in passing shocks by them; and in taking sparks from them, when electrified.

The electric effect was never perceived by us to be attended with any motion or alteration in the organs themselves, but was frequently accompanied with a little transient agitation along the cartilages which surround both organs: this is not discernible in the plump and turgid state of the animal, while he is fresh and vigorous; but as his force decays, from the relaxation of his muscles, his cartilages appear through the skin, and then the slight action along them is discovered.

May we not from all these premises conclude, that the effect of the Torpedo proceeds from a modification of the electric fluid? The Torpedo resembles the charged Phial in that characteristic point of a reciprocation between its two surfaces. Their effects are transmitted by the same mediums; than which there is not perhaps a surer criterion to determine the identity of subtile matter: They, besides, occasion the same impression on our nerves. Like effects have like causes. But it may be objected, that the effects of the Torpedo, and of the charged Phial, are not similar in all their circumstances; that the charged Phial occasions attractive or repulsive dispositions in neighbouring bodies; and that its discharge is obtained through a portion of air, and is accompanied with light and sound; nothing of which occurs with respect to the Torpedo.

The inaction of the electricity of the animal in these particulars, whilst its elastic force is so great as to transmit the effect through an extensive circuit and in its course to communicate a shock, may be a new phænomenon, but is no ways repugnant to the laws of electricity; for here too, the operations of the animal may be imitated by art.

The same quantity of electric matter, according as it is used in a dense or rare state, will produce the different consequences. For example, a small Phial, whose coated surface measures only six square inches, will, on being highly charged, contain a dense electricity capable of forcing a passage through an inch of air, and afford the phænomena of light, sound, attraction, and repulsion. But if the quantity condensed in this Phial, be made rare by communicating it to three large connected jars, whose coated surfaces shall form together an area 400 times larger than that of the Phial (I instance these jars because they are such as I use); it will, thus dilated, yield all the negative phænomena, if I may so call them, of the Torpedo; it will not now pass the hundredth part of that inch of air, which in its condensed state it sprung through with ease; it will now refuse the minute intersection in the strip of tinfoil; the spark and its attendant sound, even the attraction or repulsion of light bodies, will now be wanting; nor will a point brought however near, if not in contact, be able to draw off the charge: and yet, with this diminished elasticity, the electric matter will, to effect its equilibrium, instantly run through a considerable circuit of different conductors, perfectly continuous, and make us sensible of an impulse in its passage.

Let me here remark, that the sagacity of Mr. Cavendish in devising and his address in executing electrical experiments, led him the first to experience with artificial electricity, that a shock could be received from a charge which was unable to force a passage through the least space of air.[5]

But, after the discovery that a large area of rare electricity would imitate the effect of the Torpedo, it may be inquired, where is this large area to be found in the animal? We here approach to that veil of nature, which man cannot remove. This, however, we know, that from infinite division of parts infinite surface may arise, and even our gross optics tell us, that those singular organs, so often mentioned, consist like our electric batteries of many vessels, call them cylinders or hexagonal prisms, whose superficies taken together furnish a considerable area.

I rejoice in addressing these communications to You. He, who predicted and shewed that electricity wings the formidable bolt of the atmosphere, will hear with attention, that in the deep it speeds an humbler bolt, silent and invisible: He, who analysed the electrified Phial, will hear with pleasure that its laws prevail in animate Phials; He, who by Reason became an electrician, will hear with reverence of an instinctive electrician, gifted in his birth with a wonderful apparatus, and with the skill to use it.

However I may respect your talents as an electrician, it is certainly for knowledge of more general import, that I am impressed with that high esteem, with which I remain, Dear Sir, Your affectionate and obedient servant,   JOHN WALSH.

To Deborah Franklin

AL: Historical Society of Pennsylvania; transcript:[6] University of Virginia Library

West Wickham, the Seat of Lord Le Despencer, Bucks
My dear Child,   July 6. 1773.
I am here in my Way to Oxford, where I am going to be

5. Cavendish did not report this result until 1776 (above, XIX, 287 n). He was working toward it in 1771–73 and must have reached the conclusion to which Walsh refers, but did not begin the experiments that fully substantiated it until after this letter was written. See James C. Maxwell, ed., *The Scientific Papers of the Honourable Henry Cavendish . . . the Electrical Researches . . .* (revised by Sir Joseph Larmor; Cambridge, 1921), pp. 11–13, 211–88.

6. The transcript has minor verbal differences and is dated July 7.

present at the Installation,[7] and shall stay a few Days among my Friends there. By Capt. All who sails next Week I shall write fully to you, and to Friends in Philadelphia. This is my only Letter per Packet. Love to our Children, and to Benny Boy. I am, Thanks to God, very well and hearty, and ever Your affectionate Husband

Addressed: To / Mrs Franklin / at / Philadelphia / via N. York / per Packet / B Free FRANKLIN

Notation: Old Letters

To Samuel Cooper

LS: British Museum; letterbook draft: Library of Congress

Dear Sir, London, July 7, 1773.

I received your very valuable Favours of March 15, and April 23.[8] It rejoices me to find your Health so far restored, that your Friends can again be benefitted by your Correspondence.

The Governor was certainly out in his Politicks, if he hoped to recommend himself here by entring upon that Dispute with the Assembly. His imprudence in bringing it at all upon the Tapis, and his bad Management of it; are almost equally censured. The Council and Assembly on the other hand have by the Coolness, Clearness and Force of their Answers, gained great Reputation.

The Unanimity of our Towns in their Sentiments of Liberty, gives me great Pleasure, as it shows the generally enlighten'd State of our People's Minds, and demonstrates the Falshood of the Opinion much cultivated here by the Partisans of arbitrary Power in America, that only a small Faction among us were discontented with the late Measures. If that Unanimity can be discovered in all the Colonies, it will give much greater Weight to our future Remonstrances.[9]

7. Of the University's new chancellor, Lord North. BF attended the ceremonies with Lord Le Despencer and at his instigation, and stopped at West Wycombe both going and returning; see BF to WF below, July 14.

8. Only the earlier one survives. BF is responding to it in this and the next three paragraphs, and in the long discussion of heating the Brattle St. Church.

9. For the opinion "much cultivated here" see above, pp. 202, 224. BF's hope for unanimity had been aroused by learning of the Virginia resolves; see the following document.

I heartily wish with you that some Line could be drawn, some Bill of Rights established for America, that might secure peace between the two Countries, so necessary to the Prosperity of both. But I think little Attention is like to be afforded by our Ministers to that salutary Work, till the breach becomes greater and more alarming, and then the Difficulty of repairing it will be greater in a tenfold Proportion.

I congratulate you on the finishing of your new Meeting-House. I have considered as well as I can without being on the Spot, the Intention of warming it by some Machine in the cold and damp Seasons. It must be a matter of Difficulty to warm sensibly all the Air in so large and so lofty a Room, especially if the Fire is not kept up in it constantly, on the common Week Days as well as Sundays; For tho' the Machine be very large and made very hot, yet the Space of Air and quantity of Wall to be warmed is so great, that it must be long before any considerable Effect will be produced. Then the Air warmed below by the Machine being rarify'd and lighter will not spread among the People below as it would under a low Cieling, but will naturally rise to the Top of the Room, and can only descend again as it becomes cooler and must give Place to the succeeding warm rising Air. It will then descend by the Walls and Windows, which being very cold by the preceding Weeks Absence of Fire, will cool that descending Air so much in so long a descent, that it will fall very heavily and uncomfortably upon the Heads of all that happen to sit under it, and will proceed in cold Currents along the Floor to the warming Machine where-ever it is situated. This must continue till the Walls are warmed, for which I think one Day is by no means sufficient, and that therefore a Fire kindled in the Morning of the Sabbath will afford no Comfort to the Congregation that Day, except to a few that sit near it, and some Inconvenience to the rest from the Currents above-mentioned. If, however, your People, as they are rich, can afford it, and may be willing to indulge themselves, should chuse to keep up a constant Fire in the Winter Months, you may have from hence a Machine for the purpose, cast from the same Patterns with those now used at the Bank, or that in Lincoln's-Inn Hall, which are placed in the middle of the respective Rooms. The Smoke of these descends, and passing under ground rises in some Chimney at a distance. Yours must be a Chimney built I suppose without the House; and as it ought to draw well, to prevent your being troubled with Smoke (as they often are at the Bank) it should be on the South side; but this I fear would disfigure your Front. That at Lincoln's-Inn Hall draws better. They are in the Form of Temples, cast in Iron, with Columns, Cornishes, and every Member of elegant Architecture. And I mention casting them from the same Patterns or Moulds, because these being already made, a great deal of work and expence will thereby be saved. But if you can cast them in New-England, a large Vase, or an Antique Altar, which are more simple Forms, may answer the Purpose as well, and be more easily executed. Yet after all, when I consider the little Effect I have observed from these Machines in those great Rooms, the Complaints of People who have tried Buzaglo's Stoves in Halls, and how far your Meeting-House must exceed them in all its Dimensions, I apprehend that after a great deal of Expence, and a good Deal of Dust in the Seats and in the Pews, which they constantly occasion, you will not find your Expectations answered. And persuaded as I am, from Philosophic Considerations, that no one ever catches the Disorder we call a Cold, from cold Air, and therefore never at Meeting; I should think it rather advisable to those who cannot well bear it, to guard against the short Inconvenience of cold Feet, (which only takes place towards the end of the Service) by Basses[1] or Bear Skin Cases, to put the Legs in, or by small Stoves with a few Coals underfoot, *more majorum*.[2]

You mention the Surprize of Gentlemen to whom those Letters have been communicated, at the Restrictions with which they were accompanied, and which they suppose render them incapable of answering any important End. The great Reason of forbidding their Publication, was an Apprehension that it might put all the possessors of such Correspondence here upon their Guard, and so prevent the obtaining more of it.[3] And it was imagined that showing the Originals to so many as were named,

1. Hassocks or bags made of bast fiber.
2. In the traditional way.
3. BF is amplifying what he said when he sent the Hutchinson letters, that the person from whom he obtained them had forbidden their publication, and that he himself regretted this restriction. Above, XIX, 412.

and to a few such others as they might think fit, would be sufficient to establish the authenticity, and to spread thro' the Province so just an Estimation of the Writers, as to strip them of all their deluded Friends, and demolish effectually their Interest and Influence. The Letters might be shown even to some of the Governor's and Lieutenant Governor's Partizans; and spoken of to every body; for there was no Restraint proposed to Talking of them, but only to copying. And possibly, as distant Objects seen only through a Mist appear larger, the same may happen from the Mystery in this Case. However this may be, the Terms given with them, could only be those with which they were received. There is still some Chance of procuring more, and some still more abominable.[4]

The great Defect here is in all sorts of People a want of Attention to what passes in such remote Countries as America; an Unwillingness even to read any thing about them, if it appears a little lengthy; and a Disposition to postpone the Consideration of the Things they know they must at last consider; that so they may have time for what more immediately concerns them, and withal enjoy their Amusement and be undisturb'd in the universal Dissipation. In other Respects, tho' some of the Great regard us with a jealous Eye, and some are angry with us, the Majority of the Nation rather wish us well, and have no Desire to infringe our Liberties. And many console themselves under the Apprehensions of declining Liberty here, that they or their Posterity shall be able to find her safe and vigorous in America. With sincere and great Esteem, I am, Dear Sir, Your most obedient humble Servant   B FRANKLIN

Revd. Dr. Cooper.

To Thomas Cushing

ALS: Public Record Office; ALS (letterbook draft): Library of Congress

Sir,   London, July 7. 1773.
I am favoured with yours of April 20, and May 6. The Letters communicated to you were not merely to "satisfy the Curiosity"[5]

4. This sentence must have been a last-minute addition, for it is not in the draft.
5. Quoted from Cushing's letter above, April 20.

of any, but it was thought there might be a Use in showing them to some Friends of the Province, and even to some of the Governor's Party, for their more certain Information concerning his Conduct and Politicks, tho' the Letters were not made quite publick. I believe I have since wrote to you, that there was no Occasion to return them speedily;[6] and tho' I cannot obtain Leave as yet to suffer Copies to be taken of them, I am allowed to say that they may be shown or read to whom and as many as you think proper.[7] Mr. George Grenville, who was the Centre to which flow'd all the Correspondence inimical to America, to whomsoever directed, had these Letters put into his Hands, as the Writers probably expected or intended they should be.[8] He lent them to another, and dying before they were return'd gave an Opportunity for their falling in ours. More may possibly be obtained if these do not make too much Noise.[9]

I thank you for the Pamphlets you have sent me, containing the Controversy between the Governor and the two Houses.[1] I have distributed them where I thought they might be of Use. He makes perhaps as much of his Argument as it will bear; but has the Misfortune of being on the weak side; and so is put to Shifts and Quibbles, and the Use of much Sophistry and Artifice to give Plausibility to his Reasonings. The Council and Assembly have greatly the Advantage in point of Fairness, Perspicuity and Force. His Precedents of Acts of Parliament binding the Colonies, and our tacit Consent to those Acts, are all frivolous. Shall a

6. BF to Cushing above, June 4.

7. From here BF's draft first read: "Had not a Person died in whose hands they were, probably we should not soon have seen them. Politicians on our side the Water should take Care what they write to Ministers if they wish the World may never know it. For Great Men are sometimes very careless of such Papers. One of them not long since gave a great Quantity of American Letters to his Footman who sold them for Waste Paper. By Chance an Acquaintance of mine saw them, bought for a Trifle and sent them to me; and they have afforded me abundance of Amusement." BF struck out the whole passage in his draft and substituted the gist of the rest of the paragraph as it appears.

8. The final clause of the sentence is missing in the draft.

9. This sentence is missing in the draft.

1. For the controversy and the pamphlet see Cooper to BF above, March 15, ns. 7, 9.

Guardian who has impos'd upon, cheated and plundered a Minor under his Care, who was unable to prevent it, plead those Impositions, after his Ward has discovered them, as Precedents and Authorities for continuing them? There have been Precedents, time out of mind, for Robbing on Hounslow Heath; but the Highwayman who robb'd there yesterday, does nevertheless deserve a Hanging.[2]

I am glad to see the Resolves of the Virginia House of Burgesses. There are brave Spirits among that People. I hope their Proposals will be readily comply'd with by all the Colonies.[3] It is natural to suppose, as you do, that if the Oppressions continue, a Congress may grow out of that Correspondence. Nothing would more alarm our Ministers; but if the Colonies agree to hold a Congress, I do not see how it can be prevented.[4]

The Instruction relating to the Exemption of the Commisioners from Taxes I imagine is withdrawn; perhaps the other also, relating to the Agents; but of that I have heard nothing. I only wonder that the Governor should make such a Declaration of his Readiness to comply with an *Intimation* in acting contrary to an *Instruction*, if he had not already or did not soon expect a Repeal of those Instructions.[5] I have not and shall never use your Name on this or any similar Occasion.

2. The letter, like so many of BF's to Cushing, came into the hands of Thomas Moffatt, who added on the back one of his testy notes; it applies particularly to this and the preceding paragraph: "Begins with Evasions and Falshood relative to the Embezzled or Stoln letters of Govr. Hutchinson &c. from the Collection of the late Mr. Whatley &c. The Greater part of the Letter is Criminal and very Instigatory to weaken or Efface The Idea of Veneration for the Parliament of Great Britain by the most shocking Similitudes or Comparisons."

3. The proposals were for committees of correspondence; see Cushing to BF above, April 20.

4. BF expanded this idea below in writing to the House, July 7, the "Publick Letter" to which he refers later in this one.

5. The instructions on exempting the commissioners and on paying BF were not changed; see above, XVIII, 178 n, 242 n. On the second issue Dartmouth was firm, but on the first more flexible. He hoped that the assessors, he wrote Hutchinson on Feb. 3, would not make the relevant clause of the bill ground for doing anything to draw complaints from the commissioners and force the Governor to veto such bills in future. Public Record

I note your Directions relating to publick and private Letters, and shall not fail to observe them. At the same time I cannot but think all the Correspondence should be in the Speaker's Power, to communicate such Extracts only as he should think proper to the House. It is sometimes extreamly embarassing to an Agent to write Letters concerning his Transactions with Ministers, which Letters he knows are to be read in the House, where there may be Governor's Spies, who carry away Parts, or perhaps take Copies, that can be echo'd back hither privately, if they should not be, as sometimes they are, printed in the Votes. It is impossible to write freely in such Cases, unless he would hazard his Usefulness, and put it out of his Power to do his Country any farther Service.[6] I speak this now, not upon my own Account, being about to decline all publick Business, but for your Consideration with regard to future Agents.

And now we speak of Agents I must mention my Concern, that I should fall under so severe a Censure of the House, as that of Neglect in their Business.[7] I have submitted to the Reproof

---

Office, C.O.5/765/[250]. This implies to us, and presumably implied to Hutchinson, official acceptance of the suggestion he had made in 1771 (above, p. 174, n. 5). The commissioners had not complained for several years, he replied in April, and his veto would make more trouble than the issue was worth. Mass. Arch., XXVII, 485. On July 2 he reported that he had signed a new bill in the usual form, because the taxing issue had not arisen. C.O.5/768/360. Had he been informally assured that it would not arise? We have no evidence, but in any case Whitehall approved the bill, c. 14 of that session: *Acts Privy Coun., Col.*, V, 580. The clause in the 1769 act that had been interpreted to make the trouble reappeared verbatim in the new one: income was taxable when derived "from any trade or faculty, business or employment whatsoever." *Mass. Acts and Resolves*, V, 18, 319.

6. BF is still replying to Cushing's letter of April 20. The mounting tension, he says in effect, has brought an agent to the point where he no longer dares communicate with the whole body of his constituents (and for good reason; see the headnote on his letter to the House below, July 7). This was a far cry from the traditional role of the Massachusetts agent, as Hutchinson described it to Dartmouth, doubtless with a touch of nostalgia: the agent used to represent the General Court and correspond with the provincial secretary, who communicated each letter to the Council, and sent the Speaker a copy to transmit it to the House when it met. Mass. Arch., XXVII, 511.

7. The censure must have been in a missing letter from Cushing or the House.

without Reply in my Publick Letter, out of pure Respect. It is not decent to dispute a Father's Admonitions. But to you in private permit me to observe, that as to the two things I am blam'd for not giving the earliest Notice of, viz. the Clause in the Act relating to Dock Yards,[8] and the Appointment of Salaries for the Governor and Judges, the first only, seems to have some Foundation. I did not know, but perhaps I ought to have known, that such a Clause was intended. And yet in a Parliament that during that whole Session refused Admission to Strangers, wherein near 200 Acts were passed, it is not so easy a Matter to come at the Knowledge of the Purport of every Clause in every Act, and to give Opposition to what may affect one's Constituents, especially when it is not uncommon to smuggle Clauses into a Bill whose Title shall give no Suspicion, when an Opposition to such Clauses is apprehended. I say this is no easy matter. But had I known of this Clause it is not likely I could have prevented its passing, in the then Disposition of Government towards America, nor do I see that my giving earlier Notice of its having passed, could have been of much Service. As to the other concerning the Governor and Judges, I should hardly have thought of sending the House an Account of it, even if the Minister had mentioned it to me, as I understood from their first Letter to me, that they had already "the best Intelligence of its being determined by Administration to bestow large Salaries on the Attorney-General, Judges and Governor of the Province." I could not therefore possibly, as their Agent, "give the *first Notice* of this impending Evil." I answered, however, "that *there was no doubt* of the *Intention* of making Governors and some other Officers *independent of the People for their Support*, and that this Purpose *will be persisted in* if the American Revenue is found sufficient to defray the Salaries."[9] This Censure, tho' grievous does not so much surprize me, as I apprehended from the Beginning, that between the Friends of an old Agent, my Predecessor, who thought himself hardly us'd in his Dismission, and those of a young One impatient

8. See above, p. 124 n.

9. For the first and third quotations see above, respectively, XVII, 281; XVIII, 29. The second was doubtless from the lost letter containing the censure.

for the Succession,[10] my Situation was not likely to be a very comfortable one, as my Faults could scarce pass unobserved.

I think of leaving England in September. As soon as possible after my Arrival in America, I purpose, God willing to visit Boston, when I hope to have the Pleasure of paying my Respects to you. I shall then give every information in my Power, and offer, humbly, every Advice relating to our Affairs, not so convenient to be written, that my Situation here for so many Years may enable me to suggest for the Benefit of our Country. Some time before my Departure, I shall put your Papers into the Hands of Mr. Lee, and assist him with my Counsel while I stay, where there may be any Occasion for it. He is a Gentleman of Parts and Ability; and tho' he cannot exceed me in sincere Zeal for the Interest and Prosperity of the Province, his Youth will enable him to serve it with more Activity. I am, Sir, very respectfully, Your obliged, and most obedient humble Servant   B Franklin

Private

Honourable Thomas Cushing, Esqr

Endorsed: Benjn Franklin London July 7. 1773

To Samuel Franklin[11]

ALS: Mr. John H. Bradshaw, Lahaska, Pa. (1975); letterbook draft:[12] Library of Congress; transcript: New England Historic, Genealogical Society

Dear Cousin,   London, July 7. 1773

I received your kind Letter of Nov. 6. and was glad to hear of the Welfare of yourself and Family, which I hope continues.

10. BF had several predecessors, but is clearly referring to William Bollan. In 1762 the General Court had dismissed Bollan from the agency; in 1769 the Council appointed him, but failed then and in 1770 to have him reinstated as agent of the province. Malcolm Freiberg, "William Bollan, Agent of Massachusetts," *More Books: the Bulletin of the Boston Public Library,* 6th ser., XXIII (1948), 169–70, 180; 6 Mass. Hist. Soc. *Coll.,* IX, 214. The "young One" was Arthur Lee, who was attempting to undermine BF's agency: above, XVIII, 127–9, 213.

11. The Boston cutler who was BF's first cousin once removed: above, XIV, 215 n and subsequent vols.

12. We have silently supplied from the draft a few words now missing in the ALS.

Sally Franklin is lately married to Mr. James Pierce, a sub-stantial young Farmer at Ewell, about 13 Miles from London; a very sober industrious Man, and I think it likely to prove a good Match, as she is likewise an industrious good Girl.[1]

I would not have you be discouraged at a little Dullness of Business which is only occasional. A close Attention to your Shop, and Application to Business will always secure more than an equal Share, because every Competitor will not have those Qualities. Some of them therefore must give way to you: And the constant Growth of the Country will increase the Trade of all that steadily stand ready for it. I send you a little Piece of mine which more particularly explains these Sentiments.[2]

My love to your good Wife and Daughters, and believe me ever, Your affectionate Cousin[3]   B FRANKLIN

Mr Saml Franklin

To the Massachusetts House of Representatives

ALS (letterbook draft):[4] Library of Congress

By forwarding the Hutchinson letters Franklin had jeopardized his position in London; by writing this one he exposed himself, without knowing it, to eventual prosecution. The letter was addressed to the Speaker but intended for the House,[5] where it was not read until

1. The draft omits the final clause. BF gave Sally twenty-five guineas as a wedding present: above, XIX, 395 n.
2. For the "Dullness of Business," and the similar recipe for overcoming it that BF gave Richard Bache, see *ibid.*, pp. 100–1, 267. The "little Piece of mine" was probably "Advice to a Young Tradesman" (above, III, 306–8), included in George Fisher, *The American Instructor: or Young Man's Best Companion* . . . (Philadelphia, 1748); Samuel's reply below, Dec. 17, acknowledged a "book of advice."
3. Instead of the final paragraph the draft reads "and am ever, Your affectionate Kinsman." Samuel's second wife, née Eunice Greenleaf, bore him four daughters between 1756 and 1767: Eunice, Hannah, Sarah, and Elizabeth. *Report of the Record Commissioners of the City of Boston*, XXIV (1894), 289, 294, 301, 314.
4. We have supplied in brackets a few missing words and parts of words from the text in Sparks, *Works*, VIII, 60–7.
5. See Cushing's suggestion above, April 20, that BF distinguish what was to be communicated from what was meant for his eyes alone.

January, 1774.[6] Long before that, however, its contents became known.

The point of the letter was that the quarrel with the mother country was coming to a crisis and the time for restraint was past. The King's ministers were by now so thoroughly antagonized, Franklin argued, that they would never voluntarily redress American grievances. The argument was questionable, for Dartmouth at the time did have in mind a number of conciliatory moves.[7] But Franklin either did not know of them or ignored them as trivial. He called for a united front of all the colonies, whether achieved by a continental congress or other means, to compel Britain to recognize American rights. The impact of his letter came from this endorsement of a congress.

"The hint of a Congress is nothing new," Hutchinson wrote Dartmouth in September; "it is what they have been aiming at the two last Sessions of the General Court . . . ."[8] Their agitation was due largely to receipt of the Virginia resolves, and by summer was being actively promoted through intercolonial correspondence. Dartmouth's conciliatory proposals could not survive such a congress, the Governor realized, but opposition to it in the House of Representatives had been strong. Then Franklin's letter arrived. The next meeting of the House, Hutchinson reported, was now likely to endorse a congress. "The plausibility with which it is recommended by their Agent will I think make many converts and my chief hopes are that many of the other Colonies will not join if the proposal should be made by this."[9]

Part of Franklin's letter was condensed and reworked, with a change of emphasis, in a paragraph of the *Boston Gazette* of Sept. 27, 1773. In October Hutchinson obtained a copy of the entire document and sent it to Dartmouth.[10] Franklin believed that there was nothing

6. At the first session of the House since the previous June. Four other letters from BF and two from Dartmouth were also read: *Mass. House Jour.*, 2nd session, Jan.–March, 1774, p. 105.

7. For those dealing with the judges and with the quarrel over taxing the customs commissioners' salaries see above, respectively, pp. 223 n and 273–4 n. In addition Dartmouth had promised, once order was restored, to withdraw the troops from Boston: Public Record Office, C.O.5/765/249. He also considered returning the naval squadron to Halifax and abolishing the appellant Courts of Admiralty: Hutchinson, *History*, III, 298.

8. Mass. Arch., XXVII, 543.

9. *Ibid.*, p. 558; see also pp. 534, 557. Members of the "Party," Hutchinson had written earlier, said that they did nothing without direction from London. *Ibid.*, p. 503.

10. Crane, *Letters to the Press*, pp. 229–31, where the paragraph in the *Gaz.* is reprinted. Hutchinson, doubtless because of his own experience,

treasonable in any of his communications to Massachusetts,[11] but about this one the American Secretary thought otherwise. In June, 1774, he instructed the Governor's successor, General Gage, to obtain the original so that Franklin might be prosecuted. The manuscript was not found. Cushing, unlike whoever had started Hutchinson's letters on their way to publicity, kept Franklin's to himself; after reading them to the House, Gage reported, he "puts them in his Pocket as his own private Correspondence."[1] That pocket turned out to be private enough to protect the agent.

Sir,   London, July 7. 1773
    The Parliament is at length prorogu'd without meddling with the State of America. Their Time was much employ'd in East India Business: and perhaps it was not thought prudent to lay before them the Advices from New England, tho' some threatning Intimations had been given of such an Intention.[2] The King's firm Answer (as it is called) to our Petitions and Remonstrances, has probably been judged sufficient for the present. I forwarded that Answer to you by the last Packet, and sent a Copy of it by a Boston Ship the beginning of last Month. Therein we are told "that his Majesty has well weighed the *Subject matter*, and the *Expressions* contain'd in those Petitions; and that as he will ever attend to the *humble* Petitions of his Subjects, and be forward to redress every *real* Grievance so he is determined to support

---

seemed somewhat defensive about sending the copy. Members of the House and others had seen it, he wrote Dartmouth in his covering letter of Oct. 19, and it would be laid before the House at its next meeting; he would then have a right to it. He added the same point that BF had made to Cooper and to Cushing (above, pp. 271, 272) about concealing his source in order to obtain further letters. Mass. Arch., XXVII, 558.
    11. To Cushing below, April 16, 1774.
    1. Carter, ed., *Gage Correspondence*, I, 364; see also above, XVIII, 120 n. The British subsequently seized the bulk of Cushing's correspondence, which is now in the Public Record Office. The disappearance of this particular letter perhaps suggests that the Speaker destroyed it.
    2. See the headnote on BF to Cushing above, June 4. In that letter BF had said that the Tea Act would flout American patriotism; yet here, addressing the House, he acquits Parliament of "meddling with the State of America." The "threatning Intimations" were presumably Dartmouth's two months earlier, discussed in BF to Cushing above, May 6.

the Constitution, and resist with Firmness every Attempt to derogate from the Authority of the *supreme Legislature*."[3]

By this it seems that, some Exception is taken to the *Expressions* of the Petitions as not sufficiently humble; that the Grievances complain'd of are not thought *real* Grievances; that Parliament is deem'd the Supreme Legislature, and its Authority over the Colonies, suppos'd to be *the Constitution*. Indeed this last Idea is express'd more fully in the next Paragraph, where the Words of the Act[4] are us'd, declaring the Right of the Crown with the Advice of Parliament, to make Laws of *sufficient Force and Validity* to bind its Subjects in America *in all Cases whatsoever*.

When one considers the King's Situation, surrounded by Ministers, Councellors, and Judges learned in the Law, who are all of this Opinion; and reflect how necessary it is for him to be well with his Parliament, from whose yearly Grants his Fleets and Armies are to be supported, and the Deficiencies of his Civil List supplied, it is not to be wondered at that he should be firm in an Opinion establish'd as far as an Act of Parliament could establish it, by even the Friends of America at the Time they repeal'd the Stamp-Act; and which is so generally thought right by his Lords and Commons, that any Act of his, countenancing the contrary, would hazard his embroiling himself with those Powerful Bodies. And from hence it seems hardly to be expected from him that [he] should take any Step of that kind. The grievous Instructions indeed might be withdrawn without their observing it, if his Majesty thought fit so to do; but under the present Prejudices of all about him, it seems that this is not yet likely to be advised.[5]

The Question then arises, How are we to obtain Redress? If we look back into the Parliamentary History of this Country, we shall find that in similar Situations of the Subjects here, Redress could seldom be obtained but by withholding Aids when the Sovereign was in Distress, till the Grievances were removed.

---

3. BF is quoting, with emphases supplied, from Dartmouth's letter above, June 2, which he enclosed to Cushing on the same date and of which he sent a copy on June 4.

4. The Declaratory Act.

5. For the instructions on the crown's paying the salaries of Massachusetts officials see above, XIX, 208–9, 380–1.

Hence the rooted Custom of the Commons to keep Money Bills intirely in their own Disposition, not suffering even the Lords to meddle in Grants, either as to Quantity, Manner of raising, or even in the smallest Circumstance. This Country pretends to be collectively our Sovereign. It is now deeply in debt. Its Funds are far short of recovering their Par since the last War: Another would distress it still more. Its People diminish as well as its Credit. Men will be wanted as well as Money. The Colonies are rapidly increasing in Wealth and Numbers. In the last War they maintained an Army of 25000. A Country able to do that is no contemptible Ally. In another War they may do perhaps twice as much with equal Ease. Whenever a War happens, our Aid will be wish'd for, our Friendship desired and cultivated, our Good will courted: Then is the Time to say, *Redress our Grievances.* You take Money from us by Force, and now you ask it of voluntary Grant. You cannot have it both Ways. If you chuse to have it without our Consent, you must go on taking it that way and be content with what little you can so obtain. If you would have our free Gifts, desist from your Compulsive Methods, acknowledge our Rights, and secure our future Enjoyment of them. Our Claims will then be attended to, and our Complaints regarded. By what I perceiv'd not long since when a War was apprehended with Spain, the different Countenance put on by some Great Men here towards those who were thought to have a little Influence in America, and the Language that began to be held with regard to the then Minister for the Colonies, I am confident that if that War had taken place he would have been immediately dismiss'd, all his Measures revers'd, and every step taken to recover our Affection and procure our Assistance.[6] Thence I think it fair to conclude that similar Effects will probably be produced by similar Circumstances.

But as the Strength of an Empire depends not only on the *Union* of its Parts, but on their *Readiness* for United Exertion of their common Force: And as the Discussion of Rights may seem unseasonable in the Commencement of actual War; and the Delay it might occasion be prejudicial to the common Welfare. As like-

---

6. The reference is to Hillsborough and the Falkland Islands crisis of 1770.

wise the Refusal of one or a few Colonies, would not be so much regarded if the others granted liberally, which perhaps by various Artifices and Motives they might be prevailed on to do; and as this want of Concert would defeat the Expectation of general Redress that otherwise might be justly formed; perhaps it would be best and fairest, for the Colonies in a general Congress now in Peace to be assembled, or by means of the Correspondence lately proposed after a full and solemn Assertion and Declaration of their Rights, to engage firmly with each other that they will never grant aids to the Crown in any General War till those Rights are recogniz'd by the King and both Houses of Parliament; communicating at the same time to the Crown this their Resolution. Such a Step I imagine will bring the Dispute to a Crisis; and whether our Demands are immediately comply'd with, or compulsory Means are thought of to make us Rescind them, our Ends will finally be obtain'd, for even th[e odiu]m accomp[anyin]g such [compulsory] Attempts [will contribute to unite and strengthen us,] and in the mean time all the World will allow that our Proceeding has been honourable.[7]

No one doubts the Advantage of a strict Union between the Mother Country and the Colonies, if it may be obtain'd and preserv'd on equitable Terms. In every fair Connection each Party should find its own Interest. Britain will find hers in our joining with her in every War she makes to the greater Annoyance and Terror of her Enemies; in our Employment of her Manufacturers, and Enriching of her Merchants by our Commerce; and her Government will feel some additional Strengthening of its Hands, by the Disposition of our profitable Posts and Places. On

7. BF, at least momentarily, is changing his tune. He had been advocating *suaviter in modo, fortiter in re*, the firm assertion of rights in temperate language. Now he is picking up Cushing's remark in his letter above of April 20, that a congress might make resolution of the conflict more difficult, and is suggesting—even though the following paragraph is milder in tone—that the difficulty be risked and the crisis provoked. This advice was what American radicals were looking for. Samuel Adams promptly publicized it, in the same issue of the *Boston Gaz.* that carried the revised extract of BF's letter; and several other colonial newspapers took up the idea. Arthur Schlesinger, *Prelude to Independence: the Newspaper War on Britain, 1764–1776* (New York, 1958), p. 156.

our side, we have to expect the Protection she can afford us; and the Advantage of a common Umpire in our Disputes thereby preventing Wars we might otherwise have with each other, so that we can without Interruption go on with our Improvements and increase our Numbers. We ask no more of her, and she should not think of forcing more from us. By the Exercise of prudent Moderation on her part, mix'd with a little Kindness; and by a decent Behaviour on ours, excusing where we can excuse from a Consideration of Circumstances, and bearing a little, with the Infirmities of her Government as we would with those of an aged Parent, tho' firmly asserting our Privileges, and declaring that we mean at a proper time to vindicate them, this advantageous Union may still be long continued. We wish it, and we may endeavour it, but God will order it as to his Wisdom shall seem most suitable. The Friends of Liberty here, wish we may long preserve it on our side the Water, that they may find it there if adverse Events should destroy it here. They are therefore anxious and afraid lest we should hazard it by premature Attempts in its favour. They think we may risque much by violent Measures, and that the Risque is unnecessary, since a little Time must infallibly bring us all we demand or desire, and bring it us in Peace and Safety. I do not presume to advise. There are many wiser Men among you, and I hope you will be directed by a still superior Wisdom.

With regard to the Sentiments of People in general here concerning America, I must say that we have among them many Friends and Well-wishers. The Dissenters are all for us, and many of the Merchants and Manufacturers. There seems to be even among the Country Gentlemen a general Sense of our growing Importance, a Disapprobation of the harsh Measures with which we have been treated, and a Wish that some Means may be found of perfect Reconciliation. A few Members of Parliament in both Houses, and perhaps some in high Office have in a Degree the same Ideas, but none of these seem willing as yet to be active in our favour, lest Adversaries should take Advantage and charge it upon them as a Betraying the Interests of this Nation. In this State of things, no Endeavours of mine or our other Friends here "to obtain a Repeal of the Acts so oppressive to the Colonists or the Orders of the Crown so destructive of the

Charter [rights] of our Province in particular,"[8] can expect a sudden [succe]ss. By degrees and a judicious Improvement of Events [we may] work a Change in Minds and Measures, but otherwise such great Altera[tions are] hardly to be look'd for.

I am thankful to the House for the Mark of their kind Attention in repeating their Grant to me of Six Hundred Pounds. Whether the Instruction restraining the Governor's Assent is withdrawn or not, or is likely to be I cannot tell, having never solicited or even once mention'd it to Lord Dartmouth, being resolved to owe no Obligation on that Account to the Favour of any Minister. If from a Sense of Right, that Instruction should be recall'd and the general Principle on which it was founded is given up, all will be very well: but you can never think it worth while to employ an Agent here if his being paid or not is to depend on the Breath of a Minister, and I should think it a Situation too suspicious and therefore too dishonourable for me to remain in a single Hour. Living frugally I am under no immediate Necessity; and if I serve my Constituents faithfully tho' it should be unsuccessfully I am confident they will always have it in their Inclination and sometime or other in their Power to make their Grants effectual.[9]

A Gentleman of our Province, Capt. Calef, is come hither as an Agent for some of the Eastern Townships to obtain a Confirmation of their Lands. Sir Francis Bernard seems inclin'd to make Use of this Person's Application for promoting a Separation of that Country from your Province and making it a distinct Government, to which purpose he prepared a Draft of a Memorial for Calef to present setting forth not only the hardship of being without Security in the Property of their Improvements, but also the Distress of the People there for want of Government, that

---

8. Quoted, we assume, from the missing letter criticizing BF, to which he referred in the private letter to Cushing that accompanied this one.

9. BF's confidence was well grounded. He was reimbursed in the end, but only after Hutchinson's instructions had become inoperative; they were never withdrawn. For the deadlock they occasioned see above, XVIII, 153, 242; XIX, 209. In early June, 1773, the House and Council made another unsuccessful attempt to pay BF, £800 this time for his services through that month. *Mass. House Jour.*, 1st session, May–June, 1773, pp. 25, 41.

they were at too great a Distance from the Seat of Government in the Massachusetts to be capable of receiving the Benefits of Government from thence, and expressing their Willingness to be separated, and form'd into a new Province, &c. With this Draft Sir Francis and Mr. Calef came to me to have my Opinion. I read it, and observ'd to them that tho' I wish'd the People quieted in their Possessions and would do any thing I could to assist in obtaining the Assurance of their Property, yet as I knew the Province of the Massachusetts had a Right to that Country, of which they were justly tenacious, I must oppose that part of the Memorial if it should be presented. Sir Francis allow'd the Right, but propos'd that a great Tract of Land between Merrimack and Connecticut Rivers which had been allotted to Newhampshire might be restord to our Province by order of the Crown, as a Compensation.[1] This he said would be of more Value to us than that Eastern Country, as being nearer home, &c. I said I would mention it in my Letters, but must in the mean time oppose any Step taken in the Affair before the Sentiments of the General Court should be known as to such an Exchange if it were offer'd. Mr. Calef himself did not seem fond of the Draft, and I have not seen him, or heard any thing farther of it since, but I shall watch it.

---

1. For the complicated issue of land grants in what is now Maine, and Gov. Bernard's involvement, see above, XVIII, 138–44. John Calef (1726–1812) had been an army surgeon during the French and Indian War, and was now an Ipswich physician who frequently represented his town in the General Court; his mission for the eastern townships lasted from 1772 to 1774, and he returned on a similar errand during the War of Independence. Anne C. Boardman, "Robert Calef and Some of His Descendants," Essex Institute *Hist. Coll.*, LXXIV (1938), 386–9. Bernard had proposed, more than a year and a half before, that Massachusetts be compensated for losing eastern Maine by acquiring an equal amount of territory from New York or New Hampshire. A possible compensation, Hutchinson had then suggested, might be the tract in southwestern New Hampshire that the Bay Colony had surrendered years before. Mass. Arch., XXVII, 319; Maine Hist. Soc., *Documentary History of the State of Maine* . . . (24 vols., Portland, 1869–1916), XIV, 187–8. See also Otis G. Hammon, "The Mason Title and Its Relations to New Hampshire and Massachusetts," Amer. Antiquarian Soc. *Proc.*, XXVI (1916), 245–63; William H. Fry, *New Hampshire as a Royal Province* (New York, 1908), pp. 209, 241–64.

Be pleased to present my dutiful Respects to the House, and believe me, with sincere and great Esteem, Sir, Your most obedient and most humble Servant.   B FRANKLIN

Thos Cushing Esqr

To Samuel Mather

ALS (letterbook draft) and extract:[2] Library of Congress

Reverend Sir,   London, July 7. 1773.

By a Line of the 4th. past, I acknowledged the Receipt of your Favour of March 18. and sent you with it two Pamphlets. I now add another, a spirited Address to the Bishops who opposed the Dissenter's Petition. It is written by a Dissenting Minister at York. There is preserv'd at the End of it a little fugitive Piece of mine, written on the same Occasion.[3]

I perused your Tracts with Pleasure. I see you inherit all the various Learning of your famous Ancestors Cotton and Increase Mather both of whom I remember. The Father, Increase, I once when a Boy, heard preach at the Old South, for Mr. Pemberton, and remember his mentioning the Death of "that wicked old Persecutor of God's People Lewis the XIV." of which News had just been received, but which proved premature.[4] I was some

2. The extract includes a few words now missing from the ALS; these, as indicated, we have supplied in brackets.

3. The pamphlet, though anonymous, was by Ebenezer Radcliffe or Radcliff (above, XIV, 219 n), who although a native of Yorkshire was a minister in London: *Two Letters, Addressed to the Right Rev. Prelates, Who a Second Time Rejected the Dissenters' Bill* (2nd ed., London, 1773). The "little fugitive Piece" was included in the appendix (pp. 117–23); it was BF's "Toleration in Old and New England," printed above, XIX, 163–8. After the dissenters failed to secure relief in 1772, they renewed their efforts the next year; again the bill passed the Commons, to be again rejected by the Lords. See Anthony Lincoln, *Some Political and Social Ideas of English Dissent, 1763–1800* (Cambridge, 1938), pp. 231–5.

4. Ebenezer Pemberton (1672–1717), who often clashed with the Mathers, was the famous and irascible minister of the Old South Church; see *Sibley's Harvard Graduates*, IV, 107–13. Increase Mather inveighed against Louis XIV, presumably in 1715 (the King died on Sept. 1), for persecuting the Huguenots.

years afterwards at his House at the Northend, on some Errand to him, and remember him sitting in an easy Chair apparently very old and feeble. But Cotton I remember in the Vigour of his Preaching and Usefulness. And particularly in the Year 1723, now half a Century since, I had reason to remember, as I still do a Piece of Advice he gave me. I had been some time with him in his Study, where he condescended to entertain me, a very Youth, with some pleasant and instructive Conversation. As I was taking my Leave he accompany'd me thro' a narrow Passage at which I did not enter, and which had a Beam across it lower than my Head. He continued Talking which occasion'd me to keep my Face partly towards him as I retired, when he suddenly cry'd out, Stoop! Stoop! Not immediately understanding what he meant, I hit my Head hard against the Beam. He then added, *Let this be a Caution to you not always to hold your Head so high; Stoop, young Man, stoop—as you go through the World—and you'll miss many hard Thumps.* This was a way of hammering Instruction into one's Head: And it was so far effectual, that I have ever since remember'd it, tho' I have not always been able to practise it. By the way, permit me to ask if you are the Son or Nephew of that Gentleman?[5] for having lived so many Years far from New England, I have lost the Knowledge of some Family Connections.

You have made the most of your Argument to prove that America might be known to the Ancients.[6] The Inhabitants being totally ignorant of the use of Iron, looks, however, as if the Intercourse could never have been very considerable; and that if they are Desc[endants] of our Adam, they left the Family before [the time of Tu]balcain.[7] There is another Discovery of [it claimed] by the Norwegians, which you have not men[tioned, unless] it be under the Words "of old viewed and observed" Page [7. About] 25 Years since, Professor Kalm, a learned Sw[ede, was] with us in Pensilvania. He contended that America was discovered by their Northern People long before the Time of Columbus, which I

---

5. Son. See the note on BF to Mather above, June 4.

6. Mather's pamphlet, enclosed in his missing letter of March 18, was *An Attempt to Shew, that America Must be Known to the Ancients . . . to Which is Added an Appendix, Concerning the American Colonies, and Some Modern Managements against Them* (Boston, 1773).

7. The teacher of artificers in metal: Gen. 4:22.

doubting, he drew up and gave me sometime after a Note of those Discoveries which I send you enclos'd. It is his own Hand writing, and his own English very intelligible for the time he had been among us. The Circumstances give the Account great Appearance of Authenticity. And if one may judge by the Description of the Winter, the Country they visited should be southward of New England, supposing no Change since that time of the Climate. But if it be true as Krantz and I think other Historians tell us, that old Greenland once inhabited and populous, is now render'd un-inhabitable by Ice, it should seem that the almost perpetual northern Winter has gained ground to the Southward, and if so, perhaps more northern Countries might anciently have had Vines than can bear them in these Days.[8] The Remarks you have added, on the late Proceedings against America, are very just and judicious: and I cannot at all see any Impropriety in your making them tho' a Minister of the Gospel. This Kingdom is a good deal indebted for its Liberties to the Publick Spirit of its ancient Clergy, who join'd with the Barons in obtaining Magna Charta, and join'd heartily in forming Curses of Excommunication against the Infringers of it. There is no doubt but the Claim of Parliament of Authority to make Laws *binding on the Colonists in all Cases whatsoever*, includes an Authority to change our Religious Constitution, and establish Popery or Mahometanism if they please in its Stead: but, as you intimate *Power* does not infer *Right;* and as the Right is nothing and the *Power* (by our Increase) continually diminishing, the one will soon be as insignificant as the other. You seem only to have made a small Mistake in supposing they modestly avoided to declare they had a Right, [the] words of the Act being [that] they have, and of *right* ought to have full Power, &c.[9]

8. The extract, which omits some phrases and the whole story about Cotton Mather, ends here; from it we have provided the bracketed insertions following the previous note. Peter Kalm had been in Pennsylvania to accumulate material for his travel book; see above, xv, 147, and BF to Colden, March 5, 1773. BF's reference to Krantz was to David Cranz or Crantz, *The History of Greenland: Containing a Description of the Country, and Its Inhabitants* . . . (2 vols., London, 1767), I, 241–79.

9. In the appendix to his pamphlet Mather argued (pp. 29–34) that no one had given Parliament the authority asserted in the Declaratory Act, and that

Your Suspicion that "sundry others, besides Govr Bernard had written hither their Opinions and Counsels, encouraging the late Measures, to the Prejudice of our Country, which have been too much heeded and follow'd" is I apprehend but too well founded. You call them "*traitorous* Individuals" whence I collect, that you suppose them of our own country. There was among the twelve Apostles one Traitor who betrayed with a Kiss. It should be no Wonder therefore if among so many Thousand true Patriots as New England contains there should be found even Twelve Judases, ready to betray their Country for a few paltry Pieces of Silver. Their *Ends*, as well as their *Views*, ought to be similar. But all these Oppressions evidently work for our Good. Providence seems by every Means intent on making us a great People. May our Virtues publick and private grow with us, and be durable, that Liberty Civil and Religious, may be secur'd to our Posterity, and to all from every Part of the old World that take Refuge among us.

I have distributed the Copies of your Piece as you desired. [I can]not apprehend they can give just Cause of Offence.

Your Theological Tracts in which you discover your great Reading, are rather more out of my Walk, and therefore I shall say little of them. That on the Lord's Prayer I read with most Attention, having once myself considered a little the same Subject, and attempted a Version of the Prayer which I thought less exceptionable.[1] I have found it among my old Papers, and send it you only to show an Instance of the same Frankness in laying myself open to you, which you say you have used with regard to me. With great Esteem and my best Wishes for a long Continuance of your Usefulness, I am, Reverend Sir, Your most obedient humble Servant   B FRANKLIN

Mr Mather

---

even the act did not claim such authority by right. The colonists would not tolerate abridgment of their liberties and imposition of unjust financial burdens, he added, but with God's help would resist.

1. Mather's tract was *The Lord's Prayer: or, a New Attempt to Recover the Right Version, and Genuine Meaning, of That Prayer* (Boston, 1766). BF's own version is printed above, XV, 299–303.

To Jane Mecom   ALS (letterbook draft): Library of Congress

Dear Sister,   London, July 7. 1773.
I believe it is long since I have written any Letters to you.[2] I
hope you will excuse it. I am oppress'd with too much Writing,
and am apt to postpone when I presume upon some Indulgence.
I received duly yours of Jan. 19. Apr. 20. May 5 and May 15.[3]
Our Relations Jenkins and Paddock came to see me.[4] They
seem to be clever sensible Men.
    Is there not a little Affectation in your Apology for the In-
correctness of your Writing? Perhaps it is rather fishing for
Commendation. You write better, in my Opinion, than most
American Women. Here indeed the Ladies write generally with
more Elegance than the Gentlemen.
    By Capt. Hatch went a Trunk containing the Goods you wrote
for. I hope they will come safe to hand and please. Mrs. Stevenson
undertook the Purchasing them with great Readiness and
Pleasure. Teasdale, whom you mention as selling cheap, is broke
and gone. Perhaps he sold too cheap. But she did her best.[5]
    I congratulate you on the Marriage of your Daughter.[6] My
Love to them. I am oblig'd to good Dr. Cooper for his Prayers.
    Your Shortness of Breath might perhaps be reliev'd by eating
Honey with your Bread instead of Butter, at Breakfast.
    Young Hubbard seems a sensible Boy, and fit, I should think for
a better Business than the Sea. I am concern'd to hear of the
Illness of his good Mother.[7]

2. Only four months; see his letter above of March 9.
    3. The disappearance of all four letters leaves some of BF's subsequent
references obscure.
    4. For these two Nantucket relatives see above, Williams to BF, Feb. 15.
In his letter to Jane of March 9 BF had promised to inquire after Jenkins.
    5. For the purchase see the following document. The firm of Marmaduke
Teasdale and James Squibb, in Tavistock Street, Covent Garden, had dealt
in lace and haberdashery and gone bankrupt the year before. *Kent's Directory
. . .* (London, 1770); *Gent. Mag.*, XLII (1772), 344.
    6. For Jenny Mecom's marriage to Peter Collas the previous March, and
BF's wedding present to them, see above, XIX, 362–3 and Jenny to BF, Jan.
9, 1773.
    7. Jane's and BF's stepnephew, Thomas Hubbart, had married Judith Ray,
the sister of BF's old friend Catherine Ray Greene. The Hubbarts had seven
sons, the eldest of whom was then twenty-three: Edward W. Day, *One

If Brother John had paid that Bond, there was no Occasion to recal it for you to pay it; for I suppose he might have had Effects of our Fathers to pay it with.[8] I never heard how it was managed. Mrs. Stevenson presents her Respects, and I am ever Your affectionate Brother   B FRANKLIN

To Jonathan Williams, Sr.

LS: Pierpont Morgan Library; ALS (letterbook draft): Library of Congress

Dear Cousin,   London, July 7, 1773.

In looking over your Letters I find in that of Nov. 12, mention of a Prize of £20 which you have drawn.[9] It never came into my Hands, and I cannot find that Smith, Wright and Gray know any thing of it. If I knew the No. of the Ticket, I could enquire farther.

I am much obliged by your Care in Hall's Affair and glad you have recovered so much of that Debt, and are likely to get the rest. I hope it will be of Service to my dear Sister. The Goods for her were sent per Capt. Hatch, in a Trunk consign'd to you.[1]

I wish you Success in your new Plan of Business, and shall certainly embrace every Opportunity I may have of promoting it.[2]

Upon your Recommendation I went to see the black Poetess and offer'd her any Services I could do her. Before I left the House, I understood her Master was there and had sent her to me but did not come into the Room himself, and I thought was not

---

Thousand Years of Hubbard History . . . (New York, [1895]), p. 57. One of these brothers, turned sailor, must have called on BF in London with the news of his mother's illness.

8. See BF to Jane above, March 9.

9. What we can now identify as Williams' letter of Nov. 12, dated mistakenly August because it mentions Josiah's death, is above, XIX, 290–1. It went by Folger in the *Argo*, which cleared Boston in mid-November: *Mass. Gaz.; and the Boston Weekly News-Letter*, Nov. 19, 1772.

1. Samuel Hall's debt had been a theme of their correspondence earlier in the year. In his letter of Feb. 15 Williams had asked BF to use part of the sum recovered to buy goods for Jane Mecom's haberdashery shop. BF had done so in May, to the tune of £55 4s. 5d.: Jour., p. 48.

2. See Jonathan, Jr., to BF above, April 20.

pleased with the Visit. I should perhaps have enquired first for him; but I had heard nothing of him.[3] And I have heard nothing since of her. My Love to Cousin Grace and your Children; I am Your affectionate Uncle,   B FRANKLIN

Jonathan Williams, Esq.

Addressed: To / Jonathan Williams, Esqr / Mercht / Boston

To Jonathan Williams, Jr.

LS: American Philosophical Society; ALS (letterbook draft): Library of Congress[4]

Dear Jonathan,   London, July 7, 1773.

I rejoiced to learn by yours of Dec. 26, that your Business went on so prosperously, and that you keep Touch so well with my good Neighbour Mr. Warren.[5] I think that by persisting steadily in your Plan, you will find the Profits encrease yearly, and become at length very considerable. And all along you will have the Satisfaction of doing your Business with Ease and Safety.

Henry's Father and Mother, were at first very unhappy about

3. Phillis Wheatley (c. 1753–84) was a talented young slave of Mr. and Mrs. John Wheatley of Boston. Her earliest published poem, on the death of George Whitefield, was addressed to the Countess of Huntingdon and opened communication between the two. In the spring of 1773 Phillis accompanied the Wheatley's son Nathaniel to England, in the hope that the sea voyage would improve her failing health. In London the Countess introduced her to high circles, and she was cordially received both as a poet and as a gifted conversationalist. Her stay was brief, however, for by October she was back in Boston. A volume of her poems, which came out in London before the end of the year, was the first significant publication by a black American. *DAB*; Julian D. Mason, Jr., ed., *The Poems of Phillis Wheatley* (Chapel Hill, 1966), pp. xiv–xv, xviii. We can account for Nathaniel Wheatley's aloofness only on the supposition that he was nervous about Phillis' status. She was still a slave (*ibid.*, p. xxxvii), yet the famous judicial decision in 1772 in the Sommersett case was being widely interpreted to mean that slaves gained their freedom on touching English soil. See above, XIX, 187–8.

4. The letter is in Fevre's hand; the postscript, missing in the draft, is in BF's.

5. See above, XIX, 439–41, and Jonathan to BF below, July 29.

their naughty Boy, but are now better Satisfied.[6] He was certainly unfit for you; I hope he will do better in the Business you have provided for him. It will be good in you to keep an Eye over him, and advise him, and countenance him as far as he may deserve it.

I shall be glad if I can be serviceable to your Father in the Commission way. I delivered your Letter to Miss Barwell. She retains a great Regard for you and desires me to tell you, that it would give her Pleasure to have any Opportunity of serving you: but that it is not likely any East India Ships will be sent to America; and I cannot learn that the Company ever consign Goods there: but shall enquire farther.[7]

Mrs. Stevenson, Mr. and Mrs. Hewson and Miss Dolly Blount are all well, and desire to be kindly remembered to you. Mrs. Hewson has now two fine Boys. I am ever, Your affectionate Uncle,
B FRANKLIN

Pray make some Enquiry after Mr. Cowan, and get the enclos'd Letter to his Hands if you can.[8]

Jonathan Williams, Junr.

Addressed: To / Mr Jonathan Williams, junr. / Mercht / Boston

Endorsed: Letter from doctr Franklin July 7—1773

6. See their letters above, June 20. In this and the following paragraph BF is answering Jonathan's letter of April 20.

7. This passage is comprehensible only on the assumption that BF is sticking literally to the request in Jonathan's letter just cited. The Williamses had hoped to have the handling of tea sent on consignment directly from the Orient; BF is saying that the Company appears to have abandoned that idea. What he fails to say—for reasons that we do not venture to guess—is that American merchants were already competing in London to be named consignees for the shipments under the Tea Act; see the note on BF to Jonathan above, June 4.

8. Jonathan's reply below, Sept. 21, identifies Cowan as the purser of H.M.S. *Glasgow.* We assume that he was Lieut. Robert Cowan, commissioned in 1764: *The Commissioned Sea Officers of the Royal Navy, 1660–1815* (3 vols., [London, 1954]), I, 205; the other Cowan listed there was no longer active. This one was in all likelihood a relative of the Mrs. Cowan who had been BF's landlady in Edinburgh years before: above, VIII, 435.

From Alexander Colden ALS: American Philosophical Society

⟨General Post Office, New York, July 7, 1773: Has received Franklin's letter of April 7 by the *Lord Hyde*, packet, and is glad to know that the accounts sent on March 3 have arrived;[9] had hoped to hear by the *Duke*, packet, that they had been approved, but did not. Encloses Willing & Morris's second Bill on Harris [Herries] & Co. for £15; the first went by the *Mercury*, packet, on June 2. Also encloses the following first bills: Archimedes Georges on Curtis & Lovell, merchants of Bristol, for £113 sterling in favor of John Bours, endorsed by him and Thomas Vernon; and Captain Norris Goddard on Anthony Todd for £69 in favor of Colden.[1]

His father, who visited him last Monday, "Continues to Enjoy a Surprising State of health and flow of Spirits," and joins with him and David and Mrs. Colden[2] in sending sincere compliments.⟩

From George Morgan

ALS (letterbook draft): Pennsylvania Historical and Museum Commission.

Dear Sir   Philada. July 8th 1773

The Cause only can sufficiently appologise for the hasty Letter which I took the Liberty to trouble you with the 4th or 5th of last May, which with the one I inclosed for my Partner Mr. Samuel Wharton I hope came safe to your Hands.[3] In a Matter so interesting, I am assured that your Humanity will plead my Excuse.

9. The corrected post office accounts for 1771–72 that BF had asked for the previous December: above, XIX, 399.

1. We can identify only some of the firms and people mentioned. For Willing & Morris and Herries & Co. see Colden's letter above, June 2. John Bours was senior warden of Trinity Church, Newport, and Thomas Vernon, another warden, was also the town's postmaster. Franklin B. Dexter, *The Literary Diary of Ezra Stiles* . . . (3 vols., New York, 1901), I, 539; above, V, 451 n. Goddard was, we presume, the master of the *Lord Hyde* mentioned above, XVII, 140; the packets were the principal mail ships, and Todd was secretary of the Post Office.

2. Cadwallader Colden and his son David need no introduction; Elizabeth Colden, Alexander's wife, was the daughter of Richard Nicholls.

3. They did. See Morgan's letter above, May 4, which explains the quarrel with Wharton that is the subject of this letter, and BF's reply below, July 14.

294

It would take up too much of your Time to descend into the Particulars of Mr. Whartons Treatment of Mr. Baynton, who as he was himself a Stranger to Deceit, placed the most implicit Confidence in Mr. Wharton, who has not only betrayd his Trust in many Instances, but insultingly laugh'd at the Weakness of those who reposed it to him. This is aggravated from the Consideration of Mr. Whartons Ingratitude, which can only be equal'd by his Vanity and Cunning. I pray of you Sir to excuse this Warmth of Expression. They are serious Truths and I feel most sensibly the Effects thereof, in the Loss of one of the best of Friends.

Should Mr. [*Wharton*] be in England on Receipt hereof, permit me to beg the favour of you to give him the Perusal of it, and a Copy if he desires it, And that you will in behalf of Mr. Bayntons distress'd and numerous Orphans,[4] receive from Mr. Wharton such Instrument of Writing as he will condescend to give, declarative of (what he has ever studiously secreted from Mr. Baynton Viz) how far or what share he is interested in Mr. Whartons Negociations or Acquisitions in England. Our different numerous Letters to him (which I beg he will allow you to peruse) particularly mine dated Novr. 1769 Novr. 22d. 1771 Jany 3d and 13th, April 27th, May 17 (left open by Capt. Falconer) and Novr. 2d. 1772 and February 1st. 1773, will fully explain our Demands on this Head, None of which he has ever deign'd to reply to in an explicit Manner.

I would wish to avoid all Disputes and Difficulties with Mr. Wharton. Had he acted as a Man of honour or even common honesty, there would never have been any between Us.

Inclosed is an Extract of a Letter dated Novr. 27th 1769 from the worthy late Dr. Evans to Mr. Wharton which had he seriously consider'd and candidly complied with, Mr. Baynton would have been this day alive and in perfect Health.[5]

4. There were fifteen of them: Townsend Ward, "The Germantown Road and Its Associations," *PMHB*, VI (1882), 17 n.

5. The extract was included in the draft, with Morgan's notation that it never elicited a reply from Wharton. Baynton and Wharton, Evans wrote, "have shared deeply of Adversity, and maintain'd a cordial Friendship. Let not Prosperity dissolve the Cement and suffer Discord to intrude." Turn

Should you be able to obtain any Satisfaction from Mr. Wharton you will confer a lasting Obligation on all Mr. Bayntons Friends and particularly on Dear Sir Your most Obedient and most humble Servant   G M

To Benja. Franklin Esqr.

To Anthony Benezet   ALS (letterbook draft): Library of Congress

Dear Friend,   London, July 14. 1773
I received your Favour of April 24. with the Pamphlets for which I thank you. I am glad to hear that such humane Sentiments prevail so much more generally than heretofore,[6] that there is Reason to hope Our Colonies may in time get clear of a Practice that disgraces them, and without producing any equivalent Benefit, is dangerous to their very Existence.

I hope e're long to have the Pleasure of seeing you, and conversing with you more fully on that and other Subjects than I can now do by writing. In the mean time believe me ever Dear Friend Yours most affectionately   B F.

Mr Antho Benezet,

---

instead to Abel James for arbitration, Evans continued; Baynton would surely agree to anything that James thought reasonable.

6. On April 28 Benezet had sent Dr. Fothergill a copy of his letter to BF of April 24, now lost, and had mentioned that he was asking BF as Pa. agent to work for acceptance of the provincial act against importing slaves. With his letter to Fothergill he enclosed a number of copies of Benjamin Rush's *Address to the Inhabitants of the British Settlements, upon Slave-Keeping* (Philadelphia, 1773). George S. Brookes, *Friend Anthony Benezet* (Philadelphia, 1937), p. 303. He doubtless sent the same pamphlet to BF.

To a Committee of the Managers of the Philadelphia Silk Filature

ALS: Historical Society of Pennsylvania; letterbook draft: Library of Congress

Gentlemen,   London, July 14. 1773

Inclos'd is the Broker's Account of Sales of the last Silk, Accounts of Charges, and my Account Current. The Price is not so high as we might have expected if the Ruin of Paper Credit here had not occasioned such a Scarcity of Currency as put a Stop to a Great Part of the Silk Business as well as other Businesses that were carried on by Credit beyond their natural Bounds.[7] Two Months Time was given to the Buyers, and I have now received the Money. You may therefore draw for the Ballance of the Account £210 10s. 5½d. on me, or in Case of my Absence on Browns & Collinson, Bankers, with whom I shall leave an Order to honour your Bill.[8] I hear by several Hands that our Silk is in high Credit; we may therefore hope for rising Prices, the Manufacturers being at first doubtful of a new Commodity, not knowing till Trial has been made how it will work. I most cordially wish Success to your generous and Noble Undertaking, believing it likely to prove of great Service to our Country, and am, with great Esteem, Gentlemen, Your most obedient humble Servant

B FRANKLIN

Messrs Abel James and Benja Morgan

Addressed: To / Messrs Abel James and Benja. Morgan / at / Philadelphia / Per Capt. All

Endorsed: Letter from B Franklin dated 14th. July 1773 inclosg Acct. Sales of Silk and his Acct. Current

Copied on the Minutes

7. BF had warned the committee in his letter above, Feb. 10, that silk manufacture was in a sorry state. See also his letter to the committee of March 15 and to Evans of April 6.

8. BF bought a few pounds of the 210 pounds of silk sold. His total of the proceeds is inexact: they were £175 5s. 5½d., and the bounty, minus charges, was £35 9s. 6d. Ledger, p. 58; Jour., pp. 48–9. In November the committee drew on him for the money; see *idem.*, p. 53, and BF's acknowledgment below, Feb. 18, 1774.

To John Foxcroft

ALS (letterbook draft): Library of Congress

Dear Friend, London, July 14. 1773.

I received yours of June 7. and am glad to find by it that you are safely return'd from your Virginia Journey, having settled your Affairs there to Satisfaction,[9] and that you found your Family well at New York.

I feel for you in the Fall you had out of your Chair. I have had three of those Squelches in different Journeys, and never desire a fourth.

I do not think it was without Reason that you continu'd so long one of St. Thomas's Disciples; for there was always some Cause for doubting. Some People always ride before the Horses Head.[1] The Draft of the Patent is at length got into the Hands of the Attorney General, who must approve the Form before it passes the Seals. So one would think much more time can scarce be required to compleat the Business: But 'tis good not to be too sanguine. He may go into the Country; and the Privy Councellors likewise; and some Months pass before they get together again. Therefore if you have any Patience, use it.[2]

9. Either personal or postal affairs: Foxcroft's visits to Virginia were mentioned frequently in 1765–7, and again in 1772, but not the reasons for them.

1. Such as the congenital optimist, Samuel Wharton. For Foxcroft's earlier skepticism about the grant see above, XIX, 82.

2. He needed it as much as Foxcroft. In the spring BF had been pessimistic (to Galloway above, April 6), and he remained so even when victory seemed in sight. The Privy Council's decision the previous summer to accept the Company's petition and establish a new colony (above, XIX, 243–4 n) had encouraged Samuel Wharton to create a committee, which included BF, to expedite the final arrangements. Peter Marshall, "Lord Hillsborough, Samuel Wharton and the Ohio Grant, 1769–1775," *English Hist. Rev.*, LXXX (1965), 733. By the spring of 1773, despite rising opposition, the Board of Trade was at work on implementing the Council's decision. In a report on May 6 the Board accepted the Walpole grant as delimited in 1770 (above, XVII, 9–11; XIX, 123 n) and embodied it in a new colony, called Vandalia, which was also to include other large tracts recently ceded by the Indians, so that Vandalia extended beyond the grant on the west, south, and east. The Board made detailed recommendations for the government, the church, and landholding in the colony. The full text (miscalled a report by the Privy Council) is in Kenneth P. Bailey, ed., *The Ohio Company Papers* . . . (Arcata, Cal., 1947), pp. 263–79; see also Thomas P. Abernethy, *Western Lands and*

I suppose Mr. Finlay will be some time at Quebec in settling his Affairs. By the next Packet, you will receive a Draft of Instructions for him.[3]

In mine of Dec. 2. upon the Post Office Accounts, to Apr. 1772 I took Notice to you, that I observed I had full Credit for my Salary, but no Charge appear'd against me for Money paid on my Account to Mrs. Franklin from the Philadelphia Office. I supposed the Thirty Pounds Currency per Month was regularly paid, because I had had no Complaint from her for want of Money: and I expected to find the Charge in the Accounts of the last Year, that is to Ap. 5. 1773. But nothing of it appearing there, I am at a loss to understand it, and you take no Notice of my Observation above mention'd. The great Ballance due from that Office begins to be remark'd here, and I should have thought the Officer would for his own sake not have neglected to lessen it, by showing what he had paid on my Account.[4] Pray, my dear Friend, explain this to me.

I find by yours to Mr. Todd, that you expected soon another little One. God send my Daughter a good Time, and you a Good Boy.[5] Mrs. Stevenson is pleas'd with your Remembrance of her, and joins with Mr. and Mrs. Hewson and my self in best Wishes for you and yours. I am, ever, Yours affectionately   B FRANKLIN

Mr Foxcroft

Per Capt Osborne

---

the American Revolution (New York and London, 1937), pp. 53–4. On July 3 the Council requested the Attorney and Solicitor General to review the Board's arrangements and put them in proper legal form for the grant and the establishment of the new colony: Acts Privy Coun., Col., V, 210. For the final chapter of delays see BF to WF below, July 25.

3. Hugh Finlay, the former postmaster at Quebec, had been in England the previous autumn with a recommendation from Foxcroft, and had finally been appointed surveyor general of the colonial postal system. See above, XIX, 273, 359, 374, 415.

4. For DF's allowance from the Philadelphia post office see idem., p. 415 n. The "great Ballance" must have been Thomas Foxcroft's accounts receivable, i.e., due but not collected; the total would have been lessened by charging the allowances to BF's account.

5. The Foxcrofts already had a daughter, born in January, 1772: ibid., p. 54. The expected baby also turned out to be a girl: Foxcroft to BF, Feb. 1, 1775, Hist. Soc. of Pa.

To William Franklin   ALS (letterbook draft): Library of Congress

This letter has hitherto been published only in an extract, which omitted a long section at the beginning and a somewhat shorter one at the end.[6] The beginning is of particular interest, because in it Franklin discussed his view of settlers' rights, as opposed to the rights of the crown, in land acquired from the Indians. That view came extremely close to denying royal sovereignty.

The starting point of his discussion was a legal opinion that applied to India. In 1757 a petition from the East India Company raised the question of title to land that the Company had conquered in Bengal, and evoked an opinion from Attorney General Pratt, later Lord Camden, and Solicitor General Yorke. The lawyers distinguished between two kinds of territory, that acquired by conquest, in which the crown had both sovereignty and title to the land, and that acquired by peaceful cession, in which the crown was sovereign but did not have proprietary rights. The critical sentence that applied to the second kind was as follows: "In respect to such places as have been, or shall be acquired by treaty, or grant from the Mogul, or any of the Indian Princes, or governments, Your Majesty's letters patent are not necessary, the property of the soil vesting in the Company by the Indian grants, subject only to Your Majesty's right of sovereignty over the settlements, as English settlements, and over the inhabitants, as English subjects, *who carry with them Your Majesty's laws, whenever they form colonies, and receive Your Majesty's protection, by virtue of Your Royal Charters.*"[7]

This sentence was later applied to American Indians. It was legally applicable, however, only on two conditions: first, that the tribal hunting grounds were not conquered territory; second, that the tribes were analogous to Indian princes in possessing full sovereignty, so that they might cede their lands to the king's subjects by treaty. Neither condition had a sound basis in law. The first one ignored the background, for the lands in question were conquered because the

6. The omission explains why historians dealing with the Pratt-Yorke opinion have not considered BF's comments. Some one, we presume WTF, crossed out the first two pages of the draft and most of the third, to the point indicated below, where the extract began in *Memoirs*, II, 195–7 of the first pagination. Sparks, Bigelow, and Smyth printed the same extract. We have used WTF's text to supply in brackets words now missing in the MS.

7. Willem Bolts, *Considerations on India Affairs; Particularly Respecting the Present State of Bengal and Its Dependencies* . . . (2nd ed., London, 1772), app., p. 181; for the full opinion see pp. 179–82.

French had surrendered them in the Peace of Paris; the second one flew in the face of the accepted doctrine that savages might cede only to the king.[8] But speculators ignored such niceties. The publication of the book Franklin mentions by Willem Bolts, in March, 1772, brought the opinion and its tempting sentence into public view.[9] On April 1, 1772, some one, perhaps William Trent, "copied" the critical sentence and doctored it to make it seem more applicable to American Indians.[1] It was sent across the Atlantic and taken to the Illinois country, where speculators used it in negotiating for a large cession that the Indians eventually made to the Illinois Land Company; and by the spring of 1773 the doctored opinion was also circulating on the eastern seaboard.[2]

8. For this doctrine see the headnote on BF's essay above, March 16, "On Claims to the Soil of America."

9. The book was advertised in the March issue of the *Gent. Mag.*, XLII (1772), 140.

1. It purported to be a true copy of the original, made in London. It deleted "the Mogul," though retaining "the Indian Princes or governments" (an odd phrase for American Indians), turned "vesting in the Company" into "vesting in the Grantees," and omitted "as English settlements." See Jack M. Sosin, *Whitehall and the Wilderness*, . . . *1760–1775* (Lincoln, Neb., 1961), p. 231. The opinion was used after American independence to legitimize prerevolutionary purchases from the Indians without royal approval, and was finally struck down in a decision by Chief Justice Marshall. *Ibid.*, pp. 260–1; Shaw Livermore, *Early American Land Companies* . . . (New York and London 1939), pp. 21 n, 106.

2. Land speculation attracted devious liars, whose evidence is a quagmire for historians. Consequently the accounts of these negotiations, of the role that the opinion played in them, and of how it gained acceptance vary in detail and in interpretation. See Thomas P. Abernethy, *Western Lands and the American Revolution* (New York, 1937), pp. 116–19; Sosin, *op. cit.*, pp. 229–35, 259–67, and "The Yorke-Camden Opinion and American Land Speculators," *PMHB*, LXXXV (1961), 38–49; Gipson, *British Empire*, XI, 484–5, 487–90.

Some highly untrustworthy evidence suggests that speculators in the 1760's, including BF, knew of the Pratt-Yorke opinion. When George Croghan was in London in 1764, he mentioned years later, Pratt and Yorke assured him that "*the Opinion*" applied to America. In 1769 Pratt, then Lord Camden, and BF and others advised Trent, or so he said long afterward, that the cession made at Fort Stanwix did not need the crown's approval. Thomas P. Bailey, ed., *The Ohio Company Papers* . . . (Arcata, Cal., 1947), pp. 462, 289. The ablest lawyers in England, Wharton reported in 1771, held that title obtained from Indians was sufficient, and "every judicious Man" assured him that the crown had no right in lands on the Ohio until it paid for them; BF, he wrote in 1772, told him much the same thing. See the

William Franklin must have obtained a copy, wondered how the speculators were using it, and enclosed it in his missing letter of April 5. His father remarked that the document contained "some small variations" from the original, with which he was obviously familiar. He seems to have taken for granted that the opinion, in whatever form, applied to America.

In that case it provided a legal buttress for the view that he had long held in private and, as this letter makes clear, had expressed to Samuel Wharton as early as 1769. When colonists acquired land from the Indians, he believed, they held it as their own with no obligation to the crown.[3] But since 1769 his thinking, as he said, had gone considerably beyond that of the lawyers—and, as he did not say, beyond that of many Americans who were not lawyers at all. He now propounded the thesis that such acquisition of land gave the settlers three options: to remain under the king's sovereignty, to accept that of the Indians, or to create by right of purchase a state of their own. He accepted what he took to be the Pratt-Yorke opinion as it applied to land title, in other words, and rejected its premise that the crown remained sovereign.

Dear Son,   London, July 14. 1773.

I received yours of April 5. and suppose I must have answered it, tho' I find no such Answer in my Letter Book. I shall now however just take Notice of some Passages.

The Opinion of Pratt and Yorke when Attorney and Sollicitor General is undoubtedly a good One, so far as it allows the Indian Power of Grant in their own Lands. It has been lately printed here at large in Bolts's Book on Indian Affairs. There are some small variations in your Extract. I gave the same Opinion to Mr. Wharton when he arrived here with respect to the Retribution Grant,[4] and advised his not applying for a Confirmation, which

---

quotations from Wharton's letters in Gipson, *op. cit.*, XI, 488. Much of this evidence strains credulity. Camden was too eminent a jurist to ignore not only the legal obstacles we have mentioned but also two other facts: that the crown paid for the cession at Fort Stanwix (above, XV, 277 n) and that the Proclamation of 1763 specifically forbade private purchase without royal licence. The assurances to Wharton, except from BF, are equally suspect.

3. Above, XVI, 291–2; XVII, 385. The same idea appears in this volume in the essay, "On Claims to the Soil of America," March 16, and underlies "An Edict by the King of Prussia," Sept. 22.

4. The cession at Fort Stanwix: above, XV, 265 n, 275–9.

I thought not only unnecessary, but what would be attended with infinite Delay and Difficulty thro' the Chicane of Office. My Advice farther was to proceed immediately to sell and settle the Lands, without supposing any Occasion for such Confirmation; and he has since frequently acknowledged the Propriety of the Advice, and wished he had followed it. But he then thought Purchasers would not have been satisfy'd with the Right, and therefore fell upon the Method of Proposing the Purchase from the Crown of a large Tract in Company, that should include it, so to avoid the Question; and by reserving to all their private Rights that might be included in the great Purchase, the Property under the Retribution Grant should be secured to the Grantees. This was the Plan of our first Petition for the 2,500,000 Acres.[5]

But my Opinion, as being somewhat of a Civilian, goes a little farther than that of those great Common Lawyers, differing also in some Respects. For I think

1. That it is the natural Right of Men to quit when they please the Society or State, and the Country in which they were born, and either join with another or form a new one as they may think proper.

The Saxons thought they had this Right when they quitted Germany and established themselves in England. And if this had not always been a Right, there could at this Day have been but one Rightful Government in the World. All the rest would be but Desertions and Sub Desertions from that One, subject to be reclaim'd and punish'd for Desertion.

2. Those who thus quit a State, quit [Submission?] to its Protection, but do not therefore become its Enemies.

[3.] If they purchase Territory in another Country, it may [be only?] on Terms of submitting to the Sovereignty and Laws before established therein or, Freedom from that Sovereignty may be purchas'd with the Land. This latter I take to be the Case[?] with respect[?] to Lands purchas'd of the Indian Nations in America.[6]

4. If a Freedom from the Sovereignty is purchased with the Land, the Purchasers may either introduce there the Sovereignty

5. See above, XVI, 166–8.
6. So in the original draft. BF then made small deletions and additions, which he did not complete to form an intelligible sentence.

of their former Prince, if they chuse it as needing his Protection; or they may erect a new one of their own, if they are sufficient to their own Defence.

According to these Principles I thought the Retribution Grant to the Traders good without a Confirmation here. They having a Right to take, and Government here no Right to forbid their Taking Grants from Indians of Property on which it had previously no Claim. And I think that any Englishman or Number of Englishmen may if they please purchase Lands of an Indian Nation unite with it and become Subject to its Government; or if they do not chuse that, and their Numbers be sufficient, they may, purchasing with the Lands a Freedom from Indian Authority, erect a new State of their own.

I have heard Nothing here of the Purchase you mention in the Ilinois Country: but you see from the above that I should make no question of the Validity of such Purchases. I imagine however, that since Government begins to taste the Advantage of Selling Lands in America, it will soon begin to think of monopolising them, by some Means or other, and preventing all private Purchases.

As to Mr. Wharton's preventing your having a Share of [the] Retribution Tract, knowing nothing of your Agreement or its Foundation, I know not what to say to it. But I wonder there should be any Talk of excluding you from the Ohio Affair, having always paid up your Share of the Expences with Mr. Galloway's and my own, for which I have Receipts under the Hands of Trent and Wharton:[7] And I think it not in their Power.

Of late I have had very small Concern in Conducting the Business. I seldom see Mr. Wharton, and hear only by the bye

7. WF had mentioned in his letter above, April 30, the Whartons' offer to buy his share of the retribution tract or grant to the "suffering traders." In a missing letter he must have spoken of an attempt to deprive him of the share, presumably because he was not contributing to Wharton's and Trent's expenses as lobbyists in London. In December, 1768, he and four others had contracted to do so, but when WF received a demand for £200 he refused to pay. Bailey, *op. cit.*, pp. 205–10; Wharton and Trent to WF, July 21, 1771, APS; WF to Thomas Wharton, April 27, 1772, Hist. Soc. of Pa. The retribution tract was included in the Walpole grant (above, XVII, 8) but distinct from it. WF had a share in each, and BF's next letter, July 25, reported paying for his son's share in the Company.

what is carrying on. He is not only shy of me himself, but I suspect that thro' his means some of my other Friends are render'd cool to me. As this however is mere Suspicion I take no Notice of it. About a Fortnight since he came to me to justify himself on Account of [an] open Letter sent to him thro' my Hands by Mr. Morgan.[8] He then told [me] that only a Council was wanting to be got together to refer the Gr[ant to the] Attorney General. Yesterday I met with him and [*torn*] at [Mr. Todd's at?] Walthamstow, where we dined.[9] Messrs. Walpole [*torn*]. He then told me that with great Difficulty he had at [last completed it?] and got the Draft into the Attorney General's Hands.[1] He [*torn*] always full of the infinite Difficulties he meets with [and his skill in?] surmounting them. Mr. Walpole afterwards told [us that the? Bu]siness was now in a fair way of being speedily concluded; and his Accounts have weight with me; as I know his Interest with the Ministry has been the principal Means of getting us thus far, and on that I most rely for getting us through.[2] [*In the margin:* Tho' Wharton's Industry ought to be allow'd its Share.] Being in a mixt Company, we could not speak much of the Affair. It is reported that Col. Mercer is to be Governor and some other Officers are mentioned of whom I know nothing.[3] Some of the Partners begin to see Mr. W. in an unfavourable Light, and one of them came to me to day to communicate his Doubts about the Fairness of W.'s Proceedings, of which more in my next.[4] I shall soon begin to stir a little more in

8. The letter, enclosed in George Morgan's note to BF above, May 4, attacked Wharton's handling of his partners' affairs in England.

9. Walthamstow was the country seat of Anthony Todd, the secretary of the Post Office and an active promoter of the Walpole Company. A committee of the Privy Council had met on July 3 and referred the report from the Board of Trade to the law officers for their opinion; see above, p. 289 n.

1. The draft that Wharton gave Attorney General Thurlow is discussed at length in BF to WF below, July 25.

2. For the Hon. Thomas Walpole see above, XVI, 163 n.

3. For Mercer and his hopes and difficulties see BF to WF above, April 6. Dartmouth's cousin, William Legge, had in fact already had the offer of the governorship: *Dartmouth MSS*, I, 335.

4. The letter of July 25, in which BF elaborated on the discontent with Wharton.

the Business, apprehending it may be of use for the common Interest of the Company.

I wonder to hear by yours of Apr. 28, that the Tea Urn was without Handles. Are there not Rings or something to lift it by? If there are, those may be covered with Cane or some what that will prevent the Heat's passing to the Hand.

There can be nothing in the Story of a Present bought for the Indians. I must have heard of it, as our Shares of the Money would have been wanted.[5] I am sorry that Capt. Falconer should on my Letter sell his Interest. I am sure I did not advise it, but only caution'd him against talking or thinking too sanguinely about the Affair, it being still an Uncertainty.[6]

I wish I could have return'd with Capt. All, believing as I do, your Character of him to be a just one.[7] But some Business will detain me till the September Packet, in which I now seriously think of Embarking. Sir J.P. had Thoughts of going to Italy; and perhaps I might have taken that Journey with him, and embark'd at Leghorn.[8] But he is gone to Scotland.

There was more Craft than Friendship in my old Friend's sending to purchase your Share, which you mention in yours of April 30. Perhaps I resent it as much as you do.

I know not how to explain the Conduct of Lord Dunmore in

5. The story had something in it, but probably not what WF supposed. Wharton and a few associates, members of the Walpole Co. but operating for themselves, were working through George Croghan to collect presents for the Indians. BF's ignorance of what was going on strongly suggests that this clique was already embarked on a scheme, which Wharton later tried hard to carry through, for obtaining a tract beyond the Ohio. See Abernethy, *op. cit.*, p. 117; Peter Marshall, "Lord Hillsborough, Samuel Wharton and the Ohio Grant, 1769–1775," *English Hist. Rev.*, LXXX (1965), 736–7.

6. WF must have mentioned in a missing letter the effect of what BF had written Falconer above, Feb. 14. The Capt.'s only reason for getting out of the Company, he had implied in answering BF on May 13, was anger at the Wharton clan.

7. For Isaac All, BF's nephew by marriage, see above, XII, 31 n and subsequent vols. His ship, the *Richard Penn*, sailed on July 21: *London Chron.*, July 20–22, 1773.

8. Sir John Pringle had been BF's traveling companion on the Continent in 1766, 1767, and 1769.

granting Lands as you say on the Kanhawa. Perhaps it is a Mistake.[9]

I am glad to find by yours of May 4 that you have been able to assist Josiah Davenport a little; but vex'd that he and you should think of putting me upon a Solicitation which it is impossible for me to engage in. I am not upon Terms with Lord North to ask any such Favour [from him.] Displeased with something he said relating to America, I have never been at his Levees, since the first. Perhaps he has taken that amiss. For [the last week we] met occasionally at Lord Le Despencer's, in our Return from [Oxford, w]here I had been to attend the Solemnity of his Installation,[1] and He seem'd studiously [to avoid] speaking to me. I ought to be asham'd to say that on such [occasions] I feel myself to be as proud as any body. His Lady indeed was more [gracious. She came,] and sat down by me on the same Sopha, and condescended to enter into a Conversation with me agreably enough, as if to make me some Amends. Their Son and Daughter were with them.[2] They staid all Night, so that we din'd, supp'd, and breakfasted together, without exchanging three Sentences. But had he ever so great a Regard for me, I could not ask that Office, trifling as it is, for any Relation of mine. And detesting as I do the whole System of American Customs, believing they will one Day bring on a Breach through the Indiscretion and Insolence of those concern'd in the Collection, I should never wish to see one so near to me engag'd in that Business. If you think him capable of acting as Deputy-Secretary, I imagine you might easily obtain that for him of Mr. Morgann. He has lately been with me, is always very complaisant, and understanding I was about returning to America, requested my Interest to obtain for him the *Agency of your Province*. His Friend Sir Watkin Lewes who was formerly Candidate for the same *great Place*, is now High Sheriff of London, and

---

9. For this and the preceding paragraph see WF's letter above, April 30. WTF's printed extract begins with the next paragraph.

1. As chancellor of the university. The press reported the "Solemnity" at length: *Public Advertiser*, July 9, 10, 12; *London Chron.*, July 6–13, 1773.

2. Lady North, née Anne Speke, was as ugly as her husband but had a heart of gold. The children were presumably their eldest: George, sixteen, and Catherine Anne, thirteen. See Alan Valentine, *Lord North* (2 vols., Norman, Okla., [1967]), I, 28–9, 76, 104.

in the way of being Lord Mayor: The new Sheriffs elect, are, (could you think it?) both Americans, viz, Mr. Sayre, the New Yorker, and Mr. W. Lee, they say a Virginian, and Brother to Dr. Lee.[3]

I now come to your last, of May 31. I send you Home's Essays,[4] with a little Piece on the Principles of Vegetation, and a Parcel of Magazines and Pamphlets. We are trying to get the Bellmetal Skillets, [*in the margin:* and if they can be had in time shall send them per this Ship,] but understand they are not much us'd here.[5]

I am glad you stand so well with Lord Dartmouth. I [am] like-wise well with him, but he never spoke to me of augmenting your Salary.[6] He is truly a good Man, and wishes sincerely a good Understanding with the Colonies, but does not seem to have Strength equal to his Wishes. Between you and I, the late Measures have been, I suspect, very much the King's own, and he has in some Cases a great Share of what his Friends call *Firmness.*[7]

3. For Maurice Morgann, the absentee secretary of New Jersey, see WF to BF above, May 4. Sir Watkin Lewes (1740?–1821) was an alderman as well as sheriff, and subsequently served a term as lord mayor: Namier and Brooke, *House of Commons,* III, 40. Stephen Sayre (1736–1818) was raised on Long Island, graduated from the College of New Jersey, went to London, and became a business partner of Dennys DeBerdt; after the latter's death Sayre organized a banking house. He was popular in London, and worked steadily for the colonial cause; in September, 1770, he sent news to Boston of the existence of the Hutchinson letters. *DAB*; Cushing, *Writings of Samuel Adams,* II, 67–8. William Lee (1739–95), the brother of Arthur and Richard Henry, had gone with the former to England in 1768, and entered into partnership with Sayre and DeBerdt. William Lee and Sayre were ardent Wilksites, which accounts for their victory at the polls; two years later Lee won an even more signal victory, when he became the only American ever elected alderman. *DAB*.

4. David Hume, *Essays and Treatises on Several Subjects* ... (2 vols., London, 1772). The author hoped for an American edition; see above, XIX, 76.

5. Bell metal is a form of bronze, three or four parts of copper to one of tin. Skillets of this material had been in use earlier in the century, but were becoming less popular. N. Hudson Moore, *The Collector's Manual* ... (new ed., New York, [1935]), p. 132; J. Seymour Lindsay, *Iron & Brass Implements of the English House* (Boston and London, [1927]), p. 56. BF managed to find the skillets and two bell-metal kettles as well: to WF below, July 25.

6. See above, WF to BF, Jan. 5, and BF to WF, April 6.

7. BF's view of the King was changing. He had tried the year before to get word to him of the danger in the colonial situation (above, XIX, 243), and

Yet, by some Painstaking and proper Management, the wrong Impressions he has received may be removed, which is perhaps the only Chance America has for obtaining *soon* the Redress she aims at. This entirely to yourself.

And now we are among Great Folks, let me tell you a little of Lord Hillsborough. I went down to Oxford with and at the Instance of Lord Le Despencer, [who] is on all occasions very good to me, and seems of late very desirous of my Company. Mr. Todd too was there, who has some Attachment to Lord H. a[nd in] a Walk we were taking told me as a Secret that Lord H. was much chagrin'd at being out of Pla[ce, and] could never forgive me [for] "Writing that Pamphlet against his [report] about the Ohio. I assur'd him, says Mr. T. that I know you did not write [it and the consequence is, that] he thinks I know the contrary and wanted to im[pose upon him in your favour; and so I] find he is now displeas'd with me and for no other C[ause in the World. His friend] Bamber Gascoign too, says, that they *well know* it [was written by Dr. Franklin, who was] one of the most mischievous Men in England."[8] That same Day Lord H. called upon Lord L[e D. whose chamber and mine were together] in Queen's College. I was in the Inner Room shifting,[9] and heard his Voice, but did not then see him as he went down Stairs immediately with Lord Le Dr. who, mentioning that I was above, he return'd directly and came to me in the pleasantest Manner imaginable. "Dr. F. says he, I did not know till this Minute that you were here, and I am come back *to make you my Bow!* I am glad to see you at Oxford, and that you look so well, &c." In Return for this Extravagance I complimented him on his Son's Performance in the Theatre, tho' indeed it was but in-

in his recent letter to the House (above, July 7) he had imputed George's position to the "Prejudices of all about him." Now in private he put the onus on the sovereign himself.

8. See our note above, XIX, 123–5, which takes issue with Hillsborough and Gascoigne on the question of BF's authorship. Gascoigne (1725–91) was an M.P. and an influential member of the Board of Trade; Dartmouth had nothing to do, John Pownall wrote William Knox a few days after BF's letter, while Gascoigne was acting as "minister for America" at the Board. Namier and Brooke, *House of Commons*, II, 490–1.

9. Changing his clothes.

different; so that Account was settled. For as People say, when they are angry, if he *strikes me, I'll strike him again*. I think sometimes it may be right to say, *if he* flatters *me I'll* flatter *him again*. This is *Lex Talionis*, returning Offences in kind. His Son however (Lord Fairford) is a valuable young Man, and his Daughters Lady's Mary and Charlotte most amiable young Women.[1] My Quarrel is only with him, who of all the Men I ever met with is surely the most unequal in his Treatment of People, the most insincere, and the most wrong-headed; witness besides his various[2] Behaviour to me, his Duplicity in encouraging us to ask for more Land, when we first ask'd only for 2,500,000 Acres, ask for *enough to make a Province*, were his Words, pretending to befriend our Application, then doing every thing to defeat it, and reconciling the first to the last by saying to a Friend, that he meant to defeat it from the Beginning, and that his putting us upon asking so much was with that very View, Supposing it too much to be granted. Thus, by the way, his Mortification becomes double. He has serv'd us by the very Means he meant to destroy us, and tript up his own Heels into the Bargain.[3]

Mr. Dagge, the Solicitor, who is one of our Partners;[4] and who

1. During his Irish tour in 1771 BF had been entertained by Hillsborough's son Arthur, then Lord Kilwarlin and now Lord Fairford; see above, XIX, 18–21, 48–9. The young man had been at Magdalen, and was one of a group that delivered "elegant Latin and English verses" at the convocation on July 8 when North was installed; the next day Fairford received an honorary M.A. *Public Advertiser*, July 12, 1773. His older sister, Mary Amelia, was married within the year to James Cecil, seventh Earl (later first Marquess) of Salisbury; she was twenty-two at the time. Charlotte, the younger sister, was nineteen. *DNB* under Wills Hill.

2. Varying.

3. The extract ends here. For Hillsborough's manoeuver see above, XVII, 8. He "tript up his own Heels" because Whitehall accepted the enlargement of the request, and his opposition to it eventually drove him from office. Above, XIX, 243.

4. Henry, John, and James Dagge were brothers; all of them were solicitors and partners in the Walpole Co. Our guess is that BF's informant was Henry (*d.* 1795), who was the most prominent of the three (he was Horace Walpole's lawyer) and the most deeply involved in the land grant. See above, XVI, 167; Lewis, *Indiana Co.*, pp. 149–50; Sir John Maclean, *The Parochial and Family History of the Deanery of Trigg Minor* ... (3 vols., London, 1873), I, 295, 297.

begins of late to dislike Wharton for assuming to himself all Merit in every thing, and on other Accounts told me yesterday that the Pamphlet above mentioned was drawn up between Messrs. Walpole, Wharton and himself. That Wh. had a good deal of Cleverness in furnishing Facts, but was for every now and then for putting some Things in contrary to his Advice who was sure they would do harm; that persisting in his Opposition, Wharton was very uppish and peremptory with him, to a degree of Insolence. That Mr. Walpole too was offended with his Behaviour, and once angrily threw the Papers on the Floor saying he would have nothing more to do with the Business. That then Wh. was all Submission and Compliance; and so they went on. Dagge added, That he never had met with a Man who on the first Acquaintance struck him so advantageously as Wharton, but that he had now a very different Opinion of him, and was sure that if we did not take care he would chouse us[5] all. Dagge dines with me tomorrow, and I shall hear a little more. He says, if we succeed all is owing to Walpole. I write these Things for your Information only. Keep them *intirely* to your self.[6]

I will communicate your Postscript to Mr. Hopkinson.[7] He is in the Country at present.

Mr. Elphinstone, tho' Schoolmasters are apt to flatter the Friends of Children, was only just in speaking highly of Billy.[8] I am much satisfied both with his Learning and Behaviour, and Elphinstone seems to value himself so much on improving him that I have hesitated about sending him to Eaton, which otherwise I should be inclin'd to do. Tho' I every day hear Complaints of the Great Schools and even of the Universities, for the Relaxation

5. Trick us.

6. BF here added and then deleted a short paragraph: "If you have present Occasion for the Money receiv'd for me by Mr. Smith, you may take it, for which I enclose an Order. But remember that I shall want it on my return." The salary due him as agent was being kept in New Jersey; he had promised Joseph Smith, who had been secretary of the Assembly's committee of correspondence, to let him know what to do with it: above, Feb. 14.

7. Thomas Hopkinson had come to England in 1770 to prepare for holy orders, and was about to be ordained and return to Philadelphia: above, XVII, 215 n.

8. Since 1767 Billy, WTF, had been attending a school in Kent kept by James Elphinston, William Strahan's brother-in-law. See above, XVI, 170 n.

of all Discipline, the viciousness of the Youth, and Extravagance of the Expence. Yet imagining that the Knowledge of Men is best learnt by a Boy in a Croud of Boys, a Knowledge, which, as Pope says,

Is, tho' no Science, fairly worth the seven,[9]

I have been strongly for sending him first to Eaton and then to Oxford. But I fear the Expence will be too great for you, as they tell me he cannot live at Eaton for less than two Hundred Pounds a Year, nor at Oxford well for less than three. Perhaps I shall take him over with me, and leave you to judge for yourself when you have seen him.

I am now working closely to prepare for the Voyage, and shall allow my self no more Country Pleasure this Summer. Several Friends have urg'd me to pass some time with them, at their Country Places, particularly Mr. Sargent, M. Fitzmaurice, Mr. Steele, and Mr. Dagge, besides the Bishop of St. Asaph and Lord Le Dr.[1] whose kind Invitations I received on the same Day and send them to you as flattering a little my Vanity (and of course yours) to find my Company solicited by two Peers, a Spiritual

9.   Good sense, which only is the gift of Heav'n,
        And tho' no science, fairly worth the seven.
Alexander Pope, *Epistles to Several Persons* (*Moral Essays*), IV, 43–4. The seven were the liberal arts.

1. BF changed his mind in the case of Lord Le Despencer, whom he visited in early August. All these friends have appeared before except Mr. Steele. He was, we believe, Joshua Steele (1700–91), an Irish-born Londoner who had long been a member of the Society of Arts. He was versed in musical theory, and two years later he published a proposal for extending the system of musical notation to speech: *An Essay toward Establishing the Melody and Measure of Speech to Be Expressed and Perpetuated by Peculiar Symbols* (London, 1775). *DNB.* A copy of this work, apparently presented to BF by the author, is in the Franklin collection of the Yale University Library. On p. 91 is a MS note signed with BF's name; we are inclined to think that the note was written in pencil by him and then inked over by someone else. It describes an experiment mentioned in the book: Steele had taken down in his notation some passages in a Shakespearean play that David Garrick had recently acted, and read them to a company that included the actor and his wife as well as BF; both Garricks were greatly impressed with the accuracy of the rendering. If the note is genuine, BF and Steele knew each other before 1775. Both had by then been members of the Society of Arts for two decades, and they had a common interest in rendering sounds with symbols. These clues lead us to assume that Joshua Steele was BF's would-be host.

and a Temporal at the same time. This too will show you that if I were dispos'd to be idle I could pass my time agreably enough; for at all their Houses every one seems desirous of contenting me. Wycomb too is quite a Paradise, and Twyford another—with more Saints in it.

I inclose you a Letter Mr. Strahan left with me to send per last Packet, but being out of Town when that was dispatch'd I omitted it. I wrote to you before, that he also begins to be suspicious of W. and is much for my Staying here; but I have too many Reasons for wishing to see home.

I shall communicate to Mr. Hopkinson what you write concerning the Mission at Trenton.

The other Day Hayne's Son brought me the enclosed. I talked with him a little about his Expedition to New Jersey. [He] seems quite as silly as his Father, so that the Family consists [of] two Fools and a Madwoman. I understood from Lord D. that [they] had sent over an Attorney to procure the necessary Information to enable them to sue for the Estate; but this Simpleton tells me they have sent no body but Lord Dartmouth himself has sent over one Lieut. Webb, who formerly lived there, expressly on this Business, and has promised him if he succeeds that he shall have *Conferment*.[2]

My eyes are tired. I am ever Your affectionate Father

B. [FRANKLIN]

2. For the Hayne affair see above, XIX, 321–2. This is the first mention of a son, who to judge by BF's phrasing accompanied his father to New Jersey. Thomas Webb was a lieutenant in the 48th Foot, which had been in America from 1758 to 1763; injuries suffered at that time had forced him to retire with a small civil appointment. In the spring of 1773 or thereabouts he appealed to Lord Dartmouth for some post at New York; in July, and again the following January, he reported to the Secretary on what Mary Hayne would have to prove in order to gain the estate. *Dartmouth MSS*, II, 145, 160, 190. This background explains BF's use of conferment, in a now obsolete sense: Dartmouth conditionally promised to confer the post for which Webb was angling. But the Lieutenant's report merely confounded the confusion, because he seems to have been misled by a red herring—that Mary Hayne's supposed father, Judge Saltar, might have been the heir of a Henry Salter, who had possessed ten thousand acres of land. There had been such a man with such a tract: 1 *N.J. Arch.*, I, 414. But his line appears to have died out in the late seventeenth century, and in any case to have been wholly unconnected with that of the Judge.

It is long since I have heard from Mr. Galloway. I purpose writing to him per Sutton.[3]

Per Capt. Osborne or perhaps Sutton

To George Morgan   ALS (letterbook draft): Library of Congress

Sir,   London, July 14. 1773
   I received yours of May 4. inclosing one for Mr. Wharton.[4] I sent it to him, requesting that he would let me know what I should write to you upon it. He call'd upon me soon after, and assur'd me, that tho' there had been some Misunderstanding with Regard to the Partners, [the] Aff[ection be]tween him and Mr. Baynton, [torn] thinking they could much better be settled [torn] forborn to write about, yet his Inte[ntion had invariably?] been to do every thing that should be de[cided upon? torn] as both you and Mr. B Family would be [torn.] I condole with you on the Loss of that good Man; and am Sir, Your most obedient Servant   B F

Mr Morgan

Per Capt. Osborne

To Benjamin Rush

    ALS: Yale University Library; letterbook draft: Library of Congress

Dear Sir,   London, July 14. 1773.
   I received your Favour of May 1. with the Pamphlet for which I am obliged to you.[5] It is well written. I hope in time that the Friends to Liberty and Humanity will get the better of a Practice that has so long disgrac'd our Nation and Religion.
   A few Days after I receiv'd your Packet for M. Dubourg, I had an Opportunity of forwarding it to him by M. Poissonnier, a Physician of Paris, who kindly undertook to deliver it.[6] M.

3. Below, Aug. 3.
4. See the annotation of Morgan's letter above.
5. Rush's letter above, enclosing his pamphlet against slavery, explains most of what BF covers in this reply.
6. See above, BF to LeRoy, June 22, and to Dubourg, June 29.

314

Dubourg has been translating my Book into French. It is nearly printed, and he tells me he purposes a Copy for you.

I shall communicate your judicious Remark relating to Air transpir'd by Patients in putrid Diseases to my Friend Dr. Priestly. I hope that after having discover'd the Benefit of fresh and cool Air apply'd to the *Sick*, People will begin to suspect that possibly it may do no Harm to the *Well*. I have not seen Dr. Cullen's Book: But am glad to hear that he speaks of Catarrhs or Colds *by Contagion*. I have long been satisfy'd from Observation, that besides the general Colds now termed *Influenʒa's*,[7] which may possibly spread by Contagion as well as by a particular Quality of the Air, People often catch Cold from one another when shut up together in small close Rooms, Coaches, &c. and when sitting near and conversing so as to breathe in each others Transpiration, the Disorder being in a certain State. I think too that it is the frowzy[8] corrupt Air from animal Substances, and the perspired Matter from our Bodies, which, being long confin'd in Beds not lately used, and Clothes not lately worne, and Books long shut up in close Rooms, obtains that kind of Putridity which infects us, and occasions the Colds observed upon sleeping in, wearing, or turning over, such Beds, Clothes or Books, and not their Coldness or Dampness. From these Causes, but more from *too full Living* with too *little Exercise*, proceed in my Opinion most of the Disorders which for 100 Years past the English have called *Colds*. As to Dr. Cullen's Cold or Catarrh *à frigore*, I question whether such an one ever existed. Travelling in our severe Winters, I have suffered Cold sometimes to an Extremity only short of Freezing, but this did not make me *catch Cold*. And for Moisture, I have been in the River every Evening two or three Hours for a Fortnight together, when one would suppose I might imbibe enough of it to *take Cold* if Humidity could give it; but no such Effect followed: Boys never get Cold by Swimming. Nor are People at Sea, or who live at Bermudas, or St. Helena, where the Air must be ever moist, from the Dashing and Breaking of Waves against

7. The new and fashionable word for epidemic grippe.
8. Musty or rank. BF's interest in colds, which went back more than forty years, had recently become more lively than ever. See above, I, 252–4; IX, 339; XVIII, 197–9, 203; the two letters just cited, and BF's notes at the end of the present volume.

their Rocks on all sides, more subject to Colds than those who inhabit Parts of a Continent where the Air is dryest. Dampness may indeed assist in producing Putridity, and those Miasms which infect us with the Disorder we call a Cold, but of itself can never by a little Addition of Moisture hurt a Body filled with watry Fluids from Head to foot.

I hope our Friend's Marriage[9] will prove a happy one. Mr. and Mrs. West complain that they never hear from him. Perhaps I have as much reason to complain of him. But I forgive him because I often need the same kind of Forgiveness. With great Esteem and sincere Wishes for your Welfare, I am, Sir, Your most obedient humble Servant   B FRANKLIN

Dr. Rush

Addressed: To / Dr Rush / Philadelphia / Per Capt. Sutton

Endorsed: B. Franklin July 14 1773

To Daniel Wister

ALS (letterbook draft): Library of Congress

Dear Sir,   London, July 14. 1773

I received yours of April 30. Much Business has hitherto prevented my visiting your Creditors, with the Proposal you mention.[10] But in a Week or two I expect a little Leisure, which I shall apply to that purpose. I wish it may prove successful, as I truly compassionate your Situation. I shall soon after let you know what may be expected from them. I am, Your Friend and humble Servant   B F

Mr Daniel Wistar

Per Capt Osborne

9. That of the Rev. Thomas Coombe, Jr.
10. Wister's proposals for salvaging his wrecked fortunes.

To Richard Bache

ALS (letterbook draft): Library of Congress

Dear Son,   London, July 15. 1773

I have now before me yours of April 6, and 29, May 21. and June 1. I rejoice with you in the first place on the good News contain'd in your last, that Sally is safely delivered of another Son.[1] I hope he will prove a Blessing to you both.

I wish your new Shop Business to prove profitable, and do not doubt it if the Shop is closely attended. Will not the Brokerage Business draw you too much from it?[2]

I have sent a Case by Capt. All. My Man by Mistake mark't it EF instead of DF. In mine to your Mother[3] there is an Account of the Contents and how they are to be dispos'd of, which I recommend to your Care. I send also a Roll of Silk under the Captain's own Care.

I am pleas'd with Ben's Readiness to accomodate his new Brother. My Love to them and Sally. I wrote to your Preston Mother, and forwarded your Letter immediately.

I was not able to get ready to go with Capt. All as I wished.[4] But I think now of going in the September Packet. I am, Your affectionate Father   B FRANKLIN
Mr Bache

Per Capt. Osborne

To Deborah Franklin

ALS: American Philosophical Society; letterbook draft: Library of Congress

My dear Child,   London, July 15. 1773

I sent you per Capt. All the last Voyage some Netting Lace of our poor Cousin's Making in Buckinghamshire:[5] You have not mention'd how you liked it; but I now send the Remainder.

1. William Bache (D.3.2.), BF's second legitimate grandchild, had been born on May 31. See above, I, lxiii.
2. Richard had decided to open a shop for groceries and wine: to BF above, April 6. The disappearance of the three other letters from him to which BF refers leaves us without a clue to the brokerage business.
3. The following document.
4. See BF to WF above, July 14.
5. For Hannah Walker and her lace see BF to DF above, Feb. 14.

The Silk Committee were so good as to make me a Present of 4 pound of Raw Silk. I have had it work'd up with some Addition of the same Silk into a French Grey Ducape, which is a fashionable Colour either for an old or young Woman. I therefore send it as a Present to you and Sally, understanding there is enough to make each of you a Negligée. If you should rather incline to sell it, it is valued here at 6s. 6d. per Yard; but I hope you will wear it.[6]

Desirous of making a little Room upon my Shelves, I have filled a Case with such Books as I have no present Use for, and sent it per Capt. All. There are in the Case, besides the Curtains and Gown return'd, sundry Parcels directed,[7] which I desire Son Bache would take care to deliver; there are also two Indian Garments called *Poncho's* which I desire you to lay up till my Return, and to put the Books into my Library. Enclos'd is the Dyer's Account.[8]

I congratulate you on Sally's safe Delivery of another Son.[9] I hope he will prove another Pleasure to you. My Love to her and her Children. O how I long to see you all.

I received your kind Letters of April 6. and 28, and May 15.[1] Dr. Small often enquires how you do. Capt. Ourry is gone to Scotland. Mrs. Stevenson, Mr. and Mrs. Hewson, all present their Respects to you. I believe I told you that Mrs. Hewson has another Son.[2] Mrs. Stevenson was all along wishing for a Grand-

6. For the Committee's gift see BF's acknowledgment of it above, Feb. 10. Ducape is a heavy corded silk, and a negligée in the eighteenth century was a loose gown. DF seems to have done as BF hoped; Sally certainly did, and was delighted with the result. See their letters below, Oct. 29, 30.

7. BF's draft adds that the parcels were for the Library Company, the APS, and WF.

8. BF paid the dyer the large sum of £1 9s. 8d. for "Curtains, etc.," and £3 4s. for the Indian garments. Jour., p. 49. We have no idea what this was all about.

9. See the preceding document.

1. See DF's letter above, April 6. Those of April 28 and May 15 have been lost.

2. He was destined for considerable distinction. Thomas Tickell Hewson (d. 1848) had been born on April 9. He became a noted physician and surgeon in Philadelphia, taught at the medical school of the University of Pennsylvania, and was president of the city's College of Physicians, 1835–48. J. Thomas Scharf and Thompson Westcott, *History of Philadelphia* ... (3 vols., Philadelphia, 1884), II, 1614.

daughter for herself and another for you. When I told her your new Grandchild was a Boy as well as hers, She says, *How provoking!*

Ben is an early Scholar, not yet quite four Years old. I hope he will prove a good One. I am ever, my dear Debby Your loving Husband,   B FRANKLIN

Addressed: To / Mrs Franklin / at / Philadelphia / per / Capt All

To Joseph Smith

AL (fragment of letterbook draft):[3] Library of Congress

Sir,   London, July 15. 1773

I am much obliged by your kind Care in receiving what the Assembly have been so good as to allow me. Please to

Mr Smith

[*Franklin's memorandum:*] Wrote to Abel James and Govr. Franklin in Recommendation of Morris Birkbeck a Quaker who goes over to look for lands.[4]

Note on an Advertisement for Land on the Ohio River

The advertisement, dated July 15, 1773, and signed by George Washington at Mount Vernon, was printed in *The Maryland Journal and Baltimore Advertiser* and in the *Pennsylvania Gazette*; it solicited applications for land grants in twenty thousand acres at the mouth of the Great Kanawha River. Its authorship has been attributed to Franklin, with no evidence but with admiration for his skill in propaganda.[5]

3. The fragment has been crossed out, presumably by BF himself.

4. The recommendations have been lost. Morris Birkbeck (1734?–1816) came from Guildford and was apparently a friend of David Barclay, through whom BF might naturally have met him. Birkbeck went to America and settled for a time in Pennsylvania, became acquainted with Anthony Benezet, and returned to England in 1775. The Philadelphia meeting certified him to the meeting in Settle, Yorks., where he seems to have been particularly concerned with elementary education. George S. Brookes, *Friend Anthony Benezet* (Philadelphia, 1937), p. 358; Hinshaw, *Amer. Quaker Genealogy*, II, 466.

5. James Melvin Lee, *History of American Journalism* (Boston and New York, 1917), p. 94.

How Washington could have enlisted that skill, particularly when the tract in question lay within the area for which the Walpole Company was negotiating, is not explained.[6] The attribution is a flight of fancy.

From Edmé-Louis Daubenton

AL: American Philosophical Society

Ce 20 Juillet, 1773.

Mr. Daubenton, le Jeune, qui a l'honneur d'envoyer a Mr. Franklin par Mr. Le Roy les planches enluminées qui sont dans cette Boite, est chargé de la part de M. Le Comte de Buffon d'y joindre ce petit memoire instructif sur la maniere de conserver les oiseaux et autres objets d'histoire naturelle, et de le prier de vouloir bien lui envoyer pour le Cabinet du Roy des productions naturelles de la Pensilvanie, qui seront toutes interessantes et nouvelles pour nous, n'ayant jamais rien reçu de ce pays la, et surtout des oiseaux, qui sont les objets qui interessent le plus actuellement Mr. De Buffon pour completer son ouvrage ornithologiste.[7]

To Richard Bache

ALS (letterbook draft): Library of Congress

Dear Son,   London, July 25. 1773

I wrote to you per Capt. Osborne, and have little to add, but that I had yesterday a Line from Preston expressing their Joy on the News I had communicated to them of their new Relation,[8] that they were all well, and should write to you in a few Days via Liverpoole.

6. For the conflict between Washington's claims and those of the Walpole Company see above, BF to WF, Feb. 14, and WF to BF, April 30.

7. For the "planches enluminées" see Daubenton's earlier letter above, May 31. LeRoy took his time about forwarding the plates and Buffon's enclosure, and presumably this covering note; they did not leave Paris until autumn. See LeRoy to BF below, Nov. 29. The following summer BF forwarded to the APS the "petit memoire instructif" and Buffon's request for specimens from Pennsylvania, whereupon the Society appointed a committee to deal with the request. BF to Rush below, July 25, 1774; APS, *Early Proc.* ... (Philadelphia, 1884), p. 94.

8. William, a new grandson; see BF's earlier letter to Bache, July 15.

This will be delivered to you by Messrs. John Hewson and Nathaniel Norgrove, who are recommended to me as sober industrious young Men, and very ingenious in their Business of Calico or Linen Printing; I wish they may meet with Encouragement to carry it on among us,[1] as there is a great deal of Linen worn in our Country, and a great deal of printed goes from hence. I therefore recommend them to your Civilities and Advice, as they will be quite Strangers there. I imagine some of the neighbouring Villages will suit best for them to work in, perhaps Germantown, or Derby. I am, Your affectionate Father

B FRANKLIN

Mr Bache

To Samuel Cooper

LS: British Museum; ALS (letterbook draft): Library of Congress

Dear Sir,   London, July 25th. 1773.

I wrote to you on the 7th Instant pretty fully, and am since favor'd with yours of June 14.[2]

I am much pleased with the Proposal of the Virginia Assembly, and the respectful manner in which it has been received by ours. I think it likely to produce very salutary Effects.

I am glad to know your Opinion that those Letters came seasonably and may be of publick Utility. I accompanied them with no Restriction relating to myself; My Duty to the Province as their Agent I thought required the Communication of them as

1. The young men were well received. John Hewson, as far as we know no relative of William, was a London printer and bleacher of calicoes. Although BF is said to have persuaded him to emigrate, to have given him numerous letters of introduction, and to have arranged a leasehold for him in Pennsylvania, this is BF's only known reference to him. Hewson reached Philadelphia in September and promptly established a print works for calicoes and linens, then joined the American army in 1775; his business suffered losses thereafter, but he and it eventually throve. Nathaniel Norgrove stayed with Hewson until 1777, when he set up his own printing works; it apparently failed soon afterward. *PMHB*, XXXVII (1913), 118–19, where the reference to the leasehold is suspect and at least in part erroneous (see above, III, 23–5); Harrold E. Gillingham, "Calico and Linen Printing in Philadelphia," *ibid.*, LII (1928), 99–105, 108.

2. Cooper's letter explains the matters that BF is discussing.

far as I could; I was sensible I should make Enemies there, and perhaps might offend Government here; but those Apprehensions I disregarded. I did not expect, and hardly still expect, that my sending them could be kept a secret: But since it is so hitherto, I now wish it may continue so, because the Publication of the Letters contrary to my Engagement, has changed the Circumstances. If they serve to diminish the Influence and demolish the Power of the Parties whose Correspondence has been and would probably have continued to be so mischievous to the Interests and Rights of the Province, I shall on that Account be more easy under any Inconveniencies I may suffer, either there or here, and shall bear as well as I can the Imputation of not having taken sufficient Care to insure the Performance of my Promise.

I think Government can hardly expect to draw any future Service from such Instruments, and one would thence suppose they must soon be dismiss'd. We shall see.

I hope to be favoured with a Continuance of your Correspondence and Intelligence while I stay here; it is highly useful to me, and will be, as it always has been, pleasing every where. I am ever, Dear Sir, Your obliged and most obedient humble Servant,

B FRANKLIN

Revd. Doctor Cooper.

Addressed: To / The Revd Doctor Cooper / Boston

To Thomas Cushing

ALS: Public Record Office; letterbook draft: Library of Congress

Sir,   London, July 25. 1773.

I am favour'd with yours of June 14 and 16.[3] the latter containing some Copies of the spirited Resolves of the Committee upon the Letters. I see from your Account of the Transaction, that you

3. The annotation of those letters and of the preceding document sufficiently covers the material in this one. Thomas Moffatt, who later expressed himself on so much of BF's correspondence with Cushing, added a note in his usual vein: "This letter relates chiefly to the Embezzled letter from The American Collection of the late Mr. Whatley in which He discovers some Apprehension of Resentment from Power but none of Remorse for his Iniquity Prevarication and falshood throughout this black Transaction."

could not well prevent what was done. As to the Rumour that other Copies were come from England, I know that could not be. It was an Expedient to disengage the House. I hope the Possession of the Originals, and the Proceedings upon them will be attended with Salutary Effects to the Province, and then I shall be well pleased.

I observe what you mention, that no Person besides Dr. Cooper and one of the Committee know they came from me. I did not accompany them with any Request of being myself conceal'd; for, believing what I did to be in the Way of my Duty as Agent, tho' I had no doubt of its giving Offence, not only to the Parties expos'd, but to Administration here, I was regardless of the Consequences. However, since the Letters themselves are now copied and printed, contrary the Promise I made, I am glad my Name has not been heard on the Occasion; and as I do not see it could be of any Use to the Publick, I now wish it may continue unknown—tho' I hardly expect it. As to yours, you may rely on my never mentioning it, except that I may be oblig'd, perhaps, to show your Letter in my own Vindication, to that Person only who might otherwise think he had reason to blame me for Breach of Engagement.

It must surely be seen here, that after such a Detection of their Duplicity in pretending a Regard and Affection to the Province while they were undermining its Privileges, it is impossible for the Crown to make any good Use of their Services, and that it can never be for its Interest to employ Servants who are under such universal Odium. The Consequence one would think should be their Removal. But perhaps it will be to Titles, or to Pensions, if your Revenue can pay them.[4] I am, with great Esteem, Sir, Your most obedient humble Servant   B FRANKLIN

Private

Honble. Thomas Cushing, Esqr

4. The reference is to Gov. Bernard, who was removed to both title and pension: he received a baronetcy, and was handsomely pensioned until appointed to the new Irish Revenue Board. Mrs. Napier Higgins, *The Bernards of Abington* . . . (4 vols., London, etc., 1903–04), II, 210–11, 213. BF's sentence replaced one that he deleted in the draft: "And yet there is such a prevailing Disposition to support Officers, that I shall not wonder if this expected Consequence should never take Place."

To Samuel Danforth[5]

ALS (letterbook draft) and copy:[6] Library of Congress

Dear Sir, London, July 25. 1773.

It gave me great Pleasure to receive so chearful an Epistle from a Friend of half a Century's Standing, and to see him commencing Life anew in so valuable a Son. I hope the young Gentleman's Patent will be as [beneficial] to him as his Invention must be to the Publick.[7]

I see by the Papers that you continue to afford her your [services,] which makes me almost asham[ed of my resolutions for] Retirement. But this exile, tho[ugh an honourable one,] is become grievous to me, in so long [a separation from] my Family, Friends and Country; [all which you hap]pily enjoy, and long may you continue to enjoy them. I hope for the great Pleasure of once more seeing and conversing with you; and tho' living-on in one's Children, as we both may do, is a good thing, I cannot but fancy it might be better to continue living ourselves at the same time. I rejoice therefore in your kind Intentions of including me in the Benefits of that inestimable Stone, which curing all Diseases, even old Age itself, will enable us to see the future glorious State of our America, enjoying in full Security her own Liberties, and

5. For the judge and long-time member of the Massachusetts Council see above, XI, 255. Although that is the only other time he has appeared in these volumes, the tone of the present letter indicates that BF considered him not only an old but also a close friend.

6. The copy is in the same hand as the extract of BF to Mather above, July 7, and has enabled us to supply in the same way passages torn from the draft.

7. Thomas Danforth (1744–1820) graduated from Harvard in 1762, assisted John Winthrop for a time, read law with Judge Trowbridge, and then opened his own practice in Charlestown. In the spring of 1773 legal business took him to England, where by his own account he was offered and declined the attorney generalship of Massachusetts, and was entrusted by Lord Dartmouth with his remarkable letter of June 19, written as a private person rather than a minister, to carry to Speaker Cushing. Danforth's invention, patented a week before BF wrote, was for using cold water to condense steam generated by distillation. The young man subsequently became a Loyalist, and returned to England in 1776. Bernard Bailyn, *The Ordeal of Thomas Hutchinson* (Cambridge, 1974), p. 215; Bennet Woodcroft, *Alphabetical Index of Patentees of Inventions* ... (London, [1969]); *Sibley's Harvard Graduates*, XV, 217–20.

offering in her Bosom a Participation of them to all the Oppress'd of other Nations.[8] I anticipate the jolly Conversation we and twenty more of our Friends may have 100 Years hence on this Subject, over that well-replenish'd Bowl at Cambridge Commencement. I am, dear Sir, for an Age to come and for ever, with sincere Esteem and Respect, Your most obedient humble servant

Saml Danforth Esqr   B F.

To William Franklin   ALS (letterbook draft): Library of Congress

Dear Son,   London, July 25. 1773

I wrote to you pretty fully per Osborne,[9] since which I attended the Hearing at the Council Board against the Report of the Board of Trade on the Complaint of Mr. Livius.[1] I think I sent you a Copy of the Complaint and Answer among the Pamphlets, containing also the Report.[2] The Time was only sufficient to hear the Counsel for Govr. Wentworth and against the Report. They

8. Danforth was that great rarity in the period, an alchemist searching for the philosopher's stone. *Ibid.*, VI, 83.

9. BF's letter of July 14, above, went by Peter Osborne, master of the *Pa. Packet*, who left Deal on July 21: *London Chron.*, July 20–22, 1773.

1. The case of Peter Livius (1739–95) made a stir at the time. He was the son of a German merchant at Lisbon, but was educated in London. After a brief stay in Portugal he returned to England, where he married the daughter of Col. John Tufton Mason, a proprietor of New Hampshire and one of its greatest landholders. Livius sought his fortune in the province, and was soon a member of its Council and a judge of the Court of Common Pleas. He was dismissed from his judgeship in 1771 by Gov. Wentworth, an old acquaintance of WF (above, XIV, 159 n, 178–8), and went to England to bring charges that he hoped would procure the Governor's removal. One of the charges— of particular interest to speculators on the one hand and colonial governors on the other—was that many of Wentworth's land grants had been *ultra vires*. Livius eventually lost his case. *Acts Privy Coun., Col.*, V, 370–2; VI, 526–7, 529–36; *Board of Trade Jour.*, 1768–75, pp. 311–12, 338, 341–3, 346–7, 349–52, 356–7, 361, 364, 373; Lawrence S. Mayo, "Peter Livius the Trouble-maker," Colonial Soc. of Mass. *Pub.*, XXV (1924), 125–9; *Sibley's Harvard Graduates*, XIII, 261–70.

2. *The Memorial of Peter Livius . . . to the Lords Commissioners for Trade and Plantations; with the Governor's Answer and the Memorialist's Reply . . .* ([London,] 1773).

seem'd to make a pretty good Case of it, but there is no judging till the other side is heard, which will be next Thursday. Gilbert Francklin, whom you may remember as Partner to Anthony Bacon, is making Interest to be Governor in Case Wentworth is removed, and some of the Board of Trade are his Friends.[3] It is doubtful what the Issue will be; but the Expence must be great to the Governor tho' he should be continued, and Livius if he fails will be half ruined.[4]

I paid into the Hands of Mr. Walpole yesterday Six hundred Pounds, being for Mr. Galloway's Share, yours and mine, £200 each, which is for the Purchase-money, and the overplus towards the Charges.[5] I enclose your Receipt. The Idea given me was that the Patent will pass the Seals in a few Days, when the Money is to be paid; but I have just now learnt from the Council Office that

3. Gilbert Francklyn, or Francklin, was in partnership with Anthony Bacon, a former Marylander who was a prominent London merchant, from 1759 to about 1773: Lewis B. Namier, "Anthony Bacon, M.P.," *Jour. of Economic and Business History*, II (1929–30), 24–5. But Francklyn seems to have spent much of his time in Antigua and Tobago, and served for a while on the Tobago Council. He was a member of and propagandist for a society of West Indian planters, and wrote a number of pamphlets on the slave trade. *Acts Privy Coun., Col.*, V, 506, 574; VI, 589–91; *Board of Trade Jour.*, 1768–75, p. 263; 1776–82, pp. 376, 403, 407, 419–421; Vere L. Oliver, *The History of the Island of Antigua* ... (3 vols., London, 1894–99), I, 258; II, 371, 373; Lowell J. Ragatz, *A Guide for the Study of British Caribbean History* ... (Washington, 1932), pp. 295, 504–5. Why Francklyn should have coveted the governorship of New Hampshire we cannot imagine.

4. Livius was resilient. When he lost his case he remained in England for a time, and was then sent to Quebec as a judge. From 1776 to 1778 he was chief justice of the province; then he was dismissed by the governor as he had been in New Hampshire. Again he went to England to seek redress, this time successfully: his office was restored, but he never returned to Quebec. A. L. Burt, "The Tragedy of Chief Justice Livius," *Canadian Hist. Rev.*, V (1924), 196–212.

5. For BF's financing of WF's and Galloway's shares in the Walpole Co. see above, XIX, 140. The Company had initially offered £10,460 7s. 3d. for the tract, a fifth to be paid when the grant issued under the great seal and the rest in annual installments; but by 1773 the whole sum was to be paid on issuance. Above, XVII, 9; Kenneth P. Bailey, ed., *The Ohio Company Papers* ... (Arcata, Cal., 1947), p. 276. The Company was now confident enough of success to collect the cash. BF paid £177 16s. 10d. per share in purchase money and £22 3s. 2d. for expenses. Jour., p. 50.

the Form put into the Attorney General's Hands by Mr. Wharton, is objected to by the Attorney on Account of its making the Proprietors all joint-tenants, so that those who die will lose their Shares and the Survivors take, which the Attorney supposes could not be the Intention of the Grantees, and for these Reasons he and the Sollicitor General have return'd the Draft to the Council disapprov'd,[6] so that there must be a new Reference, for which a Council must be got together, and that can scarce be done till the next Meeting of Parliament. Before I heard this I ask'd Maj. Trent who drew the Draft. His Answer was, it was somebody Mr. Wharton got to do it, he could not tell who. Dagge is dissatisfied that he was not consulted and thinks it should have been shown to Mr. Jackson, to him, and to all of us. Blair, Clerk of the Council, made a Remark on the Occasion a little particular. That Man, says he, speaking of Wharton, is *too fine*, he outwits himself. I want to see the Draft, that I may know what this meant.[7] Keep all this to yourself.

6. Under joint tenancy the last surviving proprietor would in theory acquire all the Company's holdings; under the alternative, tenancy in common, each proprietor's heirs would acquire his rights. The law officers also took exception to the vagueness of the boundaries and of the responsibility for paying quitrents to the crown. The question of what "the Draft" was that they disapproved is discussed in the next note.

7. William Trent and Samuel Wharton need no introduction. Henry Dagge (above, p. 310 n) was a lawyer for the Company, and one of its most prominent legal members was Richard Jackson, counsel to the Board of Trade. William Blair had been clerk of the Privy Council since 1735, commissioner of stamps with one short interval since 1737, and clerk of the Signet Office since 1748; he held the first two positions in 1778, and the third until 1782. Joseph T. Haydn, *The Book of Dignities* . . . (3rd ed., London, 1894), p. 283; John Chamberlayne, *Magnae Britanniae Notitia* . . . (London, 1735), p. 42 of second pagination; *The Royal Kalendar* . . . (London, 1778), pp. 70, 132; *ibid.*, 1782, p. 108.

Blair's comment on the draft leaves us even more in the dark than BF was. The Privy Council had instructed Attorney General Thurlow and Solicitor General Wedderburn to review the report from the Board of Trade, as explained in the note on BF to Foxcroft above, July 14. The opinion that the law officers delivered on July 16, a copy of which is in the Library of Congress, gives the impression of being on that report and on nothing else; see *Acts Privy Coun., Col.*, V, 210; VI, 543, 556. BF is saying something quite different—that the opinion took exception to points that were not in the Board's report but in another document, Wharton's draft (which we have

327

I have sent you in Capt. Sutton a Box containing two Skillets and two small Kettles of Bellmetal,[8] the latter being recommended here rather than Skillets, but if you don't chuse them send them to your Sister, or one of each. The Box is fill'd up with some Pamphlets, which you may send to my House, or keep them till my Return.

There is another Box for you from Mr. Sergeant which I receiv'd with the enclos'd Note.[9] I think he told me it was to contain a little Present of Wine. My Love to Betsey. I am ever Your affectionate Father   B F.

I shall write to Mr. Galloway per the Packet of next Week.[1] My Respects to him.

To John Winthrop   ALS (letterbook draft): Library of Congress

Dear Sir   London, July 25. 73
I received your Favours of March 4 and April 19. Mr. Danforth paid me the 52*s.* you sent by him. The Vol. of Transactions I

---

not found) of a grant to the Company. BF, it appears, was partly right. The law officers ignored the large section of the report that dealt with the establishment of Vandalia, and considered only the terms of the grant. Here they objected to one new condition and two old ones. The new, joint tenancy, the Board had not mentioned and Wharton clearly had. The old were in the report, quitrents and boundaries, the latter in the exact wording that the Company had used in 1770. The opinion did not impress the Privy Council. The following October its committee responded by ignoring joint tenancy and insisting that the grant, except for a slight change in quitrents, be drawn up as the Board had proposed it. *Ibid.*, V, 210. BF was correct, this evidence suggests, in believing that Wharton introduced into the governmental machinery a draft grant of his own, which by raising the issue of joint tenancy gave Thurlow and Wedderburn a point of attack. If so the lobbyist was indeed *"too fine"*: he contributed to a delay that proved fatal. It again postponed the Company's hopes, and the rising American crisis engulfed them.

8. See above, p. 308.
9. WF had met John Sargent when in England with BF (above, VII, 321–2), and had apparently, like BF, established lasting relations with the banker.
1. The letter is below, Aug. 3.

think went in a Trunk that I sent to Mr. Jonathan Williams. I hope you receiv'd it safe.

Mr. Danforth has succeeded in obtaining his Patent.[2] I hope it will prove serviceable to himself as well as the Publick.

Dr. Priestly is now well provided for.[3] Lord Shelbourne is become his Patron, and desirous to have the Company of a Man of general Learning to read with him and superintend the Education of his Children has taken him from his Congregation at Leeds, settled £300 a year upon him for Ten Years, and £200 for Life, with a House to live in near his Country Seat. My Lord has a great Library there which the Dr. is now putting in Order,[4] and seems very happy in his new Situation. The learned Leisure he will now have, secure of a comfortable Subsistance, gives his Friends a pleasing Hope of many useful Works from his Pen. I expect him soon in town, when I shall communicate to him your Remarks on his last Book, for which I am sure he will feel himself much obliged to you.

Your Remark on the Passage of Castillioneus, will be read at the Society at their next Meeting. I thank you much for the Papers and Accounts of Damage done by Lightning which you have favour'd me with. The Conductors begin to be used here. Many Country Seats are provided with them, some Churches, the Powder Magazines at Purfleet, the Queen's House in the Park, &c. and M. Le Roy, of the Academy of Sciences at Paris, has lately given a Memoir recommending the Use of them in that Kingdom, which had been long oppos'd and obstructed by Abbé Nollet.[5] The Duke of Tuscany he says, ce Prince qui ne connoit

2. For Thomas Danforth and his patent see BF to Samuel Danforth above, July 25.

3. This and the following paragraph are in reply to Winthrop's letter above, March 4, where several matters that BF is discussing are explained. The letter of April 19 has been lost.

4. Bowood housed one of the richest private libraries in England. After Shelburne, by then Marquis of Lansdowne, died in 1805 the auction of his books took thirty-one days; his historical MSS went to the British Museum as the Lansdowne collection. *DNB*.

5. The controversy over the rods at Purfleet figured prominently in the preceding volume. The Queen's House was the former Buckingham House on St. James's Park, later incorporated into Buckingham Palace; see Henry B. Wheatley, *London Past and Present* . . . (3 vols., London, 1891), I,

pas de délassement plus agreable des soins penibles du Gouverne-ment,[6] que l'etude de la Physique, à [sic] ordonné, l'année derniere, qu'on établit de ces Barres audessus de tous les magasins à poudre de ses Etats; on dit que la République de Venise a donné les mêmes ordres, &c.

I am glad to see that you are elected into the Council, and are about to take Part in our Publick Affairs. Your Abilities, Integrity and sober Attachment to the Liberties of our Country, will be of great Use at this Tempestuous Time in conducting our little Bark into safe Harbour.[7] By the Boston News papers there seems to be among us some violent Spirits who are for an immediate Rupture. But I trust the general Prudence of our Country-men will see that by our growing Strength we advance fast to a Situation in which our Claims must be allow'd; that by a premature Struggle we may be crippled and kept down another Age; that as between Friends every Affront is not worth a Duel, between Nations every Injury not worth a War, so between the Governed and the Governing, every Mistake in Government, every Incroachment on Rights is not worth a Rebellion. Tis in my Opinion, sufficient for the present that we hold them forth on all Occasions, not giving up any of them, using at the same time every means to make them generally understood and valued by the People; cultivating a Harmony

---

291-3. The royal lightning rods had the pointed ends that BF recommended, and in 1777 the King—for political or scientific reasons—had them replaced by Benjamin Wilson's blunt-ended rods. Smyth, *Writings*, VII, 64-5; Hist. MSS Commission, *Second Report* ... (London, 1871), app., p. 13. For LeRoy's memoir see his letter above, April 19. Nollet had been, for the better part of twenty years until his death in 1770, the chief French opponent of BF's electrical theories: above, IV, 423-5, 428; XIX, 127.

6. Leopold (1747-92), the third son of Francis I and Maria Theresa and the brother of Marie Antoinette and the Emperor Joseph II, had been Grand Duke of Tuscany since 1765. The cares of government were indeed heavy for him, because in his small state he was proving himself to be one of the most effective reformers of the age.

7. Winthrop had never before held important public office. On May 26 the House elected him as one of eight new members of the Council. Three of the eight, John Adams among them, the Governor vetoed; Winthrop and four others he reluctantly accepted. *Mass. Acts and Resolves*, XVIII, 705; Hutchinson, *History*, III, 284-5. For Winthrop's subsequent political role see *Sibley's Harvard Graduates*, IX, 257-8.

among the Colonies, that their Union in the same Sentiments may give them greater Weight; remembring withal that this Protestant Country (our Mother tho' of late an unkind one) is worth preserving, and that her Weight in the Scale of Europe, and her Safety in a great degree, may depend on our Union with her. Thus conducting, I am confident, we may within a few Years, obtain every Allowance of, and every Security for, our inestimable Privileges that we can wish or desire. With great and sincere Esteem, I am ever, Dear Sir, Your most obedient humble Servant   B F

Mr Winthrop

From William Franklin   ALS: American Philosophical Society

Honoured Father,   New york July 29th. 1773
    I arrived here on Monday Evening last when I had the Pleasure of receiving yours of June 2. by the Packet. I am on my Way to Albany with Mrs. Franklin, who wanted a Jaunt this Summer on Account of her Health; and I have some Business to transact there likewise.[8]
    I am surprized the Grant was not made out when you wrote. By the May Packet Wharton wrote that every Thing would be compleated so that he should certainly leave England by the End of the Month or the Beginning of June at farthest. Mr. McRabie (Neave's Partner) has, I am told, wrote that as soon as the Grant passed the Seals, Wharton would receive as much Money for Lands in the new Colony, as would be sufficient to discharge all the Demands of Baynton & Wharton's Creditors. And Thos. Wharton has actually paid, or agreed to pay, all the Money allowed by the Trustee for the Maintenance of Wharton's Family during his Negotiations in England, which puzzles the Creditors to account for.[9]

8. The business had to do with the intricate affairs of the Burlington Co. and its land claims near Lake Otsego: William H. Mariboe, "The Life of William Franklin..." (unpublished doctoral dissertation, University of Pa., 1962), pp. 301–3, 326–7.
    9. Negotiations for the Walpole grant were proceeding at a glacial pace; see above, BF to Foxcroft, July 14, and to WF, July 25. McRabie we cannot identify, but his London firm of Richard Neave & Son (above, XII, 151 n)

331

Our Chief Justice is just returned from Rhode Island, without being able to do any Thing in Execution of the Commission he went upon, as they could obtain no Evidence worth relying on.[1] He tells me that Govr. Hutchinson is made very unhappy by the Publication of his Letters to Whately, and the consequent Treatment he has received, and talks of going to England. It is said by some that you sent the Letters over, and by others that it was Mr. Temple. I suppose it must be the latter. Govr. H. told the Chief that the Party against him [was] much elated on receiving some Letters from you [and?] you went so far as to advise them t[o be bold?] in insisting on their *Independency*. [But the?] Govr's. Party, on the other hand, are or pretend to [be] in hig[h Spirits?] at the Advices they have received from England. The Govr. is gloomy and low spirited, and seems by no means pleased with his Situation.[2]

I have not Time to add more, nor even to copy this, as the Capt. of the Sloop has just sent me Word he is waiting for me. Betsy joins in Duty with, Honoured Sir, Your ever dutiful Son

WM. FRANKLIN

Addressed: To / Dr. Franklin / Craven Street / London / per Packet

---

had acted as banker for Baynton, Wharton & Morgan since 1763 and was deeply involved in its financial difficulties. Those difficulties had gone on for years: in 1767 the creditors had chosen a board of trustees to supervise the affairs of the Philadelphia firm, but its assets were not finally liquidated until 1776. Max Savelle, *George Morgan, Colony Builder* (New York, 1932), pp. 37–41, 73–5. McRabie seems to have promised that his house, once the grant was made, would again lend money to its correspondent, presumably in return for mortgages on newly acquired western land.

1. Frederick Smyth had been chief justice of New Jersey since 1764: above, XI, 464 n. He was a member of the commission of inquiry into the *Gaspee* affair, for which see above, XIX, 379, and the note on Cooper to BF, March 15, 1773.

2. Our conjectural insertions are based on the context and the space torn away at the end of each line. For the publication of the Hutchinson letters see below, p. 539 n. The Governor was indeed unhappy. Exposure of his correspondence eroded such support as he had had, and Dartmouth had rebuked him for opening a constitutional mare's nest in the debate with the House and Council. In June he had asked leave to go to England; it was given, but did not arrive until the middle of the tea crisis. Bernard Bailyn,

From Jonathan Williams, Jr.

ALS: American Philosophical Society

Dear and honoured Sir   Boston July 29 [–Aug. 4]. 1773

I was desired to send Mrs. Stevenson 6 Boxes of Sperma Ceti Candles, but as they will not admit a less quantity than 22 lbs. [?][3] to be shipt, was obliged to send her 9: which I have shipped on board the Lydia Capt. Hood directed to you as per the inclosed Bill of Lading. Mrs. S will appropriate the amount to the Payment of an Organ I desired you to procure for me in my last:[4] such an one as you bought for Mrs. Foxcroft. I hope you will excuse the trouble I give you in the matter and shall be particularly obliged by your sending it as soon as it is finished. I inclose a Schedule of my account with Mr. Warren, that you may judge of my Conduct with regard to that Gentleman.[5] My constant aim is, and shall be, to be as punctual as I can and I think I have done my utmost endeavours. I stick to my ready money plan, and do not intend to part from it, tho' cannot do so much Business as if I trusted, but at this time that is particularly hazardous, for Goods are so very low for Cash, that no person that is able to pay will ask a

---

The Ordeal of Thomas Hutchinson (Cambridge, Mass., 1974), pp. 218–20, 250–9. BF pointed out in his reply to this letter below, Oct. 6, that all he had advised in writing to Cushing was to stand firm and to trust in America's growing strength. But he had told the Speaker more than that in his letter of May 6, quoting what he had said to Dartmouth: Parliamentary authority over the colonies could not be exercised without destroying it. That statement might well have seemed in Boston to be an assertion of de facto independence. Then how could the Governor's party have been in high spirits (if we guess the word correctly)? Perhaps because Whitehall was taking the crisis in Massachusetts seriously, and was considering coercive measures to make the House retreat from its stand. Above, p. 201; Hutchinson, *History*, III, 297.

3. The figures and the squiggle that we render as "lbs." are so blurred that we must settle for a plausible guess.

4. Of June 28. Mrs. Stevenson apparently sold the candles for £29 1s. 5d. From the proceeds BF deducted the freight and duty, £7 9s. 9d., and the cost of the organ, £16 15s., leaving a balance due of £4 16s. 8d. Jour., p. 52; Ledger, p. 67.

5. Williams had long been dealing with James Warren, BF's neighbor in Craven Street; see above, XIX, 33–4.

Credit. I therefore conclude that my Goods in my Store are better than if they were in Debts, as I always have more by me than sufficient to pay what I owe.[6] My Father gives his Duty to you and asks the favor of you to send him the following Books, Vizt

The Aurora
The Mystery of Magnum } by Jacob Behmen, and any other of his Works.
The Threefold Life

also The Works of William Law, his Appeal to all that Doubt, on Regeneration, and on divine knowledge.[7] These are not to be had in this Country, or we would not be thus troublesome: and he begs he may not be disappointed. Please to pay for them out of the Surplusage of the Candles.

Augt 4th 1773

Since writing the above, we have received your kind Favour to my Father, covering an Account of sundry Goods for my Aunt Mecom, which are not yet out of the Ship. I am much obliged by your Goodness in delivering my letter to Mrs. Barwell, as also for your kind promise of assistance relative to East India Consignments.[8] Please to make my best respects acceptable to her, with

6. For Jonathan's "ready money plan" see *idem.*, pp. 100–1.

7. The senior Williams, or perhaps a friend for whom he was agent, was exploring Christian mysticism. William Law (1686–1761), the Anglican clergyman and author of *A Serious Call to a Devout and Holy Life* ... (London, 1729), had a brief but strong influence on John and Charles Wesley; see the *DNB*. The tracts of his about which Williams was inquiring went through several editions before being included in Law's collected works (9 vols., London, 1762); the first printings were as follows: *An Appeal to All That Doubt or Disbelieve the Truths of the Gospel* ... (London, 1742); *The Grounds and Reasons of Christian Regeneration* ... (London, 1739); and *The Way to Divine Knowledge* ... (London, 1752). Law was a disciple of Jakob Böhme (1575–1624), the famous German mystic, and translated his writings. *The Works of Jacob Behmen* ... (4 vols., London, 1764–81) contains "The Aurora," the "Mysterious Magnum: or an Explanation of Genesis," and "The Threefold Life of Man."

8. Jonathan is referring to BF's letter to his father above, June 4; with it was doubtless enclosed an invoice, now lost, of goods bought for Jane Mecom's shop. The letter and goods went by the *Nicholas*, Capt. Hatch, which sailed on June 10 and arrived on July 30. *London Chron.*, June 10–12; *Boston Gaʒ.*, Aug. 2, 1773.

every gratefull acknowledgment, for the favorable reception of my letter. If I should not have time to write to Mrs. Blunt, please to remember me to her, with great respect and esteem, as also to all enquiring Friends. All are well on this side and Join in Love and Duty with Your dutifull and Affectionate Kinsman

JONA WILLIAMS JUN

Addressed: To / Doctr B Franklin

Endorsed: July 29. and Augt 4. 1773

From John Cuthbert[9]   ALS: American Philosophical Society

Sir,   Newcastle on Tyne, July 30, 1773.

The Time elapsed since I had the pleasure of seeing you at the Royal Society and receiving your Commission in regard to the Furniture of our Collieries makes me almost ashamed to sit down to answer it. As soon as I got to Newcastle I made what Enquiry I could for a proper Person to copy and design all their Utensils, and at last found one Mr. Beilby, an Ingenious Drawing-Master here who undertook it and I hope will have executed it to your satisfaction.[1] I got him Leave from the Proprietors to attend Walker our first and greatest Colliery in these parts, about five miles from hence, with an order also for the chief Agents to give him all the Assistance in their power.[2] I have laid his Drawings

9. Cuthbert (d. 1782), of Witton Castle, near Durham, an F.R.S. since 1765 and a member of the Royal Society Club and the Society of Arts, was also a governor of the Inner Temple and of Magdalen Hospital, a London institution for the relief of penitent prostitutes. At his death he was worth £2,000 a year: *Gent. Mag.,* LII (1782), 599. Whether he was directly connected with the Newcastle collieries we do not know.

1. Ralph Beilby (1744–1817) was beyond question ingenious, and much more than a drawing master. The Newcastle jeweler and silversmith made a name for himself as an engraver, and at this time was training an even more famous apprentice, Thomas Bewick. *DNB.* BF's reply below, Aug. 28, makes clear that he had commissioned the drawings for a French acquaintance who was writing a work on mining techniques.

2. The colliery at Walker was the deepest and most important in the north of England. Among its "Utensils" was a celebrated horse-powered machine for raising the coal from the floor six hundred feet below. See Robert L. Galloway, *Annals of Coal Mining and the Coal Trade* ... (London, 1898), pp. 275–6.

before several of them who say they are very exact and properly performed, and am only sorry it was not in my power to send 'em you sooner. A Call to some of my own Affairs in another County and a long Illness kept me absent from this Place near Six Months, and I did not immediately find a Conveyance for 'em on my Return. I ventur'd however to deliver 'em 'tother Day to Lady Bewicke,[3] who promis'd me to send 'em to you with the greatest Care, and proposes being in London within a Fortnight. We thought it unnecessary to give an expensive Drawing of the Fire Engine with all its Apparatus and Accoutrements, as it is not only in the shops, but in Desigulier's Experimental Philosophy.[4] I shall be happy, Sir, if they please you, and am Your most Humble Servant,   J. CUTHBERT.

Franklin's Use of "Prudential Algebra"

AD:[5] American Philosophical Society

These seemingly random jottings turn out to have more significance than at first appears. They are the only example we have yet encountered of Franklin's using his private decision-making method, which he had offered to Priestley the year before. It involved listing in separate columns the reasons for and against a given action, then striking out those that balanced each other in importance, then determining which column finally had the greater weight.[6] In the present case he did not follow the method to the letter, but it was clearly at work. He was attacking the problem that engaged him intermittently and often: had the time come to return home? He put down the reasons against in one column, the reasons for in another; instead of deleting items in

3. She was the widow, we assume, of the former sheriff of Northumberland, Sir Robert Bewicke; see John B. Burke, *A Genealogical and Heraldic Dictionary of the Landed Gentry* . . . (2 vols., London, 1851), I, 92.

4. The Newcomen engine, a forerunner of Watt's steam engine, is described at length with two full-page plates in John T. Desaguliers, *A Course of Experimental Philosophy* (3rd ed.; 2 vols., London, 1763), II, 467–90. The engine was the first effective means of pumping water from the mines, and in the past sixty years had come into wide use throughout the colliery districts.

5. On the verso of BF's draft of his letter below to John Williams, Aug. 15, and presumably antedating it; see the next note but one.

6. Above, XIX, 299–300.

both, he made crosses beside most of those in the first. What the marks meant is not clear, because he did not mention this variant to Priestley; but it is a reasonable conjecture that he was checking considerations on which he put the most emphasis. In any case the list with crosses outweighed the other, and his "algebra" persuaded him to stay.

[Before August 3?,[7] 1773]

Stay		Go
S. J. P.—Eur.[8]	×	Recover of F
Finish 5th Edn.[9]	×	Settle with Do. for Ph.O[10]
—— Piece on New Stove[11]	×	Get clear of Agys.[12]
—— Dialogue[13]	×	Repose
Settle with Mrs. S.[14]	×	Prevent Waste at h[15]

7. The date of the letters to Foxcroft, WF, and Galloway below, in which BF first mentioned his decision to stay in England. Internal evidence establishes the year beyond question.

8. In 1772 BF had been disappointed in his hope of a European trip with Sir John Pringle (above, XIX, 132); he had recently been disappointed again, when Pringle had gone instead to Scotland. Above, p. 306. The hope had been postponed, we assume, but not abandoned.

9. The latest edition of *Exper. and Obser.* was in preparation: BF to LeRoy above, March 30, and to Ingenhousz below, Sept. 30.

10. This and "Recover of F" refer to settling with John Foxcroft both their personal accounts and those for the Philadelphia post office. See above, XVIII, 91; XIX, 60–1, 273, 320, 414–15.

11. He had promised Dubourg, in his letter above of June 29, a description of his new stove; it was clearly on his mind, although he did not in fact compose it until years later.

12. The agencies for Georgia, Massachusetts, New Jersey, and Pennsylvania. He subsequently said that *the* reason for his deciding to stay was "some Events in our Colony Affairs." To Ingenhousz below, Sept. 30.

13. He had apparently begun work on what later became "A Dialogue between Britain, France, Spain, Holland, Saxony and America," which we print below in early 1775. See Crane, *Letters to the Press*, p. 283. The final form of the essay suggests by its tone that the draft in 1773, whatever it was, underwent thorough revision.

14. BF paid Mrs. Stevenson surprisingly little in 1773, but a large sum when he finally left in 1775: Ledger, pp. 12, 67. He told John Williams, in the letter cited above, that he was short of cash—perhaps too short to discharge his debt to his landlady. If so, and if she was as willing to extend credit as she seems to have been, he may have wanted to avoid a settlement at this time.

15. Our guess (the reader may have a better one) is that "h" meant "home," and that BF had in mind what he considered to be DF's extravagance; see above, XVIII, 90–1.

337

Ohio Business.[16]   Settle with H's Exrs.[17]
Pap. Money[18]   ×
Boston Agy.[19]   ×
Beccaria[20]

To Alexander Colden   ALS (letterbook draft): Library of Congress

⟨West Wycomb, at Lord Le Despencer's, August 3, 1773: Has received Colden's of June 2 enclosing seconds of "sundry Bills acknowledg'd in my last" and the first of Willing & Morris on Harris & Co. for £15. Encloses Ogle's protested bill on Anderson for £83 10s. 3d.,[1] which with charges totals £83 16s. Compliments to Mrs. Colden.⟩

To John Foxcroft   ALS (letterbook draft): Library of Congress

West Wycomb, Lord LeDespencer's, Augt. 3. 1773
Dear Sir,
I wrote to you pretty fully by Capt. All viâ Philadelphia,[2] and have not since heard from you.
I did purpose to have visited you in the September Packet, but begin to see that I must stay here one Winter more, on Account of some Publick Business of Importance.
The Ohio Grant is still unfinish'd, and like to continue so for

16. No emphasis here, perhaps because BF was no longer in the inner counsels of the Walpole Company and was pessimistic about the interminable delays in securing approval of its grant.
17. To settle with David Hall's executors the accounts that Hall, shortly before his death, had been pressing BF to settle: above, XIX, 57–8, 91–2.
18. A reminder to attend to the Pennsylvania paper money act that BF mentioned to Galloway below, Aug. 3.
19. He was free to turn over the affairs of the agency to Arthur Lee (above, XVIII, 127), but at that juncture may have been reluctant to do so.
20. He was overseeing the translation of Beccaria's *Elettricismo artificiale*; see his letter to the author below, Aug. 11.
1. See the letter BF is answering: above, p. 225.
2. Above, July 14.

some time, as the Attorney and Solicitor General in whose Hands the Patent lies for their Examination, are gone out of town.[3]

I hope to hear from you fully on the Subject of the Accounts mentioned in my last. And am ever, Dear Friend, Yours most affectionately   B FRANKLIN

Mr Foxcroft

To William Franklin   ALS (letterbook draft): Library of Congress

West Wycombe, Lord Le Despencer's Aug. 3. 1773
Dear Son,

I am com hither to spend a few Days and breathe a little fresh Air.

Nothing material has occurr'd since mine per sutton, except the final Hearing at the Cockpit relating to Gov. Wentworth, against whose Conduct the Board of Trade had reported, and the Hearing was at the Instance of his Friends against the Report. Their Lordships have not yet given their Determination, but it is thought he is in no Danger.[4]

As to the Ohio Affair, it is scarce likely to be got through this Summer, for Reasons I have already given you.[5]

Our Paper Money Act[6] not being yet considered here, together with the Massachusetts Affairs, will I believe keep me another Winter in England.

Temple is just return'd to School from his Summer Vacation. He always behaves himself so well, as to encrease my Affection for him every time he is with me. As you are like to have a considerable Landed Property, it would be well to make your Will,

3. An odd way to put it. The law officers had reported weeks before, and the next move lay with the Privy Council. See BF to WF above, July 25.

4. The hearing before the Privy Council at the Cockpit on July 29 was the second of two held on Peter Livius' complaint against Wentworth, which BF discussed in his letter of July 25. For reports of the hearings see the *London Chron.*, July 22–24, 29–31, 1773. On October 8 the complaint was dismissed by an order in council: *Dartmouth MSS*, II, 177.

5. In the letter just cited.

6. No such New Jersey act seems to have been under consideration at this time; BF was doubtless referring to the Pennsylvania act mentioned in the following document.

if you have not already done it, and secure this Property to him. Our Friend Galloway will advise you in the Manner. Whatever he may come to possess, I am persuaded he will make a good Use of it, if his Temper and Understanding do not strangely alter.

I am in this House as much at my Ease as if it was my own, and the Gardens are a Paradise. But a pleasanter Thing is the kind Countenance, the facetious[7] and very Intelligent Conversation of mine Host, who having been for many Years engaged in publick Affairs, seen all Parts of Europe, and kept the best Company in the World is himself the best existing.

I wear the Buttons (for which I thank you) on [my] Suit of light Gray, which matches them. All the Connoisseurs in natural Productions are puzzled with them not knowing anything similar.[8] With Love to Betsey, I am ever Your affectionate Father

B F

To Joseph Galloway   ALS (letterbook draft): Library of Congress

Dear Sir,   Augt. 3. 1773

I was in hopes the Acts passed at your Winter Session, particularly the Paper-money Act might have been presented so as to come under Consideration before the Recess of the Boards. But they have not yet made their Appearance.[1] I had Thoughts of returning this Fall, but have now concluded to stay another Winter, thinking my being here may be of Use when that comes under Consideration.

Inclosed I send you two or three Acts relating to America that have passed here lately. That relating to the legal Tender is

7. In the obsolete sense of polished or witty.
8. WF had in all likelihood sent his father some of the buttons that the sea carved from slate in "Button-mold Bay," like those that BF had given to Peter Collinson almost a decade before: above, XI, 182.
1. How BF had heard of them, and why they had not arrived although they had been passed the previous February, we do not know. The act, one of fifteen, authorized emitting £150,000 in bills of credit and provided for a fund to discharge the public debt. The Privy Council referred this act, with the others, to the Board of Trade in February, 1774, and it was subsequently allowed. 8 *Pa. Arch.*, VIII, 6965, 7093; *Board of Trade Jour.*, 1768–75, p. 386, 393–5; Joseph A. Ernst, *Money and Politics in America, 1755–1775* ([Chapel Hill, N.C., 1973]), pp. 304–8, 313–15.

similar to what pass'd 3 or 4 Years since in favour of New York, and which cost that Province £180 being consider'd as a private Act. It was then intimated to me, that I might upon Petition obtain such Acts for each of the Provinces I was concern'd with; but I thought it a shameful Imposition merely to accumulate Fees for the Officers of the two Houses: The Act to be amended was a publick Act, and if they had blunder'd in making it they ought to amend it gratis. I therefore would not apply. And now some of the Merchants complaining that thro' this Obstruction to the Making of Paper [Money] Trade is declining in America, and Payments difficult, they have of themselves attempted the Remedy. Mr. Jackson drew the Bill, and it was a better one, but some of the Board of Trade [torn] it, and he does not now so well like it.[2]

It is long since I have had the Favour of a Line from you. I hope your Indisposition is not returned. With great and sincere Esteem, I am ever, Dear Sir, Your most obedient humble Servant   B [FRANKLIN]

Mr Galloway

To Noble Wimberley Jones

ALS (letterbook draft): Library of Congress

Dear Sir,   London,[3] Augt. 4. 1773
I hope you continue well tho' I have not had the Pleasure of hearing from you since your Favour of Jan. 13. The Seeds I sent

2. A New York enactment in 1769 raised a legal question about the meaning of the Currency Act of 1764. In 1770 Parliament settled the question, as it applied to New York, by permitting that colony to issue bills that would be legal tender for money due the province but not for private debts. This was an admission, BF is saying, that the earlier act had been a blunder. The remedy became law in June, 1773: 13 Geo. III, c. 57, extended the 1770 statute to all the colonies. See *idem.*, pp. 282–5, 308–9; Jack M. Sosin, "Imperial Regulation of Colonial Paper Money, 1764–1773," *PMHB*, LXXXVIII (1964), 194–8; Gipson, *British Empire*, XI, 260–3. BF's earlier comments on the New York act may be found above, XVII, 121, 170–1, 174.

3. BF was actually at West Wycombe visiting Lord Le Despencer, and mail was being forwarded to him there; see BF to WF above, Aug. 3, and Fevre's notes below of Aug. 4 and 5. We have commented earlier on BF's habit, when out of town, of writing to American friends as if from London.

you last Year were not as you supposed from that Mr. Ellis who had been your Governor, but from another of the Name, Author of the enclos'd Pamphlet.[4]

I now send you a few more East India Seeds which I had from another Quarter. I hope some of them may be in a vegetating State and prove of Use. With great Esteem, I am ever, Dear Sir, Your most obedient humble Servant   B F

Noble Wimberley Jones Esqr

From Lewis Fevre[5]   ALS: American Philosophical Society

Honoured Sir,   Craven-Street, August 4, 1773.

By Monday night's Post I sent you two Parcels which contained the Acts relating to America, and five Letters or Parcels that came with the Packet: by last night's Post one Letter; all which I hope you have received. Mr. Oliphant called here this Day, and left with me a Receipt for £800 that Mr. Alexander paid Mess. Brown & Collinson on your Account.[6] Honoured Sir, I am with great Respect, Your Dutiful Servant,   L. FEVRE.

Addressed: To / Dr. Franklin.

4. See the letter to which BF is replying. The most likely pamphlet by John Ellis, given the context, is *Directions for Bringing Over Seeds and Plants, from the East Indies and Other Distant Countries, in a State of Vegetation . . .* (London, 1770).

5. BF's clerk "of French Extraction," for whom see above, XIX, 438. We suspect that he spelled his Christian name Louis, but cannot prove it; in the only two references we have found it is anglicized. He was forwarding mail because BF was visiting Lord Le Despencer; see BF to WF above, Aug 4.

6. This payment is not recorded in BF's Jour. or Ledger. It was unquestionably connected with BF's underwriting William Alexander during the financial crisis of the previous year; see above, XIX, 315–16.

From Charles Jackson[7] ALS: American Philosophical Society

⟨Wednesday, August 4, 1773: An invitation, with apologies for the short notice, to breakfast and dinner tomorrow at Hampstead.⟩

Franklin's Contributions to an Abridgment of the Book of Common Prayer

> Printed in [Baron Le Despencer,] *Abridgement of the Book of Common Prayer, and Administration of the Sacraments, and Other Rites and Ceremonies of the Church, According to the Use of the Church of England: Together with the Psalter, or Psalms of David* . . . (London, 1773), pp. iii–vii and verso of Psalter title page; "Some Heads for a Preface," Dashwood Papers, Bodleian Library; three MS fragments: American Philosophical Society.

Lord Le Despencer, who as Sir Francis Dashwood had acquired notoriety as a rake, devoted himself in later life to more sober occupations. From 1766 until his death in 1781 he was one of the postmasters general; in 1770 he was concerned with a plan for reconciliation with the colonies;[8] and shortly thereafter he became interested in altering the liturgy of the Anglican Church. "Having first reformed himself," in the words of Paul Leicester Ford, he "conceived the idea of reforming the Book of Common Prayer."[9] His method of reform was not to change but to cut: he amended nothing in the familiar order of service; he left out a great deal. By the summer of 1773 he had completed his excisions and drafted a preface to explain why he believed that they were an improvement. At some point, presumably when Franklin visited him at West Wycombe in October, 1772, he showed his work to his guest and asked for suggestions. Franklin

---

7. The comptroller of the Foreign Office in the General Post Office; see above, XIV, 301 n.

8. See above, XVII, 199. The plan, we have since learned, is in the Dashwood Papers on deposit in the Bodleian Library.

9. *Franklin Bibliography. A List of Books Written by, or Relating to Benjamin Franklin* (Brooklyn, N.Y., 1889), p. xxxvii. The quotation expresses a common scholarly attitude toward the Baron's endeavor; for a more thoughtful discussion of his motives, and of the contemporary background of reforming ideas, see Betty Kemp, *Sir Francis Dashwood: an Eighteenth-Century Independent* (New York and London, 1967), pp. 137–46, 154–7.

must have been glad to oblige. He had already turned his hand to amending the Lord's Prayer,[1] and here was a chance to improve the Church's entire liturgy. Le Despencer gave him a free hand: "Doctor Franklyn is desired to add, alter, or diminish as he shall think proper anything herein contained. LLD is by no means tenacious."[2]

But Franklin used this license sparingly. His part in the main work of abridgment, he said years later,[3] was confined to reducing the Catechism to two questions and their answers, and arranging short selections from the Psalms for reading and for singing. The implication of his statement is that the rest of the cutting was done by Le Despencer, and we have no reason to doubt that it was. The preface, the most interesting part of the volume, was the work of both men; but the Baron's rough draft indicates that he was the principal author. The three fragments in Franklin's hand are identical, except for one short passage, with the final printed text. One fragment is what remains, we believe, of a copy he made of the preface in almost its final form; the second contains a paragraph on the Catechism, which was embodied in the preface; the third is an "Advertisement" explaining how the "Singing-Psalms" were to be used. We reproduce the preface as printed, collating it in our annotation with the surviving fragments, and then the Advertisement, which was undoubtedly Franklin's handiwork.

His part in the revision was substantially finished by August 5, 1773; the volume was then in press, and was published in mid-September.[4] Its

1. See above, XV, 299–303. In the abridgment the Lord's Prayer survived uncut. It was too short to be shortened, presumably, and changes were ruled out.

2. The note is at the beginning of Le Despencer's rough draft, "Some Heads for a Preface," MS B 12/2, Dashwood Papers, for access to which we are grateful to Sir Francis Dashwood. The draft includes some of the actual abridgment, and a note on p. 7 makes clear that BF was provided with a Prayer Book in which the proposed deletions were marked, so that he had ample time to consider them.

3. To Granville Sharp in 1785: Smyth, *Writings*, IX, 358–9.

4. See the notes from Fevre and Mrs. Stevenson that immediately follow this document, and the *London Chron.*, Sept. 14–16, 1773. It has often been said that the book was printed on Le Despencer's private press at West Wycombe; see for example Kemp, *op. cit.*, p. 137. But those notes strongly indicate a London printer; and in the letter to Sharp, just cited, BF said that "the book was printed for Wilkie, in St. Paul's Church Yard." Whoever did the work was slovenly: in addition to the usual errata, part of Morning Prayer was omitted; in the Yale copy BF's extracts from the versified psalms are wildly jumbled, and in the middle of them appear two canceling leaves from Morning and Evening Prayer.

appearance aroused little interest. Some copies were given away, he remarked later, and very few sold. Most became waste paper. "In the Prayers," he concluded philosophically, "so much was retrench'd that Approbation would hardly be expected...."[5] But this was only part of the reason. The Prayer Book has proved to be resistant to change even in periods of spiritual turmoil, and in the 1770's the "fat slumbers of the Church," in Gibbon's phrase, were not yet disturbed by the twitching of reform. Even if they had been, the proposed abridgment did much more, despite the assertions of the preface, than "retrench" through eliminating superfluities. The process of condensing amounted for the orthodox to evisceration, because it struck at the core of doctrine: the Holy Ghost virtually disappeared from the Trinity, and the mediating role of Christ was reduced almost to the vanishing point. Such innovations could not be expected to impress the faithful. The God of their tradition, a far remove from the simplified deity of the abridgment, proved to be immune to simplifying.

PREFACE
[Before August 5, 1773]

The Editor of the following Abridgement of the Liturgy of the Church of England thinks it but decent and respectful to all, (more particularly to the reverend body of Clergy who adorn the Protestant Religion by their good works, preaching, and example) that he should humbly offer some reasons for such an undertaking. He addresses himself to the serious and discerning. He professes himself to be a Protestant of the Church of England, and holds in the highest veneration the doctrines of Jesus Christ. He is a

5. From the letter to Sharp cited above. BF gave a presentation copy of the book to Mrs. Christopher Baldwin, the wife of his old friend on Clapham Common. "She is not a little proud of ... your Liturgy," her husband wrote him years later, "which is her constant Sundays entertainment." Dec. 18, 1778, APS; see also Alexander Small to BF, June, 1786, APS. Her copy, though it has since disappeared, lives on in another form. It came into the hands of the Rev. Michael Lort, the noted antiquary, who in 1783 lent it as a curiosity to Shute Barrington, the newly installed Bishop of Salisbury. Barrington was enough interested to enter the deletions in a 1745 Prayer Book of his own, and to make a number of notes. This volume eventually found its way to an American owner, who mistakenly believed that he possessed the copy that BF had used for the abridgment and given to Mrs. Baldwin. *PMHB*, XXI (1897), 502. The Bishop's Prayer Book is now in the APS library, and his notes explain its early history.

sincere lover of social worship, deeply sensible of its usefulness to society; and he aims at doing some service to religion, by proposing such abbreviations and omissions in the forms of our Liturgy (retaining every thing he thinks essential) as might, if adopted, procure a more general attendance. For, besides the differing sentiments of many pious and well-disposed persons in some speculative points, who in general have a good opinion of our Church, it has often been observed and complained of, that the Morning and Evening Service, as practised in the Churches of England and elsewhere, are so long, and filled with so many repetitions, that the continued attention suitable to so serious a duty becomes impracticable, the mind wanders, and the fervency of devotion is slackened. Also the propriety of saying the same prayer more than once in the same service is doubted, as the service is thereby lengthened without apparent necessity; our Lord having given us a short prayer as an example, and censured the Heathen for thinking to be heard because of much speaking.[6] Moreover, many pious and devout Persons, whose age or infirmities will not suffer them to remain for hours in a cold church, especially in the winter season, are obliged to forego the comfort and edification they would receive by their attendance on divine service. These, by shortening the time, would be relieved: and the younger sort, who have had some principles of religion instilled into them, and who have been educated in a belief of the necessity of adoring their Maker, would probably more frequently, as well as cheerfully, attend divine service, if they were not detained so long at any one time. Also many well-disposed tradesmen, shopkeepers, artificers, and others, whose habitations are not remote from churches, could, and would (more frequently at least) find time[7] to attend divine service on other than Sundays, if the prayers were reduced into a much narrower compass. Formerly there were three services performed at different times of the day, which three services are now usually joined in one. This may suit the conveniency of the person who officiates, but is too often inconvenient and tiresome to the congregation. If this Abridgement, therefore, should ever meet with acceptance, the well-

6. Matthew 6:7.
7. The fragment of the preface in BF's hand begins here.

disposed Clergy, who are laudably desirous to encourage the *frequency* of divine service, may promote so great and good a purpose, by repeating it three times on a Sunday, without so much fatigue to themselves as at present. Suppose, at Nine o'clock, at Eleven, and at One in the Evening; and by preaching no more sermons than usual, of a moderate length; and thereby accommodate a greater number of people with convenient hours.

These were general reasons for wishing and proposing an Abridgement. In attempting it we[8] do not presume to dictate even to a single Christian: we are sensible there is a proper authority in the rulers of the Church for ordering such matters; and whenever the time shall come when it may be thought not unseasonable to revise our Liturgy, there is no doubt but every suitable improvement will be made, under the care and direction of so much learning, wisdom, and piety, in one body of men collected. Such a work as this must then be much better executed. In the mean time, this humble performance may serve to shew the practicability of shortening the service near one half, without the omission of what is essentially necessary: and we hope, moreover, that the book may be occasionally of some use to families, or private assemblies of Christians.

To give now some account of particulars. We have presumed upon this plan of Abridgement to omit the First Lesson, which is taken from the Old Testament, and retain only the Second from the New Testament; which, we apprehend, is more suitable to teach the so-much-to-be-revered doctrine of Christ, and of more immediate importance to Christians; altho' the Old Testament is allowed by all to be an accurate and concise history, and, as such, may more properly be read at home.[1]

We do not conceive it necessary for Christians to make use of

8. The shift from the third person singular, used hitherto, may indicate that BF revised the remainder of the preface.

1. This is the only passage where the wording differs substantially from BF's fragment, which reads as follows: "We have presumed upon this plan of Abridgement to leave out the first Lesson. The Old Testament is allowed by all the Sects of Christianity, to be an accurate and concise History and as such may be read at home; but we apprehend the New Testament is sufficient, and more suitable to teach the so much to be revered Doctrine of Christ, and of more immediate Importance to Christians." Le Despencer's initial reference to the Old Testament was more supercilious than in either BF's or the final

more than one creed. Therefore in this Abridgement are omitted the Nicene Creed, and that of St. Athanasius. Of the Apostles' Creed we have retained the parts that are most intelligible, and most essential.[2] And as the *Father*, *Son*, and *Holy Ghost*, are there confessedly and avowedly a part of the Belief, it does not appear necessary, after so solemn a confession, to repeat again in the Litany, the *Son* and *Holy Ghost*, as that part of the Service is otherwise very prolix.

The Psalms, being a collection of Odes, written by different persons, it hath happened that many of them are on the same subject, and repeat the same sentiments; such as those that complain of enemies and persecutors, call upon God for protection, express a confidence therein, and thank him for it when afforded. A very great part of the book consists of repetitions of this kind, which may therefore well bear abridgement. Other parts are merely historical, repeating the mention of facts more fully narrated in the preceding books, and which, relating to the ancestors of the Jews, were more interesting to them than to us. Other parts are *local*, and allude to places of which we have no knowledge, and therefore do not affect us. Others are *personal*, relating to the particular circumstances of David or Solomon, as kings; and can therefore seldom be rehearsed with any propriety by private Christians. Others imprecate, in the most bitter terms, the vengeance of God on our Adversaries, contrary to the spirit of Christianity, which commands us to love our enemies, and to pray for those that hate us, and despitefully use us. For these reasons it is to be wished, that the same liberty were, by the governors of our Church, allowed to the minister with regard to the *reading Psalms*, as is taken by the clerk, with regard to those that are to be sung, in directing the parts that he may judge most

---

version: "It is a Jewish book very curious," he wrote in his draft, "perhaps more fit for the perusal of the learned than suited to the capacitys of the general illiterate part of Mankind."

2. Two of the many parts that were considered unintelligible or unessential were the Crucifixion and the Resurrection. The Creed after pruning read:

"I believe in God the Father Almighty, Maker of Heaven and Earth: And in Jesus Christ his Son, our Lord. I believe in the Holy Ghost; The Forgiveness of Sins; and the Life Everlasting. Amen."

348

suitable to be read at the time, from the present circumstances of the congregation, or the tenor of his sermon, by saying, Let us *read* such and such parts of the Psalms named. Until this is done, our Abridgement, it is hoped, will be found to contain what may be most generally proper to be joined in by an assembly of Christian people. The Psalms are still apportioned to the days of the month, as heretofore, though the several parts for each day are generally a full third shorter.[3]

We humbly suppose the same service contained in this Abridgement might properly serve for all the Saints Days, Fasts, and Feasts, reading only the Epistle and Gospel appropriated to each day of the month.

The Communion is greatly abridged, on account of its great length; nevertheless, it is hoped and believed, that all those parts are retained which are material and necessary.[4]

3. Le Despencer's marginal note in his draft, "Doctr. Franklyns remark on the Psalms to be here inserted," indicates that BF was the principal author of this long paragraph. Much of it is incomprehensible without some familiarity with the part of the Prayer Book that BF was abridging, and the ways in which that part was customarily used. The Psalms were printed in full after the Commination, divided into roughly equal parts for each day of the month; at the end of the volume they reappeared, with a separate title page, in the old metrical version of Sternhold and Hopkins designed for singing. The minister was limited to a reading of the Psalms appointed for the day. His lay assistant, the parish clerk, selected metrical Psalms to replace canticles or to be inserted where hymns are now used; he sang each line, and the congregation repeated it. BF retained in his abridgment the familiar format of two sets of Psalms. He drastically cut, as he says, those intended to be read, but retained some part of each. He excluded more than half of those intended to be sung, and made brief extracts from the others, drawn not from Sternhold and Hopkins but from the later arrangement by Nicholas Brady and Nahum Tate, and collected into a tiny psalter with a title page of its own, on the verso of which appears the Advertisement printed below.

4. The orthodox would not have agreed. The excisions in the Communion service indicate, perhaps more clearly than any others in the book, the way in which the abridgment affected doctrine. In the words of administration, spoken by the celebrant when offering the bread and wine, the old Elizabethan formula that was, and is still, in use embodied two ideas, that Christ is present in the consecrated elements and that the Eucharist commemorates His death. The abridgment put sole emphasis on commemoration: "Take and eat this, in remembrance that Christ died, and feed on him in thy heart with thanksgiving. Drink this, in remembrance that Christ's Blood was shed, and be thankful."

Infant Baptism in Churches being performed during divine service, would greatly add to the length of that service, if it were not abridged. We have ventured, therefore, to leave out the less material parts.[5]

The Catechism, as a compendium of systematic theology, which learned divines have written folio volumes to explain, and which therefore, it may be presumed, they thought scarce intelligible without such expositions; is, perhaps, taken altogether, not so well adapted to the capacities of children as might be wished. Only those plain answers, therefore, which express our duty towards God, and our duty towards our neighbour, are retained here.[6] The rest is recommended to their reading and serious consideration, when more years shall have ripened their understanding.

The Confirmation is here shortened.

The Commination, and all cursing of mankind, is (we think) best omitted in this Abridgement.

The form of solemnization of Matrimony is often abbreviated by the officiating Minister, at his discretion. We have selected what appear to us the material parts, and which, we humbly hope, will be deemed sufficient.

The long prayers in the service for the Visitation of the Sick, seem not so proper when the afflicted person is very weak, and in distress.

The Order for the Burial of the Dead is very solemn and moving; nevertheless, to preserve the health and lives of the living, it appeared to us that this service ought particularly to be shortened. For numbers, standing in the open air with their hats off, often in tempestuous weather, during the celebration, it's great length is not only inconvenient, but may be dangerous to the attendants. We hope, therefore, that our Abridgement of it will be approved by the Rational and Prudent.

The Thanksgiving of Women, after Child-birth being, when

5. The fragment of the preface in BF's hand ends here.
6. Actually the section on the Lord's Prayer was also retained. BF's copy of this paragraph, the second MS fragment of his, is headed "A Note under the first Page of the Catechism"; he and the Baron must have decided later to embody it in the preface.

read, part of the Service of the day, we have also, in some measure, abridged that.

Having thus stated very briefly our motives and reasons, and our manner of proceeding in the prosecution of this work, we hope to be believed, when we declare the rectitude of our intentions. We mean not to lessen or prevent the Practice of Religion, but to honour and promote it. We acknowledge the excellency of our present Liturgy; and, though we have shortened it, we have not presumed to alter a word in the remaining Text; not even to substitute *who* for *which* in the Lord's Prayer, and elsewhere, altho' it would be more correct. We respect the characters of bishops, and other dignitaries of our Church; and with regard to the inferior clergy, we wish that they were more equally provided for, than by that odious and vexatious, as well as unjust method, of gathering tythes in kind, which creates animosities and litigations, to the interruption of the good harmony and respect which might otherwise subsist between the rectors and their parishioners.

And thus, conscious of upright meaning, we submit this Abridgement to the serious consideration of the prudent and dispassionate, and not to enthusiasts and bigots; being convinced in our own breasts, that this shortened method, or one of the same kind better executed, would further religion, increase unanimity, and occasion a more frequent attendance on the worship of God.

ADVERTISEMENT,
relating to the Choice of proper Psalms.

In the following Extracts from the *Singing Psalms*, we have been governed by the same Considerations as in the Abridgement of the *Reading Psalms*; which Considerations appear at large in the Preface.

And for the more easy finding such Portions of the Psalms as may be best suited to the present State of Mind and Circumstances of those who use them, we have arranged them under the following Heads; *viz.*

1. When disposed to impress the Mind with a Sense of God's

Omnipresence, Justice, and *Power,* use such Parts as you may find convenient of Extract I. which are from Psalms 11, and 39.[7]

2. In *Confession* of Sin, and expressing *Repentance,* use Parts of Psalm 51, or 90, to be found in Extract II.

3. In resolving *Amendment of Life,* use Part of Psalm 119, from Extract III.

4. For *Encouragement* in *Virtue* and *Piety,* use Parts of Psalm 1, 15, 24, 32, 34, 41, 112, 127,[8] 133, as found in Extract IV.

5. When disposed to *Prayer,* for yourself, the King, or the People, you may find what is proper in Extract V. from Psalm 19, 25, 51, 54, 67, 86, 143.

6. For expressing *Confidence in God,* his Power and Goodness, use Parts of Extract VI. from Psalm 4, 18, 23, 27, 34, 37, 46, 62, 91, 130, 146.

7. When under *Dejection of Spirit,* in *Distress,* or *Affliction,* you may find something suitable in Extract VII. from Psalms 6, 13, 22, 31, 44, 56, 69, 109.

8. In Times of *Publick Distress* from *Enemies,* see in Extract VIII. from Psalms 60, 123.

9. In Times of *Success,* Extract IX. from Psalms 9, 34.

10. When disposed to *Praise* and *Thanksgiving,* use Parts of Extract X. from Psalms 8, 19, 30, 65, 89, 92, 93, 95, 100, 103, 104, 106, 107, 111, 113, 116, 117, 136, 138, 145, 147, 149, 150.

11. When longing for a better World, and desirous to see God, use Extract XI. from Psalms 39, 42, 63, 84.

We trust the pious Christian will find some Convenience in this Selection of the Psalms, and in our Arrangement of the Parts selected.[9]

7. So in BF's draft, the third MS fragment of his, and in the printed text. The psalm in the extract is 139.

8. The extract included as well some verses from Psalm 128.

9. Bishop Barrington, in the 1745 Prayer Book described above, made the following comment: "Instead of the old version of Hopkins and Sternhold Dr. Franklyn proposes extracts from Tate's and Brady's version, under 11 heads, according to the state of mind and circumstances of the persons who use them. This appears to me a more judicious mode than leaving the whole to the choice of an Ignorant Parish Clerk."

From Lewis Fevre ALS: American Philosophical Society

Honoured Sir,   Craven-Street, August 5, 1773.

Mr. Hay desires to be informed, as soon as possible, if there are to be any Additions to the Psalms, as they have but six Pages more to do, to finish the whole.[1]

This Day Dr. Sheppherd, accompanied by Professor Allamand, called; The latter Gentleman desired me to acquaint you that he should stay three weeks in Town, and that Count Bentwick was arrived.[2] I am, Honoured Sir, with great Respect Your Dutiful Servant,   L. FEVRE.

P.S. By last night's Post I sent you two Letters; The one inclosed here, from Mr. Temple, came last night, but too late for the post, as it was past eleven when the Servant brought it.[3]

Addressed: To / Benjamin Franklin, Esq;

From Margaret Stevenson   ALS: American Philosophical Society

Dear Sir,   Thursday Augt 5 [1773]

I am much obliged, with your kind inquires, the Cheldren I thanke God, ar All weell and your D and your Lady B— hom i Dinde with a Tusday and Dannke your health, all ar well at

---

1. Hay, whoever he was, came from the printer who was completing Le Despencer's revised version of the Prayer Book, to which BF had contributed; see the preceding document.

2. Jean Allamand was a professor at the University of Leyden, and Count Bentinck was an Anglo-Dutch aristocrat who was a prominent figure in the States General; both were old acquaintances of BF. See above, respectively, XVIII, 106 n; IX, 367 n. Their companion was Antony Shepherd (1721–96), F.R.S., Plumian Professor of Astronomy at Cambridge. *DNB.*

3. The conjecture is tempting, but implausible, that the writer was John Temple. If he was involved with the Hutchinson letters, he had good cause to get in touch with BF; for news that they had been published in Boston had just arrived, and rumors were rife of how they had been obtained: *London Chron.*, July 29–31, Aug. 3–5, 1773. We are virtually convinced, however, that the letter was from WTF. After spending his vacation with his grandfather he had just returned to school: BF to WF above, Aug. 3.

Ewell.[4] I am verey well But do not expect to Continu so Long; for I have lifed opon Benns [Beans] and Backon for ten days. I have noe News, Mr. Faver has Bin to the Printers as orderd; he is writing[5] and as you request a line from me I have no grater Pleasuer, Dear Sir, then when I can oblige my Beast frinde. I shall be glad to see you come home well, which is the Sincerr wish of your fathfull Servant   MARGT STEVENSON

Addressed: Doct. Franklin

To Giambatista Beccaria[6]

Retranslated[7] from the Italian in Giuseppe A. G. S. Eandi, *Memorie istoriche intorno gli studi del padre Giambatista Beccaria* ... ([Turin,] 1783), pp. 149–50.

Dear and Reverend Sir: London 11 August 1773.

I embrace this opportunity to greet you through Signor Fromond, your most ingenious fellow countryman,[8] and to let you know that, because my ongoing commitment to various affairs precludes my doing further research in our favorite science, I believed that I could not better foster it among the English than by procuring a translation into our language of your latest,

4. Our reading of Mrs. Stevenson's scrawl, though open to doubt, is plausible. The children on whom she was reporting were her grandsons, William Hewson and his four-month-old brother Thomas. Ewell is a village south of London and not far from Streatham, where Walter Blunt had his home; if the house was between the two villages, either might have served for address. In any case Mrs. Stevenson had "Dinde" with Dorothea Blunt and Mary ("Lady") Barwell, for whom see above, XVII, 194 n.

5. Fevre's note is the preceding document.

6. For the distinguished professor of physics at Turin see above, V, 395 n and subsequent volumes.

7. We are indebted to Robert Lopez, Sterling Professor of History at Yale, for assistance in our retranslation. It differs slightly in wording but not in substance from that in Smyth, *Writings*, VI, 112.

8. Gian Francesco Fromond was a young Lombard scientist who had been visiting England as part of a European tour. Father Boscovich is said to have introduced him to BF, and this letter in turn introduced him to Beccaria. Fromond was subsequently put in charge of the Lombard physics laboratories. Antonio Pace, *Benjamin Franklin and Italy* (APS *Memoirs*, XLVII; Philadelphia, 1958), p. 36.

excellent book. This is now completed, with the help of some friends who contributed to the cost, and ready for the press.[9] May I ask you to have five hundred copies of the illustrations reproduced from your copper [plates] and sent to me to be used for the projected edition? They might come by sea from Nice, and be addressed to your Envoy Extraordinary, who will be good enough to permit it.[1] I will promptly pay, according to your direction, any charges for paper, printing, shipping, etc. If this can be done, it will save us the expense of engraving. I remain always with the greatest esteem, dear Sir, your most obedient [and] most humble servant, B. FRANKLIN.

Two Letters from Giambatista Beccaria

Incomplete drafts: American Philosophical Society

These letters were drafted in reply to Franklin's of August 11, the preceding document, and were completed at some time between receipt of that letter and early March, 1774.[2] Whether Beccaria sent them in

9. BF had put the translation of Beccaria's *Elettricismo artificiale*... [Turin, 1772] into the hands of Jean-Louis de Lolme (1741–1804), a Genevan who had been forced into exile in England in 1768, and who became well known in political circles through his *Constitution de l'Angleterre*... (Amsterdam, 1771). He had to support himself by his pen. In April, August, and October of 1773 BF paid him a total of £57 15s. for the translation, money collected by John Nourse, the bookseller who was publishing the volume, from the friends BF mentions. De Lolme later spoke of having visited BF in Craven Street some months before the latter's departure for America. Jour., pp. 47, 50–2; *The Constitution of England*... (4th ed., London, 1784), p. 525 n.

1. The engravings from *Elettricismo artificiale* were consigned to Filippo Ottone Ponte, Count of Scarnifiggi, an old pupil of Beccaria at Turin and later, as Sardinian Minister to Paris after 1777, a close observer of BF's mission. *The Royal Kalendar*... (London, 1772), p. 100; Pace, *op. cit.*, chap. v, *passim*. Scarnifiggi had left London by the time the engravings arrived (BF to Beccaria below, March 20, 1774), but his successor must have delivered them, for they were duly used in the English edition: *A Treatise upon Artificial Electricity*... (London, 1776). The volume was not published until the autumn of that year: *Public Advertiser*, Oct. 23, 1776.

2. In his reply below, March 20, 1774, BF acknowledged receipt of what appear to have been these two letters. Pace discusses the drafts (*op. cit.*, pp. 59–60, 328) and prints one of them (pp. 376–8); we tend to disagree with him on which was the earlier letter.

355

draft is not clear, but only the drafts survive; and they pose an editorial problem. His earlier letters to Franklin, which have been variously handled in preceding volumes, were by comparison finished productions and yet, as the editors' comments indicate, were far from clear.[3] The Italian's convoluted prose is hard to follow even at its best, and electrical disquisitions, as contemporaries complained, turn it into virtually a language of its own.[4] A literal translation would be gibberish. A free one is dangerous, even when supplemented by the original text; but we can see no alternative to an English rendering that takes liberty with the Italian in order to convey what we believe Beccaria meant. If we are sometimes mistaken, despite expert assistance,[5] we share the blame with the author.

Chiarissimo, e onoratissimo Signore Padrone mio singolarissimo,
   Il Signor Fremond mi ha addimandato a vostro nome, se io avea il *Tentamen* di Epino. Io ho primamente ricevuto tale Libro dal Sig. Sausseure Filosofo genevrino nel 1772, quando stava stampando L'ultimo Libro; nè allora Lo lessi, perchè io era occupatissimo, e mi fidava dell'istoria del Sig. Priestley; solamente giunto a stampare il num. 453 del libro, ovè tratto del esperienza di Richman intorno a'fili annessi ad una Lastra, La cercai in Epino; e fui sorpresso di trovarla in Epino più complicata, che non è in Priestley, per quanto mi parve allora; che fra le altre cose non intesi, che Epino per la parola catena intendea la communicazione di una faccia della Lastra col suolo.
   Ora solo La dimanda del Sig. Fremond mi ha eccitata curiosità

---

3. See above, VII, 300–15; XIII, 450–3; XIV, 41–57; XVIII, 108–10.
   4. He is long-winded and repetitive, said a reviewer of *Elettricismo artificiale*... [Turin, 1772], and his language "is often obscure, and without the plates would be unintelligible ... from the variety of words and phrases which he has been obliged to adapt, and sometimes to invent, for the explanation of the different phenomena of this new science." *Monthly Rev.*, XLVII (1772), 554. A decade later Dr. Ingenhousz characterized Beccaria's style as "dark, diffuse, and perplexed," calculated to "vex and tire the readers mind, without clearing up the difficulty"; those who extolled his works "had in reality not had the courage to get thro them." To BF, Aug. 15, 1783; APS.
   5. From Professor Robert Lopez, who provided us with literal translations, and from Professor Antonio Pace, who gave us generous and much appreciated advice on our freer renderings. Although neither is responsible for the results, we are deeply indebted to both.

sicchè ho disgiunto le carte del libro di Epino, e lo ho scorso; e universalmente vi ho trovato molto ingegno, e la sorgente vi ho divisata dell' Ipotesi Geometrica coltivata poi, e migliorata di molto dal Sig. Cavendisch. La chiamo Ipotesi geometrica, perchè a me pare, che non adegui i fenomeni fisici, e che da essi prescinda almanco in parte sollecita unicamente di misurare.

Considerata poi più attentamente la esperienza del Richman, trovo che essa non differisce dalla mia, sè non perchè in quella l'atmosfera della faccia caricata non si dovea estendere alla faccia opposta della Lastra. Epperò io stimerei bene di aggiungere La seguente nota alla parola *imperfettissima* del sopradetto num: 453.

"Considerata meglio questa sperienza, vedo, che a me riesce più complicata, perchè l'atmosfera della faccia caricata si estende alla faccia opposta della lastra; che la mia posta talle circostanza è vera; e che tolta tale circostanza, è anche vera quella del Richman.

"Annetto alla stremità del conduttore l'uncino A d'una boccia ABCDE di lunghissimo collo (Tav. VI; fig. 5); che cosi niuna estrania atmosfera si estende alla pancia della boccia. Poi annetto un elettroscopio al conduttore, che vale il filo annesso da Richman alla faccia caricata della Lamina, e ne annetto un altro all' armatura esteriore della boccia, che vale il filo annesso da richman alla faccia opposta.

"Allora impugnando io La pancia della boccia, e caricandola vedo, che insorge e cresce la divergenza per eccesso dell'elettroscopio annesso al conduttore *per l'eccesso, che ringorga dalla faccia interna della boccia.* Nè in tanto si move punto l'elettroscopio annesso alla pancia della boccia, *perchè e comunica col suolo, e ad esso non si estende niuna estrania atmosfera.*

"Compita la carica, e intralasciato lo stropicciamento del vetro, assai rapidamente insorge la divergenza dell' elettroscopio annesso alla boccia e scema la divergenza dell' elettroscopio annesso al conduttore; e sì le due divergenze mirano all'egualità. *Perchè tolta la forza attuante La carica, le elettricità contrarie scemano, e mirano all'egualità con forza proporzionata alla carica indotta; epperò scagliando del fuoco suo l'interna faccia della boccia, e sì spingendone via il fuoco del conduttore scema la divergenza dell' elettroscopio di questo; E traendo del fuoco da ogni parte la faccia esterna, epperò anche dall'elettroscopio annesso, insorge in questo la divergenza.*

"Che poi abbandonando a se la boccia le due divergenze scemando restino equali, *ciò avviene conformemente alla equalità, a cui mirano le due contrarie elettricità.*

"Che toccando alternativamente le pancia della boccia, e il conduttore, alternativamente si abbatta, e insorga (o anche cresca) la divergenza degli elettroscopii, *ciò si è spiegato trattando della scarica per alternazione.*"

Questa nota, io dicea, mi pare conveniente; ma poi mi pare affatto necessario il cambiamento del penultimo num: 992 del libro, il quale principia: *del che la ragione elle è.* Bisogna che io vaneggiassi quando lo ho scritto; tanto lo trovo scipito. Ecco come mi pare, che debba essere.

992. [*In the margin:* numeri da sostituirsi] Ed io opino, che questa particolarità della elettricità vindice negativa della Lastra sola si dicchiari con la seguente considerazione: Che la superiorità, cui abbia la elettricità in una faccia del corpo isolante sopra la elettricità della faccia opposta, ha efficacia a far comparire la omologa in essa faccia opposta (quella superiorità dico ha questa efficacia) proporzionata alla grandezza sua direttamente, e alla carica attuale del corpo inversamente.

Appicco un elettroscopio al conduttore, e uno all'armatura esteriore d'una boccia di lunghissimo collo (Tav: VI, fig. 5.) sicchè l'atmosfera del conduttore non giunga a disturbare l'elettroscopio della boccia; e trovo, che, se stropiccio per pochi momenti il vetro lasciando isolata la boccia, ciò basta perchè l'elettroscopio della boccia acquisti una grande divergenza per eccesso, e la ritenga lungamente. *Perchè la carica è nulla, e la superiorita dell'eccesso interiore è grande.*

Ma se seguo a stropicciare il vetro, e vo eccitando delle scintille dall' armatura esteriore della boccia, in verità l'elettroscopio segue a ripigliare alcuna divergenza per eccesso, ma la ripiglia ognora minore, e ognora meno rapidamente. *Perchè la carica diviene ognora maggiore, e la superiorità, cui ha il totale eccesso interno sopra il totale difetto esterno è ognora minore.*

Se repplico la sperienza; ma dopo l'eccitamento di ogni scintilla intralascio di stropicciare, la divergenza per eccesso si volge, in tale intervallo, in divergenza per diffetto tanto maggiore, e tanto più presto, quanto è maggiore il numero delle scintille già estratte; vale a dire quanto è maggiore la carica già indotta, e quanto resta minore la superiorità dell'eccesso interiore sopra il totale esteriore difetto.

Le cose consentanee accadono nella elettricità vindice universalmente. Quando disgiungo le due lastre ABab, MNmn (tav: XI, fig. 4) di fresco scaricate, allora nella faccia esteriore di ciascuna appare molto vivace e molto durevole la elettricità omologa a quella, cui per la elettricità vindice positiva ripiglia la faccia interiore. I *Perchè le due lastre appunto sono scaricate;* II *E perchè le facce interiori ripigliano elettricità molto vivaci, cospirando l'eccesso insorgente in MN ad avvalorare il difetto insorgente in ab; e reciprocamente.*

Quando ignudo una faccia della lastra sola ABab (Tav: XI, fig, 1.) similmente scaricata di fresco,

TRANSLATION

[After Aug. 11, 1773]

Most illustrious and honored Sir, my most particular Master

Signor Fromond asked me from you whether I had Aepinus' *Tentamen.* I received the book from Signor Saussure, the Genevan philosopher, in 1772 when I was publishing my latest work; and, because I was extremely busy then, I did not read it but relied upon Signor Priestley's history. Only when I came to paragraph 453 of my book, where I discuss Richmann's experiment with the wires attached to a plate, did I look for it in Aepinus;[6] where I was surprised to find it more complicated, it seemed to me at the time, than in Priestley, because among other things I did not understand that Aepinus meant by "chain" the connection between one face of the plate and the ground.

Only now has Signor Fromond's question roused my curiosity, so that I have opened the pages of Aepinus' work and gone through it. And I have in general found great talent in it, and

6. For Fromond see BF's letter above of Aug. 11, and for de Saussure XIX, 324 n. Aepinus (above, VIII, 393 n) had published his *Tentamen theoriae electritatis et magnetismi* in St. Petersburg in 1759. Beccaria's latest work, *Elettricismo artificiale,* to which the paragraph number refers, was an expansion of his earlier *Dell' elettricismo artificiale, e naturale* . . . (Turin, 1753). The experiment of Georg Richmann, the Swedish scientist, is described in Priestley, *History,* pp. 337–8.

recognized there the source of the geometric hypothesis that Mr. Cavendish later developed and greatly improved. I call it geometric hypothesis because it is solely concerned with measurement and does not, in my opinion, take physical phenomena into account but to a large degree disregards them.[7]

When I later considered Richmann's experiment more carefully, I discovered that it differed from mine only in that the atmosphere of the charged face did not extend to the opposite face of the plate. Hence I should think that the following note might usefully be appended to the words *most imperfect*[8] in the aforementioned paragraph 453:

"A closer look at that experiment shows me that mine is more complicated, because the atmosphere of the charged face extends to the opposite face of the plate. Given that condition, mine is valid; without that condition, Richmann's is also valid.

"I connect the hook, A, of a bottle with a very long neck, ABCDE, to the end of the conductor (Plate VI, fig. 5) so that no extraneous atmosphere reaches the interior of the bottle. Then I connect the conductor to an electroscope, which corresponds to the wire Richmann attached to the charged face of the plate, and the outer surface of the bottle to another electroscope, which corresponds to the wire Richmann attached to the opposite face.

"Afterward, as I hold and charge the body of the bottle, I observe that the electroscope connected with the conductor diverges increasingly *because of the surplus that flows from the internal surface of the bottle*. Meanwhile the electroscope connected with the outer surface does not move at all, *both because it communicates with the ground and because no extraneous atmosphere reaches it*.

"Once the charging is done and the rubbing discontinued, the divergence of the electroscope connected with the bottle rises

---

7. For Cavendish's paper in 1771, which consisted of a series of mathematical propositions and corollaries, see above, XIII, 544 n and Arthur J. Berry, *Henry Cavendish: His Life and Scientific Work* ([London, etc., 1960]), pp. 92–5.

8. Aepinus' account of Richmann's experiment, Beccaria had written, "è per lo manco imperfettisima." The statement was omitted in the translation that was the subject of BF's letter and of this reply. So was the note that follows and the emendation of Paragraph 992 below, both of which refer to the plates in *Elettricismo artificiale*.

extremely fast, and that of the electroscope connected with the conductor diminishes, so that the two tend to equalize. *For, once the force producing the charge is removed, the contrary electricities diminish and tend to equalize, with a force commensurate with the induced charge. As the inner face of the bottle projects some of its fire and repels that of the conductor, therefore, the divergence of the latter's electroscope decreases; and as the outer face loses fire, including that of the connected electroscope, the divergence in the latter rises.*

"When the bottle is left to itself the two divergences diminish to the equality *to which the two contrary electricities tend.*

"Touching the body of the bottle and the conductor in alternation decreases and increases the divergence of the electroscopes. *This has been explained in discussing the discharge by alternation.*"

This note, as I said, seems to me appropriate. But then a change is needed, in my opinion, in the next to last paragraph, 992, which begins "The reason for this is." I must have been out of my mind when I wrote it, so senseless does it appear to me. Here is how I think it ought to read:

"992. And this peculiarity of the plate's negative vindicating electricity[9] is, I believe, explained by the following consideration: that the imbalance between the electricity on one face of the insulating body and that on the other face has the effect (I mean the imbalance has this effect) of producing a correspondence in that other face that is directly proportionate to the amount [of the imbalance] and inversely proportionate to the body's actual charge.

"I connect an electroscope with the conductor and another with the outer surface of a bottle with a very long neck (Plate VI, fig. 5), so that the conductor's atmosphere does not disturb the bottle's electroscope. If I rub the glass for a moment, leaving the bottle insulated, this is enough to give the bottle's electroscope a large divergence by surplus, which it retains a long time. *For there is no charge, and the internal surplus is great.*

"But, if I go on rubbing the glass and exciting sparks from the

9. Beccaria's long emendation is marked in the margin, "numeri da sostituirsi," or paragraphs that should be substituted; he presumably intended to combine them in a single numbered paragraph. For "vindicating electricity" see above, XIV, 49–57, and Beccaria, *A Treatise upon Artificial Electricity . . .* (London, 1776), pp. 393–419.

bottle's exernal surface, the electroscope continues to pick up some divergence by surplus, but less and less of it and more and more slowly. *For the charge keeps growing, and the imbalance between the total inner surplus and the total outer deficiency grows steadily less.*

"If I repeat the experiment but stop rubbing after I have excited each spark, in the intervals [between them] the divergence by surplus becomes divergence by deficiency, at a speed depending on the size and frequency of the sparks obtained, in other words on the size of the induced charge and the degree of imbalance between the inner surplus and the outer deficiency.

"Corresponding phenomena invariably occur in vindicating electricity. When I disconnect the two freshly discharged plates ABab, MNmn (Plate XI, fig. 4), the electricity on the outer face of each, corresponding to the positive vindicating electricity that the inner face acquires, appears very lively and enduring (1) *because the two plates are discharged and* (2) *because the inner faces acquire very lively electricities as the increasing surplus in MN stimulates the rising deficiency in ab and vice versa.*

"When I uncover a single surface of the ABab plate (Plate XI, fig. 1), likewise freshly discharged [*remainder missing*]."

Chiarissimo, e Onoratissimo Signore, Padrone mio singolare,

Dopo che mi avete fatto addimandare di Epino, io Lo ho riletto anche la seconda volta, e oltre all'avervi inteso, come già vi ho scritto, Lo sperimento di Richman, ho notato particolarmente.

I. Che Epino conoscea, che non v'ha movimento tra' corpi uno elettrizzato L'altro no. Epperò tocca ad Epino questa determinazione, cui io attribuiva a me ne' fogli dell'atmosfera elettrica.

II. Che Epino ha addotto alcuno sperimento dell'Elettricità vindice; v[erbi] g[ratia] di stropicciare una contro L'altra due Lastre guernite di manico isolatore, le quali congiunte non segnano niuna elettricità, disgiunte segnano elettricità contrarie. Probabilmente questa sperienza Epino La ha tratta dalla sperienza di Pekino, cui ho addotta nelle sperienze dell'elettricità vindice.

III. Mi è poi piaciuta singolarmente La teoria magnetica Epiniana massime intorno al punto, che il magnetismo s'induce confacentemente alla posizione, cui hanno al sistema magnetico terrestre i corpi, che ne sono capaci. Il magnetismo indotto colla scintilla vi consente.

Universalmente poi l'opera di Epino mi è paruta molto degna. Ma la memoria del Sigr. Cawendisk mi pare superiore massime nel ridurre il valore dell'azione elettrica alla ragione inversa de'quadrati delle distanze molto prossimamente, e nel ridure conseguentemente le elettricità alle facce de' corpi.

Ma sinceramente, come io ho già scritto, non so arrestarmi nella pura attrazione e ripulsione nella parte, che risguarda i fenomeni elettrici derivativi. Il vedere l'atmosfera elettrica, che dalla faccia sovrana del vostro quadro si va grado grado estendendo, e si ripiega sotto a' margini nudi, e successivamente ne va occupando anche la parte armata dell'inferiore faccia, ed altre si fatte infinite sperienze, mi astringono a riserbare v[erbi] g[ratia] La ripulsione per La forza primitiva del fuoco elettrico.

Un amico mi ha fatto vedere l'articolo XVII dell'appendix to the montly review volume forty seventh pag. 552. Bramerei, che gli deste un'occhiata. La mia vanità mi avea voluto persuadere, che a dettare tale articolo abbia avuto parte la gelosia della plebbe, e che La menzogna vi sia entrata per qualche cosa.

Ho letto con piacere gli elogi, che Priestley dà all'elettrometro di Elsmey. Ne ho costrutto uno doppio per ogni modo. I. ABCDE, abcde sono due cartoncini, la figura de' quali risulta da un rettangolo ACDF, e da due semicerchi ABC, FED. II. Essi cartoncini sono annessi alla sommità della colonnetta GH sicchè restano paralleli, e distanti alcune linee uno dall'altro. III. La Testa G della colonnetta porta un capelletto di ottone, che regge due fini e mobilissimi perni corrispondenti a'centri v, ed v de' semicerchi. IV. A' perni sono annessi i pendoli VP, vp, &c.

Eccone i vantaggi. I. Tra due piani vicini non si dispiega niuna elettricità, e quelle che si dispiegano attorno a' margini si vogliono supporre eguali. Epperò il movimento de' pendoli non è disturbato dalla forza dell'elettricità dispiegantesi dall'unico piano di Elsmey; la quale forza mira ad allontanare il pendolo normalmente dal piano; mentre la forza, che ne dee dare la misura mira a muoverlo parallelamente al piano medesimo. II. Uso due pendoli; perchè il confronto delle loro divergenze mi serve di guida a situare l'elettrometro in modo, che sia menomamente disturbato da' corpi aggiacenti; e anche quando L'elettrometro è situato ottimamente, mi piace di prendere la semisomma delle due divergenze.

Sono parecchi anni, che uso un elettrometro per misurare le picciole elettricità atmosferiche, per le quali non serve l'elettrometro di Ensnley. Se non temerò di annoiarvi, ve ne manderò La descrizione.

Se mi occorrerà di scrivere di cose elettriche farò un picciolo ristretto di Epino, e Cawendisk &c.

Io avea scritta questa carta unicamente per memoria di materia da scrivere; ma ora ricevo La lettera d'inbarco delle 500 copie; non ho tempo a riscrivere, nè vuo differire, Epperò perdonate Chiar-[issim]o Signore alla improprietà, e al disordine di questa lettera. Le copie delle tavole sono 508 tutte unite; inoltre, siccome alcune copie della seconda tavola sono con pocha margine, v'è il supplemento.

La spesa della carta e impronto è di L piemontesi 116 soldi $7\frac{1}{2}$. Non so peranche la spesa della cassa, e del trasporto a Nizza; ne manderò la nota; E se vorrete mandarmi alcuna copia della traduzione (e poche mi basteranno) saro soddisfatto. Sono curiosissimo di sapere se il Signore Priestley ha cercato di avverare un mio sospetto

TRANSLATION

[After Aug. 11, 1773[1]]

Most illustrious and honored Sir, my particular Master,

After you asked me about Aepinus I reread him a second time;

1. This letter was also in answer to BF's of Aug. 11, and internal evidence suggests that it was the later of the two. It exists in two incomplete drafts, of which we have printed the longer; the shorter contains the same first four paragraphs in slightly abbreviated form, and then adds a sentence that is not in the other: "Quando io ho scritto di athmosfera elettrica nel 17[. .], e mi sono attribuito le scoperta di quella parte di legge, io ignorava affatto, che altri ne avesse scritto, nemmeno avea veduto le vostre sperienze attorno all' atmosfera de' cannoni." "When I wrote about atmospheric electricity in 17[. .] and attributed to myself the discovery of some of its laws, I was quite ignorant that others had written about it; and I had not heard of your experiments with the atmosphere of tubes." Beccaria was presumably referring to his work in 1753. BF's experiments were actually performed in 1755; see above, V, 516–19.

and in addition to learning from him about Richmann's experiment, as I already wrote you, I noted in particular:

I. That Aepinus realized that there is no motion between an electrified and an unelectrified body. Hence this discovery, which I ascribed to myself in writing about electrical atmosphere, belongs to Aepinus.

II. That Aepinus has noted an experiment on vindicating electricity, i.e., rubbing together two plates fitted with an insulated handle: they generate no electricity when together, and opposing electricity when separated. Aepinus probably derived this experiment from the Pekin observations,[2] which I have cited in my discussion of vindicating electricity.

III. I particularly liked Aepinus' magnetic theory, above all his point that magnetism is related to the position in the terrestrial magnetic system occupied by bodies capable of being magnetized. Magnetism caused by a spark is no exception.[3]

Aepinus' work strikes me in general as of great value. But Mr. Cavendish's seems to me even better, particularly because it reduces the effect of electrical action very nearly to the inverse of the squares of the distances, and thereby reduces the actions to the surfaces of the bodies.

Frankly, however, in my section on derivative electrical phenomena I cannot stop, as I already wrote you, with mere attraction and repulsion. Seeing the electrical atmosphere spread gradually from the upper face of your square and bend around under the bare margins, and successively fill the coated part of the lower face, and [observing] innumerable other similar experiments that have been made compel me to limit, for instance, the primordial force of the electric fire to repulsion.[4]

2. Made by Jesuits in Pekin, forwarded by them to the Imperial Academy in St. Petersburg in 1755, and published in its transactions. See Beccaria's *Treatise* cited above, p. 404; above, XIV, 49 n.

3. Beccaria seems to be referring to the effect of a spark on changing the magnetic direction of a needle, a point that he discusses in *idem.*, pp. 306–7. The translator of the *Treatise* appended a note on that passage that is also relevant to this one: "If the above paragraph, on the contents of which the author seems to lay a particular stress, had been more clearly expressed in the original, the translation of it would also have been somewhat clearer."

4. All that is apparent in this passage, at least to us, is that Beccaria was referring to what he called the "Franklin square," a sheet of glass coated on

A friend showed me the seventeenth article of the appendix to the Monthly Review, Vol. XLVII [1772], 552[-4]. I should like you to have a look at it. Vanity tries to persuade me that vulgar envy had a hand in the article, and that part of it is untrue.[5]

I read with pleasure the praise from Priestley for Elsmey's electrometer. I built a double one.[6] I: Two pieces of cardboard (ABCDE, abcde) are each composed of a rectangle (ACDF) and two half-circles (ABC,FED). II: These pieces are attached to the top of the small column (GH) so that they are parallel and a fraction of an inch[7] apart. III: The head (G) of the little column has a small brass cap, which bears two thin and extremely flexible pins connecting the centers of the half-circles (v,v). IV: To these are attached the pendulums (VP,vp), &c.

Here are the advantages. I: No electricity is released between planes so close to one another, and what is released from the margins should be considered uniform; hence the motion of the pendulums is unaffected by the electricity coming from Elsmey's single plane, which tends to drive his pendulum perpendicularly away from the plane, whereas the force to be measured tends to drive it parallel. II: I use two pendulums, because comparing their divergences helps me to place the electrometer where it will be least disturbed by adjacent bodies; and even when it is so placed I take the mean between the two divergences.

For many years I have used an electrometer to measure small amounts of atmospheric electricity, for which Ensnley's is useless. I will send you a description if it will not bore you.

---

both sides with lead, with which he had experimented; see the *Treatise*, p. 76. BF's description of the square is above, III, 356–7.

5. The reviewer, in addition to the comments quoted above on Beccaria's style, suggested that his work was largely derived from experiments in England, where the apparatus was more sophisticated and the scientists were further advanced than in Italy.

6. Priestley's account of the electrometer is printed above, XVII, 259–63. Beccaria changed "Elsmey" later in the letter to "Ensnley"—an advance toward his goal of Henly, which his translator finally achieved in the *Treatise*, p. 444 n. The MS sketch of the electrometer is in Pace, *op. cit.*, p. 377.

7. In "alcune linee" Beccaria presumably had in mind some multiple of the Paris line, a unit of measurement that was slightly less than a tenth of an inch.

Should I have occasion to write about electrical matters, I will make a brief summary of Aepinus and Cavendish, &c.

[*Postscript?*] I had composed this only as a memorandum of things to write about. But I have now received the bill of lading for the 500 copies;[8] I have no time to rewrite, and no wish to delay. Hence do forgive, most illustrious Sir, the mistakes and disorder of this letter. The copies of the plates number in all 508; because some copies of the second plate have little margin, extras have been added.

The cost of the paper and handling is £116 7s. Piedmontese. I do not yet know the charge for the box and transportation to Nice; I will send you the bill. I should be glad if you would send me some copies of the translation; a few would suffice. I am most curious to know whether Signor Priestley has tried to confirm a suspicion of mine [*remainder missing*].

To [John Williams]   ALS (draft): American Philosophical Society

The recipient of this letter can be identified with confidence. In late June Jonathan Williams, Jr., had sent papers for his Uncle John, the customs inspector, who had come to England with him and Josiah in 1770 and had remained there;[9] these must be the papers that Franklin mentions in his postscript. Other internal evidence confirms that the year was 1773: Franklin's return to town was from his visit to Lord Le Despencer, and his plan to leave for America, although he used it to turn aside Williams' request for a loan, was one that he had recently abandoned.[1]

Sir   Augt 15. [1773]
On my Return to Town I found your Note of Monday. Having for some time designed to leave England this Summer, I have

8. Beccaria was responding to BF's request, in his letter above of Aug. 11, for engravings to illustrate the translation. See BF's reply below, March 20, 1774.

9. Jonathan's letter to BF, enclosing the papers, is above, June 28. For John Williams see above, XII, 193 n; XVII, 212 n, 284.

1. Some weeks earlier he had told Cushing, WF, and Bache that he was leaving (above, July 7, 14, and 15); on Aug. 3 he had told Foxcroft, WF, and Galloway that he was staying. See also his "Prudential Algebra" on the back of the present letter: above, before Aug. 3.

either forbidden or have not calld for Remittances that would otherwise have been made to me, and among others from your Brother, so that my Cash here is lower than usual. However, to see if I could possibly accommodate you, I have taken a little time to examine what Demands may be incumbent on me to discharge before my Departure, and I never on any Occasion was more convinc'd of the Truth of the old Saying, *That our Sins and our Debts are always more than we take them to be.*[2] In short I find I shall have full Occasion for all the Money I can command here, so that without the greatest Inconvenience to my self I cannot comply with your Request; under which Circumstance you do not seem to desire it. And as I know your Brother's Punctuality, I make no doubt you will soon receive from him the Remittances he ought to make you.[3] I am, Sir, Your most obedient humble Servant   B F

Jonathan desires me to give you the Reading of the enclos'd Papers.

Franklin and William Bollan to Lord Dartmouth

ALS:[4] the William Salt Library, Stafford

This letter to the American Secretary, and the one from Franklin alone on the following day, raise an interesting question about the agents' timing. On the 20th they forwarded what had "this day come to our hands," the letter to Dartmouth from the Massachusetts House and Council; on the 21st Franklin forwarded the petition from the House, "just received," for the removal of Hutchinson and Oliver. Speaker Cushing had sent the first with his letter of June 30, and the second with that of June 25;[5] did they in fact arrive in reverse order, or did

2. A slight emendation of proverb no. 4,179 in Thomas Fuller, *Gnomologia: Adages and Proverbs* . . . (London, 1732).

3. BF added, then deleted, "the £450 of your Money which you mention he has recovered for you."

4. In Bollan's hand, perhaps because the enclosure was signed by Thomas Flucker, secretary of the Council as well as of the province, and was therefore formally Bollan's concern.

5. For the contents of each see the annotation of the two Cushing letters above.

the agents agree to present them in that order for reasons of their own? The letter was relatively conciliatory; the petition was a bomb-shell. When each was received is not clear, but there is good reason to suppose that the petition arrived first.[6] If so, Franklin may have kept it for a time to see what developed, and then decided with Bollan that the letter gave them a diplomatic way to impress Dartmouth with their constituents' good will before confronting him with the explosive petition.

S. hampton street, Covt. garden, Augt. 20th. 1773

My Lord,

The Letter herewith inclosed, from the Council and house of Representatives of the Massachusetts province to your Lordship, having this day come to our hands, we think it our duty to forward it without delay, and have the honour to be, with the greatest respect, Your Lordship's most obedient, and most humble servants   W. BOLLAN

B FRANKLIN

The rt. honble. the Earl of Dartmouth

Endorsed: Mr. Bollan 20 Aug. 1773

6. Whether it did or not depends on what ship carried it. Capt. Hall in the *Dartmouth* and Capt. Loring in the *William* sailed from Boston on June 29, and arrived in London respectively on Aug. 4 or 5 and on Aug. 18 or 19. *Mass. Gaz.; and the Boston Weekly News-Letter,* July 1, and *Lloyd's Evening Post,* Aug. 4–6, 18–20, 1773. Cushing may have sent the petition and his covering letter of June 25 in either, or very possibly in both. Hall certainly carried *a* copy of the petition, for a letter-writer in London had seen one by the 7th (——Wentworth to Rockingham, Aug. 7, 1773, Wentworth Woodhouse MSS, R1/1438, Sheffield City Libraries); if BF's copy came by the same ship, as seems probable, he had it a fortnight before he told Dartmouth that it was "just received." The letter from the House and Council was enclosed in Cushing's above of June 30, which went in duplicate. The Speaker's LS arrived late: it went by way of Liverpool, where it was postmarked Aug. 26. His ALS went by the *Neptune* out of Nantucket, and she passed Gravesend on the 17th: 6 Mass. Hist. Soc. *Coll.,* IX, 305; *Public Advertiser,* Aug. 19, 1773.

To Peter P. Burdett

ALS: Yale University Library; mutilated draft: American Philosophical Society

Burdett is one of the shadowy figures who often appear on the periphery of Franklin's circle. He lived in Derby for a time, where he was a good friend of Joseph Wright, the painter, and of John Whitehurst, the clock-maker and Franklin's acquaintance for many years.[7] Burdett first made a name for himself as a cartographer; he won a prize in 1767 for a map of Derbyshire, and some years later did the initial work on a notable map of Cheshire. In 1769 he surveyed a route for the projected Leeds and Liverpool canal, and for the next five years he lived in Liverpool. His interests were shifting to the graphic arts: he was the founder and first president of a local academy of painting and sculpture and contributed to the exhibitions of the Society of Artists, of which he was an honorary fellow. He was the pioneer in the use of aquatint in England, and developed a process for transferring aquatint engravings to pottery. He was soon experimenting with this discovery; he offered it to Frederick of Prussia and, more practically, to the Wedgwoods, who attempted for almost a year and a half to utilize his invention and then, in March of 1773, abandoned it.[8] That recent setback may well have led Burdett to consider emigrating to America as a surveyor to lay out canals, an idea that he must have broached in the missing letter that Franklin is answering. But the idea, like the earlier invention, died aborning. In 1774 Burdett, plagued by creditors, left for the Continent; there he entered the service of the Markgraf of Baden, who was delighted to find that he knew Franklin and promptly for-

---

7. Burdett undoubtedly carried the letter from Whitehurst to BF printed above, XIV, 41; in that case BF had by now known him for at least six years.

8. See Ann Finer and George Savage, eds., *The Selected Letters of Josiah Wedgwood* (London, [1965]), pp. 115–20. The best résumé of Burdett's career is in the introduction by John B. Harley and Paul Laxton to a modern facsimile reprint of the Cheshire map, *A Survey of the County Palatine of Chester: P. P. Burdett, 1777*, Historic Soc. of Lancs. and Cheshire, occasional ser., 1 (1974), 2–7; we are indebted to Dr. Harley for reviewing our headnote. See also Sir Henry T. Wood, *A History of the Society of Arts . . .* (London, 1913), p. 300; Algernon Graves, *The Society of Artists of Great Britain . . . [and] the Free Society of Artists . . .* (London, 1907), p. 43; Benedict Nicolson, *Joseph Wright of Derby . . .* (2 vols., New Haven, [1971]), I, 117–18; E. Rimbault Dibdin, "Liverpool Art and Artists in the Eighteenth Century," Vol. of the Walpole Soc., VI (1917–18), 65–6, 78.

370

warded, through him, an invitation to the American to take up residence in Baden.[9] Burdett died in Karlsruhe in 1793.

Sir, London, Augt. 21. 1773.

I find here on coming to Town your Favour of the 10th Instant. I should think a Man of your Talents a great Acquisition to the Colonies, if we could make it worth your while to remove thither. No Country, certainly, is better fitted by Nature to receive Advantage from the Arts of making Rivers navigable, and forming extensive Communications by means of short Canals between their Branches: But as yet I doubt whether their Population and internal Commerce are sufficient to bear the Expence. Mr. Ballandine, however, may in this Respect be better informed than I am. As yet there has been no Meeting of those concern'd in the intended new Colony, and I apprehend that when they have obtain'd their Patent, their first Cares must be of another kind. But since I am acquainted with your Willingness to engage in such Undertakings, on proper Encouragement, I shall omit no Opportunity of doing Justice to your Character wherever my Opinion may have any Weight, and with the more Pleasure as I am persuaded that in serving you I shall serve my Country.[1]

I should be glad to be inform'd where I can see some Sample of your new Art of Printing in Imitation of Paintings. It must be a

9. Burdett to BF below, Dec. 15, 1774.

1. Burdett had apparently suggested that he was equipped to lay out navigable waterways in the vast tract that the Walpole Co. hoped to acquire. Although BF rejected this idea, another may have been in the back of his mind: that Burdett could be useful in designing the canals of which BF's Philadelphia friends were dreaming. See above, XIX, 157–8, 278–9. John Ballendine, a Virginian, had come to England to study canals and locks, and had published in London proposals for opening the Potomac; his schemes died when he returned to America in 1774, and he reverted to his old trade of ironmaster. See [George Armoroyd,] *A Connected View of the Whole Internal Navigation of the United States* . . . (Philadelphia, 1830), pp. 208–14; Corra Bacon-Foster, "Early Chapters in the Development of the Potomac Route to the West . . . ," Columbia Hist. Soc. *Records*, XV (1912), 117–23; Kathleen Bruce, *Virginia Iron Manufacture in the Slave Era* . . . (New York, [1931]), pp. 42–50; Randolph W. Church, "John Ballendine . . . ," *Va. Cavalcade*, VIII, No. 4 (1959), 39–46; [Fairfax Harrison,] *Landmarks of Old Prince William* . . . (2 vols., Richmond, 1924), II, 427–9, 435–6, 540, 556.

most valuable Discovery.[2] With great Esteem, I am, Sir, Your
most obedient humble Servant   B FRANKLIN

Mr Burdet

Addressed: To / Mr P. P. Burdett / at / Liverpool / B Free
FRANKLIN

To Lord Dartmouth

Printed in a broadside, *Proceedings of His Majesty's Privy-Council on
the Address of the Assembly of Massachusetts-Bay, to Remove His
Governor and Lieutenant-Governor* ... [Boston, 1774]: Massachusetts
Historical Society.

MY LORD,   London, August 21, 1773.

I have just received from the House of Representatives of the
Massachusett's-Bay, their Address to the King, which I now
enclose, and send to your Lordship, with my humble request in
their behalf, that you would be pleased to present it to his Majesty
the first convenient opportunity.[3]

I have the pleasure of hearing from that province by my late
letters, that a sincere disposition prevails in the people there to
be on good terms with the Mother Country; that the Assembly
have declared their desire only to be put into the situation they
were in before the stamp act; they aim at no novelties.[4] And it is

2. "But more likely to meet with adequate Encouragement," BF added in
his draft, "on this Side the Water than on ours." In part, perhaps, because BF
omitted this qualification in the ALS, Burdett responded by sending him
samples of his work; see BF's acknowledgment of them below, Nov. 3.
Burdett never did receive adequate encouragement, as mentioned in the
headnote; and his work was so far forgotten that Paul Sandby later received
credit for having introduced the aquatint process into England in 1774.
William Sandby, *Thomas and Paul Sandby* ... (London, 1892), pp. 135–6.

3. The petition for the removal of Hutchinson and Oliver, enclosed in
Cushing to BF above, June 25, led directly to BF's humiliation before the
Privy Council five months later; see the headnote on the Council's report
below, Jan. 29, 1774. The timing of this letter to Dartmouth and the one
from BF and Bollan above, Aug. 20, is discussed in the headnote on the latter.

4. This was certainly the purport of the letter from the House that BF
and Bollan had forwarded to Dartmouth the day before; see the headnote
on Cushing to BF above, June 30. If BF had himself received letters to the
same effect, we know nothing of them.

said, that having lately discovered, as they think, the authors of their grievances to be some of their own people, their resentment against Britain is thence much abated.[5]

This good disposition of their's (will your Lordship permit me to say) may be cultivated by a favourable answer to this Address, which I therefore hope your goodness will endeavour to obtain. With the greatest respect, I have the honor to be, my Lord, &c.

B. FRANKLIN.

Agent for the House of Representatives.

To Jonathan Shipley

ALS: Yale University Library; draft: American Philosophical Society

My dear Lord,   London, Augt. 21. 1773.

Inclos'd I send a Boston Newspaper in which the Sermon is advertis'd. The Speaker of the Assembly of the Massachusets, in his Letter to me says, "The Bishop's Sermon is much liked, as it discovers a catholick Spirit, and Sentiments very favourable with regard to America." Dr. Chauncey, an ancient Dissenting Minister of Boston, writes, "The Bishop of St. Asaph's Sermon I got reprinted in 24 Hours after it came to hand. 'Tis universally received here with Approbation and Wonder, and has done much Good. It sold amazingly. A second Impression was called for in two Days."

I daily expect to hear more of it from the other Colonies.[6]

I hope the good Family all continue well and happy. With sincere Esteem and affectionate Respect I am ever Your Lordship's most obedient humble Servant   B FRANKLIN

Bishop of St. Asaph

5. This had been BF's expectation, or so he said, in sending the Hutchinson letters; and he apparently believed that events since then had proved him right.

6. For the Bishop's sermon and its dissemination in the colonies see the note on BF to Cushing above, April 3. The Speaker's acknowledgment on June 14 contained BF's first quotation; the second was in a letter now lost from the Rev. Charles Chauncy (above, XI, 255 n), for many years the pastor of the First Church in Boston.

To Thomas Cushing ALS (letterbook draft):[7] Library of Congress

Sir,   London, Augt. 24. 1773

I received duly your several Favours of June 25, 26, and 30. with the Papers enclosed.[8] My Lord Dartmouth being at his Country Seat, in Staffordshire, I transmitted to him the Address for the Removal of the Govr. and Lieut. Govr. and Mr. Bollan and I jointly transmitted the Letter to his Lordship from both Houses.[9] I delivered to Mr. Bollan one Set of the authenticated Copies of the Letters [and] we shall co-operate [in] the Business [we] are charg'd with.

I am told that the Governor has requested Leave to come home;[1] that some great Persons about the Court do not think the Letters, now they have seen them, a sufficient Foundation for the Resolves, [that therefore] it is not likely he will be remov'd, but suffered to re[sign, and that] some Provision will be made for him here.[2] But nothing [I apprehend], is likely to be done soon, as most of the great Officers of State who compose the Privy Council, are in the Country, and likely to continue there till the Parliament meets, and perhaps the above may be chiefly Conjecture.

[I have] inform'd Mr. Lee, that in Case there should be a Hearing, I was directed to engage him as Council for the Province; [and] that I had receiv'd no Money, but would advance what might be necessary; those Hearings by Council being expensive.

I purpose writing to you again per the Packet: and am, with [the] greatest Respect, Sir, Your most obedient humble Servant.

B F.

7. Portions of the letter have been torn; we supply them in brackets from the text in WTF, *Memoirs*, II, 199 of the first pagination, altering in the postscript what the editor mistakenly read as "Mr. Lewis."

8. The letter of June 25, to which BF is chiefly replying, and that of the 30th are above; the third has vanished.

9. BF's and Bollan's letters of transmittal are above, Aug. 20, 21. See also below, the Earl's acknowledgment, Aug. 25, and BF to Cushing, Sept. 1.

1. See WF to BF above, July 29.

2. Rumors were circulating that Thomas Pownall would be made a K.B. and sent to the colonies as a mediator: *Public Advertiser*, Aug. 4, 12, 1773. On Aug. 24 a correspondent in the same newspaper, which had just published the Hutchinson letters, argued that they were insufficient basis for the resolves. A reply, we believe by BF, appeared on Aug. 31; see below.

[P.S. No determination is] yet [public on the case] of [Mr. Livius against Governor W]entworth which has been a very [costly Hearing I] believe to both Sides.[3]

Honble Thos Cushing Esqr

From John Baskerville[4]   ALS: American Philosophical Society

Dear Sir,   Birmingham 24 Augt. 1773.

I am enlarging My Foundry in Order to sell Types abroad, but first to our own Colonys; in Consequence of which I beg Your good Offices in sending them to any printing Houses You approve in any part of North America. You asked Me when in Town if My Types would set with Caslon's; I can now answer Yes; within the Thickness of the paper I write on at farthest;[5] for at first seting out we strictly conform'd to the Height of his; which I did not recollect when You asked Me the question first. You will please to observe that if any Orders proceed from the Specimen; I shall expect a person appointed to receive them in London on whom I may draw for Value at three Months. I shall assert the superior Merit the publick is pleas'd to allow Me, by charging the largest Sizes two pence, and the smaller 3 or 4 pence More than Caslon's per lb as the hardness of Metal in mine (which I am strictly determined to keep to) will trebly pay that difference to the person who uses them.

I have sent 25 Specimens in a Sheet of Chinese Paper, and a Sett of the Characteristics of which I beg Your Acceptance.[6]

3. For the Livius case see BF to WF above, July 25, Aug. 3. A few days after BF wrote this letter Livius' complaint was dismissed: *Acts Privy Coun., Col.,* V, 370–5.

4. For the famous printer and BF's old friend see the biographical note above, IX, 257 n.

5. *I.e.,* provided the paper is as thick as this. The thin serifs in the type require a deep impression.

6. With the specimens BF received Baskerville's edition, the fifth, of Anthony Ashley Cooper, third Earl of Shaftesbury, *Characteristicks of Men, Manners, Opinions, Times* ... (3 vols., Birmingham, 1773). BF admired the typography, but was particularly fascinated by the huge sheet of Chinese paper, presumably rice paper, in which the specimens were wrapped. To Baskerville below, Sept. 21.

As the pleasantest Time o'Year for travelling is now approaching pray give us Your Company for a Month, and take a Bed at Easy Hill. You know all Your Friends here will rejoice to see You, and none more than Dear Sir Your obedient humble servant.   JOHN BASKERVILLE

Addressed: To / Benjamin Franklyn Esqr / Craven Street in the Strand / London

From Lord Dartmouth   Copy:[7] Library of Congress

Sir,   Sandwell, 25 August, 1773.
    I have received your Letter of the 21st. Instant, together with an Address of the House of Representatives of the Massachusets Bay, which I shall not fail to lay before the King, the next time I shall have the Honor of being admitted into his presence. I cannot help expressing to you the pleasure it gives me to hear that a sincere disposition prevails in the People of that Province to be on good terms with the Mother Country, and my earnest hope that the time is at no great distance, when every ground of uneasiness will cease, and the most perfect tranquillity and happiness be restored to the breasts of that people. I am, Sir, Your most obedient Humble Servant,   DARTMOUTH.

Benjn. Franklin Esqr.

Notation: Lord Dartmouths Answer to Dr. Franklin

From Thomas Cushing
                              LS and ALS (copy):[8] Library of Congress

Sir   Boston Augt: 26: 1773
    Since my last, which was of the 30th June past, I have been favoured with yours of 2d and 4 of June last, Inclosing Lord

---

7. In Fevre's hand except for the signature.
8. Only the postscript and signature of the LS are in Cushing's hand; he enclosed the copy (dated Aug. 22) with his letter below of Sept. 18.

Dartmouths Letter directed to yourself as agent of the late House of Representatives in answer to the Several Petitions of the House, which Letter I shall lay before them as soon as the Court meets; I hope soon to be favoured with your observations on this occasion;[1] By Capt. Lyde I had the Honor to receive a Letter from Lord Dartmouth wherein he has Condescended with great Freedom to Communicate to me his sentiments upon the State of our publick affairs. His Lordship's sentiments are truly noble and generous, they well Comport with his high station and fully Justify that Confidence which his majestys american subjects repose in his wisdom and justice. His Lordship has kindly assured me, that whenever the Province shall by a decent, temperate and dutiful Representation of such measures of Government, as may appear to her to be Injurious to her legal Rights and civil Liberties, lay a proper foundation for releif, that no man will be more ready than he will to assist and support such Representation.[2] I have wrote his Lordship upon this subject, but decency would not permit me to Use that freedom with his Lordship that you will suffer me to use with you. I heartily wish that the Letter of the two Houses to His Lordship of the 29 June Last may fully answer the purposes of the representation his Lordship has mentioned.[3] The Court now stands prorogued to the 4th of november next and, I doubt not, will be further prorogued to the middle of January next: so that it is not likely the Court (if they

1. Dartmouth's letter of June 2 and the two from BF are above. In both of his BF promised observations, but did not make them until his letter to the House of July 7.

2. Dartmouth's remarkable letter, of June 19, was written not as a minister of the crown but as a private person. In that capacity he both supported the principle of Parliamentary taxation and deplored its exercise in imposing the Townshend duties. He equally deplored, however, the "wild and extravagant" doctrines that the House had asserted in answering Gov. Hutchinson; they precluded compromise, and would have to be replaced by a "decent, temperate, and dutiful" statement of grievances if Parliament were to consider the matter. Stevens, *Facsimiles*, XXIV, no. 2025; see also Bargar, *Dartmouth*, pp. 89–90.

3. The letter from the two houses is summarized in the headnote on Cushing to BF above, June 30. Cushing enclosed with the present letter his reply to Dartmouth, discussed in the next note; see BF's answer below, Nov. 1.

were so disposed) will have it in their power to prepare and forward such a Representation before the opening of the next session of Parliament, however in case the Court should meet time Enough for that purpose, I am apprehensive many difficulties will attend the accomplishment of it: If I am not so unhappy as to misunderstand his Lordship, relative to the Representation he has mentioned, he intends a Representation of Grievances, in which the point in dispute with respect to the Right of Parliament shall be intirely waved and Kept out of sight, upon which I would observe that Every part of america are greatly Interested in the important Question which by the Governor has been moved here; The alarm is Universal; The Conduct of the late House in this interesting dispute has met with the approbation of all the Colonies; The Eyes of the whole Continent are turned upon this Province, and several Houses of assembly have appointed Committees to Correspond with a Committee appointed by the House of Burgesses of Virginia and with such other Houses of Assembly that shall Chuse Committees for that purpose; and, if I conjecture right, the Houses of assembly thro' the Continent will in general adopt the same measures, and therefore it is most probable, should a motion be made at the next sessions of the general assembly for a new Petition or Representation, that it would be immediately proposed to Consult with the other Houses of Assembly or else to appoint Committees to meet in Congress to agree upon the form of Petitioning, which I fear will make it still more difficult to restore that Harmony between both Countries so ardently wish'd for. I would therefore submit it to your Consideration, (as I have to the Consideration of his Lordship) whether it would not be more Eligible for the Parliament of Great Britain to take up american affairs upon their own principles, without any apparent attention to the applications made by the americans for redress, and from great national Consideration place america upon the same footing on which she was at the Conclusion of the late war; by this means the intangling Questions of the right of Parliament (which I humbly think for the happiness of both Countries ought never to have been agitated) will be kept out of sight, and the colonies by such a voluntary act of Justice and Benevolence will be highly gratified, and will be immediately brought to a renewall of that wonted reliance which, untill of late, they have ever had

378

on the Honor and parental affection of the British Nation.[4] I would further observe, (not from any personal pique or Prejudice to the Governor or Lieut. Governor but purely that you may Know every thing that will tend to Restore that Tranquility and Harmony so much sought for) that It appears from the proceedings of the two Houses the last session, relative to those Gentlemen, to be necessary that the Prayer of the Petition of the House to His Majesty of the 23d of June last for their removal should be granted, their usefulness is At an End, and they have entirely lost the Confidence of the People, and if they should do a thousand good offices, so far from being considered in a favourable light, they would all be Considered as Springing from some sinister View, but this I write in great Confidence and desire you would Consider it altogether of a private nature.

I have with freedom mentioned my apprehensions Concerning any further Petition or Representation for the redress of greiviances, your prudence will direct as to the propriety of Communicating them to Lord Dartmouth or any other Person. I Conclude with great Respect your most humble Servant

THOMAS CUSHING

PS. I beg the favor of your delivering the Inclosed to Lord Dartmouth

Benjamin Franklin Esqr.

Endorsed: Hon. Thos Cushing Esq. Aug. 26. 1773[5]

4. Cushing's reply to Dartmouth, on Aug. 22, tactfully reasserted the claims of the House. It had glossed over the issue of Parliament's authority, but in his opinion would never retreat from the position that it had taken. The rest of his letter said substantially what he recapitulated up to this point for BF, except that it made no mention of the committees of correspondence or the possibility of a continental congress. Stevens, *Facsimiles,* XXIV, no. 2028.

5. The endorsement is on the LS, which also has a note, badly faded, that appears to be in BF's hand: "Extract of a Letter from Thos Cushing Esq Speaker of the House of Representatives of the Massachusetts Bay to their Agent in London, dated Aug 26, 1773." The portion marked for the extract is that between our notes 1 and 4, and the final paragraph.

To John Cuthbert

ALS (draft): American Philosophical Society

Sir, London, Augt. 28. 1773.

Your Favour of July 30. came duly to hand, and I have since received and sent to France the Drawings brought to Town by Lady Bewick. I hope they were not too late to be of Use, tho' I had a Letter from M. Morand about three Months before, that he then despair'd of receiving them, and thought of publishing his Work without them.[6] I have not heard from him since I sent them; as I hoped I might before this time but shall pay upon Sight your Order on Account of the Expence you have been at, and am exceedingly oblig'd by the Care and Pains you have been so good as to take in procuring them. I hope your Health is perfectly reestablished, and am, with great Regard, Sir, Your most obedient humble Servant B FRANKLIN

Notation: Mr Cuthbert relating to the Coal mine Drawings

On the Hutchinson Letters

Printed in *The Public Advertiser*, August 31, 1773

The letters, which had been public property in Boston since the beginning of the summer, were by now attracting attention in England. On August 19th the *Public Advertiser* began to publish them, and on the 31st it printed this paragraph in the middle of a mélange of European news. Franklin cannot be proved to have been the author, but Verner Crane has pointed out strong reasons for supposing that he was.[7] No one else could have been, in fact, unless his ideas were remarkably close to Franklin's.

A Correspondent observes[8] that the Discovery of Governor

---

6. He eventually received and paid for them by sending BF four guineas for Cuthbert: Jour., p. 55. Jean-François-Clément Morand (1726–84), by training a doctor and by avocation a scientific jack-of-all-trades, was in process of publishing his *Art d'exploiter les mines de charbon de terre* (3 vols., Paris, 1768–79). The work was part of the monograph series of the Académie des sciences, *Descriptions des arts et métiers.*

7. *Letters to the Press*, pp. 231–2.

8. A common introduction in the *Public Advertiser* to a reworking of whatever the correspondent had written. The printer may have taken such

Hutchinson's and Oliver's Letters points out an easy Way of re-establishing Peace and Harmony between Great Britain and her Colonies, and consolating[9] the Confidence of the latter, by producing all the confidential Letters received from America on public Affairs, and from public Men. It is in vain to say, this would be betraying private Correspondence, since if the Truth only was written, no Man need be ashamed or afraid of its being known; and if Falshoods have been maliciously covered under the Cloak of Confidence, 'tis perfectly just the incendiary Writers should be exposed and punished. What a weak, what a wicked Plan of Government is that, which, under the Seal of Secrecy, gives Encouragement to every Species of Malice and Misrepresentation. That Government have been deceived almost to the fatal Issue of declaring War against our Colonies is certain; and it is equally certain, that it is in their Power to make an honourable Sacrifice of the wicked Authors of this dangerous Deception.

To Richard Bache   ALS (letterbook draft): Library of Congress

Dear Son,   London Sept. 1. 1773.
    I received yours of July 6, by the last Packet that is arriv'd; for we have not yet [that?] of August.
    I had thoughts of going by this Packet, but various Considerations, some publick and some private, have occurr'd inducing me to postpone my leaving England for another Season.[1]
    A Bill you drew for £27 18s. 0d. on Francis Roper, Mercht in London, has been brought to me, with a Direction annex'd to it that I should be apply'd to in case of Need. I was told that no such Person could be found or heard of. So I accepted the Bill for the Honour of the Drawer; but hope you will make no more such Drafts.
    All Friends in Craven Street are well, and rejoice in the Increase

---

liberties with this paragraph. But the style and content, except perhaps for the final sentence, sound to us like BF.

9. Either a misprint for "consolidating," as Crane thought, or consolating in the now obsolete sense of encouraging.

1. BF weighed these considerations by means of his "Prudential Algebra" above, before Aug. 3.

of [your] Family. Mrs. Stevenson is just come from a V[isit to Sally] Franklin that was, now Mrs. Pearce, where another [Increase may soon?] be expected.² Mrs. S. took her Grandson with her, [*torn*.] Temple went too, having a few Holidays on Account of [*torn*]; and being fond of Farming, as he was there and assisted in Seedtime, he was very desirous to be there at the Harvest, where he lent a helping Hand, and made himself as he does [every?]where, exceedingly welcome. Your affectionate Father

B FRANKLIN³

Mr Bache

To Alexander Colden ALS (letterbook draft): Library of Congress

⟨London, September 1, 1773: Has received Colden's of July 7, enclosing Archimedes Georges on Curtis & Lowell for £113 and Norris Goddard on Anthony Todd for £69. Is glad to hear that Colden and his family are well.⟩

To Thomas Cushing

Extract⁴ reprinted from Jared Sparks, ed., *The Works of Benjamin Franklin* . . . (10 vols., Boston, 1836–40), VIII, 83 n.

[September 1, 1773]

In my last I informed you, that the address to the King, and the letter from the General Court to Lord Dartmouth, are both transmitted to his Lordship. Enclosed are copies of his answers to Mr. Bollan and myself. There are some expressions in the close of his Lordship's letter to me, that have a favorable appearance, and therefore I take this first opportunity of communicating it.⁵

2. Sally had married James Pearce in mid-April: BF to DF above, April 6. The Pearce farm was at Ewell, near London.

3. BF added a postscript, which is now torn and indecipherable except for the single word "deliver."

4. The letter seems to be complete, as Sparks implies, except for the opening and closing salutations. The date in Sparks is confirmed by BF's reference in his next letter, Sept. 12.

5. BF's "last" to Cushing was on Aug. 24. Dartmouth's reply to Bollan, or possibly to BF and Bollan together, is missing; his reply to BF is above, Aug. 25. Cushing's letter of Dec. 10 acknowledged receipt of the Earl's answers.

To Deborah Franklin

ALS: American Philosophical Society; letterbook draft: Library of Congress

My dear Child,   London, Sept. 1. 1773

I received yours of July 5. and rejoice with you on the safe Delivery of our dear Daughter, and on our having another Grandson.

I like Ben's Kindness and Generosity to his Brother, with his Silver Spoon; and am glad he has got so well over the Measles.[6] 'Tis a precious little Fellow! How much I long to see him!

I am griev'd at the Death of good Dr. Evans. When I observe that almost every Letter I receive from you acquaints me with the Death of some Friend, I begin to fear, that when I return, I shall find myself a Stranger in my own Country; and leaving so many Friends here, it will seem leaving Home to go there.

Our Relation that made the Lace (of which I sent you a second Parcel) is special Poor, and always like to be so, therefore I paid her the usual Price, tho' she would have made it a Present.[7] It was so plain I thought you might have worne it. I am pleas'd that it suits Sally. My Love to her and hers.

Your God-Daughter, Amelia Evans that was (now Barry) has been return'd some time from Africa, but it is only lately that I knew of her Return, for being remov'd she at first miss'd finding me. She is married to a Captain of a Ship in the Turky Trade, and has been once to Turky with her Husband, and has a Son born at Smirna, a fine stout Boy, a year old, as big as her Daughter of two Years that was born in Ireland. She is a great Traveller, having now been in all the 4 Quarters of the World. Last Tuesday Mrs. Stevenson and I went to dine with her and her Husband at a little Box they live in about 2 Miles out of town. He seems a clever Man, and they appear to live comfortably, the House prettily furnish'd, and every thing neat and tidy. She suckled her Giant Boy, and you know what a little Creature she is. Her Girl, the moment I enter'd the Room, smil'd and ran to me; kept to me all the time I staid, would not go to any Body else not even to

6. See above: for the new grandson Bache to BF, July 15, and for Ben's measles XIX, 314, 393-4. The silver spoon has vanished with DF's letter.

7. For Hannah Walker's lace see BF to DF above, Feb. 14.

Father or Mother, nor suffer another little Girl, about 5, that was there playing with her, to come near me. This was thought the more extraordinary, as the Child is remarkably shy, and never went willingly to a Stranger before. It is withal so very like its Grandmother, that I am half inclin'd to think there has been a Transmigration, and that she remember'd an old Friend.[8] They din'd with me yesterday here in Craven street. Amelia sends her Duty to you and Love to Sally, with some curious Seeds she brought with her from Turky, and which I wish you would take care to propagate.

There is a new Translation of my Book at Paris, and printed there, being the 3d Edition in French. A Fifth Edition is now printing here.[9] To the French Edition they have prefix'd a Print of your old Husband, which tho' a Copy of that per Chamberlain has got so French a Countenance, that you would take him for one of that lively Nation.[1] I think you do not mind such things, or I would send you one. I am ever, my dear Debby, Your affectionate Husband   B FRANKLIN

Addressed: To / Mrs Franklin / Philadelphia / viâ N York /per Packet / B Free FRANKLIN

8. The transmigration was from Martha Hoskins Evans (d. 1748); she had been close enough to DF to have her as godmother at Amelia's christening in 1744. Amelia's daughter in turn was named Amelia. Lawrence H. Gipson, *Lewis Evans* . . . (Philadelphia, 1939), pp. 5, 80 n; for the Evans family see also above, XII, 64 n; XVI, 134–5. At the foot of the draft BF wrote "Amelia," perhaps to remind himself to write the mother.

9. Dalibard had translated and published two editions of *Exper. and Obser.*, in 1752 and 1756: *Expériences et observations sur l'électricité faites . . . en Amérique.* . . . Barbeu-Dubourg's *Œuvres* included a new translation of the 1769 edition of *Exper. and Obser.*, and a great deal of additional material. Meanwhile BF was preparing a fifth English edition, for which see above, p. 129 n.

1. The print is the frontispiece of this volume, and its provenance is explained in the list of illustrations.

To William Franklin

AL (incomplete letterbook draft): Library of Congress; remainder, except a brief passage, reprinted from William Duane, ed., *The Works of Dr. Benjamin Franklin* . . . (6 vols., Philadelphia, 1808–18), VI, 329–31;[2] three final sentences quoted in William Franklin to Joseph Galloway, November 25, 1773: American Philosophical Society

Dear Son,   London, Sept. 1 1773

I have now before me yours of July 5. and 6. The August Packet is not yet arrived.

Dr. Cooper of New York's Opinion of the Author of the Sermon, however honourable to me, is injurious to the good Bishop; and therefore I must say in Justice and Truth, that I knew nothing of his Intention to preach on the Subject, and saw not a Word of the Sermon till it was printed.[3] Possibly some preceding Conversations between us may have turn'd his Thoughts that way; but if so, that is all.

I think the Resolutions of the New England Townships must have the Effect they seem intended for,[4] viz. to show that the Discontents were really general, and their Sentiments concerning their Rights unanimous, and not the Fiction of a few Demagogues, as their Governors us'd to represent them here. And therefore not useless, tho' they should not as yet induce Goverment to acknowledge their Claims. That People probably may think it sufficient for the present to assert and hold forth their Rights, secure that sooner or later they must be admitted and acknowledg'd. The declaratory Law here, had too its Use, viz. to prevent or lessen at least a Clamour against the Ministry that repeal'd the Stamp Act, as if they had given up the Right of this Country to

2. The draft is torn in places; we have supplied in brackets, from the Duane text, the words so lost.

3. For Shipley's sermon see BF to Cushing above, April 3; the Rev. Myles Cooper clearly considered BF responsible for the ideas it contained. Cooper (1737–85), an Anglican minister who was President of King's College, was a staunch Loyalist and one of the best known clergymen in the colonies. *DAB*.

4. The resolutions were responses to the declaration of the Boston town meeting, for which see the headnote on BF's Preface above, end of February. The resolutions themselves are discussed in Richard D. Brown, *Revolutionary Politics in Massachusetts: the Boston Committee of Correspondence and the Towns, 1772–1774* (Cambridge, Mass., 1970), chap. v.

govern America. Other Use indeed it could have none, and I remember Ld. Mansfield told the Lords, wh[en upon] that Bill, that it was nugatory.⁵ To be sure, in a Dispute between two Partys about Rights, the Declaration of one Party can never be suppos'd to bind the other.

It is said there is now a [project on] foot here to form an Union with Ireland, and [that Lord Harcou]rt is to propose it at the next Meeting of [the Irish parlia]ment. The Eastern Side of Ireland are a[verse to it;] supposing that when Dublin is no longer the Seat of their Legislature it will decline, the Harbour being but indif-[ferent,] and that the western and sou[thern] Ports will rise and f[lourish] on [its] Ruins, being good in themselves and much better situ[ated for com]merce. For these same Reasons, the w[estern and southern people] are inclin'd to the Measure, and 'tis [thought it may be carried.]⁶ But these are difficult Affairs, and [usually take longer time] than the Projectors imagine. Mr. Cro[wley, the author of] several Proposals for uniting [the colonies with the mother-]Country, and who runs about much among the Ministers, tells me the Union of⁷ Ireland is only the first step towards a general union. He is for having it done by the

5. William Murray, Lord Mansfield, one of the great judges in the history of English law, was an outspoken opponent of concessions to the colonies. His speech of Feb. 24, 1766, dealt with the principle of Parliamentary authority behind the Stamp Act: Cobbett, *Parliamentary History*, XVI (1765–71), 172–7.

6. Gen. Simon Harcourt, first Earl Harcourt (1714–77), succeeded Viscount Townshend in 1772 as lord lieutenant of Ireland. *DNB*. The central issue of Irish politics at this time was a proposal, originating with Harcourt, to tax absentee landlords; see Thomas H. D. Mahoney, *Edmund Burke and Ireland* (Cambridge, Mass., 1960), pp. 50–6. Rumor linked the proposal with a design for union; see the *London Chron.*, Aug. 28–31, and the Dublin *Freeman's Jour.*, Sept. 7–9, Oct. 23–26, 1773. In November Dublin County instructed its representatives in the Irish Parliament that the demand to tax absentees was the result of local agitation in the south, and would lead directly to union and the destruction of Irish trade, manufacture, and agriculture. The plan of union was apparently a bogey created by opponents of the tax. See Thomas F. Moriarty, "The Irish Absentee Tax Controversy of 1773 . . .," APS *Proc.*, CXVIII (1974), 388–90, 393, 405.

7. The draft breaks off here. For Thomas Crowley's proposals for union see above, XV, 238.

parliament of England, without consulting the colonies, and he will warrant, he says, that if the terms proposed are equitable, they will all come in one after the other. He seems rather a little cracked upon the subject.[8]

It is said here that the famous Boston letters were sent chiefly, if not all, to the late Mr. Wheatly. They fell into my hands, and I thought it my duty to give some principal people there a sight of them, very much with this view, that when they saw the measures they complained of, took their rise in a great degree from the representations and recommendations of their own countrymen, their resentment against Britain on account of those measures might abate, as mine had done, and a reconciliation be more easily obtained. In Boston, they concealed who sent them, the better to conceal who received and communicated them. And perhaps it is as well that it should continue a secret. Being of that country myself I think those letters more heinous than you seem to think them; but you had not read them all, nor perhaps the council's remarks on them.[9] I have written to decline their agency on account of my return to America. Dr. Lee succeeds me.[1] I only keep it while I stay, which perhaps will be another winter.

I grieve to hear of the death of my good old friend Dr. Evans. I have lost so many since I left America that I begin to fear I shall find myself a stranger among strangers when I return. If so, I must come again to my friends in England.

I have heard nothing of the Ohio Affair since my last. Depend upon it no such Orders were given to build Houses at Fort Pitt. I shall as you advise exert myself in that Business more than I have done,[2] for I see 'tis necessary; and that is one Inducement to my continuing here a little longer. My respectful Compliments to

8. WF had said just the same thing: XVI, 35.

9. See the note on Williams to BF above, June 28.

1. See BF to Cushing above, July 7.

2. In the absence of the letters that BF is acknowledging, WF's point must be divined from the context. "That Business" was obviously not Fort Pitt (for which see BF to Bache above, Feb. 3) but the Walpole grant, which BF had discussed in his "last," presumably that of July 25, and his earlier letter of July 14.

Mr. Galloway, from whom I now hear very seldom.[3] I am ever your affectionate father,   B FRANKLIN

An Infallible Method to Restore Peace and Harmony

Printed in *The Public Advertiser*, September 8, 1773.[4]

Franklin had long believed that the method outlined here offered the best hope of reconciliation, but he had never before formulated his belief so concretely or expressed it so publicly. His decision to do so at this point may have been related to his recent discovery that the Massachusetts House and Council, speaking for the province, had taken the same position in their letter of June 29 to Lord Dartmouth.[5]

To the Printer *of the* Public Advertiser.

Permit me, Sir, to communicate to the Ministry, thro' the Channel of your Paper, an *infallible Method* (and but one) to silence the Clamours of the Americans; to restore Peace and Harmony between the Colonies and the Mother Country; to regain the Affections of the most loyal, and I will venture to say the most virtuous of his Majesty's Subjects, whose Assistance may one Day be necessary to preserve that Freedom, which is the Glory and Happiness of the English Nation, and without which, from the Luxury and Effeminacy which at present reigns so universally among us, is in imminent Danger of being lost forever. The Method is plain and easy: Place the Americans in the same Individual Situation they were in before that di[aboli]cal, unconstitutional, oppressive Revenue Act was formed and endeavoured to be carried into Execution by Mr. Grenville; repeal the odious Tax on Tea; supersede the Board of Commissioners; let the Governors and Judges be appointed by the Crown, and paid by the People as usual; recall the Troops, except what are absolutely necessary for the Preservation of the new-acquired Provinces; in

3. WF quoted the paragraph to this point, as explained in the source identification, as coming from a letter of "Sept. 1[?]." The digit is obscure but single, and BF apparently did not write his son again until Oct. 6; see his letter below of that date. The quotation, which we have no way of locating in the text, seems to fit here as well as anywhere.

4. The annotation in Crane, *Letters to the Press*, pp. 232–3, relates particular passages to others in BF's earlier and later writings.

5. See the headnote on Cushing to BF above, June 30, and the reference to the letter from the houses in BF to Cushing below, Nov. 1.

fine, put every Thing on its ancient Footing. The Plea of its being dishonourable to give up a Point once determined upon, is vain and nugatory: The Instances are innumerable of Repeals of Acts of Parliament, which, when passed, were thought wise and necessary. The Stamp Duty for America is a recent Instance in point. Acts of Prerogative are surely not more sacred than Acts of Parliament. I insist upon it, that nothing would redound so much to the Honour of Administration, nothing would convince Mankind that the Intentions of Government are just and equitable, equal to the little Sacrifice of Vanity and the Pride of Power to the general Welfare of the British Empire. It is asserted, that there are Emissaries from France, who endeavour to foment the Difference between Great Britain and her Colonies. Disappoint this subtle and perfidious Nation. I will venture to prophecy, that notwithstanding this little Breach, the Connexion will be as strong, perhaps stronger than ever.

It was always the Boast of the Americans, that they could claim their Original from the Kingdom of Great Britain, and their Joy upon being re-admitted to all the Privileges of Englishmen will operate as a new Cement to a grateful and generous People, which will for ever ensure their future Loyalty and Obedience.

The above is the sincere Opinion of

A *Well-Wisher to Great Britain and her Colonies.*

Rules by Which a Great Empire May Be Reduced to a Small One

Printed in *The Public Advertiser*, September 11, 1773; incomplete draft and notes:[6] American Philosophical Society

Franklin was pleased with this satire, which was a companion piece to "An Edict by the King of Prussia."[7] Both had the virtues, he believed,

6. The draft lacks the middle pages and conclusion. The notes are small additions, written on the back of an invoice from Brown & Whitefoord dated Sept. 2, 1773; we indicate where they were and were not embodied in the draft.

7. Below, under Sept. 22. For a literary analysis of the satires see Richard E. Amacher, *Benjamin Franklin* (New York, [1962]), pp. 82–8. The fullest analysis is unfortunately not in print: Francis X. Davy, "Benjamin Franklin, Satirist: the Satire of Franklin and Its Rhetoric," unpublished doctoral dissertation, Columbia University, 1958.

of brevity, comprehensiveness, and "out-of-the-way forms" that caught attention; but he preferred the "Rules" to the "Edict" for the breadth and variety of its contents and for "a kind of spirited ending of each paragraph."[8] His technique in the two was different: in this one he challenged his readers to see their government's policy through colonial eyes; in the "Edict" he jolted them with the fiction that they were colonists themselves. The two essays had a single purpose, to induce the public to take a fresh look at the American problem. When Parliament reconvened in the autumn, that problem promised to be a major subject of discussion; and the sensational demand from Massachusetts for the removal of Hutchinson and Oliver was sure, when it came before the Privy Council, to provoke a storm. Moderate counsels could never prevail unless the folly of past measures was exposed, and Franklin devoted himself to exposing it. At the top of his satirical bent he could not be ignored, and the initial public reaction to his efforts was gratifying. The issue of the *Public Advertiser* containing the "Edict" sold out immediately, and both satires were widely reprinted in England and then in America.[9]

What Franklin achieved is another matter. Satire is a poor instrument of persuasion, for the open-minded are likely to be entertained—perhaps shocked—rather than convinced, and the close-minded to be angered. He was aware of the danger. Although he hoped to turn a spotlight on colonial grievances in order to gain redress, he realized that the effect might be to make matters worse.[1] For him personally that seems to have been the effect. The government dared not mention these attacks for fear of giving them even greater publicity, he concluded later, but they accounted in great part for the official fury unleashed upon him early in 1774.[2]

The substance behind the "Rules" was scarcely new. Franklin had, in more sober fashion, made almost every point before. He touched hardly at all upon the constitutional issues that the Bostonians had set boiling, no doubt because they were difficult to treat satirically; but he marshaled most of the other themes that were his stock in trade as a controversialist. Some related to the colonies in general, some to Massachusetts in particular, and they ran the gamut from old trade restrictions and novel taxes to the oppression wrought by the army

8. BF to WF below, Oct. 6.

9. *Ibid.*; Crane, *Letters to the Press*, pp. 233–4, 236–7.

1. To WF below, Nov. 3. BF's most interesting comment on his motives was to Jane Mecom below, Nov. 1.

2. See the extract of a letter from London below, Feb. 19, 1774.

and navy; the result was, as he said, comprehensive. These themes were so familiar from long reiteration that in their usual form they might well have evoked no more than a shrug from the British public. By recasting them in the "out-of-the-way" form of satire he gave them a new bite. But the effect was short-lived. The government soon bit him in turn and then—the final irony—legislated many of his "Rules" in the Coercive Acts of 1774.

For the Public Advertiser.

RULES *by which a* GREAT EMPIRE *may be reduced to a* SMALL ONE. [Presented privately to a *late Minister,* when he entered upon his Administration; and now first published.][3]

An ancient Sage valued himself upon this, that tho' he could not fiddle, he knew how to make a *great City* of a *little one.*[4] The Science that I, a modern Simpleton, am about to communicate is the very reverse.

I address myself to all Ministers who have the Management of extensive Dominions, which from their very Greatness are become troublesome to govern, because the Multiplicity of their Affairs leaves no Time for *fiddling.*

I. In the first Place, Gentlemen, you are to consider, that a great Empire, like a great Cake, is most easily diminished at the Edges. Turn your Attention therefore first to your remotest Provinces; that as you get rid of them, the next may follow in Order.

II. That the Possibility of this Separation may always exist, take special Care the Provinces are never incorporated with the Mother Country, that they do not enjoy the same common Rights, the same Privileges in Commerce, and that they are governed by *severer* Laws, all of *your enacting,* without allowing them any Share in the Choice of the Legislators. By carefully making and preserving such Distinctions, you will (to keep to my Simile of the Cake) act like a wise Gingerbread Baker, who, to facilitate a Division, cuts his Dough half through in those Places, where, when bak'd, he would have it *broken to Pieces.*

3. When Hillsborough took office in 1768, in other words, he adopted these rules to guide his policy. Brackets are in the original.

4. The sage was Themistocles, as reported by Plutarch; BF's wording is approximated in John and William Langhorne, *Plutarch's Lives* ... (6 vols., London, 1770), I, 281.

III. These remote Provinces have perhaps been acquired, purchas'd, or conquer'd, at the *sole Expence* of the Settlers or their Ancestors, without the Aid of the Mother Country. If this should happen to increase her *Strength* by their growing Numbers ready to join in her Wars, her *Commerce* by their growing Demand for her Manufactures, or her *Naval Power* by greater Employment for her Ships and Seamen, they may probably suppose some Merit in this, and that it entitles them to some Favour; you are therefore to *forget it all*, or resent it as if they had done you Injury. If they happen to be zealous Whigs, Friends of Liberty, nurtur'd in Revolution Principles, *remember all that* to their Prejudice, and contrive to punish it: For such Principles, after a Revolution is thoroughly established, are of *no more Use*, they are even *odious* and *abominable*.[5]

IV. However peaceably your Colonies have submitted to your Government, shewn their Affection to your Interest, and patiently borne their Grievances, you are to *suppose* them always inclined to revolt, and treat them accordingly. Quarter Troops among them, who by their Insolence may *provoke* the rising of Mobs, and by their Bullets and Bayonets *suppress* them. By this Means, like the Husband who uses his Wife ill *from Suspicion*, you may in Time convert your *Suspicions* into *Realities*.

V. Remote Provinces must have *Governors*, and *Judges*, to represent the Royal Person, and execute every where the delegated Parts of his Office and Authority. You Ministers know, that much of the Strength of Government depends on the *Opinion* of the People; and much of that Opinion on the Choice of[6] Rulers placed immediately over them. If you send them wise and good Men for Governors, who study the Interest of the Colonists, and

5. BF added this passage, beginning with "If they happen," from one of the notes mentioned above. His comment must have shocked English readers as much as he intended, for the principles of the Glorious Revolution had developed differently on the two sides of the Atlantic. In England the principle of an omnicompetent crown in Parliament had largely submerged the contractual limitations on government inherent in the Bill of Rights. The colonies, where local autonomy was in tension with control from London, preserved in full force the principle that authority per se was dangerous. See Bernard Bailyn, *The Ideological Origins of the American Revolution* (Cambridge, Mass., [1967]), especially pp. 35–6, 43–7, 201–3.

6. The first portion of the surviving draft ends here.

advance their Prosperity, they will think their King wise and good, and that he wishes the Welfare of his Subjects. If you send them learned and upright Men for judges, they will think him a Lover of Justice. This may attach your Provinces more to his Government. You are therefore to be careful who you recommend for those Offices. If you can find Prodigals who have ruined their Fortunes, broken Gamesters or Stock-Jobbers, these may do well as *Governors;* for they will probably be rapacious, and provoke the People by their Extortions. Wrangling Proctors and petty-fogging Lawyers[7] too are not amiss, for they will be for ever disputing and quarrelling with their little Parliaments, if withal they should be ignorant, wrong-headed and insolent, so much the better. Attorneys Clerks and Newgate Solicitors will do for *Chief-Justices*, especially if they hold their Places *during your Pleasure*: And all will contribute to impress those ideas of your Government that are proper for a People *you would wish to renounce it.*

VI. To confirm these Impressions, and strike them deeper, whenever the Injured come to the Capital with Complaints of Mal-administration, Oppression, or Injustice, punish such Suitors with long Delay, enormous Expence, and a final Judgment in Favour of the Oppressor. This will have an admirable Effect every Way. The Trouble of future Complaints will be prevented, and Governors and Judges will be encouraged to farther Acts of Oppression and Injustice; and thence the People may become more disaffected, *and at length desperate.*

VII. When such Governors have crammed their Coffers, and made themselves so odious to the People that they can no longer remain among them with Safety to their Persons, recall and *reward* them with Pensions. You may make them *Baronets* too,[8] if that respectable Order should not think fit to resent it. All will contribute to encourage new Governors in the same Practices, and make the supreme Government *detestable.*

VIII. If when you are engaged in War, your Colonies should vie in liberal Aids of Men and Money against the common Enemy, upon your simple Requisition, and give far beyond their Abilities,

7. Proctors had their own areas of pettifoggery, the ecclesiastical and admiralty courts.
8. Sir Francis Bernard.

reflect, that a Penny taken from them by your Power is more honourable to you than a Pound presented by their Benevolence. Despise therefore their voluntary Grants, and resolve to harrass them with novel Taxes. They will probably complain to your Parliaments that they are taxed by a Body in which they have no Representative, and that this is contrary to common Right. They will petition for Redress. Let the Parliaments flout their Claims, reject their Petitions, refuse even to suffer the reading of them, and treat the Petitioners with the utmost Contempt. Nothing can have a better Effect, in producing the Alienation proposed; for though many can forgive Injuries, *none ever forgave Contempt.*

IX. In laying these Taxes, never regard the heavy Burthens those remote People already undergo, in defending their own Frontiers, supporting their own provincial Governments, making new Roads, building Bridges, Churches and other public Edifices, which in old Countries have been done to your Hands by your Ancestors, but which occasion constant Calls and Demands on the Purses of a new People. Forget the *Restraints* you lay on their Trade for *your own* Benefit, and the Advantage a *Monopoly* of this Trade gives your exacting Merchants. Think nothing of the Wealth those Merchants and your Manufacturers acquire by the Colony Commerce; their encreased Ability thereby to pay Taxes at home; their accumulating, in the Price of their Commodities, most of those Taxes, and so levying them from their consuming Customers: All this, and the Employment and Support of thousands of your Poor by the Colonists, you are *intirely to forget.* But remember to make your arbitrary Tax more grievous to your Provinces, by public Declarations importing that your Power of taxing them has *no limits*, so that when you take from them without their Consent a Shilling in the Pound, you have a clear Right to the other nineteen. This will probably weaken every Idea of *Security in their Property,* and convince them that under such a Government *they have nothing they can call their own;* which can scarce fail of producing *the happiest Consequences*![9]

X. Possibly indeed some of them might still comfort themselves, and say, "Though we have no Property, we have yet *something* left that is valuable; we have constitutional *Liberty* both

9. BF had made this point earlier in his marginalia: above, XVII, 339.

of Person and of Conscience. This King, these Lords, and these Commons, who it seems are too remote from us to know us and feel for us, cannot take from us our *Habeas Corpus* Right, or our Right of Trial *by a Jury of our Neighbours:* They cannot deprive us of the Exercise of our Religion, alter our ecclesiastical Constitutions, and compel us to be Papists if they please, or Mahometans." To annihilate this Comfort, begin by Laws to perplex their Commerce with infinite Regulations impossible to be remembered and observed; ordain Seizures of their Property for every Failure; take away the Trial of such Property by Jury, and give it to arbitrary Judges of your own appointing, and of the lowest Characters in the Country, whose Salaries and Emoluments are to arise out of the Duties or Condemnations, and whose Appointments are *during Pleasure.* Then let there be a formal Declaration of both Houses, that Opposition to your Edicts is *Treason*, and that Persons suspected of Treason in the Provinces may, according to some obsolete Law, be seized and sent to the Metropolis of the Empire for Trial; and pass an Act that those there charged with certain other Offences shall be sent away in Chains from their Friends and Country to be tried in the same Manner for Felony. Then erect a new Court of Inquisition among them, accompanied by an armed Force, with Instructions to transport all such suspected Persons, to be ruined by the Expence if they bring over Evidences to prove their Innocence, or be found guilty and hanged if they can't afford it. And lest the People should think you cannot possibly go any farther, pass another solemn declaratory Act, that "King, Lords, and Commons had, hath, and of Right ought to have, full Power and Authority to make Statutes of sufficient Force and Validity to bind the unrepresented Provinces IN ALL CASES WHATSOEVER." This will include *Spiritual* with temporal; and taken together, must operate wonderfully to your Purpose, by convincing them, that they are at present under a Power something like that spoken of in the Scriptures, which can not only *kill their Bodies*, but *damn their Souls* to all Eternity, by compelling them, if it pleases, *to worship the Devil*.[1]

XI. To make your Taxes more odious, and more likely to

---

1. BF introduced "unrepresented Provinces" into his quotation from the Declaratory Act. His Biblical reference is to Matthew 10:28.

procure Resistance, send from the Capital a Board of Officers to superintend the Collection, composed of the most *indiscreet, ill-bred* and *insolent* you can find. Let these have large Salaries out of the extorted Revenue, and live in open grating Luxury upon the Sweat and Blood of the Industrious, whom they are to worry continually with groundless and expensive Prosecutions before the above-mentioned arbitrary Revenue-Judges, all *at the Cost of the Party prosecuted* tho' acquitted, because *the King is to pay no Costs.* Let these Men *by your Order* be exempted from all the common Taxes and Burthens of the Province, though they and their Property are protected by its Laws. If any Revenue Officers are *suspected* of the least Tenderness for the People, discard them.[2] If others are justly complained of, protect and reward them. If any of the Under-officers behave so as to provoke the People to drub them, promote those to better Offices: This will encourage others to procure for themselves such profitable Drubbings, by multiplying and enlarging such Provocations, and *all with work towards the End you aim at.*

XII. Another Way to make your Tax odious, is to misapply the Produce of it. If it was originally appropriated for the *Defence* of the Provinces and the better Support of Government, and the Administration of Justice where it may be *necessary,* then apply none of it to that *Defence,* but bestow it where it is *not necessary,* in augmented Salaries or Pensions to every Governor who has distinguished himself by his Enmity to the People, and by calumniating them to their Sovereign. This will make them pay it more unwillingly, and be more apt to quarrel with those that collect it, and those that imposed it, who will quarrel again with them, and all shall contribute to your *main Purpose* of making them *weary of your Government.*

XIII. If the People of any Province have been accustomed to support their own Governors and Judges to Satisfaction, you are to apprehend that such Governors and Judges may be thereby influenced to treat the People kindly, and to do them Justice. This is another Reason for applying Part of that Revenue in larger Salaries to such Governors and Judges, given, as their Commissions are, *during your Pleasure* only, forbidding them to take any

2. A reference to John Temple, dismissed in 1770: above, XIX, 402.

Salaries from their Provinces; that thus the People may no longer hope any Kindness from their Governors, or (in Crown Cases) any Justice from their Judges. And as the Money thus mis-applied in one Province is extorted from all, probably *all will resent the Misapplication.*

XIV. If the Parliaments of your Provinces should dare to claim Rights or complain of your Administration, order them to be harass'd with repeated *Dissolutions.* If the same Men are continually return'd by new Elections, adjourn their Meetings to some Country Village where they cannot be accommodated, and there keep them *during Pleasure;* for this, you know, is your PREROGATIVE; and an excellent one it is, as you may manage it, to promote Discontents among the People, diminish their Respect, and *increase their Disaffection.*

XV. Convert the brave honest Officers of your Navy into pimping Tide-waiters and Colony Officers of the Customs. Let those who in Time of War fought gallantly in Defence of the Commerce of their Countrymen, in Peace be taught to prey upon it. Let them learn to be corrupted by great and real Smugglers; but (to shew their Diligence) scour with armed Boats every Bay, Harbour, River, Creek, Cove or Nook throughout the Coast of your Colonies, stop and detain every Coaster, every Wood-boat, every Fisherman, tumble their Cargoes, and even their Ballast, inside out and upside down; and if a Penn'orth of Pins is found un-entered, let the Whole be seized and confiscated. Thus shall the Trade of your Colonists suffer more from their Friends in Time of Peace, than it did from their Enemies in War. Then let these Boats Crews land upon every Farm in their Way, rob the Orchards, steal the Pigs and Poultry, and insult the Inhabitants. If the injured and exasperated Farmers, unable to procure other Justice, should attack the Agressors, drub them and burn their Boats, you are to call this *High Treason* and *Rebellion*, order[3] Fleets and Armies into their Country, and threaten to carry all the Offenders three thousand Miles to be hang'd, drawn and quartered. *O! this will work admirably!*

XVI. If you are told of Discontents in your Colonies, never believe that they are general, or that you have given Occasion for

3. The second portion of the surviving draft begins here.

them; therefore do not think of applying any Remedy, or of changing any offensive Measure. Redress no Grievance, lest they should be encouraged to demand the Redress of some other Grievance. Grant no Request that is just and reasonable, lest they should make another that is unreasonable. Take all your Informations of the State of the Colonies from your Governors and Officers in Enmity with them. Encourage and reward these *Leasing-makers;*[4] secrete their lying Accusations lest they should be confuted; but act upon them as the clearest Evidence, and believe nothing you hear from the Friends of the People. Suppose all *their* Complaints to be invented and promoted by a few factious Demagogues, whom if you could catch and hang, all would be quiet. Catch and hang a few of them accordingly; and the *Blood of the Martyrs* shall *work Miracles* in favour of your Purpose.

XVII. If you see *rival Nations* rejoicing at the Prospect of your Disunion with your Provinces, and endeavouring to promote it: If they translate, publish and applaud all the Complaints of your discontented Colonists,[5] at the same Time privately stimulating you to severer Measures; let not that *alarm* or offend you. Why should it? since you all mean *the same Thing*.[6]

XVIII. If any Colony should at their own Charge erect a Fortress to secure their Port against the Fleets of a foreign Enemy, get your Governor to betray that Fortress into your Hands. Never think of paying what it cost the Country, for that would *look*, at least, like some Regard for Justice; but turn it into a Citadel to awe the Inhabitants and curb their Commerce. If they should have lodged in such Fortress the very Arms they bought

4. Liars, a phrase derived from Scottish law. The part of the sentence that follows, from "secrete" to "Evidence," BF interlined in his draft from one of the notes mentioned above.

5. The controlled French press had been publishing, since the time of the Stamp Act, documentation of the developing Anglo-American quarrel; see Durand Echeverria, *Mirage in the West: a History of the French Image of American Society to 1815* (Princeton, [1957]), pp. 36–7.

6. BF added Rule XVII to his draft from one of the notes mentioned above, but deleted the opening sentence of that note: "If wretched Writers rail against your Colonists, and do their best to widen Breaches, reward them with Pensions or with Patent Places: if those are to be paid out of the Colony Revenue, and those are Colony Places, it will be the more *grating* and of course *so much the better*. And if you see," etc.

and used to aid you in your Conquests, seize them all, 'twill provoke like *Ingratitude* added to *Robbery*.[7] One admirable Effect of these Operations will be, to discourage every other Colony from erecting such Defences, and so their and your Enemies may more easily invade them, to the great Disgrace of your Government, and of course *the Furtherance of your Project*.[8]

XIX. Send Armies into their Country under Pretence of protecting the Inhabitants; but instead of garrisoning the Forts on their Frontiers with those Troops, to prevent Incursions, demolish those Forts, and order the Troops into the Heart of the Country, that the Savages may be encouraged to attack the Frontiers, and that the Troops may be protected by the Inhabitants: This will seem to proceed from your Ill will or your Ignorance, and contribute farther to produce and strengthen an Opinion among them, *that you are no longer fit to govern them*.

XX. Lastly, Invest the General of your Army in the Provinces with great and unconstitutional Powers, and free him from the Controul of even your own Civil Governors. Let him have Troops enow under his Command, with all the Fortresses in his Possession; and who knows but (like some provincial Generals in the Roman Empire, and encouraged by the universal Discontent you have produced) he may take it into his Head to set up for himself. If he should, and you have carefully practised these few *excellent Rules* of mine, take my Word for it, all the Provinces will immediately join him, and you will that Day (if you have not done it sooner) get rid of the Trouble of governing them, and all the *Plagues* attending their *Commerce* and Connection from thenceforth and for ever.   Q.E.D.

7. BF interlined this sentence in his draft from one of the notes mentioned above.

8. The second portion of the surviving draft ends here. BF returned to the subject of this paragraph in his introduction to Bernard's speeches below, Sept. 17.

To Thomas Cushing

Reprinted from William Duane, ed., *The Works of Benjamin Franklin* ... (6 vols., Philadelphia, 1808–18), VI, 331–2.

Sir,   London, Sept. 12, 1773.

The above is a copy of my last, per packet. Inclosed is the original letter therein mentioned.[9] His lordship continues in the country, but is expected (secretary Pownall tells me) the beginning of next month.

To avoid repealing the American tea duty, and yet find a vent for tea, a project is executing to send it from hence, on account of the East India company to be sold in America, agreeable to a late act, impowering the lords of the treasury to grant licences to the company to export tea thither, under certain restrictions, duty free. Some friends of government (as they are called) of Boston, New York, Philadelphia, &c. are to be favored with the commission, who undertake by their interest to carry the measure through in the colonies.[10] How the other merchants thus excluded from the tea trade will like this, I cannot foresee. Their agreement, if I remember right, was not to import tea, till the duty shall be repealed. Perhaps they will think themselves still obliged by that agreement, notwithstanding this temporary expedient; which is only to introduce the tea for the present, and may be dropped next year, and the duty again required, the granting or refusing such license from time to time remaining in the power of the treasury. And it will seem hard, while their hands are tied, to see the profits of that article all engrossed by a few particulars.[11]

9. The duplicate of BF to Cushing above, Sept. 1, is now missing. With that letter he enclosed copies of Dartmouth to Bollan, also missing, and to BF of Aug. 25. The latter must have been the original that he now enclosed.

10. For the background and development of the project that was "executing" see above, BF to Galloway, Feb. 14, to Cushing and to Williams, June 4. The Tea Act imposed certain restrictions on export, which were repeated in the licenses issued by the Treasury; see Francis S. Drake, ed., *Tea Leaves: Being a Collection of Letters and Documents Relating to the Shipment of Tea* ... *in the Year 1773* ... (Boston, 1884), pp. 249–51.

11. Is BF suggesting, in this guardedly obscure passage, that merchants should resist for economic reasons? He was well aware of other reasons: a saving of 3*d.* a pound would never serve "to overcome all the Patriotism of an American!" To Cushing above, June 4. Yet he gives no hint here of anticipating the violent popular reaction that tea would evoke. Opposition to the

Enclosed I take the liberty of sending you a small piece of mine, written to expose, in as striking a light as I could, to the nation, the absurdity of the measures towards America, and to spur the ministry if possible to a change of those measures.[1]

Please to present my duty to the house, and respects to the committee. I have the honor to be, with much esteem, sir, your most obedient humble servant, B. FRANKLIN.

From Charles Wilcox[2] ALS: American Philosophical Society

Sir   Bristol, 13th Septr. 1773.

You was so kind as to assure Me in Your Letter to Me of the 3d Febry last that if I had Occasion to trouble You, You would Serve Me. The Case now Sir is this I am apply'd to by the Heirs of one Colonel William Cole who had an Estate in Maryland and Philadelphia to recover the same for them. You will Extreamly Oblige Me Sir to let Me know if You knew any such Person. He died about 13 Years since at Coles Creek in Maryland. I beg You will excuse the Trouble I give You to answer this Letter,[3] it will be serving a poor Family and Oblige Sir Your most Humble Servant   CHAS. WILCOX

———

duty, dormant since the collapse of the nonimportation agreements in 1770, was reviving throughout the colonies; and the uproar in Boston began at about the time when BF's letter must have arrived there. See Labaree, *Tea Party*, pp. 50, 104–9.

1. Earlier editors assumed that the enclosure was the "Edict by the King of Prussia," which may not have been written yet and was certainly not in print. BF must have sent the "Rules," the preceding document; the "Edict" went with his note to Cushing below, Sept. 23.

2. An American who had arrived in Bristol earlier in the year and gone into business there. He seems to have been a middleman in the hardware trade between Birmingham and New England; see his letter to Samuel and Stephen Salisbury, April 21, 1773, Salisbury Papers, II (5), Amer. Antiquarian Soc. BF was in intermittent correspondence with him for some time; three of Wilcox's letters have survived, of which this is the first, and none of BF's.

3. We are as ignorant of Col. Cole as were Wilcox and BF. The latter apparently suggested inquiring of the Annapolis postmaster; see Wilcox's acknowledgment below, Nov. 8.

PS. A Vessell will sail in about 10 days for Phila. if you have any dispatches I will take Care to forward them

Benja Fra[nklin]

Addressed: Benja. Franklin Esqr LLD / In / Craven Street / London

'Tis Never Too Late to Mend

Printed in *The Public Advertiser*, September 14, 1773

Although Franklin was delighted with his satire, "Rules by Which a Great Empire May Be Reduced to a Small One," he was not confident that the public shared his opinion of it.[4] To draw attention to it, presumably, he inserted the following letter in the *Public Advertiser*.[5] But the essay needed no such publicity; it was making its own way, and was soon widely reprinted.[6]

To the Printer *of the* Public Advertiser.

SIR,

I HAD the Pleasure to read in your Paper of Saturday last some excellent Rules, by which a GREAT EMPIRE may be reduced to a *small One*. They are drawn up in a fine Vein of *Irony*, which is admirably supported throughout.

If the Ministry have any Sense of Shame remaining, they must blush to see their Conduct with respect to America placed in such a striking Point of Ridicule; and the ingenious Author is intitled to the Thanks both of Great Britain and the Colonies for shewing the Absurdity and bad Policy of such Conduct.

To be sensible of Error is one Step towards Amendment; no Man is infallible; and MINISTERS are but *Men;* 'tis never too late to mend, nor is it any Impeachment of our Understanding to confess that we have been mistaken; for it implies *that we are wiser Today than we were the Day before;* and surely *Individuals* need not

4. See BF to WF below, Oct. 6.
5. Crane's evidence for BF's authorship is convincing: *Letters to the Press*, p. 235 ns.
6. See BF to WF below, Nov. 3.

be ashamed publicly to retract an Error, since the LEGISLATURE itself does it every Time that it repeals one of its own Acts.[7]

But though the Americans have long been oppressed, let them not despair. The Administration of the Colonies is no longer in the Hands of a Shelburne, a Clare, or a Hillsborough; thank Heaven *that* Department is NOW entrusted to an ENGLISHMAN![8] Be it *his* Glory to *reverse* those baneful and pernicious Measures which have too long harrassed the Colonies, and have given such a Blow to the *Credit*, the *Commerce*, and the NAVAL POWER of the Mother Country. I am, SIR,

A sincere Well-wisher to GREAT BRITAIN *and her* COLONIES.

From Benjamin Rush

AL (incomplete): American Philosophical Society

Honoured Sir   [After Sept. 15, 1773[9]]

I acknowledge myself much indebted to you for the Instruction contained in your last Letter. I have met with many Facts which confirm your Opinion of the Origin of Catarhs from Cloaths, Beds, Books &c. Baron Van Swieten in his last Volume of Commentaries on Dr. Boerhave's Aphorisms[1] in treating upon

7. BF is repeating a point he had just made in his "Infallible Method": above, Sept. 8.

8. Shelburne, in the Southern Department, had been responsible for American affairs before 1768, and Clare had been president of the Board of Trade; Hillsborough, on becoming the first American Secretary in 1768, also took over Clare's position. All three were Anglo-Irish and members of the Irish peerage. BF was on excellent terms with Shelburne, and had no bias against the Irish in general. Perhaps he assumed such a bias in his readers, and wanted to emphasize Dartmouth's opportunity to break with the past.

9. Although the letter has been tentatively dated 1771 (*PMHB*, LXXVIII [1954], 12), it was clearly in answer to BF to Rush above, July 14. Four ships sailed from England around July 21, and arrived in Philadelphia on and after Sept. 15 (*London Chron.*, July 20–22; *Pa. Gaz.*, September 15, 22). Hence Rush could not have had BF's letter before mid-September.

1. Gerard van Swieten, *The Commentaries upon the Aphorisms of Dr. Herman Boërhaave ... Concerning the Knowledge and Cure of the Several Diseases Incident to Human Bodies ...* (11 vols., London, 1754–59). For Van Swieten see above, XVIII, 165 n; Hermann Boerhaave (1668–1738) was an extremely influential medical teacher at Leyden, who originated the clinical method of instruction.

403

Epidemic Diseases mentions with Astonishment a Disorder which was peculiar only to the students and Bookseller of the University of Alstorp in Switzerland.[2] May not the Origin of this be traced to the Library of the University from which all the Inhabitants of the town except the Bookseller were probably excluded? A Clergyman from Charlestown in South Carolina who had never heard of your Remark informed me lately that he had almost lost his wife by a severe Catarh which she caught by assisting him in moving his Library from One Room into Another.[3] Instances of Catarh derived and propagated from Beds, Cloathes &c. might be mentioned without Number. But I can by no means think that Catarhs should be confined to these Causes. The Cases you have mentioned I grant a little invalidate the Arguments derived from the Operation of *Cold* in producing Catarhs, but I beg Leave to add that they do not appear conclusive. Dr. Gaubius in his Pathology[4] speaks of certain remote Causes of Diseases which act only on what he calls the "predispositis." Thus a few Glasses of Wine will bring on a Fitt of the Gout upon a Man who inherits a gouty Constitution, provided he drinks them at the usual seasons of that Disorder's attacking him. The same Quantity of Wine will have no Effect upon a Man who is not predisposed, or subject to the Gout. We cannot say however from this that Wine is not One of the remote Causes of that Disorder. Putrid Diseases are brought on by Effluvia from putrefying Animal substances. The City of Edinburgh and many of the principal Cities in Spain

2. As far as we can discover there was no such place, let alone university; Rush may have had in mind the Latin school at Altdorf, in the canton of Uri.

3. The clergyman, we believe, was the Rev. William Tennent, the minister of the Independent Church in Charleston and a citizen of considerable prominence, who had married Susan Vergereau. See Newton B. Jones, "Writings of the Reverend William Tennent, 1740–1777," *S. C. Hist. Mag.*, LXI (1960), 129–45. Tennent, who had graduated from Princeton two years before Rush and must have known him there, sailed for Philadelphia in July: *S.-C. Ga**., July 12, 1773. A few months earlier Rush had turned down an offer of a thousand guineas a year to settle in Charleston: Lyman H. Butterfield, ed., *Letters of Benjamin Rush* . . . (2 vols., [Princeton,] 1951), I, 77. Tennent may possibly have been attempting, after his wife's experience, to get the Doctor to change his mind.

4. Hieronymus David Gaubius, *Institutiones pathologiae medicinalis* . . . (Leyden, 1758); for the author see above, XVIII, 165 n.

are never free from these *Effluvia* and yet we do Not find they are more subject to putrid Diseases than Other Places. It will not do to say here that the Volatile salt which is constantly extricated from these foecal Matters acts as an antisceptic and prevents putrid Diseases. The same Salt is extricated from Other putrid Matters without producing any such Effect. These Facts however by no means call in Question the Truth of that general Proposition that putrid animal Effluvia generate putrid Diseases. The Operation of Cold and moisture requires a Predisposition in the Body to produce a Disorder in it. A man with weak Lungs seldom fails of having a Cough brought on, or aggravated by wetting his feet, sitting in a damp Room, riding or walking in the night Air. A man who has had the Sensibility of his Lungs encreased by previous warm weather, a warm Room, or by speaking or singing long, or with a loud voice will seldom fail of having a Cough or Defluxion brought on his Breast, if he exposes himself immediately After any of these, to a cold Air. Cold and moisture it may be said influence the Operation of those Matters which bring on Catarhs, and thus appear to act by themselves. But it cannot be so in the present Instances. Moreover in the Histories of all Epidemics, whether Plague, small pox, putrid fevers &c. we find the operation of Cold and moisture in the most sensible Manner upon the Body either in predisposing to, preventing or changing the Type of these Diseases. But I go further; we find several Diseases actually produced by Cold such as the Rheumatism, Angina, and Pleuresy.

After much and painful Enquiry into [*remainder missing.*]

On Governor Bernard's Testimony to the Loyalty of Massachusetts[5]

Printed in *The Public Advertiser*, September 17, 1773

To the Printer *of the* Public Advertiser.

Sir,

As I gather from a very sensible Piece, entitled "RULES AND ORDERS for reducing a great Empire to a SMALL ONE," published

5. We follow Crane (*Letters to the Press*, p. 236) in attributing this to BF rather than Arthur Lee.

in your Paper of Saturday last, that the Inhabitants of the Province of the Massachusetts Bay had all their Arms (which were bought of us with their own Money, and with which they fought so successfully in our glorious Conquests in the last War) taken from them without any Consideration whatever,[6] which were in the Castle ordered out of their Hands by Lord Hillsborough a few Years ago, will you be so good as to publish the following Extracts from three of Governor Bernard's Speeches to that People? before he became their implacable Enemy, on being found out, detected and despised by them, from which (even his Testimony) it will appear how ready they were, on all Occasions, to assist us both with their Money and their Blood to the utmost of their Abilities.

⟨On Nov. 12, 1761, the Governor expressed his pleasure at the unanimity of the support that had been forthcoming from the oldest and most loyal American colony, and his confidence that both houses would do everything in their power to make his administration useful to the province. On April 24, 1762, he thanked them for their prompt compliance with every requisition, for which the credit was entirely theirs; his reward was to preside over such a public-spirited people. On May 27, 1762, he lauded the colony's war effort: never before that year had regiments been so easily and quickly raised, and provision for the King's service had been so ample that nothing more was at present required.[7]⟩

N.B. These are the People who have lately had Fleets and Armies sent among 'em, to subdue them as REBELS and TRAITORS!!!

From Thomas Cushing   ALS and LS (copy): Library of Congress

Sir   Boston Sept. 18 1773

The foregoing is Copy of my last[8] since which I have not received any of your Favors; I have lately received a Letter from

6. See Rule XVIII in the satire printed above, Sept. 11.

7. For the text of the extracts see Sparks, *Works*, IV, 466–8. BF returned to the subject of Bernard in his communication to the *Public Advertiser* below, after Oct. 30.

8. His letter of Aug. 26 above.

the Speaker of the House of Deputies of the Colony of Rhode Island desiring I would favor him with G Rome's original Letter. I have wrote him that it is returned to England. Inclosed you have a Copy of the Speaker's Letter and should be glad if you could furnish me, Mr. Bowler or Mr. Henry Merchant of Newport with the original Letter before mentioned, or if you cannot obtain leave to Send the original Letter Again, perhaps you may furnish us with an attested Copy of it, which may in some measure answer the purpose tho not so well as the original.[9] I should be glad [if] you would Inform me how far the administration have proceeded with regard to the Judges saleries, we have been Informed that the King in Council has ordered that they shall be allowed Salleries from home, but whether Warrants have as yet been even Issued for their payment is uncertain. I should be glad to know in what situation this matter is in at present.[10] I conclude with great respect Your most humble Servant   THOMAS CUSHING

9. For Metcalf Bowler see the *DAB*, and for Henry Marchant above, XVIII, 145; XIX, 212–13. George Rome was an English merchant, who had come to Newport in 1761 to collect debts for a London firm; he and Thomas Moffatt were members of a group that made itself intensely unpopular, just before the Stamp Act crisis, by seeking revocation of the Rhode Island charter. Edmund S. and Helen M. Morgan, *The Stamp Act Crisis . . .* (Chapel Hill, N.C., [1953]), pp. 47–8. Cushing's inquiry about the letter in 1767 from Rome to Moffatt, part of the Hutchinson correspondence and printed below at the end of the appendix, is the first evidence that the Speaker had returned the original MSS to BF; they have vanished, along with whatever note accompanied them. Bowler's letter, dated Aug. 20, 1773, and now in the Library of Congress, explained that Rome should be prosecuted, in the opinion of the Rhode Island House of Deputies, for having tried to promote measures that would subvert the rights of all the colonies and reduce them to slavery. A second inquiry from Bowler elicited a second request from Cushing below, Dec. 11. Whether or not BF produced the original, Rome was later haled before the House and imprisoned: Sabine, *Loyalists*, II, 237–8.

10. For the issues at stake in this controversy see above, pp. 111 n, 125 n. Royal warrants issued in August, 1772, for paying the judges' salaries had not arrived by January, 1773, when the House voted the stipends for the previous year; Hutchinson delayed his assent until he had made sure that payments by the province and the crown would not overlap. In February the House voted the judicial salaries in advance for 1773; the Governor refused assent on the ground that paying for future services was unprecedented and would defeat the King's intent. In March the House resolved that any judge who accepted a royal salary was promoting arbitrary government, and in

[*In the margin:*] Inclosed you have a Newspaper in which you have Inserted a Letter to the Cheif Justice and a paper laid before the Superior Court.[1]

Endorsed: Augst. 22. 73[2] Thos Cushing Esqr with Metcalf Bowler's Letter, Speaker of the Rh Island Assembly.

From Jonathan Williams, Jr.   ALS: National Archives

Dear and honoured sir   [Before Sept. 21, 1773[3]]

I received your kind Letter inclosing one for Mr. Cowan purser of the Glasgow, who is now at Hallifax, but as the Ship is ordered here in about 3 Weeks, shall keep 'till that time as the most certain way of getting it speedily to his hands.[4]

I am sorry to find that the East India Company do not intend to send a Ship to America, but am not the less obliged by your and Mrs. Barwells kind Intentions. Commission Business is allowed to be the safest that is transacted, and as I can attend more

---

June it declared that the judges must, on pain of impeachment, say whether they would accept. Bradford, ed., *Mass. State Papers*, pp. 365–7, 397–8; Mass. Arch., XXVII, 444–5, 452; *Mass. House Jour.*, 1st session, May–June, 1773, pp. 87–8, 94. The warrants, to judge by Cushing's inquiry, had still not arrived in September, more than a year after they had been issued.

1. The *Mass. Spy* of Sept. 16, which contained a letter attacking Chief Justice Peter Oliver for refusing to say whether he would take a royal salary, and a demand from the grand jury of the Superior Court, echoing the June resolution of the House mentioned above, that he and the other judges explain where they stood on the question.

2. Cushing misdated the copy of his letter of the 26th, mentioned in the first sentence.

3. The letter is endorsed, in a hand that might be BF's, "Date suppos'd to be about Oct. 17. 1773." Williams sent it by Capt. Benjamin Gorham, who left Boston on Sept. 21. *Mass. Gaz.*; *and the Boston Weekly News-Letter*, Sept. 23, 1773.

4. For this reference and those that follow see BF's letter above, July 7. H.M.S. *Glasgow*, of twenty guns, arrived on the American station in 1768, and achieved brief prominence in the spring of 1776 when she was engaged by an American squadron and jettisoned her dispatches. John Charnock, *Biographia navalis* . . . (6 vols., London, 1794–98), VI, 552; William B. Willcox, *Portrait of a General* . . . (New York, 1964), p. 78.

affairs than I have to employ me, I should be glad to make as many commercial concerns as I can, especially in England, as all our Trade centers there: and if they did not prove immediately so profitable, it renders a Man of such consequence, that in turn his connexion is solicited by others, and many advantageous transient affairs might fall into his hands, which for want of being known he might miss of. I am never so happy as when fully employed, for of whatever profession I might be, I should wish to be the most eminent. This I know has the appearance of ambition, but I hope I have not too much of it, and I hope also when it leads in the channel of Business 'tis not blameable, for it appears to me no extraordinary proof of Talents, to do what any one else may do, and I think the best Cobler has more merit than an ordinary merchant. For this reason I am flattered with, and fond of my superfine Cloth Trade, for I wish to be conspicuous for my knowledge in, and attention to Business as well as for preserving an unlimited Credit. I could not bear *that* should suffer, for I had rather live on bread and water and be thought an honest man, than to posses Thousands with a suspicious Character. I intend this Winter to strain every nerve to lessen my debts in England, and if in my power to pay them all, for just at this Time the credit of this Town seems to be going to general Wreck, so that it particularly Behoves me to establish mine, that after the purgation is over, I may come out with unsullied reputation, and pursue my Business with fresh Vigour.[5] 'Tis imagined that many orders from this side will be refused, and only those who can bear a scrutiny will be trusted again, by which means the Trade will get into such hands, as to enable the prosecutors of it to carry it on with satisfaction and profit. I have delivered the Letter to Henry[6] who I take care to advise with regard to his Behaviour to his master and application to his Trade which I hope and believe he will be master of and as I hear no complaints I am inclined to think he behaves very well.

5. Boston was still in the aftermath of the crisis of 1772, when credit had been drastically curtailed. See above, XIX, 101 n; Jonathan Williams, Sr., to BF, Feb. 15, 1773.
6. Mrs. Walker had sent BF some letters to forward to her son Henry; see her note above, June 20. We assume that BF had enclosed them in his letter of July 7 to Jonathan, who for some reason acknowledged only one.

Be pleased to make my best Respects acceptable to Mrs. Stevenson, Mr. and Mrs. Hewson Mrs. Blunt and all enquiring. Friends on this side are well and join in Duty and Love with Your dutifull and Affectionate Kinsman JONA WILLIAMS JUNR

By mine and several other Letters from England I find the Merchants trading to N England [have] declined shipping Tea to any of their Friends in consequence of the India Company having it in contemplation to ship Teas themselves, which leads me to think they did intend it; but you must best know what can be obtain'd, from them, and what is proper I should receive. I am (as above) J W

Addressed: To / Doctr Benja Franklin / at Mrs Stevensons In / Craven Street / Strand / London / Per Gorham

To John Baskerville   ALS (draft): American Philosophical Society

Dear Sir,   London, Sept. 21. 1773.

I duly received your Favour of the 24th past, and some time after, the Parcel containing the Specimens and your valuable Present of Shaftsbury excellently printed for which I hold myself greatly obliged to you. The Specimens I shall distribute by the first Ships among the Printers in America, and I hope to your Advantage.[7] I suppose no Orders will come unaccompanied by Bills or Money, and I would not advise you to give any Credit, especially as I think it will not be necessary.

The Sheet of Chinese Paper, is from its enormous Size a great Curiosity. I see the Marks of the Mold in it. One Side is smooth; that I imagine is the Side that was apply'd to the smooth Face of the Kiln on which it was dry'd. The little Ridges on the other Side I take to be Marks of a Brush pass'd over it to press it against that Face in places where it might be kept off by Air between, and which would otherwise prevent its receiving the Smoothness. But we will talk further of this when I have the Pleasure of seeing you.

7. See Baskerville's letter above, Aug. 24. If the specimens were distributed, none seems to have survived: William Bennett, *John Baskerville, the Birmingham Printer* . . . (2 vols., [Birmingham,] 1937–39), II, 32–3, 38.

You speak of enlarging your Foundery. Here are all the Matrices and Puncheons of James's Foundery to be sold;[8] there seem to be among them some tolerable Hebrews and Greeks, and some good Blacks.[9] I suppose you know them. Shall I buy any of them for you?

I thank you for your kind Invitation. Perhaps I may embrace it for a few Days. My best Respects to good Mrs. Baskerville, and believe me ever, with great Esteem, Your most obedient humble Servant

B F[10]

[*In another hand:*] To Baskerville

8. See Mores to BF above, June 7. Earlier editors misread the phrase as "matrices of Rumford's and James's founderies."

9. *I.e.*, black letter.

10. The two final paragraphs of the draft, with BF's initials, run across only two-thirds of the sheet. In the remaining third appears the following list, in his hand and at right angles to the draft:

Hebrews	27	at £3	81
Samaritan	2		3
Syriac	4		5
Arabic	3		7
Ethiopic	2		2
Greek	22	at 3	66
Line Capitals	7		7
Rom and Ital	16 ⎱	21 at 3	63
Do	5 ⎰		
Runic. Gothic &c.	12.	10*s.*	6
Black	13.	at 3	39
			————
			279

The list, to judge by its position on the page, seems to have been written before the draft. If the prices quoted were those at the auction in December, however, the draft preceded the list. If they were prices that were being asked earlier, on the other hand, BF may have meant to include them.

To Henry S. Woodfall[1] AL: American Philosophical Society

This note went to the recipient, then to a mutual friend, then back to Woodfall and eventually back to Craven Street. The note was on a covering sheet around the manuscript of the following document, "An Edict by the King of Prussia," and explained the typographical form that Franklin wished to have given to his satire. On the verso of the sheet Woodfall addressed it and its contents to Franklin's old friend and neighbor Caleb Whitefoord, who owned stock in the newspaper and frequently saw material submitted to it.[2] Whitefoord readdressed the cover and the manuscript to Woodfall with a request to him, written under Franklin's note, to publish the satire at once.[3] The printer did so. He then returned the cover to Franklin, and added under Whitefoord's note one of his own to explain how he had handled "the enclosed," which was either the manuscript or a clipping of the published text. This small sheet, in other words, has a great deal to say about the birth of the satire.

[Before September 22, 1773]

If Mr. Woodfall shall think fit to give the enclosed a Place in his Paper, he is requested to take Care that the Compositor observes strictly the Italicking, Capitalling and Pointing. If it is done as correctly as the *Rules for diminishing*, &c. it will be very satisfactory to his humble Servant the Author.[4]

[*Note by Whitefoord to Woodfall:*] Pray let the inclosd appear in P.A. as soon as you can conveniently. Yours &c.

1. Henry Sampson Woodfall (1739–1805) was a stormy petrel and one of the best known newspapermen of his day. He succeeded his father as printer of the *Public Advertiser* in 1760, and continued the paper for more than three decades; he turned it into an open forum that was, as he said in 1769, "what its correspondents please to make it." One of them was Junius, for whom Woodfall acted as both publisher and editor, and who involved him in his first—but far from last—trial for libel. *DNB*. Despite BF's frequent appearances in the columns of the paper, this is the only extant bit of correspondence between him and its printer.

2. Crane, *Letters to the Press*, p. xxi.

3. Crane misread Whitefoord's request as a part of BF's note (*ibid.*, p. 237), a natural error because the two men had a strikingly similar hand. For Whitefoord see above, X, 171 n.

4. This was a point on which BF felt strongly; see his letter to WF below, Oct. 6. A comparison of the text of the "Edict" with that of the "Rules" (above, Sept. 11) shows how faithfully Woodfall heeded the injunction.

[*Note by Woodfall to Franklin:*] If the enclosed had been printed as a Foreign Article I feared it would have been lost, or at least not so much attended to as it deserved.   H S W

Addressed by Woodfall: To / Caleb Whitefoord, Esq.

Addressed by Whitefoord [?]*:* To Mr. H[enry Woodfall?]

Notation by Whitefoord: Cover to K. of P.

An Edict by the King of Prussia

Printed in *The Public Advertiser*, September 22, 1773.[5]

When this famous hoax first appeared, Franklin had the pleasure of seeing it taken at face value.[6] Part of the reason, no doubt, was his shrewdness in choosing the fictional author. Frederick II of Prussia had been estranged from Britain by the Peace of Paris, and made no secret of his contempt for the country. He had recently suggested, according to an English officer at his court, sending over several regiments to protect the monarchy against radicals, and even coming himself to be king.[7] His conduct towards his Continental neighbors, as reported in London, was equally unsavory and far more relevant to Franklin's purposes: the King sent troops to keep order in his newly acquired Polish provinces and bullied the Polish Diet, issued an edict laying claim to part of the Dutch Netherlands, and then to cap the climax justified his acquisitions in Poland by asserting that they had rightfully been Prussian since the days of the Teutonic Knights.[8] His reputation with the British public, in short, was calculated to give his edict the ring of authenticity.

The document, after the preamble, is built of British materials. It consists of various Parliamentary statutes, beginning with the Restoration, which are partly quoted, partly paraphrased, and partly embel-

5. A few typographical errors have been silently corrected from the reprint in the *London Chron.*, Sept. 21–23, 1773. For the many later reprintings see Crane, *Letters to the Press*, pp. 236–7.

6. By guests of Lord Le Despencer: BF to WF below, Oct. 6.

7. *London Chron.*, Jan. 2–5, 5–9, 1773.

8. *Ibid.*, Jan. 30–Feb. 2; March 16–18, 18–20; July 31–Aug. 3, 1773. "The King of Prussia's *character*," BF commented, helped to give the "Edict" reality. To WF below, Oct. 6.

lished with Franklin's inventions.[9] He intended the "Edict" and its companion, the "Rules by Which a Great Empire May be Reduced to a Small One," as anything but persiflage. Under the surface the "Edict" was a summary of colonial grievances that went back for almost a century; King Frederick's foisting them upon Britain was what Franklin called an "out-of-the-way form" to highlight them.[1]

For the Public Advertiser.

The SUBJECT of the following Article of FOREIGN INTELLIGENCE being exceeding EXTRAORDINARY, is the Reason of its being separated from the usual Articles of *Foreign News*.[2]

Dantzick, September 5.

WE have long wondered here at the Supineness of the English Nation, under the Prussian Impositions upon its Trade entering our Port.[3] We did not till lately know the *Claims*, antient and modern, that hang over that Nation, and therefore could not suspect that it might submit to those Impositions from a Sense of *Duty*, or from Principles of *Equity*. The following *Edict*, just made public, may, if serious, throw some Light upon this Matter.

"FREDERICK, by the Grace of God, King of Prussia, &c. &c. &c. to all present and to come,* HEALTH. The Peace now enjoyed

* *A tous presens et à venir*. Orig.

---

9. BF listed some of the statutes in a concluding paragraph. In the order in which he discussed them earlier in the text they were: the Caroline Navigation Act, 12 Chas. 11, c. 18; the Iron Act of 1750, 23 Geo. 11, c. 29; the restriction on colonial wool manufacture in 10/11 Will. 111, c. 10; the Hat Act of 1732, 5 Geo. II, c. 22; and the act of 1717 for transporting felons, 4 Geo. I, c. 11. See George Simson, "Legal Sources for Franklin's 'Edict,'" *Amer. Literature*, XXXII (1960–61), 152–7.

1. See the headnote on the "Rules" above, Sept. 11. A recent writer has suggested that the germ of the "Edict" was BF's marginal comment in 1766 (above, XIII, 83), "Germany the Mother Country of this Nation"; see J. A. Leo Lemay, "Benjamin Franklin," in Everett Emerson, ed., *Major Writers of Early American Literature* ([Madison, Wis., 1972]), pp. 227–8.

2. For the printer's part in the placement of the hoax see the preceding document.

3. The free city of Dantzig, which the first partition had just separated from the nominal rule of Poland, was not yet part of Prussia; yet Prussian authorities were reportedly stopping British trade with the port: *London Chron.*, Aug. 5–7, 1773.

throughout our Dominions, having afforded us Leisure to apply ourselves to the Regulation of Commerce, the Improvement of our Finances, and at the same Time the easing our *Domestic Subjects* in their Taxes: For these Causes, and other good Considerations us thereunto moving, We hereby make known, that after having deliberated these Affairs in our Council, present our dear Brothers, and other great Officers of the State, Members of the same, WE, of our certain Knowledge, full Power and Authority Royal, have made and issued this present Edict, viz.

WHEREAS it is well known to all the World, that the first German Settlements made in the Island of Britain, were by Colonies of People, Subjects to our renowned Ducal Ancestors, and drawn from *their* Dominions, under the Conduct of Hengist, Horsa, Hella, Uffa, Cerdicus, Ida, and others; and that the said Colonies have flourished under the Protection of our august House, for Ages past, have never been *emancipated* therefrom, and yet have hitherto yielded little Profit to the same. And whereas We Ourself have in the last War fought for and defended the said Colonies against the Power of France, and thereby enabled them to make Conquests from the said Power in America, for which we have not yet received adequate Compensation.[4] And whereas it is just and expedient that a Revenue should be raised from the said Colonies in Britain towards our Indemnification; and that those who are Descendants of our antient Subjects, and thence still owe us due Obedience, should contribute to the replenishing of our Royal Coffers, as they must have done had their Ancestors remained in the Territories now to us appertaining: WE do therefore hereby ordain and command, That from and after the Date of these Presents, there shall be levied and paid to our Officers of the Customs, on all Goods, Wares and Merchandizes, and on all Grain and other Produce of the Earth exported from the said Island of Britain, and on all Goods of whatever Kind imported into the same, a *Duty* of *Four and an Half* per Cent. *ad Valorem*, for the Use of us and our Successors. And that the said Duty may more effectually be collected, We do hereby ordain, that all Ships or Vessels bound from Great Britain to any other Part of the World, or from any other Part of the World to Great

4. During the Seven Years' War Britain had provided large subsidies to Frederick.

415

Britain, shall in their respective Voyages touch at our Port of KONINGSBERG, there to be unladen, searched, and charged with the said Duties.

AND WHEREAS there have been from Time to Time discovered in the said Island of Great Britain by our Colonists there, many Mines or Beds of Iron Stone; and sundry Subjects of our antient Dominion, skilful in converting the said Stone into Metal, have in Times past transported themselves thither, carrying with them and communicating that Art; and the Inhabitants of the said Island, *presuming* that they had a natural Right to make the best Use they could of the natural Productions of their Country for their own Benefit, have not only built Furnaces for smelting the said Stone into Iron, but have erected Plating Forges, Slitting Mills, and Steel Furnaces, for the more convenient manufacturing of the same, thereby endangering a Diminution of the said Manufacture in our antient Dominion. WE *do therefore* hereby farther ordain, that from and after the Date hereof, no Mill or other Engine for Slitting or Rolling of Iron, or any Plating Forge to work with a Tilt-Hammer, or any Furnace for making Steel, shall be erected or continued in the said Island of Great Britain: And the Lord Lieutenant of every County in the said Island is hereby commanded, on Information of any such Erection within his County, to order and by Force to cause the same to be abated and destroyed, as he shall answer the Neglect thereof to Us at his Peril. But We are nevertheless graciously pleased to permit the Inhabitants of the said Island to transport their Iron into Prussia, there to be manufactured, and to them returned, they paying our Prussian Subjects for the Workmanship, with all the Costs of Commission, Freight and Risque coming and returning, any Thing herein contained to the contrary notwithstanding.

WE do not however think fit to extend this our Indulgence to the Article of *Wool*, but meaning to encourage not only the manufacturing of woollen Cloth, but also the raising of Wool in our antient Dominions, and to prevent *both*, as much as may be, in our said Island, We do hereby absolutely forbid the Transportation of Wool from thence even to the Mother Country Prussia; and that those Islanders may be farther and more effectually restrained in making any Advantage of their own Wool in the Way of Manufacture, We command that none shall be carried *out of one*

County into another, nor shall any Worsted-Bay, or Woollen-Yarn, Cloth, Says, Bays, Kerseys, Serges, Frizes, Druggets, Cloth-Serges, Shalloons, or any other Drapery Stuffs, or Woollen Manufactures whatsoever, made up or mixt with Wool in any of the said Counties, be carried into any other County, or be Water-borne even across the smallest River or Creek, on Penalty of Forfeiture of the same, together with the Boats, Carriages, Horses, &c. that shall be employed in removing them. *Nevertheless* Our loving Subjects there are hereby permitted, (if they think proper) to use all their Wool as *Manure for the Improvement of their Lands.*

AND WHEREAS the Art and Mystery of making *Hats* hath arrived at great Perfection in Prussia, and the making of Hats by our remote Subjects ought to be as much as possible restrained. And forasmuch as the Islanders before-mentioned, being in Possession of Wool, Beaver, and other Furs, have *presumptuously* conceived they had a Right to make some Advantage thereof, by manufacturing the same into Hats, to the Prejudice of our domestic Manufacture, WE do therefore hereby strictly command and ordain, that no Hats or Felts whatsoever, dyed or undyed, finished or unfinished, shall be loaden or put into or upon any Vessel, Cart, Carriage or Horse, to be transported or conveyed *out of one County* in the said Island *into another County,* or to *any other Place whatsoever,* by any Person or Persons whatsoever, on Pain of forfeiting the same, with a Penalty of *Five Hundred Pounds* Sterling for every Offence. Nor shall any Hat-maker in any of the said Counties employ more than two Apprentices, on Penalty of *Five Pounds* Sterling per Month: We intending hereby that such Hat-makers, being so restrained both in the Production and Sale of their Commodity, may find no Advantage in continuing their Business. But lest the said Islanders should suffer Inconveniency by the Want of Hats, We are farther graciously pleased to permit them to send their Beaver Furs to Prussia; and We also permit Hats made thereof to be exported from Prussia to Britain, the People thus favoured to pay all Costs and Charges of Manufacturing, Interest, Commission to Our Merchants, Insurance and Freight going and returning, as in the Case of Iron.

And lastly, Being willing farther to favour Our said Colonies in Britain, We do hereby also ordain and command, that all the

Thieves, Highway and Street-Robbers, House-breakers, Forgerers, Murderers, So[domi]tes, and Villains of every Denomination, who have forfeited their Lives to the Law in Prussia, but whom We, in Our great Clemency, do not think fit here to hang, shall be emptied out of our Gaols into the said Island of Great Britain *for the* BETTER PEOPLING *of that Country*.[5]

We flatter Ourselves that these Our Royal Regulations and Commands will be thought *just* and *reasonable* by Our much-favoured Colonists in England, the said Regulations being copied from their own Statutes of 10 and 11 Will. III. C. 10, 5 Geo. II. C. 22, 23 Geo. II. C. 29, 4 Geo. I. C. 11, and from other equitable Laws made by their Parliaments, or from Instructions given by their Princes, or from Resolutions of both Houses entered into for the GOOD *Government* of their own Colonies in Ireland and America.

And all Persons in the said Island are hereby cautioned not to oppose in any wise the Execution of this Our Edict, or any Part thereof, such Opposition being HIGH TREASON, of which all who are *suspected* shall be transported in Fetters from Britain to Prussia, there to be tried and executed according to the *Prussian Law*.[6]

Such is our Pleasure.

> Given at Potsdam this twenty-fifth Day of the Month of August, One Thousand Seven Hundred and Seventy-three, and in the Thirty-third Year of our Reign.

By the KING in his Council   RECHTMAESSIG, *Secr.*"

Some take this Edict to be merely one of the King's *Jeux d'Esprit:* Others suppose it serious, and that he means a Quarrel with England: But all here think the Assertion it concludes with, "that these Regulations are copied from Acts of the English Parliament respecting their Colonies," a very *injurious* one: it being impossible to believe, that a People distinguish'd for their *Love of Liberty*, a Nation so *wise*, so *liberal in its Sentiments*, so *just and equitable* towards its *Neighbours*, should, from mean and *injudicious* Views of *petty immediate Profit*, treat *its own Children* in a Manner so *arbitrary* and TYRANNICAL!

5. For the origin of the phrase see above, XV, 11 n.
6. An echo of the tenth rule for reducing a great empire, BF's earlier satire.

To Thomas Cushing

ALS: Public Record Office

Sir   London, Sept. 23. 1773

Nothing of Importance has occurr'd here since my last.[7] This serves chiefly to cover a Newspaper, in which I have stated a few of the American Grievances that were omitted in my Receipt for diminishing a great Empire.[8] These odd ways of presenting Matters to the publick View, sometimes occasion them to be more read, more talk'd of, and more attended to. With great Respect, I am, Sir, Your most obedient humble Servant   B FRANKLIN

Honble Thos Cushing Esqr

Endorsed: Benja Franklin Sept 23. 1773 private

To Mrs. [James?] Alcock[9]

ALS (letterbook draft): American Philosophical Society

Madam   [*C*. Sept. 24, 1773[1]]

At the Request of Dr. Hawkesworth I am to mention to you what occurr'd to me on reading the Copy of Mr. Alcock's Letter, and in Conversation with the Dr. on your Affairs.

There is no Grant of Land as yet to be obtained from those

7. Of Sept. 12, above.

8. BF was following the "Rules" with the "Edict". In this letter, Thomas Moffatt commented, "He acknowledges Himself Author of a Receipt or rather Prescription for Diminishing a Great Empire as published in a London News Paper."

9. Not much is known about her, but hints appear in this letter and elsewhere. Her friendship with the Hawkesworths and her teaching experience suggest that she had been on the staff of Mrs. Hawkesworth's school for young ladies at Bromley. Her husband had preceded her to Pennsylvania and was settled on a farm west of the Schuylkill; she joined him there the following December, and en route delivered a letter to Richard Bache from BF: Bache to BF below, Jan. 1, 1774. A James "Alcocks," who we presume was the husband, was a resident of Blockley Township, immediately west of Philadelphia, in 1774; he was on the tax list but not assessed, which implies that he was a new resident. 3 *Pa. Arch.*, XIV, 313. Other Alcocks, who may well have been some of the boys to whom BF refers in this letter, subsequently appeared in York and Chester Counties: *ibid.*, XII, 455; XXI, 87, 410, 518, 780; 5 *Pa. Arch.*, V, 573.

1. The date of BF's missing letter to Bache, just cited.

419

concern'd in the new Colony, their Grant from the Crown not having yet pass'd the Seals.[2]

With so many Children I think your Situation will be better in Pensilvania than in London. Here you cannot get them put Apprentices to learn any Business by which they may afterwards get a reputable Living, without a considerable Premium, and maintaining them in Clothes during their Apprenticeship. In Pensilvania it is otherwise, and they may be got into sober industrious Families and taught Trades on much easier Terms: And I should think it adviseable to get them all so fix'd as soon as possible, at least the Boys; for then it will be more easy for you and Mr. A. to subsist comfortably upon his Industry and yours.

I suppose that his Acquaintance with and Dexterity in Business, may induce his being engag'd in some Store as a Storekeeper, or Clerk, and in time perhaps a Partner. And as Mrs. Hawkesworth, who I take to be one of the best Judges in such Matters, has assur'd me, that no one is better qualify'd than yourself to keep a Boarding School [for] young Ladies, I should hope, that if there [is any?] Opening for such a School in America, y[ou would?] get into that Business, as soon as you can p[rovide?] and furnish a proper House. My Son and [Daugh]ter Bache, if you apply to them in my Na[me to] consult with them, will, I am sure, give you [all the?] Advice in their Power. Wishing you a good Voyage, and a happy Sight of your Husband, I am, Madam, Your most obedient humble Servant　　　　　　　　　　　　　B FRANKLIN

From Joseph Priestley　　　ALS: American Philosophical Society

Dear Sir　　　　　　　　　　　　　Calne[3] 26 Septr 1773.

With this I return you *Mr. Winthrop's letter*, according to your desire, thanking you for your endeavours to serve me in America,

2. The Walpole grant. A document among BF's papers in the APS may well contain the "Copy of Mr. Alcock's Letter" that he is here discussing. The document is addressed to Mrs. Hawkesworth. The bulk of it is an extract, with no indication of the date or author but apparently written from Philadelphia; the recipient is urged to obtain from Mr. Wharton a grant of land on the Ohio "in the Names of the Children and my self their Guardian."

3. Priestley was staying with his family in the Wiltshire village, which was on Lord Shelburne's Bowood estate. Frederick W. Gibbs, *Joseph Priestley: Revolutions of the Eighteenth Century* (New York, 1967), pp. 86–7.

though I find, as I was apprehensive, that the scheme would not answer.[4] Please to return my thanks to the professor for his candid and judicious remarks on my *History of Opticks*, which will be much improved by them, if it should come to a second edition.

Dr. Price will have informed you, that I have resumed my experiments on *air*, and with a good prospect of success. Since that I have been much more successful; but in a letter I can only confine myself to the heads of things.

The most important of the observations I have made lately is of an *alkaline*, corresponding to my *acid air*, of which an account is given in what I have already printed. This I get by treating a volatile alkali in the same manner in which I before treated the spirit of salt. As soon as the liquid begins to boil the vapour arises, and being received in a vessel filled with quick-silver, continues in the form of *air*, not condensed by cold.[5]

I imagined that a mixture of this alkaline with acid air would make a neutral, and perhaps a common air; but, instead of that, they make a beautiful white salt of a very curious nature. It immediately deliquesces and even wholly disappears upon being exposed to the open air, and if it be in a dry and deep vessel, where moisture cannot easily come at it, it wholly evaporates in dense white clouds, occasioning a very strong smell.[6]

4. The scheme of finding an academic post, which Winthrop had quashed in his letter above to BF, March 4. Priestley's wording suggests that the comfort of his berth with Lord Shelburne had not dissipated the hope of emigrating.

5. Alkaline air is in modern terms gaseous ammonia; acid (which Priestley called marine acid) air is hydrogen chloride gas; and spirit of salt is hydrochloric acid. For "what I have already printed" see above, XIX, 174. Priestley discussed his experiments on ammonia in more detail in *Experiments and Observations on Different Kinds of Air* (1st ed.; 3 vols., London, 1774–77), III, 294–6; (2nd ed., corrected; 3 vols., London, 1775–84), I, 163–77; and in *Experiments and Observations Relating to Various Branches of Natural Philosophy* . . . (2 vols., London, 1779–81), II, 218–24. He was experimenting, as appears later in the letter, with both solid and liquid volatile alkali. The solid was doubtless ammonium carbonate, then called sal volatile; the liquid was, we assume, an aqueous solution of ammonium carbonate called spirit of sal volatile.

6. Gaseous ammonia and hydrogen chloride gas, mixed with ordinary air, produce white clouds of ammonium chloride which subsequently form a deposit, then called sal ammoniac, of the same substance.

This Alkaline vapour, like the acid, is quickly imbibed by water, which thereby becomes Spirit of Sal Volatile.

Nitrous air makes this alkaline vapour turbid,[7] and perhaps generates a different salt; but I have not yet made a tenth part of the experiments that I propose to do with this new kind of air.

I have just found that spirit of wine yields air also, which is probably pure phlogiston,[8] but I have not yet made one experiment with it.

If volatile alkali, liquid or solid, be exposed to nitrous air, during its effervescence with common air, the vessel is presently filled with beautiful white clouds; and the salt is tinged blue. This explains the constitution of nitrous air, but I have no time for reasoning.[9]

This experiment appears to great advantage when a vessel, no matter how large, containing the smallest portion of volatile alkali, fluid or solid, is opened in a quantity of nitrous air, for the whole is filled almost instantly with dense white clouds.

Report says that you are about to leave us, at least for a time. If this be true, I shall be very sorry; as it will deprive me of one of the greatest satisfactions that used to make my annual visits to London agreeable. If you should leave England before winter, I should think myself very happy in an opportunity of seeing you before your departure. As I cannot conveniently come to London, I should be peculiarly happy in seeing you and Sir John Pringle, in my new situation; and I flatter myself that I could amuse you with some of my new experiments. If you can oblige me so far, give me a line to acquaint me with your intention, that I may be sure to be at home when you come. I am, Dear Sir, yours sincerely   J PRIESTLEY

7. For Priestley's work with nitrous air (nitric oxide) see above, XIX, 201–2.

8. Spirit of wine was alcohol; phlogiston, which was basic to the still predominant school of chemical thought, was conceived to be the inflammable element present in all combustible substances.

9. Gaseous ammonia, mixed with nitric oxide gas and ordinary air, produces a white cloud of ammonium nitrate. Priestley later continued this line of experimentation and outlined his reasoning about it in the second ed., cited above, of *Experiments . . . on Different Kinds of Air*, I, 204–13.

Jacques Barbeu-Dubourg: Prefaces to the Two Volumes of the *Œuvres*

"Préface" printed in Jacques Barbeu-Dubourg, ed., Œuvres de M. Franklin . . . (2 vols., Paris, 1773), I, [i]-viii; "Discours préliminaire" printed in ibid., II, [i]-viii; AD (draft of "Préface"): American Philosophical Society

For almost twenty years, since Dalibard had brought out his translations of *Experiments and Observations* in 1752 and 1756,[10] Europeans with no knowledge of English had been out of touch with Franklin's activities. During that period two more editions of the *Experiments* had appeared, each larger than the last, and another was in preparation; but few even among the philosophes could have had more than a vague idea of what the recent work involved. Dubourg, the avid publicist, decided to remedy this ignorance. He based his volumes on the latest edition of the *Experiments*, that of 1769, but added to it, along with numerous observations of his own, much new material that Franklin made available to him; about a third of the items had never before appeared in print. The translation, in consequence, revealed the American more fully than ever before, "l'étendue de ses connoissances et la Fécondité de son génie." The effect, though impossible to measure, was considerable. Dubourg reported jubilantly at the end of the year that the two volumes were being received "avec une sorte de passion favorable," and that they would exalt the reputation of America not only in France but throughout Europe.[1] If what he said was true, and it probably was, the *Œuvres* helped to create the reputation that a few years later stood Franklin and his country in such good stead.

PRÉFACE *DU TRADUCTEUR*   [Before Sept. 30, 1773[2]]

Au milieu des Sauvages de l'Amérique il s'éleva presque subitement, sur la fin du siecle dernier, une Ville dont l'enceinte n'est pas encore circonscrite, et qui ne cesse de s'étendre de jour en jour suivant les alignemens qui lui furent premiérement tracés.

Son nom est Philadelphie, et l'amour fraternel est son unique

---

10. See above, IV, 302 n, 303.

1. To BF below, Dec. 29.

2. The prefaces were undoubtedly written early in the year, if not the year before, but the only date we can assign them is when the volumes were published. In writing to Ingenhousz on Sept. 30, the following document, BF speaks of them as "lately printed" in Paris; the first review we have found of them was on Oct. 2 in *L'Année littéraire* . . . , tome V for 1773, pp. 317–50.

loi fondamentale; ses portes sont toujours ouvertes à tout le monde; et quoique son Fondateur en ait formellement exclus deux sortes d'hommes, l'athée et le fainéant, il semble que cette exclusion même n'ait été que comminatoire; car s'il existoit un athée dans le reste de l'univers, il se convertiroit en entrant dans une ville où tout est si bien; et s'il y naissoit un paresseux, ayant incessamment sous les yeux trois aimables soeurs, la richesse, la science et la vertu, qui sont les filles du travail, il prendroit bientôt de l'amour pour elles, et tâcheroit de les obtenir de leur pere.

Les Trembleurs (ou Quakers) persécutés en Angleterre, s'étant réfugiés en Amérique sous la conduit de Guillaume Pen, y fonderent cette colonie. C'étoient des hommes d'une trempe fort singuliere. L'espece d'enthousiasme, qu'un nommé Fox leur avoit communiqué, n'avoit pour objet que les vertus morales, sans aucun dogme métaphysique. Ils s'excitoient au tremblement pour consulter le Seigneur[3] sur tout ce qu'ils vouloient entreprendre; et après avoir médité sur leurs devoirs dans le plus profond recueillement, prenant leurs lumieres naturelles pour des révélations extraordinaires, ils se croyoient tous autant de prophetes et de prophetesses. Ainsi Pen crut que le ciel lui avoit inspiré d'acheter et de payer de deux côtés (du Roi d'Angleterre, et des Sauvages) le terrein désert où il vouloit bâtir sa Ville, afin que son établissement fût béni de Dieu et des hommes. Ces Trembleurs, depuis quelques années, ont beaucoup rabattu de leur enthousiasme, mais ils ont précieusement conservé leurs maximes et leurs usages; chacun présente lui-même son propre hommage à la Divinité; les femmes mêmes sont admises à prêcher parmi les hommes; tous sont réputés Prêtres et Prêtresses; tous s'appellent freres et soeurs, et se traitent constamment comme tels ....

⟨Montesquieu called Penn a true Lycurgus, and the learned authors of the *Encylopédie* have repeated this untenable comparison.[4] Judge trees by their fruit: Lycurgus formed a destructive

3. "C'étoient les hommes," Dubourg's draft reads, "les plus singuliers de l'Univers. Un nommé fox leur avoit communiqué son Enthousiasme, et ils s'excitoient aux Convulsions pour consulter le Seigneur," etc.

4. For the specific Montesquieu references see [Gonzague Truc, ed.,] *De l'Esprit des lois* (2 vols., Paris, [1961]), I, 40. The authors of the *Encyclopédie, ou dictionnaire raisonné* were undoubtedly learned, but in this case also confused; in their article on Pennsylvania they twisted Montesquieu's words to apply to the Indians rather than the Quakers.

people, who were subject to a thousand privations, never grew in number and never, in six centuries, produced a scholar or an artist of note; Penn formed a lovable people, who enjoy the good things of life, have increased a hundred fold in less than a hundred years, and combine respect for the arts and a keen interest in science with the greatest simplicity of manners.⟩

En 1746, époque mémorable dans l'histoire de la Physique par la fameuse expérience de Leyde, feu M. Collinson, de la Société royale de Londres, envoya en présent à ses bons amis de Philadelphie, un tube électrique, avec des instructions sur la maniere de s'en servir, ne doutant pas qu'ils n'en fissent un très bon usage. Ce tube, qui fut heureusement remis à M. Franklin, l'occupa tout entier pendant quelques mois, après quoi il crut devoir rendre compte à M. Collinson de ses expériences et de ses réflexions sur cette matiere.[5]

Quoique ses Lettres ne fussent pas originairement destinées à voir le jour, elles furent bientôt publiées en Anglois et traduites en François. Elles parurent aussi neuves et aussi intéressantes à Paris et à Londres qu'en Pensylvanie, et commencerent à faire connoître à l'Europe ce Philosophe Américain qui, du premier vol, déployant ses ailes sans effort, s'étoit élevé à une hauteur dont nos plus célebres Physiciens demeurerent tout étonnés.

La réputation de M. Franklin s'est toujours soutenue, toujours accrue depuis. Sans composer aucun traité en forme, son génie s'est exercé successivement sur quantité de sujets divers; et à mesure que l'occasion s'en est présentée, il a fait part de ses découvertes à ses amis dans des Lettres familieres, où il leur propose du ton le plus modeste les idées les plus lumineuses.

Ces divers morceaux, après avoir été imprimés et réimprimés séparément, ont été réunis en un Volume *in*-4°. publié à Londres, où l'on en prépare encore actuellement une édition nouvelle.[6] Mon attachement pour l'Auteur m'en a fait entreprendre la traduction, et son amitié pour moi l'a engagé à tirer de son portefeuille quelques morceaux qui n'avoient point encore paru, pour enrichir l'édition Françoise. Puissé-je me flatter que le Public ne trouvera pas trop discordantes quelques petites réflexions que j'ai

5. See the *Autobiog.*, pp. 240–3.
6. The 1769 and 1774 editions respectively.

pris la liberté d'y inserer, tantôt au commencement, et tantôt à la fin de divers articles.[7]

Ce qui me fait espérer que l'on aura quelqu'indulgence pour moi, c'est qu'on verra que les petites lettres, que j'ai eu occasion d'écrire à M. Franklin pendant le cours de cette édition, m'ont attiré des réponses qui ne le cedent au reste de l'ouvrage ni pour l'agrément, ni pour l'utilité.

Dans l'édition Angloise, les différentes matieres sont mêlées ensemble presque sans ordre; et le volume de celle-ci étant grossi de plus d'un tiers, cette espece de confusion en auroit été d'autant plus désagréable. J'ai donc cru devoir présenter séparément tout ce qui a rapport à l'Electricité; et ranger le reste ensuite, non seulement par ordre de matieres, mais encore, autant qu'il m'a été possible, dans l'ordre des dates. Ces deux Parties s'étant trouvées à peu près égales, et ayant très-peu de rapport entre elles, les amis de l'Auteur et les miens m'ont conseillé de les partager en deux Tomes, que diverses personnes aimeront mieux avoir séparément, et que les autres pourront faire relier en un seul volume.

On a placé tout au commencement le portrait de l'Auteur, et à la fin de chaque Tome les figures relatives aux objets qui y sont traités.

Une chose qui paroîtra presqu'incroyable, quoique très vraie, c'est que M. Franklin, toujours occupé d'une multitude d'affaires graves, tant publiques que particulieres, n'a jamais fait de la Physique que son délassement; connoissant aussi peu les heures perdues, que beaucoup de gens ici ne connoissent l'emploi du tems. Né avec un esprit solide, et élevé au milieu des *Quakers*,[8] il a su n'en point prendre les singularités, mais où auroit-il pris des goûts frivoles? Dévoué sans relâche au service de sa Patrie, il a été constamment chéri et révéré de ses Concitoyens, l'ame de leurs conseils au-dedans, et chargé de leurs intérêts au-dehors; présent, absent, il a toujours rempli leurs voeux, et réciproquement il a toujours sû leur inspirer tout ce qu'il a voulu pour leur bien commun. Les sciences utiles ont fait à Philadelphie, sous son

7. The three paragraphs that follow are omitted in the draft.
8. Scarcely. BF was not exposed to Quakers until he went to Philadelphia.

influence, des progrès d'une rapidité presque sans exemple; et la Société Philosophique qui s'y est formée, à laquelle toutes les Colonies voisines ont pris part, et qui l'a choisi pour Président, a donné dès la fin de sa seconde année un volume de Mémoires, où l'on voit avec admiration un si parfait accord du savoir le plus éminent avec la vertu la plus pure, qu'on trouveroit difficilement dans l'ancien monde quelque chose de comparable à ce début du monde nouveau.[9]

DISCOURS PRÉLIMINAIRE *DU TRADUCTEUR*

Ceux qui ne voyent qu'un Electricien dans M. Franklin, ne le connoissent pas à moitié. La multitude d'objets divers que comprend cette seconde Partie de ses Œuvres montre l'étendue de ses connoissances et la fécondité de son génie.

Il commence par un morceau de physique générale dans un goût tout-à-fait neuf, à mon avis. L'explication qu'il y donne de divers météores, des vents alisés, des orages, des trombes, et autres grands phénomenes de la nature, est d'une simplicité, et en même-tems d'une force de dialectique qui enchante. N'ayant pu emprunter de l'expérience qu'un premier point d'appui assez mobile, il s'élance rapidement de-là dans les régions aëriennes jusqu'à une hauteur prodigieuse, sans qu'on perde un seul moment de vue la direction du fil à l'aide duquel il s'y est élevé. Trois ou quatre savans Américains, en lui rendant toute la justice qui lui

---

9. The draft ends with some verse, presumably Dubourg's, that he was sensible enough to omit from the printed text:

Le feu du Ciel dérobé,
Et le nouveau monde eclairé
    Au flambeau de la Physique:
    L'Equation politique,
Du respect de l'Autorité
Et des droits de la liberté:
    Les Trembleurs de Philadelphie
En Philosophes transformés
    Donnant l'essor à leur genie:
Des grains en ce livre semés
    Voilà quelle moisson Franklin a recueillie.

étoit due, ont cru appercevoir quelques points défectueux dans cette brillante hypothese; mais un Dominicain, qui se croit obligé de s'éloigner en quelque chose des opinions du Docteur Angélique, ne le combat pas avec plus d'égards et de défiance de lui-même, que ces MM. n'en ont montré en attaquant M. Franklin. Quelques-uns cependant ramassent tant de forces, et les déployent avec tant d'art, que le commun des Lecteurs a de la peine à prévoir de quel côté penchera la victoire; mais notre Auteur paroît l'emporter enfin.[1]

J'ai cru devoir placer ce morceau le premier, à raison de son étendue et de son importance; je serai désormais plus fidele à l'ordre des tems.

Le plus ancien des ouvrages imprimés de M. Franklin, qui fut publié à Philadelphie en 1745, nous rappelle à nos propres foyers, pour nous apprendre à nous chauffer mieux et avec plus d'œcono-mie. Il a médité de nouveau sur la même matiere, et nous promet encore une nouvelle construction de cheminée.[2]

De la physique, M. Franklin passe tout-à-coup à des réflexions politiques sur la population.[3] Les Princes, qu'Homere appelloit les pasteurs des peuples, devroient faire leur plus sérieuse étude de cet objet, et ne sauroient en puiser la connoissance dans une source plus pure.

L'Inoculation de la petite vérole fournit la matiere des deux lettres suivantes; mais M. Franklin se contente de marquer l'intérêt qu'il y prend, en excitant ses correspondans à la traiter d'une maniere qui réponde à son importance.[4]

Dans le morceau qui suit, il se réduit également à présenter au public les conjectures plausibles d'un de ses amis sur la lumiere que rend l'eau de la mer dans certaines circonstances.[5]

1. The "savans Américains" who questioned BF's meteorological theories in the 1750's were Cadwallader Colden, John Perkins, and Jonathan Todd. For their differences with him see above, IV, 358–60, 369–73, 429–42, 452–4, 488–95; V, 124–6, 145–7, 256–8. Here and in subsequent paragraphs we cite in our series, chronologically arranged, material in the *Œuvres* to which Dubourg refers. The "morceau de physique" is above, IV, 235–43.

2. BF's account of the Philadelphia fireplace in 1744: II, 419–46; his improved construction he promised Dubourg in his letter above of Jan. 22.

3. "Observations Concerning the Increase of Mankind": IV, 225–34.

4. BF's letters from and to Perkins: IV, 336–8, 340–1.

5. The plausible conjectures were Bowdoin's: V, 113–15.

Mais on retrouve bientôt M. Franklin tout entier dans ses réponses au Gouverneur de la Nouvelle Angleterre, au sujet des changemens qu'on se proposoit de faire dans l'administration des Colonies de l'Amerique.[6] On y verra, sans doute, avec plaisir une prévoyance singuliere, et une annonce quasi prophétique des événemens futurs, fondée sur la plus profonde connoissance tant des vrais rapports des intérêts de l'un et de l'autre pays, que de la disposition des esprits, qui avoit été représentée sous un faux jour au Parlement d'Angleterre.

L'espece de bonhommie avec laquelle M. Franklin débite ensuite d'excellentes leçons œconomiques, ne paroitra peut-être pas aussi agréable ici que dans sa patrie, où ce petit sermon a fait sur les esprits de tout un peuple une impression dont il y a peu d'exemples dans l'histoire ancienne.[7]

Retournant de-là à la physique, à l'occasion des nouvelles expériences de quelques Chymistes sur le froid produit par l'évaporation des liqueurs, M. Franklin propose des conjectures très-ingénieuses, tendantes à établir une nouvelle théorie des conducteurs du feu ordinaire; et il en déduit immédiatement non-seulement l'explication peu commune de quantité de faits très-communs, mais encore une bonne observation de pratique sur le remede le plus approprié à la brûlure et aux douleurs inflammatoires.[8]

Les réflexions sur les différentes couches de terre sont d'une belle ame: celles qui suivent sur la salure originaire de la mer montrent une heureuse sagacité d'esprit; et celles qui concernent l'utilité qu'on peut retirer des cheminées pendant l'été, font également honneur à l'esprit et au coeur de M. Franklin.[9]

On sera peut-être étonné de se trouver redevable d'un nouvel instrument de musique à notre Philosophe. Cet instrument ne paroît pas fait pour produire beaucoup d'effet dans un orchestre, mais on assure qu'il porte au coeur des accens si touchans qu'il semble étonnant que les virtuoses dont Paris abonde, ne lui ayent

6. To Gov. Shirley: V, 443–7, 449–51.
7. "Father Abraham's Speech": VII, 340–50.
8. To Lining: VII, 184–90; VIII, 108–12.
9. To Pringle, Bowdoin, Peter Franklin, and Dubourg: VII, 357; VIII, 195–8; IX, 106–7; XIX, 368–9.

pas fait jusqu'ici plus d'accueil. D'un autre côté, je crains que nos Musiciens ne soient pas contens de la façon dont il parle des compositions de la musique moderne, quoique sa critique paroisse assaisonnée d'un véritable sel attique.[1]

Dans la lettre sur la propagation du son, M. Franklin est conduit à des vues neuves par des observations fines. Dans la suivante, il proteste ingénuement de son ignorance sur la cause de certaines ondulations qu'il a peut-être observées le premier, quoiqu'une infinité de gens en ayent habituellement de semblables sous leurs yeux.[2]

Ses remarques sur la profondeur des canaux navigables, et ses petites expériences à ce sujet, peuvent servir à mettre quelques Physiciens sur la voie pour déterminer avec précision le juste point de leur excavation.[3]

M. Franklin donne ensuite de bons avis à un ami, en l'exhortant à apprendre à nager, et raconte avec grace comment il traversa un vaste étang en nageant à voile.[4]

Mais que dirai-je de ses quarrés et cercles magiques?[5] Je crains que beaucoup de personnes ne s'en amusent point du tout, et que d'autres ne s'en amusent trop.

A l'égard de sa correspondance avec Mlle. Stevenson,[6] je suis persuadé que beaucoup de peres de familles desireroient un semblable Mentor à leurs filles. Sans avoir l'honneur de connoître personnellement cette *petit Philosophe*, j'ai par devers moi des preuves non équivoques des progrès qu'elle a faits sous un si grand Maître. Mais il suffit de lire les dissertations que M. Franklin lui adresse, soit au sujet des marées remarquables dans certaines rivieres, soit au sujet des moyens de se désaltérer avec l'eau de la mer, soit au sujet de l'évaporation de l'eau de quelques rivieres qui ne portent pas leur tribut à l'océan, comme on l'imagine communément, soit enfin sur la différence des couleurs par

1. To Beccaria and Dubourg: X, 126–30; XIX, 422. BF's "sel attique" was sprinkled in a different extract: XII, 164.
2. To Kames and Pringle: XII, 162–4; X, 158–60.
3. To Pringle: XV, 115–18.
4. To Neave (XV, 295–8), and to Dubourg above, under the end of March.
5. To Collinson; IV, 393–6, 399–400.
6. VIII, 455–7; IX, 117, 119–22, 212–17, 247–52, 296–7, 338–9; X, 67–8.

rapport à la chaleur, sans compter ce qu'il lui promet encore pour déterminer exactement la véritable cause des rhumes; pour juger de l'intelligence et du goût qui lui attiroient de telles lettres.

Ce que M. Franklin a daigné m'adresser au sujet de son bain d'air, et de l'abondante transpiration des corps nuds, ne peut que faire beaucoup regretter la perte du jeune Médecin qu'il avoit engagé à entreprendre une suite d'expériences à ce sujet, qui auroient pû devenir infiniment intéressantes. Il n'est pas douteux que MM. Pringle et Huck ne fussent très en état d'y suppléer, s'ils vouloient en prendre la peine, et on seroit fondé à l'espérer de leur zele pour le bien de l'humanité, si l'on ne connoissoit en même-tems la grandeur et l'importance de leurs occupations.[7]

J'avoue que, dans ce que dit M. Franklin des qualités tant corporelles que spirituelles des peuples de l'Amérique, il n'y a presque rien qui n'eût déjà été dit; mais comment, et par qui, et dans combien de contes absurdes ce peu de faits vraiment intéressants n'étoient-ils pas en quelque sorte noyés?

Quelques Lecteurs trouveront peut-être un peu forte la maniere dont s'exprime M. Franklin par rapport au Parlement d'Angleterre, au sujet des dissentions qui se sont élevées entre la Métropole et les Colonies;[8] mais il est à considérer qu'il est le Ministre accrédité de ces Colonies pour défendre leurs droits à la Cour Britannique; et l'on a vu ici, il y a environ trois ans, dans les *Ephémérides du Citoyen,* puis dans un brochure séparée, la traduction des réponses pleines de vigueur qu'il avoit faites un jour dans le Parlement, et qui avoient été imprimées immédiatement à Londres.

Si je n'avois pas craint qu'on ne pût m'imputer d'engager quelques personnes dans un double emploi, et de grossir inutilement ce volume, j'aurois été tenté d'y insérer, 1°. ces mêmes réponses au Parlement; 2°. un certain extrait du *London-Chronikle,* qui est écrit du ton le plus fin et le plus agréable, et dont on a déja la traduction à la suite des *Lettres d'un Fermier de Pensylvanie*; 3°. enfin un petit préambule exquis, fourni par notre Auteur, pour mettre à la tête du beau projet du Colonel d'Alrimple, inséré dans

7. To Dubourg in 1768 (xv, 180–1) and March 10 and May 4, 1773.

8. This and the previous paragraph refer to another letter to Dubourg: XVII, 233–4.

un des Journaux d'Agriculture de l'année derniere.[9] On auroit eu ainsi le recueil de toutes les Œuvres connues de M. Franklin.

Mais il n'est pas tems de songer à former un corps complet des œuvres d'un auteur vivant, sain de corps et d'esprit, et travaillant journellement, peut-être avec plus d'ardeur que jamais. M. Franklin est dans son automne, et c'est la saison des fruits.

Sa Patrie le rappelle; elle a des droits sur lui, mais ce ne sont pas des droits exclusifs; toute la terre est la patrie du vrai Philosophe, et il y eut peut-être moins de vraie philosophie dans l'ancien portique d'Athenes, que dans le nouveau portique de Philadelphie.

To Jan Ingenhousz

ALS (letterbook draft): American Philosophical Society

My dear Friend,   London, Sept. 30. 1773

I rejoic'd as much as any Friend could do, at the News we receiv'd here from time to time of your Successes in your Profession, and of the safe Recovery of your illustrious Patients of that most amiable Family:[1] But it griev'd us all at the same time to hear that you did not yourself enjoy Health in that Country. Surely their known Goodness will graciously give you Leave of Absence, if you have but the Courage to request it, and permit you to come and reside in England, which always agreed well with your Constitution. All your Friends here will be made happy by such an Event.

I had purposed to return to America this last Summer, but some Events in our Colony Affairs, induc'd me to stay here another Winter. Sometime in May or June next I believe I shall leave England. May I hope first to see you here once more?

9. The three items omitted were BF's examination before the House of Commons, his "Causes of the American Discontents before 1768," and the plan for benefiting the New Zealanders for which he wrote a foreword; see above, respectively XIII, 129–62, XV, 4–13, and XVIII, 215–17. Dubourg had translated and published all three, the first and third in the *Ephémérides* and the second as an appendix to Dickinson's *Lettres d'un fermier de Pensylvanie* . . . (Amsterdam [*i.e.*, Paris], 1769).

1. For the Doctor see above, XIV, 4 n. At this time he was in Vienna as physician to the imperial family. BF, it is clear from later passages in this letter, was answering one from him that is now lost.

I shall be glad to see the Work of Abbé Fontana on that Disease of Wheat.[2] As yet I have not heard that it is come to England.

Sir W. Hamilton writes from Naples, that after many Experiments, he has not been able to perceive any certain Signs of Electricity in the Torpedo. It is perhaps best that there should be two Opinions on this Subject: for that may occasion a more thorough Examination of it, and finally make us better acquainted with it.[3]

It is not difficult to construct a Needle so as to keep pointing to the Meridian of any one Place, whatever may be the Variation in that Place. But to point always to the Meridian wherever the Needle may be remov'd, is I apprehend not possible.[4]

Mr. Nairne, has, as you have heard, finished a very fine Electric Machine. I have seen Sparks from the Prime Conductor 13 Inches in length. He has added a large Battery, and produces a Discharge from it sufficiently strong to blast growing Vegetables, as Lightning is suppos'd to do. From a greater Force used, perhaps some more Discoveries may be made.[5] I am much pleas'd with the

2. Felice Fontana, *Osservazioni sopra la ruggine del grano* ... (Lucca, 1767). For Abbé Fontana (1730–1805), a distinguished naturalist and physiologist, see the *Enciclopedia italiana de scienze, lettere ed arti* ... (36 vols., [Rome], 1929–39).

3. Ingenhousz, as BF undoubtedly knew, was interested in torpedo fish, and on a visit to Leghorn had captured some, held them in his hand, and felt the shocks they gave. He wrote Sir John Pringle on Jan. 1, 1773, about this experience, and the letter was published in *Phil. Trans.*, LXV (1775), 1–4. Sir William Hamilton had been experimenting with the torpedo earlier in the year; see de Saussure to BF above, Feb. 23.

4. This paragraph is puzzling because it seems to belabor the obvious. BF must be referring to the variation of the compass needle from the true north ("the Meridian"), a phenomenon that had long been under investigation as part of the attempt to determine longitude exactly. In his missing letter Ingenhousz may have suggested constructing some instrument that, wherever located, would correct for this variation; impossible, BF seems to be saying, because the angle of variation is never the same. But this scarcely needed pointing out to Ingenhousz, who was no tyro; see his paper on magnetic needles in *Phil. Trans.*, LXIX (1779), part 2, 537–46. Contemporary methods of computing variation are discussed in Charles Hutton, *A Mathematical and Philosophical Dictionary* ... (2 vols., London, 1795), II, 637.

5. BF is referring to the electrical machine and battery that Edward Nairne, the instrument-maker, had built and subsequently described in the *Phil.*

Account you give me of your new Machine of white Velvet rubbed upon Hareskin.

Last Year the Board of Ordnance apply'd to the Royal Society here for their Opinion of the Propriety of erecting Conductors to secure the Powder Magazines at Purfleet. The Society appointed a Committee to view the Magazines and report their Advice. The Members appointed were Messrs. Cavendish, Watson, Delavall, Robertson, Wilson and myself. We accordingly after viewing them drew up a Report, recommending Conductors to each, elevated 10 feet above the Roof, and pointed at the Ends. M. Delavall did not attend, but all the rest agreed in the Report, only M. Wilson objected to pointing the Rods, asserting that blunt Ends or Knobs would be better. The Work however was finished according to our Direction. He was displeas'd that his Opinion was not followed, and has written a Pamphlet against Points.[6] I have not answered it, being averse to Dispute. But in a new Translation and Edition of my Book printed lately at Paris, 2 Vols. 4to., you will see some new Experiments of mine, with the Reasonings upon them, which satisfy'd the Committee. They are not yet printed in English, but will in a new Edition now printing at Oxford; and perhaps they will be in the next Transactions.[7]

It has been a Fashion to decry Hawkesworth's Book: but it does not deserve the Treatment it has met with. It acquaints us

---

Trans. The machine may have been a simplified and improved version of one that he had already made, on Priestley's design, for the Grand Duke of Tuscany; but the new design was clearly his own, and not the one he described in his *Directions for Using the Electrical Machine . . .* (London, 1774). On Sept. 14, 1773, he used the machine "to blast growing Vegetables." *Phil. Trans.*, LXIV (1774), part 1, 79–82, 85–7; Jack Lindsay, ed., *Autobiography of Joseph Priestley . . .* ([Bath, 1970]), p. 96. BF, who may have attended this demonstration, looked forward to further discoveries because Nairne's machine was the best means yet found to simulate lightning.

6. See above, our note on BF's marginalia, after March 21, and XIX, 260–2, 429–30.

7. The French translation was in Dubourg, *Œuvres*, I, 289–301; the English version is above, XIX, 244–55. The experiments did not appear in the *Phil. Trans.*, as far as we can discover, or in the 5th ed. of *Exper. and Obser.* (London, 1774).

with new[?] People having new Customs; and teaches us a good deal of new Knowledge.[8]

Capt. Phips is returned, not having been able to approach the Pole nearer than 81 Degrees, the Ice preventing.[9]

M. Fremont, an ingenious young Italian who was lately here, gave me a little Spy Glass of his Making upon Pere Boschovich's Principles, the Ocular Lens being a composition of different Glasses instead of the Objective.[1] It is indeed a very good one.

Sir John Pringle is return'd from Scotland, better in Health than heretofore. He always speaks of you with Respect and Affection: as does Dr. Huck[2] and all that knew you. I am ever, with the sincerest Esteem, Dear Sir, Your faithful and most obedient Servant   B F

Dr Ingenhausz

Wrote at W.W. for next week[3]

8. BF's friendship with the publisher and the author may have influenced his opinion. In June William Strahan had brought out John Hawkesworth's *An Account of the Voyages Undertaken by the Order of His Present Majesty for Making Discoveries in the Southern Hemisphere* ... (3 vols., London, 1773). The volumes were a compilation of the various explorers' accounts, reworked by the compiler and written in the first person. Critics complained of this device, among other things, because Hawkesworth intruded himself: "the usual plain texture of the nautical narrative suddenly disappears, by the insertion of some splendid philosophical *patches* of a very different manufacture." *Monthly Rev.* . . ., XLIX (1774), 138; see also the *Gent. Mag.*, XLIII (1773), 286–90; *London Chron.*, July 10–13, 1773. The best modern description of the genesis and reception of the work is in John C. Beaglehole, *The Life of Captain James Cook* (Stanford, Cal., [1974]), pp. 290–1, 439–40, 457–9.

9. For the voyage commanded by Capt. the Hon. Constantine Phipps see BF to LeRoy above, March 30. One of the purposes of the expedition was to test instruments for measuring longitude; BF may therefore have assumed that Ingenhousz would be interested in the outcome.

1. For Fromond, the young Lombard scientist, and his English visit see BF to Beccaria above, Aug. 11. The famous Jesuit mathematician and astronomer, Ruggiero Giuseppe Boscovich (1711?–87), is said to have recommended Fromond to BF; see Antonio Pace, *Benjamin Franklin and Italy* (Philadelphia, 1958), pp. 35–6, where the nature of the "little Spy Glass" is explained.

2. Dr. Richard Huck had been an acquaintance of BF for at least five years: above, XV, 172 n.

3. BF's note to himself, we suppose, to indicate that the letter was drafted at West Wycombe, to be finished in London the next week. The letter to

To Deborah Franklin   ALS: American Philosophical Society

My dear Child,   London, Oct. 6. 1773

I must, I find, stay another Winter here absent from you and my Family, but positively nothing shall prevent, God willing, my Returning in the Spring.

I had no Line from you by the last Packet, but had the Satisfaction of hearing you were well. I thank God, my Health continues; but I cannot in the course of things expect it much longer, which makes me the more anxious to be where I would chuse to die—at home.

Mrs. Stevenson and Polly send their Love to you and yours. The Children are fine. The eldest now talks every thing.[4] They are carried every day to the Park; and as they live in the same Street, the eldest calls on me sometimes to tell God-Papa little Stories of what he has seen there; His pretty Prattle makes me the more long to see our own Grandchildren. God grant me that Satisfaction, and that I may find you all well and happy. Sally should give me a Line now and then, for I love to read her Letters. I am ever, My dear Debby, Your affectionate Husband

B Franklin

Addressed: To / Mrs Franklin / at / Philadelphia / viâ N York / per Packet / B Free Franklin

To William Franklin

Reprinted from William Duane, ed., *The Works of Dr. Benjamin Franklin* . . . (6 vols., Philadelphia, 1808–18), VI, 332–4.

Dear Son,   London, October 6, 1773.

I wrote to you on the 1st of last month, since which I have received yours of July 29, from New York.

I know not what letters of mine governor H. could mean, as advising the people to insist on their independency. But whatever they were, I suppose he has sent copies of them hither, having

---

Percival below, Oct. 15, was similarly drafted at Lord Le Despencer's on Sept. 25.

4. William Hewson, Jr., was not yet two and a half.

heard some whisperings about them. I shall, however, be able at any time, to justify every thing I have written; the purport being uniformly this, that they should carefully avoid all tumults and every violent measure, and content themselves with verbally keeping up their claims, and holding forth their rights whenever occasion requires; secure, that from the growing importance of America, those claims will ere long be attended to, and acknowledged.[5] From a long and thorough consideration of the subject, I am indeed of opinion, that the parliament has no right to make any law whatever, binding on the colonies. That the king, and not the king, lords, and commons collectively, is their sovereign; and that the king with their respective parliaments, is their only legislator.[6] I know your sentiments differ from mine on these subjects. You are a thorough government man, which I do not wonder at, nor do I aim at converting you. I only wish you to act uprightly and steadily, avoiding that duplicity, which in Hutchinson, adds contempt to indignation. If you can promote the prosperity of your people, and leave them happier than you found them, whatever your political principles are, your memory will be honored.

I have written two pieces here lately for the Public Advertiser, on American affairs, designed to expose the conduct of this country towards the colonies, in a short, comprehensive, and striking view, and stated therefore in out-of-the-way forms, as most likely to take the general attention. The first was called, *Rules by which a great empire may be reduced to a small one;* the second, *An Edict of the king of Prussia.*[7] I sent you one of the first, but could not get enough of the second to spare you one, though my clerk went the next morning to the printer's, and wherever they were sold. They were all gone but two. In my own mind I preferred the first, as a composition for the quantity and variety of the matter contained, and a kind of spirited ending of each paragraph. But I find that others here generally prefer the second. I am not suspected as the author, except by one or two

5. These sentences and the final paragraph answer WF's letter of July 29. We have silently corrected a few obvious misprints in Duane's text.

6. Contrast this crisp summary of BF's views with his tentative, almost groping discussion of the same subject in his letter to WF above, XV, 75–7.

7. Above, respectively Sept. 11 and 22.

friends; and have heard the latter spoken of in the highest terms as the keenest and severest piece that has appeared here a long time. Lord Mansfield I hear said of it, that it *was very* ABLE *and very* ARTFUL indeed; and would do mischief by giving here a bad impression of the measures of government; and in the colonies, by encouraging them in their contumacy.[8] It is reprinted in the Chronicle, where you will see it, but stripped of all the capitalling and italicking, that intimate the allusions and mark the emphasis of written discourses, to bring them as near as possible to those spoken:[1] printing such a piece all in one even small character, seems to me like repeating one of Whitfield's Sermons in the monotony of a school-boy.[2] What made it the more noticed here was, that people in reading it, were, as the phrase is, *taken in,* till they had got half through it, and imagined it a real edict, to which mistake I suppose the king of Prussia's *character* must have contributed. I was down at lord Le Despencer's when the post brought that day's papers. Mr. Whitehead was there too (Paul Whitehead, the author of Manners[3]) who runs early through all the papers, and tells the company what he finds remarkable. He had them in another room, and we were chatting in the breakfast parlour, when he came running in to us, out of breath, with the paper in his hand. Here! says he, here's news for ye! *Here's the king of Prussia, claiming a right to this kingdom!* All stared, and I as much as any body; and he went on to read it. When he had read two or three paragraphs, a gentleman present said, *Damn his impudence, I dare say, we shall hear by next post that he is upon his march with one hundred thousand men to back this.* Whitehead, who is very shrewd, soon after began to smoke it, and looking in my face said,

8. For Mansfield's position see the note on BF to WF above, Sept. 1.

1. The reprint in the *London Chron.* of Sept. 21–3, on the front page, made up in prominence for what it lacked in "capitalling and italicking." For BF's earlier complaint about the *Chron.*'s handling of a contribution see above, XV, 16.

2. Whitefield's preaching style had, while draining BF's purse, aroused his vast admiration: *Autobiog.*, pp. 177–8, 180.

3. *Manners*, a satirical poem that appeared in 1739, publicized the modest talents of Paul Whitehead (1710–74); he was an intimate friend of Le Despencer when the latter was still Sir Francis Dashwood, and secretary and steward of the "monks" of Medmenham Abbey, also known as the Hell-Fire Club. *DNB.*

I'll be hanged if this is not some of your American jokes upon us. The reading went on, and ended with abundance of laughing, and a general verdict that it was a fair hit: and the piece was cut out of the paper and preserved in my lord's collection.

I don't wonder that Hutchinson should be dejected. It must be an uncomfortable thing to live among people who he is conscious universally detest him. Yet I fancy he will not have leave to come home, both because they know not well what to do with him, and because they do not very well like his conduct. I am ever your affectionate father,   B FRANKLIN.

To Jonathan Williams, Jr.

ALS: First Federal Savings & Loan Association, Boston (1958)

Dear Jonathan,   London, Oct. 6. 1773.

Inclos'd is the Receipt for the Organ which I wish safe to hand, and that it may please.[4] My Love to the Family, and to my Sister. I shall write fully to you per some Boston Ship when I have a little time.[5] I am ever, Your affectionate Friend   B FRANKLIN

To Jane Mecom

ALS: American Philosophical Society

Dear Sister,   London, Oct. 9. 1773

I have not heard from you since your Goods arriv'd. I hope they got safe to hand, and that they please.[6]

I write this Line just to let you know I am well, Thanks to God, and to cover a Paper of mine printed here, which I send because you desired I would send you what I published from time to time, and I am willing to oblige you; but often they are things out of your way so much that I omit sending them, and sometimes I forget it, and sometimes I cannot get a Copy to send, which was the Case of a Piece since this now enclos'd, viz. *An Edict of the*

---

4. See Jonathan's request in his letter above, June 28. He acknowledged receipt of the organ on Dec. 11, below.

5. BF fulfilled his promise in a letter of Nov. 1, which has since been lost; see Williams to BF below, Jan. 24, 1774.

6. See his letter above, July 7.

King of Prussia, all that were printed being gone in a few Hours.[7]
I hope you and Jenny and her Husband[8] continue well which to hear will always be a Pleasure to Your affectionate Brother

B FRANKLIN

From Joseph Priestley   ALS: American Philosophical Society

Dear Sir,   Calne 14. Oct 1773.
If I had had a frank for Mr. Johnson, I should not have given you this trouble; but Ld. Shelburne is not at home, and my covers for him are expended.[9]

I hope you received my letter, in which I gave you some account of my discovery of an *alkaline air,*[10] tho' I have not had the plea[sure of] hearing from you since. I am still busy in examining its properties and affinities, some of which are curious enough. The most remarkable observation I have made is of the manner in which it affects *alum* put into it. This substance absorbs it very fast, and then comes out perfectly white, and altogether unlike what it was; but I have not yet examined it any farther.[1]

I have also found that this alkaline air is slightly *inflammable.* This is not observed without attention, for a candle dipped into it goes out several times before there is much appearance of its

7. He was sending her "Rules by Which a Great Empire May Be Reduced to a Small One," printed above, Sept. 11. For the run on his Prussian hoax see his letter to WF above, Oct. 6.

8. The newlyweds, Jenny and Peter Collas.

9. Priestley was in frequent touch with Joseph Johnson, the London bookseller and publisher, for whom see above, XI, 258 n. BF had the franking privilege for receiving and sending letters because he was a postal official, and Shelburne because he was an M.P. (*ibid.,* pp. 39 n, 257 n). Priestley, having run out of his patron's covers, was thriftily enclosing a communication for BF to forward to Johnson.

10. Above, Sept. 26, where Priestley discussed his chemical discoveries at greater length and most of the terms used here are explained.

1. Alum is a mineral salt, aluminum sulphate combined with either potassium or ammonium; our conjecture is that Priestley was using the latter combination. For a more detailed description see his *Experiments and Observations on Different Kinds of Air* (2nd ed., corrected; 3 vols., London, 1775–84), I, 174.

inflammability. This, however, agrees with the opinion of chymists, that volatile Alkali contains phlogiston.

As you have not written to me, I hope you are planning an excursion to Calne, along with Sir John Pringle, or some of our friends. This would make me very happy. I am, with great respect, Dear Sir, yours sincerely   J PRIESTLEY.

Endorsed: Dr Priestley. Oct. 1773

To John Alleyne[2]

ALS (draft): American Philosophical Society; printed in John Alleyne, *The Legal Degrees of Marriage Stated and Considered, in a Series of Letters to a Friend* (2nd ed., London, 1775), appendix, pp. 1–2.[3]

Dear Sir,   Craven Street, 15th Oct. 1773

I have never heard upon what Principles of Policy the Law was made prohibiting the Marriage of a Man with his former Wife's Sister, nor have I ever been able to conjecture any political Inconvenience that might have been found in such Marriages, or to conceive of any moral Turpitude in them.[4] I have been personally acquainted with the Parties in two instances, both of which were happy Matches, the second Wives proving most affectionate Mothers-in-law to their Sister's Children, which indeed is so naturally to be expected that it seems to me wherever there are Children by the preceding Match, if any Law were to be made relating to such Marriages, it should rather be to enjoin than to forbid them; the Reason being stronger than that given for the Jewish Law, which enjoined the Widow to marry the Brother of a

2. For BF's young legal friend see above, xv, 182 and subsequent volumes.

3. The draft, dated Oct. 13, is in pencil and has numerous deletions and interlineations, and is so badly faded that the APS has assisted us in collating it with the printed text; the differences between the two are insignificant except for the date. That in the pamphlet was presumably in the letter as sent, and we have accordingly used it.

4. Canon law, incorporated into English law by several 16th-century statutes, prohibited on grounds of affinity a man's marriage to his deceased wife's sister. Civil process might void such a marriage when contracted, and Alleyne's pamphlet argued that Parliament should ban this process. The first edition (London, 1774) contained passages on pp. 51 and 55 about which he must have sought BF's advice before bringing out the second edition; this letter is the reply.

former Husband while there were no Children, viz. that Children might be produced who should bear the Name of the deceased Brother;[5] it being more apparently necessary to take Care of the Education of a Sister's Children already existing than to procure the Existence of Children merely that they might keep up the Name of a Brother. I am Dear Sir, Your most obedient humble Servant   B FRANKLIN

To Thomas Percival[6]

ALS (draft): American Philosophical Society; copy: National Library of Scotland

Dear Sir,   [London 15 October 1773[7]]
I have received here your Favour of September 18th. enclosing your very valuable Paper of the Numeration of Manchester.[8] Such Enquiries may be as useful as they are curious, and if once made general would greatly assist in the prudent Government of a State. In China, I have somewhere read, an Account is yearly taken of the Numbers of People, and the Quantities of Provision

5. A reference to Levirate marriage, widespread in primitive societies and prescribed in Deut. 25: 5–10; by this custom only the first-born was the dead brother's heir.

6. For the Lancashire physician and scientist see above, XVIII, 104 n.

7. The heading of the copy. The letter, so dated, appears in [Edward Percival, ed.,] *The Works, Literary, Moral, and Medical, of Thomas Percival, M.D.* . . . (4 vols., Bath and London, 1807), I, xxx–xxxiv. The draft is headed "West Wycomb, in Seat of Lord Le Despencer, Sept. 25. 1773," and mentions in the first sentence Percival's favor "of the 18th." The copy and the printed text, which are almost identical, lack BF's spelling and punctuation but are otherwise probably closer than the draft to the letter as sent. Although we print the draft we incorporate, and note when significant, changes that we believe BF made in the final version.

8. The letter has been lost, but Edward Percival presumably had a copy before him when he compiled the *Works*. He there remarks, p. xxx, that BF received with the letter "Dr. Percival's second volume of 'Essays,' &c." The essays were Percival's *Essays Medical and Experimental* . . . (2nd. ed.; 2 vols., London, 1772–73); the "&c." was either a printed or MS copy of *Observations on the State of Population in Manchester* . . . ([Manchester, 1773]), the "very valuable Paper" to which BF refers. For the sequels to it see Percival to BF below, June 21, 1774.

produc'd. This Account is transmitted to the Emperor, whose Ministers can thence foresee a Scarcity likely to happen in any Province, and from what Province it can best be supply'd in good time. To facilitate the collecting this Account, and prevent the Necessity of entring Houses, and spending time on asking and answering Questions, each House is furnish'd with a little Board to be hung without the Door during a certain time each Year, on which Board, is marked certain Words, against which the Inhabitant is to mark Number or Quantity somewhat in this Manner,[9]

Men			1	
Women	}	Persons	2	} 5
Children			2	
Rice or Wheat			5 Quarters	
Flesh			1000 lb.	

All under 16 are accounted Children, and all above as Men and Women. Any other Particulars the Government desires Information of, are occasionally mark'd on the same Boards. Thus the Officers appointed to collect the Accounts in each District, have only to pass before the Doors, and enter in their Book what they find marked on the Board without giving the least Trouble to the Family. There is a Penalty on marking falsly, and as Neighbours must know nearly the Truth of each others Account, they dare not expose themselves by a false one to each others Accusation. Perhaps such a Regulation is scarce practicable with us.

The Difference of Deaths, between 1 in 28, at Manchester and 1 in 120[1] at Monton, is surprizing. It seems to show the Unwholesomeness of the Manufacturing Life, owing perhaps to the Confinement in small Close Rooms: or in larger with Numbers, or to Poverty and want of Necessaries, or to Drinking, or to all of them. Farmers who manufacture in their own Families what they have occasion for and no more, are perhaps the happiest People and the healthiest.

9. In the copy and printed text of this letter everything but the left-hand column was deleted. The door cards were less for preventing famine than for tax-collecting, and their use was neither so widespread nor so effective as BF implies. See Ping-ti Ho, *Studies on the Population of China, 1368–1953* (Cambridge, Mass., 1959), pp. 39–46.

1. Thus in the draft and the printed text. The copy reads 68, which was Percival's actual figure in the *Observations* cited above. Monton was a village four miles from Manchester.

'Tis a curious Remark that moist Seasons are the healthiest.[2] The Gentry of England are remarkably afraid of Moisture, and of Air. But Seamen who live in perpetually moist Air, are always Healthy if they have good Provisions. The Inhabitants of Bermuda, St. Helena, and other Islands far from Continents, surrounded with Rocks against which the Waves continually dashing fill the Air with Spray and Vapour, and where no wind can arrive that does not pass over much Sea, and of course bring much Moisture, these People are remarkably healthy. And I have long thought that mere moist Air has no ill Effect on the Constitution; Tho' Air impregnated with Vapours from putrid Marshes is found pernicious, not from the Moisture but the Putridity.[3] It seems strange that a Man whose Body is compos'd in great Part of moist Fluids, whose Blood and Juices are so watery, who can swallow Quantities of Water and Small Beer daily without Inconvenience, should fancy that a little more or less Moisture in the Air should be of such Importance. But we abound in Absurdity and Inconsistency. Thus, tho' it is generally agreed that *taking the Air* is a good Thing, yet what Caution against Air, what stopping of Crevices, what wrapping-up in warm Clothes, what Shutting of Doors and Windows! even in the midst of Summer! Many London Families go out once a Day to take the Air; three or four Persons in a Coach, one perhaps Sick; these go three or four Miles or as many Turns in Hide Park, with the Glasses both up close, all breathing over and over again the same Air they brought out of Town with them in the Coach with the least change possible, and render'd worse and worse every moment. And this they call taking the Air. From many Years Observations on my self and others, I am persuaded we are on a wrong Scent in

2. For the remark, borrowed from another writer, see the reprint of the *Observations* in Percival's *Philosophical, Medical, and Experimental Essays* ... (London, 1776), pp. 20–1.

3. BF's friends shared this idea that marsh air was dangerous, and one of them had publicized it years before: John Pringle, *Observations on the Diseases of the Army* (4th ed., London, 1764), especially pp. 84–5, 179–80. Joseph Priestley and Richard Price were investigating the question, and soon supported Pringle's view in two articles, entitled respectively "On the Noxious Quality of the Effluvia of Putrid Marshes ... " and "Farther Proofs of the Insalubrity of Marshy Situations ... ," in *Phil. Trans.*, LXIV (1774), part 1, 90–8.

supposing Moist, or cold Air, the Causes of that Disorder we call a Cold. Some unknown Quality in the Air may perhaps sometimes produce Colds, as in the *Influenza:* but generally I apprehend they are the Effects of too full Living in proportion to our Exercise.[4] Excuse, if you can, my Intruding into your Province, and believe me ever, with sincere Esteem, Dear Sir, Your most obedient humble Servant   B F

Notation: To Thomas Percival.

From Jonathan Williams, Sr.

ALS: American Philosophical Society

Honoured Sir   Boston Oct 17th 1773
    I Duly received your favour by Capt. Hatch, Covering Invoice for my much Esteem'd Aunt Mecom,[5] whose Goods Came Safe to hand, I Bilive She in futer Will Supply herself with every sort of Good from our Desprate Merchants on better Terms then Can be Imported from England.
    I am favour'd with yours Feby. 7th July 7. and in Regard to my two Last Tickits one of which Drew £20—the fait of the other one I know not nor the numbers of Either, as Messr. Smith Wright & Gray Did not advice me as thay Did off the first,[6] and thay must know better than any one Can, you tell me that one of them Drew £20. and my Son knows the fait in Regard this Likewise.
    The Black Poetess master and mistress prevaild on me to mention her in my Letter but as its turnd out I am Sorry I Did.[7]
    My Brother is Still in England poor man What Can he Be about, his Oldest Son Was Vilently attack with a Disorder in his Head,

4. BF's interest in colds was particularly active this year, as shown in his letters above to Dubourg, March 10 and June 29, to LeRoy, June 22, to Rush, July 14; and in his notes on the subject at the end of this volume.
    5. The letter of June 4 above; for the invoice see the note on the letter from Jonathan, Jr., above, July 29.
    6. See BF to Williams above, July 7.
    7. Because BF, when he went to call on the slave, Phillis Wheatley, was not politely received by her master's son: *ibid.*

and Died 12 Days ago a Young man in the Prime of Life a promising Youth, cut down and is no more.[8] I thank you kindly for your kind Wishes and offer to Serve me and my son in the Commission Way. We Shall be Very Carefull not to Dishonour the Recommandations of any of our Friends. My Wife and Children Joine in Duty to you and our best Respects to Good Mrs. Stevenson and all Who Loved Our Departd [?] Son. I Expected to [have] had from Capt. Ann my Cask of Tongs and Sounds. But my man has hitherto Disopintd me, but Still promises one.[9] I am With the highest Esteem Your Dutiful Nephew and Humble Servant   JONA WILLIAMS

NB I take the Liberty to Inclose a Letter from Henry to his Father.

Addressed: To / Doctr Benja Franklin / at Mrs Stevensons / Craven Street / Strand / London

From Joseph Galloway[1]   ALS: American Philosophical Society

Dear Sir   Trevose, Bucks, Octr. 21st. 1773

Mr. John Coxe, the Son of Mr. William Coxe my Friend and Neighbour, comes to England with Intent to finish his Study of the Law at one of the Temples.[2] His good Character and close

8. John Williams, the customs inspector's son, died on Thursday evening, Oct. 7, and was to be buried on Monday afternoon. *Boston Gaz.*, Oct. 11. We have little more idea than his brother had of what the inspector was doing in London, except that he was offering advice to the government, presumably in hopes of a post, and had recently been in financial straits. *Dartmouth MSS.*, II, 81, 84, 133, 152; BF to John Williams above, Aug. 15.

9. BF's offer of service was in his letter of June 4. In that of March 9 he had acknowledged another cask of tongues and sounds.

1. BF was writing frequently to Galloway; but the Speaker, unless many of his letters have disappeared, did not reciprocate. On April 6 BF had mentioned having had no word from him. As far as we know he had thereafter only this brief note and two letters, now missing, which he acknowledged below on Nov. 3, 1773, and Feb. 18, 1774. The old friendship may have survived after the political alliance evaporated, as argued by Benjamin Newcomb in *Franklin and Galloway: a Political Partnership* (New Haven and London, 1972), pp. 234–6. But friendship, to judge by the evidence that remains, did not show itself in a two-way correspondence.

2. Galloway's neighbor, William D. Coxe, was a Philadelphia merchant and a large landholder in New Jersey; he had resigned as a stamp distributor in 1765: above, X, 213 n; XII, 256 n. His son John (1752–1824) had graduated

446

Application to the Business of his intended Profession, added to an Opinion I have entertained of his Abilities, induces me to recommend him to your Notice and Advice. Any Favors you shall be so kind as to confer on him will be adding to the Number of those already done to Dear Sir, your faithful humble Servant

JOS. GALLOWAY

Addressed: To / Benjamin Franklin Esqr / in / Craven Street / London

From Francis Maseres[3]   ALS: American Philosophical Society

Dear Sir,   Inner temple, Oct. 26, 1773.

Having had occasion to mention the Abbé Reynal's account of the European colonies, and to quote a passage from it in my French memoire written in defence of my draught of an Act of parliament for settling the laws of the province of Quebec,[4] I thought it a proper compliment to him to send him a copy of that Memoire. In return for this civility he has sent me a letter in which he acquaints me that the edition that was published last year of his

---

in 1769 from the College of Pennsylvania; in his later years he was a state and federal judge. William Nelson, *New Jersey Biographical and Genealogical Notes* ... (N.J. Hist. Soc. *Coll.*, IX; Newark, 1916), p. 87; *Catalogue of the Trustees Officers and Graduates* ... *of the University of Pennsylvania, 1749–1880* (Philadelphia, 1880), p. 30; John T. Scharf and Thompson Westcott, *History of Philadelphia* ... (3 vols., Philadelphia, 1884), II, 1531; Edward L. Clark, *A Record of the Inscriptions* ... *in the Burial-Grounds of Christ Church, Philadelphia* ... (Philadelphia, 1864), p. 603.

3. The former Attorney General of Quebec, and an F.R.S. for the past two years, had been appointed the previous August a baron of the exchequer. See above, XIX, 179; *DNB.*

4. Maseres' *Mémoire à la défense d'un plan d'acte de parlement* ... (London, 1773) quoted on pp. 52–3 a passage about the French West Indies in [Guillaume-Thomas-François Raynal], *Histoire philosophique et politique des établissemens, et du commerce des Européens dans les deux Indes* ... (4 vols., Amsterdam, 1770). The abbé Raynal (1713–96), a lapsed Jesuit, was a prolific writer on historical and political subjects and a well known philosophe. Diderot and several others contributed to the *Histoire*, which in its early editions carried on the theory advanced by de Pauw of American degeneracy: above, XIX, 197. The work was an enormous success and went through many editions.

work above mentioned was a stolen one, and very imperfect; and that he is now writing an accurate edition of it:[5] and he desires that I would assist him in that design by sending him accurate accounts of the population, the State of the trade, shipping, agriculture, produce, and other Material circumstances relating to the British colonies in North America. This I am utterly unable to do and therefore beg leave to refer him to you, who can do it better than any body I know, if your leisure and inclination permit you to take the necessary trouble to assist this writer in compleating his useful work.[6] I remain your's   F: MASERES.

Addressed: To / Dr: Benjamin Franklyn / at Mrs: Stevenson's / in Craven Street / in the Strand. / London.

From Robert Hare[7]

ALS: American Philosophical Society

Sir   Philadelphia Octr 28th: 1773.

I beg you to accept my warmest thanks for the fervor of the recommendations you favor'd me with. They are not only likely to promote my views of business but have introduc'd me into a very agreeable society and been principally instrumental in procuring the happiness I enjoy here.

I have delay'd these acknowledgements under hopes that your arrival here would give me an opportunity of making them personally and it greatly dissapoints me that I must not hope for

5. Perhaps the new 7-vol. edition published in 1774, which is said to have been supervised by the author: Maurice Tourneux, ed., *Correspondance littéraire, philosophique et critique par Grimm, Diderot, Raynal, Meister, etc.* ... (16 vols., Paris, 1877–82), x, 453. But Raynal was probably referring to the revision that occupied the next seven years and produced the 1780 edition, which was so outspoken in its criticism of the ancien régime that it drove the author into exile. Larousse, *Dictionnaire universel.*

6. Maseres apparently enclosed with this letter a list of specific queries about America that Raynal had sent him. They may have been behind BF's inquiry of Elliott, which elicited the latter's circumstantial reply below, Nov. 8. BF had the queries translated and sent to the APS, which concluded more than a year later that they did not fall within its scope. *Early Proc.* ... (Philadelphia, 1884), pp. 89, 93. Raynal's list and the translation are in BF's papers in the APS.

7. The young Londoner whom BF had recommended to Richard Bache, Coombe, Evans, and Galloway the previous spring; see his letters above, April 6.

that pleasure this year. I am Sir very respectfully Your oblig'd and obedient Servant RT HARE.

Addressed: Dr Benjan: Franklin / Craven Street / London.

From Deborah Franklin[8] ALS: American Philosophical Society

My Dear child ocktober the 29. 1773

I have bin verey much distrest a boute you as I did not [*have*] aney letter nor one word from you nor did I hear one word from aney bodey that you wrote to so I muste submit and indever to submit to what I am to bair. I did write by Capt. Folkner to you but he is gon down and when I read it over I did not like it and so if this dont send it I shante like it as I donte send you aney news nor I donte go abrode.

I shall tell you what Consernes my self our youngest Grand Son is the finest child as a live[9] he has had the Small Pox and had it verey fine and got a brod a gen Capt. All will tell you a boute him and Benj Franklin Beache but as it is so dificall to writ I have desierd him to tell you I have sente a Squerel for your friend and wish her better luck.[1] It is a verey fine one I have had verey bad luck with two thay one kild and another run a way all thow thay was bred up tame I have not a Caige as I donte know whare the man lives that makes them. My love to Salley Franklin [as] was my love to all our Cusins as thow menshond remember me to Mr. and Mrs. Weste due you ever hear aney thing of Amelly Evens as was.[2]

Thanke you for the Silke and hat it at the womans to make it

8. Although she lived more than a year longer, this is the last surviving letter from her. She seems to have written others in the late autumn, but none in 1774; BF's letter to her of Sept. 10, 1774—the last surviving one from him —complains of her nine-month silence.

9. William Bache, born on May 31.

1. In BF's letter above, Feb. 14, he had described to her the tragedy of Mungo, Georgiana Shipley's previous squirrel from Pennsylvania. Georgiana did indeed have better luck with the new one: he was still alive, at a ripe old age, almost six years later. Georgiana to BF, May 1, 1779; APS.

2. For Sally's marriage see BF to Samuel Franklin above, July 7. DF had either not yet received, or had forgotten, the long description of Amelia Evans' family in BF's letter to her above, Sept. 1.

up[3] but have it put up as you donte [*torn; illegible*] I thonke it is verey prittey what was the prise I desier to give my love to everey bodey [that?] I shold love. Billey was in towen 5 or 6 day when the child was in the Small pox Mrs. Franklin [has?] not sene him yit I am to tell a verey pritey thing a bout Ben the players is Cum to town and thay air to ackte on munday he wanted to see a play he unkill Beache[4] had given him a doler his mamah asked him wather he wold give it for a ticket or buy his Brother a necklas he sed his Brother a necklas he is a charmin child as ever was Borne my Grand children air the Beste in the world. Salley will write. I Cante write aney mor I am your afeckshone wife   D FRANKLIN

The Managers of the Pennsylvania Hospital to Franklin, David Barclay, and John Fothergill

Minutebook copy: Pennsylvania Hospital, Philadelphia

Philada. October 29th. 1773.

Esteemed Friends John Fothergill Benjamin Franklin David Barclay

We have lately received from our Friend David Barclay on Your behalf the State of the Accounts relating to the mony received by you for the Use of the Pennsa. Hospital, and of the Payment of the Bills drawn on you by the Managers, a Ballance remaining in favour of the Hospital, being £134 1s. 2d. we have drawn on you payable to our Treasurer Joseph Hillborn a Bill No. 33 dated 26th inst. for that Sum.[5]

3. For the silk see BF to DF above, July 15, and Sally's letter below, Oct. 30. Our guess is that "hat" was a slip for "had."

4. Theophylact. Richard Bache had recently taken his son on a visit to New York: Sally to BF below, Oct. 30.

5. See the Managers' letters above, Jan. 1, 4, 18, Feb. 14, and April 6. Barclay's letter to them of July 17, recorded in their minutes of Oct. 4, explained that sale of the remaining 3% annuities left the credit balance mentioned here. Hillborn, the new treasurer of the Hospital, was presumably the Quaker of that name (1732–1802) mentioned in Hinshaw, *Amer. Quaker Genealogy*, II, 374–5; he was a merchant of some prominence, and remained treasurer until 1780: J. Thomas Scharf and Thompson Westcott, *History of Philadelphia* ... (3 vols., Philadelphia, 1884), I, 273; Thomas G. Morton, *The History of the Pennsylvania Hospital* ... (Philadelphia, 1895), p. 408.

Gratefully sensible of this fresh proof of your Beneficence and Friendship in the Transaction of this Business we return you our Sincere Acknowledgments for ourselves for the Contributors and the many afflicted Objects who are the immediate partakers of this Charitable Act.

The mony arising from this Gratuity has been placed out on real Securities which is a very seasonable and acceptable Addition to our Capital Stock, the Income of which, tho' still far short of our Yearly Expences; Yet as the Institution maintains its Reputation for usefulness in many respects, and is conducted to the Satisfaction of the Contributors we have Grounds to hope will continue to merit the Attention of the Benevolent in such manner as to enable the Managers to encounter the Difficulties frequently occurring without reducing our Funds, that as the number of Patients increase our Endeavours united with the Physicians may extend the means of Relief to the diseased and impotent for whose sake this laudable Charity was instituted.

In the Course of this Year we have lost by Death our Treasurer Joseph King, two Physicians Doctr. Phineas Bond and Dr. Cadwalader Evans, and lately a Manager, Isaac Jones, all of whom were assiduous in their several Departments for the promotion of the Benefit of the Hospital. Dr. John Morgan and Dr. Charles Moore are appointed to succeed the Physicians Joseph Hillborn Treasurer, and Robt. Strettell Jones a Manager in the Room of his Father,[6] and we have no doubt will unite their Endeavours with us for the general good of the Institution under our Care. We are very respectfully Your much obliged Friends[7]

6. All these Philadelphians have appeared before, some many times and a few with little hint of who they were. They may be found above as follows: King, XIX, 366 n; Bond, II, 240 n; Evans, VII, 287 n; Isaac Jones, XI, 339 n; Morgan, IX, 374 n; Moore, X, 244 n; Robert Strettell Jones, Isaac's son, XVIII, 18 n.

7. The minutes record that the letter was signed by all the Managers present.

From Samuel Rhoads

ALS: Library of Congress

Dear Friend   Philada. October 29th 1773

Inclos'd are the Votes of the present Assembly. What happen'd last year I doubt not the Speaker has Communicated; this year they sat but a short time, chose their Officers and adjourn'd.[8]

Some Domestick Affairs of the Speakers call'd him out of Town Imiediately after he left the Chair; the Committee of Correspondance I presume will not meet till he returns. I have therefore undertaken to send the Votes, which will shew what is done.

As no new Instructions are given to the Agent no doubt the old Ones remain Valid; and he may Justly presume that it was not owing to any Neglect in the Assembly that they have not this Year given their Instructions to their Agent as formerly, But to a Confidence that he needed none. I am with great Esteem and respect thy Assured Friend   SAML RHOADS

Addressed: To / Benjamin Franklin Esqr. / Agent for / Pennsylvania / in / London

Endorsed: Saml. Rhodes Octr 29—1773

From Sarah Bache

ALS: American Philosophical Society

Dear and Honoured Sir   October 30. 1773

We are all much disapointed at your not coming home this Fall. I was in great hopes of seeing and presenting you with two of the finest Boys in the World, do not let any thing my dear Sir prevent your coming to your Family in the Spring for indeed we want you here much. I give you many thanks for the very eligant Silk,[1] I never knew what it was to be proud of a new Garment before. This I shall wear with pride and pleasure. Little William

---

8. The new Assembly met on Oct. 14; Galloway was re-elected speaker, and he, Rhoads, and others were named to the committee of correspondence. On the 15th BF was reappointed agent, and on the 16th the House adjourned until Nov. 29. 8 *Pa. Arch.*, VIII, 7023–4, 7027, 7037. The Speaker seems to have had little communication with BF, official or private; see the note on Galloway's letter above, Oct. 21. BF's reply to Rhoads's letter is below, Jan. 5, 1774.

1. See BF to DF above, July 15.

is just out of the Small Pox had it most delightfully. He is for size and temper beyond all the Boys of his age in America, how can Mrs. Stevenson wish for Girls?[2] The Boy Babies are infinitly Cleverer. I dare say by this time she would not change her youngest Grandson for a Girl. I am sure [I] would not part with Will for a Doz. Girls. I have not seen Mr. Baches letter but suppose he has given you an account of Bens manly behavour on his Journey to N. York, where He went in high expectation of meeting with you, and would have stayed for the September Packet, could they have had any hopes of your bein in her.[3] I must mention to you that I am no longer house keeper, it gave my dear Mama so much uneasiness, and the money was given to me in a manner which made it impossible to save any thing by laying in things before hand, so that my house keeping answered no good purpose, and I have the more readily given it up, tho I think it my duty, and would willingly take the care and trouble of her could I possibly please and make her happy.[4] The dining room wants new Paper, the Border which is a gold one never was put up, the handsome Picture is in it and it would make a sweet [?] room if it was new done up. We have no plates or Dishes fit to set before your Friends, and the Queens ware is thought very eligent here particularly the spriged.[5] I just mention this as it would be much cheaper for you to bring them than to get them here and you have them much handsomer. Mama has sent a Fine Fellow in Mungo's room, the Ground ones never can be tamed they say however we will try to get some and send them.[6] I have no news to write as I know very little that passes out of the nursery, where indeed its my greatest pleasure to be. After my Mother and Mr. Bache had done writing a Son of your Old

2. Young William had had smallpox "delightfully" at less than four months. Sally was replying to Mrs. Stevenson's comment that BF had quoted in the letter just cited.

3. BF had thought of returning by Capt. All in July, then by the September packet, but each time had postponed his departure. See his letters to Bache above, July 15, Sept. 1.

4. See BF to Sally above, April 6.

5. Queen's ware was the cream-colored earthenware that Josiah Wedgwood had brought to perfection in the late 1760's; sprigs are raised decorative designs.

6. For DF's new gift of squirrels see her letter above, Oct. 29.

Friend Potts of Potts Grove called to ask for a letter, mentioning his name will I know be enough,[7] and as my little Boy wants me I must conclude with love to Mrs. Stevenson, Mr. and Mrs. Hewson. I am as ever my dear Papa your Dutiful and Afectionate Daughter,   S BACHE

Reply to D. E. Q.   Copy: Library of Congress

The publication of "Rules by Which a Great Empire May Be Reduced to a Small One," signed Q.E.D., attracted considerable attention, which Franklin stimulated by two shorter contributions to the same paper.[8] On October 18 the *Public Advertiser* reprinted the "Rules," and in the issues of October 29–30 it carried a reply from some one—Sir Francis Bernard, according to Franklin—who signed himself D.E.Q. The writer gave fourteen rules of his own that the Americans, he argued, were following in order to destroy the empire.[9] The essay was an unwieldy bludgeon: the style was prolix to a degree, and the satire heavy-handed. This dart was in reply.[1]

7. John Potts (1710–68), the ironmaster and founder of Pottsgrove, now Pottstown, had nine sons. Among them were Jonathan, who accompanied Benjamin Rush to Edinburgh in 1766 to study medicine, and James, who in 1773 was preparing for the law. Isabelle James, *Memorial of Thomas Potts, Junior, . . . with an Historic-Genealogical Account of His Descendants . . .* (Cambridge, Mass., 1874), pp. 91–116, 122, 170–1, 227. BF at different times met two of the brothers in London: Thomas Potts to BF below, Aug. 1, 1774. One of the two was undoubtedly Jonathan in the late 1760's, when he was with Rush. The other, who Sally implies is leaving for England, may well have been James; the journey would have been a natural one for a fledgling lawyer.

8. See above, Sept. 11, 14, 17.

9. At the end he accused BF, without naming him, of having purloined the Hutchinson letters from William Whately. BF's connection with the affair must have been rumored in London months before his public avowal below, Dec. 25.

1. BF apparently did not publish his reply, but it bears the unmistakable stamp of his authorship. See Crane, *Letters to the Press*, p. 238. With the MS are two copies, one in the same hand and one in Fevre's, of an extract from Voltaire, which quotes a remonstrance to Louis XIII against making war on his own subjects. The quotation seems quite irrelevant to this squib; perhaps BF thought of basing another upon it.

To the Printer of the Publick Advertizer

Sir   [After Oct. 30, 1773]

D.E.Q. that is Sir F. Bernard in his long labour'd, and special dull Answer to Q.E.D. endeavours to persuade the King, that as he was his Majesty's Representative,[2] there was a great Similitude in their Characters and Conduct, and that Sir: F.'s Enemies are *Enemies of his Majesty* and of all Government.

This puts one in mind of the Chimney-sweeper condemn'd to be hang'd for Theft, who being charitably visited by a good Clergyman for whom he had work'd, said, *I hope your Honour will take my part, and get a Reprieve for me, and not let my Enemies have their Will; because it is upon your Account that they have prosecuted and sworn against me.* On my Account! How can that be? *Why, Sir, because as how, ever since they knew I was employ'd by your Honour, they resolv'd upon my Ruin: for they are Enemies to all Religion; and they hate you and me and every body in black.*   Z.Z.

To Thomas Cushing   ALS: Public Record Office

Sir,   London, Nov. 1. 1773

I duly received your Favour of the 26th of Augt. with the Letter enclos'd for Lord Dartmouth, which I immediately sent to him. As soon as he comes to Town I shall wait upon his Lordship, and discourse with him upon the Subject of it; and I shall immediately write to you what I can collect from the Conversation.[3]

In my Opinion the Letter of the two Houses of the 29th of June, proposing as a satisfactory Measure the Restoring Things to the State in which they were, at the Conclusion of the last War, is a fair and generous Offer on our Part; and my Discourse here is, that it is more than Britain has a Right to expect from us; and that if she has any Wisdom left, she will embrace it, and agree

2. D. E. Q.'s first rule was to attack the King personally; the fifth was to make similar attacks on the men he chose as colonial officials.

3. For Cushing's letter and its enclosure for Dartmouth see above, Aug. 26. BF reported to the Speaker on his conversation with the Earl in his letter below, Jan. 5, 1774.

with us immediately;[4] for that the longer she delays the Accommodation, which finally she must for her own sake procure, the worse Terms she may expect, since the Inequality of Power or Importance that at present subsists between us is daily diminishing, and our sense of our own Rights and of her Injustice continually increasing. I am the more encouraged to hold such Language, by perceiving that the general Sense of the Nation is for us; a Conviction prevailing that we have been ill-us'd, and that a Breach with us would be ruinous to this Country. The Pieces I wrote to increase and strengthen these Sentiments were more read, and talk'd of, and attended to, than usual. The first, as you will see by the enclos'd, has been call'd for and reprinted in the same Paper, besides being copied in others and in the Magazines. A long, labour'd Answer has been made to it (by Govr. Bernard as is said) which I send you. I am told it does not satisfy those in whose Justification it was written, and that a better is preparing.[5]

I think with you, that great Difficulties must attend an Attempt to make a new Representation of our Grievances in which the Point of Right should be kept out of sight, and especially as the Concurrence of so many Colonies seems now necessary. And therefore it would certainly be best and wisest for Parliament (which does not meet till after the Middle of January) to take the Matter up of themselves, and at once reduce Things to the State desired. There are not wanting some here who believe this will really be the Case: For that a new Election drawing now into View,[6] the present Members are likely to consider the Composing all Differences with America as a Measure agreable to the Trading

4. The letter of the two Houses is discussed in the headnote on Cushing to BF above, June 30; for BF's endorsement of its proposal see his "Infallible Method" above, Sept. 8.

5. The *Public Advertiser* reprinted the "Rules" on Oct. 18. The "long, labour'd Answer" attributed to Bernard, discussed in the preceding document, ended with the promise of a more finished essay in the near future.

6. Under the Septennial Act the term of the Parliament elected in 1768 would have run until the spring of 1775, but rumor of a dissolution had been circulating the previous summer; in its issue of July 1–3 the *London Chron.* had reported that a general election might be held before New Years. In fact North did not dissolve until September, 1774, and even then he caught the opposition unprepared: Bernard Donoughue, *British Politics and the American Revolution* . . . (New York and London, 1964), pp. 177–81.

and Manufacturing Part of the Nation; and that the Neglecting it may be made use of by their Opponents to their Disadvantage.

I have as yet received no Answer to the Petition for Removing the Governors.[7] I scarce expect it to be comply'd with, as it would embarras Government to provide for them otherwise, and it will be thought hard to neglect Men who have expos'd themselves by adhering to what is here call'd the Interest and Rights of *this Country*. But this is only Conjecture, as I have heard nothing certain about it. Indeed I should think continuing them in their Places would be rather a Punishment than a Favour: For what Comfort can Men have in living among a People with whom they are the Object of universal Odium?

I shall continue here one Winter longer, and use my best Endeavours, as long as I stay, for the Service of our Country. With great Esteem and Respect, I have the Honour to be, Sir, Your most obedient and most humble Servant   B FRANKLIN

Private

Honourable Thomas Cushing, Esqr

Endorsed: Benj Franklin Esqr   London   Novr. 1. 1773[8]

To Jane Mecom   ALS: American Philosophical Society

Dear Sister,   London, Nov. 1. 1773
I received your kind Letter of June 28. with great Pleasure, as it inform'd me of your Welfare.

I thank you for your good Wishes that I may be a means of restoring Harmony between the two Countries. It would make me very happy to see it, whoever was the Instrument. I had us'd all the smooth Words I could muster, and I grew tir'd of Meekness when I saw it without Effect. Of late therefore I have been saucy, and in two Papers, *Rules for reducing a great Empire to a small one;*

---

7. Hutchinson and Oliver; see Cushing to BF above, June 25.

8. Thomas Moffatt later added, in his usual vein, an endorsement of his own: "This letter encourages Opposition to Administration and promises certain Success from Perseverance and also acknowledges his sending several publications of his own composing (which are not distinguished or therefore known by any Certain Title) to Effect or Accomplish the Deliverance of America from the Oppression of Parliament."

and, *An Edict of the King of Prussia*,[9] I have held up a Looking-Glass in which some Ministers may see their ugly Faces, and the Nation its Injustice. Those Papers have been much taken Notice of, many are pleased with them, and a few very angry, who I am told will make me feel their Resentment, which I must bear as well as I can, and shall bear the better if any publick Good is done, whatever the Consequence to myself. [*In the margin:* This to yourself.] In my own private Concerns with Mankind, I have observ'd that to kick a little when under Imposition, has a good Effect. A little Sturdiness when Superiors are much in the Wrong, sometimes occasions Consideration. And there is Truth in the Old Saying, That *if you make yourself a Sheep, the Wolves will eat you.*[10]

I communicated Coz. Jenny's Verses to my little Circle of Female Friends who made the *Bouts Rimez*, and they were pleas'd to praise them. I hope she is got well home from her Visit to Nantucket.[1] My Love to her.

Your Neighbour Hall must have been pretty well advanc'd in Years when he dy'd.[2] I remember him a young Man when I was a very young Boy. In looking back how short the Time seems! I suppose that all the Passages of our Lives that we have forgotten, being so many Links taken out of the Chain, give the more distant Parts Leave as it were to come apparently nearer together.

I was glad to hear of the Ship's Arrival in which I sent your Things.[3] I hope they will prove agreable and advantageous to you. If you possibly can, try to increase your Capital, by adding the Profits. Consuming all the Profits and some of the Principal, will soon reduce it to nothing. I am ever, my dear Sister, Your very affectionate Brother   B FRANKLIN

9. Above, Sept. 11 and 22 respectively.

10. BF had used the same proverb on Cushing: above, Jan. 5.

1. Jane Mecom Collas had presumably been visiting her Nantucket relatives. This is the first hint we have had of her penchant for versifying, and the verses themselves have disappeared. For the parlor game of *bouts rimés* see above, XVIII, 272.

2. Hugh Hall had died the previous June at the age of eighty; see Van Doren, *Franklin-Mecom*, p. 142.

3. See above, BF to Jane and to Jonathan Williams, Sr., July 7; BF had news of the goods' arrival in the postscript of the letter from Jonathan, Jr., above, July 29.

To Peter P. Burdett Copy:[4] American Philosophical Society

Sir,   London, Nov. 3, 1773.

I was much pleased with the Specimens you so kindly sent me, of your new Art of Engraving. That on the China is admirable. No one would suppose it any thing but Painting.[5] I hope you meet with all the Encouragement you merit, and that the Invention will be, (what Inventions seldom are) profitable to the Inventor.

I know not who (now we speak of Inventions) pretends to that of Copper-Plate Engravings for Earthen-Ware, and am not disposed to contest the Honor of it with any body, as the Improvement in taking Impressions not directly from the Plate but from printed Paper, applicable by that means to other than flat Forms, [is] far beyond my first Idea. But I have reason to apprehend I might have given the Hint on which that Improvement was made. For more than twenty years since, I wrote to Dr. Mitchell from America, proposing to him the printing of square Tiles for ornamenting Chimnies, from Copper Plates, describing the Manner in which I thought it might be done, and advising the Borrowing from the Bookseller, the Plates that had been used in a thin Folio, called *Moral Virtue delineated*, for the Purpose. As the Dutch Delphware Tiles were much used in America, which are only or chiefly Scripture Histories, wretchedly scrawled, I wished to have those moral Prints, (which were originally taken from Horace's poetical Figures) introduced on Tiles, which being about our Chimneys, and constantly in the Eyes of Children when by the Fire-side, might give Parents an Opportunity, in explaining them, to impress moral Sentiments; and I gave Expectations of great Demand for them if executed. Dr. Mitchell wrote to me in Answer, that he had communicated my Scheme to

4. The letter, which is in Fevre's hand, continued the correspondence of the previous summer, apparently inaugurated by Burdett; see BF's letter to him above, Aug. 21.

5. This was just the point that had worried Josiah Wedgwood in 1772. When he had been trying out Burdett's process for transferring acquatints to pottery, as mentioned in the headnote on the letter just cited, he had feared that the use of printed designs might become known and impair the market for hand-painted ware. Ann Finer and George Savage, eds., *The Selected Letters of Josiah Wedgwood* (London, [1975]), p. 118.

several of the principal Artists in the Earthen Way about London, who rejected it as impracticable:[6] And it was not till some years after that I first saw an enamelled snuff-Box which I was sure was a Copper-plate, tho' the Curvature of the Form made me wonder how the Impression was taken.

I understand the China Work in Philadelphia is declined by the first Owners. Whether any others will take it up and continue it, I know not.[7]

Mr. Banks is at present engaged in preparing to publish the Botanical Discoveries of his Voyage. He employs 10 Engravers for the Plates, in which he is very curious, so as not to be quite satisfied in some Cases with the Expression given by either the Graver, Etching, or Metzotinto, particularly where there is a Wooliness or a Multitude of small Points or a Leaf. I sent him the largest of the Specimens you sent containing a Number of Sprigs.[8] I have not seen him since, to know whether your Manner would not suit some of his Plants, better than the more common Methods. With great Esteem, I am, Sir, Your most obedient humble Servant, B. FRANKLIN

6. For Dr. John Mitchell see above, II, 415 n. None of the many references to him in early volumes of this series throws any light on the exchange of letters to which BF refers, and we have failed to identify *Moral Virtue Delineated.*

7. No one else did. Bonnin & Morris had been forced out of business in 1772, and china-making was not revived in Philadelphia for half a century. Harold E. Gillingham, "Pottery, China, and Glass Making in Philadelphia," *PMHB*, LIV (1930), 117.

8. Designs in the form of sprays, normally on textiles but in this case presumably on the borders of an aquatint; Burdett had clearly sent BF a selection of his prints as well as printed china. BF hoped to interest Joseph Banks in using the new medium for his plates, which illustrated Daniel Solander's description of the specimens that he and Banks had brought back from their voyage with Cook in the *Endeavour.* We have no indication that Banks was interested. He continued to direct the work of engraving until soon after Solander's death in 1782, and then tired of the project; it was never completed. See the anonymous and unpaginated introduction to *Illustrations of Australian Plants Collected in 1770 . . . by the Right Hon. Sir Joseph Banks . . . and Dr. Daniel Solander . . .* (3 vols., London, 1905); John C. Beaglehole, ed., *The Endeavour Journal of Joseph Banks, 1768–1771* (2 vols., [London, etc., 1962]), I, 120–3.

To William Franklin

Reprinted from William Duane, ed., *The Works of Benjamin Franklin* ... (6 vols., Philadelphia, 1808–18), VI, 337–8.

Dear Son,   London, Nov. 3, 1773.

I wrote you pretty fully by the last packet, and having had no line from you of later date than the beginning of August, and little stirring here lately, I have now little to write.

In that letter I mentioned my having written two papers, of which I preferred the first, but the public the last.[9] It seems I was mistaken in judging of the public opinion; for the first was re-printed some weeks after in the same paper, the printer giving for reason, that he did it in compliance with the earnest request of many private persons, and some respectable societies; which is the more extraordinary as it had been copied in several other papers, and in the Gentleman's Magazine.[1] Such papers may seem to have a tendency to increase our divisions, but I intend a contrary effect, and hope by comprising in little room, and setting in a strong light the grievances of the colonies, more attention will be paid them by our administration, and that when their un-reasonableness is generally seen, some of them will be removed to the restoration of harmony between us.   B. FRANKLIN

To Joseph Galloway

Reprinted from William Temple Franklin, ed., *Memoirs of the Life and Writings of Benjamin Franklin, L.L.D., F.R.S., &c.* ... (3 vols., 4to, London, 1817–18), II, 200 of first pagination.

Sir,   London, Nov. 3, 1773.

There is at present great quietness here, and no prospect that the war between the Turks and Russians will spread farther in Europe.[2] The last harvest is allowed to have been generally plenti-ful in this country; and yet such was the preceding scantiness of crops, that it is thought there is no corn to spare for exportation, which continues the advantages to our corn provinces.

9. In his letter above of Oct. 6 BF discussed his two satires.

1. See the *Public Advertiser*, Oct. 18, and the *Gent. Mag.*, XLIII (1773), 441–5.

2. For the war and the first partition of Poland see above, XIX, 132.

The parliament is not to meet till after the middle of January. It is said there is a disposition to compose all differences with America before the next general election, as the trading and manufacturing part of the nation are generally our well wishers, think we have been hardly used, and apprehend ill consequences from a continuance of the measures that we complain of: and that if those measures are not changed an American interest may be spirited up at the election against the present members who are in, or friends to administration.[3] Our steady refusal to take tea from hence for several years past has made its impressions. The scheme for supplying us without repealing the act, by a temporary licence from the treasury to export tea to America free of duty, you are before this time acquainted with. I much want to hear how that tea is received. If it is rejected the act will undoubtedly be repealed, otherwise I suppose it will be continued, and when we have got into the use of the Company's tea, and the foreign correspondences that supply us at present are broken off, the licences will be discontinued, and the act enforced.[4]

I apprehend the better understanding that lately subsisted in our provincial administration will hardly be continued with the new Governor; but you will soon see.[5] I wish for the full letter you promise me by the next packet, which is now daily expected. With unalterable esteem and attachment, I am ever, my dear friend, yours most affectionately,   B. FRANKLIN.

3. BF had said much the same thing to Cushing, above, Nov. 1. The American interest that raised his hopes did not materialize; see Gipson, *British Empire*, XII, 270–2.

4. For the declining revenue from the tea duty see Labaree, *Tea Party*, p. 52. Here BF seems to be saying, as to Cushing above, p. 400, that if the tea is rejected the Tea Act will be repealed, whereas if the Company corners the market the English import duty will be restored.

5. In August, 1773, John Penn had returned after two years to replace his more popular brother Richard as lieutenant governor.

To William Brownrigg LS:[6] the Royal Society

Franklin's curiosity about the interaction of oil and water had first been aroused, as he mentions in this famous letter, by an experience on shipboard in 1757, and reawakened by another in 1762. He seems to have pondered the significance of what he had observed on those occasions, but to have done nothing further until—at some time that cannot be exactly determined—he experimented with pouring oil on a pond in Clapham Common. The result amazed him: half an acre of water became "smooth as a Looking Glass." When he and Sir John Pringle visited Brownrigg at Ormathwaite in 1772, the three repeated the experiment on Derwent Water. Franklin's interest was now fully aroused, and he continued to probe the puzzle—with John Smeaton near Leeds, in a pond in Green Park, and then in October, 1773, on a much larger scale but with inconclusive results in the waters off Spithead.[7] Meanwhile he had heard further from Brownrigg on the subject (above, Jan. 27), and this letter was his reply. In it he gathered together his observations and advanced a theory to account for the spread of oil upon water and the effect on calming waves. The theory was incomplete, just as the experiments were inconclusive; but it aroused much interest at the time and had its influence on the later study of surface tension.[8]

Dear Sir, London, Nov. 7, 1773.

Our Correspondence might be carried on for a Century with very few Letters, if you were as apt to procrastinate as myself.

6. In Fevre's hand. He also made an extract; it is with the original, and was published with a few slight verbal changes in *Phil. Trans.*, LXIV (1774), 447–60.

7. All that we know of these experiments is what BF told Brownrigg. Another that he did not mention was in October, 1772, when he was visiting Lord Shelburne at Wycombe: Pierre Edouard Lémontey, ed., *Mémoires de l'abbé Morellet* . . . (2 vols., Paris, 1821), I, 197–8.

8. The only article we know that traces the influence of BF's published letter is Charles H. Giles, "Studies in the Early History of Surface Chemistry: Franklin's Teaspoonful of Oil," *Chemistry and Industry* (Nov. 8, 1969), pp. 1616–24; see also Edward H. Davidson, "Franklin and Brownrigg," *Amer. Literature*, XXIII (1951–52), 38–56. We are most grateful to Dr. Giles and to Mr. E. E. Smith, the Hon. Secretary of the Clapham Antiquarian Soc., for providing us with information, particularly about Christopher Baldwin and the experiment at Clapham, that we have used in our annotation. We are also indebted to Dr. Giles for furnishing us the photograph of Mount Pond.

Tho'an habitual Sinner, I am now quite ashamed to observe, that this is to be an Answer to your Favour of January last.[9]

I suppose Mrs. Brownrigg did not succeed in making the Parmesan Cheese, since we have heard nothing of it.[10] But as a Philosophess, she will not be discouraged by one or two Failures. Perhaps some Circumstance is omitted in the Receipt, which by a little more Experience she may discover. The foreign Gentleman, who had learnt in England to like boiled Plumbpudding, and carried home a Receipt for making it, wondered to see it brought to his Table in the Form of a Soup. The Cook declar'd he had exactly followed the Receipt. And when that came to be examined, a small, but important Circumstance appeared to have been omitted. There was no Mention of the Bag.

I am concerned that you had not, and I fear you have not yet found time to prepare your excellent Papers for Publication. By omitting it so long, you are wanting to the World, and to your own Honour.

I thank you for the Remarks of your learned Friend at Carlisle.[1] I had when a Youth, read and smiled at Pliny's Account of a Practice among the Seamen of his Time, to still the Waves in a Storm by pouring Oil into the Sea: which he mentions, as well as the Use of Oil by the Divers. But the stilling a Tempest by throwing Vinegar into the Air had escaped me. I think with your Friend, that it has been of late too much the Mode to slight the Learning of the Ancients. The Learned too, are apt to slight too much the Knowledge of the Vulgar. The cooling by Evaporation was long an Instance of the latter.[2] This Art of smoothing the Waves with Oil, is an Instance of both.

Perhaps you may not dislike to have an Account of all I have heard, and learnt and done in this Way. Take it, if you please, as follows.

In 1757 being at Sea in a Fleet of 96 Sail bound against Louis-

9. The letter survives only in an extract: above, Jan. 27.

10. BF had presumably given her the recipe during his visit in the summer of 1772; it was the same one, we assume, that he had sent to Catherine Greene: above, XIX, 25. See also below, p. 506 n.

1. The Rev. James Farish; see the Brownrigg letter cited above. The extract begins with this sentence.

2. BF had cited examples many years before: above, VIII, 109–10.

bourg,[3] I observed the Wakes of two of the Ships to be remarkably smooth, while all the others were ruffled by the Wind, which
blew fresh. Being puzzled with this differing Appearance I at last
pointed it out to our Captain, and asked him the meaning of it?
"The Cooks, says he, have I suppose, been just emptying their
greasy Water thro' the Scuppers, which has greased the Sides of
those Ships a little;" and this Answer he gave me with an Air of
some little Contempt, as to a Person ignorant of what every Body
else knew. In my own Mind I at first slighted his Solution, tho' I
was not able to think of another. But recollecting what I had
formerly read in Pliny, I resolved to make some Experiment of
the Effect of Oil on Water when I should have Opportunity.

Afterwards being again at Sea in 1762, I first observed the
wonderful Quietness of Oil on agitated Water in the swinging
Glass Lamp I made to hang up in the Cabin, as described in my
printed Papers, page 438 of the fourth Edition.[4] This I was
continually looking at and considering, as an Appearance to me
inexplicable. An old Sea Captain, then a Passenger with me,
thought little of it, supposing it an Effect of the same kind with
that of Oil put on Water to smooth it, which he said was a
Practice of the Bermudians when they would strike Fish which
they could not see if the surface of the Water was ruffled by the
Wind. This Practice I had never before heard of, and was obliged
to him for the Information, though I thought him mistaken as to
the sameness of the Experiment, the Operations being different;
as well as the Effects. In one Case, the Water is smooth till the Oil
is put on, and then becomes agitated. In the other it is agitated
before the Oil is applied, and then becomes smooth. The same
Gentleman told me he had heard it was a Practice with the Fishermen of Lisbon when about to return into the River, (if they saw
before them too great a Surff upon the Bar, which they apprehended might fill their Boats in passing) to empty a Bottle or two
of oil into the Sea, which would suppress the Breakers and
allow them to pass safely: a Confirmation of this I have not since

3. BF and WF, on their way to England, accompanied Loudoun's expedition
against Louisbourg to the vicinity of Nantucket, where their packet left the
convoy. Above, VII, 174.

4. Above, X, 159–60. BF elaborates here on what he had then written to
Pringle.

had an Opportunity of obtaining. But discoursing of it with another Person, who had often been in the Mediterranean, I was informed that the Divers there, who when under Water in their Business, need Light, which the curling of the Surface interrupts, by the Refractions of so many little Waves, they let a small Quantity of Oil now and then out of their Mouths, which rising to the Surface smooths it, and permits the Light to come down to them.[5] All these Informations I at times revolved in my Mind, and wondered to find no mention of them in our Books of Experimental Philosophy.

At length being at Clapham, where there is, on the Common, a large Pond, which I observed to be one Day very rough with the Wind, I fetched out a Cruet of Oil, and dropt a little of it on the Water.[6] I saw it spread itself with surprising Swiftness upon the Surface, but the Effect of smoothing the Waves was not produced; for I had applied it first on the Leeward Side of the Pond where the Waves were largest, and the Wind drove my Oil back upon the Shore. I then went to the Windward Side, where they began to form; and there the Oil tho' not more than a Tea Spoonful produced an instant Calm, over a Space several yards square, which spread amazingly, and extended itself gradually till it reached the Lee Side, making all that Quarter of the Pond, perhaps half an Acre, as smooth as a Looking Glass.

After this, I contrived to take with me, whenever I went into the Country, a little Oil in the upper hollow joint of my bamboo Cane, with which I might repeat the Experiment as Opportunity should offer; and I found it constantly to succeed.

In these Experiments, one Circumstance struck me with particular Surprize. This was the sudden, wide and forcible Spreading of a Drop of Oil on the Face of the Water, which I do

5. A time-honored practice; see Pliny, *Natural History*, Book II, 234.
6. The experiment was made on Mount Pond, which had been created on the common years before by Henton Brown, BF's friend and banker (for whom see above, IX, 218 n). Brown had for neighbor Christopher Baldwin, a native of Antigua who was in business in London as a West Indian merchant; although he has not hitherto appeared except above, p. 345 n, he also was by this time a good friend of BF. Baldwin helped him with his experiment, for he twice referred to it in later years: to BF, March 5, 1779; Feb. 18, 1783. APS.

Where Franklin poured oil: Mount Pond, Clapham Common

not know that any body has hitherto considered. If a Drop of Oil is put on a polished Marble Table, or on a Looking Glass that lies horizontally; the Drop remains in its Place, spreading very little. But when put on Water it spreads instantly many feet round, becoming so thin as to produce the prismatic Colours, for a considerable Space, and beyond them so much thinner as to be invisible except in its Effect of smoothing the Waves at a much greater Distance. It seems as if a mutual Repulsion between its Particles took Place as soon as it touched the Water, and a Repulsion so strong as to act on other Bodies swimming on the Surface, as Straws, Leaves, Chips, &c. forcing them to recede every way from the Drop, as from a Center, leaving a large clear Space. The Quantity of this Force, and the Distance to which it will operate, I have not yet ascertained, but I think it a curious Enquiry, and I wish to understand whence it arises.

In our Journey to the North when we had the Pleasure of seeing you at Ormathwaite, we visited Mr. Smeaton near Leeds. Being about to shew him the smoothing Experiment on a little Pond near his House, an ingenious Pupil of his, Mr. Jessop,[7] then present, told us of an odd Appearance on that Pond, which had lately occurred to him. He was about to clean a little Cup in which he kept Oil, and he threw upon the Water some Flies that had been drowned in the Oil. These Flies presently began to move, and turned round on the Water very rapidly, as if they were vigorously alive, tho' on Examination he found they were not so. I immediately concluded that the Motion was occasioned by the Power of the Repulsion abovementioned, and that the Oil issuing gradually from the spungy Body of the Fly continued the Motion. He found some more Flies drowned in Oil, with which the Experiment was repeated before us; and to show that it was not any Effect of Life recovered by the Flies, I imitated it by little bits of oiled Chip, and Paper cut in the form of a Comma, of this size **𝟗** when the Stream of repelling Particles issuing from the

7. This is our first evidence that BF's northern tour in 1772 included a visit to John Smeaton, the famous engineer. William Jessop (d. 1814) was more than ingenious: he had been Smeaton's pupil for a decade and more, and at the time BF met him was about to branch out on his own to become one of the most eminent canal-builders of his time. See Samuel Smiles, *Lives of the Engineers* . . . (3 vols., London, 1861–62), II, 197 n.

Point, made the Comma turn round the contrary way. This is not a Chamber Experiment; for it cannot well be repeated in a Bowl or Dish of Water on a Table. A considerable Surface of Water is necessary to give Room for the Expansion of a small Quantity of Oil. In a Dish of Water if the smallest Drop of Oil be let fall in the Middle, the whole Surface is presently covered with a thin greasy Film proceeding from the Drop; but as soon as that Film has reached the Sides of the Dish, no more will issue from the Drop, but it remains in the Form of Oil, the Sides of the Dish putting a Stop to its Dissipation by prohibiting the farther Expansion of the Film.

Our Friend Sir J. Pringle being soon after in Scotland, learnt there that those employed in the Herring Fishery, could at a Distance see where the Shoals of Herrings were, by the smoothness of the Water over them, which might be occasioned possibly, he thought, by some Oiliness proceeding from their Bodies.

A Gentleman from Rhode-island[8] told me, it had been remarked that the Harbour of Newport was ever smooth while any Whaling Vessels were in it; which probably arose from hence, that the Blubber which they sometimes bring loose in the Hold, or the Leakage of their Barrels, might afford some Oil to mix with that Water which from time to time they pump out to keep the Vessel free, and that same Oil might spread over the surface of the Water in the Harbour, and prevent the forming of any Waves.

This Prevention I would thus endeavour to explain.

There seems to be no natural Repulsion between Water and Air, such as to keep them from coming into Contact with each other. Hence we find a Quantity of Air in Water, and if we extract it by means of the Air-pump; the same Water again exposed to the Air, will soon imbibe an equal Quantity.

Therefore Air in Motion, which is Wind, in passing over the smooth Surface of Water, may rub, as it were, upon that Surface, and raise it into Wrinkles, which if the Wind continues are the elements of future Waves.

The smallest Wave once raised does not immediately subside and leave the neighbouring Water quiet; but in subsiding raises nearly as much of the Water next to it, the Friction of its Parts

8. Doubtless Henry Marchant, for whom see above, x, 316 n; XVIII, 145 n.

making little Difference. Thus a Stone dropt in a Pool raises first a single Wave round itself, and leaves it by sinking to the Bottom; but that first Wave subsiding raises a second, the second a third, and so on in Circles to a great Extent.

A small Power continually operating will produce a great Action. A Finger applied to a weighty suspended Bell, can at first move it but little; if repeatedly applied, tho' with no greater Strength, the Motion increases till the Bell swings to its utmost Height and with a Force that cannot be resisted by the whole Strength of the Arm and Body. Thus the small first-raised Waves, being continually acted upon by the Wind are, (tho' the Wind does not increase in Strength) continually increased in Magnitude, rising higher and extending their Bases, so as to include a vast Mass of Water in each Wave, which in its Motion acts with great Violence.

But if there be a mutual Repulsion between the Particles of Oil, and no Attraction between Oil and Water, Oil dropt on Water will not be held together by Adhesion to the Spot whereon it falls, it will not be imbibed by the Water, it will be at Liberty to expand itself, and it will spread on a Surface that besides being smooth to the most perfect degree of Polish, prevents, perhaps by repelling the Oil, all immediate Contact, keeping it at a minute Distance from itself; and the Expansion will continue, till the mutual Repulsion between the Particles of the Oil, is weakened and reduced to nothing by their Distance.

Now I imagine that the Wind blowing over Water thus covered with a Film of Oil, cannot easily catch upon it so as to raise the first Wrinkles, but slides over it, and leaves it smooth as it finds it. It moves a little the Oil, indeed, which being between it and the water serves it to slide with, and prevents Friction as Oil does between those Parts of a Machine that would otherwise rub hard together. Hence the Oil dropt on the Windward Side of a Pond proceeds gradually to Leeward, as may be seen by the smoothness it carries with it, quite to the opposite Side. For the Wind being thus prevented from raising the first Wrinkles that I call the Elements of Waves, cannot produce Waves, which are to be made by continually acting upon and enlarging those Elements, and thus the whole Pond is calmed.

Totally therefore we might supress the Waves in any required

Place, if we could come at the Windward Place where they take their Rise. This in the Ocean can seldom if ever be done. But perhaps something may be done on particular Occasions, to moderate the Violence of the Waves, when we are in the midst of them, and prevent their Breaking where that would be inconvenient.

For when the Wind blows fresh, there are continually rising on the Back of every great Wave, a number of small ones, which roughen its Surface, and give the Wind Hold, as it were, to push it with greater Force. This Hold is diminished by preventing the Generation of those small ones. And possibly too, when a Wave's Surface is oiled, the Wind in passing over it, may rather in some degree press it down, and contribute to prevent its rising again, instead of promoting it.

This as a mere Conjecture would have little weight, if the apparent Effects of pouring Oil into the Midst of Waves, were not considerable, and as yet not otherwise accounted for.

When the Wind blows so fresh, as that the Waves are not sufficiently quick in obeying its Impulse, their Tops being thinner and lighter are pushed forward, broken and turned over in a white Foam. Common Waves lift a Vessel without entring it, but these when large sometimes break above and pour over it, doing great Damage.

That this Effect might in any degree be prevented, or the height and violence of Waves in the Sea moderated, we had no certain Account, Pliny's Authority for the Practice of Seamen in his time being slighted. But discoursing lately on this Subject with his Excellency Count Bentinck of Holland, his Son the Honble. Capt. Bentinck, and the learned Professor Allemand, (to all whom I showed the Experiment of smoothing in a Windy Day the large Piece of Water at the Head of the Green Park) a Letter was mentioned which had been received by the Count from Batavia, relating to the saving of a Dutch Ship in a Storm, by pouring Oil into the Sea. I much desired to see that Letter, and a Copy of it was promised me, which I afterwards received.[9] It is as follows.

9. The experiment in Green Park was in a large reservoir or canal, which has since been filled in: Henry B. Wheatley, *London Past and Present* (3 vols., London, 1891), II, 152. William Bentinck, Count Bentinck (1704–74), a

Extrait d'une Lettre de Mr. Tengnagel à Mr. le Comte de Bentinck, écrite de Batavia le 15 Janvier 1770. Près des Isles Paulus et Amsterdam nous essuiames un orage, qui n'eut rien d'assez particulier pour vous être marqué, si non que notre Capitaine se trouva obligé en *tournant sous le vent*,[1] de verser de l'huile contre la haute mer, pour empecher les vagues de se briser contre le navire, ce qui réussit à nous conserver et a été d'un très bon effet: comme il n'en versa qu'une petite quantité à la fois, la Compagnie doit peut-être son vaisseau à six demi-ahmes[2] d'huile d'olive: j'ai été présent quand cela s'est fait, et je ne vous aurois pas entretenu de cette circonstance, si ce n'étoit que nous avons trouvé les gens ici si prévenus contre l'expérience, que les officiers du bord ni moi n'avons fait aucune difficulté de donner un certificat de la verité sur ce chapitre.

On this Occasion I mentioned to Capt. Bentinck, a thought which had occurred to me in reading the Voyages of our late Circumnavigators, particularly where Accounts are given of pleasant and fertile Islands which they much desired to land upon, when Sickness made it more necessary, but could not effect a Landing thro' a violent Surff breaking on the Shore, which rendered it impracticable. My Idea was, that possibly by sailing to and fro at some Distance from such Lee Shore, continually pouring Oil into the Sea, the Waves might be so much depressed and lessened before they reached the Shore, as to abate the Height and Violence of the Surff and permit a Landing, which in such Circumstances was a Point of sufficient Importance to justify the Expence of Oil that might be requisite for the purpose. That

---

younger son of the first Earl of Portland and an F.R.S. since 1731, had called at Craven St. the summer before; see Fevre to BF above, Aug. 5. His son, Capt. John Albert, R.N. (1737-75), was also a count of the empire, and at this time was commanding a guardship at Portsmouth. *DNB*; Namier and Brooke, *House of Commons*, II, 83-4. For Jean Allamand, the professor at Leyden, see above, XVIII, 106 n. Allamand sent the copy to BF, who eventually thanked him for it in his letter below, Aug. 21, 1774.

1. [BF's *note*:] Suppos'd to mean, *In wearing the Ship*.
2. A considerable quantity: the ahm or aam was a liquid measure that varied locally, but at Amsterdam was equivalent to 41 gallons. For the interest that this episode aroused see van Lelyveld to BF below, Dec. 9, 1774; March 11, 1775. APS.

Gentleman, who is ever ready to promote what may be of publick Utility, (tho' his own ingenious Inventions have not always met with the Countenance they merited[3]) was so obliging as to invite me to Portsmouth, where an Opportunity would probably offer, in the course of a few Days, of making the Experiment on some of the Shores about Spithead, in which he kindly proposed to accompany me, and to give Assistance with such Boats as might be necessary. Accordingly, about the middle of October last, I went with some Friends, to Portsmouth; and a Day of Wind happening, which made a Lee-Shore between Haslar Hospital and the Point near Jillkecker;[4] we went from the Centaur with the Longboat and Barge towards that Shore. Our Disposition was this; the Longboat anchored about a $\frac{1}{4}$ of a Mile from the Shore, part of the Company were landed behind the Point, (a Place more sheltered from the Sea) who came round and placed themselves opposite to the Longboat, where they might observe the Surff, and note if any Change occurred in it upon using the Oil: Another Party in the Barge plied to Windward of the Longboat, as far from her as she was from the Shore, making Trips of about half a Mile each, pouring Oil continually out of a large Stone Bottle, thro' a Hole in the Cork somewhat bigger than a Goose Quill. The Experiment had not in the main Point the Success we wished; for no material Difference was observed in the Height or Force of the Surff upon the Shore: But those who were in the Longboat could observe a Tract of smoothed Water the whole Length of the Distance in which the Barge poured the Oil, and gradually spreading in Breadth towards the Longboat; I call it smoothed, not that it was laid level, but because tho' the Swell continued, its Surface was not roughened by the Wrinkles or smaller Waves before-mentioned, and none, or very few White-caps (or Waves whose Tops turn over in Foam) appeared in that whole Space, tho' to windward and leeward of it there were plenty; and a Wherry that came round the Point under Sail in her way to Portsmouth, seemed to turn into that Tract of choice, and to use it from End to End as a Piece of Turnpike Road.

3. Bentinck had a gift for practical mechanics, and was particularly noted for his improvement of the chain pump on shipboard. *DNB*.

4. The Gosport shore, across the harbor from Portsmouth, running southwest to Gilkicker Point.

It may be of Use to relate the Circumstances even of an Experiment that does not succeed, since they may give Hints of Amendment in future Trials: It is therefore I have been thus particular. I shall only add what I apprehend may have been the Reason of our Disappointment.

I conceive that the Operation of Oil on Water, is first to prevent the raising new Waves by the Wind, and secondly, to prevent its pushing those before raised with such Force, and consequently their Continuance of the same repeated Height, as they would have done, if their Surface were not oiled. But Oil will not prevent Waves being raised by another Power, by a Stone, for Instance, falling into a still Pool; for they then rise by the mechanical Impulse of the Stone, which the Greasiness on the surrounding Water cannot lessen or prevent, as it can prevent the Winds catching the Surface and raising it into Waves. Now Waves once raised, whether by the Wind or any other Power, have the same mechanical Operation, by which they continue to rise and fall, as a Pendulum will continue to swing, a long Time after the Force ceases to act by which the Motion was first produced. That Motion will however cease in time, but time is necessary. Therefore tho' Oil spread on an agitated Sea, may weaken the Push of the Wind on those Waves whose Surfaces are covered by it, and so by receiving less fresh Impulse, they may gradually subside; yet a considerable Time, or a Distance thro' which they will take time to move may be necessary to make the Effect sensible on any Shore in a Diminution of the Surff. For we know that when Wind ceases suddenly, the Waves it has raised do not as suddenly subside, but settle gradually and are not quite down till long after the Wind has ceased. So tho' we should by oiling them take off the Effect of Wind on Waves already raised, it is not to be expected that those Waves should be instantly levelled. The Motion they have received will for some time continue: and if the Shore is not far distant, they arrive there so soon that their Effect upon it will not be visibly diminished. Possibly therefore, if we had began our Operations at a greater Distance, the Effect might have been more sensible. And perhaps we did not pour Oil in sufficient Quantity. Future Experiments may determine this.

After my Thanks to Capt. Bentinck, for the chearful and ready

473

Aids he gave me, I ought not to omit mentioning Mr. Banks, Dr. Solander, General Carnac, and Dr. Blagdon, who all assisted at the Experiment, during that blustring unpleasant Day, with a Patience and Activity that could only be inspired by a Zeal for the Improvement of Knowledge, such especially as might possibly be of use to Men in Situations of Distress.[5]

I would wish you to communicate this to your ingenious Friend Mr. Farish, with my Respects; and believe me to be, with sincere Esteem, Dear Sir, Your most obedient humble Servant.

B FRANKLIN

Dr Brownrigg

Notation: Extract of a Letter from Benjamin Franklin LLD. and F R.S. to William Brownrigg M.D. and F.R.S. concerning the stilling of the Waves by means of Oil. Recd. May 15th, 1774

From Grey Elliott[6]

ALS: American Philosophical Society

Sir   Hammersmith 8th Novr. 1773

Agreable to my promise I take the Liberty of inclosing a State of the Produce of the Province of Georgia: it was Compiled by a Gentleman in the Customs, and is I think done with accuracy as he was assisted in it by most of the Gentlemen in trade, and every

5. The extract ended with this paragraph, which was deleted before publication. BF had been acquainted with Banks and Solander for more than two years: above, XVIII, 209. Dr. Charles Blagden (1748–1820), F.R.S., was a young friend of Banks who later became noted in medical research. *DNB.* Gen. John Carnac (1720?–74), M.P. for Leominster, had returned some years before from India, only to find that he could not get the fortune he had made there remitted to England. Namier and Brooke, *House of Commons,* II, 194. Another member of the party is said to have been the Solicitor General, Alexander Wedderburn, who a few months later blasted BF before the Privy Council. See Thomas J. Pettigrew, *Memoirs of . . . John Coakley Lettsom . . .* (3 vols., London, 1817), I, part 2, 175–6.

6. A Georgia planter (d. 1787), who had recently emigrated to London. He was originally a South Carolinian, but moved to Georgia in the late 1750's and took a prominent part in its affairs as surveyor and auditor general, then

Light in their Power given.[7] In the Year 1758 the Exports seem triffling, compared with the former and Succeeding Years, owing to the General Embargo which you may recollect took place in America that year. In the Year 1759 almost the whole Crop of Indigo made in Georgia was Shipt from Carolina, which was also the Case in 1762. In 1760 a Considerable increase appears, Chiefly in the Article of Deer Skins, which is thus to be accounted for, the Indian trade before that time was carried on almost entirely from Charlestown, altho sometimes when Vessels offered in Georgia, some small parcels of skins were shipped from thence, but scarce any had been so for two Years before: The Gentlemen concerned in that Branch in Charlestown, finding Men of property began to trade in Georgia, and fearing to Lose a Business then very profitable, Established a House in Savannah, and exported from thence. In the Years 1761 and 1762 you find the exports of that Article considerably decreased, this was owing to the Charlestown Gentlemen selling out their Stock and trade, for which they had a very considerable premium, to some Merchants in Savannah, but it being Stipulated that the purchase money should be paid in Skins and in Charlestown, from thence of Course they were

---

a member (and briefly the Speaker) of the Assembly, and finally in the decade before 1773, with one brief absence, a member of the Council. An ordinance passed on Sept. 29, 1773, appointed him alternate agent for the province, at an annual salary of £100, to act in BF's absence; see the headnote on the Ga. Commons House committee of correspondence to BF below, March 14, 1774. Elliott spent the rest of his life in England, and from 1777 till his death held minor offices in the Board of Trade and was its successor. Candler, *Ga. Col. Recs.*, VII, 811; VIII, 581; XIII, 417–18; XVI, 534; XIX, part 1, 506–8; Paul McIlvaine, *The Dead Town of Sunbury, Georgia* (Asheville, N.C., 1971), pp. 11–12; *Board of Trade Jour.*, 1776–82, p. 125; *Gent. Mag.*, LVII (1787), 548.

7. The enclosure, we assume, was the compilation by William Brown, the comptroller and searcher of customs at Savannah, which Gov. Wright had sent to Dartmouth the year before (*Dartmouth MSS*, II, 109) and which was printed as a broadside, *An Aggregate and Valuation of Exports of Produce from the Province of Georgia, with the Number of Vessels and Tonnage Employed Therein, Annually Distinguished, from the Year 1754 to 1773* ... (Savannah, [1773]). Most of the statistics were published in Oliver M. Dickerson, *The Navigation Acts and the American Revolution* (Philadelphia, 1951), pp. 26–7.

exported. After that period the exports of that Article are regular. Silk you will find a decreasing Article since Government with-drew the bounty;[8] few now except the Germans at Ebenezer breed Worms, and what little is made among them is owing to the Industry of a private Shop-keeper there. I must however observe that the imports into Great Britain have not lessened in pro-portion to the exports from Georgia, as I think at least one third of what appeared to be exported from thence while the Bounty continued, was raised by the Swiss on the Carolina side of Savannah River, and is now Shipped from Charlestown: the reason it was not exported from thence before was, that Altho they had the premium from the Society of Arts, in Carolina in common with the other Colonies, (at least I think so) yet the bounty from the Crown was confined to Georgia, and of Course they brought their Cocoons from Purysbourg[?] to the filature in Savannah. Silk cannot I think ever be a Staple while our Settle-ments are in a manner Confined to the Sea Coast, but I am persuaded it will be well worth while to encourage the Cultiva-tion, or rather raising the White Mulberry in the back Settle-ments, for many reasons too tedious to trouble you with now. Tobacco is an Article that will soon be very Considerable, above 50 hogsheads were shipped in the Vessel I came over in, and when the Lands lately Ceded by the Indians are settled, I am persuaded many thousands of hogsheads will be raised in Virginia[9] I am told the Crops rather are decreasing. The different Articles of Exports January last I have not got, but the Amount was £110,400. If any thing else in this Compilation appears worthy Your Attention and requires explanation, I shall with great pleasure as far as I can do it.

I must now beg Leave briefly to state to you the Affair of the

---

8. The bounty withdrawn was an appropriation authorized by the Privy Council, and reduced in 1766 and eliminated in 1771, for buying silk cocoons in Georgia. Trevor R. Reese, *Colonial Georgia: a Study in British Imperial Policy in the Eighteenth Century* (Athens, Ga., [1963]), p. 125. A Parliamen-tary bounty on imported raw silk took effect in 1770; see above, XVI, 200 n, where the premium from the Society of Arts, mentioned below, is also explained.

9. For the land cession to Virginia see above, XIX, 4 n.

Barony:[10] should you think it proper to take up the matter when the Boards meet, it may perhaps not be unuseful. The Barony was granted originally by the Lords proprietors of South Carolina in the Year 1716 or 1718, but not run out till the Year 1732, some time but not long, before the Charter of Georgia was granted. I must own that it appears Clearly to me that the proprietors made known to the Trustees and their Officers, their Grant and Claim, and I believe the Lines of the original Survey are yet to be Seen. The president and Assistants alotted it at different times, as you will see by the extracts from their Minutes which I took the Liberty to leave with you; and some disbanded Soldiers, of whom some are yet alive, had the Kings bounty of Land, as it was termed, alotted them within the lines in the Year 1749. After the Trustees surrendered their Charter, and the Kings Government took place, the two first Governors did not Scruple to give Grants for several Alottments under the Trustees, and within the Barony; the last of these Mr. Ellis it is to be presumed was not ignorant of the Claim, for during his Administration, an Act was passed for Quieting possessions which appears to have been and certainly was Intended to defeat it: the Claimants however remonstrated against the Act here, and it was repealed by an Order in Council, this was I think about the year 1758. When Sir James Wright Came to the Government he, having I believe been Concerned for the Claimants, would not issue Warrants, or sign any Grants for Lands within the Limits of the Claim, which by this time were pretty well known, and in the Year 1764 or 1765 or thereabouts, an Act for the Limitation of Actions being passed in Georgia, a clause was by the Legislature Inserted in it, expressly excepting the Claim of Sir Wm Baker from being affected by it.[1] Thus the matter stands; I think I mentioned to you the Offers of Composition, proposed by the Claimants to the holders of Land, which it must be acknowledged are Moderate and favorable, Yet in some

10. For the tangled background of the land claims by Sir William Baker's estate see the references cited above, XVII, 139 n.

1. The Georgia trustees surrendered their charter in 1752, and over the next two years royal government was organized. Henry Ellis was first lieutenant governor and then governor, 1757–60. The first Georgia act, in 1759, was disallowed in 1761; the second act, during Wright's governorship, was in 1767. *Acts Privy Coun., Col.*, IV, 490–2; above, XVII, 148–50.

particular cases almost Impossible to be complied with. By the Petition which I believe Mr. Knox furnished you with, the foundation of the Intended Application to the Crown thro him is clear and plain, yet he, having I presume particular reasons, misunderstood the Intent of it, and wrote to Committee of Correspondence that he wanted Authority to treat with the proprietors for the purchase, which was Certainly never Meant.[2] I had some Correspondence with the Late Mr. Linwood and Mr. Baker the Claimants on the Subject, which if you think proper, I will Communicate to you, and when Mr. Baker comes to town, should you Judge it necessary, I will with your Approbation, and by no means otherwise, have a Conversation with him on the Subject, and if he can be brought to Join, or acquiesce in the solicitation you may make for Satisfaction to be made out of the Surplus of the produce of the Ceded Lands, it may perhaps not be unserviceable;[3] but this I submit to Your better Judgment; as I will by no means Interest my self in this or any other matter relating to the province, but so far as you may approve; and I shall always be exceeding happy to have it in my power to furnish you

2. The petition originally sent to William Knox, the former agent for Georgia, had been to the Assembly from settlers threatened by the Baker claims. Knox had not addressed the crown as expected, and BF had been instructed to do so. He complied and sent home a copy of his petition, in a now lost letter of May 1, 1771. The Privy Council rejected the petition in June, 1772, on advice of the Board of Trade. *Ibid.*, pp. 138–9, 148–9, 203; XVIII, 18, 20, 158, 169–70; XIX, 95, 226–7, 257 n; Candler, *Ga. Col. Recs.*, XVII, 781; *Board of Trade Jour.*, 1768–75, pp. 274–5; *Acts Privy Coun., Col.*, V, 295–6.

3. Nicholas Linwood (d. 1773), a London wine merchant and former director of the East India Co., had been Sir William Baker's associate in the land claim: Namier and Brooke, *House of Commons*, III, 44. Mr. Baker was probably Sir William's younger son Samuel, who seems to have taken over his father's business interests. *Ibid.*, II, 42. Earlier attempts to settle the dispute, either by cash compensation to the claimants or by a grant to them of equivalent land elsewhere, had come to nothing. *Acts Privy Coun., Col.*, IV, 492; V, 295–6. The idea of compensation in land was apparently reviving. Wright had recently negotiated a cession from the Creeks and Cherokees of more than two million acres: John R. Alden, *John Stuart and the Southern Colonial Frontier . . .* (Ann Arbor, Mich., 1944), pp. 304–5. Elliott is suggesting that the "Surplus of the produce" of these lands, whatever that means, be used to buy off the Baker heirs.

with any information that may be of use while you remain in England, or Chuse to transact the Affairs of Georgia, and as this matter of the Barony is at present the most Interesting point, I could earnestly wish it may if possible be determined while you are here; as to myself I can with great truth assure you, that I am not in the least personally concerned in it.

I must now Apologize for this Long Scrawl, which I hope you will excuse. I shall be from home for some days, but should any thing I have touched upon in this Letter, require my Waiting upon you in the mean time, a Line directed for me at Hammersmith will come to my hands. I am with respect Sir Your most Obedient Humble Servant   GREY ELLIOTT

A vessel sails for Georgia in about 8 or 10 days, Should you have occasion to write.

From Charles Wilcox   ALS: American Philosophical Society

Sir   Bristol 8th, Nov'r. 1773.
    Your very Polite and Esteem'd Favor of the 5th Current, came in Course of Post yesterday, Inclosing Me one for Anto. Stewart Esqr. for which you have my Thanks.[4] It will always give Me Pleasure to be Serviceable to you here. You will give Me leave to acquaint you that the Concord Capt. Volans for Philadelphia will sail from hence about the 12th Jany. Any Letters you have for

---

4. BF's missing letter of the 5th was undoubtedly in answer to Wilcox's inquiry above, Sept. 13, about an estate in Maryland, and enclosed another letter in which BF passed on the question to the Annapolis postmaster. This was the Mr. Stewart whom we did not identify above, XVI, 185; he held the post at least from 1764 to 1774: *Md. Gaz.*, Nov. 1, 1764; Sept. 8, 1774. He was a Scot, the son of an Edinburgh attorney; see a genealogical fragment in All Hallows Parish Register (Maryland Hall of Records), I, 56–7, for which we are indebted to Mrs. Bryce Jacobsen, archivist. Stewart was a merchant and shipowner in Annapolis, who the next year acquired unwanted prominence when his brig was burned because it carried tea; he later became a Loyalist, lost his estate, and petitioned for land in Nova Scotia. "Account of the Destruction of the Brig 'Peggy Stewart' at Annapolis, 1774," *PMHB*, XXV (1901), 248–54; Gipson, *British Empire*, XII, 197–8; Sabine, *Loyalists*, II, 332–3.

that Place shall be duly taken care of, or any Thing Else you are pleas'd to reccommend to Me, be Assured Sir nothing will give Me greater Pleasure than to have very frequent Opportunitys to convince you how much I esteem you, and I beg leave in Haste to Say that I am very Respectfully Dear Sir Your most Obedient and Obliged Humble Servant CHAS: WILCOX

Benj. Franklin Esqr

Addressed: Benjn Franklin Esqr LLD / Craven Street, / London

From Samuel Cooper

AL (draft): British Museum

Dear Sir, Boston N.E. 10th. Novr. 1773.[5]

I received your valuable Favors of the 7th and 25th of July,[6] and you will please to accept the Thanks of the Committee of our Congregation as well as my own for the Trouble you have very kindly given yourself in your clear and particular Account of the warming Machines for large Rooms, and your Advice respecting our new Building, together with the truly philosophical and convincing Reasons upon which it is founded. All to whom I have read that Part of your Letter have been highly entertain'd with it; and I must particularly thank you for your Observation, that we do not receive the Disorder commonly calld a Cold from cold Air, and therefore *never at Meeting*, being proud of supporting myself with your Authority against some of our Physicians who seem to think that all the Disorders of their Patients are caught there. Your Letter has satisfy'd my whole Congregation, and we are now all determin'd to worship, and make ourselves as comfortable as may be, *More Majorum*.

After all the sollicitous Inquiries of the Governor and his Friends, respecting his Letters, etc. it still remains a Secret, from, and to whom they came. This is known here to two Persons only besides myself; and will I believe remain undiscover'd, unless

5. But the letter was not actually sent until after the Tea Party; see Cooper to BF below, Dec. 17.
6. Printed above; the letter of the 7th explains the rest of this paragraph.

further Intelligence should come from your Side the Water than I have reason to think has yet been obtain'd. Tho I cannot but admire your honest Openness in this Affair, and Negligence of any Inconveniences that might acrue to yourself in this essential Service to our injur'd Country. I have the Pleasure to find that a Confidence in your Abilities and Principles, is very far from being diminished in our House of Commons, and to assure you that one of the Members for this Town, (Mr. A—) a Correspondent of Dr. Lee's, who had the chief Hand in a Letter from the House to you, which I perceive by your Reply gave you Uneasiness, has lately express'd the warmest Esteem of you as an important and thoro' Friend to the Rights of America.[7] This Gentleman I regard, for his uncommon Zeal and Activity in Support of these Rights, but have repeatedly found Occasion in a friendly Manner to blame his excessive Jealousy in a Cause peculiarly dear to him, which has sometimes led him to treat not in the kindest Manner some of its faithful Advocates, and particularly Governor Pownall.[8] The Speaker, and many others in the House are your steady Friends, particularly Major Hawley from N. Hampton a Gentleman of the Law,[9] who speaks with uncommon Clearness and Force, and is behind no man there in Point of Influence. I mention these Things from no other Motive, than an Apprehension that at your Distance from us it might be some Satisfaction and Direction to you to know them.

7. The "Letter from the House" was the missing one, presumably from Cushing in early May, about which BF showed more asperity than uneasiness in writing to him on July 7. Samuel Adams' change of heart, as Cooper saw it, was expressed in a letter to the press the previous September; for Adams' authorship see William V. Wells, *The Life and Public Services of Samuel Adams* ... (3 vols., Boston, 1865), I, 365 n. The letter quoted BF's advice (above, XVIII, 27–9) to keep harping upon colonial rights and grievances, and referred to him as "this great man." *Boston Gaz.*, Sept. 20, 1773.

8. In the aftermath of the Boston Massacre Thomas Pownall had urged caution and moderation upon the Bostonians. His letters angered the extremists, and Adams accused him of counseling dependence on the mother country. In 1772 Pownall wrote him to ask why he "did represent me, in your public opinions, at least as a doubtful friend of the province." Frederick Griffin, *Junius Discovered* (Boston and London, 1854), pp. 297–9; see also 6 Mass. Hist. Soc. *Coll.*, IX (1897), 189–193; Mass. Arch., XXVI, 518.

9. Joseph Hawley (1723–88) had been an active and respected member of the House since 1766: *DAB*.

NOVEMBER 10, 1773

There has been an Attempt, by Mr. Sewall, (as is generally believ'd) Judg of Admiralty for N. Scotia, and our Attorney General, to vindicate the Governor's Letters, in one of our New's Papers.[1] The Sophistry made but a feeble Impression, and except among a few, rather provok'd than pacify'd.

Report of the Purfleet Committee to the Royal Society[2]

ALS: the Royal Society

Gentlemen   House of the Royal Society Novr. 18. 1773

In pursuance of your Appointment of Sepr. 9th last, we went to Purfleet, on the 14th of the same month, to view the Conductors erected on the Magazines there, and having carefully examined the same, we found them constructed agreeable to the written directions formerly given by your Committee.

H. CAVENDISH
WILLIAM WATSON
B FRANKLIN
J ROBERTSON

To the President and Council of the Royal Society

1. Jonathan Sewall (1728–96) had been attorney general since 1767 and a judge of the Halifax vice-admiralty court since 1768; *DAB*. His defense of Hutchinson was in a series of articles in the *Mass. Gaz.; and the Boston Weekly News-Letter*, signed "Philalethes"; see Carol Berkin, *Jonathan Sewall: Odyssey of an American Loyalist* (New York and London, 1974), pp. 97–100, 157; Bernard Bailyn, *The Ordeal of Thomas Hutchinson* (Cambridge, Mass., 1974), pp. 245–8.

2. This report was the aftermath of the acrimonious investigation the previous year into ways and means of protecting the magazine against lightning. Although pointed lightning rods were now installed, the controversy over them continued. See above, XIX, 154–6, 213, 232–3, 262–5, 429.

From Jacques Barbeu-Dubourg

ALS: American Philosophical Society

Mon cher Maitre,   A Paris ce 25e. 9bre. 1773

J'ai reçu le paquet que vous avez eu la bonté de m'envoyer par M. Stanley,[3] qui ne m'a point laissé son adresse, et que je n'ai pu savoir d'ailleurs. Ce paquet contenoit les Transactions philosophiques de Philadelphie, la vie de M. Collinson, et les deux dernieres pieces que vous avez publiées dans les papiers publics, et j'ai lu le tout avec le plus grand plaisir. J'aime le ton gay avec lequel vous persiflez vos *ridiculum acri fortius et melius magnas plerumque secat res.* J'ai été bien content de la reflexion de M. Collinson sur la vie champetre et les occupations du jardinage qui semblent plus assorties que toute autre avec la probité et la candeur. Je me tiens pour averti par Messieurs Otto et Morgan de cultiver des *Coronasolis,* pour tirer de l'huile de leurs semences. La machine de M. W. Henry, quoiqu'elle ne paroisse pas decrite assez clairement, m'a paru fort ingenieuse.[4] M. de Reaumur a fait part au public d'une idée assez analogue que M. Le Prince de Conti lui avoit suggerée au sujet de ses fours à poulets.[5] A propos

3. Thomas-François Stanley, a Parisian watch-maker who was some relative of Jean-Baptiste LeRoy, had been in London, doubtless on business, and BF had been helpful to him; see the following document. We know nothing more about Stanley except that he became a master in 1776 and seems to have died in 1799: G. H. Baillie, *Watchmakers and Clockmakers of the World* (London, [1929]), p. 338.

4. BF had sent his two famous satires (above, Sept. 11, 22), John Fothergill's *Some Account of the Late Peter Collinson . . .* (London, 1770), and the first volume of the APS *Trans.* (for 1769–70; Philadelphia, 1771). Dubourg's comment on the satires, that ridicule is for the most part more effective than severity in cutting to the heart of important matters, is from Horace, *Satires,* I: 10: 14–15. Collinson's reflections on country life are on p. 10 of Fothergill's volume. The remaining references are to articles in the *Trans.*: accounts by Drs. Otto and Morgan of obtaining oil from sunflower seeds (pp. 234–9) and William Henry's description of his device for maintaining an even heat in a furnace or an incubator for chicks (pp. 286–9).

5. Réaumur's method of using ovens to hatch chicks, as in ancient Egypt, is described in the beginning of his *Art de faire éclorre . . . des oiseaux domestiques de toutes especes . . .* (2 vols., Paris, 1749), where he explains (1, 5–6) that his scheme was encouraged by Philippe, duc d'Orléans, regent for Louis xv. If the volume also mentions Conti, the reference has eluded us; but Dubourg's next letter (below, Dec. 29) makes clear that that prince of

de cela j'attens avec d'autant plus d'impatience la description de votre nouveau poele que je me propose de reprendre sur la fin de l' hiver avec un ou deux amis le project de faire couver des oeufs et elever des poulets avec oeconomie sans le secours des poules couveuses.[6] Si vous aviez jamais speculé sur cela, je vous prie de me faire part de vos reflexions.

S'il y a quelque critique de votre ouvrage,[7] je n'en suis pas encore informé. On en parle tres bien de toutes parts; les feuilles periodiques en ont fait les plus grands eloges, cependant le debit n'y repond pas jusqu'icy; il est vrai que le tems des fetes de la Cour apres la saison des vacances est une circonstance tres defavorable.

Si j'ai donné mon adresse aux ecoles de Medecine, ce n'est pas que j'aye changé de demeure; c'est parceque le Bedeau de la faculté qui y demeure et qui est mon relieur, s'est chargé de tous les details, et n'avoit pas droit de faire mettre son nom au frontispice ainsi c'est de ma part un domicile d'election chez lui, comme il est d'usage commun d'elire domicile chez son procureur quand on a des procès, afin qu'il soit le premier instruit des significations qu'on recoit à ce sujet. Quant à la rue, ce n'est pas de la boucherie, mais de la bucherie, mot derivé vraisemblablement de bucher, et celui cy de buche, ou busche, et cette rue a pu etre ainsi appellée par rapport aux chantiers de bois de chauffage ou les buches sont entassées en grandes piles, lesquels chantiers sont en tres grand nombre de ce meme côté de la riviere, mais aujourd'huy un peu plus loin, parce qu'on les repousse successivement a mesure que la ville etend son enceinte.

J'ai eté fort aise de faire connoissance avec M. Fromond,[8] mais il a demeuré trop peu de tems icy. Je lui ai porté un exemplaire de

---

the blood remained actively interested in the subject. Louis-François de Bourbon, prince de Conti (1717–76), a military hero of the War of the Austrian Succession who had subsequently fallen from favor, was involved in politics as an opponent of the philosophes: Larousse, *Dictionnaire universel*.

6. BF's failure to describe the stove in his letter above, June 29, seems to have left Dubourg hoping that it could be adapted to hatching and raising chicks.

7. The *Œuvres* had at last been published.

8. For the Italian physicist see BF to WF above, Feb. 3.

vos oeuvres pour lui et un dont il a bien voulu se charger pour le P. Beccaria. J'en ai envoyé un a la societé philosophique de Roterdam par la voye d'un Chapelain de l'ambasse de Hollande (M. de la Broue) et un a la societé royale de Gottingue par le moyen de M. Zanoni.[9] Il faut esperer que M. Pickering ne tardera pas desormais d'arriver avec ceux dont il s'est chargé pour vous de si bonne grace.[1]

Quelques discussions que j'ai eu a essuyer de la part du graveur et de son imprimeur en taille douce m'ont empeché de pouvoir vous envoyer plustôt les 12 portraits[2] que l'on vous demande separement; mais enfin j'en ai fait tirer un demicent de nouveaux et je ferai partir demain la douzaine en question avec les six exemplaires que vous desirez aussi de l'ouvrage par les voitures ordinaires tout simplement, sans attendre ni chercher davantage d'occasions, attendu que cela fait un paquet suffisant pour les messageries. Je l'ai adressé a Calais a M. Audibert du Pont negociant qui vous l'expediera aussitôt pour Londres.

M. Dalibard est tres content de sa glace, quoique beaucoup plus chere que celles de ce pays cy.[3] Il vous salue et vous remercie. Lorsque vous me ferez la grace de m'envoyer quelque chose par la poste à l'avenir, il me parviendra franc de port, si vous voulez prendre la peine de mettre a votre lettre une première envelope a

9. De la Broue, whom we cannot identify, carried a copy to the Batavian Society of Experimental Science, which had elected BF to membership in 1771: above, XVIII, 100 n. Giovanni Antonio Rizzi-Zannoni (1736–1814), an Italian geographer and cartographer who had made a name for himself in Poland and Germany and was currently employed by the French government, carried a copy to the Königliche Gesellschaft der Wissenschaften, of which he had been a member since 1757. For his career see *Grande dizionario enciclopedico* ... (19 vols. to date, Turin 1966–); Aldo Blessich, "Un geografo italiano de secolo XVIII ... ," Società geografica italiana, *Bollettino*, XXXV (1898), 12–23, 56–69, 183–203, 453–66, 523–37.

1. Pickering cannot be precisely identified. He was a distant relative of Dr. John Lettsom, very likely the Isaac Pickering who appears in Betsey C. Corner and Christopher Booth, ed., *Chain of Friendship: Selected Letters of Dr. John Fothergill* ... (Cambridge, Mass., 1971), pp. 297–8, 344, 346 n, 348–9; see also Thomas J. Pettigrew, *Memoirs of the Life and Writings of the Late John Coakley Lettsom* (3 vols., London, 1817), I, 12.

2. The Martinet engraving that is the frontispiece of this volume.

3. The mirror that Mlle. Biheron had brought from London; see her letter above, June 26.

mon adresse, et de l'arreter avec tres peu de cire sans cachet; d'ajouter a cette lettre tous les papiers ou brochures qu'il vous plaira,
de recouvrir le paquet d'une bande transversale de papier d'un ou
deux pouces de large, arretée sans cachet avec un peu de cire, avec
une souscription a Monsieur Zanoni, enfin de recouvrir le tout
d'une envelope exterieure avec votre cachet, et d'y mettre
l'adresse a Monseigneur, Monseigneur le Duc d'Aiguillon, Pair
de France, et Ministre d'etat a Versailles.[4] Si le paquet faisoit un
trop gros volume, il seroit a propos d'en faire deux envois
successifs en le partageant, quoique un paquet de 8 ou 10 feuilles
d'impression puisse passer ainsi sans difficulté.

M. Le Roy lut le 13e. de ce mois a la rentrée publique de
l'Academie des siences un memoire sur les conducteurs destinés a
preserver les batimens, dont je me serois fait un devoir de vous
rendre compte en detail, s'il ne m'avoit dit qu'il vous le communi-
queroit.[5] Il pretend que M. Wilson n'etoit pas le seul de l'avis des
conducteurs sans pointe; en ce cas j'etois dans l'erreur a cet egard.

J'ai vu M. Le Marquis de Courtenvaux,[6] et diné chez lui lundi
dernier, où nous bumes a votre santé. Il a une magnifique
machine electrique, ou je compte essayer quelques experiences
dans le courant de la semaine prochaine. Je ne manquerai pas de
vous rendre compte du succès, s'il en vaut la peine. Il y a pourtant
apparence que ce ne sera pas immediatement, parce qu'il pourra
etre besoin de plusieurs seances et peutetre meme de divers pre-
paratifs, et que l'on ne fait pas toujours aller les ouvriers aussi vite
que l'on voudroit; vous devez le savoir aussi bien ou mieux
qu'un autre, d'ailleurs je ne sais peutetre pas encore bien tout ce
que j'aurai à leur demander.

J'espere que l'extrait du vieil Almanac de Pensylvanie ne sera
pas seulement applaudi icy, mais qu'il y fera du fruit.[7] Dieu le
veuille. Mademoiselle Biheron, Mademoiselle Basseporte et ma
femme m'ont chargé de vous faire bien des amitiés. Pas une d'elles

4. Dubourg had an almost obsessive interest in complex ways of sending
mail; see above, XIX, 385.

5. LeRoy had sent BF a copy of the paper months before; see his letter
above, April 19.

6. For Courtanvaux, the French soldier-scientist, see above, XV, 34 n.

7. Dubourg had included "The Way to Wealth" (above, VII, 326–50) in
the *Œuvres*, II, 171–82.

ne se portent bien; ce sont trois emplatres, mais qui vous sont bien attachées. J'ai bien peur que cela ne vous conviennent gueres.

Pour moi, je me porte bien, graces à Dieu, et si bien que j'aurois passé la mer pour aller vous trouver cet hiver, si ma femme eût eté en un etat ou je pusse la quitter. Si sa santé se raffermit nous ferons le voyage ensemble l'année prochaine, si elle veut m'en croire. J'ai l'honneur d'etre avec un tendre et inviolable attachement, Monsieur et cher Ami, Votre tres humble et tres obeissant serviteur   DUBOURG

Mes respectueuses civilités, s'il vous plait a M. Pringle.

Addressed: To / Dr. Franklin f. r. s. Deputy / Postmaster general of North America / Cravenstreet / London / for the Post office

From Jean-Baptiste LeRoy   ALS: American Philosophical Society

Lundy 29 Nov. [1773]

Je me proposois tous ces Jours cy de vous écrire Monsieur et cher confrère pour vous rendre compte d'un mémoire que j'ai lu à notre rentrée publique sur la forme des *conducteurs de la Foudre* ou *des Gardes-Tonnerre* mais malgré moi cela ne m'a pas été possible. Cependant Je crois que M. Dubourg vous en aura écrit.[8] Deux choses m'ont déterminé à cette Lecture l'une la néséssité de faire mieux connaître dans ce pays cy par une Lecture publique la necessité et les avantages de ces *Gardes-Tonnerre* l'autre de dissiper tous les nuages qui pourroient rester dans les Esprits sur leur forme. Mais Je vous en écrirai plus au long. Cette lettre n'est que pour vous prévenir que vous recevrez au premier Jour la caisse des gravures des Oiseaux de M. De Buffon qui est partie il y a deja du temps. Vous trouverez dans cette caisse les mémoires de mon frère dont j'ai déja eu l'honneur de vous parler.[9]

8. In the preceding document Dubourg merely mentioned the paper; see LeRoy to BF above, April 19.

9. For Daubenton's "planches enluminées" see his notes to BF above, May 31 and July 20. The memoirs were, we presume, Pierre LeRoy's *Précis des recherches . . . pour la détermination des longitudes en mer pour la mesure artificielle du tems . . .* (Paris, 1773).

J'y en ai mis aussi deux ou trois pour M. Walsh que vous voudrez bien lui faire remettre. J'ai pris la liberté de vous recommander dernierement par une lettre dont je l'ai chargé pour vous M. Desdouaires qui va en Angleterre pour y faire quelques éducations. C'est un homme fort honnête et à qui je vous serai bien obligé de rendre Service, si vous le pouvez.[1]

Je vous dois mille et mille remercimens pour tout ce que vous avez bien voulu faire pour mon Parent M. Stanley.[2] Il n'a cessé de me parler dans les différrentes fois que je l'ai vu de toutes vos politesses et de tout ce que vous aviez fait pour lui rendre service. Adieu Monsieur et cher confrère. Pardonnez si je vous quitte si promtement. C'est bien contre mon coeur je vous assure mais je crains que la poste ne parte sans emporter ma lettre. Vous ne doutez pas de tous les sentimens qui m'attachent à vous pour la vie

LE ROY

Addressed: To / Benjamin Franklin Esqu. / Deputy Post Master of North / America, Fellow of the Royal / Society / in Craven Street / London.

From Richard Bache

ALS: American Philosophical Society

Dear sir   30th. Novr. 1773.

I send you the inclosed that you may see the Disposition the good People of this City are in, respecting the Tea, that is hourly expected.[3] The Paper however is designed more as a Scare Crow,

1. We cannot identify M. Desdouaires, but are convinced that he was the French master who left Paris at the end of the year with Dubourg's letter to BF below, Dec. 29, and another letter, no doubt this one, from LeRoy. Although the phrase "pour y faire quelques éducations" was as awkward French two centuries ago as it would be today, we are assured on good authority, its only possible meaning is that Desdouaires intended to do some tutoring.

2. For Stanley see the preceding document.

3. He doubtless enclosed the broadside of Nov. 27, warning the Delaware pilots and the captain of the tea ship *Polly* that they would be tarred and feathered if they brought her up the river. When she arrived a month later, she turned back for England without landing the tea. Labaree, *Tea Party*, pp. 101, 156–9.

488

than any thing else. I am with Respect Dear sir Your Affectionate
son   R BACHE

Addressed: To / Doctor Benjamin Franklin / Craven Street /
London

From the Marquis de Condorcet[4]

ALS: American Philosophical Society

A paris ce 2 Xbre [1773]

Voici, mon cher et illustre confrere, quelques questions que je
prends la liberté de proposer à la Société philosophique de Philadelphie, et dont je vous supplie de vouloir bien me procurer la
reponse.[5]

1°. Si les pierres calcaires et les silex renfermant des productions
marines, ou des empreintes de productions marines, ces productions soit coquilles soit empreintes de poissons ou de végetaux
appartiennent-elles à des especes conues, et ces especes se rencontrent elles dans les mers voisines de Philadelphie ou dans des
mers eloignées? (Les analogues vivans des fossiles que nous
trouvons en france n'existent souvent que dans les mers voisines
de l'équateur.) A quelle hauteur sur les montagnes et a quelle profondeur sous la terre trouve-t-on de ces productions? Se rencon-
trent-elles egalement dans les montagnes qui ont une forme pira-
midale et dans celles dont la forme est hemi-spherique? Y'a

4. Marie-Jean-Antoine-Nicolas Caritat, marquis de Condorcet (1743–94),
was already making his name as a mathematician and writer, and had been for
several years a member of the Académie des sciences. He was a prolific contributor to its *Mémoires.* In 1773 he was assistant to its permanent secretary,
and was writing BF in that capacity; he subsequently succeeded to the office.
See the *Index biographique des membres et correspondants de l'Académie des
sciences . . .* (Paris, 1954), pp. 118–19. In later years Condorcet was one of the
most illustrious leaders and victims of the French Revolution. This letter and
BF's reply below, March 20, 1774, were clearly the first—though far from the
last—contact between "le prométhée moderne" and the man whom Voltaire
called "mon philosophe universel."
5. BF forwarded Condorcet's inquiries to the APS, along with those he had
received from Buffon and Raynal (above: Daubenton to BF, July 20; Maseres
to BF, Oct. 26); different members of the Society agreed to answer Condorcet's various queries. APS, *Early Proc. . . .* (Philadelphia, 1884), pp. 93–6.

t'on trouvé des os fossiles et à quelles especes appartiennent-ils?

2°. A-t-on pour la direction de l'aiguille aimantée des observations faites soit a Philadelphie soit dans les colonies voisines de maniere qu'on sache quels ont été dans le même lieu les changemens que cette direction a éprouvés année par année? (Les observations faites à Paris semblent indiquer que l'aiguille y décrit de grandes oscillations en sorte que sa plus grande vitesse a repondu a l'annee 1684, et à quatre degrés environs vers l'ouest, et la durée de l'oscillation serait entre un siecle et demi et deux siecles.) Si on a de bonnes observations faites à peu près année par année à Philadelphie je voudrais en avoir une table.

3°. Les hauteurs du Barometre ont elles avec les changemens de tems les mêmes rapports que dans notre Continent? Cela doit être en general mais il peut y avoir quelques singularités capables de jetter un grand jour sur la science métereologique science importante et qui est encore dans son enfance puisque nous ignorons même quelle partie dans le changemens du poids de l'atmosphere est due à l'effet des corps celestes et quelle partie est due à des causes locales, que nous n'avons que des conjectures sur les formation de la plupart des météores.

4°. Je voudrais savoir si dans les colonies anglaises, il y a des Negres qui ayant eu leur liberté y aient vecu sans se mêler avec les blancs. Si leurs enfans négres nés libres et elevés come libres ont conservé l'esprit et le caractere negre ou ont pris le caractere Europeen. Si on a vu des gens d'esprit parmi eux.

5°. Si l'on rencontre dans les plaines ou sur les montagnes de l'amerique des pierres qui come la basalte, et la pierre ponce paraissent devoir leur origine à des volcans, si on y trouve des charbons de terre, des houilles inflammables ou non inflammables, et si ces productions sont au dessus ou au dessous de quelques bancs de coquilles.

Je me flatte, mon cher et illustre confrère que [vous] voudrez bien me faire avoir une réponse à ces questions, quoique je n'aie jamais eu le bonheur de voir le promethée moderne.[6] J'ai l'honneur

6. "Prometheus der neuen Zeiten" was Immanuel Kant's phrase for BF in 1756, in the third essay on the Lisbon earthquake: *Gesammelte Schriften* ... (29 vols. to date, Berlin, 1902–), I, 472.

d'être avec l'attachement le plus inviolable, monsieur et cher confrere votre très humble et très obeissant serviteur

LE M[ARQU]IS DE CONDORCET
Sec. [de l'Aca]démie des Sciences
rue de Louis le grand.

Addressed: To / Franklin Esq. Agent / of the English colonys / London

Endorsed: M. Condorcet

From Nathaniel Falconer ALS: American Philosophical Society

Dear Sir   2d of December 1773

This will inform you of my Savef arrivall of Dover after a passage of 30 Days. I took my Leave of mrs. Franklin the Last Day of November in the morning when She mrs. Beach and the two Boys where all well.[7] I hope in a few Days to have the pleashure of takeing by the hand my best Compliments to mrs. Stevenson mrs. and mr. hewson and master Temple. I am Dear Sir your most Humble Servant   NATH FALCONER

postscript. I have not put aney of your Letters ashore for Resons I Shall Give you when we meet. Ship marrey and Elizabeth

Addressed: To / Docter Franklin / in / Craven Street Strand / London

From Caffiéri l'Ainé[8] ALS: American Philosophical Society

Monsieur   Calais le 6 xbre 1773

Jay l'honneur de vous donner avis que je vous Envoie par messieurs minet & fector de Douvres une Caisse Emballee

---

7. The Kingbird was four at the time, and his brother William was six months old. By "November" Falconer meant October: the letter is postmarked "4 DE," or Dec. 4.

8. The Directeur des postes at Calais, a position that passed down in one family for more than a century before the Revolution. For the little that is known about this particular director, which does not include his Christian names, see Jules Guiffrey, *Les Caffiéri, sculpteurs et fondeurs-ciseleurs* ... (Paris, 1877), pp. 63–5.

Contenant Librairie marquee *MF Libri* que Jay recû de Paris d'Envoy de Mr. Pankouke.[9] Vous voudrèz bien avoir la Complaisance de men accuser la reception, jay deboursè pour port de Paris à Calais passavants[1] porteurs &c. 15 livres tournois, que jay porté en Compte à messieurs minet & fector qui sen prevaudront sur vous avec leurs autres fraids. Jay l honneur d'etre avec une parfaitte Consideration, Monsieur Votre tres humble et tres obeissant Serviteur   CAFFIERI L'AINÉ

Monsieur franklin / Londres

Addressed: To / Monsr. Franquelin depute / des Colonies d' Amerique / Membre de la societé royale / et de l'academie des Sciences / de Paris In Crawen Street / *London*

From John Ellis[2]

AL: American Philosophical Society

Grays Inn 8th: Decr. 1773

Mr. Ellis presents his kindest respects to Doctor Franklin, he has seen Doctor Fothergill very lately, who is very urgent to have his thoughts on Coffee go to the press. Mr. Ellis hopes that Doctor Franklin will be so good accordingly to promise to send him his thoughts on the [?] Subject, considering it in a Political light of the advantages it would be to Government to encourage the growth of Coffee in our Islands, by Lowering the duties and excise.[3]

9. Minet & Fector was a mercantile and banking firm; the partners at the time were William Minet of London and his cousin, Peter Fector, who was in charge of the Dover Office. See William Minet, "Extracts from the Letterbook of a Dover Merchant . . . ," *Archaeologia Cantiana*, XXXII (1917), 249, 273, 278–9. Charles-Joseph Panckoucke (1736–98), the famous bookseller, editor, writer, and friend of Voltaire, was the owner of the *Mercure de France*.

1. Written authorizations to transport merchandize on which duty has been paid.

2. The eminent naturalist, with whom BF had been in touch for some time; see above, XIX, 317 n.

3. Ellis was completing *An Historical Account of Coffee, with an Engraving, and Botanical Description of the Tree* . . . (London, 1774), which was a compilation of a number of authors. Fothergill, who was among them, was eager to have the book published because he wanted to encourage the importation and consumption of coffee, which he believed was beneficial to

Mr. Ellis would be glad as soon as the Doctor has done with the french book on Coffee which Mr. Ellis lent him he would be much obliged [?] to him to return it as the [*torn*] on the Subjects which [*torn*].⁴

Addressed: To / Doctor Benj. Franklin / at Mrs. Stevensons / in Craven Street / Strand

From Jonathan Shipley   ALS: American Philosophical Society

Dear Sir   Twyford Dec: 9th. 1773
    Tho I gave my Daughter Georgiana full powers to return You our best thanks for the kind Visit You intend us, I cannot help assuring You myself that We shall be most extreamly happy to see You and hope You will come as soon and stay as long as your Affairs will permit.⁵

    Your Countrymen in N. America have done me too much honour for the little merit of meaning well. I am glad they seem to approve of moderate and conciliating measures⁶ in which I fear We shall not have the wisdom to join with them. I am, Dear Sir, Your obligd and affectionate humble Servant

                                                    J. St. Asaph

---

the emotions. R. Hingston Fox, *Dr. John Fothergill and His Friends* ... (London, 1919), pp. 63–4. By "our islands" Ellis meant those in the Caribbean and particularly, no doubt, Dominica, of which he was the agent. BF had promised to help with the book, as Ellis reminded him in a second note below, Dec. 25. But his answers of Dec. 26, 1773, and Jan. 12, 1774, indicate that help consisted of information rather than thoughts.

    4. The book was undoubtedly Antoine Galland, *De l'Origine et du progrès du café; sur un manuscrit arabe de la Bibliothèque du roi* ... (Caen, 1699), which is described at some length in Mohammed Abdel-Halim, *Antoine Galland, sa vie et son oeuvre* (Paris, 1964), pp. 247–9. Ellis apparently summarized Galland in the early pages of his own work.

    5. If the Christmas visit to Twyford took place—and we have no other evidence that it did—BF's affairs kept him from staying through the holidays. His public avowal of responsibility for the Hutchinson letters, dated Dec. 25, was at least ostensibly written from Craven St., and his note to Ellis the next day certainly was.

    6. BF's letter above of Aug. 21 had promised further news, which he had apparently sent, of American reactions to the Bishop's sermon.

493

From Thomas Cushing

LS and copy: Library of Congress

Sir   Boston December 10th 1773

I have duly received your several Favors of Augt 24 and Sept 1st. with the papers Inclosed[7] which I shall Communicate to the House as soon as they meet. Capts: Hall, Bruce and Coffin are arrived with a quantity of Tea shiped (in pursuance of a late Act of Parliament) by the East India Company to the address of Richard Clark & sons, Thos and Elisha Hutchinson, Benjamin Faneuil and Joshua Winslow Esqr. Capt. Loring is hourly expected with more of the same Article consigned to the same persons;[8] This has greatly alarmed the People here who have had several Meetings upon the Occasion, Inclosed you have a paper containing their proceedings and resolutions, by which you will perceive that they insist upon the Consignee's sending back the Tea and have determined it shall never be landed or pay any duty here.[9] The Colonists have been long complaining of the Parliament's taxing them without their Consent, they have frequently remonstrated against the exercise of a power they deem unconstitutional, Their Petitions have been neglected if not rejected, however within about Twelve or fifteen months past they have, by administration and by their Freinds in Great Britain, been led to Expect that their greiviances would be redressed and the revenue Acts repealed and from some Accounts, received the last

7. In the letter of Sept. 1; the papers were Dartmouth's answer to BF above, Aug. 25, and to Bollan, now apparently lost.

8. The *Dartmouth* and *Eleanor*, Capts. James Hall and James Bruce respectively, had already docked; the *Beaver*, Capt. Coffin, was in quarantine and did not join the others at Griffin's Wharf until the 15th, the day before the Tea Party. The *William*, Capt. Loring, never did arrive but was wrecked on Cape Cod; for the fate of her tea see Cooper to BF below, Dec. 17. For the Boston consignees see above, p. 230 n. The Hutchinsons and Clarkes, who played the principal roles, were related (young Thomas Hutchinson had married Richard Clarke's daughter) and had long been particularly obnoxious to the Sons of Liberty. By the end of November some of the consignees had left Boston, and the others had taken refuge in Castle William. See Cooper's letter just cited.

9. The minutes and resolutions of the two mass meetings on tea, Nov. 29 and 30, are printed in Mass. Hist. Soc. *Proc.*, xx (1882–83), 10–17. For a chronology of the developing crisis see the headnote on Cooper's letter just cited.

Winter from your side the Water, they had reason to expect the Tea Act would have been repealed the very last Session,[10] instead of which the Parliament, at that very Session when the People expected to have obtained releif, passed an Act impowering the East india Company to Ship their Tea to America. This they considered as a New Measure to Establish and Confirm a Tax on the Colonists, which they complained of as unjust and unrighteous, and consequently has renewed and increased their distress and it is particularly increased by this Act as it is introductive of Monopolies and of all the Consequent Evils thence arising, but their greatest Objection is from its being Manifestly intended more Effectually to secure the payment of the Duty on tea laid by an Act passed in the 7th of George the Third, which Act in it's operation deprives the Colonists of the exclusive right of taxing themselves; they further apprehend that this late Act was passed with a veiw not only to secure the Duty aforesaid but to lay a foundation of Enhancing it and in a like way, if this should succeed, to lay other Duties and that it demonstrates an indisposition in Ministry that the Parliament should grant them releif; Impressed with these sentiments the People say they have been Amused, they have been deceived and at a time when they had reason to Expect they should have been releived they find administration pursuing fresh Measures to Establish and Confirm those very Acts which if persisted in must reduce them to Abject Slavery; This is the Source of their distress, a distress that borders upon Dispair and they know not where to fly for releif, this is the

10. This betrayal of the expectation that grievances would be redressed reappears in the opening of the letter from the Mass. House committee of correspondence below, Dec. 21, and in Winthrop's letter of the 31st; the conclusion of Cooper's of the 17th referred to the administration's "fair and repeated Professions of an Intention to relieve us." What professions did the writers have in mind? Whitehall had considered some moves to ease tension (above, pp. 223 n, 273–4 n), and Dartmouth's private letter to Cushing (above, p. 377 n) had been conciliatory in tone if not in substance; BF had written optimistically during the previous winter about repeal of the tea duty (above, pp. 8–10, 98–9). But none of these straws gave ground for believing that the ministry had intended major redress. The belief may have been genuine, based on information from London of which we have found no trace; or it may have been a concoction to promote resisting the Tea Act.

Cause of the present great uneasiness and has been the occasion
of the extraordinary measures pursued by the People here and in
several of the principal Colonies, for you must observe the same
spirit prevails in Philadelphia and New York; Philadelphia began
and passed their resolutions above a month ago, New York
Catch'd it from them and so it passed on to this Government,[11]
and If Administration had put their Invention upon the utmost
Stretch to Contrive a plan of union for the Colonies, I cannot well
Conceive of any one measure that would tend more Effectually to
unite the Colonies than the present Act impowering the East
india Company to Export their Tea to America. And if they
should have it in Contemplation to Shew any marks of Resentment upon the Colonies for their Conduct relative to this matter,
It is thought, they ought to begin with the People amoung yourselves as many of them have for this three or four months past
been repeatedly notifying our merchants of this manovure and
advising them not by any means to suffer the Tea to be landed, if
they designed to preserve their freedom; they have been blowing
the Coals,[1] we have got into a flame and where it will End God
only knows. In Short, Sir, our affairs are brought to a very
Serious Crisis; and the Court party themselves, as I am Informed,
plainly see that the people are so thoroughly roused and alarmed
and discover such a determined resolution not any longer to suffer
these Impositions, that they begin to think it absolutely necessary
the measures of Administration with respect to America should be
alter'd; they find that the Spirit runs higher than in the Time of
the Stamp Act, and that the Opposition is more Systematical so
that they fear nothing less than the repeal of the revenue Acts and
a radical redress of American Greiviances will save us from a
Rupture with Great Britain which may prove fatal to both

11. The Philadelphia resolutions were actually passed on Oct. 16; opposition there and in New York developed concurrently, and in Boston a few
weeks later. See Gipson, *British Empire*, XII, 75–6; Labaree, *Tea Party*, 89–
103, 105–6.

1. Who were "they"? The only hint of an answer we have found is a
reference in Hutchinson (*History*, III, 303 n) to letters counseling resistance,
written in London in early August and received some two months later.
Cushing may also have had in mind BF's letter to him above of Sept. 12, but
that to our mind scarcely constituted "blowing the Coals."

Countries.[2] The People here are far from desiring that the Connection between Great Britain and America should be broken, *Esto Perpetua* is their ardent wish but upon terms only of Equal Liberty. May the Great Governor of the Universe overule the Councils of the Nation and direct and influence to such Measures as may be productive of such an happy Connection. This will be delivered you by Mr. John Sprague a young Gentleman who goes for London with a Veiw to Improve himself in the study of Phisic,[3] I must refer you to him for a more particular and Circumstantial account of the State of Affairs here and I recommend him to your freindly Notice. I conclude with great respect Your most humble servant   THOMAS CUSHING

(Private)

Benjamin Franklin Esqr

From Thomas Cushing   ALS: Library of Congress

Sir,   Boston Decr 11. 1773

Since the foregoing[4] I have received another Letter from the Speaker of the House of Deputies of Rhode Island and wrote at their desire, requesting that I would use my Endeavors to pro-

2. Hutchinson gave no indication, either in his correspondence at the time or in his subsequent account of the crisis, that he and his friends advocated any such surrender. They believed that agitation against the tea was confined to the Boston area, and put their hopes in strong measures: Mass. Arch., XXVII, 578–9, 581–2, 587–8; Hutchinson, *History*, III, 302–17.

3. John Sprague (1752–1800), the son of a local physician, graduated from Harvard in 1772 and, after studying medicine under his father, went to England to continue his training; but when he returned he never actively practiced. See Ebenezer Alden, *Early History of the Medical Profession in the County of Norfolk, Mass.* . . . (Boston, 1853), p. 24. Sprague sailed from Boston, with this letter and the following one, on Dec. 12 in the brig *Dolphin;* contrary winds detained her long enough for Hutchinson to have his dispatches about the Tea Party put on board on the 17th. *Mass. Gaz.; and the Boston Weekly News-Letter,* Dec. 16, 1773; Mass. Arch., XXVII, 587, 589, 600. The brig apparently arrived in England days after the ship that carried Dr. Williamson with his news of the Tea Party; see the note on Cushing to BF below, Dec. 21.

4. The copy (misdated Sept. 16) of his letter of Sept. 18 above; that letter explains what follows.

cure them G: Rome's original letter, I must therefore repeat my request to you Sir that you would be so Kind as procure and transmitt said Letter to Metcalf Bowler Esqr or Mr. Henry Merchant of Rhode Island. Therein you will much oblidge their House of Deputies. I conclude with respect Your most humble Servant   THOMAS CUSHING

To Benja: Franklin Esqr

Addressed: To / Benjamin Franklin Esqr LLD / in / London / per Favour Mr / Jhon Sprague[5] / QDC

From Jonathan Williams, Jr.

ALS: American Philosophical Society

dear and honoured Sir   Boston Decemr 11, 1773

Inclosed is a Letter from the Revd. Doctr Mather which he desired me to send to you.[6] I am much obliged by your kindness in procuring the Organ as desired which came out in good order, except the omission of one Pipe the 11th from the lef side in the second (leaden) Stop,[7] which I suppose the [maker?] forgot: I shall be obliged if you will please to send me the cost of it, as the Lady who it is for wants to know how much she must pay. She desired me to give her Respects to You, with assurances of her obligation for your care in giving Directions for the making of it. I have it not in my power to remit to Mr. Warren, if I had ever so much money, as Bills of Exchange are exceeding scearce and none to be had that I can find, and if there were any they would cost much above parr, so must endeavour to make up this debt [?] by greater Sums at once, when I have it in my power; And in order to enable me to do it I shall not order any Goods the coming Spring, for from appearances I have great Reason to beleive that

5. See the preceding document.
6. The enclosure, which has disappeared, was presumably in answer to BF's long letter to Mather above, July 7.
7. A stop is a graduated set of pipes of the same kind, giving tones of the same quality; the barrel organ commonly had two stops, one of metal and one of wooden pipes. For earlier correspondence about the organ see above, Williams' letter of June 28 and BF's reply of Oct. 6.

Trade will much alter in the course [of the] Year, and by restraining my Importation for a time, I shall be able to pursue it with vigour and Reputation, as I shall not have the Burden of a dead Stock on hand. I am (tho' much in haste) Your dutifull and Affectionate Kinsman   J WILLIAMS JUNR

Compliments to all enquiring Freinds.

Addressed: To / Benjamin Franklin LLD, FRS. / at Mrs Stevensons / In Craven Street / Strand / London / Per the Hayley / Capt Scott

From Samuel Cooper

AL (draft): British Museum

In this letter, written the day after the Tea Party, Cooper confined himself until his conclusion to narrating the developments that culminated in destruction of the tea. His narrative is difficult to follow because it is not in chronological order; to clarify it we list the actual sequence of events.

November 3: The Sons of Liberty, knowing that the tea was soon expected and that opposition was forming in New York and Philadelphia, held a popular meeting at the Liberty Tree to force the consignees to resign. When they did not appear, the mob attacked the house where they had gathered but failed to coerce them.

November 5, 6, 18: Three town meetings again demanded, to no avail, that the consignees resign.

November 17: The Clarkes' house was mobbed.

November 19, 23, 27: In three meetings the Governor's Council refused to take responsibility for the tea.

November 28: The first tea ship, the *Dartmouth*, arrived; on the 30th she docked.

November 29: An extra-legal mass meeting demanded that the tea be returned to England. The consignees who were still in town, after agreeing to have the tea stored until the Company sent further instructions, fled to Castle William.

November 30: The mass meeting reconvened. The *Dartmouth's* cargo was declared at the customs house and became liable to the Townshend duty; her master and Francis Rotch, her owner's son, agreed that the tea should be returned.

December 2: The *Eleanor* arrived and docked.

499

December 14: Another mass meeting persuaded Rotch to ask the customs authorities for clearance for the *Dartmouth* to leave; they refused.

December 15: The *Beaver* docked with the other two ships at Griffin's Wharf.

December 16: A final mass meeting heard Rotch explain why the *Dartmouth* could not sail, and instructed him to appeal to the Governor; when he reported back that he had done so without success, the mob of "Indians" formed.[8]

In his concluding comments on these events Cooper echoed a number of themes that ran through the letters of Franklin's Boston correspondents during the crisis.[9] One was surprise: Whitehall had lulled Massachusetts with promises to alleviate the situation, and then without warning had dumped tea upon it. Another was a new sense of unity: the Bostonians, now that they had answered a call to action from other colonies and been supported by other towns in the province, had the assurance of men who no longer stood alone. A third theme, closely related to the second, was recognition that the die had been cast: Whitehall was expected to react strongly, to resort to more armed force; and force would be met with determination. "We have got into a flame," as Cushing had said in his letter of the 10th, "and where it will End God only knows."

December 17, 1773.

I miss'd the Opportunity of sending you the above,[1] and am now to give you an Account of what has since happen'd among us.

Upon Information that the Tea with the American Duty upon it was certainly ship'd and might soon be expected we heard of an Opposition forming in N. York and Philadelphia, and Measures concerting there to induce a Resignation of the Consignee's. Our Patriots, determin'd to second their Brethren in the other Colonies, appointed a Meeting of the People at Liberty Tree, at Noon Day, to receive the Resignation of the Consignees for this Province: but they chose not to appear upon this Intimation at that Place. A Committee was then chosen to wait on them at the Store [of] Mr. Clark the Eldest of them, where all the Consignees

8. This chronology is derived from the description of the crisis in Labaree, *Tea Party*, pp. 109–41.

9. See particularly the letter from Cushing above, Dec. 10, and from the House committee of correspondence below, Dec. 21.

1. Cooper's letter of Nov. 10.

were met, to know if they would resign their Commission: a great Part of the Body, without a Vote for it, accompanied the Committee. The Answer was rough and peremptory—no Resignation.[2] Soon after the Governor call'd a Council, and the Consignees petition'd that the Tea upon it's Arrival might be under their Protection. The Council declin'd having any Thing to do with it.[3] A Town Meeting was legally call'd, and respectable Committees chosen, who repeatedly attempted to obtain the almost universally desir'd Resignation, but without Effect: The Consignees insisted upon landing the Tea, tho they conceded to store it, till they could hear from their Constituents.[4] We soon were inform'd, that the Consignees at N. York and Philadelphia behav'd in a soothing Manner to the People, and upon being assur'd that the Tea was still dutied here, declar'd without Reserve they would not have the lest Share in executing a Commission so disagreable to their Fellow Citizens.[5] About this Time, a Number of People assembled in the Evening before Mr. Clark's House—from which a Musket or Pistol was fired upon them, without any Damages and they in return broke his Windows and retir'd.[6]

Soon after,[7] the Consignees who consulted with Governor &c, in evr'y Step, retir'd to the Castle in Imitation of the Commissioners, and with similar Views and Hopes, no doubt, where they have remain'd ever since; except Mr. Joshua Winslow, who lately arriv'd from N Scotia, and lives at Marshfield.[8]

2. Nov. 3.

3. Nov. 19, 23, 27.

4. The meetings on Nov. 5, 6, 18; the consignees' concession on the 29th.

5. The consignees at New York washed their hands of the business, and those at Philadelphia resigned. Labaree, *Tea Party*, pp. 95–6, 99–103.

6. Nov. 17.

7. Nov. 29.

8. The customs commissioners had fled for safety to Castle William in 1768 and in 1770, and did so again during the tea crisis. Above, xv, 268 n; XVII, 189, 192–3; Labaree, *Tea Party*, p. 145. Joshua Winslow (1727–1801) had earlier spent much time in Nova Scotia, and is said to have still had a home there; but his principal residence was the Marshfield house that was subsequently Daniel Webster's. Winslow became a Loyalist and died in Quebec. Alice M. Earle, ed., *Diary of Anna Green Winslow* ... (Boston, 1894), pp. [iii], x–xv.

Upon the Arrival of the Tea, an assembly of the People was call'd; it prov'd as large as any ever known here, of which Mr. Hancock was Moderator:[9] Great Numbers from the Neighboring Towns united in it; and indeed the People in the Country have all along been equally Zealous with their Brethren in Boston in this common Cause, and there is now established a Correspondence and Union between them, never known before. The Moderator and People were strongly desirous of preserving the Tea untouch'd, for the E. India Company. They labor'd this Point with undissembled Ardor and great Patience: they consider'd however, that Landing the Tea, would ensure the Duty; that it might be smuggled from the Castle, and that the Price of Tea higher among us than to the Southward, would be an almost invincible Temptation to this. They insisted therefore it should go back in the same Bottom. They urg'd this upon the Consignees with great Earnestness, from an apprehension, that the Tea, in the present Temper of the Province, would not be safe—but in vain. They could not be perswaded to further Concession than before. The Master and Owner were then call'd, who, seing the irresistable Torrent, engag'd that the Tea should return as it came. Two other Vessels freighted with it, arrivd, and the same Engagement was made for them. There we tho't the Matter would have ended. But the Governor, Consignees, Revenue Officers &c, rais'd obstacles to this measure, and seem'd to chuse that the Tea should be destroy'd, and the Exasperation of both Countries heighten'd.[10] Another Assembly of the People

9. Nov. 29. Cooper seems to be mistaken about Hancock: he begged off being moderator, and Jonathan Williams, Sr., took his place. Mass. Arch., XXVII, 581; Labaree, *Tea Party*, p. 120.

10. All those concerned with the tea were caught in the tangles of the law. The *Dartmouth*'s cargo became liable to duty once it was declared on Nov. 30, and according to 13/14 Chas. II, c. 11, and 7/8 Wm. III, c. 22, the duty had to be paid within twenty days on pain of seizure. When the time limit expired the customs officers were free to put the cargo under guard; the consignees might then pay the duty and try to market the tea, or resign and leave the officers to auction it. The alternative, "that the Tea should return as it came," was not feasible: as long as the duty remained unpaid the ship could not legally leave Boston or dock in London. The procedure, which had been standard throughout the century, was for the customs collector to certify that duty had been paid and the ship cleared, whereupon the governor issued

was call'd, of which a Country Gentleman was Moderator.[1] The Owner of the Ship first arriv'd appear'd before them, and plead that if they held him to his Engagements to carry the Tea back He should be ruin'd, for Want of Clearances &c. He was desir'd by the People to apply to the Custom House for a Clearance, which He did and was refus'd. He was then desir'd[2] to wait on the Governor at Milton for a Pass at the Castle, which was also refus'd. The People waited for his Return till Dusk last Evening; as soon as the Governor's Refusal was known the Assembly was dissolv'd. Just before the Dissolution, two or three hundred Persons in Dress and appearance like Indians, pass'd by the old South Meeting House where the Assembly was held, gave a War Hoop, and hasten'd to the Wharf where all the Tea Ships lay, and demanding the Tea, which was given up to them without the least Resistance, they soon emptied all the Chests into the Harbor, to the Amount of about three hundred and fourty. This was done with out Injury to any other Property, or to any Man's Person; An Interloper indeed, who had found Means to fill his Pockets with Tea, upon being discover'd was stript of his Booty and his Cloaths together; and sent home naked. A remarkable Instance of Order and Justice, among Savages. When they had done their Business, they silently departed, and the Town has been remarkably quiet ever since. This was done last Evening, and had it been deferr'd a few Hours longer, the Tea, it was suppos'd would have been taken under the Protection of the Admiral, or the Castle.[3] The Governor, Collector, and Consignees, most certainly had it

---

a permit for her to pass Castle William; without clearance from the customs she might not enter a British port. Hutchinson, on whom Cooper blamed the whole imbroglio, was well aware that he could not resolve it without violating the old laws of trade, which he was sworn to uphold. Mass. Arch., XXVII, 576, 589, 595, 611; Hutchinson, *History*, III, 311–13; Labaree, *Tea Party*, pp. 139–40.

1. Dec. 14. The moderator was Samuel P. Sargent of Weston, whose role emphasized the growing solidarity of Boston and the countryside. *Ibid.*, p. 137.

2. At the final mass meeting, Dec. 16.

3. On the 14th the Governor had proposed that the ships be put under naval protection, but the consignees—presumably in fear of their lives—had refused. Hutchinson, *History*, III, 312. Rumor of this offer may have helped to precipitate the Tea Party before the twenty-day limit had expired.

in their Pow'r to have sav'd this Destruction, and return'd it undiminish'd to the Owner, in England, as the People were extremely desirous of this, did evr'y Thing in their Pow'r to accomplish it, and waited so long for this Purpose, as to run no small Risque of being frustrated in their grand Design of preventing it's being landed.

The fourth and only remaining Vessel with Tea, Capt. Loring is ashore near Cape Cod, the Cargo like to be sav'd—but what will become of this Tea bro't in that Bottom, Time will discover. We have no account that any has yet arriv'd at N.Y. or Philadelphia. It is not doubted however, that from the latter Place it will be all sent back; and should it be landed in the former, that it will remain unvended in the Fort.[4] To the warm and violent opposition made here, the People have been partly at least excited by their Brethren in those Places, and by the Merchants in London; but the Principle upon which they acted, was, a thoro Detestation of the insidious Design of Administration, to establish and increase the American Revenue upon this Article, after fair and repeated Professions of an Intention to relieve us. In what Manner it will resent the Treatment we have given to this exasperating Measure is uncertain; but thus much is certain, that the Country is united with the Town, and the Colonies with one another, in the common Cause, more firmly than ever. Should a greater military Pow'r be sent among us, it can never alter the fix'd Sentiments of the People, tho' [it] would increase the public Confusions, and tend to plunge both Countries into the most unhappy Circumstances. The Tories, or Tools of Hutchinson seem struck with a Pannic. Some of them own now the Impossibility of supporting the Measures of Administration, and a Necessity of their being chang'd. The longer the Governor is continu'd, the more plainly this Necessity will appear. In this View, there are some wise Friends to their Country, who do not

4. The fourth ship, the *William*, was wrecked off Provincetown on Dec. 10; part of the tea was salvaged, but only one chest ever reached a consumer. On the 13th Boston learned that the Governor and Council at New York had agreed to land and guard the tea there. Mass. Arch., xxvii, 587. This proved to be unnecessary because the ship, delayed by storms, did not arrive until April, 1774. She was then turned back, as the ship to Philadelphia had been at the end of 1773. Labaree, *Tea Party*, pp. 150–1, 156–9.

regret his Continuance in the Chair. The last Hope of Him and his Friends is, to govern wholly by a military Pow'r.

To Dr Franklin—In addition to a Letter of Novr 10th.

From Samuel Franklin   ALS: American Philosophical Society

Dear Sir   Boston 17th Decr, 1773.

I Received your kind Letter by Mr. Danforth with the book of advice Inclos'd,[5] for which I kindly thank you, and hope I Shall follow your good Directions. I find Still the times are hard and Dificult, but Desire to be thankfull. I Rubb along with my Neighbours. I hope Sir these Lines may find you in good health as they Leave me and my Family. My Wife and my four Daughters Joyns with me in kind Love to you and our Cozens Peirce, and we Should be glad of a few Lines from them. I Saw your Sizter Mecom a few Days ago who was better than She had been Some time. As for news, after three or four meetings of the Committes of the Near towns with a good number of the Inhabitants of Boston and our Committe they Had yesterday a grand meeting of about 5000 persons at the old South, to putt into Excecution the Sending the Ships back with the Tea and I think the Body Waited with a great deal of patience both upon the Consignees and Mr. Rotch. And finding the Governor would not give the Vessell a pass about 6 o clock the Meeting was Desolv'd and a parcell of men Calld Indians appear'd and by Nine o clock I heard that all the Tea was Destroyed by throwing it into the Sea.[6] Such Sir is the Zeal of the Body of this people against Tea that Comes with a Duty. I Shall always be verry Glad Sir to hear from you and Remain Your Loving Kinsman   SAMEL FRANKLIN

To Dr Benjamin Franklin.

Addressed: To Dr / Benjamin Franklin / in / London / per Capt Scott

5. See above: the "kind Letter" of July 7 (which also explains the later reference to "our Cozens Peirce") and BF to Danforth, July 25.

6. See the preceding document.

From [Theodore Forbes?] Leith:[7]

Printed in *Lloyd's Evening Post*, Dec. 20–22, 1773

For LLOYD'S EVENING POST.

Manner of making the PARMESAN CHEESE, *as observed by Dr.* LEITH, *and by him communicated to* B. FRANKLIN, *Esq.*

The Parmesan Cheese is not made at present in the neighbourhood of Parma, but is solely the produce of the State of Milan, and especially of the country betwixt Placentia and Milan; that made near Lodi is the most esteemed. The following account is given from an observation of the whole process, as conducted at a considerable Farmer's on the road to Lodi.

The milk of fourscore cows, which had been kept over night, was skimmed about four o'clock in the morning, and at the same time the cows were again milked, and at seven that milk also was skimmed; then the skimmed milk of both evening and morning were put together in a large copper vessel, wide at the mouth, gradually diminishing some way down, and towards the bottom it became a perfect cylinder, nearly of the diameter of the cheese they usually make. This vessel was suspended by an iron rod turning on an axis, by means of which it could be put upon, or removed from the fire at pleasure. The milk was then made blood warm, to fit it for the action of the runnet, and removing it from

---

7. BF's informant was, we assume, the Scottish doctor (1746–1819) who had received his M.D. from Edinburgh in 1768 and was by this time practicing in Greenwich. He subsequently became an F.R.S. and a member of the College of Physicians, and retired in 1806 on inheriting the family estate in Aberdeenshire. *DNB.* Although we know nothing about his acquaintance with BF, the two may have met either through William Hewson or through Benjamin Rush, who took his degree from Edinburgh at the same time as Leith. We do not know when the Scot made his tour of Italy, but he brought back information that BF had longed for earlier. "If I could find in any Italian Travels a Receipt for making Parmesan Cheese," he had remarked in 1769, "it would give me more Satisfaction than a Transcript of any Inscription from any old Stone whatever." Above, XVI, 172–3. If Leith gave him this account long before he published it, as is quite possible, BF may have reduced its gargantuan proportions in the recipes he sent Catherine Greene and Mrs. Brownrigg: above, XIX, 25; XX, 464.

the fire, runnet was put to it in the common way.[8] After waiting an hour, the coagulation was perfect, though the curd was tender, and they then broke it down by means of a stick, with a round board, of six inches in diameter fastened to the end of it; after which they broke it still more, by dividing any lumps that were formed, by a stick, through which a number of twigs were passed in different directions. The curd was then allowed to subside, and about a fifth part of the whey was taken off, and put by in a large pail; after which the vessel was again placed upon the fire, (which never was allowed to become very strong,) and kept there for an hour an[d a] half. During all this time, one of the people was constantly employed in stirring and breaking down the curd, as above described.

About half an hour after the vessel had been put upon the fire, a quantity of powdered saffron was put in without any rule but the putting as much as was sufficient to give the whey the tinge of a high-coloured Parmesan Cheese, the curd remaining for some time as white as before. They then heated the whey, so as to render it insufferable for one to retain the hand in it, by which they knew it was proper to turn the vessel from the fire. We observed, that during this process the curd underwent a considerable change; from being spongy, and not easily yielding to pressure, it now seemed to separate spontaneously from the whey, and yielded even to the slightest pressure; we also thought that the whey, in heating, acquired the peculiar smell of Parmesan Cheese. Upon the vessel being removed from the fire, and not stirred, the curd immediately separated very perfectly from the whey, and in less than half an hour they took off all the whey, unless a small pail-full, and it being still pretty hot, a quantity of the cold whey which was first removed, was poured on the curd, by which it was cooled so as to allow a person to raise it from the bottom of the vessel, where it lay already in the form of a cheese; another person then passed a coarse, loosely worked linen cloth under the curd, and brought it round on all sides; then one held the corners of the cloth, whilst another poured back nearly the whole of the whey, in order to facilitate the lifting the curd out of

8. Rennet, a curdling agent made from a calf's stomach, loses its efficacy when overheated.

this huge vessel: This was immediately done, and the curd placed in a tub, along with a pail-full of whey, and after a quarter of an hour it was placed in the mould, which consisted of a single hoop of wood, without either top or bottom, and was only kept in its proper form by means of a cord, so fitted as that by it the size of the mould might be increased or diminished, to adapt it to the quantity of curd.

The ordinary size of the Cheese made there is from two to three feet in diameter, and six to eight inches in thickness. The Cheese was left in the mould, without any weight upon it, for a quarter of an hour, to allow the whey to run out of itself, after which they remove the cloth altogether, and a board of four or five inches in thickness was laid upon it, and some time after a stone, of little more than thirty pounds in weight, was placed above the wood; all this apparatus was removed the day following, and employed for the cheese of that day. The weight being taken off, the cheese was carried into the drying-house, a tolerably cool place, though not so airy as those in this country. The second day they sprinkle some bay salt over it, and it is managed afterwards in the common way, only that when near dry, it is painted over with a substance called Rosette, of a purplish colour.

The Cheese made at that Farm weigh from fourscore to one hundred and thirty pounds at the different seasons, as they commonly make all winter over; the pound consists of twenty-eight of their ounces. The Cheese are sold for eighty or ninety Milanese livres, a livre being equal to about sevenpence-halfpenny of our money.

Men were employed entirely to conduct the business of the Farm, and we saw them also make butter from the cream they had taken off the milk, but in a very slovenly manner. The only thing worth notice was, that at the time we were there, they put pieces of ice in with the cream, as the weather was exceedingly hot; for this purpose each Farmer has his ice-house; in winter they put in warm water in the place of it.

From Thomas Cushing

ALS: Library of Congress

Sir   Boston Decr. 21. 1773

Since the Above[1] the Teas are all destroyed but as the Vessell is just upon sailing must refer for particulars to Dr. Williamson the Bearer of this whom I recommend to your Notice and to whom I must also refer you for a particular Account of the transactions here and the other Colonies relative to this affair.[2] I am with great respect your most humble servant   THOMAS CUSHING

Benjamin Franklin Esqr

From the Massachusetts House of Representatives Committee of Correspondence

LS: Library of Congress; LS: Harvard University Library; draft: Boston Public Library

Sir   Boston December 21st. 1773

It has been the Expectation of many of the Colonists that the last Session of Parliament would have put a final end to those Grievances under which they had so long been oppressed, and against which they had so long, in vain, Remonstrated. They expected that the Revenue Acts would have been Repealed and

1. The copy of his letter of Dec. 10 above.

2. For Hugh Williamson, the Philadelphia doctor and mathematician, see above, x, 266 n. He was "a reputed messenger from the people of Philadelphia," according to Hutchinson, "to promote uniformity of measures" (Mass. Arch., xxvii, 602), and presumably for that reason detoured to Boston on his way to England. He witnessed the Tea Party while waiting to sail, and carried the earliest news of it to reach London. He left on Dec. 22 on the *Hayley*, the first ship out after the great event, and was at Dover some four weeks later. *Mass. Gaz.; and the Boston Weekly News-Letter*, Dec. 23, 1773; *Public Advertiser*, Jan. 21, 1774. The *Hayley* carried not only this letter but also, we assume, the following one and Cooper's of Dec. 17; she arrived days before the *Dolphin* brought Hutchinson's dispatches. Williamson had an interview with Dartmouth and was examined before the Privy Council. Above, p. 497 n; David Hosack, "A Biographical Memoir of Hugh Williamson . . .," N.-Y. Hist. Soc. *Coll.*, III (1821), 144 n. Williamson subsequently, so the story goes, was the intermediary who obtained the Hutchinson correspondence. *Ibid.*, pp. 143-4, 151-3, [177-]9; *DAB*. Although the story is patently absurd, he may have been instrumental in obtaining the copies of two additional Hutchinson letters that BF sent Cushing with his note below, June 30, 1774.

that they should no more have had reason to complain of the
Unconstitutional exertions of Parliamentary Power: They were
naturally led to form these expectations from the Conduct of Administration,[3] who lately encouraged them with assurances, that
if all things remained quiet in America, these unhappy dissentions would soon terminate in a lasting Union. But how Sir, were
they Surprized to find they had been deceived to find that the
Parliament, at the very time they expected relief, pursued New
Measures for Effectually Securing and inhancing the oppressive
Revenues, and with this View by an Act, passed the last Session,
Impowered the East India Company to Ship their Teas to
America. From this Act, they readily saw that they had nothing
to hope from the favour of Administration, but that they rather
discovered an indisposition that the Parliament should grant them
any relief, they considered the Act as introductive to Monopolies
which besides the train of Evils that attend them in a Commercial
View are forever dangerous to Publick Liberty more especially
under the direction and Influence of Government, they also looked
upon it pregnant with new Grievances, paving the way to further
Impositions, and in it's Consequences threatning the final
destruction of American Liberties. Thrown by this Idea into a
State of Desperation, the United Voice of the People, not only in
this Province but in New York and Pensylvania, and as far as we
can learn, in all the Colonies, was, that they would never suffer
the Tea to be landed, but would prefer any Species of hazard and
danger to a tame Submission to measures, which if pursued must
reduce them to a State of Abject Slavery. Administration could
not have invented[4] a method so effectual for raising the Spirit of
the Colonies, or promoting among them an entire union of
Sentiment. At the same time People on your side the Water have

3. The draft, which is in Cushing's hand, here inserted and then deleted
"and the favourable Expectations of their Freinds on your side the water,
who lately," etc. Was this veiled reference meant to include BF? In the late
winter he had been optimistic about repeal of the tea duty; see his letters
above to Galloway, Feb. 14, and to Cushing, March 9. In any case the
hope had been widespread in Massachusetts that concessions would soon be
forthcoming, as witness Cushing's letter of Dec. 10 and Cooper's of Dec. 17.

4. The draft originally read, "Perhaps it would have been Impossible for
the wit of man, or the wisdom of Administration, to have invented," etc.

for several Months been repeatedly Informing our Merchants of this Manouver and advising them as they regarded their Sacred Rights to withstand the landing of the Teas by the most Vigorous opposition.

While the Minds of the People were impressed with these Sentiments, the Vessels arrived with the Teas, Consigned to Messrs. Richard Clark & Sons, Thomas and Elisha Hutchinson, Benjamin Faneuil and Joshua Winslow Esquires; previous to this the Town of Boston had several Meetings, in order to Induce the Consignees to resign their Trust, but to no purpose, and immediately upon the arrival of the Vessels aforesaid, that every measure possible might be taken to prevent Confusion and disorder, while the minds of all were in great agitation, the People in this and many of the neighbouring Towns Assembled in the Old South Meeting House (Faneuil Hall not being capacious enough to Contain the People that attended) to prevail with the Consignees to send back the Teas and if possible to preserve it from that Destruction, which the resentment of the People might justly lead *them* to Expect. You will see by the inclosed papers the Measures they took and the Resolves they passed; and will wonder, perhaps, that these resolves and Measures were in vain. They not only treated with the Consignees but with the owners and masters of these Vessels, but all without Success. Despairing to Effectuate any Method of Accommodation, after having tried all that could be devised to no purpose, they Dissolved the Meeting, which agreable to their constant and declared design had protected the Teas from destruction.[5] Nigh twenty days were now passed since the Arrival of one of the Tea Vessels Commanded by Capt: Hall, at which time, according to Act of Parliament, it was in the Power of the Custom House Officers to take the Teas into their own possession in order to Secure the duties, there were just grounds to think that they intended to do it the Minute the Twenty Days were expired and that they would attempt to Land them by force and overbear any opposition that might be made, by a second Effusion of Blood: under these Apprehensions, the Teas on the Evening of the 16th: Instant

5. Much of the letter to here recapitulates, in somewhat greater detail, what Cushing had written BF above, Dec. 10. For what follows see the annotation of Cooper to BF above, Dec. 17.

were destroyed by a Number of Persons unknown and in disguise. Such was the obstinacy of the Consignees their Advisers and Coadjutors, Such their Aversion to all Conceiliating Measures, that they are almost universally Condemned, and some even of the Court party among us, acknowledge that the destruction of the Teas must be imputed to these obstinate Enemies of our Liberties, who never would consent to any Method proposed for its preservation, and who perhaps wished to irritate and inflame the minds of an injured, oppressed People to measures of violence of which afterwards they hoped to make their own advantages.

The House of Representatives at the last Session appointed us a Committee to write to their Agent, in pursuance of this appointment, we have given you this Information of the present State of our affairs and doubt not you will make such an Improvement of this intelligence as shall be most for the Interest of this Province in particular and of the Colonies in General. We are with respect, Your most humble Servants   THOMAS CUSHING
             SAMUEL ADAMS
             JOHN HANCOCK
             WM: PHILLIPS[6]

Benjamin Franklin Esqr

Endorsed:[7] Papers relating to Hutchinson's Letters &c

From Seth Paddock[8]   ALS: American Philosophical Society

Dear Sir   Illing[ton, Decem]ber: 21st: 1773[9]
 I Was Very Well Received Here By our Kinsman and Family[1]

6. For William Phillips, the Boston merchant, see above, XVI, 273 n.

7. On the LS in the Library of Congress, apparently in BF's hand.

8. A Nantucket relative who, we believe, had visited BF in London months before; see BF to Jane Mecom above, July 7. In March, 1774, BF lent Paddock £15 on the latter's note: Jour., p. 53.

9. The letter is torn, but for reasons discussed in the next note we have no doubt about the place. The date is at least highly probable because of the reference to Christmas. Paddock was on an enforced vacation: his ship, the *Duke of Cumberland,* had been lost off the Scilly Islands on Sept. 22 on a voyage from New England. *Public Advertiser,* Oct. 4; *Mass. Gaz.; and the Boston Weekly News-Letter,* Dec. 2, 9, 1773.

1. We assume that these were the same as the "Mr. Foulger and Family" in Paddock's final sentence, in other words that he was staying with some of

and a Number of Gentlemen Farmers Who Intend to Settle in Ameria I have Given Them my Best Advice of the Country Which is to land att New Yourk Which is in the Center of America and a Fine Country all Round them. I Am Prevaild upon to Stay Here and Keep Christmass. I Have addressd: Mr: Benjn: Stead for His assistance for a Ship in the Carolina Trade as His Connections are Very Large in that Trade[2] and Should Be Extremely obligd: to you to Send Him a line With the Inclosd: if it is no more than To lett Him Know you are my Friend. Mr: Foulger and Family Presents their Compliments to you and Mrs. Stephenson likewise mine to that Lady and am Very Respectfully Sir your most Humble Servant   SETH PADDOCK

Addressed: To / Benjamin Franklin Esqr / Craven Street Strand / London

Franklin's Public Statement about the Hutchinson Letters   Printed in *The London Chronicle*, Dec. 23–25, 1773[3]

By the late summer of 1773 the furor aroused by the Hutchinson letters had spread from Boston to London. Franklin's role in the affair was still unknown; attention focused on who had obtained the correspondence from Thomas Whately's papers,[4] and a long controversy on this point began in the pages of the *Public Advertiser*. On September 4 an

---

his and BF's distant English relatives, and that "Mr." was the Thomas Foulger who appears a number of times in the next volume. The Nantucket Folgers came originally from Norfolk, and a family of the name had been living in Illington in 1759: above, VIII, 277. BF, to judge by Paddock's conclusion, had been in touch with them.

2. Benjamin Stead, a London merchant of Threadneedle St., had lived in South Carolina and married there before returning to England in 1759, and his home was a center for visitors from the colony; he apparently died early in 1776. Lothrop Withington, "South Carolina Gleanings in England," *S.C. Hist. and Geneal. Mag.*, IV (1903), 237; Mabel L. Webber, "Extracts from the Journal of Mrs. Ann Manigault," *ibid.*, XX (1919), 58 n, 123 n.

3. The letter was also published in the *Public Advertiser*, Dec. 27, and the *London General Evening Post*, Dec. 28.

4. For the circumstances in which the letters started on their way to BF see above, XIX, 403–4.

anonymous correspondent publicized the story that William Whately was said to be circulating among his friends, that John Temple, and no one else, had had access to the papers, and had for a time been left alone with them; in the light of Temple's character, the writer added, the conclusion was obvious. On November 25 a rebuttal appeared from a correspondent who called himself a member of Parliament: after Thomas Whately's death the letters in question had never been in William's possession; the man who had obtained them—here the writer paraphrased Franklin's argument[5]—had served the colonies and the mother country well by providing the opportunity for reconciliation. Another correspondent, under the pseudonym "Antenor," replied in the issue of December 8 by repeating the substance of the September communication and quoting a statement by Whately that Temple alone had handled the letters. The next day Temple himself entered the lists: on seeing "Antenor's" charge he had called at once upon Whately, who had categorically denied it and insisted that he had merely allowed Temple to remove some of his own letters. Whately took prompt exception. In a letter published on the 11th he vouched for "Antenor's" story as essentially correct; Temple had assured him three times, he added without comment, that he had taken no letters but his own.

Each man had now publicly given the other the lie, and a duel followed on December 11. It was a seriocomic affair; neither antagonist was a swordsman, or knew the punctilio that the code prescribed. Whately received wounds that were more embarrassing than dangerous, and was temporarily incapacitated. Stories circulated that Temple had played foul on the field of honor, and he tried to exonerate himself by giving an account, which appeared on the 18th, of what had happened; in closing he made clear that the issue behind the duel was still open.[6] At that point Franklin, who had good reason to suppose that another meeting would take place as soon as Whately recovered, published the brief statement below.

Why did a fortnight elapse between the duel and the statement? Partly, no doubt, because such a momentous step did not need to be hurried; even when the prospect arose of another duel, Whately was

5. *Ibid.*, pp. 407–8.

6. The letters to the *Public Advertiser* that we have summarized, and later ones that carried the controversy into 1774, are printed in [John Almon,] *Biographical, Literary, and Political Anecdotes* ... (3 vols., London, 1797), III, 236–73. Almon omitted a large section of the Dec. 8 letter, in which "Antenor" clearly implied that the "member of Parliament" whom he was answering was Temple.

out of harm's way for a while under the care of his surgeon. Franklin may also have been slow to learn of developments: he is said to have been out of town when Temple and Whately fought, perhaps on the Christmas visit to the Shipleys that he had planned;[7] and London gossip would have taken time to reach Hampshire. If he had learned at Twyford what was happening, he might well have cut short his stay and returned to town for the latest news. It persuaded him, whenever and wherever he heard it, to drop the secrecy that had shrouded his role for the past year, and to project himself into a controversy that was the talk of London. His decision touched off a virulent newspaper campaign against him,[8] which prepared the way for the scene a month later before the Privy Council.

To the PRINTER of the LONDON CHRONICLE.

Sir,   Craven-street, Dec. 25, 1773.

Finding that two Gentlemen have been unfortunately engaged in a Duel, about a transaction and its circumstances of which both of them are totally ignorant and innocent, I think it incumbent on me to declare (for the prevention of farther mischief, as far as such a declaration may contribute to prevent it) that I alone am the person who obtained and transmitted to Boston the letters in question. Mr. W. could not communicate them, because they were never in his possession; and, for the same reason, they could not be taken from him by Mr. T.[9] They were not of the nature of *"private letters between friends:"* They were written by public officers to persons in public station, on public affairs, and intended

---

7. Benjamin Vaughan, years later, remarked that BF was not in London when the duel occurred and did not hear of it for some time: *Political, Miscellaneous, and Philosophical Pieces . . . Written by Benj. Franklin . . .* (London, 1779), p. 339 n. For the intended visit to Twyford see Shipley to BF above, Dec. 9.

8. BF's statement also received wide publicity in America; see Crane, *Letters to the Press*, p. 239.

9. We have pointed out above (XIX, 404 n) that this letter, strictly construed, did not deny Temple a part in the affair. BF merely corroborated the correspondent in the *Public Advertiser* of Nov. 25: because William Whately had never had these particular letters, neither he nor Temple could have taken them *after* Thomas Whately's other papers came into his brother's hands. About what happened before that BF said nothing.

to procure public measures;[10] they were therefore handed to other public persons who might be influenced by them to produce those measures: Their tendency was to incense the Mother Country against her Colonies, and, by the steps recommended, to widen the breach, which they effected. The chief Caution expressed with regard to Privacy, was, to keep their contents from the *Colony Agents*, who the writers apprehended might return them, or copies of them, to America. That apprehension was, it seems, well founded; for the first Agent who laid his hands on them, thought it his duty[1] to transmit them to his Constituents.

B. FRANKLIN,
Agent for the House of Representatives of the Massachusetts-Bay.

From John Ellis[2]

AL: American Philosophical Society

Grays Inn Decr the 25th 1773

Mr. Ellis presents his respectful compliments to Dr. Franklin and begs he would return him the French Book upon Moco Coffee, as he intends to make some extracts from it. Dr. Fothergill being very desirous that the remarks upon Coffee should be speedily publishd. Hopes he will think of his kind promise of assisting therein, as it must speedily go to the press.

Addressed: To / Dr. Benjn. Franklin / at Mrs. Stevenson's / in Craven Street / Strand

10. The Lieut. Gov. and the Secretary of Mass. were corresponding with an M.P., but of course not in their official capacity. The question of whether their and Whately's positions robbed the correspondence of its private character was one hotly debated at the time; see Wedderburn's speech below, Jan. 29, 1774.

1. Here BF subsequently added a note: "Governor Hutchinson, as appears by his letters, since found and published in New England, had the same idea of *duty*, when he procured copies of Dr. Franklin's letters to the assembly, and sent them to the ministry of England." WTF, *Memoirs*, I, app., lxi. For Hutchinson's action see the headnote on BF to the Mass. House above, July 7. BF's note must have been written after the spring of 1775, when Hutchinson's correspondence was "found and published"; see Bernard Bailyn, *The Ordeal of Thomas Hutchinson* (Cambridge, Mass., 1974), pp. 334–40.

2. BF had clearly ignored Ellis' previous request above, Dec. 8. It is here repeated almost verbatim, except for the references to Moccha coffee and to BF's promise, and did elicit a prompt reply; see the following document.

To John Ellis[3]

ALS: Linnean Society, London

Dear Sir, Cravenstreet Dec. 26. 73

I return the Book you were so kind to favour me with. Upon Consideration, tho' I wish to do any thing you can be desirous I should do, I find it impossible for me to write any thing worth reading on a Subject that will be exhausted by Dr. Fothergill and yourself, who are both so much better acquainted with it. I am ever, with the greatest Respect and Esteem, Dear Sir, Your most obedient humble Servant   B FRANKLIN

Addressed: To / John Ellis Esqr / Grays Inn / Mr Griffiss No 32 Fleet market

Endorsed: Decr. the 26th 1773 Benjn. Franklin

From a Committee of the Library Company of Philadelphia

Minutebook copy: Library Company of Philadelphia

Sir, Philada. Decr. 28th 1773

In Behalf of the Directors of the Library Company of Philadelphia, we acknowledge the receipt of your sundry favours, particularly of the 22d August 1772 with the Books by Falconer; for observations upon which you will please to be referr'd to the last Page of the Inclosed.[4] Mr. Bache has likewise delivered Hawkesworth's Voyages, McPherson's Iliad and Dalrymple's Letters,[5] for which additional instance of your attention to the Interest of the Company, we present our Thanks. The Directors agree with you in Sentiment concerning the Journals of the

---

3. See the preceding document; BF's second reply is below, Jan. 12, 1774.

4. BF's letter is above, XIX, 270. The committee enclosed the list of books mentioned in Rhoads's postscript.

5. The books that BF sent the Library via Richard Bache were John Hawkesworth, *An Account of the Voyages Undertaken by the Order of His Present Majesty for Making Discoveries in the Southern Hemisphere* ... (3 vols., London, 1773); James Macpherson (the "translator" of the Ossianic poems), *The Iliad of Homer* ... (2 vols., London, 1773); and part I of vol. II of Sir John Dalrymple, *Memoirs of Great Britain and Ireland* ... (2nd ed.: 2 vols. in 3, London, 1771–88), which contained official correspondence and was published in 1773.

House of Commons as the opportunities of purchasing them at Auction are so frequent and the price so much lower. We should be glad to hear how soon the new Edition of the Encyclopaedia may be expected.[6]

The Company being in want of the Books mentioned in the inclosed Catalogue, must beg your kind assistance in procuring them (with any others you may think proper for our Collection) to be sent by the first Opportunity. We should be glad with these Books to have a sketch of our Account upon receipt of which we shall be careful immediately to remit the Balance.

Since our last the Library has been removed to a new Building called The Carpenters Hall,[7] in the Centre of the Square, in which Friends School stands; the Books (inclosed within Wire Lattices) are kept in one large Room and in another handsome Appartment the Apparatus is deposited and the Directors meet. With great Regard We are Sir Your obliged humble Servants[8]

ROBT. S JONES.

JOSIAH HEWES.

PS. The Directors some time since sent a Catalogue of the Books in the Library, which we hope got to hand.

In Case of Doctr. Franklin's Absence, the inclosed Catalogue of Books is recommended to Mr. Strachan, to be forwarded per first Opportunity for this place.[9]   SAMUEL RHOADS

Sent per the Polly, Capt. Ayres[10]

Doctr. Benjamin Franklin,

6. For the journals of the House see above, XIX, 270. The Library Co. had been interested in the *Encyclopédie* for almost three years: above, XVIII, 17, 69, 117–18; XIX, 117.

7. The now famous Philadelphia landmark had been completed in 1771. The Library's moving into it was apparently a reason why the first Continental Congress met there in 1774: Charles H. Cohen, "The Origins of Carpenters' Hall . . . ," Numismatic and Antiquarian Soc. of Philadelphia *Pub.*, XXVIII (1916–18), 124.

8. For the members of the committee see above, XVIII, 18 n; XIX, 153 n.

9. The Library's catalogue was *The Charter, Laws, and Catalogue of Books of the Library Company of Philadelphia* . . . (Philadelphia, 1770). A presenta-

(*Footnotes 9 and 10 continued on p. 519*)

From Jacques Barbeu-Dubourg

ALS: American Philosophical Society

A Paris ce 29e. Xbre. 1773

Monsieur et cher Ami

Dans le moment que je traçois cette première demie ligne on m'a annoncé une persone envoyée par M. Le Prince de Conti pour me demander si j'avois reçu la description et la figure que vous m'avez promise de votre cheminée, et me prier de lui en faire part aussitôt que je l'aurai. J'ai repondu que vous sauriez incessamment l'interêt que S.A.S. y prenoit et que des que j'aurois votre reponse a ce sujet j'aurois l'honneur d'aller lui en rendre compte. Bien d'autres moins qualifiés m'en demandent tous les jours des nouvelles.[1]

J'appris hier au soir qu'on avoit ouvert un souscription chez un Notaire pour donner un prix *au meilleur memoire sur les moyens d'ecarter le tonnerre des edifices et des individus,* sur quoi on s'en rapportera au jugement de l'Academie des sciences.[2] Reste à savoir si la souscription a peine encore annoncée se remplira facilement. Je n'en desespere pourtant pas.

Si vous prenez la peine d'ouvrir l'une des volumes du journal de Medecine que je prens la liberté de vous adresser pour M. Rush vous verrez le compte qu'on y rend des experiences de Comus sur la platine. Peutetre ne savez vous pas qui est ce Comus. C'est un joueur de gobelets fort en vogue sur les boulevards, mais fort

---

tion copy to BF, inscribed by Francis Hopkinson, is now in the Library of the APS. This was presumably the volume that BF acknowledged on Feb. 18, 1774, along with the other "Catalogue" or list of books to be bought. Strahan shipped the order at that time; see his bill below, Sept. 13, 1774.

10. The *Polly* was the tea ship; Capt. Ayres was clearly allowed to pick up letters, but the day after this one was written he was compelled to return to England with his cargo. Labaree, *Tea Party*, pp. 158–9.

1. Conti's interest in heating went back many years, and had been focused on methods of hatching chicks; see Dubourg to BF above, Nov. 25. Dubourg was still relying on, and apparently broadcasting, his friend's vague promise to send him a description of the stove; see BF's letters to him above, Jan. 22 and June 29.

2. We can find no record of such a prize in the proceedings of the Académie des sciences for the next two years.

distingué dans son espece, et qui jouit d'une consideration audessus de son etat.[3]

Vos ouvrages sont de plus en plus goûtés de tout ce qu'il y a de plus capable d'en juger dans ce pays cy et de donner le ton à la longue, mais n'ayant pas la faveur des libraires cela ne gagne pas encore beaucoup dans le public; il faut prendre patience à cet egard. Je compte que non seulement tout le monde y viendra, mais que votre patrie en profitera et sera aussi exaltée à votre occasion non seulement en france mais dans toute l'Europe qu'elle y a fait peu de sensation jusqu'a present. Beaucoup de gens commencent à s'en entretenir, et tous avec une sorte de passion favorable. Je reçois plus de complimens de ma petite preface que le plus grand ouvrage ne m'en auroit attiré dans toute ma vie. Voila ce que me vaut de planer a l'ombre de vos ailes. *O, et praesidium, et dulce decus meum*![4]

Celui qui s'est chargé de la presente, que je ne connois que depuis quelques jours qu'un ami commun me l'a adressé, a conçu le projet que je souhaite qui lui reussisse, d'aller se faire maitre de langue françoise a Londres. Il ne me paroit pas encore bien fort sur l'Anglois, mais on assure qu'il possede superieurement le talent de l'enseignement qui est une sorte de don special de la nature qui n'est pas aussi identifié qu'il sembleroit devoir l'etre avec le savoir le plus profond. Oserois-je vous demander d'avoir pour lui quelques bontés sans vous compromettre? Il a une lettre a vous remettre aussi de la part de M. Le Roy, qui le connoit peutetre depuis plus longtems ou plus à fond, et qui est d'ailleurs plus capable d'en juger.[5]

J'ai des millions de complimens a vous faire de ma femme, de Melle. Biheron et d'une multitude de gens de tout sexe et de tout

3. Comus was a pseudonym of Nicolas-Philippe Ledru (1731–1807), who had a European reputation as a sleight-of-hand artist. BF might have heard of him, for he had had a successful English tour in 1765–66; see the *Gent. Mag.*, XXXVI (1766), 207. By 1773 he was becoming interested in electricity, which he soon tried to use to cure nervous diseases: Larousse, *Dictionnaire universel* under Ledru. His account of experiments with platinum was "Expériences nouvelles sur la platine et sur différens cobalts soumis à l'étincelle électrique," *Jour. de médecine, chirurgie, pharmacie, &c.* . . . , XL (1773), 468–72.

4. Horace, *Odes*, I:1:2.

5. Undoubtedly the M. Desdouaires to whom LeRoy referred in his letter to BF above, Nov. 29.

etat. Mais soyez sûr que personne ne vous est plus sincerement attaché, ne fait de voeux plus ardens pour votre conservation et votre prosperité, ne desire plus de vous embrasser cette annee pour vous repeter que je suis de toute mon ame Tout a vous

DUBOURG

Mes respectueuses civilités, s'il vous plait, a Monsieur Pringle que Dieu conserve et benisse.

From John Winthrop

Extract:[6] Library of Congress

[December 31, 1773]

I concur perfectly with you in the Sentiments expressed in your last.[7] No considerate Person, I should think, can approve of desperate Remedies, except in desperate Cases. The People of America are extreamly agitated by the repeated Efforts of Administration to subject them to absolute Power. They have been amused with Accounts of the pacific Disposition of the Ministry, and flattered with Assurances that upon their humble Petitions all their Grievances should be redressed. They have petitioned from time to time; but their Petitions have had no other Effect than to make them feel more sensibly their own Slavery. Instead of Redress, every Year has produced some new Manoeuvre, which could have no Tendency but to irritate them more and more. The last Measure of the East India Company's sending their Tea here, subject to a Duty, seems to have given the finishing Stroke to their Patience. You will have heard of the Steps taken at Boston, New York and Philadelphia to prevent the Payment of this Duty by sending the Tea back to its Owners. But as this was found impossible at Boston, the Destruction of the Tea was the Consequence.[8] What the Event of these Commotions will be, God only knows. The People thro' the Colonies appear immoveably fix'd in their Resolution, that the Tea Duty shall never be paid; and if

6. From the last page of BF's draft of his "Tract Relative to the Affair of Hutchinson's Letters," where the date is given.
7. Above, July 25.
8. See Cooper to BF above, Dec. 17.

the Ministry are determin'd to inforce these Measures, I dread the Consequences: I verily fear they will turn America into a Field of Blood. But I will hope for the best.

On a Proposed Act to Prevent Emigration

Copy:[9] Library of Congress

The rate of emigration to America from Scotland and Ireland, particularly Ulster, increased rapidly in the years immediately before 1775. Rising rents were a principal cause, along with the unemployment that in Scotland followed the financial crisis of 1772 and in Ireland the collapse of the linen trade.[10] By 1773 the drain of population was causing concern. In November a correspondent in *The Public Advertiser*, calling himself Britannus, proposed a Parliamentary ban on emigration; on December 21 another correspondent, or the same with another pseudonym, expressed surprise that no one heeded the idea.[11]

Franklin did. He had long been interested in the growth of population, and had recently concluded that restraints put upon emigrating from Great Britain violated the subject's natural rights. His tour of Ireland and Scotland in 1771 had exposed him to the shocking conditions of those to whom such restraints chiefly applied.[1] The argument that peasants should be kept at home to protect them from the misery of life in America was calculated to rouse his dissent; and in the following reply to Britannus, apparently never published, he deftly combined solicitude for their present situation with propaganda for settling in America.

To the Printer of the Publick Advertiser

Sir,   [December?, 1773]
You give us in your Paper of Tuesday, the 16th of November,

9. In Fevre's hand.
10. See Ian C. C. Graham, *Colonists from Scotland: Emigration to North America, 1707–1783* (Ithaca, N.Y., [1956]), especially pp. 21, 23–42, 46–89; R. J. Dickson, *Ulster Emigration to Colonial America, 1718–1775* (London, [1966]), especially chap. v.
11. Crane, *Letters to the Press*, pp. 238–9. Although the idea was not confined to one newspaper, it gained little momentum. The government contented itself with administrative efforts to discourage emigration, which was not formally banned in Scotland until 1775; in Ireland no effective restraints were imposed. Graham, Dickson, *op. cit.*, pp. 96–100 and 194–200 respectively.
1. See above, XVII, 39, 399–400; XIX, 7, 71.

what is called "the Plan of an Act to be proposed at the next Meeting of Parliament to prevent the Emigration of our People." I know not from what Authority it comes, but as it is very circumstantial, I must suppose some such Plan may be really under Consideration, and that this is thrown out to feel the Pulse of the Publick. I shall therefore, with your leave, give my Sentiments of it in your Paper.

During a Century and half that Englishmen have been at Liberty to remove if they pleased to America, we have heard of no Law to restrain that Liberty, and confine them as Prisoners in this Island. Nor do we perceive any ill Effects produced by their Emigration. Our Estates far from diminishing in Value thro' a Want of Tenants, have been in that Period more than doubled; the Lands in general are better cultivated; their increased Produce finds ready Sale at an advanced Price, and the Complaint has for some time been, not that we want Mouths to consume our Meat, but that we want Meat for our Number of Mouths.

Why then is such a restraining Law *now* thought necessary? A Paragraph in the same Paper from the *Edinburgh Courant* may perhaps throw some Light upon this Question. We are there told "that 1500 People have emigrated to America from the Shire of Sutherland within these two Years, and carried with them £7500 Sterling; which exceeds a Years Rent of the whole County; and that the single Consideration of the *Misery* which most of these People *must suffer* in America, independent of the Loss of Men and Money to the Mother Country, should engage the Attention not only of the *landed Interest, but of Administration.*" The humane Writer of this Paragraph, may, I fancy, console himself, with the Reflection, that perhaps the apprehended future Sufferings of those Emigrants will never exist: for that it was probably the authentic Accounts they had received from Friends already settled there, of the Felicity to be enjoyed in that Country, with a thorough Knowledge of their own Misery at home, which induced their Removal. And, as a Politician, he may be comforted by assuring himself, that if they really meet with greater Misery in America, their future Letters lamenting it, will be more credited than the *Edinburgh Courant*, and effectually without a Law put a Stop to the Emigration. It seems some of the Scottish Chiefs, who delight no longer to live upon their Estates in the honourable

Independence they were born to, among their respecting Tenants, but chuse rather a Life of Luxury, tho' among the Dependants of a Court, have lately raised their Rents most grievously to support the Expence. The Consuming of those Rents in London, tho' equally prejudicial to the poor County of *Sutherland,* no Edinburgh Newspaper complains of; but now that the oppressed Tenants take Flight and carry with them what might have supported the Landlords London Magnificence, he begins to *feel* for the MOTHER-COUNTRY, and its enormous *Loss* of £7500 carried to her Colonies! *Administration* is called upon to remedy the Evil, by another Abridgement of ENGLISH LIBERTY.[2] And surely Administration should do something for these Gentry, as they do any thing for Administration.

But is there not an easier Remedy? Let them return to their Family Seats, live among their People, and instead of fleecing and skinning, patronize and cherish them; promote their Interest, encourage their Industry, and make their Situation comfortable. If the poor Folks are happier at home than they can be abroad, they will not lightly be prevailed with to cross the Ocean. But can their Lord blame them for leaving home in search of better Living, when he first sets them the Example?

I would consider the proposed Law,

1st. As to the NECESSITY of it.

2dly. The PRACTICABILITY.

3dly. The POLICY, if practicable.

and 4thly. The JUSTICE of it.

Pray spare me room for a few Words on each of these Heads.

1st. As to the *Necessity* of it.

If any Country has more People than can be comfortably subsisted in it, some of those who are incommoded, may be induced to emigrate. As long as the new Situation shall be *far* preferable to the old, the Emigration may possibly continue. But when many of those who at home interfered with others of the same Rank, (in the Competition for Farms, Shops, Business, Offices, and other Means of Subsistence) are gradually withdrawn, the Inconvenience of that Competition ceases; the Number

2. An allusion to a phrase, by then notorious, in one of Hutchinson's published letters: above, XIX, 402.

remaining no longer half starve each other, they find they can now subsist comfortably, and tho' perhaps not quite so well as those who have left them, yet the inbred Attachment to a native Country is sufficient to overbalance a moderate Difference, and thus the Emigration ceases naturally. The Waters of the Ocean may move in Currents from one Quarter of the Globe to another, as they happen in some places to be accumulated and in others diminished; but no Law beyond the Law of Gravity, is necessary to prevent their Abandoning any Coast entirely. Thus the different Degrees of Happiness of different Countries and Situations find or rather make their Level by the flowing of People from one to another, and where that Level is once found, the Removals cease. Add to this, that even a real Deficiency of People in any Country occasioned by a wasting War or Pestilence, is speedily supply'd by earlier and of course more prolific Marriages, encouraged by the greater Facility of obtaining the Means of Subsistence. So that a Country half depopulated would soon be repeopled, till the Means of Subsistence were equalled by the Population. All Encrease beyond that Point must perish, or flow off into more favourable Situations. Such Overflowings there have been of Mankind in all Ages, or we should not now have had so many Nations. But to apprehend absolute Depopulation from that Cause, and call for a Law to prevent it, is calling for a Law to stop the Thames, lest its Waters, by what leave it daily at Gravesend, should be quite exhausted. Such a Law therefore I do not conceive to be *Necessary*.

2dly. As to the Practicability.

When I consider the Attempts of this kind that have been made, first in the time of Archbishop Laud, by Orders of Council, to stop the Puritans who were flying from his Persecutions, into New-England, and next by Louis XIV, to retain in his Kingdom the persecuted Huguenots; and how ineffectual all the Power of our Crown, with which the Archbishop armed himself, and all the more absolute Power of that great French Monarch, were, to obtain the End for which they were exerted.[3] When I consider

3. William Laud's attempts to curb emigration through the Privy Council, particularly in 1634 and 1638, were ineffective; so were Louis XIV's efforts, when he revoked the Edict of Nantes, to keep Huguenots from leaving France.

too, the extent of Coast to be guarded, and the Multitude of Cruizers necessary effectually to make a Prison of the Island for this confinement of free Englishmen, who naturally love Liberty, and would probably by the very Restraint be more stimulated to break thro' it, I cannot but think such a Law IMPRACTICABLE. The Offices would not be applied to for Licences, the Ports would not be used for Embarcation. And yet the People disposed to leave us would, as the Puritans did, get away by Shipfuls.

3dly. As to the *Policy* of the Law.

Since, as I have shewn, there is no Danger of depopulating Britain, but that the Places of those who depart will soon be filled up equal to the Means of obtaining a Livelihood, let us see whether there are not some general *Advantages* to be expected from the present Emigration. The new Settlers in America, finding plenty of Subsistence, and Land easily acquired whereon to seat their Children, seldom postpone Marriage thro' fear of Poverty. Their natural Increase is therefore in a proportion far beyond what it would have been if they had remained here.[4] New Farms are daily every where forming in those immense Forests, new Towns and Villages rising; hence a growing Demand for our Merchandise, to the greater Employment of our Manufacturers and the enriching of our Merchants. By this natural Increase of People, the Strength of the Empire is increased; Men are multiplied out of whom new Armies may be formed on Occasion, or the old recruited. The long extended Sea Coast too, of that vast Country, the great maritime Commerce of its Parts with each other, its many navigable Rivers and Lakes, and its plentiful Fisheries, breed multitudes of Seamen, besides those created and supported by its Voyages to Europe; a thriving Nursery this, for the manning of our Fleets in time of War, and maintaining our Importance among foreign Nations, by that Navy which is also our best Security against invasions from our Enemies. An Extension of Empire by Conquest of inhabited Countries is not

4. Recent studies tend to support BF's contention that marriages were contracted earlier in the New World than the Old, resulting in larger families; see, for example, the tables in Robert V. Wells, "Quaker Marriage Patterns in a Colonial Perspective," 3 *W&MQ*, XXIX (1972), 429, 438.

so easily obtained, it is not so easily secured, it alarms more the neighbouring States, it is more subject to Revolts, and more apt to occasion new Wars. The Increase of Dominion by Colonies proceeding from yourselves, and by the natural Growth of your own People, cannot be complained of by your Neighbours as an Injury, none have a right to be offended with it. Your new Possessions are therefore more secure, they are more cheaply gained, they are attached to your Nation by natural Alliance and Affection, and thus they afford an additional Strength more certainly to be depended on, than any that can be acquired by a Conquering Power, tho' at an immense Expence of Blood and Treasure. These methinks are national Advantages that more than equiponderate with the Inconveniencies suffered by a few Scotch or Irish Landlords, who perhaps may only find it necessary to abate a little of their present Luxury, or of those advanced Rents they now so unfeelingly demand. From these Considerations, I think I may conclude that the restraining Law proposed, would if practicable be IMPOLITIC.

4thly. As to the *Justice* of it.

I apprehend that every Briton who is made unhappy at home, has a Right to remove from any Part of his King's Dominions into those of any other Prince where he can be happier. If this should be denied me, at least it will be allowed that he has a Right to remove into any other Part of the same Dominions. For by this Right so many Scotchmen remove into England, easing their own Country of its supernumeraries, and benefitting ours by their Industry. And this is the Case with those who go to America. Will not these Scottish Lairds be satisfied unless a Law passes to pin down all Tenants to the Estate they are born on, (*adscriptitii glebae*[5]) to be bought and sold with it? God has given to the Beasts of the Forest and to the Birds of the Air a Right when their Subsistence fails in one Country, to migrate into another, where they can get a more comfortable Living; and shall Man be denied a Privilege enjoyed by Brutes, merely to gratify a few avaricious Landlords? Must Misery be made *permanent*, and suffered by *many* for the Emolument of One? While the Increase

5. Serfs bound to the land.

527

of Human Beings is prevented, and thousands of their Offspring stifled as it were in the Birth, that this petty Pharaoh may enjoy an *Excess* of Opulence? God commands to increase and replenish the Earth: The proposed Law would forbid increasing, and confine Britons to their present Number, keeping half that Number too, in wretchedness. The Common People of Britain and of Ireland, contributed by the Taxes they paid, and by the Blood they lost, to the Success of that War, which brought into our Hands the vast unpeopled Territories of North America; a Country favoured by Heaven with all the Advantages of Soil and Climate; Germans are now pouring into it, to take Possession of it, and fill it with their Posterity; and shall Britons, and Irelanders, who have a much better Right to it, be forbidden a Share of it, and instead of enjoying there the Plenty and Happiness that might reward their Industry, be compelled to remain here in Poverty and Misery? Considerations such as these persuade me, that the proposed Law would be both UNJUST and INHUMAN.

If then it is *unnecessary, impracticable, impolitic,* and *unjust,* I hope our Parliament will never receive the Bill, but leave Landlords to their own Remedy, an Abatement of Rents and Frugality of Living; and leave the Liberties of Britons and Irishmen at least as extensive as it found them. I am, Sir, Yours &c.

A Friend to the Poor.

Notation: Paper written in England by B F to discourage the intended Act for preventing Emigration

From Sir John Pringle   AL: Historical Society of Pennsylvania

Monday evening [December, 1773?[6]]

Dr. Pringle's Compliments to Dr. Franklin and if he is to be at

---

6. Pringle enclosed a proof page of his pamphlet, *A Discourse on the Different Kinds of Air* . . . (London, 1774). He had delivered the discourse, as president of the Royal Society, at the presentation of the Copley Medal to Priestley on November 30, 1773; the pamphlet was reviewed the following February in the *Gent. Mag.,* XLIV (1774), 81. This note was therefore written between the end of November and the publication date, and December seems a likely time.

home this evening and at leisure Dr. P. will wait upon him and play at chess.

Mean while Dr. P. returns Dr. F. the French letter which he was to shew to C. Castries [?]. He sends him a small piece upon Electricity, sometime ago sent to Dr. P. from Germany, but which Dr. P. has not yet perused: Also sends Dr. F. the first sheet of his 4to edition in order for giving the measure to the intended Vignette.[7]

Notes on Colds[8]

AD (draft): Library of Congress

These notes defy editing. They are hard to decipher; the ink has now faded in places to illegibility. They are on loose sheets of paper with no hint of their sequence, and frequent marginal additions have to be interpolated by guesswork. No internal evidence suggests a date, if indeed the sheets were all written at the same time. Previous editors, although they handled the notes in different ways, usually said or implied that they belonged in 1773; we follow that conjecture merely because we have no ground for a better one.[9] Last but not least, Franklin's meaning is often obscure and even impenetrable. His jot-

---

7. We cannot identify the French letter. As for Castries, if our reading of the name is correct, it is tempting to think he was the son of the marquis de Castries, minister of marine during part of BF's French mission; but unfortunately the young man (he was seventeen) was known as the comte de Charlus, and we have no evidence that he had recently been in England or Pringle in France. The "small piece" on electricity was, we assume, that which Ingenhousz mentioned in his letter to BF below, May 12, 1774. The vignette was a printer's decoration on the first page of the *Discourse*; Sir John presumably wanted BF's professional opinion.

8. One loose sheet among the notes contains only a heading, "Hints concerning what is called Catching of Cold," which may possibly have been BF's intended title.

9. The notes first appeared, with no clue to their date, in WTF, *Memoirs* (3rd ed.; 6 vols., London, 1818–19), VI, 239–52, from which we have supplied in brackets a few words now missing or indecipherable; and in Sparks, *Works*, VI, 387–97. In Sparks's 2nd ed. (6 vols., Boston, 1840) he reprinted the notes between a letter of late June and one of early July, 1773 (VI, 387–97), a clear implication that they were written at that time; he gave no reasons. Bigelow and Smyth followed suit: *Works*, V, 154–65; *Writings*, VI, 62–72. Whenever BF drafted the notes, 1773 was a year when the subject of colds was much on his mind; see the final note on BF to Percival above, Oct. 15.

tings were for himself, like his marginalia, but here they were no more than reminders—he knew of what, if we do not—for a treatise that he never got around to writing.[1] They need little annotation. When they seem incomprehensible, we dare not conjecture what he had in mind; when they are clear, they are for the modern reader a mixture of medical fact and myth that requires no explanation.

[1773?]

Definition of a Cold.

Query.

It is a Siziness[2] and thickness of the Blood, whereby the smaller Vessels are obstructed, and the Perspirable Matter retained, which being retained offends both by its Quantity and Quality; By Quantity as it overfills the Vessels; and by its Quality, as Part of it is acrid, and being retained produces Coughs and Sneesing by Irritation.

How this Siziness is produc'd.

1. By being long expos'd in a Cold Air, without Exercise; cold thickens Glew.
2. By a diminish'd Perspiration, either 1. from breathing and living in moist Air, which will not take away the P.M.[3] [*in the margin:* Mem. Costiveness after much Bathing. Facts.] or 2. from a clogging of the Pores by clammy Sweat dry'd on and fastning down the Scales of the Skin; or 3. by Cold constringing[4] the Pores partially or totally, sleeping or waking, or 4. by having [to] eat foods of too gross Particles for free Perspiration as Oisters, Pork, Ducks, &c.
3. By Repletion, as when more is thrown into the Habit[5] by eating and Drinking, than common Perspiration is capable of Discharging in due time [*in the margin:* Mem. In an approaching Cold, more water made than usual]; whence the Vessels are distended beyond their Spring, and the Quantity of contained Fluids that should be briskly moved to preserve or acquire a due Thinness, is too weighty for

1. See above, XVIII, 203 n.
2. Viscosity.
3. Perspirable matter.
4. Constricting.
5. An obsolete term for the body.

their Force, whence a slow Motion, thence viscidity. This Repletion is encreased by a Constipation of the Belly happening at the same time.

4. By cooling suddenly in the Air after Exercise. Exercise quickening the Circulation, produces more perspirable Matter in a given time, than is produced in Rest. And tho' more is likewise usually discharg'd during Exercise, yet on sudden quitting of Exercise and standing in the Air, the Circulation and Production of PM. still continuing some time, the over Quantity is retain'd. Safer to go into Water not too cold.

4 Reapers.

4. By particular Effluvia in the Air, from some unknown Cause. General Colds thro'out a Country. By being in a Coach close or small Room with a Person had a Cold.

5. By Relaxation of the Solids, from a Warm and moist Air, so that they are too weak to give due Motion to the Fluids.

Of Partial Colds, affecting parts of the Body.

Causes of Feverishness attending Colds.

Ill Consequences often attending Colds, as Pleurisies, Consumptions &c. Some never take Cold, some frequently. Causes of the Difference.

Present Remedies for a Cold, should be warming, diluting bracing.

Means of preventing Colds, Temperance, Choice of Meats and Drinks, warm Rooms, and Lodging and Clothing in Winter dry Air, Care to keep the Belly open, and frequent Discharge of Water, warm Bathing to cleanse the Skin. Rubbing after Sweat, especially in the Spring.

Difficulties that first put me on thinking on this Subject.

Query.

People get cold by less and not by more viz

by putting on a damp Shirt, on a dry Body	Yes
by putting a dry Shirt on a wet Body, tho' this wets the shirt ten times more	No
by Sitting in a Room, where the Floor has been new wash'd	Yes
by going into a River, and staying there an Hour (No Sheets so wet)	No

by Wetting the Feet only	Yes
by Wetting all the Clothes thro' to the Body, and wearing them a whole Day	No
by Sitting in a Room against a Crevice	Yes
by Sitting as long in the open Air	No

Few of these Causes take Place, if vessels are kept Empty.

Reapers in Pensilva.
  Drinking cold Water when they are hot
    If it makes them sweat, they are safe
    If not, they fall ill and some die
  People hot, should drink by Spoonfulls, the Reason.

Taking Cold. The Disorder only call'd so in English, and in no other Language.

American Indians, in the Woods, and the Whites in Imitation of them, lie with their Feet to the Fire in frosty Nights on the Ground, and take no Cold while they can keep their Feet warm.

Feet and Hands apt to be Cold in that Disorder, and why. Is it the Siziness, or the greater Evaporation?

Hottentots grease themselves, occasions other Evacuations more plentiful. Greasing keeps the body warm bad to hold Water too long. Parts colder when first uncloath'd than afterwards. Why?

It was a Disgrace among the ancient Persians to cough or spit. Probably as it argu'd Intemperance.

Vessels when too full leak. Quicksilver thro' Leather.

Thin Fluid leak'd evaporates. Corners of Eyes, &c. Sizy will not all evaporate. What's left corrupts. Hence Consumption. Hectic Fevers from Absorption of Putrid Pus. It ferments the Blood like Yeast.

People seldom get Cold at Sea tho' Sleep in Wet Clothes. Constant Exercise Moderate Living. Bad Cooks. Yet Air's very moist. Wet floors. Sea surrounding, &c.

Exercise cures a Cold. Bishop Williams riding seventy Miles, from London or Exeter to Salisbury.

Bark good for a Cold taken Early.

Particular Parts more accustomed to discharge the insulating persp[irable] Matter, as under the Arms in some, Feet in others, &c.

Exp[erimen]t of two Rasors [?].

Every Pain or Disorder now ascrib'd to a Cold.

It is the Covering Excuse of all Intemperance.

Numbers of People in a close Room and exercising there, fill the Air with putrid Particles.

People kill'd by House of Commons, breathing the Air thro' Holes in Cieling.

Think they get Cold by coming out of such hot Rooms they get them by being in.

Those that live in hotter Rooms, (Stoves) get no Colds.

Germans and all the northern People.

Alderman and Turtle.

People remark they were very well before a Cold and eat hearty. Wonder how they catch'd it.

Signs of Temperance

Mouth not clammy after Sleep.

Saliva thin and watery.

Eyelids not stuck together with hard Glue.

Voice clear.

No Flegm to raise.

Advice for Mode of general Temperance without appearing too singular. Supper not bad after preparatory light Dinner. May be rectify'd by slight Breakfast next Morning. He must be too full that one Excess will much disorder.

Time of Great Meal mended of late. After Dinner not fit for Business. Variation of Compass. One Hour in 20 Years.

Causes of Colds Primary and Secondary

People often don't get Cold where they think they do, but do where they think they do not. Colds of different kinds, putrid and plethoric.

People from the Country get Cold when they come to London and Why? Full Living with moist Air. London Air generally moist why? Much [putrid Air in] London. River, etc.

Cooks and Doctors should change Maxims.

Commonsense more common among the common Scotch.

1773

Those who dont compare cannot conceive the Difference between themselves and themselves in full [or spare] Living.

Wet Newspapers, why give Colds.

Old Librarys, and damp old Books.

Putrid Animal Matter, in Paper. Size.

Courts should not sit after Dinner. Juries fast, a good Inst[i-tutio]n.

Chess: Impatience of Deliberation because more difficult Writing. &c.

Most Follies arise from full Feeding. Reasons pro and con not all present. Temperate Nations wisest. Dining Entertainments bad. Rem[nant?]s of Barbarism. Expensive. Full feeding of Children stupifies. Fasting strengthens Reason rather than subdues Passion.

One Mark of Siziness in the Blood, and a Disposition to what is called a Cold, is a Froth standing on the Urine.

Scarce any Air abroad so unwholesome as Air in a c[lose] Room often breath'd.

Warm Air dissolves more Moisture than cold. In hot Countries Men wrap themselves in wet Sheets to sleep.

A general Service to redeem People from the slavish Fear of getting Cold, by showing them where the Danger is not and that where it is, 'tis in their Power to avoid it.

Surfeit, an Expression formerly us'd, now laid aside.

Costiveness occasioning Colds, how to be prevented.

Colds formerly called Rheums and Catarrhs.

Particular Foods said to engender Rheums.[6]

6. At this point WTF interpolated, in the first printing of the notes cited above, a passage that is not now among the original drafts; later editors followed suit. We assume that the passage is genuine and that the MS has since been lost. In WTF's text it reads:

"Quere. Is Mr. Wood more or less subject to catch cold since he betook himself to his low diet?

Answer (by Mr. Wood). He now finds himself *much more* healthy, and *much less* liable to catch cold. What few colds he now catches are so very slight that he is not sensible of them, but from the urine, which is then not so clear.

I caused the above question to be asked Mr. Wood, and obtained the answer. It is the Mr. Wood who lives upon a pound of flour in a pudding.

B. FRANKLIN"

About Mr. Wood we know little, and that indirectly. Although BF makes

Dampier, speaking of the Customs of the People at Mindanao, p. 330, says, "You see abundance of People in the River from Morning till Night washing their Bodies or Clothes. If they come into the River purposely to wash their Clothes, they strip and stand naked till they have done; then put them on and march out again."[7]

The Coats of the Vessel are a kind of Network, which contains the Fluids only when not so press'd as to enlarge the Pores of the Net, or when the Fluids are not so press'd as to break the Cohesion of the Globules or Particles, so as to make them small enough to come through. When the Vessels are full, occasioned by a Course of full Living, they labour in carrying on the Circulation; their Spring or Power of Contraction and Compressing the Fluids they contain, being overstrain'd is weaken'd, the Circulation proceeds more slowly, the Fluids thicken and become more gluey, both for want of due churning and because less Heat is produc'd in the Body. Such a Body requires more Aid of Clothing and Fire to preserve its warmth.

If a Person in that State of Body walks a Mile or two or uses any other Exercise that warms him, the Fluids are rarified by the Heat,

---

him sound like a character in Mother Goose, he was in fact a miller, in the service of the Earl of Essex, whom BF met through Sir John Pringle. Until middle age Wood indulged his gargantuan appetite to the ruin of his health; then his pudding diet worked a miraculous cure. See *The Annual Register . . .*, XV (1772), 94–6 of second pagination, and the letter, probably from Jean-Baptiste LeRoy, quoted by Gilbert Chinard in "The Strange Fortunes of Two Volumes of the 'Transactions,'" APS *Year Book*, 1944, pp. 84–5.

7. William Dampier, *A New Voyage round the World . . .* (4th ed.; 3 vols., London, 1699–1703), I, 330. All previous editors included at this point a paragraph, endorsed on the back "Catching Cold," that is among BF's notes but not in his hand; it is an extract from [John Gregory,] *A Comparative View of the State and Faculties of Man with Those of the Animal World* (3rd ed., London, 1766), pp. 51–2: "All that Class of Diseases which arise from catching cold, is found only among the civilized part of Mankind. An old Roman, or an Indian, in the Pursuit of war or hunting, would plunge into a River whilst in a profuse Sweat, without fear, and without danger. The greater care we take to prevent catching Cold by the various contrivances of modern Luxury, the more we become subject to it. We can guard against Cold only by rendering ourselves superiour to its Influence. There is a striking instance of this in the vigorous Constitutions of Children who go thinly clad in all Seasons and weathers."

distend the Vessels still more, and the thinner Parts of the Fluids in tender Places force out thro' the Pores of the Vessels in form of a gluey Water, viz. at the Eyes, within the Nose, and within the Lungs. This in moderate Exercise.

If the Exercise is increas'd it comes thro' every Pore in the Skin and is called Sweat.

The more volatile Parts of this extravasated Fluid, evaporate and flie off in the Air; the gluey Part remains thickens and hardens more or less as it becomes more or less dry; in the Nose and on the Lungs where Air is continually coming and going it soon becomes a Mucus, but can hardly grow dryer because surrounded with moist Parts, and supplyed with more Moisture. What ouzes out of the Corners of the Eye when shut, or in Sleep, hardens into what is called a kind of Gum, being in fact dry Glue.

This in a Morning almost stiks the Eyelids together.

With such Mucous Matter the Nose is some times almost stopped, and must be cleared by strong Blowing.

In the Windpipe and on the Lungs it gathers and is impacted, so as sometimes to induce a continual Coughing and Hawking to discharge it.

If not easily discharg'd but remaining long adhering to the Lungs, it corrupts and inflames the Parts it is in contact with [*in the margin:* Even behind the Ears and between other Parts of the Body so constantly in contact that the perspirable Matter, Sweat, &c. cannot easily escape from between them, the Skin is influenc'd by it, and a partial Putrefaction begins to take place], they corrupt and ulcerate. The Vessels being thus wounded discharge greater and continual Quantities. Hence Consumptions.

Part of the corrupted Matter absorb'd again by the Vessels and mix'd with the Blood occasions Hectic Fevers.

When the Body has sweated, not from a dissolution of Fluids, but from the Force above mention'd, as the Sweat dries off, some clammy Substance remains in the Pores, which closes many of them wholly or in part.

The subsequent Perspiration is hereby lessened.

The Perspirable Matter consists of Parts approaching to Putrefaction, and therefore destin'd by Nature to be thrown off, that living Bodies might not putrify, which otherwise from their Warmth and Moisture they would be apt to do. [*In the margin:*

The more Food eaten the more corrupted Particles to perspire.]
These corrupting Particles if continually thrown off, the remainder of the Body continues uncorrupt, or approaches no nearer to a State of Putrefaction. Just as in Boiling Water, no greater degree of Heat than the Boiling Heat can be requir'd; because the Particles that grow hotter, as fast as they become so, flie off in Vapour.

But if the Vapour could be retain'd Water might be made much hotter, perhaps red hot, as Oil may, which is not so subject to Evaporation. So if the Perspirable Matter is retain'd, it remixes with the Blood, and produces first a slight putrid Fever attending always what we call a Cold, and when retain'd in a great Degree more mischievous putrid Diseases.

In hot Countries, Exercise of Body with the Heat of the Climate create much of this putrid perspirable Matter, which ought to be discharg'd. A check in those Countries very pernicious. Putrid Malignant Violent Fevers and speedy Death the Consequence.

Its Discharge is also check'd another Way, besides that of closing the Pores, viz. by being in an Air already full of it, as in close Rooms containing great Numbers of People, Playhouses, Ball Rooms, &c.

For Air containing a Quantity of any kind of Vapour, becomes thereby less capable of imbibing more of that Vapour, and finally will take no more of it.

If the Air will not take it off from the Body it must remain in the Body; and the Perspiration is as effectually stopt and the perspirable Matter as certainly retain'd as if the Pores were all stopt.

A Lock of wet Wool contain'd in a Nutmeg Grater, may dry, parting with its Moisture thro' the Holes of the Grater. But if you stop all those Holes with Wax it will never dry.

Nor if expos'd to the open Air will it dry when the Air is as moist as itself. On the contrary if already dry, and expos'd to moist Air, it would acquire Moisture.

Thus People in Rooms heated by a Multitude of People, find their own Bodies heated, thence the quantity of perspirable Matter is increased that should be discharged but the Air not being changed grows so full of the same Matter, that it will receive no more. So the Body must retain it. The Consequence is, that next Day, perhaps sooner, a slight putrid Fever comes on, with all the Marks of what we call a Cold, and the Disorder is suppos'd to be got by coming out of a Warm Room, whereas it was really taken while in that Room.

Putrid Ferments beget their likes. Small Pox. Wet rotten Paper, containing corrupt Glue. The Cold Fever communicable by the Breath to others, &c.

Urine retain'd occasions Sneezing &c.

Coughing and Spitting continually Marks of Intemperance.

People eat much more than is necessary.

Proportionable Nourishment and strength is not drawn from great Eating.

The succeeding Meals force the preceding thro' half undigested.

Small Meals continue longer in the Body, and are more thoroughly digested.

The Vessels being roomy can bear and receive without Hurt an accidental Excess.

They can convert[?][8] more easily.

There is less Quantity of corrupting Particles produc'd.

Putrid Fish very bad.

Black [Hole in the Indies.]

From Anthony Todd

AL: American Philosophical Society

⟨1773? A note in the third person: thanks Franklin "for the Paragraphs which seem to be perfectly right"; the New York packet will sail, wind permitting, when tonight's mail reaches Falmouth.⟩

8. The word is almost illegible. Earlier editors read it as "concrete," which BF would have had to have written "concret"; but no meaning of that verb makes sense in context.

Appendix: The Hutchinson Letters

Printed in *The Representation of Governor Hutchinson and Others, Contained in Certain Letters Transmitted to England, and Afterwards Returned from Thence, and Laid before the General Assembly of the Massachusetts-Bay . . . (Boston, 1773).*

The letters from Hutchinson, Oliver, and others, when they were printed in Boston in June, 1773,[9] had such an impact on Franklin's career that we are publishing them as an appendix to this volume of his papers. They do not fall within our usual rubric, because they had no bearing on his actions or thoughts at the time they were written; for that reason we keep our annotation to a minimum.[10] But the letters have not

9. The steps by which the letters were publicized can be established partly from items in the press, partly from the Court records, legislative Council (State House, Boston), xxx, and the *Mass. House Jour.*, 1st session, May–June, 1773. On June 2, after the galleries had been cleared, Samuel Adams read the letters to the House of Representatives. On the 9th, when copies were being compared with the originals before the House, the galleries were opened and "a great concourse of people attended to hear their contents, who were filled with abhorrence of the measures proposed . . ." by the writers. *Mass. Spy*, June 10. On the 15th the House ordered the letters printed for the members, who had copies the next day. A title page was added, presumably at this time, and the pamphlet was published on the 17th. Simultaneously its contents began to be serialized in the *Spy*, but the committee of correspondence did not disseminate copies throughout the colony until the 22nd. *Ibid.*, June 17; Thomas R. Adams, *American Independence: the Growth of an Idea* . . . (Providence, R.I., 1965), pp. 72–3. This five-day interval is puzzling. Hutchinson's later account in his *History*, III, 287–94, although innocent of dates, seems to say that the day of publication was close to the 21st or 28th. The 21st would explain the delay, but only in the face of the evidence we have cited.

10. Most of the important subjects that the letters touch upon have been covered in previous volumes and may be found through the indices; we confine ourselves to those that have not been mentioned. A fully annotated edition is projected for the near future, as pamphlet no. 40 in the third volume of Bernard Bailyn's *Pamphlets of the American Revolution, 1750–1776*. For further information about the events that were the setting of the letters see John H. Cary, *Joseph Warren* . . . (Urbana, Ill., 1961); Charles M. Andrews, *The Boston Merchants and the Non-importation Movement* (New York, [1968]); Richard D. Brown, *Revolutionary Politics in Massachusetts* . . . (Cambridge, Mass., 1970); Hiller B. Zobel, *The Boston Massacre* (New York, [1970]); and Labaree, *Tea Party*.

been reprinted in more than a century,[1] and they played a key role in the last fifteen months of Franklin's British mission. They led directly to the petition from the Massachusetts House for the removal of the Governor and Lieutenant Governor; the petition, in turn, produced the hearing before the Privy Council in January, 1774, at which Solicitor General Wedderburn used the letters as text for a tongue-lashing that was the one great public humiliation of Franklin's life.[2] The chickens that had been dispatched to Boston under a pledge of secrecy came home to roost in London in a blaze of attention.

We have already discussed the mysterious circumstances in which Franklin acquired the correspondence, and said something about its contents.[3] Hutchinson and Oliver were important local officials at that time, it must be remembered, but did not become governor and lieutenant governor until 1771. Their conduct thereafter was irrelevant to the petition, which charged them solely with having written letters, in 1767–69, that "tended" to deter the King from hearing the grievances of his colony and to exacerbate friction between it and the mother country. In those years the violence and threats that were in the air of Boston gave many of its citizens good reason to be disturbed. The framework of society seemed to be dissolving, and conservatives naturally looked to Britain to restore order, by force if need be; where else could they look? The writers repeatedly made clear, however, that they did not blame the people at large, but only a few firebrands among them.

When Hutchinson and Oliver painted the situation in the darkest colors, as they certainly did, the reason may have been that they saw it that way; or they may have exaggerated for the purpose of provoking British intervention. They harp on five interrelated forms of intervention that they would clearly welcome: the customs commissioners require protection; something must be done to counteract the non-importation agreements; the governor should receive a salary from the

1. The letters appeared in 1773–4 in a number of editions, of which the most complete is that which we have used; for the others see Adams, *op. cit.,* pp. 72–5. The only later appearance of the correspondence, to the best of our knowledge, was in a reprint of a pamphlet published in 1774: [Israel Mauduit, ed.,] *Franklin before the Privy Council, White Hall Chapel, London, 1774, on Behalf of the Province of Massachusetts, to Advocate the Removal of Hutchinson and Oliver* (Philadelphia, 1859), pp. 17–51; another printing in 1860 has the same pagination. Mauduit defended the writers in a long critique of their letters.

2. See below, Jan. 29, 1774.

3. Above, XIX, 402–7.

crown to strengthen his hand; troops are needed to maintain order; constitutional changes may be advisable. Although few specific remedies are suggested, the call for strong measures is unmistakable.

No one with a traditional view of the constitution doubted that such measures were well within the government's legal authority. Franklin and his constituents, on the other hand, believed that asking for them was attempting to subvert the constitution, and the petition charged Hutchinson and Oliver, in effect, with having made that attempt.[4] Was the charge well founded? Franklin obviously thought so, or he would never have sent the letters in the first place; and their reception in Boston proves that many Americans agreed with him. Others did not, and in England the prevalent view was just the opposite: that the letters were private and innocuous, and that Franklin had played the part of a vicious trouble-maker. This clash of opinion has persisted for two centuries.[5] The letters are open to diverse interpretations, and still challenge readers to form their own.

Sir,   Boston, 18th June 1768.

As you allow me the honour of your correspondence, I may not omit acquainting you with so remarkable an event as the withdraw of the commissioners of the customs and most of the other officers under them from the town on board the Romney, with an intent to remove from thence to the castle.

In the evening of the 10th a sloop belonging to Mr. Hancock, a representative for Boston, and a wealthy merchant, of great influence over the populace, was seized by the collector and comptroller for a very notorious breach of the acts of trade, and, after seizure taken into custody by the officer of the Romney man of war, and remov'd under command of her guns. It is pretended that the removal and not the seizure incensed the people. It seems

4. For the difference in constitutional viewpoint reflected here see *idem.*, pp. 8–10.

5. Historians who take a kindly view of BF's role are Ellen E. Brennan, *Plural Office-Holding in Massachusetts, 1760–1780* . . . (Chapel Hill, N.C., 1945); John C. Miller, *Sam Adams: Pioneer in Propaganda* (Stanford, Cal., 1960); and Gerard B. Warden, *Boston, 1689–1776* (Boston, [1970]). For a sympathetic view of Oliver and Hutchinson see their biographies in *Sibley's Harvard Graduates*, VII, 383–413, and VIII, 149–217; James K. Hosmer, *The Life of Thomas Hutchinson* . . . (Boston, 1896); Gipson, *British Empire*, XII; Bernard Bailyn, *The Ordeal of Thomas Hutchinson* (Cambridge, Mass., 1974); and Carol Berkin, *Jonathan Sewall* . . . (New York and London, 1974).

not very material which it was. A mob was immediately rais'd, the Officers insulted, bruis'd and much hurt, and the windows of some of their houses broke; a boat belonging to the collector burnt in triumph, and many threats utter'd against the commissioners and their officers: no notice being taken of their extravagance in the time of it, nor any endeavours by any authority except the governor, the next day to discover and punish the offenders; and there being a rumour of a higher mob intended monday (the 13th) in the evening the commissioners, *four of them*, thought themselves altogether unsafe, being destitute of protection, and remov'd with their families to the Romney, and there remain and hold their board, and next week intend to do the same, and also open the custom-house at the castle. The governor press'd the council to assist him with their advice, but they declin'd and evaded calling it a brush or small disturbance by boys and negroes, not considering *how much it must be resented in England* that the officers of the crown should think themselves obliged to quit the place of their residence and go on board a King's ship for safety, and all the internal authority of the province take no notice of it. The town of Boston have had repeated meetings, and by their votes declared the commissioners and their officers a great grievance, and yesterday instructed their representatives to endeavor that enquiry should be made by the assembly whether any person by writing or in any other way had encouraged the sending troops here, there being some alarming reports that troops are expected, but have not taken any measures to discountenance the promoters of the late proceedings; but on the contrary appointed one or more of the actors or abettors on a committee appointed to wait on the governor, and to desire him to order the man of war out of the harbour.

Ignorant as they be, yet the heads of a Boston town-meeting influence all public measures.

It is not possible this anarchy should last always. Mr. Hallowell who will be the bearer of this tells me he has the honor of being personally known to you. I beg leave to refer you to him for a more full account. I am, with great esteem, Sir, your most humble and obedient servant,   THO. HUTCHINSON.

Sir,   Boston, August 1768.

It is very necessary other information should be had in England of the present state of the commissioners of the customs than what common fame will bring to you or what you will receive from most of the letters which go from hence, people in general being prejudiced by many false reports and misrepresentations concerning them. Seven eighths of the people of the country suppose the board itself to be unconstitutional and cannot be undeceived and brought to believe that a board has existed in England all this century, and that the board established here has no new powers given to it. Our incendiaries know it but they industriously and very wickedly publish the contrary. As much pains has been taken to prejudice the country against the persons of the commissioners and their characters have been misrepresented and cruelly treated especially since their confinement at the castle where they are not so likely to hear what is said of them and are not so able to confute it.

It is not pretended they need not to have withdrawn, that Mr. Williams had stood his ground without any injury although the mob beset his house, &c. There never was that spirit raised against the under officers as against the commissioners, I *mean four of them.*[6] They had a public affront offered them by the town of Boston who refused to give the use of their hall for a public dinner unless it was stipulated that the commissioners should not be invited. An affront of the same nature at the motion of Mr. Hancock was offered by a company of cadets. Soon after a vessel of Mr. Hancock's being seized the officers were mobb'd and the commissioners were informed they were threatned. I own I was in pain for them. I do not believe if the mob had seized them, there was any authority able and willing to have rescued them. After they had withdrawn the town signified to the governor by a message that it was expected or desired they should not return. It was then the general voice that it would not be safe for them to return. After all this the sons of liberty say they deserted or abdicated.

The other officers of the customs in general either did not leave

6. John Williams was the inspector general of customs; see above, XII, 193 n. The fifth commissioner was John Temple.

the town or soon returned to it. Some of them seem to be discontented with the commissioners. Great pains have been taken to increase the discontent. Their office by these means is rendered extremely burdensome. Every thing they do is found fault with, and yet no particular illegality or even irregularity mentioned. There is too much hauteur some of their officers say in the treatment they receive. They say they treat their officers as the commissioners treat their officers in England and require no greater deference. After all it is not the persons but the office of the commissioners which has raised this spirit, and the distinction made between the commissioners is because it has been given out that four of them were in favor of the new establishment and the *fifth was not.* If Mr. Hallowell arrived safe he can inform you many circumstances relative to this distinction which I very willingly excuse myself from mentioning.

I know of no burden brought upon the fair trader by the new establishment. The illicit trader finds the risque greater than it used to be, especially in the port where the board is constantly held. Another circumstance which increases the prejudice is this; the new duties happened to take place just about the time the commissioners arrived. People have absurdly connected the duties and board of commissioners, and suppose we should have had no additional duties if there had been no board to have the charge of collecting them. With all the aid you can give to the officers of the crown they will have enough to do to maintain the authority of government and to carry the laws into execution. If they are discountenanced, neglected or fail of support from you, they must submit to every thing the present opposers of government think fit to require of them.

There is no office under greater discouragements than that of the commissioners. Some of my friends recommended me to the ministry. I think myself very happy that I am not one. Indeed it would have been incompatible with my post as chief justice, and I must have declined it, and I should do it although no greater salary had been affixed to the chief justices place than the small pittance allowed by the province.

From my acquaintance with the commissioners I have conceived a personal esteem for them, but my chief inducement to make this representation to you is in regard to the public interest which I am sure will suffer if the opposition carry their point against them. I am with very great esteem, Sir, your most obedient humble servant,   THO. HUTCHINSON.

August 10. Yesterday at a meeting of the merchants it was agreed by all present to give no more orders for goods from England, nor receive any on commission until the late acts are repealed. And it is said all except sixteen in the town have subscribed an engagement of that tenor. I hope the subscription will be printed that I may transmit it to you.

Dear Sir,   Boston, 4th October 1768.
     I was absent upon one of our circuits when Mr. Byles arrived. Since my return I have received from him your obliging letter of 31st July. I never dared to think what the resentment of the nation would be upon Hallowell's arrival. It is not strange that measures should be immediately taken to reduce the colonies to their former state of government and order, but that the national funds should be effected by it is to me a little mysterious and surprizing. Principles of government absurd enough, spread thro' all the colonies; but I cannot think that in any colony, people of any consideration have ever been so mad as to think of a revolt. Many of the common people have been in a frenzy, and talk'd of dying in defence of their liberties, and have spoke and printed what is highly criminal, and too many of rank above the vulgar, and some *in public posts* have countenanced and encouraged them untill they increased so much in their numbers and in their opinion of their importance as to submit to government no further than they thought proper. The legislative powers have been influenced by them, and the executive powers intirely lost their force. There has been continual danger of mobs and insurrections, but they would have spent all their force within ourselves, the officers of the Crown and some of the few friends who dared to stand by them possibly might have been knock'd in the head, and some such fatal event would probably have brought the people to their senses. For four or five weeks past the distemper has been growing, and I confess I have not been without some apprehensions for myself, but my friends have had more for me, and I have had

repeated and frequent notices from them from different quarters, *one of the last I will inclose to you.*[7] In this state of things there was no security but quitting my posts, which nothing but the last extremity would justify. As chief justice for two years after our first disorders I kept the grand juries tollerably well to their duty. The last spring there had been several riots, and a most infamous libel had been published in one of the papers, which I enlarged upon, and the grand jury had determined to make presentments, but the attorney-general not attending them the first day, Otis and his creatures who were alarmed and frightned exerted themselves the next day and prevailed upon so many of the jury to change their voices, that there was not a sufficient number left to find a bill.[8] They have been ever since more enraged against me than ever. At the desire of the governor I committed to writing the charge while it lay in my memory, and as I have no further use for it I will inclose it as it may give you some idea of our judicatories.

Whilst we were in this state, news came of two regiments being ordered from Halifax, and soon after two more from Ireland. The minds of people were more and more agitated, broad hints were given that the troops should never land, a barrel of tar was placed upon the beacon, in the night to be fired to bring in the country when the troops appeared, and all the authority of the government was not strong enough to remove it. The town of Boston met and passed a number of weak but very criminal votes; and as the governor declined calling an assembly they sent circular letters to all the towns and districts to send a person each that there might be a general consultation at so extraordinary a crisis. They met and spent a week, made themselves ridiculous, and then dissolv'd themselves, after a message or two to the governor which he refused to receive; a petition to the King which I dare say *their agents* will never be allow'd to present, and a result which they have published ill-natured and impotent.

In this confusion the troops from Halifax arrived. I never was much afraid of the people's taking arms, but I was apprehensive

7. [*Note in the pamphlet:*] See the following Letter.
8. The libel was primarily an attack on Gov. Bernard; see Bailyn, *Ordeal of Thomas Hutchinson,* pp. 119–20.

of violence from the mob, it being their last chance before the troops could land. As the prospect of revenge became more certain their courage abated in proportion. Two regiments are landed, but a new grievance is now rais'd. The troops are by act of parliament to be quartered no where else but in the barracks until they are full. There are barracks enough at the castle to hold both regiments. It is therefore against the act to bring any of them into town. This was started by the council in their answer to the governor, which to make themselves popular, they in an unprecedented way published and have alarmed all the province; for although none but the most contracted minds could put such a construction upon the act, yet after this declaration of the council nine tenths of the people suppose it just. I wish the act had been better express'd, but it is absurd to suppose the parliament intended to take from the King the direction of his forces by confining them to a place where any of the colonies might think fit to build barracks. It is besides ungrateful, for it is known to many that this provision was brought into the bill after it had been framed without it, from meer favor to the colonies. I hear the commander in chief has provided barracks or quarters, but a doubt still remains with some of the council, whether they are to furnish the articles required, unless the men are in the province barracks, and they are to determine upon it to day.

The government has been so long in the hands of the populace that it must come out of them by degrees, at least it will be a work of time to bring the people back to just notions of the nature of government.

Mr. Pepperrell a young gentleman of good character, and grandson and principal heir to the late Sir William Pepperrell being bound to London, I shall deliver this letter to him, as it will be too bulky for postage, and desire him to wait upon you with it. I am with very great esteem, Sir, your most humble and most obedient servant,   THO. HUTCHINSON.

APPENDIX

Sir,   Sept. 14. 1768.[9]
The great esteem I have for you in every point of light, perhaps
renders my fears and doubts for the safety of your person greater
than they ought to be; however if that is an error it certainly
results from true friendship, naturally jealous. Last night I was
informed by a gentleman of my acquaintance, who had his information from one intimate with and knowing to the infernal
purposes of the sons of liberty as they falsely stile themselves, that
he verily believ'd, from the terrible threats and menaces by those
catalines against you, that your life is greatly in danger. This
informant I know is under obligations to you and is a man of
veracity. He express'd himself with concern for you, and the
gentleman acquainting me with this horrid circumstance, assured
me he was very uneasy till you had notice. I should have done
myself the honor of waiting on you but am necessarily prevented.
The duty I owed to you as a friend and to the publick as a member
of society, would not suffer me to rest till I had put your honor
upon your guard; for tho' this may be a false alarm, nothing
would have given me greater pain, if any accident had happen'd,
and I had been silent. If possible I will see you to morrow, and let
you know further into this black affair. And am with the sincerest
friendship and respect, your honor's most obedient, and most
humble servant.   ROB. AUCHMUTY.

To the hon'ble Thomas Hutchinson,

Dear Sir,   Boston, 10th December 1768.
I am just now informed that a number of the council, perhaps 8
or 10 who live in and near this town, have met together and agreed
upon a long address or petition to parliament,[1] and that it will be
sent by this ship to Mr. Bollan to be presented. Mr. Danforth who
is president of the council told the governor upon enquiry, that it
was sent to him to sign, and he supposed the rest of the council
who had met together would sign after him in order, but he had

9. Enclosed with the preceding letter. For the writer, Robert Auchmuty
(d. 1788), see the *DAB*. He was a prominent Boston lawyer and judge of the
Vice-Admiralty Court, and subsequently a member of the *Gaspee* commission.
1. Against the Townshend Acts.

548

since found that they had wrote over his name *by order of council*, which makes it appear to be an act of council. This may be a low piece of cunning in him, but be it as it may, it's proper it should be known that the whole is no more than the doings of a part of the council only, although even that is not very material, since, if they had all been present without the governor's summons the meeting would have been irregular and unconstitutional, and ought to be discountenanced and censured. I suppose there is no instance of the privy council's meeting and doing business without the king's presence or special direction, except in committees upon such business as by his majesty's order has been referr'd to them by an act of council, and I have known no instance here without the governor until within three or four months past.

I thought it very necessary the circumstances of this proceeding should be known, tho' if there be no necessity for it, I think it would be best it should not be known that the intelligence comes from me. I am with very great regard, Sir, your most humble and most obedient Servant,   THO. HUTCHINSON.

Dear Sir,   Boston, 20th January 1769.

You have laid me under very great obligations by the very clear and full account of proceedings in parliament, which I received from you by Capt. Scott. You have also done much service to the people of the province. For a day or two after the ship arrived, the enemies of government gave out that their friends in parliament were increasing, and all things would be soon on the old footing; in other words that all acts reposing duties would be repealed, the commissioners board dissolved, the customs put on the old footing, and *illicit* trade be carried on with little or no hazard. It was very fortunate that I had it in my power to prevent such a false representation from spreading through the province. I have been very cautious of using your name, but I have been very free in publishing abroad the substance of your letter, and declaring that I had my intelligence from the best authority, and have in a great measure defeated the ill design in raising and attempting to spread so groundless a report. What marks of resentment the parliament will show, whether they will be upon the province in general or particular persons, is extremely uncertain, but that they will be placed somewere is most certain, and I add, because *I think it ought to be so* that those who have been most steady in preserving the constitution and opposing the licenciousness of such as call themselves sons of liberty will certainly meet with favor and encouragement.

This is most certainly a crisis. I really wish that there may not have been the least degree of severity beyond what is absolutely necessary to maintain, I think I may say to you the *dependance* which a colony ought to have upon the parent State; but if no measures shall have been taken to secure this dependance, or nothing more than some declaratory acts or resolves, *it is all over with us*. The friends of government will be utterly disheartned, and the friends of anarchy will be afraid of nothing be it ever so extravagant.

The last vessel from London had a quick passage. We expect to be in suspense for the three or four next weeks and then to hear our fate. I never think of the measures necessary for the peace and good order of the colonies without pain. There must be an abridgment of what are called English liberties. I relieve myself by considering that in a remove from the state of nature to the most perfect state of government there must be a great restraint of natural liberty. I doubt whether it is possible to project a system of government in which a colony 3000 miles distant from the parent state shall enjoy all the liberty of the parent state. I am certain I have never yet see the projection. I wish the good of the colony when I wish to see some further restraint of liberty rather than the connexion with the parent state should be broken; for I am sure such a breach must prove the ruin of the colony. Pardon me this excursion, it really proceeds from the state of mind into which our perplexed affairs often throw me. I have the honor to be with very great esteem, Sir, your most humble and most obedient servant,

THO. HUTCHINSON.

Dear Sir, Boston, 20th October, 1769.

I thank you for your last favor of July 18th. I fancy in my last to you about two months ago I have answered the greatest part of it.

My opinion upon the combination of the merchants, I gave you very fully. How long they will be able to continue them if parliament should not interpose is uncertain. In most articles they may another year, and you run the risque of their substituting when they are put to their shifts something of their own in the place of what they used to have from you, and which they will never return to you for. But it is not possible that provision for dissolving these combinations and subjecting all who do not renounce them to penalties adequate to the offence should not be made the first week the parliament meets. Certainly all parties will unite in so extraordinary case if they never do in any other. So much has been said upon the repeal of the duties laid by the last act, that it will render it very difficult to keep people's minds quiet if that should be refused them. They deserve punishment you will say, but laying or continuing taxes upon all cannot be thought equal, seeing many will be punished who are not offenders. *Penalties of another kind seem better adapted.*

I have been tolerably treated since the governor's departure, no other charge being made against me in our scandalous newspapers except my bad principles in matters of government, and this charge has had little effect, and a great many friends promise me support.

I must beg the favor of you to keep secret every thing I write, until we are in a more settled state, for the party here either by their *agent* or by some of their emissaries in London, have sent them every report or rumour of the contents of letters wrote from hence.[2] I hope we shall see better times both here and in England. I am, with great esteem, Sir, your most obedient servant,

THO. HUTCHINSON.

Sir, Boston, 7th May 1767.
I am indebted to you for the obliging manner in which you receiv'd my recommendation of my good friend Mr. Paxton, as well as for the account you are pleased to send me of the situation of affairs in the mother country.

2. Nervousness about this danger at this time was understandable. William Bollan, the Council's agent, had recently procured some letters of Gov. Bernard and sent them to Boston; see above, XVI, 129 n.

I am very sorry that the colonies give you so much employment, and it is impossible to say how long it will be before things settle into quiet among us. We have some here who have been so busy in fomenting the late disturbances, that they may now think it needful for their own security to keep up the spirit. They have plumed themselves much upon the victory they have gained, and the support they have since met with; nor could any thing better shew what they would still be at, than the manner in which by their own account published in the news-papers last August they celebrated the 14th of that month, as the first anniversary commemoration of what they had done at the tree of liberty on that day the year before.[3] Here a number of respectable gentlemen as they inform us now met, and among other toasts drank general Paoli, and the spark of liberty kindled in Spain. I am now speaking of a few individuals only, the body of the people are well disposed, yet when you come to see the journal of the house of representatives the last session, I fear you will think that the same spirit has seized our public counsels. I can however fairly say thus much in behalf of the government, that the last house was packed by means of a public proscription just before the election, of the greatest part of those who had appeared in the preceding session in the support of government: their names were published in an inflammatory news-paper, and their constituents made to believe they were about to sell them for slaves. Writs are now out for a new assembly, but I cannot answer for the choice: I hope however that the people in general are in a better temper; yet the moderate men have been so browbeaten in the house, and found themselves so insignificant there the last year, that some of them will voluntary decline coming again. I thinks this looks too much like a despair of the common-wealth, and cannot be justified on patriotic principles.

The election of counsellors was carried the last year as might have been expected from such an house. The officers of the crown and the judges of the superior court were excluded. And I hear that it is the design of some who expect to be returned members

3. The celebration was the first anniversary of the riot on Aug. 14, 1765. "What they had done at the tree of liberty" was destroy Andrew Oliver's office and attack his house. See Edmund S. and Helen M. Morgan, *The Stamp Act Crisis* . . . (Chapel Hill, N.C., [1953]), pp. 123–4.

of the house this year to make sure work at the ensuing election of counsellors, by excluding, if they can, the gentlemen of the council (who by charter remain such 'till others are chosen in their room) from any share in the choice, tho' they have always had their voice in it hitherto from the first arrival of the charter. If the house do this, they will have it in their power to model the council as they please, and throw all the powers of government into the hands of the people, unless the governor should again exert his negative as he did the last year.

You have doubtless seen some of the curious messages from the late house to the governor, and can't but have observed with how little decency they have attacked both the governor and the lieutenant governor. They have also in effect forced the council to declare themselves parties in the quarrel they had against the latter in a matter of mere indifference. In their message to the governor of the 31st of January they have explicitly charged the lieutenant governor (a gentleman to whom they are more indebted than to any one man in the government) with "ambition and lust of power", merely for paying a compliment to the governor agreeable to ancient usage, by attending him to court and being present in the council-chamber when he made his speech at the opening of the session; at which time they go on to say, "none but the general court and their servants are intended to be present", still holding out to the people the servants of the crown as objects of insignificance, ranking the secretary with their door-keeper, as servants of the assembly; for the secretary with his clerks and the door-keeper are the only persons present with the assembly on these occasions.

The officers of the crown being thus lessen'd in the eyes of the people, takes off their weight and influence, and the balance will of course turn in favor of the people, and what makes them still more insignificant is their dependance on the people for a necessary support: If something were left to the goodwill of the people, yet nature should be sure of a support. The governor's salary has for about 35 years past been pretty well understood to be a thousand pound a year sterling. When this sum was first agreed to, it was very well; but an increase of wealth since has brought along with it an increase of luxury, so that what was sufficient to keep up a proper distinction and support the dignity of a governor then, may well be supposed to be insufficient for the purpose now. The lieutenant governor has no appointments as such: the captaincy of Castle-William which may be worth £120 sterling a year is looked upon indeed as an appendage to his commission, and the late lieutenant governor enjoyed no other appointment: he lived a retired life upon his own estate in the country, and was easy. The present lieutenant governor indeed has other appointments, but the people are quarrelling with him for it, and will not suffer him to be easy unless he will retire also.

The secretary may have something more than £200 a year sterling, but has for the two last years been allowed £60 lawful money a year less than had been usual for divers years preceding, tho' he had convinced the house by their committee that without this deduction he would have had no more than £250 sterling per annum in fees, perquisites and salary altogether, which is not the one half of his annual expence.

The crown did by charter reserve to itself the appointment of a governor, lieutenant governor and secretary: the design of this was without doubt to maintain some kind of balance between the powers of the crown and of the people; but if officers are not in some measure independent of the people (for it is difficult to serve two masters) they will sometimes have a hard struggle between duty to the crown and a regard to self, which must be a very disagreeable situation to them, as well as a weakening to the authority of government. The officers of the crown are very few and are therefore the more easily provided for without burdening the people: *and such provision I look upon as necessary to the restoration and support of the King's authority.*

But it may be said how can any new measures be taken without raising new disturbances? The manufacturers in England will rise again and defeat the measures of government. This game 'tis true has been played once and succeeded, and it has been asserted here, that it is in the power of the colonies at any time to raise a rebellion in England by refusing to send for their manufactures. For my own part I do not believe this. The merchants in England, and I don't know but those in London and Bristol only, might always govern in this matter and quiet the manufacturer. The merchant's view is always to his own interest. As the trade is now managed, the dealer here sends to the merchant in England for his goods;

upon these goods the English merchant puts a profit of 10 or more probably of 15 per cent when he sends them to his employer in America. The merchant is so jealous of foregoing this profit, that an American trader cannot well purchase the goods he wants of the manufacturer; for should the merchant know that the manufacturer had supplied an American, he would take off no more of his wares. The merchants therefore having this profit in view will by one means or other secure it. They know the goods which the American market demands, and may therefore safely take them off from the manufacturer, tho' they should have no orders for shipping them this year or perhaps the next; and I dare say, it would not be longer before the Americans would clamour for a supply of goods from England, for it is vain to think they can supply themselves. The merchant might then put an advanced price upon his goods, and possibly be able to make his own terms; or if it should be thought the goods would not bear an advanced price to indemnify him, it might be worth while for the government to agree with the merchants before hand to allow them a premium equivalent to the advance of their stock, and *then the game would be over.*

I have wrote with freedom in confidence of my name's not being used on the occasion. For though I have wrote nothing but what in my conscience I think an American may upon just principles advance, and what a servant of the crown ought upon all proper occasions to suggest, yet the many prejudices I have to combat with may render it unfit it should be made public.

I communicated to governor Bernard what you mentioned concerning him, who desires me to present you his compliments, and let you know that he is obliged to you for the expressions of your regard for his injured character. I am with great respect, Sir, your most obedient and most humble servant,   ANDW. Oliver.

I ask your acceptance of a journal of the last session which is put up in a box directed to the secretary of the board of trade.

Sir,   Boston, 11 May, 1768.
I am this moment favored with your very obliging letter by Capt. Jarvis of the 2d March, which I have but just time to

acknowledge, as this is the day given out for the ship to sail. I wrote you the 23d of February in reply to your letter of the 28th December, that of the 12th February which you refer to in this of the 2d of March is not yet come to hand. You lay me, sir, under the greatest obligations as well for the interesting account of public affairs which you are from time to time pleased to transmit me, as for your steady attention to my private concerns. I shall always have the most grateful sense of Mr. Grenville's intentions of favor also, whether I ever reap any benefit from them or not. Without a proper support afforded to the king's officers, the respect due to government will of course fail; yet I cannot say whether under the present circumstances, and considering the temper the people are now in, an additional provision for me would be of real benefit to me personally or not. It has been given out that no person who receives a stipend from the government at home, shall live in the country. Government here wants some *effectual* support: No sooner was it known that the lieut. governor had a provision of £200 a year made for him out of the revenue, than he was advised in the Boston Gazette to resign all pretensions to a seat in council, either with or without a voice. The temper of the people may be surely learnt from that infamous paper; it is the very thing that forms their temper; for if they are not in the temper of the writer at the time of the publication, yet it is looked upon as the ORACLE, and they soon bring their temper to it. Some of the latest of them are very expressive, I will not trouble you with sending them, as I imagine they somehow or other find their way to you: But I cannot but apprehend from these papers and from hints that are thrown out, that if the petition of the House to his Majesty and their letters to divers noble Lords should fail of success, some people will be mad enough to go to extremities. The commissioners of the customs have already been openly affronted, the governor's company of Cadets have come to a resolution not to wait on him (as usual) on the day of General Election the 25th instant if those gentlemen are of the company. And the Town of Boston have passed a Vote that Faneuil-Hall (in which the governor and his company usually dine on that day) shall not be opened to him if the commissioners are invited to dine with him. A list of counsellors has within a few days past been printed and dispersed by way of sneer on Lord

Shelburne's letter,[4] made up of king's officers; which list, the writer says, if adopted at the next general election may take away all grounds of complaint, and may possibly prove a healing and very salutary measure. The lieutenant governor is at the head of this list, they have done me the honor to put me next, the commissioners of the customs are all in the list except *Mr. Temple*, and to compleat the list, they have added some of the waiters. I never thought 'till very lately that they acted upon any *settled plan*, nor do I now think they have 'till of late; a few, a very few, among us have planned the present measures, and the government has been too weak to subdue their turbulent spirits. Our situation is not rightly known; but it is a matter worthy of the most serious attention. I am with the greatest respect, Sir, your most obedient and most humble Servant, ANDW. OLIVER.

I shall take proper care to forward your Letter to Mr. Ingersol. He had received your last.

Sir,   Boston, 13th February, 1769.

I have your very obliging favor of the 4th of October. I find myself constrained as well by this letter as by my son and daughter Spooner's letters since, to render you my most sincere thanks for the very polite notice you have taken of them; and I pray my most respectful compliments to the good lady your mother, whose friendly reception of them at Nonsuch has, I find engaged the warmest esteem and respect. He hath wrote us that he had a prospect of succeeding in the business he went upon; but the last letter we had was from her of the 23d of November, acquainting us that he had been very ill, but was getting better.[5] She writes as a person overcome with a sense of the kindness they

4. In 1767 Hutchinson had been attacked in the House and excluded from sitting *ex officio* on the Council; Shelburne's letter praised him and criticized the action of the House. See Hutchinson, *History*, III, 127–8, 133–4.

5. In 1762 Margaret Oliver had married John Spooner, a young Boston merchant but already a widower. *Sibley's Harvard Graduates*, VII, 385, 392; Thomas Spooner, *Records of William Spooner ... and His Descendants* (Cincinnati, 1883), p. 346 n. The husband apparently did not recover from his illness, and died before the year was out.

had met with, in a place where they were strangers, on this trying occasion.

You have heard of the arrival of the King's troops, the quiet reception they met with among us was not at all surprizing to me. I am sorry there was any occasion for sending them. From the address of the gentlemen of the council to General Gage, it might be supposed there was none. I have seen a letter from our friend Ingersoll with this paraphrase upon it. "We hope that your Excellency observing with your own eyes *now* the troops are among us, our peaceable and quiet behavior, will be convinced that wicked G——r B——d told a fib in saying, We were not so before they came." I have given you the sense of a stranger on a single paragraph of this address, because I suspected my own opinion of it, 'till I found it thus confirm'd. If you have the newspapers containing the address, your own good sense will lead you to make some other remarks upon it, as well as to trace the influence under which it seems to have been penned. The disturbers of our peace take great advantage of such aids from people in office and power. The lieutenant governor has communicated to me your letter containing an account of the debates in parliament on the first day of the session: We soon expect their decision on American affairs, some I doubt not with fear and trembling. Yet I have very lately had occasion to know, that be the determination of parliament what it will, it is the determination of some to agree to no terms that shall remove us from our old foundation. This confirms me in an opinion that I have taken up a long time since, that if there be no way to take off the original incendiaries, they will continue to instill their poison into the minds of the people through the vehicle of the BOSTON GAZETTE.

In your letter to the lieutenant governor you observe upon two defects in our constitution, the popular election of the Council, and the return of Juries by the Towns. The first of these arises from the Charter itself; the latter from our provincial Laws. The method of appointing our Grand Juries lies open to management. Whoever pleases, nominates them at our town-meeting; by this means one who was suppos'd to be a principal in the Riots of the 10th of June last, was upon that Jury whose business it was to inquire into them: But the provincial legislature hath made sufficient provision for the return of Petit Juries by their act of

23d Geo. 2d, which requires the several towns to take lists of all persons liable by law to serve, and forming them into two classes, put their names written on separate papers into two different boxes, one for the superior court and the other for the inferior: And when veniries are issued, the number therein required are to be drawn out in open town-meeting, no person to serve oftner than once in three years. The method of appointing Grand Juries appears indeed defective; but if the other is not it may be imputed to the times rather than to the defect of the laws, that neither the Grand Juries nor the Petit Juries have of late answered the expectations of government.

As to the appointment of the council, I am of opinion that neither the popular elections in this province, nor their appointment in what are called the royal governments by the King's mandamus, are free from exceptions, especially if the council as a legislative body is intended to answer the idea of the house of lords in the British legislature. There they are suppos'd to be a free and independent body, and on their being such the strength and firmness of the constitution does very much depend: whereas the election or appointment of the councils in the manner before mentioned renders them altogether dependent on their constituents. The King is the fountain of honour, and as such the peers of the realm derive their honours from him; but then they hold them by a surer tenure than the provincial counsellors who are appointed by mandamus. On the other hand, our popular elections very often expose them to contempt; for nothing is more common than for the representatives, when they find the council a little untractable at the close of the year, to remind them that May is at hand.

It may be accounted by the colonies as dangerous to admit of any alterations in their charters, as it is by the governors in the church to make any in the establishment; yet to make the resemblance as near as may be to the British parliament, some alteration is necessary. It is not requisite that I know of, that a counsellor shou'd be a freeholder; his residence according to the charter is a sufficient qualification; for that provides only, that he be an inhabitant of or proprietor of lands within the district for which he is chosen: Whereas the peers of the realm sit in the house of lords, as I take it, in virtue of their baronies. If there should be a reform of any of the colony charters with a view to keep up the resemblance of the three estates in England, the legislative council shou'd consist of men of landed estates; but as our landed estates here are small at present, the yearly value of £100 sterling per annum might in some of them at least be a sufficient qualification. As our estates are partable after the decease of the proprietor, the honour could not be continued in families as in England: it might however be continued in the appointee *quom diu bene se gesserit*, and proof be required of some mal-practice before a suspicion or removal. Bankruptcy also might be another ground for removal. A small legislative council might answer the purposes of government; but it might tend to weaken that levelling principle, which is cherish'd by the present popular constitution, to have an honorary order establish'd, out of which the council shou'd be appointed. There is no way now to put a man of fortune above the common level, and exempt him from being chosen by the people into the lower offices, but his being appointed a justice of the peace; this is frequently done when there is no kind of expectation of his undertaking the trust, and has its inconveniences. For remedy hereof it might be expedient to have an order of Patricians or Esquires instituted, to be all men of fortune or good landed estates, and appointed by the governor with the advice of council, and enroll'd in the secretary's office, who shou'd be exempted from the lower offices in government as the justices now are; and to have the legislative council (*which in the first instance might be nominated by the Crown*) from time to time fill'd up as vacancies happen out of this order of men, who, if the order consisted only of men of landed estates, might elect, as the Scottish peers do, only reserving to the King's governor a negative on such choice. The King in this case wou'd be still acknowledged as the fountain of honour, as having in the first instance the appointment of the persons enroll'd, out of whom the council are to be chosen, and finally having a negative on the choice. Or, the King might have the immediate appointment by mandamus as at present in the royal governments. As the gentlemen of the council would rank above the body from which they are taken, they might bear a title one degree above that of esquire. Besides this legislative council, a privy council might be establish'd, to consist of some or all of those persons who constitute the legislative council, and of other persons members of the house of representatives or otherwise of note and distinction; which wou'd extend the honours of government, and afford opportunity of distinguishing men of character and reputation, the expectation of which wou'd make government more respectable.

I wou'd not trouble you with these reveries of mine, were I not assured of your readiness to forgive the communication, although you could apply it to no good purpose.

Mr. Spooner sent me a pamphlet under a blank cover, intituled, *"the state of the nation"*.[6] I run over it by myself before I had heard any one mention it, and tho't I cou'd evidently mark the sentiments of some of my friends. By what I have since heard and seen, it looks as if I was not mistaken. Your right honorable friend I trust will not be offended if I call him mine, I am sure you will not when I term you such, I have settled it for a long time in my own mind that without a representation in the supreme legislature, there cannot be that union between the head and the members as to produce a healthful constitution of the whole body. I have doubted whether this union could be perfected by the first experiment. The plan here exhibited seems to be formed in generous and moderate principles, and bids the fairest of any I have yet seen to be adopted. Such a great design may as in painting require frequent touching before it becomes a piece highly finish'd; and after all may require the miliorating hand of time to make it please universally. Thus the British constitution consider'd as without the colonies attain'd it's glory. The book I had sent me is in such request, that I have not been able to keep it long enough by me, to consider it in all its parts. I wish to hear how it is receiv'd in the house of commons. I find by the publications both of governor Pownall and Mr. Bollan, that they each of them adopt the idea of an union and representation, and I think it must more and more prevail. The argument against it from local inconveniency, must as it appears to me be more than balanc'd by greater inconveniencies on the other side the question, the great difficulty will be in the terms of union. I add no more, as I fear I have already trespass'd much on your time and patience, but that I am, Sir, your obliged and most obedient humble Servant,

ANDW. OLIVER.

6. [William Knox,] *The Present State of the Nation: Particularly with Respect to Its Trade, Finances, &c.* . . . . (London, 1768).

Sir,   New-York, 12th August, 1769.

I have been in this city for some time past executing (with others) his Majesty's commission for settling the boundary between this province and that of New-Jersey. I left Boston the 11th July, since which my advices from London have come to me very imperfect; but as my friend Mr. Thompson writes me that he had drawn up my case and with your approbation laid it before the D. of Grafton, I think it needful once more to mention this business to you.

There was a time when I thought the authority of government might have been easily restored; but while it's friends and the officers of the crown are left to an abject dependance on these very people who are *undermining it's authority;* and while these are suffered not only to go unpunished, but on the contrary meet with all kind of support and encouragement, it cannot be expected that you will ever again recover that respect which the colonies had been wont to pay the parent state. Government at home will deceive itself, if it imagines that the taking off the duty on glass, paper and painter's colors will work a reconciliation, and nothing more than this, as I can learn, is proposed in Ld. H's late circular letter. It is the principle that is now disputed; the combination against importation extends to tea, although it comes cheaper than ever, as well as to the other forementioned articles. In Virginia it is extended lately to wines; and I have heard one of the first leaders in these measures in Boston say, that we should never be upon a proper footing 'till all the revenue acts from the 15th Charles 2d were repealed. Our assembly in the Massachusetts may have been more illiberal than others in their public messages and resolves; yet we have some people among us still who dare to speak in favor of government: But here I do not find so much as one, unless it be some of the King's servants; and yet my business here leads me to associate with the best. They universally approve of the combination against importing of goods from Great-Britain, unless the revenue acts are repealed, which appears to me little less than assuming a negative on all acts of parliament which they do not like! They say expressly, we are bound by none made since our emigration, but such as our own convenience we choose to submit to; such for instance as that for establishing a post-office. The Bill of Rights and the Habeas Corpus Acts, they say are only declaratory of the common law which we brought with us.

Under such circumstance as these, why should I wish to expose myself to popular resentment? Were I to receive any thing out of the revenue, I must expect to be abused for it. Nor do I find that our chief justice has received the £200 granted him for that service; and yet the assembly have this year withheld his usual grant, most probably because he has such a warrant from the crown.

With regard to my negociations with Mr. Rogers, I did in conformity to your opinion make an apology to Mr. Secretary Pownall for mentioning it, and there submitted it. I hear it has been since talk'd of; but unless I could be assured in one shape or other of £300 per annum, with the other office, I would not chuse to quit what I have. I have no ambition to be distinguished, if I am only to be held up as a mark of popular envy or resentment. I was in hopes before now through the intervention of your good offices to have received some mark of favor from your good friend; but the time is not yet come to expect it through that channel! I will however rely on your friendship, whenever you can with propriety appear in forwarding my interest, or preventing any thing that may prove injurious to it.

If Mr. R. has interest enough to obtain the secretary's place, I shall upon receiving proper security think myself in honour bound to second his views, though I have none at present from him but a conditional note he formerly wrote me. If he is not like to succeed, and my son Daniel could have my place, I would be content unless affairs take a different turn to resign in his favor, whether administration should think proper to make any further provision for me or not. And yet I never thought of withdrawing myself from the service, while there appeared to me any prospect of my being able to promote it.

If I have wrote with freedom, I consider I am writing to a friend, and that I am perfectly safe in opening myself to you. I am, with great respect, Sir, your most obedient, humble servant,

ANDW. OLIVER.

Dear Sir,　　　　　On board his Majesty's Ship Romney, Boston
Harbour, 20th June, 68.

The commissioners of the customs have met with every insult since their arrival at Boston, and at last have been obliged to seek protection on board his Majesty's ship Romney: Mr. Hallowell, the comptroller of the customs who will have the honor to deliver you this Letter, will inform you of many particulars; he is sent by the Board with their letters to Government. Unless we have immediately two or three regiments, 'tis the opinion of all the friends to government, that Boston *will be in open rebellion.* I have the honor to be with the greatest respect and warmest regard, Dear Sir, Your most faithful and oblig'd servant,

CHAS. PAXTON.[7]

My Dear Sir,　　　　　　　　Boston, Decem. 12th 1768.

I Wrote you a few days ago, and did not then think of troubling you upon any private affair of mine, at least not so suddenly; but within this day or two, I have had a conversation with Mr. Oliver, secretary of the province, the design of which was my succeeding to the post he holds from the crown, upon the idea, that provision would be made for governor Bernard, and the lieutenant governor would succeed to the chair, then the secretary is desirous of being lieutenant governor, and if in any way, three hundred pounds a year could be annexed to the appointment. You are sensible the appointment is in one department, and the grant of money in another; now the present lieutenant governor has an assignment of £200 a year upon the customs here; he has not received any thing from it as yet, and is doubtful if he shall; he has no doubt of its lapse to the crown, if he has the chair; if then by any interest that sum could be assigned to Mr. Oliver as lieutenant governor, and if he should be allowed (as has been usual for all lieutenant governors) to hold the command of the castle, that would be another £100. This would compleat the secretary's views; and he thinks his public services, the injuries he has received in that service, and the favorable sentiments entertained of him by

7. For this customs commissioner see above, XIV, 120 n.

government, may lead him to these views, and he hopes for the interest of his friends. The place of secretary is worth £300 a year, but is a provincial grant at present, so that it will not allow to be quartered on: And as I had view upon the place when I was in England, and went so far as to converse with several men of interest upon it, tho' I never had an opportunity to mention it to you after I recovered my illness, I hope you will allow me your influence, and by extending it at the treasury, to facilitate the assignment of the £200 a year, it will be serving the secretary, and it will very much oblige me. The secretary is advanced in life, tho' much more so in health, which has been much impaired by the injuries he received, and he wishes to quit the more active scenes; he considers this as a kind of *otium cum dignitate*, and from merits one may think he has a claim to it. I will mention to you the gentlemen, who are acquainted with my views and whose favourable approbation I have had. Governor Pownall, Mr. John Pownall, and Dr. Franklin. My lord Hillsborough is not unacquainted with it. I have since I have been here, wrote Mr. Jackson upon the subject, and have by this vessel wrote Mr. Mauduit. I think my character stands fair. I have not been without application to public affairs, and have acquired some knowledge of our provincial affairs, and notwithstanding our many free conversations in England, I am considered here as on government side, for which I have been often traduced both publickly and privately, and very lately have had two or three slaps. The governor and lieutenant governor are fully acquainted with the negociation, and I meet their approbation; all is upon the idea the governor is provided for, and there shall by any means be a vacancy of the lieut. governor's place. I have gone so far, as to say to some of my friends, that rather than not succeed I would agree to pay the secretary £100 a year out of the office to make up £300, provided he could obtain only the assignment of £200, but the other proposal would to be sure be most eligible. I scarce know any apology to make for troubling you upon the subject; the friendship you shewed me in London, and the favourable expressions you made use of to the lieut. governor in my behalf encourage me, besides a sort of egotism, which inclines men to think what they wish to be real. I submit myself to the enquiries of any of my countrymen in England, but I should wish the matter may be secret 'till it is effected. I am with very great respect and regard, my dear sir, Your most obedient, and most humble servant,

NATH. ROGERS.[8]

Sir,   N. London, February 7, 1768.

Notwithstanding of my having written to you very often, and at much length of late, and that I am upon the point of setting out for Boston with the first weather fit for travelling, yet I cannot refrain from troubling you with a few lines about the 8th and 9th letters of the Farmer, which I now inclose you. They are oracular here and make rapid deep impressions, and who is there at this time here, if capable, that may undertake to contradict or expose these agreeable seasonable epistolary Sophisms? Relief, Support and Recompence so long and so much expected, hop'd and wish'd for, seems too tardy and slow paid. Vigour and resolution seems to be exhausted in G. Britain, or bestowed upon improper and more trivial objects, than the subjection or obedience of America. Excuse these out-pourings of melancholly and despondency in a very dreary day, when the weather alters and the sun shines abroad, perhaps I may see through a brighter or more agreeable medium, but believe me the prospect is now bad and unpromising, but however it may prove, I desire and pray you to be assured that I am, Sir, your most obedient and most humble servant,

THOMAS MOFFAT.[9]

I will also trouble you from Boston.

Sir,   N. London, Nov. 15, 1768.

By Mr. Byles I am favoured with your most obliging letter of the second of August last, for which together with your extraordinary civility to Mr. Byles I truly thank you: I could not really think of such a person going from hence without shewing him to

8. Hutchinson's nephew. See above, XVI, 66 n; Bailyn, *Ordeal of Thomas Hutchinson*, pp. 135, 183.
9. See above, XI, 191 n and subsequent vols.

you, as a parson or minister of his way and turn of thinking may be considered as of the comit [comet?] kind here, which leads me to say somewhat abruptly if not improperly to you, that it seems to me here as if the universities of Scotland had conspired to distinguish all the firebrand incendiary preachers of this country with plumes of honorary degrees and titles, which in truth are only so many mortifications to the friends of G. Britain or lovers of letters, who cannot help being touch'd and chagrin'd at the too frequent profusion of honour and titles conferr'd from Scotland upon the leading preachers of sedition. I wish this affair of literary prostitution from my native country may induce you to speak of it to some of that nation with whom I know you are intimate, that may think of preventing it for the future.

As to Boston, the great theatre of action, I have been silent for some time past only for want of certain intelligence, as every day generally produc'd new rumours without any or much foundation in truth, but since the arrival of the two regiments with Col. Dalrymple all has been quiet there. I now flatter myself that measures of vigour will be pursued and maintained here, and I impatiently wish to hear that your friend is in power and confidence again, but that is indeed a point I have much expectation, desire and faith in. As you have express'd heretofore to me inclination of knowing the proceedings of the Rhode Island assembly respecting compensation to the sufferers in the riot of Newport, I now trouble you with a copy of my letter of this day to the lords of the treasury, which mutatis mutandis, is the same with that also to the Earl of Hillsborough of the same date with a copy of the narrative and letter to Lord Shelburne.

My Lords,   N. London, Nov. 14th, 1768.

Again I presume upon troubling your lordships with as short an account as may be written of what has very lately pass'd in the G. assembly of Rhode Island colony, in reference to their granting of a compensation to the sufferers from the riot of Newport 1765, as resolved on in the British parliament and very graciously recommended from his Majesty to the governor and company of that colony by his principal secretary of state.

Tired out and greatly mortified with a long course of frequent fruitless and a very expensive attendance upon the G. assembly, I had resolved above a year ago to solicit them no more: but at the intercession of my fellow sufferer Mr. Howard chief justice of North Carolina, I was again prevailed upon to go to Newport in September last, where and when the assembly then met and I had sufficient influence to engage the speaker of the house of deputies to move several times for reading a petition of Mr. Howard's, with an estimate of his loss solemnly sworn to and authenticated by a notary publick with every necessary prescribed form. The speaker also urged upon the house because of my attending from another colony upon that account only, but the deputies would neither consent to hear Mr. Howard's petition nor receive his estimate.

Immediately after this refusal a message was sent from the upper house of magistrates requesting the lower house to enter now upon the riot of Newport by immediately impowering the high sheriff to impannel a jury of inquisition to assertain and repair the loss of Dr. Moffatt, Mr. Howard and Mr. Johnson, but the house of deputies could not listen nor agree to any part of this proposal from the upper house.

About the middle of last I wrote a most respectful letter to the governor of Rhode Island and inclosed to his honor the estimate of my loss in the Newport riot sworn to before and attested by a magistrate here requesting the favor of the governor to lay the same before the ensuing assembly. The governor writes on the seventh of this month "that at the last session of assembly he presented my estimate and read my letter in a great committee of both houses of assembly but could not prevail to have it consider'd then;" and adds "that he will endeavour to bring it in again next February."

Under the strongest impressions of assurance the G. Assembly of Rhode Island never will recompence the suffered in the riot of Newport, may I again presume to implore your lordships interposition and influence to obtain a recompence for the sufferers in Rhode Island from some more effectual and certain channel than that of depending any longer upon the duty or justice of the G. Assembly in that colony. And my lords may I yet farther presume in writing to your lordships to add that by endeavouring to restore in some measure what I lost in that riot I am now sadly sensible that I have not overvalued the same in my estimate, as also that if I am not compensated by the interest, generosity and equity of your lordships, I can never expect to be possess'd of half the value I then lost, as the office of a comptroler here I now hold, had but a very inconsiderable salary with small perquisites. I am, My lords, &c. &c.   T. M.

In my last letter which I hope you have received, as I address'd it to the care of your brother, I then touch'd upon sir Wm. Johnson's being here some weeks in quest of health, and of the pleasure Mr. Stewart and I enjoy'd with him; as also that lord Charles Grenville Montague was here en passant with his lady; and I also then intimated to you our happiness in Mr. Harrison the collector of Boston having accepted Mr. Stewart's warm invitation to come here after the very flagrant riot at Boston, in which he had been so greatly insulted, abus'd and hurt, who came here with his lady, son and daughter, and staid a fortnight: when we planned and regulated all these colonies into a system which I could wish to see effected. Since which Mr. Stewart has visited Mr. Harrison at Boston at the time when Mrs. Harrison with their son and daughter sailed for London as a place of perfect safety and liberty. Mr. Harrison's son is capable and promising, but was cruelly us'd by the mob of Boston, which will I hope incline Mr. Harrison's friends or rather the friends of government to provide suitably for so young a sufferer. I could not easily within the compass of a letter to you say the pleasure I have felt in observing the strict union and friendship that subsists and is now rivetted between Mr. Harrison and Mr. Stewart upon principles of the truest honor and virtue, both of whom well understand and sincerely wish the true interest of G. Britain and all her colonies, especially in the cardinal articles of legislation and government, as also in the subaltern or lesser points of taxation and revenue from which objects no attachments, connections or views will or ever can sway the one or the other. As I have been accustomed to write to you with a plainness and freedom which I flatter myself has not been disagreeable, so therefore I would farther say of Mr. Stewart that he married in an opulent popular and commercial family, some of whom perhaps may be supposed to have more oblique interest than may be consistent with regulation or a due submission to the laws of G. Britain, so it is with a peculiar and very sensible satisfaction that I can assure you his spirit address and conduct in so nice a situation deserves the greatest praise and commendation, as it has perhaps been or may be very influential on some of the best among them, even to a better way of thinking and acting. By the inclos'd you will know that Mr. Stewart now writes to Mr. Grenville, and mentions somewhat of his application for leave of absence from the Treasury board, which I only wish him to succeed in because I think Mr. Harrison and him really the most capable persons here to throw light upon many transactions here which cannot be communicated in letters or any written representation to satisfaction or proper advantage. If Mr. Stewart obtains leave to return home I shall be unhappy enough by his absence. Two years are now elapsed since I came here, a great part of which has been spent in anxiously wishing for the genius of Britain to awake and vindicate her supreme jurisdiction and authority impiously questioned and denied in colonies so very lately redeemed from hostile incursions and encroachments, but I believe the time is now come, and I rejoice in its approach. I wish you every felicity with the preferment and employment you like best, and am Sir, Your most obedient humble Servant,

THOMAS MOFFAT.

Sir,   Boston, December 15. 1768.

In November last I wrote you from N. London, and inserted in that letter a copy of what I had written to the lords of the treasury and the Earl of Hillsborough, relative to the compensation of the sufferers in the riot at Newport 1765. I hope and very much wish that letter may have come to your hand, because in it you will see how strictly and soon I follow your counsel in making affidation to the estimate of my loss, which as I apprehended made not the least impression nor could make upon the general assembly of Rhode-Island, because there was not I believe a member in either house that did not think and believe my loss exceeded the estimate frequently laid before them to no purpose. I thank you therefore for the kind and good advice which I instantly followed, and which I think has finished this long and tedious transaction on this side of the atlantick, which has not only been ineffectual but attended with much trouble and expence to me. How or in what light it may be now considered by administration or parliament I cannot at this time and distance judge, far less determine. Sometimes I flatter myself that a resolve of the British senate will not be allowed to be thus scorned and trampled upon; at other times I despond and think the object too small for attention; and as there were but three sufferers in Rhode-Island colony, two of them to my great pleasure and triumph are now amply and very honorably provided for, I sometimes imagine that compensation may drop and be forgot, and indeed if it was not for the confidence which I have in you and some others in the house of commons, I should certainly despair of any recompence, and which upon recollection I must acknowledge as criminal in a very great degree, because of its having been resolved on in the parliament of Great-Britain that such sufferers should be compensated: And I am not conscious that I have omitted, delayed or neglected any part of my duty in the course of negociating it here in America.

A few days ago I came here chiefly to see and enjoy my friend collector Harrison that we might open bosoms to one another upon the great scene and field of affairs in this country, the face of which is only alter'd apparently here from the arrival of the King's troops and ships, which have indeed restored a very certain security and tranquility, and prevented if not put a final period to their most pestilent town-meetings. There is nor can be no real alteration in the sentiment or disposition of the prime disturbers. This is but an interval or truce procur'd from the dread of a bayonet. The special and catholick remedy deriv'd from and founded in an acknowledgement of the British supremacy and legislation over America manifested under the exercise of a more firm, regular and consistent plan of civil government, must come from the decrees of the British parliament, otherwise the country and particularly N. England, will soon and forever be in perpetual anarchy and disobedience. The anxiety and distress of the few here that are well affected to government before the arrival of the troops and ships was very great, and in my opinion will be greater if vigorous, salutary and proper measures are not adopted in parliament.

All here seem anxious and impatient to know the complexion

and temper of the British parliament, and what is very unaccountable if not incredible, the sons of liberty here so called are elevated with hope and assurance that their claims and pretensions will be receiv'd and recogniz'd, as they affect to phrase it, but if I err not, this presumption of hope may have arisen or been cherished in a great measure by some visits of an officer of high military rank from N. York to some of the most popular and violent ringleaders here, and I wish that I could say to you that the most mischievous here had not been countenanced also by a person of another and very different station.

I find that in consequence of and under an apprehension of unsettled, unsafe times here, Mr. Harrison has thought it best that Mrs. Harrison, his son and daughter, should go to London, as a place of true liberty and safety, and as I hope they will be arrived before this reaches you, and as I formerly mentioned to you Mr. Harrison's son as a young sufferer very roughly handled upon the 10th of June, so if you incline to see and discourse him for intelligence or any other motive, Mr. Hallowell of this town can easily bring him to you.

If any thing remarkable occurs here during my stay I shall not fail to write to you again. I am, sir, your most obedient and most humble servant, THOMAS MOFFAT.

Sir, Narraganset, 22d December 1767.[1]

I am now withdrawn to my little country villa, where, tho' I am more retired from the busy world, yet I am still invelop'd with uneasy reflections for a turbulent, degenerate, ungrateful continent, and the opposition I have met with in my indefatigable endeavours to secure our property in this colony, but hitherto without success. The times are so corrupted and the conflict of parties so predominant, that faction is blind, or shuts her eyes to the most evident truths that cross her designs, and believes in any absurdities that assists to accomplish her purposes under the prostitution and prostration of an infatuated government. Judge then, my dear sir, in what a critical situation the fortunes of we poor Europeans must be among them.

1. Enclosed with the preceding letter. For the writer, George Rome, see the note on Cushing to BF above, Sept. 18.

We have not been able to recover our property for years past, how great soever our exigencies may have been, unless we soothed them into a compliance: We are unwilling to enter into a litiscontestation with them, because the perversion of their iniquitous courts of justice are so great, that experience has convinced us we had better loose half, to obtain the other quietly, than pursue compulsory measures: We are also afraid to apply to a British parliament for relief, as none can be effectually administered without a change of government, and a better administration of justice introduced; and was it known here, that we made such application home, not only our fortunes would be in greater jeopardy, but our lives endangered by it before any salutary regulations cou'd take place. We are sensible of the goodness of the KING and PARLIAMENT, but how far, or in what space of time our grievance, as a few individuals, might weigh against the influence of a charter government, we are at a loss to determine.

In 1761, I arrived in America, which circumstance you probably remember well: With great industry, caution and circumspection, I have not only reduced our demands, and regulated our connections in some measure, but kept my head out of a HALTER which you had the honor to grace. (Pray Doctor how did it feel? The subject is stale, but I must be a little funny with you on the occasion.) Much still remains to be done, and after all my best endeavours, my constituents, from a moderate calculation, cannot lose less than £50,000 sterling, by the baneful constitution of this colony, and the corruption of their courts of judicature. *It is really a very affecting and melancholly consideration.*

Under a deep sense of the infirmities of their constitution; the innovations which they have gradually interwoven among themselves; and stimulated by every act of forbearance, lenity and patience, we have indulged our correspondents until deluges of bankruptceys have ensued, insolvent acts liberated them from our just demands, and finally, had our indisputable accounts refused admission for our proportion of the small remains, until colony creditors were first paid, and the whole absorbed. We have had vessels made over to us for the satisfaction of debts, and after bills of sales were executed, carried off in open violence and force by Capt. Snip-snap of Mr. No body's appointment, and when we sued him for damages, recover'd a louse. We have in our turn been sued in our absence, and condemned *ex parte* in large sums for imaginary damages, for which we can neither obtain a trial, nor redress. They refuse us an appeal to the king in council; the money must be paid when their executions become returnable; and were we to carry it home by way of complaint, it would cost us two or three hundred pounds sterling to prosecute, and after all, when his Majesty's decrees comes over in our favour, and refunding the money can no longer be evaded, I expect their effects will be secreted, their body's released by the insolvent act, and our money, both principal, interest and expences irrecoverably gone. Is not our case grievous? We have in actions founded upon notes of hand, been cast in their courts of judicature. We have appeal'd to his Majesty in council for redress, got their verdicts reversed, and obtain'd the King's decrees for our money, but *that is all;* for altho' I have had them by me twelve months, and employed two eminent lawyers to enforce them into execution conformable to the colony law, yet we have not been able to recover a single shilling, tho' we have danced after their courts and assembly's above THIRTY DAYS, *in vain* to accomplish that purpose only: Consider my dear sir, what expence, vexation, and loss of time this must be to us, and whether we have not just cause of complaint.

We have also in vain waited with great impatience for years past, in hopes his Majesty wou'd have nominated his judges, and other executive officers in every colony in America, which wou'd in a great measure remove the cause of our complaint. Nothing can be more necessary than a speedy regulation in this, and constituting it a regal government; and nothing is of such important use to a nation, as that men who excel in *wisdom* and *virtue* should be encouraged to undertake the business of government: But the iniquitous course of their courts of justice in this colony, deter such men from serving the public, or if they do so, unless patronized at home, their wisdom and virtue are turned against them with such malignity, that it is more safe to be *infamous* than renown'd. The principal exception I have met with here, is James Helmes, Esq; who was chosen chief justice by the general assembly at last election. He accepted his appointment, distinguishes himself by capacity and application, and seems neither afraid nor ashamed to administer impartial justice to *all,* even to the native and residing creditors of the mother country. I have known him grant them temporary relief by writs of error, &c. when both he, and they, were overruled by the partiality of the court; and in vain, tho' with great candour and force, plead with the rest of the bench, that for the honour of the colony, and their own reputation, they ought never to pay less regard to the decrees of his Majesty in council, because the property was determined in Great Britain, than to their own. I have also heard him with *resolution and firmness*, when he discovered the court to be *immoderately partial*, order his name to be inrol'd, as dissenting from the verdict. For such honesty and candour, I am persuaded he will be deposed at next election, unless they should be still in hopes of making a convert of him.

I wish it was in my power to prevent every American from suffering for the cause of integrity, and their mother country; *he*, in an especial manner, should not only be *protected* and *supported*, but appear among the first promotions. Is there no gentleman of public spirit at home, that would be pleased to be an instrument of elevating a man of his principals and probity? or is it become fashionable for vice to be countenanced with impunity, and every trace of virtue past over unnoticed! God forbid.

The colonies have originally been wrong founded. They ought all to have been regal governments, and every executive officer appointed by the King. Until that is effected, and they are properly regulated, they will never be beneficial to themselves, nor good subjects to Great-Britain. You see with what contempt they already treat the acts of parliament for regulating their trade, and enter into the most public, illegal and affronting combinations to obtain a repeal, by again imposing upon the British merchants and manufacturers, and all under the cloak of *retrenching their expences*, by avoiding every *unnecessary superfluity*. Were that really the case, I am sure I wou'd, and also every other British subject, esteem them for it; but the fact is, they obtain'd a repeal of the stamp act by mercantile influence, and they are now endeavouring by the same artifice and finesse to repeal the acts of trade, and obtain a total exemption from all taxation. Were it otherways, and they sincerely disposed to stop the importation of every unnecessary superfluity, without affronting the British legislation, by their public, general, and illegal combinations, they might accomplish their purposes with much more *decency*, and suppress it more effectually by the acts of their own legislation, imposing such duties upon their importation here,[2] as might either occasion a total prohibition, or confine the consumption of them to particular individuals that can afford to buy, by which measures they would also raise a considerable colony REVENUE, and ease the poorer inhabitants in the tax they now pay: But the temper of the country is exceedingly *factious*, and prone to sedition; they are growing more *imperious, haughty*, nay *insolent* every day, and in a short space, unless wholsome regulations take place, the spirit they have inkindled, and the conceptions of government they have imbibed, will be more grievous to the mother country than ever the ostracism was to the Athenians.

A bridle at present, may accomplish more than a rod hereafter; for the malignant poison of the times, like a general pestilence, spreads beyond conception; and if the British parliament are too late in their regulations, neglect measures seven years, which are essentially necessary now, shou'd they then be able to stifle their commotions, it will only be a temporary extinction, consequently, every hour's indulgence will answer no other purpose than enable them in a more effectual manner to sow seeds of dissension to be rekindled whenever they are in a capacity to oppose the mother country and render themselves independent of her.

Have they not already in the most public manner shewn their opposition to the measures of parliament in the affair of the late stamp act? Don't they now with equal violence and audacity, in both public papers and conversation, declare the parliamentary regulations in their acts of trade to be illegal and a mere nullity? What further proofs do we wait for, of either their good or bad disposition? Did you ever hear of any colonies, *in their infant state*, teach the science of tyranny, *reduced into rules*,[3] over every subject that discountenanced their measures in opposition to the mother country, *in a more imperious manner than they have done these four years past?* Have they not made use of every stroke of policy (in

2. [*Note in the pamphlet:*] I mean foreign growth, or fabrications; but if on British, it wou'd be more pardonable than their present system.
3. [*Note in the pamphlet:*] The Committee to the Sons of Liberty, &c.

their way) to avail themselves of the dark purposes of their independence, and suffered no restraint of conscience, or fear, not even the guilt of threatening *to excite a civil war*, and *revolt*, if not indulged with an unlimited trade, without restraint; and British protection, without expence? for that is the english of it. Is this their true, or mistaken portrait? SAY. If it is their true one, ought not such pernicious maxims of policy? Such wicked discipline? Such ingratitude? Such dissimulation? Such perfidy? Such violent, ruthless and sanguinary councils, where a Cleon bears rule, and an Aristides cannot be endured, to be crushed in embryo? If not, the alternative cannot avoid producing such a government, as will ere long throw the whole kingdom into the utmost confusion, endanger the life, liberty and property of every good subject, and again expose them to the merciless assassination of a rabble.

I am sensible that in all political disputes, especially in America, a man may see some things to blame on both sides, and so much to fear, which ever faction should conquer, as to be justified in not intermedling with either; but in matters of such vast importance as the present, wherein we have suffer'd so much, still deeply interested, and by which the peace and tranquility of the nation is at stake; it is difficult to conceal ones emotions from a friend, and remain a tranquil spectator on a theatre of such chicanery and colusion, as will inevitably (if not checked, and may sooner happen than is imagin'd by many) chill the blood of many a true Briton.

It may be true policy, in some cases, to tame the fiercest spirit of popular liberty, not by blows, or by chains, but by soothing her into a willing obedience, and making her kiss the very hand that restrains her; but such policy wou'd be a very unsuitable potion to cure the malady of the present times. They are too much corrupted; and already so intoxicated with their own importance, as to make a wrong use of lenient measures. They construe them into their own natural rights, and a timidity in the mother country. They consider themselves a little bigger than the *frog* in the *fable*, and that G. Britain can never long grapple with their huge territory of 1500 miles frontier, already populous, and increasing with such celerity, as to double their numbers once in *twenty-five years*. This is not perfectly consonant with my idea of the matter, tho' such calculation has been made; and admitting it

577

to be erroneous, yet, as they believe it, it has the same evil effect, and possesses the imaginations of the people with such a degree of insanity and enthusiasm, as there is hardly any thing more common than to hear them boast of particular colonies that can raise on a short notice *an hundred thousand fighting men, to oppose the force of Great-Britain;* certain it is, that they increase in numbers by emigration &c. very fast, and are become such a body of people, with such extensive territory, as require every bud of their genius and disposition to be narrowly watched, and pruned with great judgment, otherways they may become not only troublesome to Great Britain, but enemies to themselves. Now is the critical season. They are still like some raw giddy youth just emerging into the world in a corrupt degenerate age. A parent, or a guardian, is therefore still necessary; and if well managed, they will soon arrive at such maturity as to become obedient, dutiful children; but if neglected long, the rod of chastisement will be so much longer necessary as to become too burthensome, and must be dropt with the colonies. They almost consider themselves as a separate people from Great Britain already.

Last month while I was attending the General Assembly, the Governor sent a written message to the lower house, importing his intentions of a resignation at the next election, assigning for reasons, the fumes in the colony and party spirit were so high, and that bribery and corruption were so predominant, that neither *life*, *liberty* nor *property* were safe, &c. &c. &c. Now Sir, whether the Governor's intentions as exhibited in this open, public declaration, was real, or *feign'd* to answer political purposes; it still evinces their decrepid state; the prostitution of government; and melancholly situation of every good subject: For it cannot be supposed by any candid inquisitor, that a declaration of that nature, and form, would, if not true, been deliver'd by a Governor to a whole legislative body, in order to emancipate himself. If this truth is granted, and this allow'd to be their unhappy situation, how much is it the duty of every good man, and what language is sufficient to paint in an effectual manner, this internal imbecility of an English colony (in many other respects favourably situated for trade and commerce, one of the safest, largest, and most commodious harbours in all America, or perhaps in all Europe, accessible at all seasons, situated in a fine climate, and abounding with fertile soil), to the maternal bowels of compassion, in order that she may seasonably, if she thinks it necessary to interpose, regulate, and wipe away their pernicious CHARTER, render'd obnoxious by the abuse of it.

I am afraid I have tired your patience with a subject that must give pain to every impartial friend to Great-Britain and her colonies. When I took up my pen, I only intended to have communicated the out-lines of such of my perplexities (without diping so far into political matter) as I tho't would atone for, or excuse my long silence, and excite your compassion and advice.

Our friend Robinson is gone to Boston to join the commissioners. My compliments to Colr Stuart. May I ask the favour of you both to come and eat a xmas dinner with me at batchelor's hall, and celebrate the festivity of the season with me in Narraganset woods. A covy of partridges, or bevy of quails, will be entertainment for the colr and me, while the pike and pearch ponds amuse you. Should business or pre-ingagements prevent me that pleasure, permit me to ask the favour of your earliest intelligence of the proceedings of parliament; and of your opinion whether our case is not so great as to excite their compassion and interposition were it known. This narration, together with your own knowledge of many of the facts, and the disposition of the colonies in general, will refresh your memory, and enable you to form a judgment. Relief from home seems so tedious, especially to us who have suffered so much, like to suffer more, and unacquainted with their reasons of delay, that I am quite impatient.

Above twelve months ago, I received from three Gentlemen in London (in trust for several others) exemplified accounts for a balance of about twenty-six-thousand pounds sterling, mostly due from this colony, not £50 of which shall I ever be able to recover without compulsive measures, and what is still worse, my lawyer advises me from all thoughts of prosecution, unless a change of government ensues. I am therefore obliged to send them his opinion (in justification of my own conduct) in lieu of money ten years due. Poor Satisfaction! Our consolation must be in a British parliament. Every other avenue is rendered impregnable by their subtilty, and degeneracy, and we can no longer depend upon a people who are so unthankful for our indulgences, and the lenity of their mother country. I wish you the compliments of the approaching season, and a succession of many happy new years. I am Sir, with much regard, Your most humble Servant,

G. ROME.

Index

Compiled by Mary L. Hart, Jennifer Lovejoy, and Joy G. Sylvester

---

[1] Entries under this heading in previous volumes have been so gargantuan as to be unusable. In the present and future volumes we limit entries to (1) items that cannot readily be found under BF's correspondents, organizations with which he was connected, etc.; (2) cross-references by title and pseudonym to his writings mentioned in the volume.

Independence: (*cont.*)
333 n, 436–7; possibility of, for colonies,
391, 398, 496–7
India: army of, in battle of Plassey, 10 n;
Lord Clive's defense of conduct in,
227; Pratt-Yorke opinion on land tenure
in, 300
Indiana Company: wf's share in, 185 n;
grant to, and Walpole Co. petition,
302–3
Indians, Indian affairs: colonists' tenure in
land acquired from, xxxiii, 117, 119,
120, 300–1, 302, 303–4; land cession to
Ill. Land Co. by, 301; effort to purchase
land from, beyond the Ohio, 306 n; and
demolition of forts on frontiers, 399;
in *Encyclopédie*, 424 n; Pauw's theory of
degeneracy of, 447 n; fur trade with, in
Ga., 475; and catching cold, 532; mentioned, 209. *See also* Cherokee Indians;
Creek Indians; Six Nations.
Indigo, Ga. exports, 475
Ingenhousz, Dr. Jan: experiments on,
interest in torpedo fish, 260 n, 433 n,
529 n; on Beccaria's prose style, 356 n;
bf suggests move to England, 432;
practices in Vienna, 432; paper on magnetic needles, 433 n; electrical machine
of, 434; letter to, 432–5; mentioned, 423 n
Inoculation, bf on, 428
"Inquiry in the Principles of Vital Motion"
(C. Colden): bf to read, 33 n, 220–1
Inslee, Samuel: *London Chron.* for, 37;
prints *N.-Y. Gaz.*, 37 n
Institutiones pathologiae medicinalis . . .
(Gaubius), on causes of disease, 404
Instructions, royal: and tax exemption of
Mass. customs commissioners, 8, 173–4,
273; on bf's Mass. salary, 17, 174, 284;
to Dinwiddie, Dunmore, on land grants,
61, 186 n; constitutional role, 82; past
colonial obedience to, 85; Hillsborough's
use of, 86; on *Gaspee* commission, 110;
on census of colonies, 148 n; effect on
colonial assemblies, 204 n; and appointment of colonial agents, 273; on royal
payment of Mass. officials, 279–80; in
bf's "Edict," 418
Ireland: bf's trip to (1771), 156 n, 310 n,
522; rumored union with Britain, 386;
controversy on absentee tax, 386 n; C.
Townshend, Harcourt lord lieutenants
of, 386 n; collapse of linen trade, 522;
proposed law to prohibit emigration
from, 522, 527–8. *See also* Commons,
Irish House of; Dublin.
Ireland, S. (weaver), and silk for R.
Garrigues, 68
Irish, bf's attitude toward, 403 n

Iron: and magnetism, 105–6; as conductor,
171; mentioned, 287
Iron Act (1750), in bf's "Edict," 414 n,
416, 418
*Isaaci Newtoni . . . opuscula mathematica,
philosophica et philologica* . . . (Castillon),
Winthrop paper on, 92, 329
Italy: bf's possible visit to, 306; scientific
advancement in, 366 n

Jack, for wf, 146, 149
Jackson, Mr. and Mrs., mentioned, 256
Jackson, Charles: invites bf, 343; letter
from, 343
Jackson, Richard: and ownership of
Delaware islands, 18; and Pa. acts
(1771, 1772), 109; and Walpole Co.,
327; and possible amendment of Cur-
rency Act, 341; mentioned, 197
Jacob, Joseph: and bf's method of making
carriage wheels, 157 n, 158 n; *Animadversions on the Use of Broad Wheels*,
158 n; *Observations on the Structure and
Draft of Wheel-Carriages*, 158 n
Jamaica, erroneous report on lightning
damage in, 4–5, 5 n, 88, 91 n
Jamaica Plain, Mass., barn in, ignited by
lightning, 93
James, Abel: and purchase of land for
Phila. Silk Filature, 15 n; on Phila.
Silk Filature committee, 43, 108, 297;
and Baynton, Wharton, Morgan quarrel,
296 n; M. Birkbeck recommended to,
319; letter to, 319
James, John, type foundry of: disposal of,
231–2, 411; bf buys type, 231 n
James, Mrs. John, and disposal of James's
type foundry, 231–2
Jardin des Plantes: specimens for, 320;
mentioned, 219
Jefferson, Thomas, mentioned, 157 n
Jenkins, Capt.: carries mail, 74, 140 n;
commands *Minerva*, 74 n; visits bf,
74 n, 290; mentioned, 98 n, 100
Jenkins, Benjamin, mentioned, 74 n
Jenkins, Charles, mentioned, 74 n
Jenkins, Seth, mentioned, 74 n, 100 n
Jenkins, Thomas, marriage to Judith
Folger, 74 n
Jesser, Mr., and search for E. Holland, 20 n,
153
Jessop, William, and bf's experiment with
oil on water, 467
Jesuits, electrical experiments of, in Pekin,
362, 365
Johnson, Joseph, Priestley writes to, via
bf, 440
Johnston (Johnson), James, letter to, 45:
mentioned, 186

615